Early Literacy in Action

Early Literacy in Action

The Language-Focused Curriculum for Preschool

by

Betty H. Bunce, Ph.D., CCC-SLP
Language Acquisition Preschool
Department of Speech-Language-Hearing
University of Kansas
Lawrence

·P A U L·H·
BROOKES
PUBLISHING C?®

Baltimore • London • Sydney

Paul H. Brookes Publishing Co.
Post Office Box 10624
Baltimore, Maryland 21285-0624
USA

www.brookespublishing.com

Typeset by Barton Matheson Willse & Worthington, Baltimore, Maryland.
Manufactured in the United States of America by
Versa Press, Inc., East Peoria, Illinois.

The individuals described in this book are composites or real people whose situations have been masked and are based on the authors' experiences. Names and identifying details have been changed to protect confidentiality.

The photographs that appear throughout the book are used by permission of the individuals pictured or their parents or guardians.

Library of Congress Cataloging-in-Publication Data

Bunce, Betty H.
Early literacy in action: The language-focused curriculum for preschool / by Betty H. Bunce.
   p.   cm.
   Includes bibliographical references and index.
   ISBN-13: 978-1-55766-922-3
   ISBN-10: 1-55766-922-8
   1. Language arts (Preschool). 2. Education, Preschool—Curricula. 3. Speech therapy for children.
   I. Title.

LB1140.5.L3B86 2008
372.6—dc22

2007037651

British Library Cataloguing in Publication data are available from the British Library.

2012   2011   2010   2009   2008

10   9   8   7   6   5   4   3   2   1

Contents

About the Author

Betty H. Bunce, Ph.D., CCC-SLP, Director, Language Acquisition Preschool (LAP); Clinical Professor, Department of Speech-Language-Hearing, University of Kansas, 1000 Sunnyside Avenue, Lawrence, KS 66045

Dr. Bunce was born and raised in a bilingual, bicultural community in southern Colorado. She earned a bachelor's degree in education from the University of Colorado, a master's degree in speech education from Temple University, and a doctoral degree in child language from the University of Kansas. She received her Certificate of Clinical Competence in Speech-Language Pathology in 1977. Dr. Bunce has taught kindergarten and preschool-age children and has worked as a school speech-language pathologist. She has also taught coursework at the university level in reading and language arts, early childhood education, multicultural issues, and speech-language pathology. She was the Kansas Speech-Language-Hearing Association nominee for the American Speech-Language-Hearing Foundation Frank R. Kleffner Award in 1997.

Dr. Bunce has written several chapters and articles on preschool education, bilingual and bicultural children, referential communication, and intervention techniques for both preschool- and elementary-age children. She has presented workshops to practitioners in the fields of early childhood education, reading intervention, and speech-language pathology and has presented papers at several international, national, and state association conventions. She is the director of the LAP at the University of Kansas, where an important part of her job is to train speech-language pathology graduate students in conducting naturalistic language intervention in classroom settings. Dr. Bunce's fields of scientific interest include preschool education, English as a second language, reading intervention, and relationships between oral language abilities and literacy skills. Her most recent research has focused on naturalistic intervention techniques and their effectiveness.

Contributors

Laura Justice, Ph.D.
Professor
School of Teaching and Learning
The Ohio State University
231 Arps Hall
1945 North High Street
Columbus, OH 43210

Khara L. Pence, Ph.D.
Research Assistant Professor
Curry School of Education
University of Virginia
315 Old Ivy Way, Suite 102
Charlottesville, VA 22903

Alice K. Wiggins, M.Ed.
Project Director
Research Faculty
University of Virginia
Box 400873
Charlottesville, VA 22904

Foreword

The preschool years are among the most productive times in a person's life. During this short period of time, children master the fundamentals of language, social interactions with peers and adults, and basic cognitive skills, all of which serve as the bedrock for later reading skill, academic achievement, and life-changing personal and professional success. Adults who care for and teach children of this age have a golden opportunity and great responsibility for guiding children during this rich period of development.

Young children manage to make great changes in a short time while going about their natural proclivities—playing with each other and with their toys, interacting with the things and events around them, and focusing attention for brief intervals on particular things or people. They talk, laugh, explore, and show surprise at unlikely events or things. They learn how to talk politely, how to have an argument, how to relate a story of what happened to them recently or a long time ago, and how to describe if they aren't feeling well. They learn to recognize their names and realize that marks on paper can be interpreted as a bill for payment of food or a story about magical characters. They do all of this in a natural, effortless manner, quite unlike the effort needed when an adult tries to learn a new language. Preschoolers don't "study" in order to learn new things; they go about the business of interacting with their world and their interactions provide the scaffolding for their development. At the same time, there are large individual differences in how well they do this—some children thrive whereas others have more modest developmental gains.

The challenge for adults who teach children of this age is how to harness children's natural interests and instincts in the service of enhancing their language, social, cognitive, and emerging literacy skills. Although the accomplishments of young children seem obvious and transparent, the obviousness masks a great deal of precision and detail in how the growth plays out and the ways in which growth can get "stuck" or "derailed" in particular areas. It requires a well-educated and well-trained adult with well-informed powers of observation and interaction to establish an effective learning environment for young children. It requires years of experience to hone such ability into a distilled form for the purpose of teaching others how to teach young children.

This volume provides a rich roadmap for a naturalistic, child-friendly preschool curriculum that is based on sound scientific principles and empirical evidence of positive outcomes for children. The core dimension is language, because it serves as the linchpin for social, cognitive, and literacy development—children with good language skills have a real advantage on the other dimensions as well. The language-focused curriculum (LFC) was established in 1985, more than 20 years ago, as a demonstration project funded by the U.S. Department of Education. The initial 10 years have been summarized (Rice, 1995). The LFC has been in continuous operation since then, and is tested daily in the realities of a teaching/research/service setting affiliated with the University of Kansas and the local public school system.

The author of this volume, Dr. Betty Bunce, has refined the curricular plans in the toughest consumer market: that of preschool children who come to their classrooms expecting to find interesting and fun things to do in an atmosphere that respects their dignity, intelligence, and enthusiasm. Parents can observe the classroom and provide feedback as well as share observations with Dr. Bunce and the other teaching staff. The reader will find 40 weeks of field-tested curriculum plans with demonstrated effectiveness for enhancing children's language, social, cognitive, and literacy development. Dr. Bunce has done a brilliant job of laying out the details of design and implementation that scaffold an array of "natural" activities in a classroom setting.

Dr. Laura Justice, along with Dr. Khara L. Pence and Alice K. Wiggins, provide a chapter with important discussion and documentation for preparing preschool teachers to implement the LFC using language stimulation techniques (LSTs). Although the LFC builds on natural adult/child verbal interactions using LSTs, the "naturalness" of child-centered interactions sometimes seems unnatural in classroom settings. Some teachers find that LSTs take some practice to get used to, but once the shift is made it can become so automatic that teachers wonder that it had to be taught. Dr. Justice's study demonstrates impressive gains in teachers' use of the methods after a short training period. There is an important caveat: follow-up reminders help consolidate long-term use.

In the broader world of educational policy, there is a spotlight on teaching methods and effectiveness with a strong emphasis on evidence-based methods and outcomes. This extends to the long-standing questions and debates about the cost-effectiveness of preschool education. Further, there is ongoing discussion of the desirability of teaching children with special needs, such as speech/language impairment, in general education classroom settings. From my perspective, these issues have been with us for a long time and will continue to be discussed and debated. This volume and the years of scholarship and empirical evaluation that it represents are a vital resource for the design and implementation of a classroom-based preschool curriculum that meets the highest professional standards and the daily challenges of our young child consumers. It is with great pride and enthusiasm that I recommend this volume, on behalf of the many well-trained and highly skilled persons who taught and were trained in the Language Acquisition Preschool over the years, the marvelous children who brought their enthusiasm to each class, and the parents who supported and benefited from the program.

Mabel L. Rice, Ph.D.
Fred and Virginia Merrill Distinguished Professor of Advanced Studies
Former Language Acquisition Preschool Director
University of Kansas
Lawrence

REFERENCE

Rice, M.L. (1995). Creating a language-focused curriculum for preschool children. In M.L. Rice & K.A. Wilcox (Eds.), *Building a language-focused curriculum for the preschool classroom: A foundation for lifelong communication* (Vol. I). Baltimore: Paul H. Brookes Publishing Co.

Preface

Over the last 20 years, the educational field has focused more and more on early intervention and the importance of language and literacy learning during the preschool years (see Guralnick, 1997, for an overview of the effectiveness of early intervention; Stipek et al., 1998, for an account of the differences a program makes in preparing young children for school; Snow, Burns, & Griffin, 1998; and Dickinson & Tabors, 2001, for information on language and literacy connections and preschool programming). These two interests, providing early intervention for children with language impairments and providing good language and literacy programming for all children, led to the development of the language-focused curriculum (LFC). The LFC, which was developed in the Language Acquisition Preschool (LAP) at the University of Kansas, aimed at providing quality preschool programming for all children, including those with speech and language impairments, those with English as their second language, and those with typical language development.

From the beginning, LAP has had three major objectives: 1) to provide services to young children, 2) to be a training site for students in speech-language pathology and early childhood education, and 3) to facilitate research. The development of the curriculum began in 1985, when Mabel Rice and Kim Wilcox started the LAP with funding as a 3-year demonstration program (Department of Education Award #GOO863079). Subsequently, LAP has received financial support from the University of Kansas and from an additional grant for 5 years from the Kansas Early Childhood Research Institute (OSEP Award #HO24U80001). Since 1994, other funding has also been provided through the local school district (USD 497) in the form of a salary for one teacher. In return, some of the children with speech and language impairments have received school-mandated services at LAP.

The principles, or criteria, of the LFC are

1. The curriculum should enable *all* preschool children to benefit from activities to enhance their language acquisition; children with better verbal skills are better prepared for school entry.
2. The curriculum should adhere to the principles of children's language acquisition.
3. Many of the time-honored practices for children's preparation for school entry should be followed, along with developmentally appropriate practice regarding cognitive and social development.
4. Care should be taken to educate children with speech and language impairments in a classroom with their typically developing peers in the least restrictive environment.
5. Staff should ensure that children with language intervention needs are not separated from the group in ways that highlight their limitations; therefore, children should not be identified for individual therapy sessions outside of the room.
6. Parental involvement should be recognized as an important component of any efforts to develop children's language, social, and cognitive skills (Rice, 1995).

In 1995, two books were published describing the LFC. Volume I provided an overview of the program, including some of the research information (Rice & Wilcox, 1995), and Volume II provided planning guides with specific lesson plans for implementation of the curriculum (Bunce, 1995). Since the publication of those volumes, many papers, workshops, articles, and book chapters have described the LFC and the research associated with it (e.g., Bunce, 1998, 1999, 2003; Bunce, Rice, & Wilcox, 2000; Hadley & Rice, 1993; Rice, 1993, 1998; Rice, Wilcox, Bunce, & Liebhaver, 1989; Watkins & Bunce, 1996).

This book is primarily a revision of the earlier second volume on the curriculum. It is intended for speech-language pathologists and early childhood educators who work with preschool-age children. The activities in it have been field-tested with more than 500 children over the 20 years that the LAP has been in existence. In addition, the activities have been used in both public schools and university training programs in several states.

The majority of the revisions in this book involve the addition of 40 weeks of curriculum plans, including weekly themes, suggested story selections, dramatic play and art activities, and group lesson plans laid out in a week-by-week manner. It also includes an overview of the sequence of activities for the entire year in the form of monthly planning guides. The revision was driven by the need to provide more detailed information on themes, lesson plans, and teaching strategies so that novice teachers could more effectively implement the curriculum. The use of the weekly thematic units provides an overall structure for preschool programming, yet it allows flexibility in the development of activities appropriate for children with varying competencies. Language and literacy goals are the major focus of the curriculum; however, cognitive, motor, and social skills are also emphasized. An individual lesson or activity may facilitate the development of several areas simultaneously. As teachers gain experience using the curriculum, they can adapt it to meet the needs of individual children while honoring the overall principles of the curriculum.

The book is organized into three parts. Part I, Foundations of the Language-Focused Curriculum (Chapters 1–5), offers an introduction to the general philosophy of the LFC and information on the structure and underlying theoretical guidelines for implementing the curriculum. It also contains information on implementing language intervention and a discussion of outcomes. Chapter 1 provides guidelines concerning language learning, curriculum development, and classroom management. Chapter 2 addresses reasons for having both teacher-led and child-centered activities and for having activities that are routine and those that vary daily. In addition, this chapter explains the focus and use of dramatic play activities. The chapter concludes with a detailed sample schedule that explains the different types of daily activities and the goals of each. Chapter 3 focuses on how to provide intervention within the classroom setting. Definitions and descriptions of language-facilitating intervention techniques are provided. Examples from children enrolled in LAP illustrate the way this type of speech and language therapy can be embedded into daily classroom activities. Chapter 4, written by Laura Justice, Alice K. Wiggins, and Khara L. Pence, addresses how the LFC was implemented in several Head Start classrooms in urban and rural Virginia. Chapter 5 discusses information on speech and language outcomes and progress monitoring.

Part II provides detailed lessons for 40 weeks. It also includes an overview of the sequence of activities for the entire year. The lesson plans are divided into two main sections, with 20 weeks of lessons for a fall semester and 20 weeks for a spring semester. Each week's lesson plans include a suggested newsletter for parents about the upcoming week's activities; the overall weekly plan, including a list of suggested props and materials; the daily plan, with suggestions on how to facilitate specific vocabulary, structure, sounds, social skills, concepts, and motor skills; and specific activity plans for each day's dramatic play, art, and group lessons.

The last section of the book, Part III, contains two appendixes and a bibliography of the children's stories used in the lesson plans. Appendix A has blank forms for curriculum planning so that programs can adapt the lessons to meet the specific needs of their children. These forms include a monthly calendar guide, a weekly planning guide, a daily planning guide, and activity plans for dramatic play, art, and group activities. Appendix B contains a blank version of the Learning Observation Guide tool described in Chapter 5. The bibliography of children's books follows Appendix B.

REFERENCES

Bunce, B.H. (1995). *Building a language-focused curriculum for the preschool classroom: A planning guide* (Vol. II). Baltimore: Paul H. Brookes Publishing Co.

Bunce, B. (1998, March). *Implementing naturalistic language intervention.* Paper presented at the Cimarron Conference on Communication Disorders, Okalahoma State University, Stillwater.

Bunce, B. (1999, April). *Using a language-focused curriculum in a preschool classroom.* Paper presented at the Core Knowledge National Conference, Orlando, FL.

Bunce, B.H. (2003). Children with culturally diverse backgrounds. In L. McCormick, D. Frome-Loeb, & R. Schiefelbusch (Eds.), *Early language intervention: Supporting children in inclusive settings* (2nd ed., pp. 367–407). Boston: Allyn & Bacon.

Bunce, B.H., Rice, M.L., & Wilcox, K.A. (2000, October). *Language Acquisition Preschool update: Celebrating 15 years of curriculum development, intervention, research, and training.* Paper presented at the Kansas Speech-Language-Hearing Association Convention, Wichita.

Dickinson, D.K., & Tabors, P.O. (Eds.). (2001). *Beginning literacy with language: Young children learning at home and school.* Baltimore: Paul H. Brookes Publishing Co.

Guralnick, M.J. (1997). *The effectiveness of early intervention.* Baltimore: Paul H. Brookes Publishing Co.

Hadley, P.A., & Rice, M.L. (1993). Parental judgments of preschoolers' speech and language development: A resource for assessment and IEP planning. *Seminars in Speech and Language, 14,* 278–288.

Rice, M.L. (1993). "Don't talk to him: He's weird": A social consequences account of language and social interactions. In A.P. Kaiser & D.B. Gray (Eds.), *Enhancing children's communication: Research foundations for intervention* (pp. 139–158). Baltimore: Paul H. Brookes Publishing Co.

Rice, M.L. (1995). Creating a language-focused curriculum for preschool children. In M.L. Rice & K.A. Wilcox (Eds.), *Building a language-focused curriculum for the preschool classroom: A foundation for lifelong communication* (Vol. I). Baltimore: Paul H. Brookes Publishing Co.

Rice, M.L. (1998, May). *Preschool language intervention in group settings: Principles, practices, and precedents.* Paper presented at the Speech Pathology Australia National Conference, Perth.

Rice, M.L., & Wilcox, K.A. (Eds.). (1995). *Building a language-focused curriculum for the preschool classroom: A foundation for lifelong communication* (Vol. I). Baltimore: Paul H. Brookes Publishing Co.

Rice, M.L., Wilcox, K.A., Bunce, B.H., & Liebhaver, G.K. (1989, October). *LAP: A model preschool for language disordered and ESL children.* Paper presented at the Kansas Speech-Language-Hearing Association meeting, Lawrence.

Snow, C.E., Burns, M.S., & Griffin, P. (Eds.). (1998). *Preventing reading difficulties in young children.* Washington, DC: National Academies Press.

Stipek, D., Feiler, R., Bykler, P., Ryan, R., Milburn, S., & Salmon, S.M. (1998). Good beginnings: What differences does a program make in preparing young children for school? *Journal of Applied Developmental Psychology, 67*(2), 153–167.

Watkins, R.V., & Bunce, B.H. (1996). Natural literacy: Theory and practice for preschool intervention programs. *Topics in Early Childhood Special Education, 6*(2), 191–212.

Acknowledgments

This book could not have been developed without the support of many people. I acknowledge the contributions of my colleagues, graduate students, and of course the children who participated in the field testing of the activities. In particular, I thank Mabel Rice, Kim Wilcox, Neil Kinsey, Jane Wegner, and Laura Justice for their continuing support of the language-focused curriculum and of the Language Acquisition Preschool. I also want to thank my colleagues at USD 497 for their participation and support. The children have taught all of us much about how to implement a language-focused curriculum. We pass this knowledge on to you.

I

Foundations of the Language-Focused Curriculum

This section includes five chapters addressing different aspects of the language-focused curriculum (LFC). In Chapter 1, the general philosophy and underlying assumptions of the curriculum are described. In addition, basic assumptions regarding children's learning are outlined. The curriculum supports the concept that children construct their own knowledge with the facilitation of adults or more competent peers in an environment designed to foster learning. In Chapter 2, the curriculum structure is presented. Major components of the LFC structure involve classification of both teacher-led and child-centered activities. There are activities that occur routinely and activities that change daily. Emphasis is given to implementing daily child-centered dramatic play activities. This chapter concludes with a detailed schedule that outlines goals and implementation of different types of daily activities. In Chapter 3, the focus is on the provision of speech and language intervention in a classroom setting. Definitions and descriptions of language-facilitating intervention techniques are provided. Examples from children enrolled in the Language Acquisition Preschool (LAP) are used to illustrate the way speech and language therapy can be embedded into daily classroom activities. Chapter 4 describes the training of teachers to use the LFC. This training occurred at the University of Virginia as part of a research project under the direction of Laura Justice. Finally, Chapter 5 discusses some of the ways the children's progress was monitored in the LAP, as well as some of the outcomes from research completed at the University of Kansas.

General Philosophy of the Language-Focused Curriculum

It is Construction Worker Day in the preschool classroom. During center time, several children are in the dramatic play area wearing hard hats and tool belts. Some children are pounding wooden pegs into the cardboard extensions attached to the playhouse. Others are using plastic saws or screwdrivers or building with cardboard bricks. Still other children are playing in the manipulative area with cars, trucks, miniature toys, LEGOs, or Bristle Blocks. Some children have chosen to paint pictures in the art area, and others are looking at books or doing puzzles in the quiet area or participating in the writing center.

At center time, the children choose the activities they wish to participate in as well as the level of that participation. The adults' role is to encourage children to participate in an activity and to support that participation. In addition, adults provide appropriate language facilitation and other supports to promote successful interaction among children and to increase children's learning of vocabulary, linguistic structure, speech sound productions, cognitive concepts, and motor and literacy skills.

This is a scenario from a classroom using the LFC. The emphasis on language in this curriculum relates to a fundamental belief that oral language skills support important development in cognitive and social skills as well as literacy skills. Therefore, this curriculum not only focuses on the development of language skills but also provides many opportunities for social, cognitive, emergent literacy, and motor skill development. An individual lesson or activity may facilitate the development of several of these areas simultaneously, and the embedded nature of the activities in the language-focused curriculum encourages optimal development in children.

The curriculum is designed for 3- to 5-year-old children. Children are viewed as active learners who construct their own knowledge. Teachers, speech-language pathologists, and other staff teach or facilitate learning by providing an environment and opportunities that encourage children to explore and experiment with materials and procedures. Children's responses are not viewed as right or wrong; rather, they are analyzed to provide information for further experimentation and refinement of skills. Teachers also teach by modeling, providing feedback, and interacting with children both verbally and nonverbally. They also encourage children to learn from their peers through interaction and observation.

The LFC, developed at the LAP at the University of Kansas, was designed for 4 half days per week. The activities provided in this volume are for a 4-day week; however, the curriculum can be easily adapted to 3 or 5 days per week. In LAP, there are two sessions each day, with children enrolled in either the morning or the afternoon session. The classroom includes children with speech and language impairments, children developing language typically, and children learning English as a second language. Eighteen to 20 children attend each session, with each of these three groups of children approximately equally represented.

Language intervention is provided in a least restrictive environment during natural interactions in the classroom setting. The LFC is based on the belief that the most effective language teaching occurs throughout the entire curriculum. All children are viewed as candidates for language enhancement, and language teaching is most effective when it focuses on the interests of individual children. The challenge to adults is to embed targeted linguistic forms (e.g., grammar terms, sounds, vocabulary) in naturally occurring interactions so that language input is functional for the child. Adults must convey the targeted linguistic forms without being obtrusive or violating children's communicative intent. On a more specific level, targeted therapy structures for children with speech and language impairments are implemented and negotiated with the children during daily classroom activities.

The LAP's classroom staff consists of a teacher who is also a speech-language pathologist, an assistant teacher with early childhood training, and speech-language clinicians in training. Although the clinicians add to the adult–child ratio, the curriculum is designed for implementation by two qualified personnel. It is possible to have other professionals, such as occupational therapists, also provide therapy in the classroom. This LFC model has been adapted to other settings, including those for children with multiple disabilities (Bunce et al., 1995).

ASSUMPTIONS ABOUT CHILDREN AND LANGUAGE LEARNING

Rice (1998) has described a model of specific language learning principles that guide the language-focused curriculum. This model is called the concentrated normative model (CNM). The concentrated aspect relates to the specific emphasis placed on language and the highlighting of specific language skills. The normative aspect of the model emphasizes the developmental potential of young children. The operational guidelines for the model are as follows:

1. *Language intervention is best provided in a meaningful social context.* This type of environment is most likely to generate meaningful language that a child can generalize to other settings. This guideline suggests that language teaching should take place in a classroom with a number of children interacting with one another as well as with adults.

2. *Language facilitation occurs throughout the entire preschool curriculum.* Rather than isolate language teaching into a special activity time, adults should encourage children's communication during a variety of activities, and different activities should be constructed to elicit different kinds of competencies.

3. *The language curriculum is rooted in content themes.* A general theme allows for consistency in the topic of conversation and a coherence of cognitive constructs. For example, if the theme for the week is construction, individual activities might focus on various ways of building things, the people who build, what people build with, and so forth. This topic can be addressed, for example, in play materials, art activities, and storybooks for consistency and continuity across a day's activities.

4. *Language begins with the child.* Language instruction is most effective when it is child centered and child initiated. This guideline is an extension of the belief that children are not *taught* language but construct it from their daily experiences. (This principle will be elaborated on later in this chapter.)

5. *Verbal interaction is encouraged.* Children have many opportunities to practice their language skills in real interactions with other children and adults. The curriculum provides many opportunities for talking and much to talk about.

6. *Nonovert language learning and overt responses are encouraged.* Children do not need to practice out loud while they are working out new linguistic rules. In fact, much

of their initial comprehension may occur with few external signs of new knowledge. Therefore, it is not necessary for children to always respond to a teacher's input.

7. *Children's utterances are accorded functional value.* If children's utterances are treated as meaningful attempts to communicate, they are more likely to achieve that status.

8. *Valuable learning can arise from child–child interactions.* Therefore, children are provided with ample opportunities to interact with one another spontaneously. For example, a child's negotiation with another child for a favorite toy offers a meaningful occasion for learning how to ask politely or how to justify one's needs. It can make a big difference whether a child says, "Gimme that" or "If you let me have that, I'll let you play with my new truck." The authenticity of this kind of learning situation is nearly impossible to simulate in adult–child interactions.

9. *Parents are valuable partners in language programming.* Parents are the most important people in young children's lives, and they are the most powerful catalysts of communication development. Therefore, parents should be part of the teaching team. This does not mean that they should be language trainers in the conventional sense. If adults do not teach that way in the classroom, they should not expect parents to practice drill material at home. Rather, parents can help teachers and therapists understand children's interests and family activities, which can then be incorporated into classroom discussions and activities.

10. *Routine parent evaluations are an integral part of the LFC.* A parent evaluation form can be generated and used as a structured way to collect parental input. In addition, parent notebooks facilitate ongoing communication with staff members. Parents are also encouraged to meet with staff members if they have concerns or questions. Two formal parent group meetings are scheduled each year to address parental concerns. Individual conferences are also scheduled each year, providing opportunities for parents to evaluate the program as well as their child's progress. Also, the children present a program at the end of each semester for the parents. This allows the parents to enjoy their child's accomplishments and to meet informally with one another.

These principles affect how adults provide intervention for children with speech and language impairments. For example, in the LAP, intervention is provided in the classroom. A variety of intervention techniques are described in Chapter 3. These techniques emphasize following children's interests and providing models and focused contrasts of targeted language structures, which may be sounds, specific grammatical structures, vocabulary words, or appropriate conversational skills with peers. In addition, in their interactions with children, adults expand or recast children's utterances in a naturalistic manner to provide additional models of the target forms and content. More than one child may be involved in these interactions. For example, as two children play with a ball, the adult might model the "is verbing" structure several times as the play proceeds (e.g., "Jasmine is rolling the ball"; "Look, Sara is bouncing the ball. She is bouncing it high"). The children hear the structure that is describing their own actions. Many models can be provided within a typically occurring activity without disrupting the activity. Opportunities for children to respond to these models are given, but verbal responses are not required. This child-centered intervention uses naturally occurring interactions to provide the focus and content of the intervention.

This style of interaction contrasts with the traditional therapy session, which involves one adult and one child with the adult providing the content and focus of the therapy. Typically, the adult models the language structure for the child, has the child respond, and then judges the correctness of the child's response. For example, the focus of the therapy may be to improve production of the "is verbing" structure (e.g., *is walking*). The adult might present action pictures and ask the child to describe the pictures; the adult may or may not model the answer for the child. The child responds and the adult then acknowledges whether the response is correct or incorrect. Some children have difficulty staying on task in this situation; others may learn to respond to the pictures but not to use the structure in conversational speech.

Although it is possible to provide child-centered therapy in one-to-one settings, it is more difficult. For example, a therapist in a one-to-one therapy session out of the classroom may follow the child's topic of conversation, but there are fewer activities for the child to choose from in such a setting than in the classroom setting. Also, there are usually only two participants, the adult and the child, so additional input from a peer is not available. To a great degree, the traditional therapy model assumes that language acquisition is adult directed. We believe, however, that language development is child directed and that it is the job of the teacher and/or speech-language pathologist to maximize the opportunities for a child to discover how language works.

ADDITIONAL GUIDELINES UNDERLYING THE LANGUAGE-FOCUSED CURRICULUM

There are several other guidelines that underlie or expand on the principles on which the language-focused curriculum is based. Although described here as independent concepts, these guidelines are interrelated and are part of a philosophy that views the child's role as knowledge constructor and the teacher's role as facilitator of the constructive process.

Supporting the Development of Language and Communication

For a curriculum to support the development of language and communication skills, opportunities for both child–child and child–adult communication must exist. Curriculum activities must allow for a variety of conversational interactions with a number of participants on topics of interest to the children. A highly directive environment in which children are expected to listen and not talk for extended periods of time is not conducive to facilitating a full range of language and communication skills. When children are allowed to choose their activities and play partners, such as during center times, a number of communication opportunities arise. Other typical activities, such as snack time, outdoor play, and sharing time, can also be effective in stimulating communicative interactions.

Using Developmentally Appropriate Activities

Providing opportunities to interact is just the first step in developing a program to facilitate language and learning. Developmentally appropriate activities are needed to provide a framework for these interactions and to enhance children's language, cognitive, motor, and personal/social skills. Developmentally appropriate activities for 3- to 5-year-old children encourage children to learn through active exploration of materials and settings. This exploration may involve both verbal and physical manipulations. Hands-on, experiential manipulations of materials rather than paper-and-pencil tasks are important for this age group. For instance, dramatic play, manipulation of blocks and puzzles, experimentation with art and other materials, and interactive story reading are appropriate activities to foster cognitive, language, literacy, social, and motor skills. As children actively engage in an activity, the teacher provides scaffolding (i.e., the framework and support for the activity). Scaffolding may take a variety of forms, which vary in the amount of support provided. Providing examples, materials, situations, comments, and demonstrations are all effective methods of scaffolding.

Respecting Individual Differences

Individual differences among children are viewed as positive. Each child has a unique contribution to make to the classroom, an ideal that is fostered by providing a supportive environment that allows children to express their own personalities and interests. All children have their own learning style and rate of learning, and each is provided opportunities to learn in the way most helpful to him or her. Not all children are expected to do every activity or to carry out activities in the same manner. Likewise, family and cultural differences are respected. Family contributions to the curriculum are encouraged and vary widely according to individual preferences.

Fostering Children's Self-Esteem

Children's self-esteem is valued; its growth is fostered in the classroom by giving children as much control over their participation in activities as possible. During center time and outdoor playtime, children can choose the activities they want to participate in. They can also decide to what degree they will engage in these activities. This includes the right to be passive participants, although children's participation in new activities is encouraged and supported by teachers. Activities can be modified to help children achieve success; each successful activity builds children's confidence in their abilities and fosters a willingness to try other new activities. Further encouragement toward competence is provided throughout the day by allowing children to, for instance, get a drink of water whenever they are thirsty, pour more juice for themselves at snack time, and attend to toileting needs without teacher direction or permission. However, teacher support is readily available when needed. During transitions between activities, children are expected to entertain themselves independently. For example, some children finish their snacks more quickly than others. If they are finished, they may read books or work on puzzles in the quiet area while they wait for others to finish. This enables children to make choices and exercise self-control. All of these opportunities help children become self-confident and competent individuals who can take care of their own needs.

Emphasizing Child-Centered Activities

For children to construct their own knowledge, child-centered activities must be a primary focus of the curriculum. In the LAP, approximately two thirds of the school day is devoted to child-centered activities. These activities take place during arrival, center time, and outdoor playtime. During child-centered activities, children play an active role in choosing and directing their activities. The teacher goes to where the children are engaged rather than calling the children to come to him or her. Therefore, the teacher follows the children's lead and joins their activities. The teacher may step out of an interaction when facilitation is no longer needed or to interact with another child or group of children. Often, the teacher may be following the lead of several children as they play together, drawing different children into an interaction when appropriate. For example, if several children are building a house, the teacher might hand a block to a child who is standing nearby and watching the others play. By giving the child an appropriate prop, the teacher assists the child in joining the group. In this manner, interactions among children are encouraged. There are usually many child–child, as well as teacher–child, interactions during child-centered activities.

Facilitating Learning Through Teacher-Led Group Activities

Teacher-led activities are also important in facilitating language and learning. During these activities, the teacher engages the attention of a group of children at various times throughout the day for approximately 10 minutes at a time. In the LAP, these activities occur during circle time, storytime, sharing time, large- and small-group time, and music time (see Chapter 2 for a sample daily schedule). Some of these activities involve daily events (e.g., roll call during circle time); others involve the presentation of new information (e.g., classifying according to shape or learning about a particular letter–sound correspondence during group time). In these group activities, the teacher gives children explicit instructions on when to talk and when to listen. Even though the teacher is more directive during these group activities, the children do participate in the interactions with verbal and nonverbal initiations (e.g., questions, body movements) and responses to the teacher.

Advocating the Process of Learning

Activities are designed to be process oriented rather than product oriented. This means that children's learning is more important than the evidence of that learning. For example, children's experimentation with materials to make an art project outweighs the importance of how the finished project looks. However, as children experiment and practice—whether with art materials or language—the form of the production usually improves. Errors are not viewed as requiring immediate correction but rather as stages in the learning process. Most activities and materials offered in the classroom are open ended, offering children greater opportunities for exploration and creation. Materials with a single purpose, such as worksheets, are not well suited to a process-oriented program. Again, the teacher's role is not to transmit knowledge that must be portrayed in a certain way; rather, the teacher facilitates children's construction of their own knowledge.

Fostering the Natural Development of Language and Literacy

In the language-focused classroom, children's understanding of the relationships between language and literacy are fostered through naturally occurring activities. Rather than requiring children to memorize the alphabet, practice writing their names on a worksheet, or learn phonics, teachers provide opportunities for children to learn these skills in the context of everyday activities. For example, children learn to recognize their names during roll call or from labels on their coat cubbies. They learn the letters of the alphabet by singing a song and later by pairing the letters in the song to the alphabet letters displayed in the room. Still later, children begin to recognize the individual letters in their names, as well as in the names of their classmates, as they see these names displayed on artwork and snack or attendance charts. During dramatic play activities, children may note words on pretend canned goods, make shopping lists by copying words, "read" to their babies, take telephone messages, and practice many other literacy skills. After repeated readings of a story, children often are able to retell it accurately and begin to recognize individual words. The children have access to writing materials and may "write" words, letters, and stories. Invented spelling is accepted, although correct spelling is modeled on signs, labels, children's name cards, and so forth. After special activities, such as a field trip to the fire station, a group story is often written describing the activity. In these ways, language and literacy relationships are formed naturally, with children's interests being the primary driving force (see Watkins & Bunce, 1996, for a description of natural literacy activities combining both phonological awareness and whole-language orientations).

Encouraging the Natural Development of Inquiry and Math Concepts

Inquiry and mathematical skills are facilitated in much the same manner as language and literacy relationships. Opportunities for observing, manipulating, and experimenting with objects and events occur during daily activities and routines. The teacher's role is to facilitate children's ability to observe, question, manipulate, and experiment. For example, children might test the ability of objects to roll during outdoor playtime with balls and tricycles and during center time with art materials, such as cardboard tubes, beads, and round macaroni wheels, or with round and tubular wooden blocks. Children's understanding of counting and number concepts can be fostered during calendar time, when each day's date is discussed, or during child-centered activities, when manipulatives can be counted. Snack time is a particularly good time to foster one-to-one matching and number concepts as crackers and juice are distributed to each child. Simple addition concepts can be taught as children have seconds on the crackers. They can take two or three more crackers, adding them to the ones they already have. Simple subtraction concepts can be taught as the children eat their crackers (e.g., first they had five crackers, then they ate one, and now they have four). Other concepts, such as size and shape or quantity (e.g., more or less), can be incorporated naturally throughout the curricular activities.

Viewing Parents as Central to the Program

Close communication with children's families is important for a variety of reasons. First, families are the primary social agents for children. As such they are the most knowledgeable about their children's communicative interests and needs. Parents (or other primary caregivers) and teachers provide one another with important information about children's needs and progress. Second, the transfer of skills learned in the classroom to other settings can be fostered by knowledgeable parents and other family members. This means that parents and family members should be aware of children's activities and help foster the skills in the home and in other settings outside the program.

Close communication between school and family can be achieved in a variety of ways. Parents and teachers may have daily contact when a child is dropped off and picked up at the school or center. They may also hold conferences, both in person and over the telephone. A third way to communicate is through a newsletter specifying the curricular activities for each week (see the newsletters at the beginning of each set of weekly plans in Section II). These communications help ensure that parents are aware of what is *going* to happen rather than what has already occurred. This means that they can ask their children specific questions about their day rather than a general "What did you do today?" (and receive the typical answer: "Nothing!"). This can help them facilitate their children's talk about their activities. They can ask such questions as "How did you make the pudding?" and "What does a vet do?" Parents of children with speech and language impairments can exchange information with speech-language personnel in many of these same ways—personal contact, telephone calls, notes describing weekly progress at school or at home—as well as through individualized education program (IEP) meetings and/or progress reports at the end of each semester.

OVERALL GUIDELINES FOR CLASSROOM MANAGEMENT

There are several strategies that can foster good classroom environment. These strategies range from having a defined schedule of activities, varying the types of activities, having an established routine, and supporting interactions between children and between children and adults. In addition, minimizing wait time between activities is especially important because of children's relatively short attention spans.

Use a Schedule of Activities

A schedule of activities lends structure to the curriculum and helps children know what to expect and how to behave. A well-paced combination of teacher-led and child-centered activities prevents children from having to sit still for long periods of time and maintains their interest in learning. Interested, motivated children who are active in their own learning are less likely to misbehave than those who are bored or disinterested. It is also important in developing a schedule to consider such factors as when children need to have a snack, change activities, and move around. For example, having snack time just after outdoor play provides children with replenishing food and drink after being active, a time to calm down after strenuous outdoor play, and important maintenance of energy. Scheduling music at the end of the day provides an opportunity for the children to express themselves through songs and motions. It is an activity in which all children can participate, and the day can end on a positive note.

Provide a Variety of Activities

To accommodate different children's interests and abilities, a variety of activities should be available during both teacher-led and child-centered activities. Children who are interested in and willing to try an activity will learn from their participation. Children who can succeed at an activity are more likely to want to continue that activity and to talk about it.

Those who have difficulty with an activity, on the other hand, may become bored and frustrated. By having alternative activities available, all children are able to find something that interests them. This variety also facilitates classroom management, as children who are actively involved in learning are less likely to need redirection.

It is also important to provide for a variety of levels of participation within an activity, particularly during teacher-led group activities for which all children may not have the same level of knowledge. For example, during a sequencing activity involving different colored patterns, one child may be asked to match a model; another child may be asked to continue the pattern (e.g., two red blocks, two green blocks, two red blocks). Still other children might be asked to recreate the pattern from memory. All of these activities involve sequencing based on color, yet the demands of each task vary. With varying task demands, children at different levels are more likely to attend to the task and to succeed.

An example of varying task levels during child-centered activities is the number and kind of centers offering different levels of participation. A child can play alone with a known toy, book, or art activity, or the child can play with others in the dramatic play area.

Establish Routines

Routines for classroom management are helpful for both children and teachers. Routines help children predict what will happen next. After they have learned a routine, they know what to do without much teacher direction. Teachers can then attend to individual children without having to give constant direction to all. Visual schedules and social stories, originally developed for use with children with autism, may be helpful for other young children—particularly those with language impairments—in learning classroom routines. (See Quill, 1997, for descriptions of visual schedules and other visual strategies for understanding classroom routines and activities; see Gray, 2003, for the use and development of social stories.)

The ability to follow a routine also helps children develop self-discipline and competence. Picking up toys can be taught during cleanup time by helping children perform the activity until assistance is no longer necessary. These self-help tasks are particularly appealing and helpful for children with speech and language impairments and those who are learning English as a second language because they can be accomplished without any talking. The children can demonstrate nonverbal competence without having to demonstrate verbal competence. The competence displayed by children in attending to their own needs also helps in classroom management.

Observe and Join in Children's Play

To fully understand children's interests and capabilities, adults need to observe children's interactions with materials and one another. They can then support children's interests and skills by providing language or other input and additional materials. After observing, teachers can join children's activity by playing either directly with them or side by side. Joining children's activities allows teachers to help develop children's schema and demonstrate additional ways of interacting or playing with an object. Playing with or alongside children also shows interest in them and gives adults a way to provide language or other input.

When interacting with children, adults should place themselves on the children's level. Doing so shows children that the adults are interested in what they are saying and doing. It also helps the adults understand the children's perspective.

Staff can extend children's focus by demonstrating additional ways to play with the items they are interested in. Some children may need support or modeling from an adult or a peer to manipulate objects in a more advanced way (e.g., stacking or sequencing blocks) or to extend a dramatic play experience. Also, the additional input may provide children the needed confidence to try new things.

Child–child interactions should also be encouraged. Some children have difficulty responding to or initiating interaction with other children and may need adults' support in joining the play of others and in making friends. Also, children may learn as much (or more) from child models as they do from adult models.

Help Children Know How to Act During Teacher-Led Activities

When conducting teacher-led activities, teachers can use a variety of techniques to attract and maintain children's attention. For example, they might develop a routine to have children gather for or leave circle time, have children sit where others will not distract them, focus on or comment positively on children's behavior, use eye contact and body language to help children stay focused, and vary the tempo and pitch of their voice during the activity. Children can be easily distracted and need help in knowing how to listen in a group activity. Attracting their attention helps them focus.

In a teacher-led group activity, children should be encouraged, though not demanded, to raise their hand before the adult responds to them. Children ages 3–5 are just learning these types of school conventions and procedures. They may forget what they wanted to say and stop responding if they have to remember to raise their hand first. Typically, the form of raising hands is secondary to the concept being taught. When more than one child wants to respond, the teacher can use a hand signal or sign to indicate to some children to wait while the teacher verbally calls on another child. This helps children understand that the teacher is aware that they want to respond, and they may be more willing to wait their turn.

Adults should vary the way they ask children to respond. For example, one child might respond nonverbally by pointing, while another child might respond only verbally. Children attend better when they cannot predict when they will need to respond. Also, more children might participate if they can respond nonverbally at first. Calling on children in a random fashion instead of going around a circle in order may help keep the children's attention.

Minimize Wait Time

Minimizing wait time is also important in classroom management. Children respond differently to transitions and move at different paces. Those who are quick to comply should not be punished by waiting aimlessly for those who are slower. For example, instead of having all children wait at the snack table until everyone has finished, staff should let the children clean up their place as they finish eating and then get a book to read. If children are waiting in line, teachers can initiate fingerplays or songs.

All of the underlying guidelines discussed in this chapter regarding language learning, curriculum development, and classroom management influence how a classroom using an LFC is conducted. The preschool child is an active learner, and classroom routine and structure must support the constructive process of active learning. Specific details on the structure of the curriculum used in the LAP are outlined in Chapter 2.

Curriculum Structure
for Naturalistic Learning

The basic principles of the LFC discussed in the previous chapter help shape the classroom structure. This chapter outlines the general types of activities included in the LFC structure. General lesson formats for child-centered and teacher-led activities are also described. (Specific details about lesson plans and ways to develop an LFC are given in Section II.) A major focus of the curriculum structure is the center time activities, particularly dramatic play. The rationale for including dramatic play activities is discussed in detail in this chapter, followed by descriptions of the other major daily activities and the roles of both children and adults during activities. This chapter also provides a brief description of how emergent literacy activities are embedded within both child-centered and teacher-led activities and how adults can facilitate language and learning. A sample schedule and a description of activities typically used in the LAP illustrate the overall structure of the LFC.

GENERAL CATEGORIES OF ACTIVITIES

The LFC was created before some of the research was done on child-initiated learning and instruction and on balancing direct and indirect teaching styles. However, several articles and program reviews of the type of structure and activities used in the LFC have subsequently supported their use (see Schweinhart & Weikart, 1988, on the importance of child-initiated learning; Stipek et al., 1998, for a comparison of direct instruction versus child-initiated instruction; and Connor, Morrison, & Slominski, 2006, on the importance of teacher–child managed learning and providing a balance of explicit and implicit learning activities).

Activities in the LFC can be categorized as those that change daily (or frequently) and those that are routine. In addition, each of the activities can be categorized as primarily either child centered or teacher led. For example, a dramatic play activity typically changes daily and is primarily child centered (e.g., playing construction workers). The group activity also may change daily but is teacher led (e.g., a classification activity). Sharing time is a routine activity that is teacher led, whereas snack time is a routine activity that is child centered. Sharing is a show-and-tell activity that follows a prescribed format wherein the teacher assists one child to ask another child questions about an object. Table 2.1 illustrates possible cross-categorization of the different activities.

Changing versus Routine Activities

It is important to have both activities that change and activities that are routine. The activities that change daily provide new information to the children and enable them to learn new concepts, vocabulary, and language structure. They challenge children's cognitive, language, social, and motor skills. They also are interesting to children because of their

Table 2.1. Classification of activities

	Teacher led	Child centered
Change daily	Small/large group time Storytime Music time	Dramatic play Art/Science
Routine	Circle time Sharing time	Arrival time Snack time Outside time Block/manipulative area Quiet area

novelty. Routine activities, on the other hand, provide known structure and a level of comfort for children. The children know what to expect from the routine activities and can predict what they are expected to do or say. These activities allow them to practice skills within a known format. Many children with speech and language impairments and those who are learning English as a second language will first begin to participate verbally during routine activities, such as sharing time or snack time, when functional language forms are similar from day to day. A balance of both kinds of activities is needed to provide an appropriate learning environment for all children.

Child-Centered versus Teacher-Led Activities

It is also necessary to have a balance between activities that are child centered and those that are teacher led. Child-centered activities allow children to focus on their own interests. As adults talk about what children are doing, children hear language describing their own activities and are more likely to talk about the activities. Children's own language is also more likely to be understood if they are talking about something they are doing. This is particularly important when children's speech is difficult to understand. Teachers (or other children) will more readily understand what a child is saying when the talk is focused on the child's own activity. Also, children who are interested in an activity are more likely to stay on task and persist even if difficulties arise.

However, it is also essential to help children make new discoveries and teach them new information. Teacher-led activities allow teachers to present new concepts and build on what children already know. Although adults control the pace during teacher-led activities, children are encouraged to participate, and they learn to listen and follow directions. Often, children incorporate concepts that have been introduced in a teacher-led activity into their own child-centered activities.

GENERAL FORMAT OF ACTIVITIES

A variety of child-centered activities and teacher-led activities are scheduled during each preschool day. Typically the day starts with a brief child-centered time during arrival and then shifts to a teacher-led circle time. This alternation of activities continues throughout the day with the longest period of time (center time and outdoor play) being child centered.

Child-Centered Activities

During child-centered activities, children are free to choose the activities in which they want to participate. They also are free to choose their level of participation, which may range from observing the play of others to actively interacting with materials and peers. Teachers act as facilitators during child-centered activities. In this role, teachers must be aware of each child's level of competence and provide appropriate structure and materials; they must also be ready to change the structure, materials, or activities based on a child's interest and needs. Supporting a child's interest may involve finding needed extra materials and/or helping children problem-solve.

Teacher-Led Activities

A general format usually guides teacher-led activities so children know what is expected. For example, circle time typically begins with a standard roll call and ends with a description of upcoming center activities. Storytime consists of a brief discussion of the title and what the story might be about before the story is read.

To begin teacher-led group activities, the teacher presents an introductory task. This may be done by giving a demonstration (e.g., showing a videotape, manipulating an object). The teacher may also introduce a task by posing a problem, either verbally ("Does a nail float?") or by demonstration (e.g., showing that an object will not fit into another if turned a particular way). Interaction between the children and teacher (or between two children) then develops the concept through the children's manipulation and exploration of the task. The children respond by suggesting solutions or answers, which are then tried by the teacher or other children. The teacher encourages the children to make predictions, try new ideas, and demonstrate their knowledge both verbally and nonverbally. Finally, when appropriate, the group completes a brief summary task or project.

This general format can be used with a variety of group activities. For instance, the group may act out a story, perform a science experiment, or recite the alphabet. (See Section II for specific group lesson plans.)

USE OF DRAMATIC PLAY ACTIVITIES

Dramatic play activities form a basis for the LFC because they facilitate language, literacy, social, and cognitive development, as explained in this section.

Fostering Language Skills

Several scholars (e.g., French, Lucariello, Seidman, & Nelson, 1985; Pellegrini, 1984; Pellegrini & Galda, 2000) have noted that dramatic play activities can facilitate preschool children's language abilities, particularly in the production of imaginative language, the use of pronouns, and the use of displaced references (i.e., talking about objects or actions not present in the environment—"then and there" topics). French et al. also noted that in non-scripted play settings (e.g., playing with blocks), children's language usually focused on object talk and discussions about objects and actions taking place in the "here and now." Non-scripted play settings, then, involve play where there is no specific event structure or overarching sequence of actions, actors, or props to represent a specific context or goal. Scripted play involves a representation of an event with an ordered sequence of actions organized around a goal. There are usually actors, actions, and props. For example, children may have a script for playing school or going out to eat. This way the children know what actions might occur, the sequence of the actions, typical props used, and the main actors.

Lucariello, Kyratzis, and Engel (1986) suggested that children can learn new syntactic and semantic forms to perform the same function when acting out a script. This may be because the language is embedded in a familiar routine. For example, many children have watched their parents place an order and pay in a fast-food restaurant and therefore they are able to reproduce this in play. Likewise, when a grocery store theme is used in play, children are familiar with pushing a cart, choosing items, and paying for these items. The new language knowledge in turn may facilitate the development of new script knowledge. Vedeler (1997) noted that in her study, the children's language was more advanced syntactically and there was use of more explicit references (vocabulary) in dramatic play activities than in any other play activity. Although most of these studies have involved typically developing children, evidence suggests that the use of scripts and/or routines may facilitate the development of language abilities in children with language impairments as well (e.g., Constable, 1986; Goldstein & Cisar, 1992; Lederer, 2002).

New vocabulary terms can be made understandable to children within the dramatic play context. For example, the term *archaeologist* might not be a term children are typically exposed to, but it becomes understandable when they are pretending to go on a archaeological dig as part of a weekly theme on exploration. Instead of being directly taught in isolation, the term is used in context. Though children may not fully understand a term, with its repeated use within a context their knowledge about a concept can be further developed. (See Dickinson, 1984, and Dickinson & Tabors, 2001, for information on "rare" words. See Rice,1990, for information on preschoolers' Quick Incidental Learning of Words [QUIL].)

Facilitating Emergent Literacy Skills

Dramatic play activities foster emergent literacy skills in a variety of ways. First, dramatic play expands children's world knowledge, which may help support later reading comprehension. For example, by playing pioneers with pretend covered wagons and horses, children can "travel" to a new area. This may later help children better understand a story such as *Little House on the Prairie*. Dramatic play activities may be particularly instrumental in helping children learn new vocabulary, which also can affect later reading knowledge. Second, a variety of printed materials are often part of a dramatic play activity, such as signs or logos (e.g., from fast-food restaurants), labels (e.g., *grocery store*), sign-in registers (e.g., motel or fitness center activities), and other props (e.g., a typewriter or notebook for an office worker, books for a library). These make children aware of the many uses of literacy in their environment. Sometimes the emergent literacy skills are central to the dramatic play activity, and other times they are more incidental. In any case, teachers can facilitate these skills as children interact with the props and with one another.

Several researchers have investigated the effect of dramatic play activities on developing literacy skills (e.g., Christie & Stone, 1999; Davidson, 1996; Ferguson, 1999; Pellegrini & Galda, 2000; Roskos & Christie, 2000.) Davidson (1996) explained four ways of integrating literacy into a dramatic play activity. One way is to have the dramatic play theme itself focus on a writing or reading activity, such as a newspaper office or a library theme. Second, emergent literacy might be embedded in the activity rather than the major focus. For example, a doctor's office theme might include a receptionist's book for writing down names of patients or a prescription pad for writing prescriptions. These activities are not necessary to the central activity but offer an additional way for children to expand on literacy skills and to recognize literacy in their environment. A third way involves the incidental use of literacy. In this use, the teacher might suggest a literacy activity in response to a child's play. For example, the teacher might suggest that a child make a sign to advertise the child's new artwork at the art show, or that the child "read" to another child when playing "babysitter." The fourth way of integrating literacy into a dramatic play activity is responding when a child initiates the activity. For example, a child might start to write another child a letter while on a pretend trip. The teacher can quickly provide a model or help by spelling requested words.

Encouraging Social Interaction

In addition to language and literacy skills, dramatic play activities encourage social interaction (Lederer, 2002; Sawyer, 1997). As children establish their theme and enact their roles, they talk with each other, play different roles, and interact with many different partners. More talking, particularly among peers, occurs in this area than in the block, art, or quiet areas (Pellegrini, 1984). The dramatic play theme facilitates these conversations among children. There is some indication that if children share a theme or script, the interaction will be sustained longer than in nonscripted interactions, although this view is controversial (Nelson, 1981; Nelson & Seidman, 1984). Nelson suggested that one reason for this is that children may use their understanding of a particular script to guide their social interactions. Also, the interactions are based on real-world scenarios, which may allow for generalization of both linguistic and social interaction skills to and from school and home environments.

Expanding Knowledge and Organizational Skills

Dramatic play activities also allow children to extend the knowledge they gain when observing a script by enacting it themselves (e.g., observing a guest speaker, such as a veterinarian, and then playing at being a veterinarian). Children may acquire a basic structure of a particular script after an initial experience with it. The scripts then become elaborated each time they are repeated (Fivush & Slackman, 1986). Thus, script frameworks may be one way children organize and extend their knowledge. In addition, Bergen (2002) noted that there is a developing body of evidence that high-quality pretend play is important in problem solving and in facilitating perspective taking.

Strengths of Different Types of Dramatic Play Activities

Different dramatic play activities have different strengths for developing language, social, cognitive, and motor skills. Some dramatic play is interactive, with defined roles (e.g., fast-food restaurant). These activities are often rich in verbal exchanges and lend themselves to promoting discourse. Other dramatic play activities may be strong in vocabulary development or classification activities as well as in interaction. For example, a grocery store script lends itself to classification activities (e.g., identifying fruits, meat, cereals) and provides a known theme for interaction. Some dramatic play activities emphasize sequential development of the action. For example, going on a picnic might involve preparing the lunch basket, getting to the park, eating the lunch, and going home. Other dramatic play activities are action oriented and provide many opportunities to practice and develop verb, adverb, and adjective structures. Firefighting and car-racing activities are examples of action-oriented dramatic play. Still other dramatic play activities, such as mechanic or construction play, promote problem solving. In these activities, the adult or child can present a problem to be solved (e.g., how to fix windows, shingle a roof, or put together a car), and all can help find a solution. Finally, some dramatic play activities promote the development of both gross and fine motor skills. Hammering with a plastic hammer to make sure a shingle is glued or turning a plastic screw when building a car are examples of the use of a variety of muscle movements.

It is important to note that within each type of dramatic play some verbal and/or social interaction does take place. Children learn to share desired items and to get their needs met in socially accepted ways. The shy child is supported in interactions with others; often, pretending itself allows the child to experiment with roles and dialogues. Dramatic play activities can entice a child to take a risk to learn by getting involved. In developing dramatic play activities, then, it is important that teachers take advantage of the particular strengths of each type of dramatic play in facilitating language, social, cognitive, and motor skills.

COMPONENTS OF DRAMATIC PLAY

A dramatic play activity has four major components: theme, props, roles, and verbal exchanges.

Theme

It is important that children have a sense of the overall theme involved in a dramatic play activity. If they have no idea what is involved in a particular dramatic play, they will usually choose not to participate. This does not mean, however, that only activities thoroughly familiar to children can be used. It does mean that for unfamiliar themes, more involved introductions may be necessary during circle time before the children take part in the play. This introduction may involve listening to and asking questions of a guest speaker, viewing a brief video clip (e.g., activities on a farm or at a rodeo), reading a story (e.g., about an airplane trip), and/or having adults and, when possible, children act out various roles to illustrate the overall theme.

As children become more familiar with a particular dramatic play activity, they enjoy playing a variety of roles. They know what to expect and can perform the roles. However, children may become so familiar with a particular dramatic play that they become bored with it. Adding novelty to familiar dramatic play often increases children's interest in participating. This novelty can often be achieved by adding new or different props or a new focus to the activity. For example, instead of just fishing, children might go ice fishing or go on a picnic where fishing is just one of the activities.

Props

Props are an important aspect of successful dramatic play activities. They provide contextual support for the dramatic play, help children identify particular roles, and to some extent, define the dramatic play. Props that can be manipulated in some way appear to be the most popular with children. It is not necessary to have actual objects or even miniature representations of the actual objects; however, it is necessary to have objects that can be used to perform the appropriate functions. It is also important that props have the distinctive features of the objects they are being used to symbolize. For example, a chair with a man's tie can become a car with a seatbelt, particularly if a Frisbee (or a round plastic lid) is used as a steering wheel. A seat, a seatbelt, and a steering wheel form some of the key features of a car. If the car is part of a "mechanic" dramatic play, key features might also include having a hood that can be raised, with some kind of "engine" inside; a box (or actual toy vehicle) with a liftable lid might be used to represent the car. For a dramatic play involving fishing, a fishing pole can be made with a stick and a string with a magnet on the end. Children use the magnet to catch paper fish, each of which has a metal paper clip attached. Having the fish in a container or on a blue area (e.g., a blanket) to define a lake or pond adds to the reality of the dramatic play activity.

The use of objects to represent other objects in dramatic play often adds to the fun. One child might use a toilet paper tube as a flashlight. It becomes a flashlight because it is so designated and because the child uses it that way. The use of props in this way fosters imaginative play. Props also provide motivation and interest. Sometimes a child will be drawn into play interactions because of the props. For example, the opportunity to experiment with a typewriter or computer keyboard may entice a child to be part of an "office" dramatic play.

Props also stimulate the need for negotiation. A favorite prop will often need to be shared. Teachers and/or peers can model specific ways to get access to a favorite object, which helps children expand their ability to get their needs met. Over the course of the semester or year, children can repeatedly practice their verbal negotiation skills in getting a turn using various props.

Roles

Another component in a dramatic play activity is the number of different roles that can be assumed. In most dramatic play activities, there are a variety of roles available. For example, when playing "house" there might be parents, children, neighbors, and pets. "Doctor" play might involve doctors, nurses, parents, sick children, receptionists, and so forth. Having a variety of roles in a particular dramatic play is important because it allows several children to play together and promotes the use of a variety of linguistic structures. It also allows children to change roles and switch identities. Children can elaborate on a particular role and even extend the dramatic play. For example, playing house may extend to going shopping to obtain food to cook for supper. The roles of cashier and other grocery store personnel can then be added. We have found that at least 3–4 roles or activities must be present for a sustained dramatic play.

Verbal Exchanges

The verbal exchanges involved in dramatic play activities are varied. The same role in a particular activity might elicit long, complex sentences from some children and just one word from others. For example, in playing fast-food restaurant, one child cashier might say, "That will be $10 for your hamburger, french fries, and drink," and another child in the same role might just say, "Money." Therefore, children do not have to be able to use multiword sentences to participate in a dramatic play activity. In addition, one child may do primarily nonverbal acting, whereas another child may verbally act out a role. Usually, children will participate in the dramatic play both nonverbally and verbally. For example, when playing "mechanic," a child may pretend to fix a car through actions but will verbally explain to another child why the car will not run. (A common explanation is that it needs a new battery!) Child-produced "sound effects" are common in some dramatic play activities.

Much language facilitation can take place through verbal interactions during dramatic play times. It is through the verbal exchanges that an adult (or another child) may provide models not only for the content and form of language but also for its use. The adult or peer may model the role by using the props and acting the part. For example, an adult may report to the child "mechanic" that something is wrong with his or her car by saying "My car needs to be fixed. I think it needs a new battery." The child might respond nonverbally by pretending to change the battery or verbally by saying something like "Let me look at the car," "Let me get a new battery," "It will take 5 hours," or "I need some tools." The adult can switch roles with the child to provide models for additional types and forms of responses.

IMPLEMENTING DRAMATIC PLAY ACTIVITIES

There are several steps involved in implementing dramatic play activities. First, the activity must be introduced to the children. For this introduction, the teacher may model or act out portions of a dramatic play, including children in the action whenever possible. Videotapes or books may give the children a visual image of an unfamiliar theme, such as a rodeo. Guest speakers, such as parents, may demonstrate activities by using props and actions rather than just telling the children about a topic. For instance, a beautician might use a doll to show how she washes and styles (or even cuts!) hair. Questions from the teachers and children can facilitate the demonstrations. Props to be used in the dramatic play activity should be part of the demonstration whenever a new theme is presented.

Second, props are arranged in the dramatic play area to set the context or scene of the action. An assistant teacher can arrange these props while the children are having circle time, or the props can be arranged earlier. It is usually best to arrange the easily portable props just before center time. We have found it best to have the dramatic play props and area available only during center time. (Other areas, such as the art, block, and quiet centers, can be open during transition times.) A major reason for having the dramatic play activity available only during center time is that the activity typically requires an introduction or demonstration. The main transition time, during which the children play in the other three areas, occurs during arrival time—before the children have been introduced to the dramatic play activity. Also, because the novelty of the activity helps keep the children's interest, it is important that they do not always have access to all of the props all of the time. (For similar reasons, the center time art project is different from the art activities available during arrival time.)

Third, the children develop the theme in a manner meaningful to them. While playing "pizza parlor," for example, a child may pretend to pick up a telephone and order a pizza to be delivered, adding an unplanned dimension to the dramatic play.

Fourth, adults participate in the dramatic play activity by modeling roles while following the children's lead. In the above example, an adult may grab a chair and a paper plate steering wheel to create a delivery car and pretend to be a driver delivering a pizza to a customer.

Fifth, children decide their level of participation in a dramatic play activity—even whether they want to participate at all. A child might observe the dramatic play setting from another area before deciding to become involved in it. Observational learning is encouraged, and overt responses are not required of children. If a dramatic play activity is overwhelming to some children, they must have the option to leave and go to another play center, such as the less threatening book and quiet area. Having the option to leave or to watch an activity gives children control over their participation, which helps them remain motivated to learn.

A variety of accommodations can be made in dramatic play activities for children who use sign language or augmentative and alternative communication (AAC) devices. A list of new sign vocabulary for a particular dramatic play may need to be posted or vocabulary programmed on an AAC device.

OTHER CENTER TIME ACTIVITIES

The three other activities typically available to children during center time are located in the art/science, manipulative or block, and "quiet" areas. A fourth area could be added, consisting of writing materials or computers. The writing area could also be part of the quiet area. As mentioned previously, the dramatic play and art activities change daily, whereas activities in the manipulative, quiet, and writing/computer (if available) areas remain relatively stable. The children, therefore, have a choice of two areas with new activities and 2–3 areas with familiar activities. One of the beliefs on which the LAP is based is that language, literacy, social, cognitive, and motor skills can be facilitated in each of the learning areas, although from day to day there may be differences in each area in the types of language used or the types of social, cognitive, and motor skills focused on. It is our experience that most children enjoy playing in all of the areas and that by the time their first semester is completed, they are usually participating in all areas at some time during the day or over a week's time.

Art/Science Area

The art activity changes each day, so it is introduced at the end of circle time following the introduction of the dramatic play activity. The introduction usually consists of demonstrating the use of the art materials and tools. Art activities often reflect the daily theme. One way this is accomplished is to have the children make a prop that can be used in the dramatic play. For example, children might make binoculars to use in an "African safari" dramatic play or a "camping and hiking" dramatic play. Another way to incorporate the theme is to have children make a picture out of items associated with a particular dramatic play. For example, the children might make a "doctor kit" by gluing Q-tips, cotton balls, and tongue depressors onto paper. During the weekly theme of "Discovering Things We Do with Our Hands," one child was observed detailing the hands on a simple figure, laboriously counting each finger as she painted. At times, the children's art product may relate to the dramatic play activity, such as car or vehicle rubbings for car racing day or an animal puppet for circus day. Often, however, some art activities do not have an end product. For example, during playdough activities children use cookie cutters, wooden craft sticks, and their hands to manipulate the playdough. At the end of center time, the playdough is rolled into a big ball and stored for future use.

Science concepts can also be introduced and reinforced at the art table. For example, as children paint they learn that mixing two colors together makes a new color (e.g., red and yellow make orange). Some projects may involve a change of state, such as cornstarch and water constructions. Children can form objects with the mixture, but when they are finished the object will melt. Other science concepts involve learning about shapes, sizes, and textures, particularly when making collages. Art projects might also involve representing different life-stage sequences, such as making or drawing caterpillars, then cocoons, and then butterflies.

Language and social interaction at the art table will vary with the children and with the type of activity. Children often work individually on a particular project (although group murals are also done). They may choose not to talk to others while they are painting, pasting, cutting, or developing their own project; they may talk only to request needed supplies. Other children may do a lot of conversing and readily discuss their art projects with other children or with adults.

Various types of art activities demand different fine motor abilities. Cutting with scissors uses different muscles and coordination than painting or pasting activities. It is important to offer a range of art activities that allow for different motor skill levels so that all children can benefit from participating.

It is also important to give children opportunities to be creative. They learn much about their world when given opportunities to experiment. They learn about shape, form, texture, and color when making designs. Art activities provide opportunities for children to use and expand their language, social, fine motor, and cognitive skills.

Block or Manipulative Area

A block or manipulative area often includes many types of blocks and other manipulative toys, such as miniature furniture, toy cars and trucks, animals, and dolls. The area also might also include a dollhouse, garage, and barn. Occasionally, items can be added to or taken away from the area, but in general, several kinds of blocks and miniature toys should be available consistently every day. Additional items relating to specific dramatic play activities may be added to the block area. For example, a miniature space ship and station might be added to the block area during a "Discovering Space" theme.

In the block area, children can play alone, beside other children, or with other children. They might simply stack blocks or create an entire miniature town or farm. The amount and kind of language used in the block area will vary depending on what the children are doing and on their level of language competence. The motor control needed to play with the items also varies with the type of toys used. Play with LEGO blocks tends to be an individual or a side-by-side activity requiring fine motor skills; large cardboard bricks generally encourage children to cooperate in building a cave or house to crawl into or out of. A variety of cognitive skills are also facilitated in the block area. Experimenting with blocks of different sizes and shapes helps children learn about relationships among large, medium, and small objects or relationships between different shapes (e.g., two right triangles of the same dimensions make a square when put together). Problem solving is promoted; for example, children determine how to build the fourth wall of a house out of small blocks because all of the large blocks are already in use. Activities in the block area can help foster the development of language, social, motor, and cognitive skills.

Quiet Area

Activities in a quiet area might involve reading and looking at storybooks, working on puzzles, playing board games, or writing on a chalkboard. A children's size book rack can display books so that children can easily see them. Books can be rotated occasionally, with some corresponding with the weekly theme. Books read during storytime can later be put in the book rack so the children can look at them again or have an adult reread them. It is important that the books contain both male and female characters from different ethnic groups in a variety of roles. The children may insist that a few of their favorite stories be kept available. There should be a variety of story formats, including those with labeling, rhyming, repetition, or complex storylines. Nonfiction books should also be included. Books showing artwork in the form of photographs, collages, pencil drawings, watercolors, block prints, or chalk drawings will broaden children's horizons. A large wooden crate turned on its side and filled with pillows provides a quiet, comfortable place to look at books or share secrets with a friend or a stuffed animal. A large beanbag chair could also be used as a quiet place to sit with friends and look at books. The children may look at books together, by themselves, or with an adult. Adults may read a story to one child or a small group of children but will often follow a child's lead and encourage the child to tell the story, labeling pictures when necessary.

Puzzles should vary in difficulty and be changed periodically. Children may work on puzzles by themselves or with others, discussing where a specific piece fits. One "puzzle" in this area could be a LEGO wall board, which is similar to a LEGO table but is mounted on the wall. At the bottom of the board is a container that stores the LEGOs, which are of different colors and designs and can be used to make a variety of patterns. The children tend to work independently or side by side at such a board and frequently match colors or shapes as they work. Work on puzzles facilitates eye–hand coordination, fine motor skills, problem solving, and figure-ground skills. A variety of board games, such as card games, memory games, and matching games, can be available for individual or joint play. The children can choose a game and play it on the floor or at a small table. Turn taking is often an important skill learned when playing board games.

A chalkboard located in the quiet area provides opportunities for the children to draw or write. Children enjoy drawing and/or writing their name or alphabet letters with colored chalk. Younger children may simply cover the board with color, learning to control arm and hand movements, which will enable them to write letters later. Children may work at the chalkboard in pairs, which requires negotiations for space or turn taking. If a chalkboard is not available, teachers can set up a writing center with a variety of paper and writing tools, including pencils and markers. Activities in the quiet area facilitate language, preacademic, motor, social, and cognitive skills.

Individualized Literacy Time

The purpose of this activity is to provide children with a personalized reading vocabulary made up of words they want to learn to read. This activity probably should not begin until the second or third month of school so that children have time to experience earlier developing emergent literacy skills, such as beginning awareness that print has meaning, some alphabet recognition, and recognition of their own name. This activity integrates the alphabetic principle (which the children are learning during some of the group activities) with the concept that reading is getting meaning from print. It provides a way for children to become aware that combinations of letters mean something and that different combinations stand for different words. This is not a required activity, although children who will be going to kindergarten soon should be encouraged to participate.

During the word for the day activity, individual children select a word they want to know how to read. The adult writes the selected word on an index card, repeats the word, names the letters, and then gives it to the child to keep in a reading envelope. The child may take the envelope home to show his or her parents, or the envelope can be kept at school. The next day, if the child can label the word, a new word is added to the envelope. Children can keep adding words as long as they are interested. After a child has accumulated about 10 words, the adult can encourage the child to select a verb and begin to form sentences with the words. Some common words selected by children are *Mom, Dad, dinosaur, Grandma, car, jump(s)*, and *like(s)*. However, each child's list is different and is based on what he or she wants to learn to read. Sometimes children learn other children's words as they watch one another's selections. A typical early sentence, arranged by manipulating the index cards, might be *Dinosaur jumps* or *Mom likes Grandma*. If the sentence requires an article, the teacher can point this out to the child and add it. After several sentences are read, these sentences can be written in a book for children to read. Most children enjoy participating in this activity and will learn anywhere from 5 words to 50. In general, children leave LAP knowing an average of 15 words and can read them on word cards and in short sentences written in a construction paper book.

The word card activity can be done during various times of the day. For example, some children could participate during arrival time, others during center time, and still others during transition times (such as playtime after snack). Three to four children at a time may be involved. A specific word card center could also be set up in the classroom.

Goal Facilitation During Center Time

During center time, adults facilitate the following goals:

- *Language goals* by modeling appropriate vocabulary and syntactic structures, modeling appropriate sounds/phonology, commenting on children's actions, maintaining/supporting conversations, asking open questions

- *Literacy goals* by modeling reading of signs/logos/labels, helping children write their name on art projects, encouraging writing activities, writing and helping children read word cards, reading to a child or group of children
- *Social goals* by facilitating peer–peer interaction as well as adult–child interaction, demonstrating/acting out roles in dramatic play, modeling negotiating skills
- *Cognitive goals* by modeling problem solving, helping to categorize items, facilitating concepts such as *same* or *different*
- *Motor goals* by modeling how to use props, assisting in writing children's names, modeling/assisting with use of art materials, helping develop pincer grip, encouraging sensory tolerance for a variety of textures

IMPLEMENTING TEACHER-LED ACTIVITIES

Teacher-led activities may vary in whether an activity is a routine activity or if it is one that changes daily. However, all of the teacher-led activities are under the control of the teacher. It is the teacher who determines the topic/focus of the activity and who participates.

Circle Time

A standard format is generally used for circle time; however, after children have adapted to the routine, it should be varied slightly to add interest or impart new knowledge. Also, it is helpful to children to have a visual schedule to review the day's activities (e.g., circle, centers, story, sharing, outdoor play, snack, group, and music). A standard format might include the following activities.

Roll Call

When it is time for circle, the children find a place to sit. The teacher displays the card with the name of the "helper of the day" (child whose name card is on the top of the pile), then takes attendance by presenting cards with the children's names on them. For the first 2–3 months, the cards are presented with each child's first name revealed. By November, the cards are presented with the first letter uncovered, and children guess whose name it is. The teacher slowly reveals the rest of the letters until the name is correctly guessed. This could be done with just a few names at a time. By November, the teacher begins to pair the initial sound of the child's name with the letter that begins the name. This could also be done with a few names at a time or with only the card belonging to the helper of the day. During the late fall or in the spring, the number of syllables in a child's name or in the name of the month may be tapped out as part of the roll call activity.

Calendar Activity

The helper of the day leads the rest of the children in counting the days of the month until that day's number is reached. The helper then places the number in the appropriate place on the calendar. The helper goes up the column to the day of the week. Children say the "day of the week" chant, chanting that particular day louder. Pictures can be added to denote weather or special activity.

Introduction of Centers

The teacher demonstrates the art activity for the day, then the dramatic play activity. The children might go to the dramatic play area to watch the teacher and helper demonstrate the day's activity, including possible scripts. After the demonstration, the group returns to the circle area, and the teacher dismisses the children to play in the quiet area, block/manipulative area, art area, and/or dramatic play or any other area that is set up (e.g., computer area).

During circle time, adults facilitate the following goals:

- *Language goals* by providing information about the day's activities
- *Literacy goals* by reading children's names or noting the letters/sounds in names or other words; by noting the number of syllables in a name, the day, or the month by clapping out the syllables
- *Social goals* by helping children learn to take turns to speak
- *Cognitive goals* by providing appropriate directions, modeling problem solving, counting, and encouraging number recognition
- *Motor goals* by demonstrating the use of art or dramatic play materials

Storytime

The teacher reads the story ahead of time to develop appropriate questions to stimulate the children's interest and responses and to provide a purpose for the reading. In some cases, specific vocabulary could be previewed with children. Teachers should use a guided reading format when reading to children. The teacher presents the book, noting the title and author (also the illustrator, if appropriate), using a finger to point to words as appropriate. The children are asked what they think the story is about.

As the story is read, the teacher stops to show the pictures and discuss what is happening. If a Big Book is used, the words of the story are indicated as they are read. The teacher brings to children's attention the characters, setting, and sequence of events. Children are encouraged to comment or to join in if a repetitive line or rhyme is part of the story. At the end of the story, the teacher summarizes what was read or asks children to retell parts of the story and/or evaluate the story.

One way to highlight story grammar is to act out a story. The teacher can choose a few children to act out the story using simple props. The teacher narrates the story, pausing to let children provide the dialogue or action. As children act out the parts, they begin to understand that a story has characters, a setting, dialogue, events, a climax, and a resolution. Stories that are easy to act out have short, repetitive dialogue lines, such as those in *Are You My Mother?* or *Goldilocks and the Three Bears*. The stories should be relatively familiar to the children. Nursery rhymes can also be acted out.

During storytime, adults facilitate the following goals:

- *Language goals* by modeling appropriate vocabulary and syntactic structures, modeling appropriate sounds/phonology, expanding on children's comments, maintaining/supporting conversations, and asking open questions
- *Literacy goals* by reading a story, presenting a variety of stories and story grammar (e.g., fairy tales, rhyming or repetitive stories, adventure stories, informational stories), helping children practice rhyming or choral reading, and helping children understand the story or act out a story
- *Social goals* by facilitating peer–peer interaction as well as adult–child interaction, demonstrating/acting out roles in a story, and modeling negotiating skills
- *Cognitive goals* by modeling problem solving, helping to categorize items, helping to learn concepts such as print has meaning and books have titles and are written by someone
- *Motor goals* by helping children put items away and encouraging them to move to circle area and sit down

Sharing Time

Sharing time teaches children to ask and answer questions within a real context. The ability to ask questions provides a way for children to obtain information both in and outside of the classroom. A child asking a question such as "What do you have?" almost always gets a response from an adult or another child. This response provides new vocabulary knowledge about items in which the child is interested. This ability may be particularly helpful for the child who has language impairments because this child may need many more presentations of a vocabulary word before acquiring it than does the typically developing child (Rice, Oetting, Marquis, Bode, & Pae, 1994).

If possible, the class should be divided for sharing time into two or three groups of children, with one adult with each group. Two children come up to the front of the group, each standing on one side of the teacher. The teacher prompts the child on the left to ask the child on the right three questions about the object the second child has for sharing time. The three questions are "What do you have?" "What do you do with it?" and "Where did you get it?" The questions can be simplified to "What have?" or "Have?"; "What do?" or "Do?"; and "Where get?" or "Get?" This enables most of the children to ask the questions. When necessary, the teacher can model a question or an answer for the children. Other questions might also be asked, such as "What color is it?" "What's its name?" and so forth.

The second child responds to each question in turn. After the sequence of questions are asked and answered, the teacher can help children note particular features of an item (e.g., color, shape, use) or the specific name of the item, and/or literacy features such as a title of a book, a logo, or a sign or symbol that is on the item.

After the questions are answered and the item shown to the other children, the child on the right sits down and the child on the left moves to the right side of the teacher to now be the one who answers. A new child comes up to be the questioner. This changing of positions is important in highlighting the roles of the questioner and responder. The cycle continues until the child who first answered the questions acts as the last questioner. All of the children can take part in the sharing activity. If a child has not brought an item from home, he or she might share a favorite item from the classroom. If they desire, children may also tell about an event rather than show an object. As the year proceeds, children will learn to ask and answer questions with less and less teacher support.

During sharing time, adults facilitate the following goals:

- *Language goals* by modeling appropriate questions and answers, expanding on children's comments, and maintaining/supporting conversations
- *Literacy goals* by supporting children in telling about/describing an object or event, and noting print on an item
- *Social goals* by facilitating peer–peer interaction as well as adult–child interaction
- *Cognitive goals* by noting features of items and labeling categories ("That's blue, just like the color of the Jamie's car")
- *Motor goals* by displaying toy items and demonstrating item use

Group Time

Appropriate activities and lessons help keep the children's attention during group time and foster learning. The format typically includes an introduction, the main lesson or skill practice, and a summary. The teacher should have all necessary materials ready. The pace is quick and the lesson focused, with the introduction taking only 1–2 minutes, the skill practice around 5–10 minutes, and the summary 1–2 minutes. The teacher plans for various levels of difficulty for each concept so that each child can succeed.

Group lessons are focused on emergent literacy, math, or other cognitive activities. The main types of lessons and general procedures are explained in the following sections. For specific activities of each type, see the lesson plans in Section II.

General Alphabet Procedures

The teacher writes the letter targeted for learning in both upper- and lowercase on whiteboard or poster paper. The teacher introduces the target letter and emphasizes the target letter sound(s). A variety of common words can be given as examples of the various sounds associated with the target letters. For vowels, the short and long sounds are usually the focus, although the teacher should mention that the letter has several sounds. The teacher directs the children's attention to the alphabet picture displays around the room.

Children whose names begin with the target sound are invited to write the target letter on the whiteboard (or poster paper). In the early part of the year, children typically write only the uppercase letters. Lowercase letters can be practiced on an individual basis. The children are asked to generate words that begin with the target letter. The teacher can provide pictures or items as needed to support the children's participation. A picture dictionary can also be used. Children can practice writing the target letter on individual chalkboards or paper. The activity ends with a review of the words that were generated, with the teacher emphasizing the target sound.

Variations to General Procedures

Other word activities during group time include the following:

- *Rhyming activities:* Children replace the initial letter in words with the same ending, such as *hat, bat,* and *cat.*
- *Discrimination activities:* Children compare two words and say whether they are the same *(bed, bed)* or different *(red, bed).*
- *Vowel sounds:* Children discriminate between long and short vowel sounds said by the teacher, with support provided as needed.
- *Syllables:* Children and teacher tap out words to determine the number of syllables in the word.
- *Deletion activities:* Children say the word that results when part of a longer word is deleted (e.g., *cowboy* without *boy* is *cow*).

Classification Activities

The teacher gathers items that can be placed in one of two categories, along with tubs or another means of sorting the items. The teacher introduces the classification concept by placing the items into the appropriate tub (e.g., all of the farm animals in one tub, zoo animals in another). Items can be removed and children asked to place the items in the correct tubs. They can also use additional items. Cueing is provided as needed for individual children to be successful.

Labeling/Matching Activities

Specific items to be matched are displayed and labeled (e.g., *circle*). Children then choose an item that matches the target item and places it with the target. The matching items may be an exact match or may be a match based on a specific category (e.g., two blue cars, a car and a truck representing a vehicle category). A variety of items are available, and cues are given as needed for individual children.

- *Number writing:* The teacher holds up a number card or writes a number on a whiteboard. The teacher or a child traces the number while saying a rhyme that describes how to write the number. As the children watch, the teacher then writes the number. Children practice writing the number on individual chalkboards or paper, with assistance as needed. The number can be paired with the correct number of items as a review.
- *Sequencing activities:* A variety of sequencing activities occur, from the typical classroom schedule and routines to stories to specific sequencing group activities. These activities help children understand that there is an order to many things and provide a beginning understanding of such terms as *first, next,* and *last.* Children learning to sequence items may need different levels of support. For example, after the teacher introduces the pattern (e.g., two red blocks, two green blocks, two red blocks), some children could add to the pattern, other children could match the pattern, and still other children could create the pattern from memory.

During group time, adults facilitate the following goals:

- *Language goals* by modeling appropriate vocabulary and syntactic structures, modeling appropriate sounds/phonology, expanding on children's comments, maintaining/supporting conversations, and asking open questions
- *Literacy goals* by presenting letters and sounds of the letters, focusing on the alphabetic principle; writing the alphabet; writing down children's dictated experience stories; noting that print has meaning; and acting out stories
- *Social goals* by facilitating peer–peer interaction as well as adult–child interaction, demonstrating/acting out roles in a story, and modeling negotiating skills
- *Cognitive goals* by modeling problem solving; helping to categorize items; and teaching concepts such as sequencing, classification (including same/different), size and shape, counting, and number recognition
- *Motor goals* by assisting children in finding a place to sit and helping them sit in circle or on a chair or mat, assisting children in manipulating materials

Music Time

The teacher has the target song and approximately 5–6 other songs or fingerplays ready. The teacher introduces the song by singing it through and then encourages the children to join in. The teacher may need to sing a line at a time when introducing a new song. After singing a song two or three times, the group sings a different song. Recordings, fingerplays, and action songs, such as "The Hokey Pokey," can be sung during music time as well. A classroom book of songs that are frequently used may be developed.

Two or three different kinds of instruments can be available to children as they sing (e.g., shakers, sticks, bells). The teacher divides the children into smaller groups. The teacher demonstrates the various instruments and hands them out so that each group of children have one kind of instrument. The teacher puts on the music and signals each group of children to play their instruments.

During music time, adults facilitate the following goals:

- *Language goals* by modeling appropriate song melody, modeling vocabulary and syntactic structures, modeling appropriate sounds/phonology, expanding on children's comments, and giving directions for children to follow (e.g., doing hand motions to songs)
- *Literacy goals* by singing the alphabet song, using songs such as "Bingo" to teach deletion of sounds, and using rhyming songs to teach sound patterns
- *Social goals* by facilitating peer–peer interaction as well as adult–child interaction, facilitating choral singing, and modeling negotiating skills
- *Cognitive goals* by modeling problem solving, sequencing skills, and classification skills ("Choose an animal song"); helping children remember the sequence in a song; and noting what the song is about
- *Motor goals* by helping children follow rhythms and song and fingerplay actions; encouraging children to play instruments and sing

ARRIVAL, OUTSIDE, AND SNACK TIME

Arrival and outside play time are routine activities that occur daily. They are also child-centered times in that the children can choose what they want to do and choose their level of participation. Snack time is also a routine activity. Snack time is a combination of both a teacher-led and child-centered activity in that there is a prescribed format that directed by the teacher and followed by the children (e.g., when to start eating, have many crackers one can have for seconds). However, the topic of conversations may be teacher led or child centered.

Arrival Time

Before children arrive, teachers make sure that available centers are stocked for arrival time play and that notes or newsletters are in children's cubbies. As each child arrives, teachers briefly greet the child and parent. The helper of the day is chosen. That child flicks the lights (or uses another signal) when it is time to put away toys and go to the next activity. The helper gets to lead the roll call and calendar activity. The helper is also the line leader when going to and from outdoor play.

When children arrive, they check in, find their cubby, hang up their personal items, and choose an area in which to play. Children can choose from activities in four areas:

1. *Art activities* include drawing, cutting, pasting, and writing names.
2. *Block/manipulative activities* include playing with large and small blocks, LEGOs, Bristle Blocks, large and small cars and trucks, train and train tracks, people figures, animals, houses, etc. The housekeeping area might also be open for children to play in.
3. *Quiet activities* include looking at books alone or with others, identifying letters or words, sharing a book or puzzle, and problem-solving how to do a puzzle.
4. *Writing activities and games* include copying letters, writing on chalkboards/whiteboards, and playing matching games or simple board games. The computer could also be available, and children could receive their individual word for the day from an adult at the word card center.

Outdoor Playtime

A standard format should be used for lining up to go outside, with the helper of the day acting as line leader. A taped line on the floor to indicate where children stand may be helpful. During outdoor time, children choose what to do and the level of their participation. Adults monitor the children's safety and encourage them to play on the equipment appropriately. They also play with children, following their lead. They encourage children to interact with one another and facilitate group games, such as "Duck, Duck, Goose." In addition to motor skills, adults can use this time to facilitate language, social, and cognitive skills. They can comment on the children's activities using verbs, encourage peer interaction using redirections, prompted initiations, and other language facilitation techniques (see Chapter 3), and help with problem solving. Drawing children's attention to signs and symbols outdoors, writing letters in the sand, and so forth, can also facilitate literacy skills.

During outdoor time, adults facilitate the following goals:

- *Language goals* by modeling appropriate vocabulary and syntactic structures, modeling appropriate sounds/phonology, commenting on children's actions, maintaining/supporting conversations, and asking open questions
- *Literacy goals* by supporting children in telling about/describing an object or event, and noting print on an item
- *Social goals* facilitating peer–peer interaction as well as adult–child interaction, and modeling or facilitating negotiation skills
- *Cognitive goals* by noting features of items, helping children understand game rules, and labeling categories ("That's blue, just like the color of the Jamie's car")
- *Motor goals* by encouraging large motor movement, motor planning, catching a ball, sliding, and riding a tricycle/other toy equipment

Snack Time

Snack could be prepared by an adult with child assistance (a snack helper could also be chosen each day). A special snack song could be sung (and signed, if desired) to indicate when it is time to eat. Teachers assist children in washing their hands and finding their chairs. Small pitchers enable children to pour their own juice. Children can also control whether they have seconds by asking that the dish be passed to them.

During snack time, teachers can model and teach how to ask for things politely and encourage children to request food items from peers, not just adults. They also chat with children and facilitate the pouring of juice and passing of the cracker plate for seconds. They facilitate simple addition and subtraction skills by noting the number of crackers and what happens if one is eaten (re-counting the crackers if necessary), and how many crackers are added when children take a second helping. They may help children note other features of the crackers, such as size and shape.

During snack time, adults facilitate the following goals:

- *Language goals* by modeling appropriate vocabulary and syntactic structures, commenting on their own or a child's actions, maintaining/supporting conversations, asking open questions, using polite terms
- *Literacy goals* by supporting children in telling about/describing an object or event, noting print on an item
- *Social goals* facilitating peer–peer interaction as well as adult–child interaction, modeling or facilitating negotiation skills ("More crackers, please")
- *Cognitive goals* by noting features of items; labeling categories; modeling counting and other beginning math skills, such as addition and subtraction ("I have three crackers. I eat one, and now I have two left")
- *Motor goals* by assisting children in pouring juice, passing the cracker plate, taking only one or two crackers at a time

FACILITATING LANGUAGE AND LEARNING DURING ACTIVITIES

Language and learning are facilitated during both child-centered and teacher-led activities. During the child-centered activities, the facilitation may be implicit or indirect. During the teacher-led activities, the facilitation may employ more explicit or direct teaching strategies.

Child-Centered Activities

During dramatic play activities, adult facilitation may involve providing verbal scripts (i.e., modeling), responding to children's speech productions, finding additional props, problem-solving how to construct an important prop, facilitating peer–peer interactions, and in general surrounding children with the language necessary to achieve their needs and wants. Emergent literacy skills may also be fostered by the type of dramatic play activity (e.g., library, office worker) or the kind of props made available (e.g., books, clipboards).

During play in the block area, teachers can facilitate language and learning by commenting on both children's and adults' actions, responding to an individual child's requests and comments, providing additional blocks, noting arrangements, and adding appropriate toys (e.g., small cars, animals, people). Emergent literacy can be encouraged by noting letters or alphabet blocks or by arranging blocks to form letters. In the art area, facilitation of language and learning may include demonstrating procedures to be used, providing models for children, or providing help with cutting, gluing, and painting. In addition, emergent literacy skills can be fostered by helping children sign their artwork, write down their dictations about their creations, or provide word cards to copy. Language may be facilitated by describing what children are doing with the materials, responding to their initiations, expanding or recasting children's utterances (see Chapter 3), and in general carrying on a conversation with children. In the quiet area, adults might facilitate language and learning by helping children complete a puzzle, match letters or numbers, or play a classification game or board game, or they might read a story to one or more children.

Facilitating language and learning also takes place during outdoor time as children and adults interact through group games or in one-to-one play. Again, adults may expand and recast children's utterances and comment on children's actions and their own. Cognitive skills can be fostered through observing the properties of natural objects together. For example, adults and children might note that sand can be poured, plants have leaves and seeds and some also have thorns, pine cones are prickly, and so forth. The properties of manipulative toys can also be noted (e.g., tricycles have pedals and can roll). Group games, such as "Duck, Duck, Goose," help children learn to follow rules and participate in a group. Children develop their motor skills through using outdoor play equipment, such as pouring sand, batting balls, throwing and catching balls, riding tricycles, and climbing. Social skills are fostered through sharing and negotiating for play equipment.

Teacher-Led Activities

During teacher-led activities, the children listen to the teacher as a group. Children learn how to respond both nonverbally, by pointing or raising their hand, and/or verbally as directed by the teacher. As a facilitator of children's learning, the teacher must be able to vary the demands of each task to meet children's differing needs and skill levels. Instead of asking each child to perform the same task, the teacher may ask some children to perform alternative tasks that achieve a similar goal. There may also be group participation, such as answering a question in unison or counting to find out the day's date. The children's participation at storytime may vary with the type of story read or told, whether from a book, on a felt board, or with a puppet. For example, children may join in on rhyming words when a rhyming book is read.

A TYPICAL DAY IN THE LANGUAGE ACQUISITION PRESCHOOL

A sample daily schedule from the LAP (shown in Table 2.2) illustrates how all of the components of the LFC can be incorporated into a program. A brief description of each activity taken from the LAP curriculum manual (Bunce & Liebhaber, 1989) is presented below. In addition, the roles and expectations for children and for adults are outlined.

Arrival Time

Teachers greet children and parents upon arrival, and then each child receives a brief health check (e.g., throat examined, stomach and limbs checked for rashes). This is a child care licensing requirement. Children who appear ill are sent home. The health check is also a good language learning opportunity as the teacher can briefly label body parts while checking them. During the process, children can tell the teacher something that happened at home, and because parents are present they can explain or elaborate on what children say so the teacher can understand (e.g., "It was Uncle Joe who came, not Uncle 'Soe'").

After the children are checked in, they have a 15-minute play period—an opportunity to greet their friends and acclimate themselves to the classroom for the day. They may play in the block/manipulative and/or quiet areas, draw pictures at the art table, or learn a word at the word card ("word for the day") center.

Circle Time

During the 10–15-minute circle time, the teacher welcomes the children and takes roll, or attendance, by holding up 3" × 5" index cards on which the children's names are written. Children raise their hand upon seeing their name on the card. Initially, the teacher will say the name as each card is displayed, but later in the year the card is presented alone.

After each child has responded to roll call, the helper of the day places his or her card on a special chart. The helper of the day is determined by the name card on top of the pile. (At the end of the day that child's card is placed on the bottom of the pile.) The teacher then introduces the theme and activities for the day. Finally, the children choose the center area in which they will participate first. In addition to language skills, many of the circle time activities focus on emergent literacy activities and emergent math skills, such as recognizing the letters in children's names, recognizing days of the week, counting, and so on.

Table 2.2. Sample daily schedule

A.M. time	P.M. time	Activity name	Activity description
8:30–8:45	1:00–1:15	Arrival	Teachers do health checks. Children engage in free play (art, block and manipulative, and books and puzzles areas open).
8:45–9:00	1:15–1:30	Circle Time	Children and teachers greet each other, discuss helper of the day, today's day, and topic for the day. Children choose where they will play.
9:00–9:50	1:30–2:20	Play Areas	Children play at any of the four centers: art, block and manipulative, books and puzzles, or dramatic play.
9:50–10:05	2:20–2:35	Cleanup/Storytime	Children clean up the toys and then listen to a story.
10:05–10:15	2:35–2:45	Sharing Time	Children gather in the circle area to share information or toys. They take turns being the questioner and responder.
10:15-10:45	2:45–3:15	Outside Time	Children play on outdoor equipment, play in the sand, or participate in organized group games.
11:00–11:15	3:30–3:45	Small/Large Group Time	Different activities are planned for each day. Sometimes the children gather in small groups during this time; on other days, the whole class participates in a group project.
11:15–11:30	3:45–4:00	Music Time and Dismissal	Children sing songs, play instruments, and/or dance. They sing the good-bye song and are dismissed.

During circle time, children are encouraged to do the following:

- Participate
- Take turns talking
- Listen to others
- Ask questions
- Recognize their own and others' names
- Practice counting skills
- Make decisions about which activity to join

Center Time

Center time lasts approximately 45–50 minutes. During this time, children can choose to play in any of the centers: art/science, block or manipulative area, quiet area, writing area, or dramatic play area. The children are free to pursue their interests in any of these areas. Some children play in all of the areas during center time; others remain in one or two. This is a child-centered time during which children choose their level of participation in an activity. The teachers follow the children's lead and model participation while stimulating verbal interactions among the children, modeling speech and language skills, and encouraging the use of context-appropriate verbal skills. Center time is also an opportunity to foster literacy, concept learning, fine and gross motor skills, and social interaction.

During center time, children are encouraged to do the following:

- Choose their own activities
- Explore everyday scripts
- Explore new scripts
- Learn new concepts

- Develop verbal interactive skills, vocabulary, grammar, and discourse competencies appropriate for enacting the script
- Play with other children
- Take turns with toys
- Ask for what they want
- Be creative
- Develop fine and gross motor skills
- "Read" signs, write numbers, and practice other emergent literacy skills

Cleanup/Storytime

To signal the end of center time, the helper of the day flashes the classroom lights. The children then help clean up by putting away the props, toys, and blocks; cleaning up the art table; and putting away the books and puzzles. The children then gather for storytime. Cleanup time provides a transition time to the next activity and helps the children sort items and follow teachers' instructions.

Storytime lasts approximately 10 minutes each day. Stories or poems are read or told to the children using children's literature books, puppets, and/or the felt board. Throughout the story, the children are asked to predict what will happen, provide some of the dialogue, and in general interact with the story. Sometimes favorite nursery rhymes or stories are acted out. Occasionally, children will make up a story that the teacher writes down. Sometimes a story will be read in another language and then retold in English. Short videotaped stories may sometimes be incorporated into storytime.

During cleanup and storytime, children are encouraged to do the following:

- Help with cleanup
- Follow directions/routine
- Listen to the story
- Learn to comprehend verbal information
- Respond appropriately to the story
- Note repetitive lines
- Enjoy the story
- Begin to develop knowledge of story grammar

Sharing Time

After storytime, the children gather together for a 10–15-minute sharing time. One child asks another child about the item he or she has brought to share. Each child has the opportunity to be both the questioner and the responder (i.e., the one who shares). Sharing time helps the children learn how to talk about a familiar item and how to ask and answer questions.

During sharing time, children are encouraged to do the following:

- Ask questions
- Speak to the group
- Listen to others
- Answer questions

Outside Time

Outside time lasts approximately 30 minutes. The children line up with the helper of the day in the lead and walk single file down to the play yard. The playground equipment includes slides, a merry-go-round, a climbing platform, rope ladders, a sliding pole, and a sand area.

There are also several styles of tricycles available. The children share the playground with other preschool classes, which helps them learn to negotiate for turns and allows them to play with children other than those who attend the LAP. Children develop their gross motor skills by climbing ropes and stairs, sliding down poles and slides, riding, running, jumping, digging, throwing, catching, and so forth. These different actions encourage the use of different verb structures as well as adverbs and adjectives. Sometimes teachers lead group games, such as "Duck, Duck, Goose," "Red Light/Green Light," "Simon Says," and "Mother (Father), May I?"

During outside time, children are encouraged to do the following:

- Experiment with sand and sand toys
- Climb on climbing toys
- Ride tricycles and scooters
- Negotiate for turns
- Run and generally have fun
- Play cooperatively (e.g., throw and catch balls)
- Observe changes in nature

Snack Time

When the children come in from outside, they wash their hands to get ready for snack time. One adult monitors the bathroom and helps children with toileting and hand washing. During snack time, the children sit at tables and enjoy a snack (e.g., crackers and juice). There is at least one adult at each table. During snack time, children practice politeness by waiting until all are seated and by asking other children for more crackers or juice as needed. The routine phrase "More crackers, please" is often one of the first phrases learned by children with speech and language impairments and children who are learning English as a second language. The phrase can be expanded to "May I have more, please?" Some children communicate by signing "crackers, please" or "more."

Snack time is also a good time for children to use counting skills and perform simple addition and subtraction. One child might have five crackers but after eating one will note that only four crackers remain. Another child will count to three as he or she takes three more crackers from the tray. Other children will comment that when three crackers are added to the one on their napkin, they have four crackers. The children often comment on the shape of the crackers, noting that some are round like circles, some are square or rectangular, and occasionally some are triangular. During snack time activities, language, cognitive, and emergent math skills can be fostered.

During snack time, children are encouraged to do the following:

- Wait until everyone is seated at the table before starting to eat
- Engage in appropriate conversation with tablemates
- Use good table manners
- Ask for more juice or crackers using appropriate words, including "please" and "thank you"
- Pour their own juice
- Take turns washing hands after snack time
- Clean up after themselves

Group Time

Group time lasts approximately 10–15 minutes and consists of activities that vary from day to day. The children may form small groups for a small-group time, or the whole class may participate together in large-group activities. Activities may involve experiments (e.g., mixing colors and seeing what happens, deciding which items sink or float, cooking pudding), sorting and matching activities, and/or sequencing activities involving repeated patterns.

Children may compose a summary chart of what happened during the experiments, with the teacher writing the information on a big chart. Class thank-you notes to visitors are also composed during group time. Often the children will each draw a picture or add their name to the note. Short alphabet and phonic lessons, as well as mathematical and inquiry activities, are presented during group time (see Section II for specific group lesson plans). Therefore, group activities foster development of language skills, emergent literacy skills, cognitive skills, and interaction/participation skills.

During group time, children are encouraged to do the following:

- Pay attention
- Learn to comprehend verbal information
- Participate
- Learn key vocabulary and concepts
- Ask questions
- Generate ideas and sentences
- Learn alphabet letters and letter–sound correspondence
- Learn number concepts
- Follow directions

Music Time

Music time occurs during the last 10–15 minutes of the day. It is a time when the children can relax and have fun singing. Many of the songs have actions or fingerplays to accompany them, and rhythm instruments are sometimes used. Favorite songs are sung over and over. Music activities are particularly good to end the day because all of the children can participate. For some children with limited language competency, music time is the first time they begin to participate actively in an activity. Doing actions, making the motions to fingerplays, or singing in a group may be less threatening than talking. Also, singing in a group is a fun way to learn to follow directions, learn words to a song, and learn about music.

During music time, children are encouraged to do the following:

- Participate
- Enjoy different melodies
- Enjoy different rhythms
- Follow directions and patterns
- Learn and enjoy rhymes

After music time, the children sing a good-bye song. When the song is completed, the children are released to their parents.

SUMMARY

The LFC used in the LAP and described in this chapter is designed to foster language and learning for 3- to 5-year-old children with varying levels of linguistic competence. Language intervention and enhancement are provided in a least restrictive environment during natural interactions. It is within these communicative interactions that children learn new language content, forms, and uses. A thematic approach is used for curricular activities. In particular, the dramatic play, art, storytime, group, and music activities are designed to develop the day's theme. Although language development is viewed as central to the learning process, developmentally appropriate activities are also utilized to facilitate cognitive, literacy, motor, and social skills.

3

Language Intervention in the Language-Focused Curriculum

Children with speech and language impairments may need more intense language stimulation than is provided by the general language facilitation guidelines outlined in Chapter 2. Several scholars have suggested that children with specific language impairment (SLI) learn in a manner similar to children whose language development is typical; however, children with language impairments need many more presentations of the target vocabulary or structures to reach the same level of competency (Gray, 2003; Rice, Oetting, Marquis, Bode, & Pae, 1994). For example, Rice, Buhr, and Nemeth (1990), using a story presented to children on videotape, found that children with typical language development needed four presentations of a new word before they could identify it correctly. Children with SLI also learned the new words through the video format, but they needed more presentations. Rice et al. (1994) found that children with SLI had gains in word learning comparable to their peers when they received 10 presentations of the words. Gray (2003) suggested that children with SLI may need at least twice as many presentations of a new word as do children with typical development and that learning the word first in comprehension is important.

Although children with SLI may need more information and more frequency of language input, they often receive less (Rice, 1993; Silliman & Wilkinson, 1991). Part of the reason for this is that they are often not active participants in verbal exchanges and may not initiate interactions or respond when addressed. This lack of initiation or response limits some potential stimulation. For example, a child who asks, "What's this?" will receive a great deal of information about objects in the environment. A child who is not able to ask questions or fails to ask them will not receive the same amount of information. Similarly, a child who responds when spoken to encourages the speaker to continue the interaction. If the child makes no response, the interaction usually ends, and this limits the opportunities to learn more about communication and language. In programs with an LFC, however, children with speech and language impairments receive much stimulation or input even when they fail to respond. The stimulation is provided by both adults and other children. Children with speech and language impairments are not required to produce verbal language, although they are provided with many opportunities to do so. The focus of this chapter is on describing specific language interventions for children with speech and language impairments using an LFC based on a concentrated normative model. This model, as described in detail by Rice (1998), proposes that intervention be provided in a naturalistic setting to capitalize on children's developmental momentum and also provide a concentrated focus on or highlight specific language skills (see also Bunce & Watkins, 1995).

SPECIFIC LANGUAGE INTERVENTION STRATEGIES

Providing language opportunities in a rich and stimulating environment and encouraging the use of language are central to all other strategies for linguistic enhancement. However, providing a stimulating environment is not enough. Other strategies are needed to focus children's attention on linguistic forms and uses. Leonard (1981) and others have come to label these strategies as *focused stimulation* (Ellis Weismer & Robertson, 2006; Fey, 1986). These strategies are also sometimes labeled *indirect strategies* because they are usually embedded within an ongoing interaction or communication. These strategies or invention techniques include *focused contrasts, modeling, event casts, open questions, expansions, recasts, redirects and prompted initiations*, and *scripted play*. A variety of studies support the use of these indirect techniques to improve lexical learning; understanding and production of grammar features; phonology; and the use of language in social situations (Camarata, Nelson, & Camarata, 1994; Gillum, Camarata, Nelson, & Camarata, 2003; Girolametto, Pearce, & Weitzman, 1997; Kouri, 2005; Proctor-Williams, Fey, & Loeb, 2001; Rice, Buhr, & Nemeth, 1990; Robertson & Ellis Weismer, 1999; Schuele, Rice, & Wilcox, 1995; Smith & Camarata, 1999).

Focused Contrasts

A *focused contrast* is a production by an adult that highlights contrastive differences in speech sounds, lexical items, and/or syntactic structures. This technique works on two levels. The first level is one of corrective feedback, in which negative evidence is provided to the child. Focused contrasts make explicit the error versus the correct form in a manner that allows the child to recognize the differences. The procedure can be a brief focusing of attention on the crucial features in an interaction, or it can involve several exchanges. For example, the adult might say to the child, "You said 'Otay,' but I say 'Okay'" to focus the child's attention on the differences between the production of /t/ versus /k/. The exchange might continue with the teacher writing a *t* and then a *k* on the chalkboard to further emphasize the contrast.

The second level involves modeled contrasts in adult talk. These verbal productions or contrasts are embedded in the ongoing descriptions. For example, if the plural marker /s/ is the target, both the singular form and the plural form would be used. With a child who is playing with cars, the clinician could request one car and then ask for two other cars. Gestures to indicate what was desired would accompany the verbal requests. During play, the adult would continue to contrast the forms. The focused contrasts highlight for the child features that are relevant or crucial to the distinction to be made. To some extent, other strategies (e.g., modeling, event casts, expansions, recasts, scripted play) provide focused contrasts to help the child attend to the crucial features of the targeted linguistic form. These two levels, corrective feedback and modeled contrasts, may be especially well suited to advancing the language skills of children with speech and language impairments and children learning English as their second language.

Modeling

One frequently used language facilitation strategy is *modeling*, or giving the child a model of a target sound, word, or form. Models such as these often contain structures that the child does not yet produce. The child is offered the opportunity to repeat or respond to the model but is not required to do so. Models are most often incorporated in naturally occurring interactions, although extra emphasis or stress may be placed on particular features to highlight them. Models usually take the form of a statement or comment. For example, if the structure "is verbing" is the target, the adult would use this form in describing what the child or other children are doing. The adult might say, "Sara is jumping" or "Now she is running."

Event Casts

Event casts provide an ongoing description of an activity and are similar to the voice-over description of athletic events provided by sports broadcasters. Teachers and other adults frequently use event casts (see Heath, 1986) as a means of language enrichment. Event casts can be used by adults during relatively teacher-directed times of the day; for example, in a group pudding-making activity, the teacher might narrate the event with "I'm opening the package, and now I'm pouring the mix into the bowl. Now, it's time for the milk. I'll put the milk in. What should I do now? Okay, stir it. I'll get out all the lumps." Furthermore, a classroom adult can use event casts during play with children who are quiet, hesitant, or shy in the classroom setting. Describing a child's play actions or one's own activities can promote language production by the child.

Event casts serve two facilitative functions. First, event casts provide a sort of language "bath," insofar as they can accompany and describe ongoing activities. This language bath allows children to hear language pertinent to ongoing events. Second, event casts can be used to encourage children to use oral problem-solving strategies by modeling their use. As the classroom teacher solves a bridge-building problem, for example, she can narrate her activities: "I wonder if this block will fit. No, it's too big. Oh, maybe if I turn it around. Yes, now it fits." This oral problem-solving model can assist children in learning to use such a strategy in working through their own daily challenges.

A cautionary note should be added here regarding the use of event casts. Although event casts are useful in describing ongoing activities, constant or highly frequent use of this intervention strategy can result in an adult-dominated classroom language environment. Thus, event casts are best used sparingly, during moments when descriptions of events or activities are desired. The descriptions can provide a means for children to connect events and language and may be particularly helpful in modeling problem-solving strategies.

Open Questions

Open questions are questions that have a variety of possible answers. Examples of open questions include "What do you think will happen next?" "Why do you think that happened?" and "What do you think we should do next?" Open questions contrast with "test," or closed, questions. Test questions usually demand a specific answer, often consisting of one- or two-word utterances. Examples of test questions include "What color is this?" and "What is this?" There is pressure to respond and to respond "correctly." Test questions are appropriate for testing a child's knowledge but are not necessarily a good way to facilitate language acquisition. Because open questions are real questions to which the adult does not necessarily know the answer, there is less pressure to provide a specific response. If a child draws a picture and then shows it to the adult, more language may be generated by the child if the adult says, "Can you tell me about your picture?" than if the adult says, "What's that?"

Expansions

Expansions occur when the adult repeats a child's utterance, filling in the missing features. For example, if a child omits a verb ending, as in the phrase "He ride bus," the adult could respond by saying "Yes, he rides the bus." Expansions serve two purposes. First, they affirm that the child has communicated effectively; second, they provide a model for achieving more adult-like forms.

Recasts

A *recast* is a conversational adjustment through which basic semantic information is retained while syntactic structure is altered (Baker & Nelson, 1984; Camarata & Nelson, 2006; Camarata, Nelson, & Camarata, 1994). Children's utterances can be recast by changing the grammatical form but maintaining meaning. For example, the utterance "He walks home now" could be recast as, "You're right. He is walking home." Thus, a recast 1) is temporally adjacent to the child's original utterance, 2) maintains the basic meaning of the child's utterance, and 3) changes one or more elements of the original utterance. Recasts are believed to promote linguistic development because they maintain the child's original ideas or meaning and present them in grammatically altered sentences. Thus, the child's attention may be drawn to the new forms or words expressed. The use of recasts shows alternative ways to form sentences without disrupting communication. Recasting is a natural response that does not appear artificial or contrived and does not disrupt conversational interactions with young children. Several authors have suggested that high-frequency presentations of target-specific recasts is important in intervention (Camarata & Nelson, 2006; Fey, Cleave, Long, & Hughes, 1993; Fey & Loeb, 2002). This emphasis on frequency of presentation is reminiscent of the finding from vocabulary studies mentioned earlier that children with language impairments appear to need more presentations of the target word than do children with typical development. Conversational recasts, then, may be one way to provide the necessary frequency without disrupting communication. Thus, recasting can be tailored to a specific child's goals. However, it can also be used in a more general manner to promote linguistic abilities, including grammar, phonology, and intelligibility (see Camarata & Nelson, 2006).

Another way recasts can be incorporated into the language of the classroom is for teachers and other classroom staff to recast their own utterances. This technique is particularly useful in teacher-directed moments of the classroom day. The teacher simply provides pairs of original and recast sentences in his or her language (e.g., "Today is Tuesday. It's Tuesday" or "Mike's drinking his juice. He's drinking apple juice"). These sentence pairs can aid children in recognizing relations between varied syntactic forms expressing the same meanings and highlight new words and their meanings. In addition, teachers can occasionally incorporate this technique into reading or talking about the text of stories (e.g., "The monster is catching the boys. He's catching them").

Redirects and Prompted Initiations

Two intervention techniques that can be used to encourage children's interactions with one another are *redirects* and *prompted initiations* (see Schuele, Rice, & Wilcox, 1995, on the use of redirects to increase peer interaction). A redirect occurs when the child approaches an adult and makes a request that could be made to another child. For example, a child waiting for a turn on a swing might approach an adult and say, "My turn on the swing." In this situation, the adult would typically redirect the child's initiation by suggesting that the child talk with the individual on the swing. In some cases, additional assistance could be provided in the form of a model (e.g., "Tell Jill, 'It's my turn'"). An alternative situation is one involving a prompted initiation in which the child does not make the initial request to the adult. Instead, the adult initially suggests or prompts the child to approach another child to play or request an item. These redirecting and prompting techniques can assist children with language impairments to learn to initiate interactions and effect change directly instead of relying on an adult as the mediator. In this way, interactions between children are promoted.

Scripted Play

Scripted play is a valuable intervention procedure because it provides opportunities for verbal communication within a meaningful context (Neeley, Neeley, Justen, & Tipton-Sumner, 2001). A script (Constable, 1986; Nelson, 1981, 1986) is a representation of an event, an ordered sequence of actions organized around a goal and including actors, actions, and props. For example, most people have a script for eating at a restaurant, which would include the sequence of events of ordering, eating, and paying; the script would also involve people who are eating, waiters or waitresses, and a cashier. Scripts do allow variations, but these generally center on the same goal. There are both similarities and differences in eating at a fast-food restaurant and in having dinner at an expensive restaurant.

Use of Scripts Throughout the Day

The notion of scripts as event representations is used throughout the classroom day in preschools such as the LAP. Familiar daily routines, such as arrival time, circle time, and snack time, develop into scripted event representations for young children. This familiarity acts as a basis upon which language experiences can be built. Children know that they will eat during snack time; this stimulates discussion of what the daily snack is, who brought it, how it was prepared, and other possible variations on the general snack theme.

In addition to their general use to provide structure for the daily routine, scripts are inherent to the LFC center time. More specifically, each day a particular dramatic play activity is available for children to select. Dramatic play activities involve using scripts for such things as everyday events (e.g., grocery shopping, gardening, cooking, cleaning), certain special events (e.g., vacation, camping, fishing), and occupations (e.g., mechanic, veterinarian, electrician). This list provides only a small sample of possible dramatic play activities. (Section II of this book provides many more scripted play activity suggestions within the weekly lessons plans.)

Dramatic Play Activities

Scripted dramatic play activities are designed to enhance children's world knowledge and the language that accompanies it. Typically, preschool children require some background, introduction, and priming for the dramatic play script of the day. This is generally provided by a discussion and/or demonstration prior to the actual activity; that is, the roles are introduced, the use of props is demonstrated, and the basic goal(s) are discussed. Children will frequently contribute their existing knowledge of the script during such discussion. The comments "Our cat was sick" and "He got a shot" were heard during the introduction to a veterinarian play script. After even an initial introduction to a new script, children begin to build a skeletal event representation for a particular activity and carry out a dramatic play script with limited adult direction and/or intervention.

Language Exchanges Between Peers

From the perspective of language intervention, scripted dramatic play activities serve a variety of functions. First, and perhaps foremost, they stimulate language exchanges, particularly exchanges between children. As children assume roles in dramatic play interactions—for example, as customers or cashiers and veterinarians or pet owners—they practice verbal negotiation skills as they exchange essential props. One of the children with typically developing language skills might request the cash register with utterances such as "My turn for the register" or "Can I have a turn now, please?" Children with language impairments may begin by making no verbal request at all, then advance to a primitive request such as "Gimme that," and ultimately arrive at more sophisticated polite forms such as "Can I use that, please?" Hearing the verbal negotiations of typically developing children and practicing with the accurate models provide an optimal learning ground for children with language impairments. An occasional adult model or recast is typically all that is needed to set the wheels of dramatic play negotiations in motion.

In a more general sense, dramatic play activities are central to the facilitation of social interactive skills. More than any other time during the LAP day, the dramatic play activity is built on interaction and is difficult, if not impossible, to carry out without conversational exchange. By nature, dramatic play activities encourage children to initiate conversations with peers and adults and to respond to peer and adult initiations. The familiar, repetitive structure of dramatic play activity scripts enhances the likelihood of interactive success for children with language impairments. After hearing a teacher or peer (acting as a waiter) say repeatedly, "Do you want more coffee?" the child with a language impairment can take the waiter role and initiate with "More coffee?" In this way, the roles and structure of dramatic play scripts assist the social interactive skills of children with language impairments.

Scripts as an Intervention Strategy

Scripted dramatic play activities constitute a key language intervention strategy used in the concentrated normative model of classroom activities. Opportunities for verbal communication about both familiar and unfamiliar objects and events arise during these activities. Children can practice social interactive skills, particularly child–child interactions, in this context, and these activities capitalize on the interactions of children with special needs with their typically developing peers. Also, it is during these activities that children can practice language form (including speech sounds) as well as function and use. Furthermore, adults can provide focused linguistic input about events and objects of interest to children during scripted play activities.

IMPLEMENTATION OF INTERVENTION

Intervention goals are to be achieved during preschool activities. As described above, in LAP, the intervention procedures used by the teacher and/or clinicians are a variety of verbal productions including focused contrasts, modeling, event casts, open questions, expansions, recasts, redirects and prompted initiations, and scripted play. Commands, requests, and test questions can be used to find out a child's present level of performance but are not considered facilitative for acquiring new language forms. Some of these intervention techniques are controlled by the adults in the sense that adults can employ them at any time; others are controlled by the children. For example, an adult can provide a model for a child whenever it is appropriate. However, an adult cannot expand a child's production unless the child has first said something. To that extent, the use of expansions by the adult is under the child's control. The following case study provides an example of testing, goal setting, intervention techniques, and plans for a child attending the LAP.

Making a Therapy Plan

An essential factor in planning for intervention in a classroom setting is that the plan be flexible. This is necessary because much of the intervention will be completed during child-centered activities, when the adult is following the child's interests. The adult, therefore, cannot be sure which activity will be the focus of the child's attention. Planning for therapy is important in preparing the adult to take advantage of the types of communicative opportunities that might arise in the classroom.

Another factor in planning for therapy is to maintain a focus on a specific child's goals and objectives. By making tentative plans of action based on information about the daily themes and activities, the adult will be more likely to provide appropriate input and note relevant output. Therefore, to incorporate speech and language goals in classroom interaction, the adult should do the following:

1. Read curriculum plans for each day of the week, focusing on the Language and Literacy Skills Facilitated section.

2. Identify the target child's speech and language goals that relate to the week's activities and could be incorporated into daily events.

3. Complete a therapy guide.

Figure 3.1 provides an example of a sample therapy guide. It includes the child's target language skills and optimum times during the day for intervention (see When to Emphasize Target Skills). Possible intervention strategies (see How to Emphasize Target Skills) are generated to highlight how these skills will be facilitated. The therapy guide also lists any special materials that will be needed (see Special Props and/or Materials). Finally, after intervention has begun, notes are made about what actually happened (see Documentation of Progress [What Happened?]). Specific data relating to the child's objectives, such as longest sentence produced, production of target structures, and peer interaction successes, are of particular interest.

Child: Suzie _____

Clinician: Laura _____

Date: 9/23 _____

Theme: Transportation (airplane) _____

Target Language Skill(s):

1. Increase use of specific vocabulary (focus on nouns, verbs, adjective, and locatives)

2. Increase number of initiations with peers

3. Increase use of present progressive (-ing)

When to Emphasize Target Skills:

During center time, snack time, outdoor play, and free time

How to Emphasize Target Skills:

Provide *focused contrasts, event casts, modeling* to elicit target structures; *expand/recast* child utterances by

- *Describing* what he is doing and providing labels for objects, actions, and locations: "Suzie, you're buy*ing* a ticket; Laura *bought* a ticket" (model of *-ing* and focused contrast between *buying* and *bought*). "You are the pilot," "You are mak*ing* an airplane," "He is fly*ing* the airplane fast," "It is land*ing* on the ground" (event casts and models).

- *Joining in* the activities and also *describing* what the clinician is doing: "I like to go on airplane trips," "I want a large Coke" (models), " My seatbelt is on," "Suzie's is off" (focused recast).

- *Commenting on* and *expanding* child utterances: Suzie: "Belt off," Laura: "Yes, your belt is off," to "My belt is off, too."

- Encouraging *requesting* from a peer or teacher during snack time, art, and sharing time; encouraging peer interaction through sharing the role of pilot or flight attendant; *redirecting* child to peers when appropriate.

Special Props and/or Materials:

Utilize play materials child is using in dramatic play, art, block, or quiet areas.

Documentation of Progress (What Happened?):

(Describe on back of sheet success/failure of therapy procedures.)

- Suzie used -ing form three times (omitted it several other times for a total correct use of 3/10)

- By the end of center time, Suzie used the term *pilot* twice instead of just pointing when she wanted to be the pilot. Suzie appeared to understand the term *behind* because she got behind another child on command while waiting for a turn.

- Suzie verbally initiated two times to an adult during a 10-minute observation.

Figure 3.1. Sample therapy guide.

INTERVENTION CASE STUDY: TOM

Three-year-old Tom speaks primarily in one-word utterances. (His mean length of utterance [MLU] is 1.22.) Tom's words are usually intelligible, and he appears to understand much of what is said to him. He is shy when interacting with peers, preferring to watch rather than to play with them. He usually pays attention to the teacher during group activities and responds nonverbally to adult directions.

The Peabody Picture Vocabulary Test–III (Dunn & Dunn, 1997) requires the child to choose a target picture from four choices. On this test, Tom achieved a raw score of 10, a standard score equivalent of 78 (mean = 100 +/– 15), and a percentile rank of 7. On the receptive section of the Reynell Developmental Language Scales–U.S. Edition (Reynell & Gruber, 1990), the child is required to listen to a variety of requests and demonstrate his or her understanding through manipulation of toy objects. Tom received a raw score of 31, a standard score of 74 (mean = 100 +/– 15), and a percentile rank of 5. On the expressive section of the Reynell Development Language Scales–U.S. Edition, which requires the child to label items, define words, and describe pictures, Tom achieved a raw score of 12 and a standard score of below 63, which rates him below the first percentile. On the Goldman-Fristoe Test of Articulation 2 (GFTA; Goldman & Fristoe, 2000) (administered imitatively), Tom scored at the 28th percentile, which is within low-normal limits.

Therapy Goals for Tom

Long-term therapy outcomes for Tom consist of the following :

1. Increase vocabulary knowledge
2. Increase mean length of utterances
3. Increase appropriate peer interactions

    Tom's short-term goals consist of the following:

1. By the end of the semester, Tom will understand and produce 20 new nouns and 10 new verbs at a level of 80% correct as measured by classroom probes. (Words will be chosen from classroom themes and activities.)
2. By the end of the semester, Tom's MLU–Morphemes will increase to 2.5 as measured by a language sample.
3. By the end of the semester, Tom will produce the following morphemes at the 80% criterion level: "on," "in," and "-ing" as measured by language sampling.
4. By the end of the semester, Tom will increase his initiations and responses to peers to a least 5 (5 initiations and at least 5 responses) as measured by the Social Interactive Coding System (Rice, Sell, & Hadley, 1990) during a 10-minute sample.

The goals for Tom, then, are to increase vocabulary knowledge, length and complexity of utterances, and appropriate peer interactions.

Therapy Examples for Tom During Classroom Activities

The following examples of classroom intervention include both general language facilitation techniques as well as specific intervention techniques. When possible, a specific focus on Tom and his intervention goals will be presented. The description will follow the classroom schedule of activities.

Arrival Time

The child in the case study, Tom, is playing with the blocks and farm animals. As he plays, the teacher describes what Tom is doing. Verbal responses from Tom are invited but not required. A number of specific vocabulary words can be used during the activities. Targeted grammatical structures are underlined in the examples that follow. In addition, many opportunities for assisting appropriate peer interactions arise.

*   Models: "You are build_ing_ a fence. A big fence. The cows can't get out. The cow is jump_ing._ He is jump_ing_ over the fence. He is _on_ the ground now."
*   Focused contrasts: "He's not _in_ the truck. He's _on_ the ground."
*   Expansions: When the child says, "Block," the adult could say, "Big block," "Two blocks," "More blocks," or "Blocks _in_ tub," depending on the child's meaning.
*   Prompted initiations: "Ask Mary for a block. Say, 'May I have a block, please?'"

Dramatic Play/ Center Time

Tom is pretending to be the veterinarian and has a toy doctor kit available. Again, a number of specific vocabulary words can be used. Underlining highlights the grammatical morphemes targeted for this child.

- Models: "My doggie's sick. Give him a shot," "Is my dog OK?" "Help my dog," and "Thank you for helping my dog."
- Expansions: If the child says, "Hurt," the adult could say, "Doggie is hurt."
- Prompted initiations: "Go ask Bobby for a turn. Say, 'May I have a turn, please?'"
- Open questions: If the adult asks, "Where can we go?" the child might say, "Vet." The adult could then say, "OK, we'll go to the vet" or "We're driving to the vet." (These are both expansions and acknowledgments.)
- Redirects: If the child says, "Want car," the adult could redirect the child to a peer with, "Tell Charlie, 'Car, please.'"

Art/Science Area: Tom is decorating a Valentine bag.

- Models: "Paper is red or pink," "Cutting out the heart," "You're pasting," and "You're putting it on the bag."
- Expansions: If the child says, "Cut," the adult could expand this with, "Cutting the paper."
- Prompted initiations: The adult could say, "Ask Gary. Say, 'More glue, please.'"
- Open questions: The adult might ask, "What color do you want?" When the child points one out, the adult could provide a model such as, "You want red."

Quiet Time

Tom is working with a puzzle and later gets a book for the clinician to read.

- Models: "You're putting the sun on the top. The dog goes here [pointing to a place on the puzzle]. It's at the bottom of the puzzle."
- Expansions: If the child says, "Pig here," the adult might say, "The pig goes here."
- Open questions: The adult could ask, "What's happening?" The child might respond, "Boy ride," to which the adult might reply with an expansion, such as "Boy is riding a bike."

Block Area: Tom is playing with blocks and little cars.

- Models: "You're stacking blocks. The blocks are falling."
- Expansions: If the child says, "Car hit," the adult might say, "The cars are hitting."

Storytime

Storytime is a teacher-directed time during which short stories are read and sometimes acted out. Stories may focus on labeling to present new vocabulary, or they may be adventure stories, which provide an introduction to story grammar. Adventure stories often have the following sequence: 1) character introduction, 2) several events, 3) climax, and 4) resolution. Many children's stories are home–adventure–home stories, in which the character's adventure begins at home, his or her adventures lead elsewhere, and then the character returns home and is safe.

Stories with repetitive lines also can be effective in teaching language structure and in helping children predict future events. These stories can provide a way for children to be involved in storytelling. As a line is read repeatedly, the children can join in. Acting out familiar stories helps children understand a story's sequence and provides a way to demonstrate knowledge of the story's grammar. Use of dialogue from a story can help children like Tom produce or practice new sentence structures.

Adult: Teddy bear, teddy bear, what do you see? I see _____ looking at me.

Tom: Look me.

Sharing Time

Sharing time helps children learn how to ask and answer questions. As a child shows the class something brought from home, another child asks three routine questions about the item ("What do you have?" "What do you do with it?" and "Where did you get it?"). Later, additional questions are encouraged. The routine questions are important as they provide support for the child who has limited language, and the routine itself helps both children know what to do and say. More important, these questions can help children learn more information about their environments outside of the classroom. Adults and other children usually respond to someone who asks them, "What do you have?" or "What's that?" The children's exposure to new vocabulary is thus increased, and they have learned one way to initiate interactions.

Transition Times

Transition times can also be used as language-learning opportunities. For example, it is very easy to find out if children understand the use of certain grammatical forms, such as the un-contractible copula (*to be* used as a main verb and in situations in which it cannot be contracted to the *'s* form). One time to do this is when the children are getting ready to go outside. The teacher can ask such questions as "Who is ready?" Children who are in line with their coats on can respond with "I am" or "He is." Requests for help in putting on outdoor clothes can be a good time to provide labels for clothing items or body parts: "Put your hand in the mitten," "Let's zip up your coat," "You need your hat to cover your ears," and so forth. In Tom's case, the new vocabulary can be emphasized as well as the form (e.g., hand *in* the mitten).

Outside Time

Outside time activities provide many opportunities to model, expand, prompt, and redirect children's verbal productions. In particular, adults can teach a variety of verbs (e.g., *run, jump, skip, ride, slide, dig, climb, build*) and prepositions (e.g., *in, through, on, down, under, on top of, in front of, behind*). Variation in the complexity of the language can be made: "Mary is slid<u>ing</u> down the slide" and "Suzie is rid<u>ing</u> the bike on the road" versus "Climb ladder" and "Dig in sand." In Tom's case, both of these types of sentences would be appropriate. Turn taking can also be highlighted during outside time. Prompted initiations, such as "Tell Joe, 'My turn, please,'" can help a child begin to negotiate for a turn on a bike or another piece of equipment.

Snack Time

Snack time provides many activities to model, expand, prompt, and redirect children's verbal productions. It is also a time to teach politeness (e.g., "Please pass the juice," "May I have more crackers, please?"). Number skills can also be taught. For example, a teacher can say, "You have five crackers. Now you ate one. How many do you have left?" or "How many crackers do you have?" or "You can have two more crackers." It is also a time to encourage peer–peer exchanges. This can be done through prompted initiations. If the adult says to the child, "Why don't you ask Suzie to pass the juice," the child might say to Suzie, "Suzie, please pass the juice"). Peer interaction can be encouraged through redirects. The child might say to an adult, "I need more," and the adult can redirect with, "Ask Suzie to hand you the crackers." Then the child might say to Suzie, "Hand me the crackers, please." In Tom's case, the redirection may be shortened to "More, please." Peer-to-peer conversations can be encouraged by just allowing them to occur. Letting children sit by their special friends also encourages them to talk to each other.

Group Time

Group time is a teacher-directed activity in which new vocabulary and concepts can be introduced to the children. The lessons may involve matching, labeling, classification, and sequencing activities, or they may involve learning the alphabet and number concepts. During group time, the teacher can support children in their participation to ensure success. Activities can easily be manipulated to allow for different skill levels. For example, one child may be asked to identify the object that is different from the others. The object may be a car with the other choices being blocks. A different child might have to identify a blue car from a choice of three other cars or identify a big red car from a group of cars that are different sizes and colors. In Tom's case, the targeted vocabulary might be a location term, so Tom would be asked to identify the item that is in the box (versus beside or under the box).

During group activities, the teacher uses appropriate language facilitation strategies, which include modeling appropriate vocabulary and structure and prompting and expanding children's initiations and responses. For a classification activity, the teacher can model the appropriate verbal and nonverbal responses and then have the children perform the appropriate responses with a new item. Using open questions can be effective in helping children learn to problem-solve or to focus on a specific feature. For example, the teacher might ask, "How can we find out how many ribs Smiley [the skeleton] has?" At least one child will usually respond by saying, "Count them." The teacher can then count or have a child help count.

Music Time

Music time is an opportunity to have fun singing and doing rhythm activities with other children. The songs are short and often repetitive so that children can easily learn them. The melody and rhythm help in learning the songs. Also, the children can often respond nonverbally by clapping or imitating the teacher's hand motions. Some children first begin to speak when singing or doing fingerplays. For example, in a traditional song such as "Old MacDonald Had a Farm," children can initially participate by just making the appropriate animal sounds. Later, they can join in singing the whole song. Tom would be one of the children who would start with imitating the different animal sounds. Songs and fingerplays also could be helpful in expanding Tom's vocabulary knowledge. Many songs use a variety of action words and labels. For example, the song "Going on a Bear Hunt" discusses crossing a bridge, swimming in a river, climbing a cliff, and so forth.

SUMMARY

The description of intervention provided in this chapter illustrates how children with speech and language impairments can receive a concentrated normative model of intervention with typical preschool activities. Strategies for facilitating language learning in the classroom setting hinge on providing an environment in which many opportunities for natural language use and interaction occur. There must be opportunities for both child–child and adult–child talk. There also needs to be a balance between activities that provide new information and new responses and activities that are routine and support and extend old knowledge.

4

Research on the Language-Focused Curriculum

Teacher Training and Implementation Fidelity

Laura Justice, Alice K. Wiggins, and Khara L. Pence

There is currently an unprecedented amount of attention on promoting the quality of children's language-learning experiences in preschool classrooms. This is particularly true for those programs, such as Head Start, that serve children who are at risk for future academic difficulties due to the effects of childhood poverty. The LFC offers a systematic, comprehensive approach to elevating the quality of the preschool classroom's language-learning environment. It also provides explicit guidance to educators for promoting both incidental and direct instruction across a range of language dimensions (e.g., grammatical structures, lexical concepts, social skills) and other important school readiness indicators (e.g., problem solving, reasoning). It is thus an important tool for educators and administrators who are vested in promoting preschool children's language-learning experiences in the classroom. Also, in light of current tensions among preschool educators and administrators on how best to strike a balance between explicit promotion of preacademic skills and the use of developmentally appropriate practice (DAP), the LFC is noteworthy in its emphasis on the use of dramatic play as a critical mechanism for teachers to explicitly promote a host of critical readiness skills.

The LFC is well grounded in contemporary social-interactionist theory of how children learn language within social contexts. Nonetheless, the current educational climate emphasizes the importance of educators' adherence to the tenets of evidence-based practice (EBP), in which decisions concerning the use of specific educational techniques and approaches are based not only on one's consideration of theory but also on evidence derived from experimental research (see Stanovich & Stanovich, 2003). This press for EBP extends throughout all facets of schooling practices to include all grade levels (preschool to high school) and content areas. With respect to preschool education, most of the attention has focused on identifying evidence-based approaches to facilitating young children's language acquisition and emergent literacy skills. This is due to the critical integrative linkages of these skills to later academic outcomes (particularly in reading) as well as some evidence

The Preschool Curriculum Evaluation Research (PCER) program, funded by the U.S. Department of Education's Institute of Education Sciences (IES), includes a national evaluation study conducted by RTI International and Mathematica Policy Research (MPR) as well as complementary research studies conducted by each grantee. The findings reported here are based on the complementary research activities carried out by research personnel at the University of Virginia under the PCER program (Grant #R305J030084). These findings may differ from the results reported for the PCER national evaluation study. The findings presented in this chapter sought to answer complementary research questions. The content of this publication does not necessarily reflect the views or policies of the PCER Consortium, including IES, RTI, and MPR, nor does mention of trade names, commercial products, or organizations imply endorsement by the U.S. Department of Education.

showing that early deficits in language and literacy development can be attenuated with intensive early interventions, including participation in high-quality preschool programming (e.g., Karoly, Kilburn, & Cannon, 2005).

To add to this body of research, specifically that which is focused explicitly on identifying effective interventions that promote young children's language and literacy skills, the U.S. Department of Education's Institute of Education Sciences (IES) supported the establishment of the Preschool Curriculum Evaluation Research (PCER) Consortium, of which we were members. The individual members of this consortium received financial support from IES to conduct rigorous large-scale longitudinal effectiveness studies of commercial preschool curricula between 2002 and 2007. As members of this consortium, we conducted two separate studies of the LFC that together involved over 400 preschool children in 30 classrooms as well as the teachers and assistants staffing these classrooms. The children in these classrooms met eligibility criteria for participating in at-risk programs and, for the most part, met eligibility based on family income (i.e., they resided in homes for which the annual household income was below federal poverty guidelines). As a group, these children had significant needs in the area of language, as indicated through formal language screenings conducted by our team. For example, in our 2nd year of implementing the language-focused curriculum, in which we worked with teachers and children in 16 preschool classrooms, we administered The Fluharty Preschool Speech and Language Screening Test–Second Edition (Fluharty-2; Fluharty, 2001) in the fall of the academic year to 147 children. On the Sequencing Events subtest, 45% of children had standard scores less than or equal to 1 standard deviation below the mean (≤ 1 SD); likewise, on the Describing Actions subtest, 54% of children performed in this range. These data illustrate both the substantial and negative effects of poverty on children's language development; they also provide telling evidence concerning the need to ensure the quality of these children's preschool learning environments if the educational community is to reduce the impact of poverty on children's long-term academic outcomes.

The teachers in these classrooms formed a heterogeneous group, as is characteristic of the preschool teaching workforce in general. For instance, some of our teachers were in their first year of teaching, whereas others had taught for many years. Some teachers had little education beyond a high school diploma; others had graduate degrees. Some taught in Head Start programs administered through county human services programs, and others taught in state-funded prekindergarten programs affiliated with elementary schools. Compensation for some teachers was at the current minimum wage standards; compensation for others was consistent with that of local schoolteachers. Undoubtedly, some of our teachers were excited about using a new, language-rich curriculum, whereas others were decidedly more hesitant—if not, on occasion, downright resistant. At least in part, this resistance was precipitated by the fact that many of the teachers were veteran users of another preschool curriculum and were comfortable with its use. Also, the curriculum in use had little explicit focus on language; consequently, the teachers were generally unfamiliar with (and perhaps even threatened by) the host of novel concepts so central to implementation of the LFC in their classrooms. Indeed, we found that many of the teachers with whom we worked over a 2-year period needed to update their knowledge of language development and language stimulation approaches.

As part of our research activities, which were designed to study not only the overall effectiveness of the LFC but also how the use of this curriculum influences the quality of teacher instruction, we developed a comprehensive training and technical assistance program for teachers implementing the LFC to ensure that they could implement the curriculum as author Betty Bunce intended it to be implemented. This involved developing a 3-day training workshop for teachers as well as follow-up refresher trainings, purchasing materials for teachers that they needed for implementing certain lessons (e.g., specific props for dramatic play activities, certain storybooks), responding to ongoing teacher questions about implementation (e.g., how much they could change certain lessons and still adhere to the curriculum), monitoring teachers' fidelity of implementation to specific aspects of the curriculum and giving feedback on their fidelity, and so forth. In the remainder of this chapter, we will detail some of our research findings concerning teacher implementation of various elements of the LFC as well as our more general thoughts on how teachers can be most effectively trained and supported to use the LFC in their classrooms. We include a detailed discussion of how stakeholder support can be heightened through all phases of curriculum implementation.

PROFESSIONAL DEVELOPMENT TRAINING: DESIGNING TEACHERS' WORKSHOP EXPERIENCE

Over a 2-year period, we trained two cohorts of preschool teachers in the use of the LFC. Our approach was to provide a comprehensive workshop to teachers prior to start of the academic year, provide a refresher workshop midway through the year, and also provide technical assistance on an ongoing basis.

The 3-day project kickoff workshop was conducted 2–3 weeks prior to the start of the academic year and was designed to familiarize the participants with the scope, sequence, and structure of the LFC. The workshop was designed in consideration of best practices and available research regarding adult learning and factors that influence the success of professional development. Such factors include close proximity in timing between the training and participants' implementation of the training material, inclusion of modeling in the presentation of workshop content, and active learning opportunities emphasizing participant practice and feedback as opposed to a focus on didactic learning opportunities (see Bandura, 1986). Workshop content comprised three general components: an overview of language and literacy development, theoretical overview of the LFC, and modeling and practice of LFC instructional processes and activity contexts. We describe each of these three components in turn.

Overview of Language and Literacy Development

In the overview of language and literacy development, we explained the difference between *communication, speech,* and *language,* reviewed important language milestones for young children, and provided an introduction to *language domains* (e.g., semantics, morphology, phonology, pragmatics). At least some of the teacher participants had never had a course on language development, and this information was very new to them and provided an important foundation to concepts crucial for implementing the LFC. For other teachers, even those with a stronger academic background in language development, this introductory section provided an important refresher of concepts they had learned some time ago during teacher training. The overview of language and literacy development was designed to help teachers and their assistants understand the importance of language development and its relationship to later school achievement, including literacy development. This component of the training was primarily didactic in nature; however, we encouraged participants to ask questions and provide examples from their own classrooms that they perceived to be relevant to the content.

Perhaps the greatest challenge in this initial segment of training was introducing teachers to linguistic terms that form the core of the LFC objectives—terms like *verb phrase structures, pronouns, adjectives, prepositions,* and *phonemes.* Research has shown that even university graduate students in education and speech-language pathology have challenges understanding these terms (Justice & Ezell, 1999), thus it should have been no surprise to our research team that our participating teachers (many of whom were not college graduates) would have little knowledge of these terms. We gave teachers some exercises to help them understand these concepts.

Theoretical Overview of the Language-Focused Curriculum

The second component of the workshop included a theoretical overview of the curriculum, which was designed to illustrate how the LFC is aligned to DAP and to bolster participants' understanding of the importance of supporting young children's language development. In the first year of our implementation, Betty Bunce provided this component of training; in the second year, we conducted this element ourselves using material in the LFC manual. For this component, teachers and their assistants received an outline of curriculum and lesson plan structures that illustrated how the weekly and daily themes should be used to support classroom activities. Teachers were also presented with curriculum objectives and targets for each objective (e.g., language skills, emergent literacy skills, cognitive skills), and they learned how they could incorporate each objective within a given classroom activity context.

In this second part of training, we differentiated the two core aspects of the LFC for teachers, which we came to refer to as 1) activity contexts and 2) instructional processes. Activity contexts comprise the elements of the curriculum that organized children's daily experiences in the classroom through a variety of activities (e.g., art, dramatic play, storytime, large group). Instructional processes comprise the interactive language experiences occurring between teachers and pupils. Concerning the latter, the LFC emphasizes teachers' use of language facilitation techniques (e.g., recasts, open questions, event casts, prompted initiations), which we came to refer to as language stimulation techniques (LSTs). Teachers learned about these techniques from a series of video clips showing how each strategy might be used within a variety of classroom activity contexts.

Modeling and Practice

For the third component of the training workshop, teachers and assistants worked in small groups to plan a thematic lesson that included activities for each of the routines in the LFC daily structure (e.g., music, art, dramatic play). They were encouraged to incorporate LSTs into their lesson plans as well. Each group then modeled the dramatic play portion of their lesson plan using appropriate props and LSTs. We provided guidance and feedback to the participants and encouraged each group to solicit additional suggestions and feedback from peers.

PROMOTING STAKEHOLDER COMMITMENT

A review of recent literature on curriculum implementation reveals some common themes regarding factors that relate to implementation success. Such factors include providing effective professional development (discussed above), encouraging stakeholder involvement, addressing resistance to change, ensuring provision of resources, providing ongoing support, monitoring implementation fidelity, and providing follow-up professional development (Haynes, 1998; Keys, 2005; Sobeck, Abbey, & Agius, 2006). Stakeholder involvement is crucial to any change process, including implementation of a new curriculum. Involving stakeholders in a change process involves gathering information about the individual needs of the stakeholders, providing stakeholders with expectations regarding the change, and promoting stakeholders' support for and acceptance of the change (Anderson & Anderson, 2001).

When asking preschool teachers to adopt a new curriculum, particularly one as comprehensive as the LFC, ensuring stakeholder involvement is an important consideration. We encouraged stakeholder involvement to the extent possible given the constraints of our experimental design. For instance, administrators at one Head Start Center that was involved with our LFC implementation project for 2 years sat "at the table" with our research team from the very start of grant development. Along the way, we provided periodic presentations to administrative teams and governing boards of directors, emphasizing the collaborative nature of the curriculum evaluation. With respect to teachers as stakeholders, although we had preselected the LFC as the curriculum to be implemented and evaluated, through the informed consent process teachers had the opportunity to choose whether or not to participate in the study. In addition, administrators participated in all training workshops so that they would be familiar with the curriculum and would be able to support teachers and assistants in their implementation of the curriculum. We also gathered information about the individual needs of stakeholders by encouraging teachers, assistants, and administrators to voice their concerns to us throughout the implementation process. Such opportunities also assisted us in addressing any resistance to the new curriculum.

Addressing Resistance to Change

We addressed participants' resistance to change in a number of ways. One area in which our implementation met resistance was with lesson plan content. The LFC lesson plans are intended to provide a guideline for the structure and content of specific lessons. However, for the purposes of our research study, we required strict levels of adherence to the lesson plans to ensure that any between-subjects (i.e., between-condition) effects could be attributed to the curriculum rather than to other extraneous factors; this requirement also ensured replicability. Consequently, we requested that teachers implement the lesson plans exactly as they were presented in the LFC manual (Bunce, 1995a). Many teachers demonstrated some degree of resistance to this request, for valid reasons. For example, some teachers expressed concern that using the preplanned lessons and sequence would provide them with less flexibility to meet the individual needs of their children. Other teachers expressed that they had accumulated favorite activities that were not included as part of the LFC lessons. An additional challenge was that one program was not permitted to use food for activities other than eating, which precluded them from offering several art activities that used pasta or cereal for stringing or pasting. Through open communication and conversations with the teachers, we were able to alleviate some of these challenges with a compromise that allowed teachers to replace LFC lessons with lessons of their own as long as the lessons aligned with the theme and supported the objectives of the LFC. In contexts other than an experimental-design research study, such modifications would ordinarily be permissible. Whenever teachers modified an activity or lesson, we asked that they document and submit the modification to our project staff.

Another area of resistance was the daily change of the LFC dramatic play scenarios. As readers of this book are aware, the LFC requires daily, weekly, and monthly rotation of themes and includes some fairly elaborate schemes for dramatic play. Many of our participating teachers had existing daily routines that were similar to the LFC routines and activities, and all of our teachers included dramatic play as part of their daily center activities. However, none of the participating teachers had previously rotated dramatic play scenarios more than a few times during the school year. In fact, most teachers maintained a "housekeeping" dramatic play scenario all year long. Some teachers were surprised at the requirement and frustrated by the effort required to rotate the dramatic play scenario on a daily basis. As with challenges regarding lesson plans, open communication—along with the provision of most of the materials needed for thematic rotations—allowed us to resolve most of the resistance related to the dramatic play activity context. Providing teachers with these materials was made possible by our federal grant support.

We should also emphasize, however, that other teachers went above and beyond the requirements for implementing each new dramatic play scenario. For instance, during the "car wash" scenario, one teacher rolled up the carpets in her classroom and let the children wash their bikes with real soap and water. For the "gardening" scenario, the same teacher filled a baby pool with potting soil and trays of live pansies. She let the children "shop" at the garden center and plant their own flowers. Although these activities are commendable and provided the children with authentic learning opportunities, the LFC does not stipulate that teachers must implement each scenario with this level of detail and complexity. We did stress to the teachers that they should balance the complexity of their activities across the week, for example, by introducing new props throughout the week. We also encouraged teachers to rely on books and stories to assist in providing detail and building context, and to allow the dramatic play props and materials to be more open ended (e.g., to use a rectangular block as a telephone). Another way we attempted to alleviate resistance to the daily dramatic play change was to encourage teachers at the same facility to coordinate their weekly schedules in a manner that allowed them to rotate the dramatic play scenarios and materials from one room to another at the end of each day.

In the second year of the study, in which we worked with 16 preschool teachers to implement the LFC, we built in more flexibility on thematic rotations by allowing teachers to rotate the dramatic play scenarios on a weekly rather than daily basis. We felt this was necessary to maintain the buy-in of our teachers who appreciated the thematic variation afforded by the LFC but were overwhelmed by daily rotation of themes. We did, however, encourage teachers to increase the complexity of each scenario as the week progressed. For example, for a "doctor's office" dramatic play scenario, teachers might have children bring their dolls to see the doctor on Monday, add a receptionist role to the setting on Tuesday and have children sign in, add an X-ray technician or nurse to the scenario on Wednesday, and so on.

Providing Resources

Throughout the curriculum implementation, we also ensured adequate provision of resources, a key factor in influencing the success of implementation. Provision of sufficient resources sends the message to teachers that change is a priority and that it is valued and supported. During our implementation, participating teachers received enough materials to implement each thematic scenario. We provided teachers with a wide variety of dramatic play props, including realistic toy props (e.g., walkie-talkies, cameras, tools), open-ended props (e.g., blocks, fabric), and costumes. We also provided teachers with a variety of arts and crafts supplies and one or two books aligned to each theme in the LFC.

Ensuring Technical Support

We also provided teachers with ongoing technical support as needed. Each week, teachers submitted weekly LFC lesson plans to our project staff and noted any additions or modifications they had made to the original plans. Teachers also asked questions about the appropriateness of changes they were unsure about. Teacher implementation of the curriculum activity contexts was relatively strong as measured by their adherence to the LFC lesson plans. Implementation fidelity was also measured three times per year using a curriculum fidelity checklist and transcriptions of videotaped classroom observations recorded during the same three visits as the fidelity checklist. By collecting ongoing data concerning how well teachers were able to implement the various elements of the LFC, we could provide relatively timely support to them over the course of the academic year.

MEASURING IMPLEMENTATION FIDELITY

Measurement of implementation fidelity is a critical component of intervention research, but it is also important to supporting a user's achievement of full implementation of a new intervention. *Implementation fidelity* refers to one's adherence to using new techniques, methods, or strategies. The LFC is a complex curriculum that requires teachers to use specific instructional processes (the LSTs), and undoubtedly, monitoring of fidelity is critical to helping teachers achieve full implementation.

The Language-Focused Curriculum Fidelity Checklist

For research purposes, we developed the LFC Fidelity Checklist, which was administered by trained observers in our LFC classrooms three times annually (fall, winter, and spring). The checklist contains 45 items and was developed by examining core LFC features (see the appendix following this chapter). The checklist is organized into seven sections. The first section focuses on instructional processes. (Note that the LST *scripted play* was not included on the checklist because it is specific to the dramatic play activity context.). Items are scored on a scale of 0–3, with 0 points indicating that the LST was not observed, 1 point indicating that

Table 4.1.   Percentage of items observed for activity context categories of the Language-Focused Curriculum Fidelity Checklist for teachers in fall of the academic year

Category	Percentage of items observed M (SD)
Daily structure	85 (15)
Dramatic play	89 (13)
Art	98 (4)
Story	83 (23)
Group	92 (20)
Music	86 (18)

it was observed one time, 2 points indicating that it was observed a few times (i.e., two to three times), and 3 points indicating that it was observed many times (i.e., four or more times).

The remaining six sections include 38 items that focus on the following LFC activity contexts: daily structure, dramatic play, art, story, group, and music. Each item receives a dichotomous rating based on whether the indicator was observed or not observed. A score is calculated for each category by dividing the number of items observed by the total number of items possible (proportion of items observed = number of items observed/total number of items).

To determine the internal consistency of the two sections of the LFC Fidelity Checklist, Cronbach's alpha was computed separately for the instructional process and activity context sections of the checklist for the fall, winter, and spring fidelity observations. Coefficients were acceptable for the instructional process items: 0.67 in the fall, 0.79 in the winter, and 0.80 in the spring. For the 38 activity context items, Cronbach's alpha was also acceptable: 0.98 in the fall, 0.91 in the winter, and 0.88 in the spring. Interrater reliability was examined by having two coders independently score the checklist in two classrooms in the second year of the PCER study. For the seven process items, the two coders' average agreement was 93%; for the 38 activity context items, the average agreement was 97%. These data indicate that the LFC Fidelity Checklist can be administered reliably.

Teacher Use of Activity Contexts

Our use of the LFC checklist over 2 years of research was informative as we considered the process of change in the classroom as teachers used a new, complex language-rich curriculum. Specifically, we found that teachers' implementation of LFC activity contexts was strong in the fall of the academic year (within 4–6 weeks following the training workshop). The percentage of checklist items observed for each of the six LFC activity contexts is presented in Table 4.1. Data show that teachers exhibited adherence to at least 85% of the items in each of the six activity context categories measured by the LFC checklist, even after a relatively short training workshop. Teachers may have demonstrated high adherence to the LFC activity contexts because implementation was tangible and clearly specified in the LFC lesson plans.

In our implementation of the LFC with seven preschool teachers in the 2003–2004 academic year, our initial 3-day workshop training focused primarily on orienting teachers to the activity contexts of the LFC and adherence to its general lesson plan structure. For many of these teachers, use of the LFC required a reorganization of the classroom day, use of new materials (including a thematic approach), and adherence to a new lesson plan structure. Consequently, we focused most of the initial workshop training on helping teachers integrate the LFC activity contexts into their classrooms (approximately 1 day of this training was spent describing the eight LSTs to the teachers). As noted, teachers showed high adherence in the fall of the year to these elements of the LFC.

Teacher Use of Language Stimulation Techniques

Teacher fidelity to implementation of the LSTs, however, was not as readily achieved. Not surprisingly, in our initial observation of teacher implementation of the LFC, which occurred about 4–6 weeks into the academic year, we found that teacher use of many of the individual LSTs was overall quite low. In fact, in a 24-minute videotaped and transcribed observation of teachers in the seven LFC classrooms, of the 2,322 utterances recorded, only 837 (36%) were LSTs. Some LSTs occurred at much higher rates than others, and there was considerable variability among teachers. The following figures show the average frequency of six of the eight LSTs observed in each of the seven classrooms. (Note: We did not code for scripted play because this technique is specific to the dramatic play context. Due to the similarity of expansions and recasts, we collapsed these two categories to form a single category termed *recasts*. For the same reason, we also collapsed prompted initiations and redirects to form a single category termed *redirects*.)

- Models: average of 65 (range: 22–111)
- Recasts: average of 30 (range: 9–52)
- Open questions: average of 16 (range: 1–53)
- Event casts: average of 5 (range: 1–13)
- Prompted initiations/redirects: average of 1 (range: 0–6)
- Focused contrasts: average of 1 (range: 0–4)

Increasing Teacher Use of Language Stimulation Techniques

As Bunce discusses in Chapter 5, the effectiveness of the LFC rests, in large part, on the extent to which classroom environments provide children with opportunities to experience language instruction in meaningful social contexts that extend across the entire preschool curriculum. Consequently, use of the LFC involves implementation and maintenance of two complementary mechanisms through which children's language skills are accelerated: 1) activity contexts and 2) LSTs. The latter *relational processes* serve as the mechanism through which children's language skills are accelerated, and teacher use of these techniques serves an important complement to the rich, stimulating linguistic environment provided by the activity contexts of the LFC.

We were not particularly surprised at the findings on LSTs, given reports in the extant literature suggesting that 1) the language-learning environment of preschool classrooms is often mediocre and that 2) there is considerable variation among programs in the language-learning supports available to pupils (see Justice, Mashburn, Hamre, & Pianta, 2007). Nonetheless, we recognized that teacher use of the LSTs was a critical mechanism of the LFC, and we gave serious thought as to how we might increase teacher use of the majority of the LSTs. We looked at the published literature on professional development for preschool teachers, particularly studies of teacher implementation of conversational techniques (rather than scripted lesson plans), given our interest in improving relational processes within the classroom. We found several studies by Girolametto and his colleagues to be particularly informative (see Girolametto & Weitzman, 2002; Girolametto, Weitzman, & Greenberg, 2003). These studies described systematic approaches for improving teachers' implementation of interactive conversational processes in preschool classrooms and described specific professional development techniques they have used effectively. In light of the research findings from this corpus of work, our team organized a refresher training for our LFC teachers, which we delivered in January of the academic year. During this training, which was approximately 4 hours long, we reviewed each of the LSTs, modeled their use, and then had teachers sit at individual computer monitors to observe videotapes of themselves in their classrooms to rate the frequency with which they used the LSTs. After their observations were completed, we held a large-group debriefing session, during which

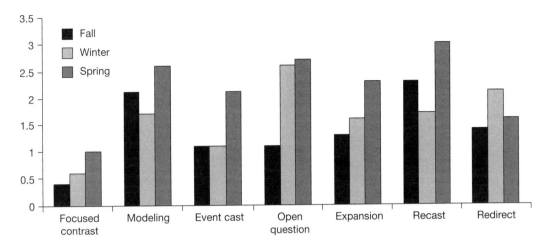

Figure 4.1. Ratings on the Language-Focused Curriculum Fidelity Checklist for teacher use of seven language stimulation techniques.

teachers reflected on their observations and discussed specific ways in which they could increase use of LSTs during various classroom activities.

The observation conducted in the LFC classrooms subsequent to this refresher, in May, showed a gradual increase in teacher use of the majority of the LSTs. Figure 4.1 shows ratings on the LFC Fidelity Checklist for teacher use of seven of the eight LSTs (again, scripted play is omitted). These data show that spring ratings for each LST were higher than fall and winter ratings, suggesting the value of using focused refresher trainings featuring video observation and opportunity for teacher reflection for improving teacher implementation of this component of the LFC.

ADDITIONAL PROFESSIONAL DEVELOPMENT TECHNIQUES

Although our research team used only one refresher training, other studies (e.g., Girolametto et al., 2003; Wasik, Bond, & Hindman, 2006) suggest that teacher participation in ongoing trainings—perhaps as often as once per month during an academic year—that allow them to practice conversational techniques are an important mechanism for facilitating teacher growth in this area. These studies also suggest that in-class modeling and practice with side-by-side coaching provided by expert teachers are viable techniques for improving teacher implementation of quality conversational techniques. Surely, these professional development techniques can be used with the LFC to provide teachers with more opportunities to practice LSTs and engage with other implementing teachers as they take on the challenge of heightening children's language-learning experiences.

Language-Focused Curriculum
Fidelity Checklist

Directions

The Language-Focused Curriculum (LFC) Fidelity Checklist is designed to assess the extent to which the LFC is implemented in each of the 14 classrooms (both treatment and control) participating in the PCER study. The LFC Fidelity Checklist should be completed over the course of 30 minutes and should follow a 2-hour long observation of LFC language stimulation techniques.

Observers should indicate with a plus (+) sign that a particular behavior has occurred when clear evidence is observed.

Observers should obtain teacher reports for items marked with an asterisk (*) if the behaviors are not directly observable.

Observers should position themselves as to be as unobtrusive as possible, yet should be able to clearly hear the teacher (or assistant) interacting with the children.

General observation information

Observer initials _____   Observation start time _____

Observation date _____   Observation end time _____

Scorer initials _____   Classroom teacher name _____

Adheres to LFC guidelines for teacher-child interaction through the following:

_____ Teacher displays print labels of objects in the classroom

_____ Teacher allows and participates in extended conversation with the students

_____ Teacher uses focused contrasts

_____ Teacher uses modeling

_____ Teacher uses event casting

_____ Teacher uses open questions

_____ Teacher uses expansions

_____ Teacher uses recasts

_____ Teacher uses redirects and prompted initiations

_____ Recognizes all child utterances for their communicative value regardless of accuracy

Adheres to the DAILY STRUCTURE of the LFC through the following:

_____ Rotates between child-centered and teacher-directed activities

_____ Organizes daily lessons around a particular theme, per the LFC manual

_____ Provides explicit structure to the daily dramatic play, art centers, and the large group session

Adheres to LFC guidelines for DRAMATIC PLAY through the following:

_____ Clear space is dedicated to dramatic play

_____ The dramatic play area has enough room for at least 4–6 children to play at one time

_____ Teacher and/or assistant are present in the dramatic play area

_____ Teacher and/or assistant present schemas related to the dramatic play theme

_____ The dramatic play is centered around a theme per the lesson plan

_____ Teacher demonstrates 3 or 4 possible roles for children

_____ Teacher prepares materials and environment in advance

_____ Dramatic play props are readily available for the children

_____ New settings are created daily*

Adheres to LFC guidelines for ART through the following:

_____ The art lesson changes daily per the lesson plan*

_____ Teacher prepares materials and environment in advance to facilitate flow of activities

_____ Art area has a table with 4–6 chairs

_____ The teacher makes a variety of materials accessible to children

_____ The teacher/assistant engages with children during the art activity

Adheres to LFC guidelines for STORY through the following:

_____ Large- or small-group story occurs

_____ Story is related to the daily theme

_____ Children are asked to predict what will happen in the story

_____ Children are asked to help tell the story

_____ Teacher delivers the story in an engaging manner

Adheres to LFC guidelines for GROUP through the following:

_____ A clear large group session exists

_____ The group session lasts between 10–15 minutes

_____ Group activities vary daily per lesson plan*

Adheres to LFC guidelines for MUSIC through the following:

_____ Song is related to the daily theme

Overview of Speech and Language Outcomes and Progress Monitoring

Ted entered the classroom at age 3 not talking, although he did produce many vowel sounds. He appeared to understand most of what was said to him and communicated using a variety of vocalizations and gestures. Subsequent testing confirmed that his receptive language scores were within typical limits but that his expressive language skills were below the 1st percentile. Ted fit the diagnosis of specific language impairment. Ted had received infant–toddler services for 6 months prior to his entry into the classroom.

Ted's initial goals focused on communication; they included extending his mean length of utterance using signs and/or words and increasing the number of sounds he produced. After approximately 4 months in the program, Ted began to use one- and two-word combinations, sometimes using signs, sometimes using a combination of words and signs. He made requests and protests, answered questions, and made comments. Most of his communication was to adults, but he began to play beside and occasionally with other children. One of his first word combinations was "What have," which he used during the sharing time routine. As Ted's expressive language progressed, his use of signs became less frequent until he rarely used any. As his language skills progressed, his conversations with other children increased.

Two years later, Ted's expressive language was approaching typical limits (14th percentile on the Reynell Developmental Language Scales). His articulation skills also were within low-normal limits (20th percentile); however, his intelligibility was below that expected of a 5-year-old (90% intelligible versus almost 100% expected for most 5-year-olds). His receptive language skills remained a strength (55th percentile on the Reynell). Ted enjoyed many of the emergent literacy activities in the classroom. He could identify the letters of the alphabet and knew many of the associated sounds. He also had a reading vocabulary of 15–20 words and could write his name. He was an active participant in classroom discussions and had two close friends. He was enrolled in kindergarten, and by the beginning of first grade Ted no longer had an IEP.

Walter came to the classroom with a diagnosis of autism. He initially communicated through various gestures, sounds, and some words. He was sensitive to touch, protesting when he was touched, particularly with a "soft" touch. He also did not like to touch a variety of sensory items, such as fingerpaint or playdough. He sometimes protested the washing of his hands. He initially had difficulty understanding classroom routine and refused to participate in many of the activities. Through collaboration with the local school district and Walter's parents, an IEP was written. Walter received occupational therapy services in the classroom from local school district personnel and communication intervention from the LAP staff members.

Slowly, Walter began to make progress. A variety of supports were used to help this child be successful in the LAP classroom. These included the use of visual scheduling to preview each day's activities, preview of the story to be read, and preview of the dramatic play and art activities available during center time and the later group activities. Social stories were also used to help him understand what to do. As Walter began to understand what the activities were and what his role could be, he began to be an active participant.

At the end of 2 years, Walter was attending during group time, could identify the alphabet, knew most of the letter–sound correspondences, and was beginning to read. His mean length of utterance was 4.14, up from 1.9 at entry 2 years earlier. He routinely used six- and seven-word utterances and typically responded to peers by joining the action or, occasionally, suggesting a play activity. He moved from the LAP area for kindergarten, but updates from his mother indicated that he performed well in kindergarten with minimal supports. At the end of first grade, Walter was reading at grade level, although he did require some support in interaction with peers and in completing all of his assignments. He did well if he was provided with visual schedules, demonstrations, and previewing of upcoming new activities.

These two case studies provide information on the effectiveness of the intervention integrated into the LFC for two individuals. However, even though there have been many other success stories for children with speech and language impairments using this curriculum, this type of information is only a beginning in documenting its effectiveness. This chapter will review some of the more formal data collected and discussed in Rice and Hadley (1995) and Wilcox and Morris (1995) regarding intervention in the LAP classroom. Different methods of monitoring progress will be described, along with a study focusing on the reading skills in third and fourth grade of former LAP children and a brief study regarding the progress of the children learning English as a second language. The chapter provides only a snapshot of children's progress, as resources have not been sufficient to permit the study of the 504 children who have been enrolled in the program over the last 22 years.

There are several difficulties to be addressed in evaluating intervention in the preschool-age population. First, speech and language is a developmental process, and children may vary in their development and still be within typical limits. Therefore, it is necessary to control for this developmental process before answering questions about an individual child's improvement. A crucial question is whether the child improved because of the intervention or maturation. Second, it is difficult to compare results across programs because of the many variables regarding curricula, children, and the severity and type of speech and language diagnoses. Third, there could be other environmental adjustments that contribute to a change in outcome that is not related to preschool programming. Finally, what constitutes effectiveness? Is it improvement in speech and language skills, communication, or social skills? Academic achievement? Achievement of "typical" status?

SPEECH AND LANGUAGE OUTCOMES

Initially, the effectiveness of the LFC and the associated concentrated normative model of language intervention was addressed by examining the standardized test scores of children when they first entered the LAP program and comparing these to their scores when they left the program. Standardized test scores were used to address the issue of maturation, particularly because there was no control group. This is a stringent standard for documenting improvement, because children could improve greatly in raw score points but remain at the same standard score due to their increase in age and the expectation that older children would get more items correct. In fact, that would be a typical outcome, particularly for children within normal limits in speech and language. For example, assume that a child's standard score mean on the Peabody Picture Vocabulary Test–Revised (PPVT-R; Dunn & Dunn, 1981) (mean = 100 +/– 15) was 100. That score would be attained by the child's achieving a raw score of 48 at age 3. Over the course of a typical learning curve, the child would need to achieve a raw score of 83 in order to remain at the standard score of 100 at age 5. The child would have made a substantial gain in the number of words he or she understood, yet that gain would not necessarily be revealed by the standard score. The child would be progressing in a typical fashion based on normative information.

Therefore, it is possible that improvement likely due to intervention could be made yet not be revealed by standard scores. In fact, in order to achieve gains in standard scores, children must have an increased learning rate. It might be predicted that children with impairments would continue to fall behind other children their age due to their slower learning rate. Therefore, children might have made good progress by remaining at the same standard score. In spite of the possibility of gains not being revealed through the use of standard scores, the scores were used as one way to document effectiveness in the LAP, where the LFC was used.

The specific tests for receptive language were the PPVT-R (Dunn & Dunn, 1981) and the comprehension subtest of the Reynell Developmental Language Scales (Reynell & Gruber, 1991). On the comprehension subtest of the Reynell, the examiner initially asks children to identify single objects by pointing to them. Later, children are asked to follow

Table 5.1. Language gains for the typically developing children and children with specific language impairment (SLI)

Measure	n	Standard scores		
		Entry	Exit	Average gain
Typically developing group	29			
Peabody Picture Vocabulary Test–Revised (PPVT-R)		100.52	107.48	6.97
Reynell Receptive		101.55	106.59	5.03
Reynell Expressive		96.03	104.62	8.59
Mean length of utterance (MLU) standard score		NA	NA	NA
Group with SLI	36			
PPVT-R		83.47	94.81	11.33
Reynell Receptive		78.53	88.25	9.72
Reynell Expressive		71.61	82.39	10.78
MLU standard score		76.56	85.39	8.83

From Rice, M.L., & Hadley, P.A. (1995). Language outcomes of the language-focused curriculum. In M.L. Rice & K.A. Wilcox (Eds.), *Building a language-focused curriculum for the preschool classroom: A foundation for lifelong communication* (p. 162). Baltimore: Paul H. Brookes Publishing Co., reprinted by permission.

increasingly complex sets of directions involving the manipulation of a variety of items (e.g., "Put the doll on the chair, find the long red pencil, give me all of the animals except the black pig"). Specific tests for expressive language included the GFTA (Goldman & Fristoe, 2000) and the expression subtest of the Reynell. The expression subtest involves labeling items, defining words, and describing pictures. In later years, newer versions of these tests were used. In addition, language sampling was completed each semester to provide information on the gains in the mean length of utterance of children with speech and language impairments. These scores were standardized so they could be compared to other test scores.

Rice and Hadley (1995) reported on the language outcomes for 65 children enrolled in the LAP over a 6-year period. Thus, the program outcomes are based on the individual outcomes for these children. There were 36 children with SLI, and the other 29 children were enrolled as typically developing language comparisons.

Rice and Hadley (1995) reported the data in two ways. First, they presented overall information about the standard scores and gains made by the two groups. They divided the intervention group into different profiles to discuss more specific information regarding this group. As can be seen from the group data shown in Table 5.1, the children with typical development made standard score gains of 5 to 8½ points. The average performance of this group shifted upwards from average to slightly above average. The children with SLI, as a group, also made gains in standard scores, ranging from 8½ points to 11 points. This group initially scored below average on all four measures and at exit scored within typical limits on three of the four measures. Therefore, these children as a group had an accelerated rate of learning.

However, this might not be the case for all children. Children with SLI vary in the nature and severity of their language difficulties. Rice and Hadley (1995) provided additional information about these children by placing them into one of three profiles. The first profile consisted of children with good receptive language but impairments in speech and expressive language. Nine children fit this profile, labeled Profile E (expressive language impairments). The second profile consisted of children with good speech skills but impairments in receptive and expressive language. Nine children also fit this profile, labeled Profile L (language-only impairments). The final profile consisted of children who had impairments in all three areas: speech, receptive language, and expressive language.

Table 5.2.   Language gains for children in different specific language impairment (SLI) profiles

Measure	n	Standard scores		Average gain
		Entry	Exit	
Profile E: Expressive language impairments	9			
Peabody Picture Vocabulary Test–Revised (PPVT-R)		100.78	109.11	8.33
Reynell Receptive		100.22	108.44	8.22
Reynell Expressive		76.44	94.44	18.00
Mean length of utterance (MLU) standard score		73.00	86.95	13.95
Profile L: Language-only impairments	9			
PPVT-R		78.67	92.89	14.22
Reynell Receptive		69.78	89.44	19.66
Reynell Expressive		78.44	79.44	1.00
MLU standard score		89.20	92.65	3.45
Profile G: Global impairments in speech and language	18			
PPVT-R		77.22	88.61	11.39
Reynell Receptive		72.06	77.56	5.50
Reynell Expressive		65.78	77.83	12.05
MLU standard score		72.55	80.95	8.40

From Rice, M.L., & Hadley, P.A. (1995). Language outcomes of the language-focused curriculum. In M.L. Rice & K.A. Wilcox (Eds.), *Building a language-focused curriculum for the preschool classroom: A foundation for lifelong communication* (p. 164). Baltimore: Paul H. Brookes Publishing Co., reprinted by permission.

This profile was labeled G (global impairments in speech and language), and 18 children fit this profile.

As Rice and Hadley (1995) noted, the children in these different profiles made differential gains (see Table 5.2). Overall, children whose scores increased the most were the children who had the lowest scores and therefore had more room for improvement. The children in Profile E (expressive language impairments) made gains in their receptive language similar to those made by the children with typical development. They made the greatest gain in expressive language, the focus of their intervention. Speech data reported from Wilcox and Morris (1995) indicated that this group of children gained 6.9 percentile points as measured by the GFTA, with an average entry score of 4.6 percentile and an exit score of 11.5 percentile. The children in Profile L (language-only impairments) made the greatest gains in receptive language skills and maintained their standing in expressive language (as discussed earlier, to maintain their standard score children must continue to develop). The children also maintained their good speech skills, achieving a percentile ranking of 45 on entry and exit as measured by the GFTA. It may be that much of the children's effort was in improving their understanding of language and that this understanding was needed before they could make substantial improvement in expressive language. In any case, longer periods of intervention appear to be needed for children with both receptive and expressive language impairments before they can make substantial improvement in expressive language, at least as measured by standardized testing. The children in Profile G (global impairments, speech and language impairments), made substantial progress in all areas, with gains ranging from 5 to 12 points. This included gains in speech skills of 9 percentile points on the GFTA. According to Wilcox and Morris, these children had an average entry percentile of 3.1 and an exit percentile of 12.1. However, only in receptive one-word vocabulary did children achieve an average score within typical limits. Although they did make improvement, they remained below age expectations in speech, receptive, and expressive language.

In sum, the children with SLI made differential progress in their language skills, but overall, all improved in their communication abilities. In addition, these children appeared to be learning at an accelerated rate; most of them substantially improved their standard score. The only group of children who maintained or only slightly improved their standard

Table 5.3. Sample format for notebook observations

Date	Child's initials	Context (e.g., Dramatic Play, Art, Group, Outdoor)	What happened?
3/8/07	BB	Dramatic Play—Pioneers	Child used device to request a turn riding in the wagon.
3/10/07	BB	Outdoor Play	Child followed verbal directions to stop running and come stand in line to go inside. No physical prompts were needed.

score were those in Profile L, the language-only group, who had difficulty with both receptive and expressive language skills. Children in this group improved their standard scores for receptive language but maintained or only slightly improved their expressive language skills as measured by standard scores. However, they had to make increases in their raw scores to maintain their standard scores. Overall, these assessments reveal that children with SLI and children with typical development did benefit from receiving instruction using the LFC and concentrated normative model of intervention.

INFORMAL TRACKING OF PROGRESS

A variety of tools are used to track the progress of children in the LAP. These tools range from making daily notes in observation notebooks to using goal cards to track improvement on individual goals on a semester basis. Language sampling is done at least twice a semester for children with speech and language impairments. The Learning Observation Guide (LOG; see Chapter 5 Appendix for a filled-in version of this log; a blank version of the LOG can be found in Appendix B in the back of the book) could also be used to track a specific child's improvement or to document behavior in preparation for a meeting with parents or school officials.

Observation Notebooks

Both general classroom observation notebooks and, on occasion, individual observation booklets are used. General observation notebooks provide a place for teachers to note gains or areas of concern for children that might be forgotten if not written down. Examples of observations include a child's success in making friends, a child's use of words to negotiate with a peer, the length of time a child attended to a task, and so forth. Individual observation notebooks are used for some children so that small gains or information noted by all staff members can be collected in one document. Information might include words spoken, participation in an activity, or use of an augmentative device. See Table 5.3 for an example of the format used.

Often, teachers keep a booklet to track children's motor development to support the goals developed by the school occupational therapist. The numbered goals for children with motor goals are listed at the top of the page. In addition to the date, the goal number is noted. This gives the occupational therapist additional classroom data about children's progress on specific fine motor goals.

Goal Cards

Each semester the speech and language goals for the children with language impairments are posted in an inconspicuous place in the classroom, such as inside a cabinet door, so all staff members can easily see them. These semester goals are taken from children's IEPs or treatment plans developed with their parents. The goals are written on 4" × 6" index cards. One side of the goal card lists the child's name; the current semester; the number and types of goals; and whether the goals are met, improved, or not met. The specific goal categories

Child: _____		Semester: _____	Clinician: _____	
Goal type	Number of goals	No change	Improvement	Met
Phonologic	_____	_____	_____	_____
Semantic	_____	_____	_____	_____
Syntactic	_____	_____	_____	_____
Pragmatic	_____	_____	_____	_____
Preacademic	_____	_____	_____	_____
Totals	_____	_____	_____	_____

Figure 5.1.   Front side of blank goal card.

are phonologic, semantic, syntactic, and pragmatic. Occasionally, preacademic goals might be listed as well. Figure 5.1 shows the front of a blank goal card.

The specific goals for the semester are written on the back side of the card along with the child's and clinician's initials. The back side of the card is then posted. The back of a filled-out card might look like that shown in Figure 5.2.

At the end of the semester, teachers complete the front side of the cards to provide a quick overview of children's progress. Figure 5.3 shows a sample.

The numbers entered on the front of the cards may be compiled to chart progress over a specific period of time for a particular group of children or for a particular child. An overall count lets teachers observe a general trend of whether children are meeting their goals, improving, or showing no improvement. For example, the goals of five children with SLI were monitored over the 2 years they were in the program. (Although the same goals might be addressed over the 2 years, they are monitored each semester; therefore, the total number of goals may include the same goals counted more than once and/or new goals.) Each of the five children had 4 semesters of intervention. The number of goals addressed ranged from four to seven each semester. The total number of goals addressed for the five children over 4 semesters was 104. Sixteen of the goals showed no improvement (at least for one semester), 44 showed improvement, and 44 were met. Therefore, 85 percent of goals showed improvement or were met and 15 percent showed no change, at least for one semester.

Table 5.4 shows the goal card information for one child over 4 semesters. This information indicates that goal improvement might not be attained the first semester a goal is addressed.

Katie
1. Will produce /k/ and /f/ in final position with 75% accuracy in words as measured by teacher probes. (These are actually two goals).
2. Will follow 10 nonroutine two-step, two-feature directions with 70% accuracy as measured by teacher probes; for example, "Pick up the *little, brown* bear and put it *beside* the *big* box." (The steps refer to the verbs in the sentences and the features refer to the descriptors of the noun and/or specificity of placement, such as *beside* or *on top of* an object).
3. Will increase the number of initiations to peers to five, with at least one interaction involving two or more turns during a 5-minute observation during free play.
4. Will increase the number of responses to peers to five, with at least one interaction involving two turns during a 5-minute observation.

Figure 5.2.   Sample completed back of goal card.

Child: _Katie_		Semester: _Fall 2006_	Clinician: _Lana_	
Goal type	Number of goals	No change	Improvement	Met
Phonologic	2	_____	1	1
Semantic	1	_____	_____	1
Syntactic	_____	_____	_____	_____
Pragmatic	_____	_____	_____	_____
Preacademic	2	_____	1	1
Totals	5	_____	2	3

Figure 5.3. Sample completed front side of goal card.

There are other reasons a child may not seem to improve in a skill during a particular semester. For example, the first semester a child is enrolled in the program, he or she may be acclimating to the classroom, making gains not necessarily being addressed (e.g., preacademic learning), or making gains in receptive language but not in expressive language. In addition, just because progress is monitored every 3 months does not mean that this is the learning time frame for a particular child. It is also possible for a child to improve in one

Table 5.4. Sample child's goal attainment over 4 semesters

Goal type	Number of goals for each semester	No change	Improvement	Met
Semester 1				
Phonological	2		1	1
Semantic	1	1		
Syntactic	2	1		1
Pragmatic				
Total	**5**	**2**	**1**	**2**
Semester 2				
Phonological	2	1 (new goal)	1	
Semantic	1	1		
Syntactic	1		1	
Pragmatic				
Total	**4**	**2**	**2**	**0**
Semester 3				
Phonological	4	2 (new goals)	2	
Semantic	1			1
Syntactic	1		1	
Pragmatic				
Total	**6**	**2**	**3**	**1**
Semester 4				
Phonological	4		3	1
Semantic				
Syntactic	2		1 (new)	1
Pragmatic				
Total	**6**	**0**	**4**	**2**
Overall totals	**21**	**6**	**10**	**5**

area and not another. For example, the child may make great gains in increasing the length of utterances and in grammar terms but not much gain in improving production of certain error sounds, at least for that semester. Finally, a child may appear to make not improvement in an area for 1 or 2 semesters and then make a jump in skills seemingly all at once. Learning is not always linear.

Language Sampling

Each semester, language sampling is completed at the beginning and end of the semester as one means of tracking progress of children with speech and language impairments. The Systematic Analysis of Language Transcripts (SALT; Miller & Chapman, 1984–2000), a computer program developed by colleagues at the Language Analysis Lab in Madison, Wisconsin, has been used to analyze the samples. Typically, the child and the clinician play in a small room with a variety of toys and items of interest to the child. The goal of the language sampling is to note the growth in expressive language skills relating to an increase in the length of the child's utterances and an increase in the number of different words used. Growth in the use of grammar terms, pronoun usage, and other language forms could also be noted. Children who attend the program for 2 years might have as many as 9–10 language samples taken. However, some children have fewer samples, particularly if they entered the program with fewer than 50 spoken words.

· · · · · · · · · **BILLY'S ENROLLMENT** ·

Billy was initially enrolled at age 3, transitioning from an infant–toddler program where he had received speech and language services for 9 months. At the time of enrollment, he was nonverbal but did produce approximately six vowels sounds and four consonants. He communicated primarily with gestures, some signs, and vocalizations primarily consisting of vowels sounds. His receptive language was below typical; however, he did score at the 9th percentile on the Peabody Picture Vocabulary Test–Third Edition (PPVT-III; Dunn & Dunn, 1997) and at the 8th percentile on the receptive section of the Reynell. Billy attended the program for 8 semesters (including two summers). Language sampling was begun in his third semester of enrollment. Table 5.5 shows the results of Billy's language sampling for 6 semesters.

Although Billy was still below typical limits in his mean length of utterances (children his age typically have an MLU in morphemes of 5.88 +/-.54), he was able to converse with other children, make comments, ask questions, and generally participate in all activities in the classroom. His intelligibility was also of concern in that he was 85% intelligible by the end of his enrollment in the preschool. At that time he was scoring within typical limits on the PPVT-III (37th percentile) and on the receptive section of the Reynell (17th percentile). His scores on the expressive section of the Reynell were at the 1st percentile. Billy tended to use nonspecific terms when describing pictures and had some difficulty in defining words. He was at the 8th percentile on the GFTA. Therefore, Billy left the program with some expressive language needs; however, he was communicating verbally and was an active learner who often asked questions. He also had good emergent literacy skills; that is, he knew the alphabet and sound associations, could write his name and most of the letters of the alphabet, and could read approximately 10–12 words. He had made great progress from being essentially nonverbal to being an active conversationalist.

Table 5.5.   Language sampling for sample child for 6 semesters

Age (in years and months)	Length of sample (in utterances)	Mean length of utterance	Number of different words (50 utterances)	Number of total words (50 utterances)
3:6	71	1.41	18	71
3:9	18	1.55	20	81
4:1	67	2.60	41	77
4:4	65	2.52	64	110
4:6	65	4.45	95	226
4:9	55	4.31	86	201

Table 5.6. Description of children in specific language impairment (SLI) and peer model (PM) groups at follow-up testing

Child	Sex	Age (in years and months)	Time in Language Acquisition Preschool (in semesters)	Type of impairment	Grade
SLI-A	Male	8:8	7	Mild–Moderate Expressive	3
SLI-B	Female	8:5	5	Severe Expressive	3
SLI-C	Female	9:7	7	Moderate Receptive and Expressive	4
SLI-D	Male	10:0	3	Moderate Receptive and Expressive	4
PM-A	Male	9:6	5	NA	3
PM-B	Male	9:4	2.5	NA	3
PM-C	Male	9:10	7	NA	4
PM-D	Male	8:6	2	NA	2[a]

[a]Child repeated kindergarten (parents were concerned about attention and fine motor development and chose to have child repeat).

LATER SCHOOL ACHIEVEMENT

Due to limited resources, it was not possible to follow many of the children enrolled in the LAP as they continued with their education. However, as part of a thesis project (Lyons, 2000), an attempt was made to contact children previously enrolled in the preschool when they were in the third and fourth grades. The purpose of the project was to note their achievement in reading and vocabulary skills. Eight families agreed to participate. Four of the children had received speech and language intervention in the preschool (SLI group) and four children were typical peer models (PM group). All had been enrolled in the preschool during the same 2–3 years. The length of attendance in the preschool for the children with SLI was 3–7 semesters; the length of attendance for the peer models was 2–7 semesters. At the time of the study, the children in the SLI group ranged in age from 8 years, 5 months to10 years; the children in the PM group ranged in age from 8 years, 6 months to 9 years, 10 months. See Table 5.6 for further descriptive information.

All children's speech and language skills were assessed upon entrance to the preschool using four assessment instruments: the GFTA, the PPVT-R, and the receptive and expressive subtests of the Reynell. Scores are considered within typical limits if they are at the 16th percentile or better. All of the test scores have a mean standard score of 100 and a standard deviation of 15 with the exception of the GFTA, which provides only percentiles.

The children with SLI varied in their abilities, with two children having only expressive language difficulties (Profile E) and two children with both receptive and expressive language impairments (Profile G, global impairments). There was also variation within these two classifications. One child was nonverbal yet had relatively good receptive language. She was placed into an expressive-only group with a child who had some verbal productions. Another child had relatively good receptive vocabulary skills yet exhibited difficulty with receptive language as well as expressive language. This child therefore fit Profile G, even though part of receptive language was within low typical limits. Table 5.7 provides information about the children's entrance assessment information.

For the follow-up study, the children's vocabulary and reading skills were assessed using the following instruments. First, receptive vocabulary skills were evaluated using the PPVT-III. Then, overall reading skills were assessed using the Gray Oral Reading Tests–Third Edition (GORT-3; Wiederholt & Bryant, 1992). The children's ability to identify real

Table 5.7. Percentiles and standard scores (SS) for specific language impairment (SLI) and peer model (PM) groups at preschool entry

Child	Goldman-Fristoe Test of Articulation (GFTA) Percentile	Peabody Picture Vocabulary Test–Revised (PPVT-R)		Reynell Receptive		Reynell Expressive	
		Percentile	SS	Percentile	SS	Percentile	SS
SLI-A	12th	22nd	88	19th	86	12th	81
SLI-B	No response[a]	12th	82	65th	106	No response[a]	No response[a]
SLI-C	2nd	32nd	93	6th	75	8th	77
SLI-D	1st	7th	78	9th	79	3rd	70
PM-A	21st	26th	90	17th	85	21st	87
PM-B	84th	42nd	97	43rd	97	29th	91
PM-C	98th	50th	100	52nd	101	43rd	97
PM-D	20th	55th	102	33rd	93	43rd	97

[a]Child was nonverbal at time of entry into preschool.

words and decode (sound out) nonsense words was evaluated using the word identification and word attack subtests of the Woodcock Reading Mastery Test–Revised (WRMT-R; Woodcock, 1987). See Table 5.8 for specific percentiles and standard scores achieved by each child.

All of the children in both groups scored within typical limits on vocabulary. The children in the SLI group ranged from a percentile rank of 32–73 (standard scores of 93–108), with an average standard score of 100. The PM group's scores ranged from percentile ranks of 55–91 (standard scores of 102–120), with an average standard score of 111. With the exception of one child in the SLI group, all children scored within typical limits in overall reading. The SLI group ranged from the 12th percentile to the 50th, with an average being 34.5 percentile (standard scores of 82–100). The PM group ranged from the 27th percentile to the 73rd, with an average of 50. The children with typical development did average a higher standard score (99.5 versus 93.25) than the children with SLI. A similar situation occurred for the word identification subtests, with all children scoring within normal limits except for the same child mentioned above, who scored below typical limits on the overall reading assessment. The children in the SLI group had standard scores from 83 to 100, with an average of 91; the children in the PM group scored from 98 to 111, with an average of 105. The word attack subtest appeared to be the hardest task, particularly for the children in the SLI group. Two of the four children in this group scored below typical limits on this task (standard scores of 83 and 72), whereas all four of the children in the PM group scored within normal limits, with scores ranging from 90 to 112.

Table 5.8. Percentiles and standard scores (SS) for specific language impairment (SLI) and peer model (PM) groups at follow-up testing

Child	Peabody Picture Vocabulary Test–Third Edition (PPVT-III)		Gray Oral Reading Tests–Third Edition (GORT-3)		Word identification		Word attack	
	Percentile	SS	Percentile	SS	Percentile	SS	Percentile	SS
SLI-A	73	109	34	94	50	100	61	104
SLI-B	32	93	42	97	16	85	13	83
SLI-C	32	93	12	82	13	83	3	72
SLI-D	70	108	50	100	39	96	17	86
PM-A	55	102	42	97	76	110	25	90
PM-B	68	107	58	103	54	101	34	94
PM-C	84	115	73	107	76	111	79	112
PM-D	91	120	27	91	45	98	48	99

Table 5.9. Percentiles and standard scores (SS) of children with specific language impairment (SLI) and school peers (SP)

Child	Peabody Picture Vocabulary Test–Third Edition (PPVT-III)		Gray Oral Reading Tests–Third Edition (GORT-3)		Word identification		Word attack	
	Percentile	SS	Percentile	SS	Percentile	SS	Percentile	SS
SLI-A	73	109	34	94	50	100	61	104
SP-A1	88	118	88	118	53	101	20	87
SP-A2	84	115	88	118	97	129	96	127
SLI-B	32	93	42	97	16	85	13	83
SP-B1	73	109	88	118	64	105	10	81
SP-B2	82	114	79	112	92	121	86	116
SLI-C	32	93	12	82	13	83	3	72
SP-C1	86	116	96	127	90	119	89	118
SP-C2	66	106	99	136	74	110	50	100
SLI-D	70	108	50	100	39	96	17	86
SP-D1	98	130	73	109	87	117	68	107
SP-D2	34	94	8	79	29	92	33	93

In addition to comparing the scores of children with SLI with those of their typically developing peers who had attended the LAP preschool, it was of interest to compare them with the vocabulary and reading scores of the children who were in the same third- or fourth-grade class as the children with SLI. These children would have received, in general, the same instruction from the same teachers as the target children, at least during the year they were studied. Many had been in the same classes throughout their school enrollment. Two children of the same sex were recruited from each of the target children's classroom. Therefore, the child identified as SLI-A had two school peers, SPA-1 and SPA-2; the child identified as SLI-B had two school peers, SPB-1 and SPB-2; and so forth. The school peer participants had no history of speech, language, or hearing problems. The first two children whose parents signed and returned the permission papers were selected to be the school peer subjects. It was not expected that the children with SLI would perform as well as their school peers on measures of reading and vocabulary, but comparisons between the two groups would provide some information about the reading skills of the rest of the children in the class. The school peers were administered the same test protocol described earlier. See Table 5.9 for a comparison of test results for children with SLI and school peers.

In general, the school peers performed better on the reading and vocabulary measures than the children with a history of SLI. Many of the former scored in the above to high average range on many of the tests. However, the lowest score on the GORT-3 was a school peer, SPD-2, who scored at the 8th percentile. The lowest score by a child with SLI was at the 12th percentile on the GORT-3. It was interesting to note that the pattern across tests was different for these two children. The child with SLI had low word attack scores, indicating difficulty with decoding, whereas the school peer had scores within typical limits on the word attack and word identification subtests. It appears that this child's decoding skill was also within typical limits, so the child's lower scores on the GORT-3 may have been due to difficulties with comprehension. All of the other children tested (peer models, school peers, and children with SLI) scored within normal limits on the GORT-3.

Overall, the children with SLI in preschool had made good progress in their vocabulary and reading skills. In the area of vocabulary, they had improved from entry percentile scores in preschool of 22nd, 12th, 32nd, and 7th (standard scores of 88, 82, 93, and 78) respectively to 72nd, 32nd, 32nd, and 70th (standard scores of 109, 93, 93, and 108) in elementary school. In grade school, vocabulary was a relative strength for all of the children with SLI. Three of the four children scored above the 34th percentile in overall reading (34th, 42nd, and 50th percentile). One child, SLI-C, scored below typical limits at the 12th percentile. This child was one of the two children who had impairments in speech and receptive and expressive language (global impairments). The other child with SLI who had impairments in all areas did well in the overall reading (42nd percentile) but scored below typical limits on the word attack subtest of the Woodcock (13th percentile).

The peer models scored within typical limits on all testing. It is interesting to note that vocabulary scores for these children also had improved since entry into preschool, from an average score of the 43rd percentile to an average score of the 74th percentile in grade school.

The school peers also scored within typical limits on all testing, with the exception of one who scored at the 8th percentile on overall reading. Many of the school peers performed the highest on the tests. These children may have been the best readers in the class. Although we wanted average readers, we chose to take the first children who returned permission slips that were the same sex as the target child with SLI.

OUTCOMES OF CHILDREN LEARNING ENGLISH AS A SECOND LANGUAGE

About one third of the children who enroll in the LAP are learning English as their second language during their time in the program. Many of the children have limited English skills because they have recently arrived in the United States. Others have resided in the United States for a lengthier time or were even born here but come from a family that speaks a language other than English in the home. Whatever the reason, these children have limited experience with hearing and using English.

To date, children from all over the globe have attended the LAP. Twenty different languages have been represented, including Japanese, Korean, Mandarin, Taiwanese, Farsi, Urdu, Hindi, Arabic, French, German, Serbo-Croatian, Polish, Russian, Danish, Spanish, and Portuguese. One or both parents of most of these children are either students or faculty members at the University of Kansas.

Most families plan to return to their homeland, so the parents want their children to be bilingual. LAP staff encourages parents to continue to speak their native language at home while the program focuses on helping the children learn English. These children are considered sequential bilingual speakers as they are learning English after learning their first language.

As described in Bunce (1995b; 2003), strategies for facilitating children's acquisition of English hinge on providing an environment for natural language and interaction to occur. Some of the language-learning techniques that have appeared helpful for children are modeling, focused contrasts, expansions and recasts, and scripted play (see Chapter 3). The major focus is to provide *comprehensible* input so children would understand what was expected and would begin to develop an understanding of English vocabulary, structure, and use. The structure of the curriculum helps to provide the context for learning. Modeling by other children, as well as adult facilitation, is important to the children's understanding of the classroom activities. The initial focus, then, is on receptive language.

As mentioned in Bunce (1995b), the children often have different learning styles. Some of them immediately try to speak, sometimes using their native language and sometimes imitating much of what is said to them. Other children go through a silent period and then begin to speak in short, often well-formed, sentences. Both of these learning styles have been reported in the literature on learning English as a second language (Bunce, 1995b; Savilli-Troike 1988; Wong-Fillmore, 1989). It is interesting that, in general, neither style seems better than the other at helping children learn English. However, often a child who immediately imitates will sometimes, after a month or so, have a short silent period and then begin to use shorter but more spontaneous utterances.

Most of the children are able to communicate in English after a semester and follow the classroom routine. They also readily participate in all of the activities. Only one child, as mentioned in Bunce (1995b), did not continue to progress in English skills beyond speaking in one- to two-word utterances. When asked in Korean why he did not speak more En-

Table 5.10. Demographics of eight Language Acquisition Preschool children learning English as a second language

Child	Native language	Age at enrollment (in months)	Age at sample (in months)	Length of enrollment (in months)
1	Spanish	35	66	31
2	Mandarin	31	66	35
3	Serbo-Croatian	31	54	23
4	Indonesian	38	60	22
5	Mandarin	42	52	10
6	Japanese	57	64	7
7	Polish	51	62	11
8	Mandarin	47	61	14

glish, the child answered that since his sister was in the class, she could tell him what to do. Also, he knew that he would soon be going back to Korea, so he did not think he needed to learn English!

Occasionally, a child whose parents speak a language other than English is delayed in his or her first language. If this child is enrolled in the LAP, he or she is evaluated, primarily in the first language, and an intervention plan is developed. Typically the intervention is provided in English; however, suggestions for facilitating the home language are provided to the parents. Parents typically request the intervention be in English because they want the child to attend American public school while they are in the United States. Interestingly, as a child's English skills improve, often parents will report improvement in the home language, too.

One study, in the form of a thesis (Shirk, 1993), examined the development of English skills in eight children in the LAP who were learning English as a second language. The languages spoken in the home varied. Three of the children spoke Mandarin; the others spoke Serbo-Croatian, Indonesian, Japanese, Polish, and Spanish. The length of time in the preschool varied from 7 to 35 months. The reason for the variation in time spent in the preschool was that some families were in the United States for a shorter time and left after a couple of semesters. Other families stayed for several semesters. Table 5.10 shows demographic information for each of these eight children.

The English language abilities of the eight children were examined using raw and standardized scores on several assessment instruments. The tests were standardized in English, so they were used for descriptive purposes for a comparison to English-language speakers the same age as the children. The PPVT-R and the Reynell were completed during the last month of the children's enrollment in the LAP (see Table 5.11). Language samples were also taken in the last month of enrollment.

Table 5.11. Test scores of eight Language Acquisition Preschool children learning English as a second language

Child	Peabody Picture Vocabulary Test–Revised (PPVT-R)		Reynell Receptive		Reynell Expressive		Mean length of utterance
	Raw score	Standard score	Raw score	Standard score	Raw score	Standard score	
1	65	104	61	97	53	93	3.51
2	47	89	57	82	53	95	4.04
3	39	85	57	93	52	95	5.03
4	58	101	53	64	42	64	2.75
5	11	55	29	63	23	63	2.75
6	11	40	31	63	30	63	1.40
7	44	84	51	65	40	64	4.51
8	30	72	56	84	49	85	3.31

In general, assessment results indicated that the longer the enrollment in preschool, the better the children's language skills. For the four children enrolled for 22 months or more, the scores approached norms for monolingual children, at least for receptive vocabulary. For the three who were enrolled the longest, this held true for the other assessments, too. In addition, the mean length of utterance (MLU) ranged from 3.51 to 5.03 for these three children. One of the children who had been enrolled for 11 months also did well on the receptive vocabulary and had an MLU of 4.51. However, this child often used some four-word routine phrases, which may have artificially raised his average length of utterance. For example, he would frequently say, "I want ____, please." The child who had been enrolled for the shortest period of time was just beginning to use English and had the lowest scores. Nevertheless, all of the children responded to others in English and were able to follow the classroom routine. Also, they participated in all of the activities.

The child from Indonesia and the one from Japan returned to their home countries upon leaving the LAP, and no further information about their achievement is available. The other children attended the local public schools following their enrollment in the preschool. These children received only minimal support from the school in the form of consultation from an ESL teacher to the classroom teacher. According to follow-up information from parents, all of the children attending the local schools were succeeding academically. It must be noted that the children learning English in the LAP primarily had parents who were attending college or who were university professors. The emphasis on learning and academics was strong within the family setting.

Filled-in Example of
Learning Observation Guide (LOG)

Learning Observation Guide (LOG)

Individual Observation of Developmental
Skills in Relationship to the
Language-Focused Curriculum

Skills Include:
Motor
Social
Language
Cognition
Emergent Literacy

Use to Develop:
Present Level of Progress
Classroom Accommodations
Individualized Interventions

Date(s) of Observation: <u>1-29-07 to 2-08-07</u>   Name: <u>James</u>

LEARNING OBSERVATION GUIDE (LOG)

Children who are 3–5 years old are developing skills in many areas, including motor, social, language, cognitive, and emergent literacy.

All children have the right to a general curriculum. Children's development of skills within the language-focused curriculum can be assessed by relating them to the four types of activities: 1) those that change daily and are teacher led, 2) those that are routine and teacher led, 3) those that change daily and are child centered, and 4) those that are routine and child centered. The activities are assessed as to whether there is a need to modify classroom procedures to accommodate a child or whether there needs to be individualized intervention devised.

	Teacher Led	Child Centered
Changes Daily	Group time Storytime Music time	Dramatic play Art
Routine	Circle time Sharing time	Arrival time Snack time Outside playtime Block area Quiet area

Directions: Observe the child as he/she participates in activities across the curriculum. Observations may take place over a 1–2 week period of time. Use the forms to provide an overall summary of observations of a child's areas of need within the four categories of activities during the week-long observation period. A scale of 1–7 is used to judge behavior that is typical versus that where there is need to make curriculum adaptations or where there is need for individualized interventions. A rating of 5 and above indicates typical behavior; a rating of 3–4 may signal a need for some accommodations; and a rating of 1 or 2 indicates individualized interventions are needed.

1	2	3	4	5	6	7
Major Concerns		Some Concerns		Typical		Above Average

Date(s) of Observation: 1-29-07 to 2-08-07   Name: James

CHANGE DAILY/TEACHER-LED ACTIVITIES
(Story, Group, Music)

Rating	Activity Focus	NOTES
	General Motor Skills	
4	Sitting on floor/chair	Prefers sitting in booster chair
5	Posture righting response	
4	Manipulation of own body/space	OK in chair; on rug may "invade" space
3	Manipulation of materials	Some difficulty with small items
	General Social Skills/Attention	
3	Listening to teacher/children	Distractible at times; seems to withdraw
3	Following directions	Needs repetition or several models
3	**Appropriate initiating/responding**	With support
4	Turn-taking skills	Needs encouragement to respond
	General Language Skills	
2	Vocabulary understanding	Needs demonstration or several models
2	Vocabulary production	Tends to use the same words
5	Speech	Speech is understandable
2	Language structure	Uses short sentences (1–3 words)
	General Cognitive Skills	
4	Imitation	Willing to try
3	Matching	Can match exact items
3	Sequencing	Needs support
3	Classification	Needs some support
2	Problem solving	Needs models and repetition
	Emergent Literacy Skills	
4	Left–right orientation	Beginning to demonstrate knowledge
3	Story grammar (types)	Beginning to respond to different genres
4	Phonemic awareness (e.g., rhyming, sound matching)	Can do many activities with support
3	Alphabet knowledge	Knows about half of the alphabet
3	Sight word recognition	Beginning to note words in stories

Date(s) of Observation: <u>1-29-07 to 2-08-07</u>   Name: <u>James</u>

ROUTINE/TEACHER-LED ACTIVITIES

Rating	Activity Focus	NOTES
	General Motor Skills	
5	Sitting on floor/chair	Prefers booster chair to sitting on rug
4	Manipulation of own body/space	Sometimes bumps others
3	Manipulation of materials	Some difficulty in placing small items
	General Social Skills/Attention	
5	Listening to teacher/children	Responds well to routine
5	Responding when called upon	Does well with routine questions
4	Initiating (e.g. sharing questions)	Can ask two out of three questions
4	Turn-taking skills	Needs teacher support at times
	General Language Skills	
2	Vocabulary comprehension	Needs support and models
2	Vocabulary production	Little variety in vocabulary usage
4	Speech	Usually can be understood
2	Language structure	One or two-word utterances
2	Requesting/commenting	Usually with gestures
	General Cognitive Skills	
4	Imitation	Generally will attempt task
3	Matching	Needs support
5	Sequencing (e.g., calendar, sharing question format)	Can follow sequence of activities (often checks visual schedule)
2	Decision making	Slow to respond in making choices
	Emergent Literacy Skills	
4	Recognizing names (e.g., roll call)	Recognizes names about half of the time
3	Rote counting	Can count to 3 consistently
2	Identifying numbers	Beginning to identify numbers 1–5
3	Letter identification	Recognizes 12 letters
5	Name-sign recognition	Knows his own name, knows other children's names

Date(s) of Observation: 1-29-07 to 2-08-07   Name: James

CHANGE DAILY/CHILD-CENTERED ACTIVITIES

Rating	Activity Focus	NOTES
	Fine Motor Skills	
5	Tactile stimulation tolerance	OK
2	Pencil grip	Often uses whole hand grip
2	Pencil/marker control (e.g., drawing)	Makes lines; beginning to make circles
2	Cutting	Rarely cuts; can snip if adult holds paper
3	Pasting	May use too much paste
4	Knob rotation, stacking, pouring	At times needs support/model
3	Manipulation of toys/props/body	Has difficulty manipulating small items
	General Social Skills	
2	Sharing materials with peers	Tends to grab; may yell
2	Turn-taking skills	Needs assistance
2	Appropriate initiating/responding	Rarely initiates to peers; may respond nonverbally
	General Language Skills	
2	Commenting/describing	Beginning to comment
2	Making requests	Makes requests verbally with gestures
2	Negotiating	Beginning to share when adult facilitates
2	Sentence structure	Uses verb-object; subject-verb
2	Vocabulary	Often uses the same words
4	Speech sounds	Most speech sound intelligible
	General Cognitive Skills	
3	Imitation/matching	Will imitate models; can do simple puzzles
2	Sequencing of action/schemes	Can include two action/schemes
2	Classifying/pattern recognition	Beginning to classify similar objects
2	Problem solving	Needs support in making choices
	Emergent Literacy Skills	
3	Pretend play (e.g., pioneer, space)	Likes dramatic play (talks on phone, feeds baby)
2	Writing letters/words /numbers	Interested in writing name; will seek help

Date(s) of Observation: 1-29-07   Name: James

ROUTINE/CHILD-CENTERED ACTIVITIES
(Arrival, Block, Quiet, Outdoor, Snack)

Rating	Activity Focus	NOTES
	General Motor Skills	
5	Movement changes (e.g., sit/stand)	Usually OK
3	Sequencing of actions	Needs support for more than two sequences
4	Chewing/swallowing	Needs extra time for snack; slow eater
4	Carrying/pouring	May need help
3	Running, sliding	May need help in sliding
4	Hopping, jumping	Can jump; some difficulty with hopping
4	Pedaling, spinning	Recently learned to pedal
	Social Skills	
4	Listening to others	Usually polite; not sure understands
3	Initiating/responding appropriate	Will respond sometimes to peers
3	Sharing toys/objects	May ignore requests or will cry if can't have toy
	General Language Skills	
2	Verb structures	Tends to use general verbs
2	Prepositions (in/under/between)	Beginning to use prepositions
4	Politeness terms	Very polite with adults
2	Question/answer forms	Rarely asks or answers questions
2	Size/shape/quantity/color terms	Rarely uses
	General Cognitive Skills	
3	Matching/imitation/observing	Somewhat inconsistent
3	Creativity	Likes to play with a variety of toys
3	Sequencing	Can put nesting doll together
3	Classification/pattern recognition	Likes to play games with zoo animals
2	Problem solving	Needs support
	Emergent Literacy Skills	
3	Names on chairs/cubbies	Can locate cubby; needs help finding chair
2	Recognition of common words (stop)	Rarely does this
2	Writing on paper/chalkboard	Will occasionally write on chalkboard

Date(s) of Observation: <u>1-29-07 to 2-08-07</u>   Name: <u>James</u>

SUMMARY

Divide total score by number of observations per category to get average rating per category.

        5+ = No Concerns
        3–4 = Some Concerns—*at risk (accommodations may help)*
        1–2 = Major Concerns *(intervention needed)*

	Total Score	Number of Observations	Average Rating	Level of Concern
Motor Skills	76	76/21 =	3.62	Some Concerns
Social Skills/Attention	47	47/14 =	3.36	Some Concerns
Language Skills	49	49/20 =	2.45	Major Concerns
Cognitive Skills	52	52/18 =	2.89	Major Concerns
Emergent Literacy Skills	46	46/15 =	3.07	Some Concerns

Any discrepancies in skills between activities that change daily and routine activities?

James shows similar behavior during either activity.

James is somewhat more successful socially in routine activities.

Any discrepancies in skills between activities that are teacher led and those that are child centered?

James consistently needed more support in child-centered activities.

James may also need support in making choices or in tasks requiring problem-solving skills.

Summary of strengths:

James has strengths in gross motor skills, speech development, interacting with adults, willingness to try an activity, and response to models and demonstration.

Summary of weaknesses:

Some concerns: Fine motor skills, peer interaction

Major concerns: Areas of receptive and expressive language, areas of sequencing, problem-solving skills

II

Lesson Plans

T his section of the book contains 40 weeks of lesson plans, organized month by month. There are 4 days of lessons per week. For programs meeting 3 days a week, one day's plans can be dropped. For programs meeting 5 days a week, staff members can plan an additional day based on the theme (see blank planning guides and lesson plans in Appendix A), or they may choose to repeat or review a day's lesson. For day programs, some of the timing of the activities may need to be extended and/or additional activities added.

ORGANIZATION OF THE CURRICULUM

Each month of plans is preceded by an overview of the theme and the activities that will change daily—that is, dramatic play, art, story, group, and music activities. The Monthly Planning Guide shows at a glance all of the lessons for these activities for one month.

Each week of lessons begins with the Weekly Planning Guide, showing the theme and changing activities for that week. Also included in the Weekly Planning Guide is a list of suggested props and materials for each day of the week, as well as a space to include notes. There is also a newsletter for the week that can be given to parents. Parents should receive the newsletter at the beginning of the week so they know what will be happening in the classroom. Parents are more likely to ask specific questions about a child's day if they are aware of the activities, and specific questions are more likely to elicit answers from a child. Contrast "What did you do today?" ("Nothing") with "What did you do when you were playing farmer?" ("We planted carrots!"). In this way, some of the vocabulary and concepts children are encountering in the center can be carried over to the home environment. Parents are also more likely to understand a child whose speech is sometimes unintelligible if they know the topic of the day's activities.

The Daily Planning Guide comes next. The Daily Planning Guide identifies the language and literacy, social, cognitive, and motor skills to be facilitated during the day's activities. Following the Daily Planning Guide are detailed plans for each day's dramatic play, art, and group activities.

USING THE LESSON PLANS

Facilitate the children's role play and expand their use of language. Emphasis on different structures and/or vocabulary may be necessary depending on each child's needs and abilities. You might model appropriate scripts, ask open questions, expand or recast a child's productions, redirect a child to request items from another child, use a modification of a cloze procedure to provide contrastive feedback, or provide confirmative feedback to a particular child.

FALL SEMESTER

September

MONTHLY PLANNING GUIDE

Activities	Monday	Tuesday	Wednesday	Thursday
Week 1 — Class Favorites				
Dramatic Play	Water Play	House	Fast-Food Restaurant	Camping
Art	Watercolor Painting	Drawings	Playdough	Cheerios Art
Group	Things in Water	Hot/Cold	Letter *A*	The Color Blue
Story	*Rainbow Fish*	*If You Give a Mouse a Cookie*	*Will I Have a Friend?*	*We're Going on a Bear Hunt*
Song	"Five Little Ducks"	"I'm a Little Teapot"	"Peanut Butter and Jelly"	"A-Camping We Will Go"
Week 2 — Places in the Community				
Dramatic Play	Doctor's Office	Beauty Shop/Barber Shop	Service Station	Grocery Store
Art	Chalk Drawings	Shaving Cream Fingerpainting	Car Track Painting	Food Collage
Group	Body Parts	Letter *B*	Sound Sequencing	Big and Little
Story	*Going to the Doctor*	*Count*	*Go, Dog. Go!*	*Little Fish, Big Fish*
Song	"The Hokey Pokey"	"The Alphabet Song"	"If You're Happy and You Know It"	"I Like to Eat Apples and Bananas"
Week 3 — Transportation				
Dramatic Play	Airplanes	Boats	Car Racing	Delivery Trucks
Art	Paper Airplanes	Meat Tray Boats	Vehicle Rubbings	Easel Painting
Group	Shapes—Circle	Same or Different	Letter *C*	Circle Collage
Story	*We're Taking an Airplane Trip*	*Mr. Gumpy's Outing*	*Wheels*	*The Truck Book*
Song	"I'm a Little Airplane"	"Row, Row, Row Your Boat"	"C is for Cookie"	"Wheels on the Bus"
Week 4 — Occupations				
Dramatic Play	Construction Worker	Veterinarian	Office Worker	Firefighter
Art	Craft Stick Construction	Paper Bag Puppets	Drawings	Playdough
Group	Shapes—Square	Caring for a Pet	Letter *D*	Fire Safety Rules
Story	*A House is a House for Me*	*Moses the Kitten*	*A Letter to Amy*	*The Fire Engine*
Song	"Johnny Works with One Hammer"	"Five Little Monkeys"	"The Alphabet Song"	"Hurry, Hurry, Drive the Fire Truck"
Week 5 — Food				
Dramatic Play	Farm	Pizza Parlor	Grocery Store	House (Cooking)
Art	Cotton Ball Chickens	Pizza Art	Coffee Filter Painting	Macaroni Necklaces
Group	Square/Circle Classification	Act out a Story	Fruits and Vegetables	Letter *E*
Story	*Growing Vegetable Soup*	*The Three Bears*	*Whiskerville Grocery*	*It Looked Like Spilt Milk*
Song	"Old MacDonald Had a Farm"	"I Wish I Were a Pepperoni Pizza"	"I Like to Eat Apples and Bananas"	"Who Stole the Cookie?"

WEEKLY PLANNING GUIDE

	Dramatic Play	Art	Group	Story	Song
Monday *Suggested Props and Materials*	Water Play *Water table, water toys, tubs, smocks*	Watercolor Painting *Watercolor paints, paper, smocks, markers*	Things in Water *Items that do and do not go in water, two tubs or mats*	*Rainbow Fish*	"Five Little Ducks"
Tuesday *Suggested Props and Materials*	House *House setting, dishes, beds, kitchen, table, dolls, clothes, couch or other cozy child-sized furniture, food items*	Drawings *Paper, markers, colored pencils*	Hot/Cold *Items or pictures of items that can be classified as hot or cold*	*If You Give A Mouse a Cookie*	"I'm a Little Teapot"
Wednesday *Suggested Props and Materials*	Fast-Food Restaurant *Fast-food restaurant scenario, play food, counter, cash register, dolls, dishes, stove, tables, trays, pretend soft drink machine*	Playdough *Playdough, cookie cutters, rolling pins*	Letter *A* *Objects and pictures of objects beginning with A, picture dictionary, alphabet chart*	*Will I Have a Friend?*	"Peanut Butter and Jelly"
Thursday *Suggested Props and Materials*	Camping *Camping scenario, tent, sleeping bags, bear's "den," bear, bridge, fish, blue sheet (for water), fishing poles, wooden logs (e.g., Lincoln Logs for fire), grill*	Cheerios Art *Cheerios, outline of a bear or a tent*	The Color Blue *Blue items*	*We're Going on a Bear Hunt*	"A-Camping We Will Go"

MY NOTES

NEWSLETTER

Vol. 1, No. 1

Date: _____

Class Favorites

Monday

Today the children can enjoy water play activities during dramatic play. The children will be painting with watercolors in art. *Rainbow Fish* is the story of the day. During group time, the children will find pictures or objects that can be found in water. They will end their day in music with the song "Five Little Ducks."

Tuesday

Today the children will be playing house in dramatic play. The children will pretend to take care of babies, cook food, and clean. They will make drawings in art. *If You Give a Mouse a Cookie* is the story for Tuesday. During group time, the children will learn about things that are hot or cold. Our featured song is "I'm a Little Teapot."

Wednesday

Fast food is the theme for today's dramatic play. The children will pretend to be workers and customers in a fast-food restaurant. There will be playdough in art. The story is *Will I Have a Friend?* During group time, the children will be introduced to the letter *A*. The special song of the day is "Peanut Butter and Jelly."

Thursday

Today our fun will involve pretending to go camping. The children will pretend to put up a tent in the wilderness, cook over a campfire, and look for animals in the woods. The children will do Cheerios outlines in art. *We're Going on a Bear Hunt* is the story. During group time, the children will focus on the color blue. Please have your child wear something blue to school today. "A-Camping We Will Go" is the day's special song.

Monday

Dramatic Play	Art	Group	Story	Song
Water Play	Watercolor Painting	Things in Water	*Rainbow Fish*	"Five Little Ducks"

DAILY PLANNING GUIDE

Language and Literacy Skills Facilitated

Vocabulary: *water, splash, drip, fish, walrus, water pump, shell, shark, net, sink, float, boat, sailboat*

Verb phrase structures: *is splashing, was splashing; sails, is sailing, sailed; rides, rode; swims, swam*

Adjective/object descriptions: *wet/dry ___, fast/slow___, big/little___*

Question structures: *what, how, where, when, who, what if, why, how many, which one*

Pronouns: *I, you, he, she, we, they, my, your, him, her, his, our, their, me, us, them*

Prepositions: *in, on, under, over, near, beneath, next to, beside, around, inside, outside*

Sounds: */s/ sink, swim, sit, pass, eats; /f/ fish, off, float; /k/ keep, sink*

Noting print has meaning: names on chairs, on cubbies, signs in dramatic play, words in books and on chalkboard

Noting sound–symbol associations: What sound does _____ start with?

Writing: letters, names, words

Social Skills Facilitated

Initiating interaction with peers and adults; responding to questions and requests from peers and adults

Negotiating with peers for toys and materials

Group cooperation: waiting for a turn in a group, taking a turn at the appropriate time

Cognitive Skills Facilitated

Problem-solving skills: what things go in water/what things do not

Classification skills: things in water

Sequencing skills: story, songs

Narrative/story structure: adventure

Motor Skills Facilitated

Large motor: outdoor play activities—jumping, running, hopping, pedaling, climbing

Small motor: writing, drawing, gluing, painting

DRAMATIC PLAY **Water Play**

Type of Activity: Central

Objectives
1. Learn new, and employ familiar, vocabulary
2. Learn new, and employ a variety of, syntactic constructions
3. Interact with peers
4. Sequence familiar routines
5. Expand conceptual knowledge of the world

Settings
- Water table
- Wading pool

Props
- Smocks
- Water pump
- Cups
- Toy boats
- Sponges
- Strainers
- Toy people
- Rubber and plastic water toys (e.g., fish, seal, walrus, worms)

Roles
- Scientists
- Laboratory technicians

General Description of Activity

Water is put in the water table and in a wading pool. The children can experiment with various textures of objects as they play in the water. Some of the water toys are rough (e.g., play swordfish, walrus), some of them are smooth (e.g., various toy boats), some are sticky (e.g., play worms, small fish used as pretend bait), some are soft (e.g., blow-up toys), and some are hard (e.g., water pump). Another area can be set up with tubs and sponges for children to see how a sponge feels with and without water in it.

Verbal Productions

Level of linguistic complexity varies with the role or competency of the child playing the role.
- "This fish feels squishy" or "Fish soft"
- "Look, if you take the air out, the boat sinks"; "Look, sink"; or "Boat sink"
- "You splashed me" or "Splash"
- "I did not mean to—sorry" or "Sorry"

Adult Facilitative Role

The adult is to facilitate role play and help expand language and literacy skills. Typical actions or strategies to use include

Playing a role: "I am a scientist. I study fish."

Modeling a statement: "That is a big fish."

Expanding a child's utterance: "Boat floating" to "A little boat is floating."

Redirecting a child to a peer: "Ask Johnny for a turn. Say, 'May I have a turn, please?'"

Providing a literacy model: "The sign says *water.*"

ART : **Watercolor Painting**

Objectives
1. Express creativity
2. Develop small motor skills (e.g., drawing, painting, cutting, pasting)
3. Practice turn-taking skills
4. Converse with peers and adults

Materials
- Watercolor paints
- Tubs of water
- Brushes
- White construction paper

General Description of Activity

Lay out white construction paper, watercolor paint boxes, and brushes on the art table. Place tubs of water to clean the brushes above the paper. The children put on smocks and sit down in front of the paper, paint box, and water tub. Each child selects a brush, wets it, and chooses the paint color. The children paint on the paper, rinsing the brush before selecting a new color. Children can paint a collage of colors, animals, people, scenery, and so on. You may want to be close by so children can talk about their paintings.

GROUP **Things in Water**

Objectives
1. Improve listening skills
2. Increase conceptual knowledge
3. Learn appropriate group-interaction skills
4. Practice turn-taking skills

Materials
- Tub filled with water
- Mat
- Objects that go in water (e.g., toy boats, toy fish, shells)
- Objects that do not go in water (e.g., paper, toy cars, doll bed, chair)
- Pictures of objects that go in water (e.g., seaweed, shells, fishing pole, boats)
- Pictures of objects that do not go in water (e.g., house, radio)
- Towels

General Description of Activity

Place a tub of water on a mat on the floor. Next to the mat have a variety of objects, some that can go in water and some that should not be placed in water. Hold up a toy boat and a piece of paper, and ask the children to choose which object can be found in or on water. Following the children's response, ask one child to place the boat in the water.

Group Participation

Continue to hold up two objects and ask individual children to choose which one goes in water. After several children have had a turn, remove the tub of water. Ask the children to sort pictures of objects according to whether they are found in water or not. Place those that are found in water in one pile and those not found in water in a different pile.

Variation

As sorting pictures of objects is best suited for older children, younger children could sort a variety of objects.

Summary/Transition Activity

Review the category of objects that go in water by quickly holding up a few pictures from the "water" pile.

Tuesday

Dramatic Play	Art	Group	Story	Song
House	Drawings	Hot/Cold	*If You Give a Mouse a Cookie*	"I'm a Little Teapot"

DAILY PLANNING GUIDE

Language and Literacy Skills Facilitated

Vocabulary: *cook, house, food, soup, stew, muffins, babies, wash, table, clean, button, zip, teeth, toothbrush, diaper, towel, bottle, dish, cup*

Verb phrase structures: *is cooking, was cooking, cooks, cooked, fixes, fixed, makes, made, do you have ___?, eats, ate, has eaten, washes, washed*

Adjective/object descriptions: *good food, hot/cold food, sweet/tart fruit, green vegetables, red apple, yellow banana, dirty/clean baby*

Question structures: *what, how, where, when, who, what if, why, how many, which one*

Pronouns: *I, you, he, she, we, they, my, your, him, her, his, our, their, me, us, them*

Prepositions: *in, on, under, over, near, beneath, next to, beside, around, inside, outside*

Sounds: /k/ *cook, cooking, make;* /l/ *lick, Jell-o, yell;* /s/ *see, cooks;* /r/ *roof, carrot, bar*

Noting print has meaning: names on chairs and cubbies, signs in dramatic play, words in books and on chalkboard

Noting sound–symbol associations: What sounds does ____ start with?

Writing: letters, names, words

Social Skills Facilitated

Initiating interaction with peers and adults; responding to questions and requests from peers and adults

Negotiating with peers for toys and materials

Group cooperation: waiting for a turn in a group, taking a turn at the appropriate time

Cognitive Skills Facilitated

Problem-solving skills: how take care of babies

Classification skills: things that are hot or cold

Sequencing skills: story, songs

Narrative/story structure: prediction

Motor Skills Facilitated

Large motor: outdoor play activities—jumping, running, hopping, pedaling, climbing

Small motor: writing, drawing, gluing, squeezing, swirling

DRAMATIC PLAY **House**

Type of Activity: Central

Objectives
1. Learn new, and employ familiar, vocabulary
2. Learn new, and employ a variety of, syntactic constructions
3. Interact with peers
4. Sequence familiar routines
5. Expand conceptual knowledge of the world

Settings
- Kitchen area
- Dining rooms
- Bedrooms
- Family rooms
- House (child-sized wooden house or a house made out of a refrigerator box—optional)

Props
- Play refrigerator
- Play sink
- Beds
- Play food
- Mops and brooms
- Cupboards
- Dishes
- Dolls
- Baby bottles
- Play vacuum
- Play stove
- Pots and pans
- Tablecloths (optional)
- Party decorations (optional)

Roles
- Mothers
- Fathers
- Babies and other children
- Party guests (optional)

General Description of Activity

In the housekeeping center, set up a pretend house or apartment, including a kitchen. Here, the children can clean the house, take care of babies, cook food, set the table, make table decorations, and prepare for a party.

Verbal Productions

Level of linguistic complexity varies with role or competency of child playing the role.
- "It's time to cook dinner" or "Cook now"
- "Clean the table" or "Clean"
- "Use the broom to sweep the floor" or "Sweep here"
- "I'll do it later" or "Okay"
- "The baby is hungry, please get the bottle" or "Baby crying"
- "Do you want some more food?" or "Food?"
- "I'm glad you came" or "Hi, come in"

Adult Facilitative Role

The adult is to facilitate role play and help expand language and literacy skills. Typical actions or strategies to use include

Playing a role: "I am the sister. I want to dress the baby."

Modeling a statement: "That is the baby's bottle."

Recasting a child's utterance: "He is eating" to "He eats a lot."

Contrasting two sounds: "Do you mean the word *pin* or the word *bin*?"

Using a cloze procedure: "I have one bottle; you have two ____ (bottles)."

ART ACTIVITY PLAN : **Drawings**

Objectives
1. Express creativity
2. Develop small motor skills (e.g., drawing, painting, cutting, pasting)
3. Practice turn-taking skills
4. Converse with peers and adults

Materials
- Paper (white or colored)
- Crayons
- Markers
- Watered-down tempera paint (optional)

General Description of Activity

Provide the children with paper and a selection of crayons and/or markers. Let the children draw anything they want. Drawings could be of themselves, their family, their pets, different scenes, designs, rainbows, and so on.

Children can turn their crayon drawings into crayon washes by painting over the pictures with a light coat of tempera paint (watered down). The paint will not stick to the crayon but will fill in where there are no crayon marks to make a background of color.

GROUP **Hot/Cold**

Objectives
1. Improve listening skills
2. Increase conceptual knowledge
3. Learn appropriate group-interaction skills
4. Practice turn-taking skills

Materials
- Ice cube and dish
- Play stove
- Hot water in a cup
- Play refrigerator
- Pictures of cold foods (or plastic cold food items)
- Pictures of hot foods (or plastic hot food items)

General Description of Activity

Place an ice cube in a dish in front of the children, along with a cup of water that has been heated in a microwave oven or on a stove so that the children can see the steam. Label the ice cube as something cold and the hot water as something hot. Have each child touch the ice cube (but not the water). Tell children that the class is going to sort things that are usually hot and things that are usually cold by putting them either on the play stove or in the play refrigerator (brought over from the housekeeping area).

Ask the children if soup is usually hot or cold. After the children answer "hot," have one child place a picture of a bowl of soup on the play stove. Next, ask whether ice cream is hot or cold. After the children answer "cold," have another child place a picture of an ice cream cone in the play refrigerator. Note that the concept of "hot" should be associated with *not* touching.

Group Participation

Give half of the children pictures of hot foods and the other half pictures of cold foods. Each child comes up to the front of the class and puts his or her picture on the stove or in the refrigerator, depending on which kind of food is depicted in his or her picture.

Variation: Use plastic food items instead of pictures.

Summary/Transition Activity

After everyone has participated, review each pictured item on the stove or in the refrigerator by labeling it as hot or cold (e.g., "hot coffee," "cold milk").

Wednesday

Dramatic Play	Art	Group	Story	Song
Fast-Food Restaurant	Playdough	Letter *A*	*Will I Have a Friend?*	"Peanut Butter and Jelly"

DAILY PLANNING GUIDE

Language and Literacy Skills Facilitated

Vocabulary: *fast food, hamburger, french fries, soft drinks, shakes, wrappers, cartons, cook, cashier, customer, order*

Verb phrase structures: *place__s an order, buy__s a hamburger, pay__s money, eat out, __is mak__ing a burger, serv__ed the customer, flipp__ed a burger, choose__s a drink*

Adjective/object descriptions: *large drink, small hamburger, paper hat, red cup*

Question structures: *what, how, where, when, who, what if, why, how many, which one*

Pronouns: *I, you, he, she, we, they, my, your, him, her, his, our, their, me, us, them*

Prepositions: *in, on, under, over, near, beneath, next to, beside, around, inside, outside (in the cash register, on the plate, near the stove)*

Sounds: /b/ __burger, __bag, /f/ __french __fries, __food

Noting print has meaning: names on chairs and cubbies, signs in dramatic play, words in books and on chalkboard

Noting sound–symbol associations: What sound does _____ start with?

Writing: letters, names, words

Social Skills Facilitated

Initiating interaction with peers and adults; responding to questions and requests from peers and adults

Negotiating with peers for toys and materials

Waiting for a turn in a group, taking a turn at the appropriate time

Cognitive Skills Facilitated

Problem-solving skills: setting up a restaurant, remembering items

Classification skills: learning about the letter *A*

Sequencing skills: putting a hamburger together in a certain order, singing a song

Narrative/story structure: adventure

Motor Skills Facilitated

Large motor: outdoor play activities—jumping, running, hopping, pedaling, climbing

Small motor: writing, drawing, gluing

DRAMATIC PLAY **Fast-Food Restaurant**

Type of Activity: Central

Objectives
1. Learn new, and employ familiar, vocabulary
2. Learn new, and employ a variety of, syntactic constructions
3. Interact with peers
4. Sequence familiar routines
5. Expand conceptual knowledge of the world

Settings
- Counter (or facsimile)
- Kitchen
- Eating area (booths or tables and chairs)
- Drive-up window (optional)

Props
- Cash register(s)
- Play money
- Dishes (plastic or Styrofoam)
- Soda pop dispenser (box lid with pretend levers)
- Posted menu
- Variety of play food (e.g., hamburgers, french fries)
- Play "kids' meals" (small boxes with little toys and play food inside)
- Paper bags
- Trays
- Dolls
- Walkie-talkie for drive-thru cashier
- Pretend cars

Roles
- Customers
- Custodians
- Cooks
- Drive-thru cashier
- Cashiers

General Description of Activity

Children act out working and eating at a fast-food restaurant. They may have customers order food at a counter from a posted list of items. Cashiers could ring up the food order on a cash register, then place the prepared food on a tray or in a bag. The customer would pay for the food and either consume it at a table or booth or take it somewhere else to eat it. The restaurant might serve hamburgers, hot dogs, chicken sandwiches, roast beef sandwiches, french fries, salads, pizza, and so forth. Drinks may include soda pop, milk, coffee, milkshakes, and so forth. The dishes and utensils could be made of plastic or Styrofoam. The customers could bus their own dishes.

Verbal Productions

Level of linguistic complexity varies with the role or competency of the child playing the role.
- "May I take your order?" or "Yes?"
- "I want a hamburger, french fries, and a Coke" or "Coke, please"
- "He is cooking the french fries now" or "Cooking now"

Adult Facilitative Role

The adult is to facilitate role play and help expand language and literacy skills. Typical actions or strategies to use include

Playing a role: "Would you like a hamburger and french fries?"

Modeling a statement: "The customer wants a refill."

Expanding a child's utterance: "Big one" to "That is a big bag."

Redirecting a child to a peer: "Ask him if you can take a turn on the cash register."

Helping a child read the menu: "The menu says *Coke* and *hamburger*."

ART **Playdough**

Objectives
1. Express creativity
2. Develop small motor skills (e.g., drawing, painting, cutting, pasting)
3. Practice turn-taking skills
4. Converse with peers and adults

Materials
- Smocks
- Cookie cutters
- Cutting boards
- Playdough
- Presses
- Rolling pins
- Flat wooden sticks

General Description of Activity

Children wash their hands and put on smocks to explore playdough on the art table, using various presses, cutters, rolling pins, wooden craft sticks, and other tools. Children can make pretend food or any other objects out of the dough by rolling, cutting, or making pressing motions. They can form animals or people by rolling a main body and then adding heads, arms, and legs. Yarn can be used for hair (if children want to take their creations home). When children are finished, they roll the dough into a ball, wash their hands, and take off and fold their smock.

GROUP **Letter *A***

Objectives
1. Improve listening skills
2. Recognize letters of the alphabet and their sounds
3. Practice appropriate group-interaction skills
4. Practice turn-taking skills

Materials
- Alphabet chart and other alphabet displays
- Blackboard and chalk or poster paper and markers
- Pictures of objects (or objects themselves) with names that begin with *A*
- Picture dictionary (or an alphabet video dictionary)

General Description of Activity

Have the class sing the alphabet song while you point to the letters on an alphabet chart. Then write the letter *A* in both upper- and lowercase on the blackboard (or on poster paper) and tell the children, "The letter *A* has several sounds, but one of them is __ (/Æ/) like the beginning sound of *apple* or *ant*. The other sound is (/eI/), which sounds like its name, as in a word like *ate*." Then direct the children's attention to the alphabet picture displays around the room.

Group Participation

Ask if anyone's name starts with *A* (e.g., Angie, Andrew, April), and have those children write the letter *A* on the blackboard. Also have two or three children whose names do not begin with *A* write the letter *A* on the blackboard. As the children write the uppercase *A*, provide verbal guidance: "Start at the top and go down at a slant. Now, start at the top and go down at a slant the other way. Draw a line across the middle to connect the two other lines." If necessary, help the children write the letter. Then ask children to think of words that begin with *A*. Write the words they offer on the blackboard and draw quick sketches (when possible) of the suggested words. If children suggest a word that does not begin with *A*, say, "No, that begins with _____," and say the two sounds so that children can compare them. Although the focus is on the short and long *A* sounds, you can accept children's suggested words that begin with other *A* sounds (e.g., *airplane*). To help children who cannot think of any words participate in the activity, prompt them with pictures or objects representing words that begin with *A*. (Pictures or objects can be handed out at the beginning of the lesson or as the lesson proceeds.) Additional words can be sought in a picture dictionary if the group has difficulty arriving at words beginning with *A*.

Summary/Transition Activity

After about 10–15 words have been suggested, review the words, emphasizing the *A* sound.

Thursday

Dramatic Play	Art	Group	Story	Song
Camping	Cheerios Art	The Color Blue	*We're Going on a Bear Hunt*	"A-Camping We Will Go"

DAILY PLANNING GUIDE

Language and Literary Skills Facilitated

Vocabulary: *tent, campfire, stick, marshmallow, backpack, sleeping bag, hike, bear, deer, animals, trees, mountains, trail*

Verb phrase structures: *roast<u>s</u> marshmallows, <u>is</u> roast<u>ing</u> hot dogs, roast<u>ed</u> marshmallows, sleep<u>s</u> in a tent, <u>is</u> sleep<u>ing</u>, <u>slept</u> in a tent, hike<u>s</u>, hik<u>ed</u>, lights a fire, <u>lit</u> a fire*

Adjective/object descriptions: *big _____, little_____, hot_____, sleepy_____, hungry_____, yellow_____, blue_____*

Question structures: *what, how, where, when, who, what if, why, how many, which one*

Pronouns: *I, you, he, she, we, they, my, your, him, her, his, our, their, me, us, them*

Prepositions: *in, on, under, over, near, beneath, next to, beside, around, inside, outside*

Sounds: /k/ <u>c</u>ook; /l/ <u>l</u>ight, ye<u>ll</u>ow, ba<u>ll</u>; /z/ <u>z</u>ipper, ball<u>s</u>; /r/ <u>r</u>oast, bea<u>r</u>; /f/ <u>f</u>ire, o<u>ff</u>

Noting print has meaning: names on chairs and cubbies, signs in dramatic play, words in books and on chalkboard

Noting sound–symbol associations: What sound does _____ start with?

Writing: letters, names, words

Social Skills Facilitated

Initiating interaction with peers and adults; responding to questions and requests from peers and adults

Negotiating with peers for toys and materials

Waiting for a turn in a group, taking a turn at the appropriate time

Cognitive Skills Facilitated

Problem-solving skills: things that are blue

Classification skills: things we take on a camping trip

Sequencing skills: songs, stories

Narrative/story structure: repetitive line story

Motor Skills Facilitated

Large motor: outdoor play activities—jumping, running, hopping, pedaling, climbing

Small motor: writing, drawing, gluing, painting

DRAMATIC PLAY **Camping**

Type of Activity: Central

Objectives
1. Learn new, and employ familiar, vocabulary
2. Learn new, and employ a variety of, syntactic constructions
3. Interact with peers
4. Sequence familiar routines
5. Expand conceptual knowledge of the world

Settings
- Campground
- Hiking area
- Lake
- Ranger station
- Mountains

Props
- Tent(s)
- Sleeping bags
- Campfire (wooden blocks)
- Grill
- Picnic items (e.g., basket, food, paper plates, utensils)
- Fishing poles (with magnets attached to catch the fish)
- Marshmallows (cotton balls on sticks)
- Boats
- Fish (with paper clips attached)
- Backpacks
- Maps
- Play forest animals (e.g., bears, raccoons, rabbits)

Roles
- Campers (family members)
- Fishermen and women
- Hikers
- Ranger

General Description of Activity

Children act out camping trips and activities. Children might choose to camp at a lake, in the mountains, or in a camping area. They might sleep in tents or under the stars in sleeping bags. They could cook their food over a wood fire or pack a lunch and go hiking or fishing. The class might establish a ranger station so families can get maps that show them where to camp.

Verbal Productions

Level of linguistic complexity varies with the role or competency of the child playing the role.
- "I am packing a lunch for the picnic" or "Picnic"
- "Let's unroll our sleeping bags" or "Let's sleep"
- "Fix the tent, please" or "My turn, please"
- "John is walking too fast" or "Too fast"
- "You missed the trail" or "Missed it"

Adult Facilitative Role

The adult is to facilitate role play and help expand language and literacy skills. Typical actions or strategies to use include

Playing a role: "I want to set up the tent."

Modeling a statement: "There is the river. Let's catch some fish."

Recasting a child's utterance: "He want to go" to "He wanted to go with you."

Contrasting two sounds: "Did you say 'tap' or 'cap'?"

ART **Cheerios Art**

Objectives
1. Express creativity
2. Develop small motor skills (e.g., drawing, painting, cutting, pasting)
3. Practice turn-taking skills
4. Converse with peers and adults

Materials
- Cheerios
- Glue
- Several pieces of paper with rectangles, circles, squares, or triangles drawn on them

General Description of Activity

Before the children arrive, draw different shapes with markers on pieces of paper. The children outline the shapes by gluing or pasting Cheerios on the lines. Children may make other pictures with the Cheerios by either following lines or arranging them free-form.

Variation

Have children draw their own shapes and then glue or paste the Cheerios on the lines.

GROUP **The Color Blue**

Objectives
1. Improve listening skills
2. Increase conceptual knowledge
3. Practice appropriate group-interaction skills
4. Practice turn-taking skills

Materials
- Blue paper
- Blue construction paper badges for those children who are not wearing blue
- An assortment of blue objects
- Tub labeled *blue*, written on blue paper
- Two red objects
- Two yellow objects

General Description of Activity

On the first Thursday of September, gather an assortment of objects that are blue, red, and yellow. At group time, hold up a piece of blue construction paper, labeling the color as *blue*. Place the paper in a tub marked with a blue label. The children look around the room to find other items that are blue. After identifying several items, the children then look at the assortment of items. One child then chooses a blue object from the pile of assorted objects and places it in the blue tub.

Group Participation

Other children take turns choosing an item that is blue and placing it in the blue tub.

Variation

Use objects of various shades of blue. Some children might discriminate between light blue and dark blue; for those who don't, ask them just to find a blue item.

Summary/Transition Activity

Because it is "blue" day and all the children are wearing something blue, dismiss the children one by one by asking them to point to the blue color on their clothes. Similar activities can be done for other colors and can be organized according to the color assigned for the day (see the lesson plans on yellow [Week 6] and red [Week 11]). At LAP, the children wear a particular color on Thursdays of every month. The primary colors are addressed in the fall semester: September is blue month, October is yellow month, and November/December is red month. The secondary colors are addressed in the spring semester: January is orange month, February is purple month, and March is green month. Other colors can be chosen for April and May.

WEEKLY PLANNING GUIDE

	Dramatic Play	Art	Group	Story	Song
Monday *Suggested Props and Materials*	Doctor's Office *Doctor's office scenario, doctor kits, scrubs, waiting area, white sheets, telephones, calendar, pencil*	Chalk Drawings *Chalk, black or dark construction paper*	Body Parts *Doll or skeleton for labeling body parts*	*Going to the Doctor*	"The Hokey Pokey"
Tuesday *Suggested Props and Materials*	Beauty Shop/ Barber Shop *Beauty shop scenario, hair dryers, curlers, pretend scissors, smocks, individual combs (with children's names on them, optional), shaving cream and containers, plastic chips for pretend razors, containers for water, water with small paintbrushes for pretend fingernail polish*	Shaving Cream Fingerpainting *Shaving cream, formboards, smocks*	Letter *B* *Objects and pictures beginning with B, slates or paper for writing letters*	*Count*	"The Alphabet Song"
Wednesday *Suggested Props and Materials*	Service Station *Gas station scenario, gas pumps, car wash (optional), mechanic tools, tracks, riding cars, taped road*	Car Track Painting *Paint, miniature cars, construction paper*	Sound Sequencing *Drum for tapping out rhythms*	*Go, Dog. Go!*	"If You're Happy and You Know It"
Thursday *Suggested Props and Materials*	Grocery Store *Grocery store scenario, cash registers, shelves, carts, pretend food and other items, bags, items that are big or little, two tubs*	Food Collage *Magazine pictures of food, paper, glue*	Big and Little *Items that are big or little, two tubs*	*Little Fish, Big Fish*	"I Like to Eat Apples and Bananas"

MY NOTES

NEWSLETTER

Vol. 1, No. 2

Date: _____

Places in the Community

Monday

The doctor's office is the dramatic play theme for today. The children will be taking care of people who are "sick" or "injured." In art, we will be making chalk-drawn "X-rays." The children will read *Going to the Doctor* during storytime. They will identify different body parts during group using a doll (or a skeleton). In music, the children will sing "The Hokey Pokey."

Tuesday

Today the children will be stylists or the customers at a beauty salon or barber shop. During dramatic play, they can have their hair "washed" and styled and get their nails manicured. At the barber shop, children might get a haircut or a shave. At the art table, they will enjoy shaving cream fingerpainting. The class will read *Count* during storytime. The focus will be on the letter *B* during group time. We will end the day by singing "The Alphabet Song."

Wednesday

Today the classroom becomes a service station, with cars and gas pumps and a mechanics' area. In art, the children will make car track paintings. Our story today is *Go, Dog. Go!* At group time, children will practice their listening skills by imitating the sound patterns tapped by the teacher on a drum. For example, the teacher might tap out the following rhythm: *tap, tap (pause) tap, tap, tap (pause) tap,* and ask a child to try to imitate that rhythm. Our featured song is "If You're Happy and You Know It."

Thursday

Today the children get to be grocery store workers and customers. There will also be shelves to stock. In art, they will make a food collage by finding pictures of food in magazines and cutting them out. They will paste the pictures on paper plates. The story for today is *Little Fish, Big Fish*. At group time, we will be classifying objects as things that are BIG and things that are LITTLE. Today's theme song is "I Like to Eat Apples and Bananas."

Monday

Dramatic Play	Art	Group	Story	Song
Doctor's Office	Chalk Drawings	Body Parts	*Going to the Doctor*	"The Hokey Pokey"

DAILY PLANNING GUIDE

Language and Literacy Skills Facilitated

Vocabulary: *doctor, nurse, paramedic, ambulance, stethoscope, thermometer, fever, cast, X-ray, oxygen, accident, vehicle, arm, leg, ankle, bandage, forehead, hospital*

Verb phrase structures: *is carrying the stretcher, drove the ambulance, rides, examines, gave oxygen, sets the leg*

Adjective/object descriptions: *broken leg, big ambulance, loud siren*

Question structures: *what, how, where, when, who, what if, why, how many, which one*

Pronouns: *I, you, he, she, we, they, my, your, him, her, his, our, their, me, us, them*

Prepositions: *in, on, under, over, near, beneath, next to, beside, around, inside, outside*

Sounds: /k/ <u>c</u>arry, do<u>c</u>tor, bro<u>ke</u>; /s/ <u>s</u>et, in<u>s</u>ide, u<u>s</u>, ambulan<u>ce</u>

Noting print has meaning: names on chairs and on cubbies, signs in dramatic play, words in books and on chalkboard

Noting sound–symbol associations: What sound does _____ start with?

Writing: letters, names, words

Social Skills Facilitated

Initiating interaction with peers and adults; responding to questions and requests from peers and adults

Negotiating with peers for toys and materials

Group cooperation: waiting for a turn in a group, taking a turn at the appropriate time

Cognitive Skills Facilitated

Problem-solving skills: What does a doctor do?

Classification skills: things in an doctor's office, body parts

Sequencing skills: story, songs

Narrative/story structure: labeling, adventure

Motor Skills Facilitated

Large motor: outdoor play activities—jumping, running, hopping, pedaling, climbing

Small motor: writing, drawing, gluing, cutting

DRAMATIC PLAY **Doctor's Office**

Type of Activity: Central

Objectives
1. Learn new, and employ familiar, vocabulary
2. Learn new, and employ a variety of, syntactic constructions
3. Interact with peers
4. Sequence familiar routines
5. Expand conceptual knowledge of the world

Settings
- Several examination rooms
- Waiting room
- Patients' "homes"

Props
- Table with a telephone and appointment book
- Several tables or mats to represent examination rooms
- Doctor kits
- Bandages
- X-ray machine
- Telephone in area representing patients' "homes"

Roles
- Doctor
- Patient
- Nurse
- Parent
- Receptionist

General Description of Activity

A doctor's office with several examination rooms and a waiting room is set up. Children who are patients call the receptionist and make an appointment. When it is time for their appointment, they go into the examination room with the doctor. He or she examines them by looking into their mouth, ears, and eyes; checking reflexes; checking muscle tone; listening with the stethoscope; and so forth. A patient might have a broken bone that needs to be X-rayed, set in a cast, and wrapped with a bandage.

Verbal Productions

Level of linguistic complexity varies with the role or competency of the child playing the role.
- "Open your mouth, please" or "Open mouth"
- "Where does it hurt?" or "Hurt?"
- "I don't feel good. My tummy hurts" or "I sick"

Adult Facilitative Role

The adult is to facilitate role play and help expand language and literacy skills. Typical actions or strategies to use include

Playing a role: "Open your mouth and say 'ah.'"

Modeling a statement: "You can be the doctor, and I will be the nurse."

Modeling how to write another child's name: "Write Suzie's name this way."

Asking open questions: "What medicine should the baby have?"

Recasting the present with past tense: "I play with Mary" to "Yes, you played with Mary for a long time."

ART **Chalk Drawings**

Objectives
1. Express creativity
2. Develop small motor skills (e.g., drawing, painting, cutting, pasting)
3. Practice turn-taking skills
4. Converse with peers and adults

Materials
- Black construction paper
- White chalk
- Other chalk available
- Chalk fixative (sprayed on to keep pictures from smudging)

General Description of Activity

The children are given black construction paper and white chalk to draw pictures on the paper. Some children might like to draw X-ray pictures by making line drawings of skeleton-like people. Some of the X-ray pictures could be of "broken" arms and then could be incorporated into the dramatic play. (The artists could be the "radiologists.") Other children might want to draw general pictures that have nothing to do with the X-ray activity.

GROUP **Body Parts**

Objectives
1. Improve listening skills
2. Increase conceptual knowledge
3. Learn appropriate group-interaction skills
4. Practice turn-taking skills

Materials
- Doll
- List of body parts
- Riddles about body parts

General Description of Activity

Hold up a doll and tell the children that they are going to take turns finding and labeling different parts of the doll.

Group Participation

Ask one child to point to the doll's arm. Ask other children to find the doll's wrist, toes, head, eyes, and so on. Then point to a body part on the doll (or on a child) and have a child label it.

Variation

Make this activity a guessing game by saying something like "I'm thinking of a body part that you point with. What is it?" The children can take turns guessing the riddle or can point to the answer on the doll. Continue with other body parts. The guessing game could be embedded within the activity to provide a more difficult task for some children who find the original requests too easy.

Summary/Transition Activity

Hold up the doll again. Quickly have the children shout out the correct label as you point to the doll's hair, eyes, arm, hand, leg, toes, and so on.

Tuesday

Dramatic Play	Art	Group	Story	Song
Beauty Shop/ Barber Shop	Shaving Cream Fingerpainting	Letter *B*	*Count*	"The Alphabet Song"

DAILY PLANNING GUIDE

Language and Literacy Skills Facilitated

Vocabulary: *comb, brush, hair, wash, cut, set, curl, dry, blow-dry, fix, shave, shaving cream, emery board, customer, appointment*

Verb phrase structures: *curls her hair, is curling, curled; dries, is drying, dried, will dry; cuts, is cutting, cut*

Adjective/object descriptions: *soft/hard ____, wet/dry hair, cold/hot ____, long/short hair, rough/smooth ____*

Question structures: *what, how, where, when, who, what if, why, how many, which one*

Pronouns: *I, you, he, she, we, they, my, your, him, her, his, our, their, me, us, them*

Prepositions: *in, on, under, over, near, beneath, next to, beside, around, inside, outside*

Sounds: /k/ *cut, back;* /s/ *set, cuts;* /sh/ *shave, brush;* /l/ *long, curl*

Noting print has meaning: names on chairs and on cubbies, signs in dramatic play, words in books and on chalkboard

Noting sound–symbol associations: What sound does _____ start with?

Writing: letters, names, words

Social Skills Facilitated

Initiating interaction with peers and adults; responding to questions and requests from peers and adults

Negotiating with peers for toys and materials

Group cooperation: waiting for a turn in a group, taking a turn at the appropriate time

Cognitive Skills Facilitated

Problem-solving skills: how to fix hair

Classification skills: things found in a beauty shop

Sequencing skills: songs, stories

Narrative/story structure: labeling

Motor Skills Facilitated

Large motor: outdoor play activities—jumping, running, hopping, pedaling, climbing

Small motor: writing, drawing, gluing

DRAMATIC PLAY **Beauty Shop/Barber Shop**

Type of Activity: Central

Objectives
1. Learn new, and employ familiar, vocabulary
2. Learn new, and employ a variety of, syntactic constructions
3. Interact with peers
4. Sequence familiar routines
5. Expand conceptual knowledge of the world

Settings
- Salon chair
  (use a highchair for dolls to sit in)
- Chairs (for children)
- Sink to "wash" hair
- Reception area with telephone, appointment book, and pencil or crayon
- Barber chair
- Manicurist's table

Props
- Curlers and clips
- Combs (put children's names on the combs so that they use only theirs, and disinfect at the end of play)
- Mirrors
- Fingernail polish bottles (filled with water)
- Small paintbrushes to apply "fingernail polish" (water)
- Pretend shampoo and conditioner
- Pretend hair spray
- Pretend hair dryer (made out of two toilet paper rolls and a cottage cheese container, with a twisted pipe cleaner to represent the cord)
- Plastic strips (pretend razors)
- Shaving cream
- Smocks (typically used when children paint)
- Pretend nail polish remover
- Nail files
- Towels
- Toy cash register
- Pretend money

Roles
- Customers
- Barber
- Receptionist
- Manicurist
- Beautician

General Description of Activity

Children play beauty/barber shop and pretend to get their hair shampooed, cut, dried, and styled. They also might get a manicure (hair salon) or a shave (barber shop). Children can use their fingers in a cutting motion to pretend to cut hair.

Verbal Productions

Level of linguistic complexity varies with role or complexity of the child playing the role.
- "I'm washing her hair" or "Wash hair"
- "Do you want your hair to be cut?" or "Cut?"
- "Your hair is wet" or "Wet"
- "Cut my hair, please" or "Cut hair"
- "He is shaving" or "He shaved"

Adult Facilitative Role

The adult is to facilitate role play and help expand language and literacy skills. Typical actions or strategies to use include

Playing a role: "Do you want a hair cut or just a shampoo?"

Modeling a statement: "I like shaving cream. It is sticky."

Modeling phonological awareness: "That's right that 'big' and 'baby' both start with 'buh.'"

Expanding a child's utterance: "Want shaving" to "You want the shaving cream."

Providing a cloze procedure: "Here is one curler. Here are five _____ (curlers)."

Providing confirmatory feedback: "That's right. It is bigger."

ART **Shaving Cream Fingerpainting**

Objectives
1. Express creativity
2. Develop small motor skills (e.g., drawing, painting, cutting, pasting)
3. Practice turn-taking skills
4. Converse with peers and adults

Materials
- Shaving cream
- Formboards
- Wooden craft sticks
- Other tools for "drawing" in the cream

General Description of Activity

Put a dab of shaving cream on each child's formboard. The children can use their hands and fingers to smear the cream all over the board, then use their fingers to draw and write in the shaving cream. The children can also make abstract designs, make full handprints, or use their fingers to practice writing letters or numbers. Fingerpainting is a good excuse to get messy and gooey. Some children love this; others may need some coaxing to get their fingers dirty.

GROUP **Letter B**

Objectives
1. Improve listening skills
2. Increase knowledge of the alphabet and sounds
3. Learn appropriate group-interaction skills
4. Practice turn-taking skills

Materials
- Alphabet chart and other alphabet displays
- Blackboard and chalk or poster paper and markers
- Pictures of objects (or objects themselves) with names that begin with B
- Picture dictionary (or an alphabet video dictionary)

General Description of Activity

Write an upper- and a lowercase letter B on the blackboard (or on poster paper) and give children several examples of words that begin with B, emphasizing the /b/ sound at the beginning of the words. (You might also hold up pictures of objects (or objects themselves) with names that begin with B.) Direct the children's attention to the alphabet picture displays around the room.

Group Participation

Ask if anyone's name starts with B (e.g., Betty, Bryn). Those children write the letter B on the blackboard (or poster paper). Give two or three other children the opportunity to write the letter B on the blackboard as well. As children write, provide verbal guidance: "Start at the top, draw a line straight down, go to the top again, make a circle to the middle of the line, make another circle from the middle to the bottom of the line." If necessary, help children write the letter. Some of the other children can practice writing a B in the air with their fingers (or, use individual chalkboards). Then ask the children to think of words that begin with B. Write the words they offer on the blackboard, drawing quick sketches (when possible) of the suggested words. If a child suggests a word that does not begin with B, say, "No, that begins with a ___," and say the two sounds so children can compare them. To help children who cannot think of any words participate in the activity, prompt them with pictures or objects representing words that begin with B. (Cards or objects can be handed out at the beginning of the lesson or as the lesson proceeds.) Additional words can be sought in a picture dictionary if the class has difficulty arriving at words that begin with B.

Summary/Transition Activity

After about 10–15 words have been suggested, review the words, emphasizing the /b/ sound.

Wednesday

Dramatic Play	Art	Group	Story	Song
Service Station	Car Track Painting	Sound Sequencing	*Go, Dog. Go!*	"If You're Happy and You Know It"

DAILY PLANNING GUIDE

Language and Literacy Skills Facilitated

Vocabulary: *transportation, vehicle, car, track, garage, mechanic, truck, finish, battery, brakes, ignition, hose, tools, engine, wheels, shapes, rectangle, square, circle, triangle*

Verb phrase structures: *works, is working, crashed the car, pushed it, was racing, starts, stopped, fixed the car*

Adjective/object descriptions: *broken part, dead battery, big/little*

Question structures: *what, how, where, when, who, what if, why, how many, which one*

Pronouns: *I, you, he, she, we, they, my, your, him, her, his, our, their, me, us, them*

Prepositions: *in, on, under, over, near, beneath, next to, beside, around, inside, outside*

Sounds: /r/ *race, starter, car;* /s/ *see, misses, miss;* /sh/ *shape, finish;* blends: *flag, truck, start*

Noting print has meaning: names on chairs and on cubbies, signs in dramatic play, words in books and on chalkboard

Noting sound–symbol associations: What sound does _____ start with?

Writing: letters, names, words

Social Skills Facilitated

Initiating interaction with peers and adults; responding to questions and requests from peers and adults

Negotiating with peers for toys and materials

Group cooperation: waiting for a turn in a group, taking a turn at the appropriate time

Cognitive Skills Facilitated

Problem-solving skills: how to fix the cars

Classification skills: kinds of tools

Sequencing skills: song, art, sound patterns

Narrative/story structure: rhyming book

Motor Skills Facilitated

Large motor: outdoor play activities—jumping, running, hopping, pedaling, climbing

Small motor: writing, drawing, gluing

DRAMATIC PLAY Service Station

Type of Activity: Related

Objectives
1. Learn new, and employ familiar, vocabulary
2. Learn new, and employ a variety of, syntactic constructions
3. Interact with peers
4. Sequence familiar routines
5. Expand conceptual knowledge of the world

Settings
- Garage/repair shop
- Desk
- Cashier's station
- Gas pumps
- Car lift (cardboard blocks holding a plastic truck high enough for a child to slide under)
- Parts counter or store (optional)

Props
- Appointment book and pencil or crayon
- Toy cash register
- Pretend money
- Hoses for pumps
- Car with hood (can be made out of cardboard)
- Dashboard
- Tools
- Pretend battery
- Pretend computer
- Pretend cans for oil change
- Play telephones
- Pretend parts to sell (optional)

Roles
- Mechanics
- Customers
- Receptionist
- Sales clerk
- Cashier

General Description of Activity

Children take their vehicles to a gas station or garage to be repaired, gassed up, or tuned up. The oil in the car may need to be changed or the battery recharged. Customers can call ahead and make appointments. In one area, a receptionist/cashier desk is arranged. Another area might have a wooden or cardboard facsimile of a car with a hood that opens so that the mechanics can work under the hood if needed. Also, blocks or a vehicle Erector Set may be placed in one area to build cars. An optional activity is to have a parts counter or store.

Verbal Productions

Level of linguistic complexity varies with the role or competency of the child playing the role.
- "May I please have the wrench?" or "Wrench, please"
- "Please start the car now" or "Start"
- "My car needs a new battery" or "Battery"

Adult Facilitative Role

The adult is to facilitate role play and help expand language and literacy skills. Typical actions or strategies to use include

Playing a role: "Do you want me to fix the tire now?"

Modeling a statement: "The mechanic works the engine."

Modeling the reading of a sign: "That sign says *park here*."

Open questions: "Which tool do you need?"

Recasting present tense with present progressive: "He drives fast" to "He is driving."

ART **Car Track Painting**

Objectives
1. Express creativity
2. Develop small motor skills (e.g., drawing, painting, cutting, pasting)
3. Practice turn-taking skills
4. Converse with peers and adults

Materials
- 8" × 11" pieces of construction paper (at least one piece per child)
- Three or four colors of tempera paint
- Smocks
- Small die-cast cars
- Shallow containers to hold the paint and cars (e.g., Styrofoam meat trays)

General Description of Activity

The children each don a smock before sitting at the art table. Give each child an 8" × 11" piece of construction paper. On the art table are several shallow containers (e.g., small Styrofoam meat trays) containing tempera paints of various colors (one color per container) and small die-cast cars. The children dip the wheels of the cars into the paint and then roll the car along their paper to make designs. Before changing to a different color, the children return the cars they had been using to their original paint container.

GROUP **Sound Sequencing**

Objectives
1. Improve listening skills
2. Increase ability to recognize and sequence patterns
3. Learn appropriate group-interaction skills
4. Practice turn-taking skills

Materials
- Drum
- Keyboard (optional)

General Description of Activity

Place a drum in front of the children. Tap out a simple pattern while the children listen, then repeat the pattern while they listen again. Invite one child to come up to the front of the class and try to make the same pattern. If necessary, give assistance.

Group Participation

Play a different pattern and have another child try to match it. Continue until all the children have had at least one turn. The patterns can vary from two short taps to complicated patterns involving a series of taps grouped in two or three sequences. For example, one pattern might be *tap-tap* (pause) *tap*. Another might be *tap-tap-tap* (pause) *tap-tap*. Other sample patterns include the following:

tap-tap (pause) *tap-tap*

tap-tap-tap (pause) *tap*

tap (pause) *tap-tap*

loud tap (pause), soft tap

two loud taps (pause), two soft taps

Variation

Set a rhythm on a keyboard and have the children clap to the rhythm.

Summary/Transition Activity

Play one more pattern and have the children clap the pattern, or play a rhythm from a song that will be sung during music time and have the children clap out that rhythm.

Thursday

Dramatic Play	Art	Group	Story	Song
Grocery Store	Food Collage	Big and Little	*Little Fish, Big Fish*	"I Like to Eat Apples and Bananas"

DAILY PLANNING GUIDE

Language and Literacy Skills Facilitated

Vocabulary: *groceries, cart, cereal, shop, checker, buy, sell, bag, sack, shelf, money, change*

Verb phrase structures: *eat<u>s</u>, <u>is</u> eat<u>ing</u>, <u>ate</u>, <u>has eaten</u>, push<u>es</u>, <u>is</u> push<u>ing</u>, push<u>ed</u>, buy<u>s</u>, <u>bought</u>, check<u>s</u>, <u>is</u> check<u>ing</u>, check<u>ed</u>*

Adjective/object descriptions: *big/little bag, full/empty shelf*

Question structures: *what, how, where, when, who, what if, why, how many, which one*

Pronouns: *I, you, he, she, we, they, my, your, him, her, his, our, their, me, us, them*

Prepositions: *in, on, under, over, near, beneath, next to, beside, around, inside, outside*

Sounds: /sh/ <u>sh</u>elf, pu<u>sh</u>; /k/ <u>c</u>art, sa<u>ck</u>; /s/ <u>s</u>ell, cart<u>s</u>

Noting print has meaning: names on chairs and on cubbies, signs in dramatic play, words in books and on chalkboard

Noting sound–symbol associations: What sound does _____ start with?

Writing: letters, names, words

Social Skills Facilitated

Initiating interaction with peers and adults; responding to questions and requests from peers and adults

Negotiating with peers for toys and materials

Group cooperation: waiting for a turn in a group, taking a turn at the appropriate time

Cognitive Skills Facilitated

Problem-solving skills: what to buy

Classification skills: fruits, vegetables, meats; big and little

Sequencing skills: songs, story

Narrative/story structure: labeling

Motor Skills Facilitated

Large motor: outdoor play activities—jumping, running, hopping, pedaling, climbing

Small motor: writing, drawing, gluing

DRAMATIC PLAY **Grocery Store**

Type of Activity: Sequential

Objectives
1. Learn new, and employ familiar, vocabulary
2. Learn new, and employ a variety of, syntactic constructions
3. Interact with peers
4. Sequence familiar routines
5. Expand conceptual knowledge of the world

Settings
- Grocery store
- Shelves and aisles
- Check-out stand
- Customers' homes

Props
- Shelves
- Canned goods and other food items
- Fruit and vegetable area
- Grocery bags
- Pretend money
- Pretend credit cards
- Pretend coupons
- Shopping carts
- Pretend cash register
- Pencil and paper for making lists
- Table for checkout area

Roles
- Shoppers
- Cashiers
- Stockers
- Baggers

General Description of Activity

The children pretend to be grocery shopping. They can make lists, take their "children" with them, choose the items on the list to put in their carts, pay, bag their groceries, and go home. Other children can be the grocery store workers. Some can keep the shelves stocked; others can be checkers and baggers.

Verbal Productions

Level of linguistic complexity varies with the role or the competency of the child playing the role.
- "Will that be all? Your total is $5" or "All? $5!"
- "Milk, please" or "Milk"
- "Do you have any cereal?" or "Want cereal"

Adult Facilitative Role

The adult is to facilitate role play and help expand language and literacy skills. Typical actions or strategies to use include

Playing a role: "That will be $5."

Modeling the reading of a sign: "That sign says *milk*."

Expanding a child's utterance: "Want cart" to "I want the big cart, please."

Redirecting a child to a peer: "Ask Mary for a turn. Say, 'May I have a turn, please?'"

ART **Food Collage**

Objectives
1. Express creativity
2. Develop small motor skills (e.g., drawing, painting, cutting, pasting)
3. Practice turn-taking skills
4. Converse with peers and adults

Materials
- White paper plates or construction paper
- Scissors
- Magazines (with pictures of food)
- Newspapers (food ads)

General Description of Activity

Children cut out pictures of food from magazines or newspapers advertisements. The children then paste these pictures on round white paper plates (or construction paper) to make a food collage. Children can choose from a variety of food pictures. Assist older children in making a picture of the different food groups.

GROUP **Big and Little**

Objectives
1. Improve listening skills
2. Increase conceptual knowledge
3. Learn appropriate group-interaction skills
4. Practice turn-taking skills

Materials
- Big tub
- Little tub
- 10 pairs of items of different sizes
- Doll (optional)

General Description of Activity

Place a big tub and a little tub in front of the children. Hold up a big object and a little object (e.g., a big toy horse and a little toy horse). Tell the children they are going to help sort some big things and little things into big and little tubs. Then illustrate by putting the big object in the big tub and the little object in the little tub.

Group Participation

Hold up other items that are the same except for size, and have different children put the items in the two tubs. Ask them to tell why they put the items where they did ("I put it there because it is a big ____ or a little ____"). The class proceeds through several item pairs. Have a variety of sizes available so that the children begin to understand that it is the comparison between the items that determines whether something is big or not. (For later lessons, the terms *large* and *small* may be used.)

Summary/Transition Activity

Have two children come to the front of the classroom. Ask the rest of the children to say which of the two children is big and which is little. The child who is little sits down. Another child who is taller than the "big" child comes up. Again the children decide who is bigger. Finally, you (or another adult) stand by the last child and ask who is bigger. (Another way would be to have the big child sit down, then you place a doll by the little child and ask, "Now who is bigger?") Be careful not to choose the smallest child in the class or a child who is particularly sensitive about his or her size. (A variation of this task would be to keep the two children at the front of the class and add a still bigger child to focus on the concepts of *big, bigger, biggest*.)

WEEKLY PLANNING GUIDE

	Dramatic Play	Art	Group	Story	Song
Monday *Suggested Props and Materials*	Airplanes *Airplane scenario, pilot and co-pilot area of plane, passenger area (chairs with ties for seat belts), carts, trays, dishes, play food, tickets and ticket counter, computer, luggage*	Paper Airplanes *Paper for folding, paper clips, markers*	Shapes—Circle *Circle shapes, individual chalkboards and chalk (optional)*	*We're Taking an Airplane Trip*	"I'm a Little Airplane"
Tuesday *Suggested Props and Materials*	Boats *Boat scenario, gift shop, swimming area, shuffleboard area, dining area*	Meat Tray Boats *Meat trays, wooden craft sticks, paper triangles, glue, tape*	Same or Different *Five exactly matched pairs of objects, 10 other objects (e.g., cars, dolls, boats, balls, blocks), two tubs or mats (optional)*	*Mr. Gumpy's Outing*	"Row, Row, Row Your Boat"
Wednesday *Suggested Props and Materials*	Car Racing *Racetrack scenario, car tracks, cars, concession stand, spectator stand (folded gym mats to make risers), chairs, mechanic area, tools*	Vehicle Rubbings *Vehicle cutouts for rubbings, paper, crayons with no paper covering, markers*	Letter C *Objects or pictures of objects starting with C, picture dictionary, alphabet chart, individual chalkboards and chalk*	*Wheels*	"C is for Cookie"
Thursday *Suggested Props and Materials*	Delivery Trucks *Delivery truck scenario, dispatch area, store area, warehouse area, taped road, "trucks" (cardboard boxes tied to child with men's ties, paper plate for steering wheel), mechanic's area (optional)*	Easel Painting *Easel, easel paint, brushes*	Circle Collage *Circles for collage, poster board with figure drawn on it (holding up one hand), figure is covered with a sheet of paper*	*The Truck Book*	"Wheels on the Bus"

MY NOTES

NEWSLETTER

Vol. 1, No. 3

Date: _____

Transportation

Monday The children will make paper airplanes in art and take airplane trips in dramatic play. They will pretend to be pilots, co-pilots, passengers and flight attendants. They will hear the story *We're Taking an Airplane Trip*. During group time, the children will focus on the circle shape. The day ends with the song "I'm a Little Airplane."

Tuesday The children will pretend to be on a fishing boat. They can be the fishermen, the captain, the crew, or the passengers. In art, they will make boats out of meat trays. They will read *Mr. Gumpy's Outing* during storytime. Group discussion will be about things that are the same and things that are different. Our theme song in music is "Row, Row, Row Your Boat."

Wednesday Today is all about racing cars. The children will be fixing cars and racing cars down the racetrack during dramatic play. They may also be the spectators or the concession stand operators. Children will do vehicle rubbings in art. *Wheels* is the story of the day. Group discussion will be about the letter *C*. Music will include the song "C is for Cookie."

Thursday Today the children will be driving delivery trucks to make deliveries from the warehouse to the toy store. They can pretend to be the truck drivers, the warehouse workers, or the store clerks. They will do easel paintings in art. The story today is *The Truck Book*. The focus at group will be on making a circle collage. At music, we will sing "Wheels on the Bus."

Dramatic Play	Art	Group	Story	Song
Airplanes	Paper Airplanes	Shapes—Circle	*We're Taking an Airplane Trip*	"I'm a Little Airplane"

Monday

DAILY PLANNING GUIDE

Language and Literacy Skills Facilitated

Vocabulary: *transportation, airplane, pilot, flight attendant, baggage, suitcase, take-off, landing, seat belt, security check, ticket, seat, passenger, beverage, cockpit*

Verb phrase structures: *fasten your seatbelt, land_s_ the plane, _is_ land_ing_, land_ed_, _flew_ the plane, serv_ed_ food, check_ed_ baggage, Who's going on the plane? I _am_* (uncontractible auxiliary verb), *I'_m_ flying* (contractible auxiliary)

Adjective/object descriptions: *large plane, small plane, big suitcase, little bag, carry-on bag, blue ____, red ____, purple ____*

Question structures: *what, how, where, when, who, what if, why, how many, which one*

Pronouns: *I, you, he, she, we, they, my, your, him, her, his, our, their, me, us, them*

Prepositions: *in, on, under, over, near, beneath, next to, beside, around, inside, outside*

Sounds: */l/ _l_ands, pi_l_ot, fi_ll_; /r/ _r_ide, ca_r_; /s/ _s_it, talk_s_; /k/ _c_arry, ti_ck_et, pa_ck_; /f/ _f_ive, o_ff_*

Noting print has meaning: names on chairs and on cubbies, signs in dramatic play, words in books and on chalkboards

Noting sound–symbol associations: What sound does _____ start with?

Writing: letters, names, words

Social Skills Facilitated

Initiating interaction with peers and adults; responding to questions and requests from peers and adults

Negotiating with peers for toys and materials

Group cooperation: waiting for a turn in a group, taking a turn at the appropriate time

Cognitive Skills Facilitated

Problem-solving skills: how to fold a paper to make an airplane

Classification skills: shapes—circles

Sequencing skills: songs, stories

Narrative/story structure: adventure

Motor Skills Facilitated

Large motor: outdoor play activities—jumping, running, hopping, pedaling, climbing

Small motor: writing, drawing, gluing, folding

DRAMATIC PLAY **Airplanes**

Type of Activity: Central

Objectives
1. Learn new, and employ familiar, vocabulary
2. Learn new, and employ a variety of, syntactic constructions
3. Interact with peers
4. Sequence familiar routines
5. Expand conceptual knowledge of the world

Settings
- Airport
- Airplane facsimile (chairs arranged in rows behind a "cab," where a play dashboard is set up)
- Ticket office or counter
- Kitchen
- Cockpit
- Baggage claim area (optional)
- Metal detector (optional)

Props
- Tickets
- Chairs with seatbelts (men's ties can be used for seatbelts)
- Dashboard
- Luggage
- Food and drinks
- Trays
- Carts
- Dolls
- Pretend money
- Dishes

Roles
- Pilot and co-pilot
- Clerks at the ticket counter
- Security people
- Flight attendants
- Passengers

General Description of Activity

Children take a pretend airplane trip, including purchasing a ticket, checking baggage at the counter, going through a security check, and finding a seat on the airplane. They must store their carry-on luggage under a seat and fasten their seatbelts before take-off. Food and beverages can be served by children acting as flight attendants. Upon arrival, the passengers can claim their baggage in the baggage area.

Verbal Productions

Level of linguistic complexity varies with the role or competency of child playing the role.
- "We're coming in for a landing, so fasten your seatbelts" or "Plane's landing"
- "Do you want a drink?" or "Drink?"
- "May I see your ticket?" or "Ticket?"

Adult Facilitative Role

The adult is to facilitate role play and help expand language and literacy skills. Typical actions or strategies to use include

Playing a role: "Fasten your seatbelts. We are ready for take off."

Modeling a statement: "The mechanic says he has to fix the engine."

Expanding a child's utterance: "I want ticket" to "I want a ticket to Kansas City."

Asking an open question: "How can we fix this?"

ART **Paper Airplanes**

Objectives
1. Express creativity
2. Develop small motor skills (e.g., drawing, painting, cutting, folding)
3. Practice turn-taking skills
4. Converse with peers and adults

Materials
- 8" × 10" paper (or other size)
- Crayons
- Paper clips
- Stickers
- Markers

General Description of Activity

Children decorate a piece of paper to make into a paper airplane with markers, crayons, and/or stickers. The adult assists the children in folding the paper to make an airplane. First, fold the paper in half lengthwise. Then fold a top edge down until it is even with the folded bottom to form a triangle shape. Turn paper over and fold the other side the same way so that one third of the paper is slanted and ends in a point. Clip a paper clip to the point of the triangle (the nose of the airplane) to hold the plane together and to provide appropriate weight so that the airplane will fly. Fold the rest of the top edge even with the bottom fold. Make a crease. Let go of the paper so it sticks out to make a wing. Turn the paper over and fold the other side in the same way. The paper airplane is ready to fly. (Other paper folding can be done to form other styles of airplanes).

GROUP **Shapes—Circle**

Objectives

1. Improve listening skills
2. Increase conceptual knowledge
3. Learn appropriate group-interaction skills
4. Practice turn-taking skills

Materials

- Colored tape
- Square cutout
- Circle cutouts in a variety of sizes
- Triangle cutout

General Description of Activity

Using colored tape (or masking tape), outline a large circle and a small circle on the floor in front of the children. Trace around each shape with your index finger as you label each circle as either large and small. Hold up a circle cutout and say, "This is a circle—a large circle. I'm going to put it in the large circle area."

Group Participation

Have the children, one at a time, place one of the circle cutouts in either the large or the small circle area. Ask some of the children to make circles in the air.

Variation

Have a child place a foot in one of the circles on the floor and a hand in the other. Another child could put a knee in one circle and head in another, and so forth.

Note

Having two circle areas (large and small) allows you to make different types of requests. One child can be asked to label the shape as a circle and helped to place it in the appropriate outline. Another child can be asked to identify the large circle and focus on both the shape and the size of the cutout. The activity, then, can be used to review the concepts of *large* and *small* as the new concept of shapes is introduced.

Summary/Transition Activity

Hold up a circle cutout and a square cutout and ask children to identify the circle. Hold up a circle cutout and a triangle cutout and again ask which is the circle.

Tuesday

Dramatic Play	Art	Group	Story	Song
Boats	Meat Tray Boats	Same or Different	*Mr. Gumpy's Outing*	"Row, Row, Row, Your Boat"

DAILY PLANNING GUIDE

Language and Literacy Skills Facilitated

Vocabulary: *sink, float, water, fish, boat, liner, rowboat, shark, sea, ocean, waves, swim*

Verb phrase structures: *is fishing, catches, floated, swam, has a fish, has gone sailing, rode in a boat, Who is going fishing, I am* (uncontractible auxiliary), *Who is the biggest, I am* (auxiliary verb)

Adjective/object descriptions: *big ____, little ____, high water, low water, tiny ____, green ____, blue ____*

Question structures: *what, how, where, when, who, what if, why, how many, which one*

Pronouns: *I, you, he, she, we, they, my, your, him, her, his, our, their, me, us, them*

Prepositions: *in, on, under, over, near, beneath, next to, beside, around, inside, outside*

Sounds: /f/ *fish*; /s/ *sail, boats*; /l/ *little, pail*; /r/ *rowboat, far*; /k/ *catch, sink*; /sh/ *ship, fish*

Noting print has meaning: names on chairs and on cubbies, signs in dramatic play, words in books and on chalkboards

Noting sound–symbol symbol associations: What sound does ____ start with?

Writing: letters, names, words

Social Skills Facilitated

Initiating interaction with peers and adults; responding to questions and requests from peers and adults

Negotiating with peers for toys and materials

Group cooperation: waiting for a turn in a group, taking a turn at the appropriate time

Cognitive Skills Facilitated

Problem-solving skills: how to make a boat, how to fish

Classification skills: things that are the same or different

Sequencing skills: songs, stories

Narrative/story structure: adventure

Motor Skills Facilitated

Large motor: outdoor play activities—jumping, running, hopping, pedaling, climbing

Small motor: writing, drawing, gluing, fingerpainting

DRAMATIC PLAY **Boats**

Type of Activity: Central

Objectives
1. Learn new, and employ familiar, vocabulary
2. Learn new, and employ a variety of, syntactic constructions
3. Interact with peers
4. Sequence familiar routines
5. Expand conceptual knowledge of the world

Settings
- Water table, filled with water
- Wading pool, filled with water
- Boat facsimile
- Fishing area (designated by blue cloth or a taped-off area)

Props
- Toy boats
- Toy people
- Various rubber sea animals (e.g., seals, whales, sharks, fish)
- Wooden or cardboard boat and submarine
- Paper fish (with paper clips attached)
- Fishing poles (with magnets attached to catch the fish)
- Pails
- Pretend grill (to cook the fish)
- Picnic items (e.g., basket, food, paper plates, utensils)
- Blue satin sheet (optional)

Roles
- Fishermen and women
- Boat captain
- Operator(s) of the toy boats, toy people, and toy animals

General Description of Activity

Children learn that boats are used on the water to travel from one place to another and that people often fish from boats. Toy boats, toy people, and toy sea animals can be used in the water table to represent boats on an ocean. A fishing boat area can be set up so that children can catch "fish." A cardboard box could be used to make a submarine or a boat that goes under the "water." The activity could be extended by having a picnic and "cooking" the fish.

Verbal Productions

Level of linguistic complexity varies with the role or competency of the child playing the role.
- "I caught a fish" or "Fish"
- "My boat can float with all these people in it" or "My boat"
- "I'm the captain. You sit here" or "You sit"
- "It's sinking" or "Sink"

Adult Facilitative Role

The adult is to facilitate role play and help expand language and literacy skills. Typical actions or strategies to use include

Playing a role: "Cast off! We are ready to sail."

Modeling rhyming: "Hey, the words *boat* and *float* rhyme."

Expanding a child's utterance: "Me fish" to "That's my fish."

Contrasting two sounds: "Is the word *fish* or *dish*?"

ART : **Meat Tray Boats**

Objectives
1. Express creativity
2. Develop small motor skills (e.g., drawing, painting, cutting, pasting)
3. To practice turn-taking skills
4. To converse with peers and adults

Materials
- Styrofoam meat trays
- Wooden craft sticks
- Precut construction paper triangles
- Glue
- Stickers or other decorations
- Tape

General Description of Activity

Place Styrofoam trays on the art table along with wooden craft sticks, stickers, construction paper, and glue. The children can decorate the tray, glue the precut triangle to the stick to make a sail, and push the stick into the middle of the Styrofoam tray to make the boat. The stick may need to be taped to the tray. Optional: Children can sail their boats in the "lake" (water table or tub filled with water).

GROUP **Same or Different**

Objectives
1. Improve listening skills
2. Increase conceptual knowledge
3. Learn appropriate group-interaction skills
4. Practice turn-taking skills

Materials
- Five exactly matched pairs of objects
- 10 other objects (e.g., cars, dolls, boats, balls, blocks)
- Two tubs (optional)

General Description of Activity

Hold up two objects that are exactly the same and talk about what is the same about them. Place the objects in one pile or tub and hold up two new objects that are different from each other (e.g., a car and a boat). Label these as *different* and put them in another pile or tub.

Group Participation

Continue to present pairs of objects to the children. Have one child decide whether each pair of objects is the same or different and place the objects in the appropriate pile or tub. Start out with objects that are exactly the same or are quite different from each other. Proceed to objects that vary somewhat but that can still be labeled as the same (e.g., different-colored cars are still cars). Focus on the fact that items can be the same even when they are not alike in *every* way. Things do not have to be an exact match to be the same. The label is important in setting up a category.

Variation

To extend this activity, demonstrate that objects can be the same in some ways and different in other ways; for example, two cars might be different because they are different colors or different sizes, but they are both cars.

Summary/Transition Activity

Review the meaning of the words *same* and *different*: *Same* describes things that are alike in some way and *different* describes things that are not alike.

Wednesday

Dramatic Play	Art	Group	Story	Song
Car Racing	Vehicle Rubbings	Letter *C*	*Wheels*	"C is for Cookie"

DAILY PLANNING GUIDE

Language and Literacy Skills Facilitated

Vocabulary: *transportation, vehicle, car, track, ramp, garage, truck, win, lose, flag, start, finish, wheels, square*

Verb phrase structures: *go<u>es</u> fast, win<u>s</u> the race, crash<u>ed</u> the car, push<u>ed</u> it, <u>was</u> rac<u>ing</u>, start<u>s</u>, stopp<u>ed</u>, won, <u>were</u> los<u>ing</u>*

Adjective/object descriptions: *race car, fast ____, slow ___, big/little ___, yellow flag, checkered flag*

Question structures: *what, how, where, when, who, what if, why, how many, which one*

Pronouns: *I, you, he, she, we, they, my, your, him, her, his, our, their, me, us, them*

Prepositions: *in, on, under, over, near, beneath, next to, beside, around, inside, outside*

Sounds: /r/ *<u>r</u>ace, sta<u>r</u>ter, ca<u>r</u>;* /s/ *<u>s</u>ee, mi<u>ss</u>es, ra<u>c</u>e;* /f/ *<u>f</u>ast, of<u>f</u>;* /sh/ *<u>sh</u>ape, fini<u>sh</u>;* blends: *<u>fl</u>ag, <u>tr</u>uck, <u>st</u>art*

Noting print has meaning: names on chairs and on cubbies, signs in dramatic play, words in books and on chalkboards

Noting sound–symbol associations: What sound does _____ start with?

Writing: letters, names, words

Social Skills Facilitated

Initiating interaction with peers and adults; responding to questions and requests from peers and adults

Negotiating with peers for toys and materials

Group cooperation: waiting for a turn in a group, taking a turn at the appropriate time

Cognitive Skills Facilitated

Problem-solving skills: how to set up the tracks

Classification skills: vehicles/nonvehicles

Sequencing skills: song, racing the cars, art

Narrative/story structure: labeling

Motor Skills Facilitated

Large motor: outdoor play activities—jumping, running, hopping, pedaling, climbing

Small motor: writing, drawing, gluing, rubbings

DRAMATIC PLAY Car Racing

Type of Activity: Related

Objectives
1. Learn new, and employ familiar, vocabulary
2. Learn new, and employ a variety of, syntactic constructions
3. Interact with peers
4. Sequence familiar routines
5. Expand conceptual knowledge of the world

Settings
- Three or four different track areas (one with two tracks elevated on one end and other tracks that form circles or ovals)
- Garage or pit area
- Spectator area
- Portable slide elevated on one end (optional—another track)
- Concession stand (optional)

Props
- Assortment of toy cars
- Tracks
- Electric tracks (optional)
- Checkered flag
- Play stopwatch
- Chairs for spectators
- Tools (e.g., wrench, screwdriver, pretend batteries)
- Pretend drink machine
- Cups
- Pretend cotton candy (optional)

Roles
- Drivers
- Mechanics
- Timers or judges
- Spectators
- Concession stand workers

General Description of Activity

Arrange several tracks for the toy cars to race on, an area for the cars to be worked on, and an area for spectators. Children play the roles of drivers, mechanics, timers, and spectators. The drivers race the cars by releasing two cars simultaneously and watching as they race down the tracks, which are elevated on one end. (Electric tracks could also be used, particularly for children with physical disabilities so that they could press the switches.) The activity could be expanded to include concession stands.

Verbal Productions

Level of linguistic complexity varies with the role or competency of the child playing the role.
- "Get your cars ready" or "Ready"
- "Your car needs a new engine" or "New car"
- "That car went very fast" or "Fast car"
- "I fixed it" or "Fix"

Adult Facilitative Role

The adult is to facilitate role play and help expand language and literacy skills. Typical actions or strategies to use include

Playing a role: "I am the starter, so get ready, get set, go."

Modeling a statement: "The spectators sit in the stands."

Redirecting a child to a peer: "Ask James if you can race the cars."

Providing confirmatory feedback: "That's right, it is the car." (Child usually says "tar.")

ART **Vehicle Rubbings**

Objectives
1. Express creativity
2. Develop small motor skills (e.g., drawing, painting, rubbing, cutting, pasting)
3. Practice turn-taking skills
4. Converse with peers and adults

Materials
- Newsprint or tracing paper
- Variety of cardboard cutouts in vehicle shapes
- Crayons with paper removed
- Container to hold crayons
- Brick wall, sidewalk, and other interesting textures for outdoor rubbings (optional)

General Description of Activity

Have the children place one or more of the vehicle cutouts under a piece of paper. Holding a crayon (with the paper covering removed) or a piece of chalk on one side, they rub over the paper back and forth until the shape of the object appears on their paper. Children can use several colors and different arrangements of objects under the paper to make a variety of pictures.

Variation

Tape large pieces of paper to a brick wall for children to make crayon rubbings. A sidewalk or manhole cover would also produce interesting rubbings.

GROUP : **Letter *C***

Objectives

1. Improve listening skills
2. Increase knowledge of the alphabet
3. Learn appropriate group-interaction skills
4. Practice turn-taking skills

Materials

- Alphabet chart and other alphabet displays
- Blackboard and chalk or poster paper and markers
- Pictures of objects (or objects themselves) with names that that begin with *C*

General Description of Activity

Invite two or three children to the front of the class to sing the alphabet song. Point to the letters on the alphabet chart as the song is sung, then write an upper- and a lowercase *C* on the blackboard (or poster paper). Give several examples of words that begin with *C*, emphasizing the /k/ sound at the beginning of the words. (You might also hold up objects or pictures of objects whose names begin with *C*.) Tell the children that sometimes *C* says another sound: /s/. Give some examples using picture cards. Direct the children's attention to the alphabet picture displays around the room.

Group Participation

Ask if anyone's name starts with *C* (e.g., Courtney, Carissa, Carlos, Cecilia), and have those children write the letter *C* on the board. Also have two or three other children whose names do not begin with *C* write the letter *C* on the blackboard. Provide verbal guidance as children write the letter: "Start at the top and draw a curved line, like half of a circle." If necessary, help children write the letter. Some of the children can practice writing *C* in the air with their fingers (or use individual chalkboards). Ask the children to think of words that begin with *C*. Write the words they offer on the blackboard and draw quick sketches (when possible) of the suggested words. If a child suggests a word that does not begin with *C*, say, "No, that begins with a _____" and say the sound along with the /k/ and /s/ sounds so children can compare them. To help children who cannot think of any words participate in the activity, prompt them with pictures of objects or objects representing words that begin with *C*. (Cards or objects can be handed out at the beginning of the lesson or as the lesson proceeds.) Additional words can be sought in a picture dictionary if the group has difficulty arriving at words that begin with *C*.

Summary/Transition Activity

After about 10–15 words have been suggested, review the words, emphasizing the /k/ sound. You might give children cards or adhesive notes with the upper- and lowercase letter *C* written on them as they identify the letter or the sound. The children can take the cards or notes home.

Variation

Scatter several adhesive notes with either an upper- or a lowercase *C* written on them around the room. Ask children, one at a time, to find the capital *C* or the lowercase *c*.

Thursday

Dramatic Play	Art	Group	Story	Song
Delivery Trucks	Easel Painting	Circle Collage	*The Truck Book*	"Wheels on the Bus"

DAILY PLANNING GUIDE

Language and Literacy Skills Facilitated

Vocabulary: *delivery truck, warehouse, goods, load, gas station, gas pump, road, highway, ramp, park, slow, fast*

Verb phrase structures: *load<u>s</u>, <u>was</u> stack<u>ing</u>, unload<u>ed</u>, deliver<u>s</u>, gas<u>es</u> up, back<u>ed</u> up, <u>drove</u>, Who stopp<u>ed</u>, I <u>did</u>*

Adjective/object descriptions: *big ____, little ____, heavy ____, light ____*

Question structures: *what, how, where, when, who, what if, why, how many, which one*

Pronouns: *I, you, he, she, we, they, my, your, him, her, his, our, their, me, us, them*

Prepositions: *in, on, under, over, near, beneath, next to, beside, around, inside, outside*

Sounds: /k/ *<u>k</u>ey, ti<u>ck</u>et, tru<u>ck</u>;* /r/ *<u>r</u>oad, na<u>rr</u>ow, deliver;* /s/ *<u>s</u>end, out<u>s</u>ide, ga<u>s</u>;* blends: *<u>sl</u>ow, <u>st</u>ack, <u>tr</u>ip*

Noting print has meaning: names on chairs and on cubbies, signs in dramatic play, words in books and on chalkboard

Noting sound–symbol associations: What sound does a _____ start with?

Writing: letters, names, words

Social Skills Facilitated

Initiating with peers and adults; responding to questions and requests from peers and adults

Negotiating with peers for toys and materials

Group cooperation: waiting for a turn in a group, taking a turn at the appropriate time

Cognitive Skills Facilitated

Problem-solving skills: how to load the truck

Classification skills: things that are circles, types of trucks

Sequencing skills: songs, story

Narrative/story structure: labeling book

Motor Skills Facilitated

Large motor: outdoor play activities—jumping, running, hopping, pedaling, climbing

Small motor: writing, drawing, gluing

DRAMATIC PLAY **Delivery Trucks**

Type of Activity: Central

Objectives
1. Learn new, and employ familiar, vocabulary
2. Learn new, and employ a variety of, syntactic constructions
3. Interact with peers
4. Sequence familiar routines
5. Expand conceptual knowledge of the world

Settings
- Warehouse
- Gas station (optional)
- Loading areas
- Roads
- Various stores

Props
- Masking tape (to mark the road)
- Cardboard boxes
- Small lids or paper plates (for steering wheels)
- Variety of goods (e.g., fruits and vegetables, toys, books)
- Motorcycles (optional—made from yardsticks with paper circles attached to both ends)
- Hose (optional—for gas)
- Pretend road signs
- Pad and pencil or crayon (to note shipments)
- Pretend money
- Cash register
- Police hat (optional)

Roles
- Drivers
- Warehouse workers
- Unloaders
- Store clerks
- Police officers (optional—see below)
- Gas station/garage attendants (optional—see below)

General Description of Activity

Children learn that delivery trucks pick up goods and transport them to new locations and that the goods are often stored in a warehouse. The children take turns being the truck. The child who is the truck gets the trailer (a cardboard box) tied around his or her waist. The child backs up to the warehouse (child-sized house or other designated area). Other children load the "truck" up, and the child drives around the room following the road (delineated by masking tape) until he or she reaches the unloading place (bookcases). An extension of this activity is to add a store area to receive the goods, police officers on motorcycles to make sure the drivers drive safely, or a gas station where trucks must fuel up.

Verbal Productions

Level of linguistic complexity varies with the role or competency of the child playing the role.
- "I'm ready to be loaded. Give me those boxes" or "Load up"
- "I want a table delivered tomorrow" or "Need a table"
- "You were going too fast. Here's your ticket" or "Too fast. Here's ticket"

Adult Facilitative Role

The adult is to facilitate role play and help expand language and literacy skills. Typical actions or strategies to use include

Playing a role: "I am the factory worker. Back your truck into the loading zone."

Modeling a statement: "The truck is going very fast."

Using a cloze procedure: "This truck is big, but this truck is even _____ (bigger)."

Expanding a child's utterance: "I drive a truck" to "I am driving the truck."

ART **Easel Painting**

Objectives
1. Express creativity
2. Develop small motor skills (e.g., drawing, painting, cutting, pasting)
3. Practice turn-taking skills
4. Converse with peers and adults

Materials
- Smocks
- Different colors of tempera
- Paint cups to hold the paint
- Large paintbrushes
- 9" × 12" or 12" × 18" paper
- Drying rack or other area for drying

General Description of Activity

Set up two easel boards with a large piece of paper clipped to each. Set out two to four cups filled with tempera paint and a paintbrush in each cup. (It is helpful to have cup covers with holes in them for the brushes. As children dip the brushes into the paint and pull them through the hole, some of the excess paint is removed. It is also helpful to place the easel over plastic or newspaper so that the paint drips do not stain the floor.)

Children put on their smocks, dip the brush into the paint, and paint shapes, objects, or anything else they want. Sometimes children will paint a picture and then experiment by painting other colors on top. Let the children experiment with the tempera for some projects. Sometimes you might have the children tell you about their painting, and you can label it for display. (Let the children decide if they want their paintings displayed.) Have a designated area for drying the pictures, such as a wooden clothes rack.

Note

This is a large muscle activity, particularly appropriate for young children (3 years and up).

GROUP **Circle Collage**

Objectives

1. Improve listening skills
2. Increase conceptual knowledge
3. Learn appropriate group-interaction skills
4. Practice turn-taking skills

Materials

- Different-sized circles cut out of various colors of construction paper
- A small clown figure with hand extended, drawn on a large piece of poster board
- Paper to cover the clown figure except hand.

General Description of Activity

Hold up a piece of construction paper cut in the shape of a circle. Ask the children, "What shape is this?" After they respond with "circle," paste the circle onto the poster board (at the bottom of which is the clown figure, covered so that the children cannot see it). Then pass out one paper circle to each child.

Group Participation

Ask one child what shape he or she has. When the child says "circle," have the child come up and paste the circle onto the poster board. To make the activity more challenging for some children, have them label both the color and shape or the size and shape (have them compare their circle to another child's and decide if it is a big or little circle). After all of the children have pasted their circles, draw lines from each circle down to the figure's hand so that it looks as if the figure is holding a bunch of balloons. Remove the paper hiding the figure and show the children the collage they have helped make.

Summary/Transition Activity

Have the children count the number of circles (balloons) the clown figure is holding.

WEEKLY PLANNING GUIDE

	Dramatic Play	Art	Group	Story	Song
Monday *Suggested Props and Materials*	Construction Worker *Construction worker scenario, cardboard box houses, tools, tool belt, shingles, pegs, wallpaper*	Craft Stick Construction *Wooden craft sticks, markers, paper, glue*	Shapes—Square *Various sizes/colors of square-shaped cutouts, several small and large circle-shaped cutouts, small chalkboard or paper (optional), chalk or markers (optional)*	*A House Is a House for Me*	"Johnny Works with One Hammer"
Tuesday *Suggested Props and Materials*	Veterinarian *Veterinarian scenario, doctor kits, desk, phones, cages, examining rooms, pretend pet food, bowls, leashes*	Paper Bag Puppets *Paper bags, cutouts (e.g., eyes, noses, mouths), glue*	Caring for a Pet *List of items pets need, water dish, pet food (can have both cat and dog food), food dish, leash and collar, cage or doghouses*	*Moses the Kitten*	"Five Little Monkeys"
Wednesday *Suggested Props and Materials*	Office Worker *Office worker scenario, desks, phones, computer keyboards, typewriters, folders, hole punch, stapler, binders, envelopes, stationery, pens, pencils, desk calendars*	Drawings *Paper (white or colored), crayons, markers, watered-down tempera paint (optional)*	Letter *D* *Alphabet chart, blackboard and chalk or poster paper and markers, pictures of objects (or objects themselves) with names that begin with D, picture dictionary*	*A Letter to Amy*	"The Alphabet Song"
Thursday *Suggested Props and Materials*	Firefighter *Fire station scenario (include dispatch office, sleeping area), houses, pretend fire engine with pretend removable hoses, mats, pole (optional), phones*	Playdough *Playdough, rolling pins, cookie cutters*	Fire Safety Rules *List of fire safety rules; pictures of children crawling and touching a door; pictures of children stopping, dropping, and rolling to put out a fire on their clothing; play telephones; a list of children's addresses*	*The Fire Engine*	"Hurry, Hurry, Drive the Fire Truck"

MY NOTES

NEWSLETTER

Vol. 1, No. 4

Date: _____

Occupations

Monday
The children will spend their day pretending to work at a construction site. In dramatic play they will use hammers, saws, and other tools. Art time will be spent constructing houses out of wooden craft sticks. *A House Is a House for Me* is the story for today, and group discussion will be about the square shape. The action song is "Johnny Works with One Hammer."

Tuesday
Today the dramatic play setting will be a veterinarian's office. The children can be the vet, the owner of the pets, or the receptionist/assistant. In art, they will make paper bag puppets. *Moses the Kitten* is our story for the day. During group time, we will discuss how to take care of pets. We will learn that pets need food, water, and a safe place to sleep. Our featured song is "Five Little Monkeys."

Wednesday
The work that people do in an office will be the dramatic play theme today. The children will be busy typing, answering the phone, and using office materials. They will make drawings in art today. Our story for Thursday is *A Letter to Amy*. During group time, children will learn about the letter *D*. "The Alphabet Song" will be the song of the day.

Thursday
Today the children will learn all about being a firefighter. They will pretend to be dispatchers or the ones driving the fire truck or fighting the fire. They might even be the ones who are being "saved." In art, we will make hoses and other items out of playdough. The story will be *The Fire Engine*. Fire safety will be discussed during group time. Our song of the day will be "Hurry, Hurry, Drive the Fire Truck."

		Monday		
Dramatic Play	Art	Group	Story	Song
Construction Worker	Craft Stick Construction	Shapes—Square	*A House Is a House for Me*	"Johnny Works with One Hammer"

DAILY PLANNING GUIDE

Language and Literacy Skills Facilitated

Vocabulary: *construction, build, building, hammer, nail, fix, roof, pound, hammer, saw, make, work, hard hat, safety, paint*

Verb phrase structures: *is building, constructed, built, hammered, Who is building? I am, makes, carries*

Adjective/object descriptions: *large/small ____, heavy/light ____, hard/soft material*

Question structures: *what, how, where, when, who, what if, why, how many, which one*

Pronouns: *I, you, he, she, we, they, my, your, him, her, his, our, their, me, us, them*

Prepositions: *in, on, under, over, near, beneath, next to, beside, around, inside, outside*

Sounds: /f/ *fix, fun, off;* /s/ *size, walks;* /k/ *construct, can, make*

Noting print has meaning: names on chairs and on cubbies, signs in dramatic play, words in books and on chalkboard

Noting sound–symbol associations: What sound does _____ start with?

Writing: letters, names, words

Social Skills Facilitated

Initiating interaction with peers and adults; responding to questions and requests from peers and adults

Negotiating with peers for toys and materials

Group cooperation: waiting for a turn in a group, taking a turn at the appropriate time

Cognitive Skills Facilitated

Problem-solving skills: how to make a building

Classification skills: tools we use to construct things

Sequencing skills: songs, steps in building, stories

Narrative/story structure: rhyming

Motor Skills Facilitated

Large motor: outdoor play activities—jumping, running, hopping, pedaling, climbing

Small motor: writing, drawing, gluing, pounding

DRAMATIC PLAY **Construction Worker**

Type of Activity: Related

Objectives
1. Learn new, and employ familiar, vocabulary
2. Learn new, and employ a variety of, syntactic constructions
3. Interact with peers
4. Sequence familiar routines
5. Expand conceptual knowledge of the world

Settings
- Street (area of the floor marked with masking tape) lined with houses made from a variety of materials (e.g., blocks, cardboard)

Props
- Playhouse
- Cardboard box additions that can be taped to the playhouse
- LEGOs
- Blocks
- Play bricks
- Paper strips of various colors for roof or siding
- Glue

- Tools (e.g., plastic hammers, wrenches, saws, screwdrivers, screws)
- Tool belts
- Pegs for pounding (wooden clothespins that can be pounded into cardboard)
- Play hardhats
- Masking tape
- Telephones

Roles
- Carpenters
- Architects

- Homeowners
- Other construction workers

General Description of Activity

Children participate in a construction/repair dramatic play involving putting together different materials to make buildings. A variety of materials can be used. One area can be set up for constructing buildings with LEGOs or other blocks. Another area can be designated for a new addition to the playhouse (using big boxes). A third area can utilize play bricks and boxes to make another house. The children can problem-solve how to construct houses or apartments by rearranging the boxes, bricks, and blocks. (Some of the houses could be doll-size; others could be large enough for the children to play in).

Houses may also need to be repaired. Children can replace a roof by making "shingles" out of paper bag strips. The strips could be laid on top of cardboard. (You might suggest that children start at the outer edge and overlay the shingles so that "rain" will roll off the roof and not under the shingles.) The children can put new siding on a house by using strips of colored paper and glue, and they could even put up wallpaper on the inside of a house.

Verbal Productions

Level of linguistic competency varies with the role or competency of the child playing the role.
- "I'm building a big house" or "Me build house"
- "We need to make that side higher. Call the carpenter" or "Higher"
- "Look, I pounded the nail into the wall" or "Look"

Adult Facilitative Role

Playing a role: "I am a painter, so give me the brush, please."

Modeling a statement: "That roof is leaking."

Expanding a child's utterance: "Saw hard" to "Sawing is hard work."

Redirecting a child to a peer: "Ask Johnny if he needs a hammer."

ART **Craft Stick Construction**

Objectives
1. Express creativity
2. Develop small motor skills (e.g., drawing, painting, cutting, pasting)
3. Practice turn-taking skills
4. Converse with peers and adults

Materials
- Large and small wooden craft sticks
- White glue
- Markers
- Yarn

- Paper of various sizes and colors (small pieces and pieces 12" × 14" in case children want to paste their sticks on the paper)
- Child scissors

General Description of Activity

Lay out large and small wooden craft sticks. Let the children glue them together to form a variety of constructions. They can make triangle shapes or "log" cabins, or form "people" or animals (or anything else). Have items such as yarn, markers, and constructions paper available for the children to use in their constructions.

GROUP **Shapes—Square**

Objectives

1. Improve listening skills
2. Increase conceptual knowledge
3. Learn appropriate group-interaction skills
4. Practice turn-taking skills

Materials

- Colored tape
- Various sizes/colors of square-shaped cutouts
- Several small and large circle-shaped cutouts
- Small chalkboard or paper (optional)
- Chalk or markers (optional)

General Description of Activity

Using colored tape, outline a large square and a small square on the floor in front of the children. These new shapes join the large and small circles previously outlined on the floor. Trace one of the square outlines on the floor or trace a square cutout, noting that a square has four sides and four corners and that the sides are all the same length.

Group Participation

Ask different children to find the large or small square by standing on it or by putting a large or small square cutout on the appropriate outline. Vary the level of difficulty. For instance, you might ask one child to identify a shape (e.g., square or circle) and another child to find a shape that is a certain size and color (e.g., "Find a large green square"). You could also vary the activity by having children place a hand on one shape and a foot on another. If necessary, have the children do this activity in smaller groups.

Variation

Have the children draw shapes (square and circle) on small chalkboards or on paper.

Summary/Transition Activity

Review the shapes by pointing to or standing on them or by holding up a shape cutout and having the children quickly label them in unison.

Tuesday

Dramatic Play	Art	Group	Story	Song
Veterinarian	Paper Bag Puppets	Caring for a Pet	*Moses the Kitten*	"Five Little Monkeys"

DAILY PLANNING GUIDE

Language and Literacy Skills Facilitated

Vocabulary: *dog, cats, birds, gerbils, Dalmatians, pets, sick, vet, shot, bandage, medicine, phone, appointment, fleas, rabies shot*

Verb phrase structures: *gives a shot, is taking the pet to the vet, fed the dog, gave medicine, petted the dog, took an X-ray*

Adjective/object descriptions: *examining table, high fever, sick cat, yellow cat, big dog, little rabbit*

Question structures: *what, how, where, when, who, what if, why, how many, which one*

Pronouns: *I, you, he, she, we, they, my, your, him, her, his, our, their, me, us, them*

Prepositions: *in, on, under, over, near, beneath, next to, beside, around, inside, outside*

Sounds: /v/ *vet, gave;* /f/ *fed, fever, off;* /r/ *rabbit, far*

Noting print has meaning: names on chairs and on cubbies, signs in dramatic play, words in books and on chalkboard

Noting sound–symbol associations: What sound does _____ start with?

Writing: letters, names, words

Social Skills Facilitated

Initiating interaction with peers and adults; responding to questions and requests from peers and adults

Negotiating with peers for toys and materials

Group cooperation: waiting for a turn in a group, taking a turn at the appropriate time

Cognitive Skills Facilitated

Problem-solving skills: how to take care of our pets

Classification skills: things a vet uses

Sequencing skills: songs, stories

Narrative/story structure: adventure

Motor Skills Facilitated

Large motor: outdoor play activities—jumping, running, hopping, pedaling, climbing

Small motor: writing, drawing, gluing, cutting

DRAMATIC PLAY Veterinarian

Type of Activity: Central

Objectives
1. Learn new, and employ familiar, vocabulary
2. Learn new, and employ a variety of, syntactic constructions
3. Interact with peers
4. Sequence familiar routines
5. Expand conceptual knowledge of the world

Settings
- Reception/waiting area
- Examining rooms
- Cages/kennels

Props
- Chairs in the reception area
- Reception desk
- Play telephone
- Doctor kit collage
- White coats
- Stuffed animals
- Pet food
- X-ray machine
- Chalk pictures (simulating X-rays)
- Play cash register
- Play money

Roles
- Veterinarians
- Animals
- Receptionist
- Kennel attendants
- Customers

General Description of Activity

Children bring their sick or injured animals to the veterinarian for treatment. There might be a waiting room set up, with a receptionist to assist pet owners. The vet's office might include an examining table, a sink, pet supplies, medicines, syringes, cotton balls, and other medical supplies. There might be cages for animals that must stay overnight.

Verbal Productions

Level of linguistic complexity varies with role or competency of the child playing the role.
- "What's wrong with your cat?" or "What matter?"
- "He needs a shot" or "Cat sick"
- "Your dog needs some stitches" or "Need stitches"
- "Your cat has fleas and needs a flea bath," "Fleas," or "Needs bath"
- "The doctor will see you now" or "You're next"

Adult Facilitative Role

The adult is to facilitate role play and help expand language and literacy skills. Typical actions or strategies to use include

Playing a role: "I am the vet. Your little cat is sick."

Modeling a statement: "That cage is too small. Put your dog in the big cage."

Redirecting a child to a peer: "Tell Johnny to give you the medicine."

Using a cloze procedure: "Here is one basket; here are two _____ (baskets)."

Recasting a child's utterance: "That his dog" to "You're right, that is his big dog."

Identifying rhyming words: "Yes, 'pet' and 'vet' rhyme."

ART **Paper Bag Puppets**

Objectives
1. Express creativity
2. Develop small motor skills (e.g., drawing, painting, cutting, pasting)
3. Practice turn-taking skills
4. Converse with peers and adults

Materials
- Paper bags, one for each child
- Construction paper
- Scissors
- Construction cutouts for facial features, such as circles, triangles, and so on
- Glue or paste

General Description of Activity

Children make paper bag puppets by decorating small brown paper bags. The puppet might be a pet or other creature. The base fold of the paper bag will be the face so that when the child's hand is placed inside the bag, the fold can be used to open and close the mouth. Children may glue red construction paper inside the fold to represent the tongue. Other construction paper cutouts can be used for facial features, such as ears, a nose, and a mouth, or children can use markers to draw in the facial features. Yarn can be used for fur. When the puppets are finished, the children can stick their hands into the bag and make their puppets "talk."

GROUP : **Caring for a Pet**

Objectives
1. Improve listening skills
2. Increase conceptual knowledge
3. Learn appropriate group-interaction skills
4. Practice turn-taking skills

Materials
- Water dish
- Pet food (can have both cat and dog food)
- Food dish
- Leash and collar
- Cage or doghouses
- Bird cage (optional)
- Aquarium (optional)
- Fish food (optional)

General Description of Activity

Set water dishes, food dishes, collars and leashes, and cages in front of the children. Ask "Who uses these?" After children have responded (e.g., "dogs," "cats," "pets"), tell the children that they will be talking about taking care of a pet.

Group Participation

Hold up a food dish, and have one child come to the front of the class to put some cat or dog food in it. Remind children that animals need food. You might ask, "Why do animals need food?" or "What food do you feed your pet?" Ask the children what else pets need, and have another child fill a water dish. Have the group discuss different places that pets sleep and pets' need for some kind of shelter. Also discuss what to do if a pet gets sick or needs shots and how a pet gets exercise. Continue to ask the children about their pets' needs (e.g., love, attention) until each child has had a chance to speak.

Variation

You could also discuss the care of other kinds of pets, (e.g., fish, hamster, birds). For example, a fish would need an aquarium, a hamster would need a maze, a bird would need a cage, and so forth.

Summary/Transition Activity

Review the items a pet needs, pointing to each item as it is mentioned (e.g., food and food dish, water, cage or house, leash).

Wednesday

Dramatic Play	Art	Group	Story	Song
Office Worker	Drawings	Letter *D*	*A Letter to Amy*	"The Alphabet Song"

DAILY PLANNING GUIDE

Language and Literacy Skills Facilitated

Vocabulary: *office, mail, letter, typewriter, computer, bills, tape, paper clip, stapler, three-hole punch, file, envelope, file cabinet, secretary, telephone, paste, folder, glue, copier, adding machine*

Verb phrase structures: *is/was typing, types, typed, Who's typing? I am, (uncontractible auxiliary verb) punching, punches, punched, is/was calling, calls, called*

Adjective/object descriptions: *fast/slow typing, big/little _____, two-hole/three-hole punch*

Question structures: *what, how, where, when, who, what if, why, how many, which one*

Pronouns: *I, you, he, she, we, they, my, your, him, her, his, our, their, me, us, them*

Prepositions: *in, on, under, over, near, beneath, next to, beside, around, inside, outside*

Sounds: */t/ type, computer, letter, at; /k/ call, ticket, back; /l/ lick, calling, bill*

Noting print has meaning: names on chairs and on cubbies, signs in dramatic play, words in books and on chalkboard

Noting sound–symbol associations: What sound does _____ start with?

Writing: letters, names, words

Social Skills Facilitated

Initiating interaction with peers and adults; responding to questions and requests from peers and adults

Negotiating with peers for toys and materials

Group cooperation: waiting for a turn in a group, taking a turn at the appropriate time

Cognitive Skills Facilitated

Problem-solving skills: What does an office worker do?

Classification skills: things in an office, things that hold paper

Sequencing skills: story, songs, alphabet

Narrative/story structure: adventure

Motor Skills Facilitated

Large motor: outdoor play activities—jumping, running, hopping, pedaling, climbing

Small motor: writing, drawing, gluing, stapling, cutting

DRAMATIC PLAY Office Worker

Type of Activity: Related

Objectives
1. Learn new, and employ familiar, vocabulary
2. Learn new, and employ a variety of, syntactic constructions
3. Interact with peers
4. Sequence familiar routines
5. Expand conceptual knowledge of the world

Settings
- Offices
- Reception area
- Break room area
- Conference room
- Elevator

Props
- Desks and chairs
- Play telephones
- Paper
- Rubber bands
- Pretend (or real) stapler
- Lists
- Folders
- Computers, typewriters, or keyboards
- Envelopes
- Stamps and scale
- Pencils or crayons
- Wastebasket
- Mop and broom
- Pretend coffeemaker

Roles
- Receptionist
- Custodian
- Office workers
- Boss

General Description of Activity

Children pretend to be people who work in an office. They might use computers or typewriters to write letters and reports. They can sit at a desk and answer a telephone, have meetings, make notes, address and weigh envelopes, staple papers together, and put papers in file folders or notebooks. They might dictate notes to other office workers or play a receptionist who answers the telephone and makes appointments.

Verbal Productions

Level of linguistic complexity varies with the role or the competency of the child playing the role.
- "Here's your file" or "Need file"
- "I want a turn on the computer now" or "My turn"
- "He typed a *J* for my name" or "*J*"
- "She stapled all of the papers" or "Staple papers"

Adult Facilitative Role

The adult is to facilitate role play and help expand language and literacy skills. Typical actions or strategies to use include

Playing a role: "Yes, Mr. Jones is in. Can I make an appointment?"

Modeling how to write another child's name: "Write John's name this way." (Show card or physically help.)

Modeling a statement: "It's my turn on the computer."

Expanding a child's utterance: "I type now" to "Can I type now?"

ART : **Drawings**

Objectives
1. Express creativity
2. Develop small motor skills (e.g., drawing, painting, cutting, pasting)
3. Practice turn-taking skills
4. Converse with peers and adults

Materials
- Paper (white or colored)
- Crayons
- Markers
- Watered-down tempera paint (optional)

General Description of Activity

Provide children with paper and a selection of crayons and/or markers and let them draw anything they want. They might draw themselves, their family, their pets, scenes, designs, rainbows, and so on. The children can describe pictures to the adult who writes down description.

Children can turn their crayon drawings into crayon washes by painting over the pictures with a light coat of tempera paint (watered-down paint). The paint will not stick to the crayon but will fill in where there are no crayon marks to make a background of color.

GROUP **Letter *D***

Objectives
1. Improve listening skills
2. Increase knowledge of the alphabet
3. Learn appropriate group-interaction skills
4. To practice turn-taking skills

Materials
- Alphabet chart and other alphabet displays
- Blackboard and chalk or poster paper and markers
- Pictures of objects (or objects themselves) with names that begin with *D*

General Description of Activity

Invite two or three children to the front to sing the alphabet song. Point to the letters on the alphabet chart as the song is sung, and then write an upper- and a lowercase *D* on the blackboard (or poster paper). Give several examples of words that begin with *D*, emphasizing the /d/ sound at the beginning of the words. (You might hold up objects or pictures of objects whose names begin with *D*.) Direct the children's attention to the alphabet picture displays around the room.

Group Participation

Ask if anyone's name starts with *D* (e.g., David, Damien, Delaney). Those children write the letter *D* on the board. Also ask two or three other children to write the letter *D* on the blackboard. Provide verbal guidance: "Start at the top and draw a curved line like half of a circle." If necessary, help the children write the letter. Some of the children can practice writing *D* in the air with their fingers (or on individual chalkboards). Ask the children to think of words that begin with *D*. Write the words they offer on the blackboard and draw quick sketches (when possible) of the suggested words. If a child suggests a word that does not begin with *D*, say, "No, that begins with a ____," and say the two sounds so children can compare them. To help children who cannot think of any words, prompt them with pictures of objects representing words that begin with *D*. (Pictures can be handed out at the beginning of the lesson or as the lesson proceeds.) Additional words can be sought in a picture dictionary if the group has difficulty arriving at words that begin with *D*.

Summary/Transition Activity

After about 10–15 words have been suggested, review the words, emphasizing the /d/ sound. You can also give the children cards or adhesive notes with upper- and lowercase letters *D* written on them as children identify the letter or the sound. The children can then take the cards or notes home.

Variation

Scatter several adhesive notes with either an upper- or a lowercase *D* written on them around the room. Ask children, one at a time, to find the capital *D* or the lowercase *d*.

Thursday

Dramatic Play	Art	Group	Story	Song
Firefighter	Playdough	Fire Safety Rules	*The Fire Engine*	"Hurry, Hurry, Drive the Fire Truck"

DAILY PLANNING GUIDE

Language and Literacy Skills Facilitated

Vocabulary: *fire, firefighter, hose, fire engine, ladder truck, siren, pole, uniform, protective clothing, face mask, oxygen, flames, smoke, fire hydrant, ashes, dispatch officer*

Verb phrase structures: *put out the fire, ride in the truck, turn on siren, honk horn, turn on hose, douse fire, dispatch the truck*

Adjective/object descriptions: *hot fire, cold ashes, red truck, green truck, loud siren, gray smoke, black smoke*

Question structures: *what, how, where, when, who, what if, why, how many, which one*

Pronouns: *I, you, he, she, we, they, my, your, him, her, his, our, their, me, us, them*

Prepositions: *in, on, under, over, near, beneath, next to, beside, around, inside, outside*

Sounds: */f/ fire, firefighter; /s/ safety, sirens*

Noting print has meaning: names on chairs and on cubbies, signs in dramatic play, words in books and on chalkboard

Noting sound–symbol associations: What sound does _____ start with?

Writing: letters, names, words

Social Skills Facilitated

Initiating interaction with peers and adults; responding to questions and requests from peers and adults

Negotiating with peers for toys and materials

Group cooperation: waiting for a turn in a group, taking a turn at the appropriate time

Cognitive Skills Facilitated

Problem-solving skills: safety rules, how/when to call 911

Classification skills: What's in a fire truck?

Sequencing skills: songs and fingerplays

Narrative/story structure: labeling

Motor Skills Facilitated

Large motor: outdoor play activities—jumping, running, hopping, pedaling, climbing

Small motor: writing, drawing, gluing

DRAMATIC PLAY **Firefighter**

Type of Activity: Sequential

Objectives
1. Learn new, and employ familiar, vocabulary
2. Learn new, and employ a variety of, syntactic constructions
3. Interact with peers
4. Sequence familiar routines
5. Expand conceptual knowledge of the world

Settings
- Fire station
- Dispatch office
- Houses (made from dismantled cardboard boxes)
- Roads (marked with masking tape)

Props
- Fire engine (made from boxes with cardboard tubes for hoses)
- Pretend fire hydrants
- Mats for beds
- Pole (optional)
- Hats and other uniform paraphernalia (rubber painting smocks can be used for fireproof jackets)
- Pretend telephones
- Microphones (made from toilet paper rolls)
- Sirens (flashlights with siren feature) (optional)

Roles
- Firefighters
- Fire chief
- Fire engine driver
- Homeowners
- Dispatch officers

General Description of Activity

Children play firefighter by staying at a fire station, sliding down a pole when there is an alarm, getting in the fire engine, arriving at the fire, and putting it out. A siren may be used to warn traffic to get out of the way so the firefighters can get to the fire. After putting out a fire, children can go back to the fire station and put their equipment away. (If possible, have real firefighters come to the classroom to talk about their jobs and show children their equipment.)

Verbal Productions

Level of linguistic complexity varies with the role or competency of the child playing the role.
- "I'm the fire chief" or "Chief"
- "My house is on fire. Come to 124 Lawrence Street" or "Fire! Come!"
- "It's my turn to drive the truck" or "Turn, please"
- "We are sleeping at the fire station in case there is a fire" or "Sleeping here"

Adult Facilitative Role

The adult is to facilitate role play and help expand language and literacy skills. Typical actions or strategies to use include

Playing a role: "Let's go. The fire is at 800 Elm Street."

Modeling phonological awareness: "That's right. The words *fire* and *fighter* both start with *F*."

Expanding a child's utterance: "It hot" to "It is hot; we better not touch."

Using an open question: "How did the fire start?"

ART **Playdough**

Objectives
1. Express creativity
2. Develop small motor skills (e.g., drawing, painting, cutting, pasting)
3. Practice turn-taking skills
4. Converse with peers and adults

Materials
- Smocks
- Playdough
- Rolling pins
- Playdough cutters
- Playdough presses
- Flat wooden craft sticks

General Description of Activity

Children wash their hands and put on smocks to play with the playdough. They can use presses, cutters, rolling pins, and wooden craft sticks to make pretend food, animals, or any other objects out of the dough by using rolling, cutting, or pressing motions. They can form animals or people by rolling a body and then adding a head, arms, and legs. Yarn can be used for hair (if children want to take home their creations). When the children are finished, they can roll the dough into a ball, wash their hands, and take off and fold their smocks.

GROUP ACTIVITY PLAN **Fire Safety Rules**

Objectives
1. Improve listening skills
2. Increase conceptual knowledge
3. Learn appropriate group-interaction skills
4. Practice turn-taking skills

Materials
- Pictures of children crawling and touching a door
- Pictures of children stopping, dropping, and rolling to put out a fire on their clothing
- Play telephones

General Description of Activity

Ask the children what they should do if the fire alarm at the preschool center sounds. Discuss what they should do if their house catches on fire. Facilitate a conversation about crawling on the floor and touching doors to see if they are hot before opening them. You might show pictures of children following this procedure. Also discuss calling 911 and giving their names and addresses to the dispatcher.

Group Participation

Have some of the children practice crawling and touching a door before opening it. Ask the group what the children should do if the door is hot. In addition, talk about having a place for family members to gather outside if the family's house catches on fire. Explain that this helps everyone know where each person is. Have some children practice calling 911 on play telephones.

Finally, have the children discuss what to do if their clothing catches on fire. Some children could demonstrate the "stop, drop, and roll" technique (i.e., the children *stop* moving, *drop* to the ground, and *roll* over and over to put out the fire on their clothes). Show pictures of children doing the stop, drop, and roll technique.

Variation

Plan and carry out a real fire drill. Make sure children understand what will happen and what they are to do.

Summary/Transition Activity

Review what to do in case of a fire at school or at home and if children's clothing catches on fire.

WEEKLY PLANNING GUIDE

	Dramatic Play	Art	Group	Story	Song
Monday *Suggested Props and Materials*	Farm *Farm scenario, barn facsimile, animals, sand area with tractors, pretend vegetables*	Cotton Ball Chickens *Cotton balls, chicken outlines, glue, markers*	Square/Circle Classification *Square and round objects and/or pictures and construction paper outlines to designate classification*	*Growing Vegetable Soup*	"Old MacDonald Had a Farm"
Tuesday *Suggested Props and Materials*	Pizza Parlor *Pizza parlor scenario, pizza booths, cash register, pizza ingredients, kitchen area, menus, soft drink area*	Pizza Art *Pizza ingredients cutouts, paper plates, glue*	Act out a Story *Props to act out story (e.g., three bowls, three chairs, three mats)*	*The Three Bears*	"I Wish I Were a Pepperoni Pizza"
Wednesday *Suggested Props and Materials*	Grocery Store *Grocery store scenario, grocery shelves, refrigerator, cash register, vegetables and other food items, carts, bags, counters, play money*	Coffee Filter Painting *Coffee filters, watercolor paints, brushes, water*	Fruits and Vegetables *Pretend fruits and vegetables, tubs or mats*	*Whiskerville Grocery*	"I Like to Eat Apples and Bananas"
Thursday *Suggested Props and Materials*	House (Cooking) *Housekeeping area (includes stove, refrigerator, table and chairs, doll beds, etc.), dishes, utensils, pretend food, dolls, bottles, blankets*	Macaroni Necklaces *Macaroni, containers for macaroni, yarn, tape*	Letter *E* *Objects and pictures of items beginning with E, alphabet chart, dictionary*	*It Looked Like Spilt Milk*	"Who Stole the Cookie?"

MY NOTES

NEWSLETTER

Vol. 1, No. 5

Date: _____

Food

Monday

Today the children will pretend to be farmers and learn about growing things. They will drive tractors, harvest fruit, and take care of animals. In art, the children will make "cotton ball chickens." Our story for today is *Growing Vegetable Soup*. At group time, the children will classify shapes—circles and squares. Our song for the day is "Old MacDonald Had a Farm."

Tuesday

Today the classroom becomes a pizza parlor. The children will order pizzas, cook pizzas, serve pizzas, and clean up the restaurant. They may be the cashier or the delivery person. In art, the children will make paper plate pizzas. The story today is *The Three Bears*. At group time, we will act out the story of the three bears. During music, we will sing "I Wish I Were a Pepperoni Pizza."

Wednesday

The classroom turns into a grocery store today. The children can be the customers, the clerks, the stockers, or even the bakers. In art, the children will make coffee filter paintings. *Whiskerville Grocery* is the story for today. At group time, the children will classify foods as either fruits and vegetables. Our fun song is "I Like to Eat Apples and Bananas."

Thursday

Today the children focus on cooking food while playing house. They will make sure their babies have plenty to eat. They will also be busy doing other housekeeping chores. In art, the children will make macaroni necklaces. *It Looked Like Spilt Milk* is the story for today. The featured letter is *E*, for egg and elephant. "Who Stole the Cookie?" is the song.

Monday

Dramatic Play	Art	Group	Story	Song
Farm	Cotton Ball Chickens	Square/Circle Classification	*Growing Vegetable Soup*	"Old MacDonald Had a Farm"

DAILY PLANNING GUIDE

Language and Literacy Skills Facilitated

Vocabulary: *farm, barn, cow, horse, pig, feed, hay, fence, corral, milk, pail, silo, pen, tractor, corn, wheat, potatoes, apples, vegetables*

Verb phrase structures: *feeds, is feeding, fed the animals, milks, milked the cow, is baling the hay, stacked the hay, plants the corn, planted the corn, is harvesting the wheat, harvested the wheat/corn, plowing the fields, plowed*

Adjective/object descriptions: *big/little _____, hungry _____, milking pail, white/brown cow; yellow/____ chicken*

Question structures: *what, how, where, when, who, what if, why, how many, which one*

Pronouns: *I, you, he, she, we, they, my, your, him, her, his, our, their, me, us, them*

Prepositions: *in, on, under, over, near, beneath, next to, beside, around, inside, outside*

Sounds: /k/ cow, chicken, milk; /f/ farm, off; /m/ milk, hammer, them

Noting print has meaning: names on chairs and on cubbies, signs in dramatic play, words in books and on chalkboards

Noting sound–symbol associations: What sound does _____ start with?

Writing: letters, names, words

Social Skills Facilitated

Initiating interaction with peers and adults; responding to questions and requests from peers and adults

Negotiating with peers for toys and materials

Group cooperation: waiting for a turn in a group, taking a turn at the appropriate time

Cognitive Skills Facilitated

Problem-solving skills: how to pretend to be a farmer, take turns

Classification skills: square/circle

Sequencing skills: story, song

Narrative/story structure: labeling story

Motor Skills Facilitated

Large motor: outdoor play activities—jumping, running, hopping, pedaling, climbing

Small motor: writing, drawing, cutting, pasting

DRAMATIC PLAY **Farm**

Type of Activity: Central

Objectives
1. Learn new, and employ familiar, vocabulary
2. Learn new, and employ a variety of, syntactic constructions
3. Interact with peers
4. Sequence familiar routines
5. Expand conceptual knowledge of the world

Settings
- Farm house (playhouse or dismantled cardboard boxes)
- Barn (playhouse or dismantled cardboard boxes)
- Field (floor area marked with masking tape or pretend fences)
- Planting area (wading pool filled with sand or soil)

Props
- Pretend tractor
- Pretend machinery
- Cow to be milked (latex gloves filled with milky water)
- Horses (yardsticks)
- Blocks for fencing
- Farm animals (stuffed animals)
- Hats
- Pretend seeds
- Scarecrow
- Cardboard trees (with removable Ping-Pong balls for fruit)

Roles
- Farmer(s)
- Farmer's helper(s)
- Farm animals (the children pretend to be animals)
- Tractor operator
- Other machinery operators
- Milker (optional)
- Fruit pickers (optional)

General Description of Activity

Children act out the different roles and activities found on a farm. There may be animals to care for, such as cows, horses, pigs, and chickens. Children may grow crops or run a dairy farm. Different types of activities can be designed around the farm theme. For example, this week the focus is on food, so provide an area with soil in which to plant and then harvest crops. (Painted Ping-Pong balls can become apples to be harvested, particularly if Velcro is attached so that the balls will stick to a cardboard tree.) Pretend tractors and other machinery could also be available.

Verbal Productions

Level of linguistic complexity varies with the role or the competency of the child playing the role.
- "It's my turn to feed the chickens" or "Feed chickens"
- "I plowed the field and then planted the corn" or "I plowed the field"
- "He is milking the cow" or "Milk cow"

Adult Facilitative Role

The adult is to facilitate role play and help expand language and literacy skills. Typical actions or strategies to use include

Playing a role: "I am a farmer. I grow crops."

Modeling a statement: "I am playing with the tractor."

Expanding a child's utterance: "He plant the seed" to "Yes, he planted the seed in the ground."

Contrasting two sounds: "Did you say 'seed' or 'feed?'"

Redirecting a child to a peer: "Ask her for a turn on the tractor. Say, 'May I have a turn, please?'"

ART : **Cotton Ball Chickens**

Objectives
1. Express creativity
2. Develop small motor skills (e.g., drawing, painting, cutting, pasting)
3. Practice turn-taking skills
4. Converse with peers and adults

Materials
- Chicken outline
- Yellow cotton balls (if not available, color white cotton balls by putting dry tempera paint in a paper bag with the white cotton balls and shaking the bag)
- Glue
- Crayons

143

General Description of Activity

Give children a piece of paper with an outline of a chicken on it. The children glue yellow cotton balls inside the chicken to make feathers. They may draw or paste a beak onto the chicken outline. They may also draw grass or make fences or anything else on their paper.

GROUP **Square/Circle Classification**

Objectives

1. Improve listening skills
2. Increase conceptual knowledge
3. Learn appropriate group-interaction skills
4. Practice turn-taking skills

Materials

- Colored tape
- Various sizes/colors of square-shaped cutouts or objects
- Several small and large circle-shaped cutouts or objects
- Small chalkboard or paper (optional)
- Chalk or markers (optional)

General Description of Activity

Using colored tape, outline a large and a small square and a large and a small circle on the floor in front of the children. Trace one of the square outlines on the floor, or a square cutout, and remind the children that a square has four sides and four corners and that the sides are all the same length. Pick up two pieces of paper, one a square and one a circle. Ask a child to put the square paper in the square on the floor.

Group Participation

Ask different children to place different sizes of paper that are either square or round on the appropriate shape on the floor. Present an object to each child that has either a square side (like a block) or a round shape (like a ball). Ask children to decide if they have a square shape or a round shape (circle). Vary the level of difficulty. For instance, you might ask one child to identify just the shape he or she has (e.g., square or circle). You might ask another child to find a shape or an object that is a particular size and color (e.g., "Find a large green square"). The children could also suggest objects that are around the room. For example, the clock on the wall has a round shape. If necessary, do this activity in small groups.

Variation

Have the children draw shapes (squares/circles) on small chalkboards or on paper.

Summary/Transition Activity

Review the shapes by pointing to or standing on them or by holding up shape cutouts and having the children quickly label them in unison.

Tuesday

Dramatic Play	Art	Group	Story	Song
Pizza Parlor	Pizza Art	Act out a Story	*The Three Bears*	"I Wish I Were a Pepperoni Pizza"

DAILY PLANNING GUIDE

Language and Literacy Skills Facilitated

Vocabulary: *soft drinks, pizza, spaghetti, shakes, wrappers, boxes, cook, cashier, customer, order, pizza parlor, pizza delivery*

Verb phrase structures: *place<u>s</u> an order, buy<u>s</u> a pizza, pay<u>s</u> money, eat out, <u>is</u> mak<u>ing</u> a pizza, serv<u>ed</u> the customer, serv<u>ed</u> a pizza, choose<u>s</u> a drink, <u>are</u> mak<u>ing</u> pizzas*

Adjective/object descriptions: *large drink, small pizza, paper hat, red cup*

Question structures: *what, how, where, when, who, what if, why, how many, which one*

Pronouns: *I, you, he, she, we, they, my, your, him, her, his, our, their, me, us, them*

Prepositions: *in the cash register, on the plate, near the stove, in the oven (in, on, under, over, near, beneath, next to, beside, around, inside, outside)*

Sounds: /p/ *<u>p</u>aper hat, wra<u>pp</u>er*

Noting print has meaning: names on chairs and on cubbies, signs in dramatic play, words in books and on chalkboard

Noting sound–symbol associations: What sound does _____ start with?

Writing: letters, names, words

Social Skills Facilitated

Initiating interaction with peers and adults; responding to questions and requests from peers and adults.

Negotiating with peers for toys and materials

Group cooperation: waiting for a turn in a group, taking a turn at the appropriate time

Cognitive Skills Facilitated

Problem-solving skills: setting up a restaurant, remembering items

Classification skills: items to put on a pizza

Sequencing skills: putting a pizza together, words to song, acting out the story

Narrative/story structure: home–adventure–home story

Motor Skills Facilitated

Large motor: outdoor play activities—jumping, running, hopping, pedaling, climbing

Small motor: writing, drawing, gluing

DRAMATIC PLAY: Pizza Parlor

Type of Activity: Central

Objectives
1. Learn new, and employ familiar, vocabulary
2. Learn new, and employ a variety of, syntactic constructions
3. Interact with peers
4. Sequence familiar routines
5. Expand conceptual knowledge of the world

Settings
- Restaurant kitchen
- Carry-out window
- Dining area
- Salad bar (optional)
- Counter

Props
- Tables and chairs
- Menus
- Pretend pizzas (plastic facsimiles or cardboard circles for pizza crusts; variety of cutouts for toppings, such as pepperoni, green peppers, and mushrooms; pieces of yellow yarn for cheese)
- Dishes and cups
- Trays
- Pretend soda pop dispenser
- Pretend cash register
- Pretend money
- Order form and pencils
- Delivery van (optional)
- Roads (area of floor marked with masking tape—optional)
- English muffins, real pizza toppings, and microwave oven (optional)

Roles
- Customers
- Waiters and waitresses
- Cashier
- Cooks
- Delivery van driver (optional)

General Description of Activity

Children run a pizza parlor. The waiter or waitress seats the guests and gives them menus. The guests order their pizzas, with various toppings, and possibly other items, such as spaghetti or bread sticks. Children who are the cooks must construct the pizzas, which are then taken to the customers by the waiter or waitress. A pizza delivery van can also be used to deliver pizzas to homes. Note: Real pizzas can be made at snack time by using English muffins as the crust. The children can add different toppings and cook the pizzas in a microwave oven.

Verbal Productions

Level of linguistic complexity varies with the role or competency of the child playing the role.
- "We have two kinds of pizza, pepperoni and cheese. Which do you want?" or "Which one?"
- "Cheese?" or "More pizza"
- "You ate my pizza" or "My pizza!"
- "You bought two pizzas and I bought one" or "One pizza"

Adult Facilitative Role

The adult is to facilitate role play and help expand language and literacy skills. Typical actions or strategies to use include

Playing a role: "Do you want a large or medium pizza?"

Modeling a statement: "That is the pepperoni pizza. This is the cheese pizza."

Asking open questions: "How do you want your pizza?"

Recasting present progressive tense with past tense: "He is baking the pizza" to "Yes, he baked that pizza in the oven."

Modeling the reading of the menu: "That menu says *large pepperoni*."

ART **Pizza Art**

Objectives
1. Express creativity
2. Develop small motor skills (e.g., drawing, painting, cutting, pasting)
3. Practice turn-taking skills
4. Converse with peers and adults

Materials
- Paper plates
- Construction paper cutouts for pizza ingredients: large red circles (for tomato sauce), gray mushrooms, green peppers, white onions, small red circles (for pepperoni), yellow yarn (for cheese)
- Glue sticks

General Description of Activity

Children glue construction paper "pizza ingredients" onto a paper plate "crust" to make their own pizza art. They can paste red circles for tomato sauce and then precut mushrooms, green peppers, pepperoni, onions, and cheese (yellow yarn). They could also cut out their own ingredients. Option: Pizzas could be served in dramatic play activities.

GROUP | **Act out a Story: *The Three Bears***

Objectives
1. Improve listening skills
2. Increase sequencing ability
3. Increase knowledge of storytelling
4. Learn appropriate group-interaction skills
5. Practice turn-taking skills

Materials
- Book(s)
- Three chairs (one small, one medium, and one large)
- Three bowls (one small, one medium, and one large)
- Three mats (one small, one medium, and one large)

General Description of Activity

Summarize the story of *The Three Bears*.

Group Participation

Assign children roles from the story. Assure the children who are not chosen the first time that everyone will have a turn and that they have the very important job of being a good listening audience. Narrate the story as the children act it out. They should say as many of the lines as they can, with prompts given when needed. Repeat the story with new actors until all the children have had a turn.

Summary/Transition Activity

Compliment the children's acting. Discuss other stories the children would like to act out another day.

		Wednesday		
Dramatic Play	**Art**	**Group**	**Story**	**Song**
Grocery Store	Coffee Filter Painting	Fruits and Vegetables	*Whiskerville Grocery*	"I Like to Eat Apples and Bananas"

DAILY PLANNING GUIDE

Language and Literacy Skills Facilitated

Vocabulary: *groceries, cart, cereal, shop, checker, buy, sell, bag, sack, shelf, money, change*

Verb phrase structures: *eats, is eating, ate, has eaten, pushes, is pushing, pushed, buys, bought, checks, is checking, checked*

Adjective/object descriptions: *big/little bag, full/empty shelf*

Question structures: *what, how, where, when, who, what if, why, how many, which one*

Pronouns: *I, you, he, she, we, they, my, your, him, her, his, our, their, me, us, them*

Prepositions: *in, on, under, over, near, beneath, next to, beside, around, inside, outside*

Sounds: /sh/ *shelf, push*; /k/ *cart, sack*; /s/ *sell, carts*

Noting print has meaning: names on chairs and on cubbies, signs in dramatic play, words in books and on chalkboard

Noting sound–symbol associations: What sound does _____ start with?

Writing: letters, names, words

Social Skills Facilitated

Initiating interaction with peers and adults; responding to questions and requests from peers and adults

Negotiating with peers for toys and materials

Group cooperation: waiting for a turn in a group, taking a turn at the appropriate time

Cognitive Skills Facilitated

Problem-solving skills: what to buy

Classification skills: fruits, vegetables, meats

Sequencing skills: songs, story

Narrative/story structure: adventure

Motor Skills Facilitated

Large motor: outdoor play activities—jumping, running, hopping, pedaling, climbing

Small motor: writing, drawing, gluing

DRAMATIC PLAY : **Grocery Store**

Type of Activity: Sequential

Objectives
1. Learn new, and employ familiar, vocabulary
2. Learn new, and employ a variety of, syntactic constructions
3. Interact with peers
4. Sequence familiar routines
5. Expand conceptual knowledge of the world

148

Settings
- Grocery store
- Customers' homes
- Shelves and aisles
- Check-out stand

Props
- Shelves
- Canned goods and other food items
- Fruit and vegetable area
- Pretend cash register
- Pretend money
- Pretend credit cards
- Pretend coupons
- Shopping carts
- Grocery bags
- Pencil and paper for making lists
- Table for checkout area

Roles
- Shoppers
- Baggers
- Cashiers
- Stockers

General Description of Activity

The children pretend to go grocery shopping. They can make lists, take their "children" with them, choose the items on the list to put in their carts, pay, bag the groceries, and go home to put their items away. Other children can be the grocery store workers. Some keep the shelves stocked, and others are checkers and baggers.

Verbal Productions

- "Will that be all? Your total is $5" or "All? Five!"
- "Milk, please" or "Milk"
- "Do you have any cereal?" or "Want cereal"

Adult Facilitative Role

The adult is to facilitate role play and help expand language and literacy skills. Typical actions or strategies to use include

Playing a role: "That will be $2 for the apples."

Modeling the /s/ sound: "She wants tomato soup."

Modeling vocabulary: "That is called a cauliflower and that is called an orange."

Modeling the reading of a sign: "The sign says *grocery store*."

Expanding a child's utterance: "My cart" to "May I have the cart, please?"

ART **Coffee Filter Painting**

Objectives
1. Express creativity
2. Develop small motor skills (e.g., drawing, painting, cutting, pasting)
3. Practice turn-taking skills
4. Converse with peers and adults

Materials
- Watercolor paints
- Brushes
- Coffee filters
- Containers of water for rinsing brushes
- Smocks
- Green construction paper (optional)
- Scissors
- Glue sticks (optional)
- Bulletin board (optional)

General Description of Activity

Children paint with watercolors on flattened coffee filters. The porous paper allows the paint to run, creating interesting designs.

Variation 1

Fold the coffee filter and have children paint on one side of it. When it is opened, the colors will have formed a design throughout the filter.

Variation 2

Have children glue the coffee filter paintings to paper stems created from green construction paper to make flowers. Display the flowers on a large bulletin board for a "flower garden."

GROUP **Fruits and Vegetables**

Objectives
1. Improve listening skills
2. Increase conceptual knowledge
3. Learn appropriate group-interaction skills
4. Practice turn-taking skills

Materials
- Plastic fruits (e.g., apple)
- Plastic vegetables (e.g., carrot)
- Two tubs

General Description of Activity

Hold up a plastic apple and a plastic carrot and ask the children to tell you which one is the fruit and which is the vegetable. If they do not know or do not respond, label each item and put each in a different tub.

Group Participation

Give each child a plastic fruit or vegetable. One at a time, each child labels the item as a fruit or a vegetable and places it into the appropriate tub. If a child makes an error, remove the item from the tub and have the child place it in the correct tub.

Variation

Rather than give each child an item, have children choose their own item from an assortment. (Explain that the tomato is often labeled as a vegetable; however, it is really a fruit.)

Summary/Transition Activity

Ask the group to name the items in the fruit category and then name the items in the vegetable category.

Thursday

Dramatic Play	Art	Group	Story	Song
House (Cooking)	Macaroni Necklaces	Letter *E*	*It Looked Like Spilt Milk*	"Who Stole the Cookie?"

DAILY PLANNING GUIDE

Language and Literacy Skills Facilitated

Vocabulary: *clean, dust, vacuum, sweep, broom, cook, house, food, soup, stew, muffins, babies, wash, table*

Verb phrase structures: *is cleaning, was dusting, vacuumed, is cooking, was cooking, cooks, cooked, fixes, fixed, makes, made, do you have ____?, eats, ate, has eaten, washes, washed*

Adjective/object descriptions: *dusty, good food, hot/cold food, red apple, yellow banana, dirty/clean baby*

Question structures: *what, how, where, when, who, what if, why, how many, which one*

Pronouns: *I, you, he, she, we, they, my, your, him, her, his, our, their, me, us, them*

Prepositions: *in, on, under, over, near, beneath, next to, beside, around, inside, outside*

Sounds: /k/ *cook, cooking, make;* /l/ *lick, Jell-o, yell;* /s/ *see, cooks;* /r/ *roof, carrot, bar*

Noting print has meaning: names on chairs and on cubbies, signs in dramatic play, words in books and on chalkboard

Noting sound–symbol associations: What sound does _____ start with?

Writing: letters, names, words

Social Skills Facilitated

Initiating interaction with peers and adults; responding to questions and requests from peers and adults

Negotiating with peers for toys and materials

Group cooperation: waiting for a turn in a group, taking a turn at the appropriate time

Cognitive Skills Facilitated

Problem-solving skills: how to clean, dust, vacuum, cook

Classification skills: things we use to care for ourselves

Sequencing skills: story, songs

Narrative/story structure: rhyming, repetitive lines

Motor Skills Facilitated

Large motor: outdoor play activities—jumping, running, hopping, pedaling, climbing

Small motor: writing, drawing, gluing, squeezing, swirling, sweeping

DRAMATIC PLAY **House (Cooking)**

Type of Activity: Central

Objectives
1. Learn new, and employ familiar, vocabulary
2. Learn new, and employ a variety of, syntactic constructions
3. Interact with peers
4. Sequence familiar routines
5. Expand conceptual knowledge of the world

Settings
- Kitchen area
- Dining rooms
- Bedrooms
- Family rooms
- House (toy house or dismantled cardboard box—optional)

Props
- Play refrigerator
- Cupboards
- Play stove
- Play sink
- Dishes
- Pots and pans
- Beds
- Dolls
- Pretend food
- Baby bottles
- Mops and brooms
- Pretend vacuum
- Tablecloths (optional)
- Party decorations (optional)

Roles
- Mothers
- Fathers
- Babies and other children
- Party guests (optional)

General Description of Activity

The housekeeping center is where the children can set up a pretend house or apartment, including a kitchen. Here the children can clean the house, take care of babies, cook food, set the table, make table decorations, and prepare for a party.

Verbal Productions

Level of linguistic complexity varies with the role or competency of the child playing the role.
- "It's time to cook dinner" or "Cook now"
- "Clean the table" or "Clean"
- "Use the broom to sweep the floor" or "Sweep here"
- "I'll do it later" or "Okay"
- "The baby is hungry; please get the bottle" or "Baby crying"
- "Do you want some more food?" or "More food?"
- "I'm glad you came" or "Hi, come in"

Adult Facilitative Role

The adult is to facilitate role play and help expand language and literacy skills. Typical actions or strategies to use include

Playing a role: "You be the mom, and I will be the sister."

Using a cloze procedure: "This is a big plate, and that is the little _____ (plate)."

Modeling a statement: "I am making chocolate chip cookies."

Event cast: "The baby is crying, so she is going to feed him. He is hungry when he wakes up. She will get the bottle, and soon he will stop crying."

Contrasting two sounds: "Did you say 'took the food' or 'c̲ook the food?'"

ART **Macaroni Necklaces**

Objectives
1. Express creativity
2. Develop small motor skills (e.g., drawing, painting, cutting, pasting)
3. Practice turn-taking skills
4. Converse with peers and adults

Materials
- Different kinds of macaroni (with holes big enough for a string to go through)
- String or yarn (with one end wrapped in tape to make threading easier)
- Pieces of paper
- Straws (cut up in 1" pieces)

General Description of Activity

Children make necklaces by stringing different kinds of macaroni. The macaroni can be dyed different colors. They can use small pieces of construction paper or straws cut to different lengths to string between the macaroni pieces. Tie one piece of macaroni to one end of the string so that the others will not fall off the string after they are strung.

GROUP **Letter E**

Objectives
1. Improve listening skills
2. Increase knowledge of the alphabet and sounds
3. Learn appropriate group-interaction skills
4. Practice turn-taking skills

Materials
- Blackboard and chalk
- Pairs of pictures of objects (or objects themselves) whose names begin with E, such as envelope and eat, elephant and eel, Eddie and Elaine, and Eskimo and eagle
- Poster paper (optional)

General Description of Activity

Writes an upper- and a lowercase letter E on the blackboard (or on poster paper). Tell the children, "E has several sounds. You hear one of them when the letter sounds like its name ('eeee'), as in the word *easy*. Another sound is like the name *Emily* or the word *elephant*. Can you hear this different ('ehh') sound?" Have the children practice saying the long and short E sounds.

Group Participation

Invite two children to the front of the class. Give each a picture of an object (or the object itself) with a name that begins with E. One child's picture (or object) should begin with the long E sound and the other with the short E sound. Ask the children to verbally label their pictures or objects for the class. Help them elongate the long or short E sound, as appropriate. Have the children place their pictures (or objects) in separate piles, beginning a pile for each of the E sounds. Continue having two children come to the front to take a turn at naming E words and placing the pictures (or objects) in the correct piles.

Summary/Transition Activity

Review the long and short vowels sounds of E by saying the sounds one last time and holding up representative pictures.

October

Activities	Monday	Tuesday	Wednesday	Thursday
Week 6 — The Five Senses				
Dramatic Play	Beauty Shop/Barber Shop (Touch)	Television Studio (Sight)	Health Clinic (Hearing)	Bakery (Taste/Smell)
Art	Shaving Cream Fingerpaint	Drawings	Rainmakers	Gingerbread Men
Group	Feely Bag	Watch a Video (*Are You My Mother?*)	Sound Bingo	Letter *F*
Story	*My Five Senses*	*I Was Walking Down the Road*	*The Grumpy Morning* (story on tape)	*The Gingerbread Man*
Song	"Head, Shoulders, Knees, and Toes"	"There's Something in My Pocket"	"Do Your Ears Hang Low?"	"Do You Know the Muffin Man?"
Week 7 — Vacation				
Dramatic Play	Airplane	Motel	Amusement Park	Boat/Cruise Ship
Art	Kites	Post Cards	Mickey Mouse Ears	Easel Painting
Group	Letter *G*	Color Yellow	Loud and Soft	How to Write a *2*
Story	*Going on a Plane*	*Ira Sleeps Over*	*Where the Wild Things Are*	*The Greedy Grey Octopus*
Song	"Going to Kentucky"	"Five in a Bed"	"It's a Small World"	"All the Little Fishies"
Week 8 — All About Fall				
Dramatic Play	Fall Cleaning	Fall Sports (Baseball)	Harvest	State Fair
Art	Leaf Rubbings	Chalk Pictures with Liquid Starch	Tissue Paper Leaf Collage	Doghouse and Dog Prints
Group	Leaf Classification	Number Recognition	Letter *H*	Act out a Story (*The Little Red Hen*)
Story	*Red Leaf, Yellow Leaf*	*Who's Counting*	*The Little Red Hen*	*Raccoons and Ripe Corn*
Song	"Five Little Leaves"	"Take Me out to the Ballgame"	"Way Down Yonder in the Paw Paw Patch"	"Five Little Ducks"
Week 9 — Places in the Community				
Dramatic Play	School	Laundromat	Doctor's Office	Fitness Center
Art	Popcorn Letters	Watercolor Paintings	Doctor Kit Collages	Self-Portraits
Group	Shapes—Triangles	Oddity Match	Emergency Information	Letter *I*
Story	*Grover Goes to School*	*A Pocket for Corduroy*	*Jenny's in the Hospital*	*Bearobics*
Song	"The Alphabet Song"	"Here We Go 'Round the Mulberry Bush"	"Five Little Monkeys"	"Teddy Bear, Teddy Bear, Turn Around"
Week 10 — Halloween				
Dramatic Play	Grocery Store	Construction Worker	Halloween House Decorating	Halloween Parade
Art	Halloween Bags	Jack-o'-lanterns	Ghosts, Bats, and Skeletons	(No art)
Group	Decorating Pumpkins	Letter *J*	Bones in a Skeleton	Trick-or-Treat Safety
Story	*It's Pumpkin Time*	*Trick or Treat, Little Critter*	*Halloween Day*	*Trick or Treat Faces*
Song	"Did You Ever See a Pumpkin?"	"Three Little Witches"	"Five Little Pumpkins"	Review Halloween songs

```
............................................
:          WEEKLY PLANNING GUIDE           :
............................................
```

	Dramatic Play	Art	Group	Story	Song
Monday *Suggested Props and Materials*	Beauty Shop/ Barber Shop (Touch) *Beauty shop scenario, individual combs, pretend shampoo, pretend hair dryer, pretend scissors, curlers, emery boards, shaving cream, plastic chips, containers for water and shaving cream, tissue, pretend fingernail polish (water in a container) and brushes*	Shaving Cream Fingerpaint *Form boards, shaving cream*	Feely Bag *Items for feely bag, feely box, or sack*	*My Five Senses*	"Head, Shoulders, Knees, and Toes"
Tuesday *Suggested Props and Materials*	Television Studio (Sight) *Television studio scenario, pretend video cameras, stage, puppets, newsroom, weather map, video, master board*	Drawings *White paper, colored pencils, construction paper for frames (optional)*	Watch a Video (*Are You My Mother?*) *Video (e.g., Are You My Mother?)*	*I Was Walking Down the Road*	"There's Something in My Pocket"
Wednesday *Suggested Props and Materials*	Health Clinic (Hearing) *Health clinic scenario, doctor kits, hearing booth, vision screening area*	Rainmakers *Toilet paper rolls, grass seed for rainmakers, tape, markers to decorate*	Sound Bingo *Sound Bingo game (or other listening game)*	*The Grumpy Morning* (story on tape)	"Do Your Ears Hang Low?"
Thursday *Suggested Props and Materials*	Bakery (Taste/Smell) *Bakery scenario, baked goods, shelves, oven, cash register, counter*	Gingerbread Men *Paper cutouts of gingerbread men, paper items to decorate with, or prepared dough and decorations for making real cookies*	Letter *F* *Picture or items that begin with the letter F, alphabet chart, picture dictionary*	*The Gingerbread Man*	"Do You Know the Muffin Man?"

NEWSLETTER

Vol. 1, No. 6

Date: _____

The Five Senses

Monday

For our *touch* theme, the children will be workers and clients in a beauty shop or a barber shop during dramatic play. In art, painting with shaving cream will enhance our touch theme. The children will read the story *My Five Senses* during storytime. During group time, the children will reach into a bag and tell us what they can feel inside it. "Head, Shoulders, Knees, and Toes" is one of the songs during music.

Tuesday

Today's dramatic play activity will be about the sense of *sight.* The children will work at a television studio. In art, the children will make drawings. Our story will be *I Was Walking Down the Road.* Group time will be spent watching a video. One of the songs in music will be "There's Something in My Pocket."

Wednesday

Today, *hearing* will be the sense the children will be learning about. For dramatic play, they will work at or be patients in the health clinic where hearing is checked. Art will also feature sound as the children construct rainmakers. The children will listen to a story on tape during storytime. We will play a sound game and guess what we hear during group time (Sound Bingo). "Do Your Ears Hang Low?" will be one of the songs we sing in music.

Thursday

The children will learn about *taste* and *smell* today. They will work in a bakery during dramatic play. We will also bake real cookies to eat at snack time. At art, we will decorate a gingerbread man. The book will be *The Gingerbread Man.* Group time will be spent learning about the letter *F,* for *fun.* "Do You Know the Muffin Man?" will be one of the songs included at music time.

Monday

Dramatic Play	Art	Group	Story	Song
Beauty Shop/ Barber Shop (Touch)	Shaving Cream Fingerpaint	Feely Bag	*My Five Senses*	"Head, Shoulders, Knees, and Toes"

DAILY PLANNING GUIDE

Language and Literacy Skills Facilitated

Vocabulary: *comb, brush, hair, wash, cut, set, curl, dry, blow-dry, fix, shave, shaving cream, emery board, customer, appointment*

Verb phrase structures: *curls her hair, is curling, curled; dries, is drying, dried, will dry; cuts, is cutting, cut*

Adjective/object descriptions: *soft/hard ____, wet/dry hair, cold/hot ____, long/short hair, rough/smooth ____*

Question structures: *what, how, where, when, who, what if, why, how many, which one*

Pronouns: *I, you, he, she, we, they, my, your, him, her, his, our, their, me, us, them*

Prepositions: *in, on, under, over, near, beneath, next to, beside, around, inside, outside*

Sounds: */k/ cut, back; /s/ set, cuts; /sh/ shave, brush; /l/ long, curl*

Noting print has meaning: names on chairs and on cubbies, signs in dramatic play, words in books and on chalkboard

Noting sound–symbol associations: What sound does _____ start with?

Writing: letters, names, words

Social Skills Facilitated

Initiating interaction with peers and adults; responding to questions and requests from peers and adults

Negotiating with peers for toys and materials

Group cooperation: waiting for a turn in a group, taking a turn at the appropriate time

Cognitive Skills Facilitated

Problem-solving skills: how to fix hair

Classification skills: things found in a beauty shop

Sequencing skills: stories, songs

Narrative/story structure: labeling

Motor Skills Facilitated

Large motor: outdoor play activities—jumping, running, hopping, pedaling, climbing

Small motor: writing, drawing, gluing

DRAMATIC PLAY : **Beauty Shop/Barber Shop (Touch)**

Type of Activity: Central

Objectives
1. Learn new, and employ familiar, vocabulary
2. Learn new, and employ a variety of, syntactic constructions
3. Interact with peers
4. Sequence familiar routines
5. Expand conceptual knowledge of the world

Settings
- Salon chair (use a highchair for dolls to sit in)
- Chairs (for children)
- Sink to "wash" hair
- Reception area with telephone, appointment book, and pencil or crayon
- Barber chair
- Manicurist's table

Props
- Curlers and clips
- Combs (put children's names on the combs so that they use only theirs, and disinfect at the end of play)
- Mirrors
- Fingernail polish bottles (filled with water)
- Pretend shampoo and conditioner
- Pretend hair spray
- Pretend hair dryer (made out of two toilet paper rolls and a cottage cheese container, with a twisted pipe cleaner to represent the cord)
- Plastic strips (razors)
- Shaving cream
- Smocks (typically used when children paint)
- Pretend nail polish remover
- Nail files
- Towels
- Toy cash register
- Pretend money

Roles
- Customers
- Receptionist
- Beautician
- Barber
- Manicurist

General Description of Activity

Children play beauty/barber shop and get their hair shampooed, cut, dried, and styled. They also might get a manicure (hair salon) or a shave (barber shop). Children can use their fingers in a cutting motion to pretend to cut hair.

Verbal Productions

Level of linguistic complexity varies with the role or competency of the child playing the role.

- "I'm washing her hair" or "Wash hair"
- "Do you want your hair cut?" or "Cut?"
- "Your hair is wet" or "Wet"
- "Cut my hair, please" or "Cut hair"
- "He is shaving" or "He shaved"

Adult Facilitative Role

The adult is to facilitate role play and help expand language and literacy skills. Typical actions or strategies to use include

Playing a role: "I would like a shampoo, please."

Modeling a statement: "The customer wants a manicure."

Contrasting error and correct structure: "He have scissors" to "Oh, you mean he has scissors."

Redirecting a child to a peer: "Say, 'Have you seen the hair dryer?'"

Identifying rhyming words: "Yes, the words chair and hair rhyme."

ART Shaving Cream Fingerpaint

Objectives
1. Express creativity
2. Develop small motor skills (e.g., drawing, painting, cutting, pasting)
3. Practice turn-taking skills
4. Converse with peers and adults

Materials
- Shaving cream
- Formboards
- Wooden craft sticks
- Other tools for "drawing" in the shaving cream

General Description of Activity

Put a dab of shaving cream on each child's formboard. The children can use their hands and fingers to smear the cream all over the board, then use their fingers to draw and write in the shaving cream. The children can also make abstract designs, make full handprints, or use their fingers to practice writing letters or numbers. Fingerpainting is a good excuse to get messy and gooey. Some children love this; others may need some coaxing to get their fingers dirty.

GROUP **Feely Bag**

Objectives

1. Improve listening skills
2. Increase conceptual knowledge
3. Learn appropriate group-interaction skills
4. Practice turn-taking skills

Materials

- Drawstring bags (or boxes), one per group of children
- 10–20 toy objects in the bags (e.g., Nerf ball, spool, car, cup, boat, bead, cotton ball, sandpaper, different types of plastic food)

General Description of Activity

Tell the children that this week they are going to be learning about different senses. Hold up a "feely" bag that has a drawstring top and contains several objects. Tell the children that they are going to try to guess what an object is by using their sense of touch. To demonstrate, have a staff member put a hand into the bag and, without looking, try to identify an object. He or she problem-solves out loud by saying something like "It feels sort of round, it is soft, I know—it is a Nerf ball!"

Group Participation

Invite one child to come to the front of the class and try to identify an object by feeling it in the bag. The child makes a guess and then holds up the object so all can see. Other children come one at a time and try to identify the objects by touch. After identifying an object, a child can either put it back in the bag or set it aside. In order to facilitate turn taking, have children do this activity in two or three small groups.

Variation

Instead of putting the object aside or back in the bag after it has been identified, children could categorize the object and make piles for those that feel rough, smooth, sharp, sticky, and so on.

Summary/Transition Activity

Ask children, "What was easy and what was hard about guessing the object?" Then ask, "What sense were we using to guess the object?" Remind the children that the sense of touch is only one of the senses we have.

Tuesday

Dramatic Play	Art	Group	Story	Song
Television Studio (Sight)	Drawings	Watch a Video (*Are You My Mother?*)	*I Was Walking Down the Road*	"There's Something in My Pocket"

DAILY PLANNING GUIDE

Language and Literacy Skills Facilitated

Vocabulary: *actor, actress, producer, director, camera, commercial, stage, television, film, puppet, story, act out*

Verb phrase structures: *is acting, acts, acted, was filming, filmed, is smiling, smiled, cried, cries*

Adjective/object descriptions: *hot lights, small stage, big/little camera, funny show, sad/happy puppet*

Question structures: *what, how, where, when, who, what if, why, how many, which one*

Pronouns: *I, you, he, she, we, they, my, your, him, her, his, our, their, me, us, them*

Prepositions: *in, on, under, over, near, beneath, next to, beside, around, inside, outside*

Sounds: /f/ *film, often, off;* /s/ *see, inside, laughs;* /r/ *run, camera, car*

Noting print has meaning: names on chairs and on cubbies, signs in dramatic play, words in books and on chalkboard

Noting sound–symbol associations: What sound does _____ start with?

Writing: letters, names, words

Social Skills Facilitated

Initiating interaction with peers and adults; responding to questions and requests from peers and adults

Negotiating with peers for toys and materials

Group cooperation: waiting for a turn in a group, taking a turn at the appropriate time

Cognitive Skills Facilitated

Problem-solving skills: how to make a television show

Classification skills: things used in a television studio; things we see

Sequencing skills: stories, songs

Narrative/story structure: repetitive line story

Motor Skills Facilitated

Large motor: outdoor play activities—jumping, running, hopping, pedaling, climbing

Small motor: writing, drawing, gluing

DRAMATIC PLAY **Television Studio (Sight)**

Type of Activity: Central

Objectives
1. Learn new, and employ familiar, vocabulary
2. Learn new, and employ a variety of, syntactic constructions
3. Interact with peers
4. Sequence familiar routines
5. Expand conceptual knowledge of the world

Settings
- Stage
- Camera area
- Costume and prop area
- Dressing room
- Master booth (technician area)
- Puppet stage (optional)

Props
- Video cameras (plastic facsimiles or a video box with an attached paper towel roll, mounted on a tripod)
- Costumes
- Pretend makeup
- Scenery and props for story to be acted out
- Puppets
- Master board (a box with levers and buttons to represent a sound and videoboard)
- Television monitors (shoeboxes with a side cut out and a picture pasted over the cutout area)

Roles
- Director
- Producer
- Actors
- Camera people
- Costume/prop director
- Makeup artist

General Description of Activity

If possible, show children a videotape featuring behind-the-scenes activities at a local television studio. Discuss the various roles of the director, producer, actors, and camera people. Suggest and describe stories that the children could act out in the dramatic play area. They can go to the "studio," which has been arranged with "cameras," a stage, props, and an area for the technicians. A puppet show may also be performed. Children can pretend to videotape a show, act in a show, put on a puppet show, work with television equipment, and so forth.

Verbal Productions

Level of linguistic complexity varies with the role or competency of the child playing the role.
- "Stand there and pretend to be the wolf" or "You be wolf"
- "I'll huff and puff and blow your house in" or "Huff and puff"
- "Today we will have sunny weather" or "Sunny"
- "It's my turn to have the camera" or "My turn"

Adult Facilitative Role

The adult is to facilitate role play and help expand language and literacy skills. Typical actions or strategies to use include

Playing a role: "I am the camera man. I will run the video."

Modeling a structure (present progressive): "He is filming the puppet show."

Modeling a sound (/s/): "We use our sense of sight to see things."

Expanding a child's utterance: "A big puppet" to "Yes, that is a big puppet."

Provide confirmatory feedback: "You're right, the dog puppet is brown and white."

ART **Drawings**

Objectives
1. Express creativity
2. Develop small motor skills (e.g., drawing, painting, cutting, pasting)
3. Practice turn-taking skills
4. Converse with peers and adults

Materials
- Paper (white or colored)
- Crayons
- Markers
- Watered-down tempera paint (optional)

General Description of Activity

Provide the children with paper and a selection of crayons and/or markers. Let the children draw anything they want. Drawings could be of themselves, their family, their pets, different scenes, designs, rainbows, and so on.

Crayon drawings can become "crayon washes" when the pictures are painted over with a light coat of tempera paint (watered-down paint). The paint will not stick to the crayon but will fill in where there are no crayon marks to make a background of color.

GROUP : **Watch a Video (*Are You My Mother?*)**

Objectives
1. Improve listening skills
2. Increase sequencing ability
3. Increase knowledge of storytelling
4. Learn appropriate group-interaction skills
5. Practice turn-taking skills

Materials
- Videotape of *Are You My Mother?*
- Props for the stories

General Description of Activity

The children view a video of a classic story.

Group Participation

Quickly summarize the story, and choose children to act out the story, if there is time. Assign children roles from the story and give them simple props if appropriate. Narrate the story as the children act it out. They should say as many of the lines as they can, with prompts given when needed. Repeat the story with new actors until all the children have had turns.

Summary/Transition Activity

Compliment the children's acting, and ask the children about other stories they would like to act out another day.

Wednesday

Dramatic Play	Art	Group	Story	Song
Health Clinic (Hearing)	Rainmakers	Sound Bingo	*The Grumpy Morning* (story on tape)	"Do Your Ears Hang Low?"

DAILY PLANNING GUIDE

Language and Literacy Skills Facilitated

Vocabulary: *doctor, nurse, paramedic, ambulance, stethoscope, thermometer, fever, cast, X-ray, oxygen, accident, vehicle, arm, leg, ankle, bandage, forehead, hospital*

Verb phrase structures: <u>is</u> carry<u>ing</u> the stretcher, <u>drove</u> the ambulance, ride<u>s</u>, examine<u>s</u>, <u>gave</u> oxygen, set<u>s</u> the leg

Adjective/object descriptions: *broken leg, big ambulance, loud siren*

Question structures: *what, how, where, when, who, what if, why, how many, which one*

Pronouns: *I, you, he, she, we, they, my, your, him, her, his, our, their, me, us, them*

Prepositions: *in, on, under, over, near, beneath, next to, beside, around, inside, outside*

Sounds: /k/ <u>c</u>arry, do<u>c</u>tor, bro<u>k</u>e; /s/ <u>s</u>et, in<u>s</u>ide, u<u>s</u>, ambulan<u>ce</u>

Noting print has meaning: names on chairs and on cubbies, signs in dramatic plays, words in books and on chalkboard

Noting sound–symbol associations: What sound does _____ start with?

Writing: letters, names, words

Social Skills Facilitated

Initiating interaction with peers and adults; responding to questions and requests from peers and adults

Negotiating with peers for toys and materials

Group cooperation: waiting for a turn in a group, taking a turn at the appropriate time

Cognitive Skills Facilitated

Problem-solving skills: What does a doctor do?

Classification skills: things in a doctor's office, body parts

Sequencing skills: story, songs

Narrative/story structure: adventure

Motor Skills Facilitated

Large motor: outdoor play activities—jumping, running, hopping, pedaling, climbing

Small motor: writing, drawing, gluing, cutting

DRAMATIC PLAY **Health Clinic (Hearing)**

Type of Activity: Central

Objectives
1. Learn new, and employ familiar, vocabulary
2. Learn new, and employ a variety of, syntactic constructions
3. Interact with peers
4. Sequence familiar routines
5. Expand conceptual knowledge of the world

Settings
- Waiting room
- Examination rooms
- Patients' "homes"

Props
- Waiting room chairs
- Magazines and toys for waiting room
- Table with a play telephone, appointment book, and pencil or crayon
- Several tables or mats to represent examination rooms
- Doctor kits
- Eye chart
- Pretend audiometer (box with knobs and earphones attached)
- X-ray machine and chalk drawings
- Patients' "homes," including play telephones

Roles
- Doctors
- Nurses
- Ophthalmologist
- Audiologist
- X-ray technician
- Receptionist
- Patients
- Parents

General Description of Activity

Children operate a health clinic consisting of a waiting room and several examination rooms where a variety of health professionals (e.g., doctors, nurses, ophthalmologists, audiologists) see patients. People call the receptionist and make appointments to be examined. The doctor or nurse examines the patient (a doll or another child) by looking into the mouth, ears, and eyes; checking reflexes and muscle tone; listening with the stethoscope; and so forth. Eyesight is tested by having the patient read an eye chart. Pretend hearing tests can be done. A patient might have a broken bone that needs to be X-rayed, set in a cast, and/or wrapped with a bandage.

Verbal Productions

Level of linguistic complexity varies with the role or competency of the child playing the role.
- "Open your mouth, please" or "Open mouth"
- "Where does it hurt?" or "Hurt?"
- "I can see all of the letters" or "See letters"
- "I don't feel good. My tummy hurts" or "I sick"
- "Raise your hand when you hear the beep" or "Raise hand"

Adult Facilitative Role

The adult is to facilitate role play and help expand language and literacy skills. Typical actions or strategies to use include

Playing a role: "I am an audiologist. I test hearing. Can you hear the beep?"

Modeling the /l/ sound: "You listen for the beep. Then put the little block in the box."

Expanding a child's utterance: "Ask Joan if she wants her hearing tested. Say, 'Can I test your hearing, Joan?'"

ART **Rainmakers**

Objectives
1. Express creativity
2. Develop small motor skills (e.g., drawing, painting, cutting, pasting)
3. To practice turn-taking skills
4. To converse with peers and adults

Materials
- Toilet paper rolls or paper towel rolls
- Dry beans or other small items (e.g., Cheerios)
- Small containers to hold the beans
- Markers or crayons
- Tape

General Description of Activity

Give each child a toilet paper roll to use to create a rainmaker. He or she may decorate the roll with crayons or markers. Tape one end shut after the child has finished decorating the roll, and have the child place a few dry beans or other small items (e.g., Cheerios, grass seed) inside the roll. Tape the other end shut and have the child shake the roll. The noise will sound like rain.

GROUP **Sound Bingo**

Objectives
1. Improve listening skills
2. Increase sequencing ability
3. Learn appropriate group-interaction skills
4. Practice turn-taking skills

Materials
- Tape recorder
- Sound Bingo game
- Markers and cards

General Description of Activity

Tell children that they will be using their listening ears today to identify sounds they hear on the tape recorder. They will look at cards with pictures and when they hear a sound that matches the picture, they will place a marker on that picture. When the children have identified all pictures in a row or column, they can say "Bingo." Pass out the Bingo cards and the markers, one card for two children.

Group Participation

The children listen to the sounds and place their markers on the appropriate pictures. Support the children as necessary, helping them identify the particular sounds heard. The game can be played several times.

Variation

Play a different sound game.

Summary/Transition Activity

Review some of the sounds and pictures, then gather up the cards and markers.

Thursday

Dramatic Play	Art	Group	Story	Song
Bakery (Taste/Smell)	Gingerbread Men	Letter *F*	*The Gingerbread Man*	"Do You Know the Muffin Man?"

DAILY PLANNING GUIDE

Language and Literacy Skills Facilitated

Vocabulary: *doughnuts, cookies, bread, eat, bake, dough, rolls, pies, chocolate, nuts, rolling pin, oven*

Verb phrase structures: *is/are baking, baked, cooked, rolled, rolls, was/were making*

Adjective/object descriptions: *fancy/plain cookies, big/little, gooey, chocolate chip cookies*

Question structures: *what, how, where, when, who, what if, why, how many, which one*

Pronouns: *I, you, he, she, we, they, my, your, him, her, his, our, their, me, us, them*

Prepositions: *in, on, under, over, near, beneath, next to, beside, around, inside, outside*

Sounds: */k/ cake, baking; /s/ sift, walks; /f/ finds, off*

Noting print has meaning: names on chairs and on cubbies, signs in dramatic play, words in books and on chalkboard

Noting sound–symbol associations: What sound does _____ start with?

Writing: letters, names, words

Social Skills Facilitated

Initiating interaction with peers and adults; responding to questions and requests from peers and adults

Negotiating with peers for toys and materials

Group cooperation: waiting for a turn in a group, taking a turn at the appropriate time

Cognitive Skills Facilitated

Problem-solving skills: how to run a bakery

Classification skills: things in a bakery

Sequencing skills: story, songs

Narrative/story structure: adventure (classic tale)

Motor Skills Facilitated

Large motor: outdoor play activities—jumping, running, hopping, pedaling, climbing

Small motor: writing, drawing, gluing

DRAMATIC PLAY **Bakery (Taste/Smell)**

Type of Activity: Central

Objectives
1. Learn new, and employ familiar, vocabulary
2. Learn new, and employ a variety of, syntactic constructions
3. Interact with peers
4. Sequence familiar routines
5. Expand conceptual knowledge of the world

Settings
- Stove, oven (kitchen area)
- Sand/water table filled with flour, or flour in tubs
- Counter area with display case (bookshelves)
- Eating area with tables and chairs

Props
- Pretend food (e.g., cookies, cakes, breads, pies)
- Flour (two 5-lb. bags or as needed)
- Sifters, measuring cups, measuring spoons, baking tins
- Cash register and money
- Dishes
- Aprons, chef hats (optional)

Roles
- Bakers
- Cashiers
- Customers
- Custodians

General Description of Activity

Children operate a bakery, making and offering for sale food items such as doughnuts, breads, and cookies. They can pretend to make the food items using a pretend stove and oven and then display them in a display case. Other children can act as customers to buy the food. The bakery might have an eating area and sell additional items, such as sandwiches.

As most bakery items are made from flour, one area can be set up so that the children can sift real flour and use measuring cups. This area might be similar to a sand/water table area, with flour replacing the sand. The flour could be placed in dish tubs and then in the empty sand/water table so that the flour is less likely to spill on the floor.

Children could also make real cookies in a separate area by decorating premade cookie dough and having an adult bake the cookies in a toaster oven (not in the classroom). Children can eat the cookies at snack time.

Verbal Productions

Level of linguistic complexity varies with the role or competency of the child playing the role.

- "I want to buy a doughnut and two cookies" or "Want cookie"
- "The flour feels soft, but it is making my nose itch" or "Flour soft"
- "Look, the flour is coming out of the sifter" or "Flour out"

Adult Facilitative Role

The adult is to facilitate role play and help expand language and literacy skills. Typical actions or strategies to use include

Playing a role: "Do you want some cookies? They are $2."

Providing a literacy model: "The sign says *cakes*."

Contrasting two sounds (focus contrast): "Did you say 'bake' or 'cake'?"

Recasting a child's utterance: "He plays with flour" to "Yes, he played with the flour in the bowl."

ART : **Gingerbread Men**

Objectives
1. Express creativity
2. Develop small motor skills (e.g., drawing, painting, cutting, pasting)
3. Practice turn-taking skills
4. Converse with peers and adults

Materials
- "Gingerbread men" cut from brown construction paper, one for each child
- Small circle cutouts
- Small triangle and square cutouts
- Yarn
- Other paper and scissors
- Glue

General Description of Activity

Have the children decorate the cutout gingerbread characters by gluing or pasting small pieces of construction paper cut in various shapes onto the figures. The shapes should be placed in separate containers so that children can easily choose the shapes they want. Children can also use other items to decorate, such as yarn, extra paper and scissors to make more cutouts, and markers. As the children glue these items on their gingerbread man, point out the circle, square, and triangle shapes they are using.

GROUP **Letter *F***

Objectives
1. Improve listening skills
2. Increase knowledge of the alphabet and sounds
3. Learn appropriate group-interaction skills
4. Practice turn-taking skills

Materials
- Alphabet chart and other alphabet displays
- Blackboard and chalk or poster paper and markers
- Pictures of objects (or objects themselves) with names that begin with *F*
- Picture dictionary (or an alphabet video dictionary)

General Description of Activity

Write an upper- and a lowercase letter *F* on the blackboard (or on poster paper) and give several examples of words that begin with *F*. Emphasize the /f/ or "fff" sound at the beginning of the words. You might hold up pictures of objects (or objects themselves) with names that begin with *F*. Direct the children's attention to the alphabet picture displays around the room.

Group Participation

Ask if anyone's name starts with *F* (e.g., Francis, Felipe, Felicia), and have those children write the letter *F* on the blackboard (or poster paper). Also have two or three other children write the letter *F* on the blackboard. Provide verbal guidance as children form the letter: "Start at the top, draw a line straight down, go to the top again and draw a line to the right, go to the middle and draw a line to the right." If necessary, help children write the letter. Some of the other children can practice writing *F* in the air with their fingers (or on individual chalkboards). Then ask the children to think of words that begin with *F*. Write the words they offer on the blackboard, drawing quick sketches (when possible) of the suggested words. If a child suggests a word that does not begin with *F*, say, "No, that begins with ___," and say the two sounds so children can compare them. To help children who cannot think of any words, prompt them with pictures or objects representing words that start with *F*. (Pictures or objects can be handed out at the beginning of the lesson or as the lesson proceeds.) Additional words can be sought in a picture dictionary if the group has difficulty arriving at words that begin with *F*.

Summary/Transition Activity

After about 10–15 words have been suggested, review the words, emphasizing the *F* sound.

WEEKLY PLANNING GUIDE

	Dramatic Play	Art	Group	Story	Song
Monday *Suggested Props and Materials*	Airplane *Airplane scenario, pilot area, seats, seatbelts, carts, suitcases, ticket area, baggage claim*	Kites *Paper, markers, glue, wooden craft sticks*	Letter G *Pictures and objects beginning with letter G, slates and chalk or paper and markers*	*Going on a Plane*	"Going to Kentucky"
Tuesday *Suggested Props and Materials*	Motel *Motel scenario, check-in counter, rooms, housecleaning equipment, pool*	Post Cards *Index cards (3" × 4" or 5" × 8"), glue, pictures, markers, chalkboard with message*	Color Yellow *Yellow paper, yellow badges (for those children who are not wearing yellow), different yellow objects, tub labeled yellow, tub labeled blue, four blue objects*	*Ira Sleeps Over*	"Five in a Bed"
Wednesday *Suggested Props and Materials*	Amusement Park *Amusement park scenario, ticket booth, tickets, different rides or games (e.g., ring toss, bean bag throw, "fishing")*	Mickey Mouse Ears *Black circles, black headband, glue, glitter (optional)*	Loud and Soft *Drum, triangle (optional), other instruments (optional), tape of different songs, audiotape or compact disc player*	*Where the Wild Things Are*	"It's a Small World"
Thursday *Suggested Props and Materials*	Boat/Cruise Ship *Boat/cruise ship scenario, captain's area, eating area, pretend food, dishes, pretend money, sleeping area, gift store, swimming area*	Easel Painting *Easels, paint, brushes, paper, smocks*	How to Write a 2 *Cards with 2 on them; individual chalkboards and chalk, paper and pencils (optional), or white board and markers; number line*	*The Greedy Grey Octopus*	"All the Little Fishies"

MY NOTES

NEWSLETTER

Vol. 1, No. 7

Date: _____

Vacation

Monday

All aboard for a ride on an airplane! The children will pretend to work on the plane and be passengers during dramatic play. They will make and decorate kites at the art center. *Going on a Plane* is the story for Monday. During group time, the children will learn about the letter *G*. The theme song for music will be "Going to Kentucky."

Tuesday

Children continue their vacation theme today by staying in a motel. They will help guests check in or be guests during dramatic play. They will make post cards in art. At storytime, the children will read *Ira Sleeps Over*. During group time, the children will learn about the color yellow. Please have your child wear something yellow today. Our featured song is "Five in the Bed."

Wednesday

Amusement park is the theme today for dramatic play. The children will ride on exciting "rides" and eat snack foods. At the art center, the children will make Mickey Mouse ears. The story is the *Where the Wild Things Are*. During group time, the children will explore things that are loud and things that are soft. "It's a Small World" will be a featured song during music time.

Thursday

The children will be walking up the gangplank to get on the cruise ship during dramatic play. They will enjoy shipboard activities and good food. In art, the children will paint at the easels. Our story for the day is *The Greedy Grey Octopus*. During group time, the children will learn how to write a *2*. We will sing "All the Little Fishies" as one of our songs during music time.

Monday

Dramatic Play	Art	Group	Story	Song
Airplane	Kites	Letter G	*Going on a Plane*	"Going to Kentucky"

DAILY PLANNING GUIDE

Language and Literacy Skills Facilitated

Vocabulary: *transportation, airplane, pilot, flight attendant, baggage, suitcase, take-off, landing, seat belt, security check, ticket, seat, passenger, beverage, cockpit*

Verb phrase structures: *fasten your seatbelt, land<u>s</u> the plane, <u>is</u> land<u>ing</u>, land<u>ed</u>, <u>flew</u> the plane, serv<u>ed</u> food, check<u>ed</u> baggage, who's going on the plane? I <u>am</u>* (uncontractible auxiliary verb), *I'<u>m</u> fly<u>ing</u>* (contractible auxiliary)

Adjective/object descriptions: *large plane, small plane, big suitcase, little bag, carry-on bag, blue ____, red ____, purple ____*

Question structures: *what, how, where, when, who, what if, why, how many, which one*

Pronouns: *I, you, he, she, we, they, my, your, him, her, his, our, their, me, us, them*

Prepositions: *in, on, under, over, near, beneath, next to, beside, around, inside, outside*

Sounds: /l/ *<u>l</u>ands, pi<u>l</u>ot, fi<u>ll</u>;* /r/ *<u>r</u>ide, ca<u>r</u>;* /s/ *<u>s</u>it, talk<u>s</u>;* /k/ *<u>c</u>arry, ti<u>ck</u>et, pa<u>ck</u>;* /f/ *<u>f</u>ive, o<u>ff</u>*

Noting print has meaning: names on chairs and in cubbies, signs in dramatic play, words in books and on chalkboard

Noting sound–symbol associations: What sound does ____ start with?

Writing: letters, names, words

Social Skills Facilitated

Initiating interaction with peers and adults; responding to questions and requests from peers and adults

Negotiating with peers for toys and materials

Group cooperation: waiting for a turn in a group, taking a turn at the appropriate time

Cognitive Skills Facilitated

Problem-solving skills: how to make kites, what to take on a trip

Classification skills: things that begin with letter *G*

Sequencing skills: songs, stories

Narrative/story structure: informational/adventure

Motor Skills Facilitated

Large motor: outdoor play activities—jumping, running, hopping, pedaling, climbing

Small motor: writing, drawing, gluing, folding

DRAMATIC PLAY : **Airplane**

Type of Activity: Central

Objectives
1. Learn new, and employ familiar, vocabulary
2. Learn new, and employ a variety of, syntactic constructions
3. Interact with peers
4. Sequence familiar routines
5. Expand conceptual knowledge of the world

Settings
- Airport
- Ticket office or counter
- Kitchen
- Cockpit
- Metal detector (optional)
- Airplane facsimile (chairs arranged in rows behind a "cab," where a play dashboard is set up)
- Baggage claim area (optional)

Props
- Tickets
- Chairs with seatbelts (men's ties can be used for seatbelts)
- Dishes
- Luggage
- Food and drinks
- Trays
- Carts
- Dolls
- Pretend money

Roles
- Pilot and co-pilot
- Flight attendants
- Clerks at the ticket counter
- Passengers
- Security people

General Description of Activity

Children take a pretend airplane trip, including purchasing a ticket, checking baggage at the counter, going through a security check, and finding a seat on the airplane. They must store their carry-on luggage under a seat and fasten their seatbelts before take-off. Food and beverages can be served by children acting as flight attendants. Upon arrival, the passengers can claim their baggage in the baggage area.

Verbal Productions

Level of linguistic complexity varies with the role or competency of the child playing the role.

- "We're coming in for a landing, so fasten your seatbelts" or "Plane's landing"
- "Do you want a drink?" or "Drink?"
- "May I see your ticket?" or "Ticket?"

Adult Facilitative Role

The adult is to facilitate role play and help expand language and literacy skills. Typical actions or strategies to use include

Playing a role: "I am a pilot. I fly a plane."

Event casting: "Johnny is flying the plane, and Jane is putting on her seatbelt. I think they are going to California. Look, Sally is the flight attendant. She is giving Jane a drink."

Asking open questions: "Where do you think this plane is going? Where would you like to go on vacation?"

Using a cloze procedure: "I have one bag and you have two ____ (bags)."

ART : **Kites**

Objectives
1. Express creativity
2. Develop small motor skills (e.g., constructing, pasting, drawing, cutting)
4. Practice turn-taking skills
5. Converse with peers and adults

Materials
- Wooden craft sticks, two for each kite
- Paper cut in diamond shape to fit on the craft-stick kite frame, one for each kite
- Markers or crayons
- Stickers (optional, for decoration)
- Yarn
- Small scraps of paper

General Description of Activity

Children glue two wooden craft sticks together in the form of a cross. They then paste the diamond-shaped paper to the wooden craft sticks. They can decorate the paper, add yarn to make a tail for the kite, and glue small bits of paper to the tail for decoration. They attach another piece of yarn or string to the kite frame. The kites are now ready to fly.

GROUP | **Letter *G***

Objectives

1. Improve listening skills
2. Increase knowledge of the alphabet and sounds
3. Learn appropriate group-interaction skills
4. Practice turn-taking skills

Materials

- Alphabet chart and other alphabet displays
- Blackboard and chalk or poster paper and markers
- Pictures of objects (or objects themselves) with names that begin with G
- Picture dictionary (or an alphabet video dictionary)

General Description of Activity

Write an upper- and a lowercase letter *G* on the blackboard (or on poster paper) and give several examples of words that begin with *G*, emphasizing the /g/ sound at the beginning of the words. You might hold up pictures of objects (or objects themselves) with names that begin with *G*. Direct the children's attention to the alphabet picture displays around the room.

Group Participation

Ask if anyone's name starts with *G* (e.g., Garrison, Gabriella), and have those children write the letter *G* on the blackboard (or poster paper). Also have two or three children whose names do not begin with *G* write the letter *G* on the blackboard. Provides verbal guidance as children write the letter: "Start at the top, draw a curved line like part of a circle and put a line on the end". If necessary, help children write the letter. Some of the other children can practice writing *G* in the air with their fingers (or on individual chalkboards). Then ask the children to think of words that begin with *G*. Write the words they offer on the blackboard, drawing quick sketches (when possible) of the suggested words. If a child suggests a word that does not begin with *G*, say, "No, that begins with ___," and say the two sounds so that children can compare them. To help children who cannot think of any words, prompt them with pictures or objects representing *G* words. (Pictures or objects can be handed out at the beginning of the lesson or as the lesson proceeds.) Additional words can be sought in a picture dictionary if the group has difficulty arriving at words that begin with *G*.

Summary/Transition Activity

After about 10–15 words have been suggested, review the words, emphasizing the /g/ sound.

Tuesday

Dramatic Play	Art	Group	Story	Song
Motel	Post Cards	Color Yellow	*Ira Sleeps Over*	"Five in a Bed"

DAILY PLANNING GUIDE

Language and Literacy Skills Facilitated

Vocabulary: *motel, beds, check-in, check-out, key, clerk, maid, room service, suitcase, swimming suit, travel*

Verb phrase structures: *travel<u>ed</u>, <u>is</u> checking in, check<u>ing</u> out, check<u>ed</u> out, <u>is</u> clean<u>ing</u> rooms, <u>are</u> mak<u>ing</u> beds, swimm<u>ing</u> in the pool, pack<u>ed</u>*

Adjective/object descriptions: *room key, big ____, little ___, red ____, blue ____*

Question structures: *what, how, where, when, who, what if, why, how many, which one*

Pronouns: *I, you, he, she, we, they, my, your, him, her, his, our, their, me, us, them*

Prepositions: *in, on, under, over, near, beneath, next to, beside, around, inside, outside*

Sounds: /l/ <u>l</u>ight, de<u>l</u>ight, poo<u>l</u>; /f/ <u>f</u>ind, of<u>f</u>

Noting print has meaning: names on chairs and on cubbies, signs in dramatic play, words in books and on chalkboard

Noting sound–symbol associations: What sound does _____ start with?

Writing: letters, names, words

Social Skills Facilitated

Initiating interaction with peers and adults; responding to questions and requests from peers and adults

Negotiating with peers for toys and materials

Group cooperation: waiting for a turn in a group, taking a turn at the appropriate time

Cognitive Skills Facilitated

Problem-solving skills: What things are yellow?

Classification skills: things in a motel

Sequencing skills: dramatic play (travel, check in, stay, check out)

Narrative/story structure: adventure

Motor Skills Facilitated

Large motor: outdoor play activities—jumping, running, hopping, pedaling, climbing

Small motor: writing, drawing, gluing

DRAMATIC PLAY **Motel**

Type of Activity: Central

Objectives
1. Learn new, and employ familiar, vocabulary
2. Learn new, and employ a variety of, syntactic constructions
3. Interact with peers
4. Sequence familiar routines
5. Expand conceptual knowledge of the world

Settings
- Check-in desk
- Bathroom areas

- Different rooms with mats for beds

- Pool
- Restaurant (optional)

Props
- Beds and pillows
- Play telephones
- Television sets (shoeboxes with a side cut out and a picture pasted over the cutout area)
- Registration book

- Pretend cash register
- Pretend money
- Pretend credit cards
- Keys
- Dolls (for babies)
- Towels
- Toothbrushes
- Brooms and mops

- Restaurant tables
- Play dishes
- Pretend food
- Suitcases
- Clothes
- Blue sheet or wading pool (the "pool")

Roles
- Clerks
- Customers
- Maids

- Room service attendants
- Lifeguard

- Waiters and waitresses (optional)
- Cooks (optional)

General Description of Activity

Children pretend they are staying at a motel while on a trip. Their rooms might have beds, television sets, and telephones. There might be a pool available and also a restaurant attached to the motel. Children can check in, go to their rooms, unpack their clothes, go out to eat (or order room service), come back to their rooms, go swimming in the pool, make telephone calls, and then sleep. They can then awake, check out, and continue their trip. They might want to stay for several days in the motel!

Verbal Productions

Level of linguistic complexity varies with the role or competency of the child playing the role.
- "May I have a room, please?" or "Room?"
- "I'm going to call for tickets" or "I calling"
- "She cleaned this room yesterday" or "Clean room"
- "Do you want your room cleaned now?" or "Clean now?"
- "No, I'm sleeping" or "No, sleep"

Adult Facilitative Role

The adult is to facilitate role play and help expand language and literacy skills. Typical actions or strategies to use include

Playing a role: "Are you staying one or two nights?"

Expanding a child's utterance: "You sleep bed there" to "Yes, I will sleep in the bed here and you can sleep in the bed there."

Identifying rhyming words: "Yes, the words *bed, red*, and *fed* all rhyme."

Modeling a statement/vocabulary: "A motel is a place with beds where you can sleep when you travel."

ART : **Post Cards**

Objectives
1. Express creativity
2. Develop small motor skills (e.g., drawing, painting, cutting, pasting skills)
3. Practice turn-taking skills
4. Converse with peers and adults

Materials
- Sissors
- A variety of magazines, particularly travel magazines or those with scenery
- Glue or paste

- Index cards (3" × 5" or 4" × 6")
- Markers or crayons
- Chalkboard and chalk or a word chart with words for children to copy

General Description of Activity

Children cut out pictures from magazines and glue them on one side of an index card. They then "write" messages to their family and friends on the other side of their cards. It is helpful to have messages such as *Dear Mom and Dad, I am having fun*, and *Love*, written on a chalkboard (or a chart) for the children to copy.

GROUP **Color Yellow**

Objectives
1. Improve listening skills
2. Increase conceptual knowledge
3. Learn appropriate group-interaction skills
4. Practice turn-taking skills

Materials
- Yellow paper
- Yellow badges (for those children who are not wearing yellow)
- Variety of yellow objects
- Four blue objects
- Two red objects
- Tub with yellow label and *yellow* written on it
- Tub with blue label and *blue* written on it

General Description of Activity

On the first Thursday of October, hold up a yellow piece of construction paper and label the color as *yellow*. Ask the children to look around the room or at the red, blue, and yellow objects you have collected to find other items that are yellow. Then have one child choose an object that is yellow and place it in the tub labeled *yellow*.

Group Participation

Other children take turns choosing an item that is yellow from a selection of red, yellow, and blue objects. The children place the yellow objects in the yellow tub. Occasionally, ask a child to choose a blue item and place it in the blue tub.

Variation

Ask the children to discriminate between different shades of yellow (e.g., pale yellow, bright yellow)

Summary/Transition Activity

Because it is "yellow day" and all the children are wearing something yellow, dismiss the children one by one by asking them to point to the yellow on their clothes.

Wednesday

Dramatic Play	Art	Group	Story	Song
Amusement Park	Mickey Mouse Ears	Loud and Soft	*Where the Wild Things Are*	"It's a Small World"

DAILY PLANNING GUIDE

Language and Literacy Skills Facilitated

Vocabulary: *ticket, amusement park, hot dogs, hamburgers, ring toss, mural, whirlie, target*

Verb phrase structures: <u>ride</u> *the whirlie*, <u>spin</u> *around*, <u>eat</u> *hot dogs*, <u>throw</u> *the ball at the target*, <u>buy</u> *tickets*, <u>draw</u>, <u>write</u>

Adjective/object descriptions: *big ___, little ___, large ___, small ___, fast ___, slow ___, red ___, blue ___, yellow ___*

Question structures: *what, how, where, when, who, what if, why, how many, which one*

Pronouns: *I, you, he, she, we, they, my, your, him, her, his, our, their, me, us, them*

Prepositions: *in, on, under, over, near, beneath, next to, beside, around, inside, outside*

Noting print has meaning: on chair and on cubbies, signs in dramatic play, words in books and on chalkboard

Noting sound–symbol associations: What sound does _____ start with?

Writing: letters, names, words

Social Skills Facilitated

Initiating interaction with peers and adults; responding to questions and requests from peers and adults

Negotiating with peers for toys and materials

Group cooperation: waiting for a turn in a group, taking a turn at the appropriate time

Cognitive Skills Facilitated

Problem-solving skills: what to do in an amusement park, how to hit the ring toss pole

Classification skills: things in a amusement park, things that are loud/soft

Sequencing skills: story, songs

Narrative/story structure: adventure

Motor Skills Facilitated

Large motor: outdoor play activities—jumping, running, hopping, pedaling, climbing

Small motor: writing, drawing, gluing, painting

DRAMATIC PLAY **Amusement Park**

Type of Activity: Central

Objectives
1. Learn new, and employ familiar, vocabulary
2. Learn new, and employ a variety of, syntactic constructions
3. Interact with peers
4. Sequence familiar routines
5. Expand conceptual knowledge of the world

Settings	• Various rides (e.g., Sit 'N Spin, miniature trampolines)	• Ticket office • Concession areas
Props	• Tickets • Bowling ball and pins • Bean bag toss • Pretend roller coaster (made from boxes)	• Target board and balls with Velcro adhesive so they stick to the target • Pretend food (e.g., hot dogs, sodas, ice cream, cotton candy) • Two cash registers • Pretend money
Roles	• Customers • Park workers (to run the games and the rides)	• Ticket sellers • Concession stand workers

General Description of Activity

An amusement park has several rides and other activities in which the children can participate. In this dramatic play, the children may circulate among activities. There might be concession stands where they can purchase food items, such as hot dogs, or they might bring a picnic to the park. The park might have a train for transportation from one area to another.

Verbal Productions

Level of linguistic complexity varies with the role or competency of the child playing the role.

- "I want a ride on the roller coaster, please" or "Want ride"

- "She needs a ticket" or "Ticket"

- "It's his turn" or "Turn, please"

Adult Facilitative Role

The adult is to facilitate role play and help expand language and literacy skills. Typical actions or strategies to use include

Playing a role: "I would like two tickets for the bean bag throw."

Expanding a child's utterance: "Throw" to "Yes, throw that ball in the hole."

Redirecting a child to a peer: "Ask him for the ring."

Modeling phonological awareness: "The words *big*, *ball*, and *box* all start with the /b/ sound."

Providing a literacy model: "That sign says *tickets*."

ART **Mickey Mouse Ears**

Objectives	1. Express creativity 2. Develop small motor skills (e.g., drawing, painting, cutting, pasting) 3. Practice turn-taking skills 4. Converse with peers and adults
Materials	• Black strips for headbands • Black circles approximately 2 inches in diameter • Black circles outlined in white chalk for children to cut out • Glue • Scissors

General Description of Activity

The children make black headbands and attach two round circles to represent Mickey Mouse's ears. Some children can cut out the circles themselves; others can paste cutout circles to the black head-bands.

GROUP **Loud and Soft**

Objectives
1. Improve listening skills
2. Increase conceptual knowledge
3. Learn appropriate group-interaction skills
4. Practice turn-taking skills

Materials
- Drum
- Triangle (optional)
- Other instruments (optional)

General Description of Activity

Place a drum in the middle of the floor and hit it hard so that the sound is *loud*. Then hit it softly so that the sound is *soft*. Label each sound as it is made. Then do the same with a triangle (musical instrument), reversing the *loud* and *soft* if desired.

Group Participation

Invite children up to hit the drum (or triangle or other instrument) either hard or softly. Ask whether the sound is loud or soft. Then ask a child to speak softly (or loudly), and have the class decide if the child's voice was loud or soft. Tell the class to yell when you raise your hand high and whisper when you lower your hand.

Summary/Transition Activity

Review the terms *loud* and *soft*. Have children sing a familiar song (e.g., "The Alphabet Song") loudly when you raise your hand and softly when your lower your hand.

Thursday

Dramatic Play	Art	Group	Story	Song
Boat/Cruise Ship	Easel Painting	How to Write a 2	*The Greedy Grey Octopus*	"All the Little Fishies"

DAILY PLANNING GUIDE

Language and Literacy Skills Facilitated

Vocabulary: *sink, float, water, fish, boat, liner, rowboat, cruise, shark, sea, ocean, waves, swim*

Verb phrase structures: *is fish<u>ing</u>, catch<u>es</u>, float<u>ed</u>, <u>swam</u>, <u>has</u> a fish, <u>has gone</u> sail<u>ing</u>, <u>rode</u> in a boat, who is going fishing, I <u>am</u> (uncontractible auxiliary), who is the biggest, I <u>am</u> (uncontractible auxiliary)*

Adjective/object descriptions: *big ____, little ____, high water, low water, tiny ____, green ____, blue ____*

Question structures: *what, how, where, when, who, what if, why, how many, which one*

Pronouns: *I, you, he, she, we, they, my, your, him, her, his, our, their, me, us, them*

Prepositions: *in, on, under, over, near, beneath, next to, beside, around, inside, outside*

Sounds: /f/ <u>f</u>ish; /s/ <u>s</u>ail, boat<u>s</u>; /l/ <u>l</u>ittle, pai<u>l</u>; /r/ <u>r</u>owboat, fa<u>r</u>; /k/ <u>c</u>atch, sin<u>k</u>; /sh/ <u>sh</u>ip, fi<u>sh</u>

Noting print has meaning: names on chairs and on cubbies, signs in dramatic play, words in books and on chalkboard

Noting sound–symbol associations: What sound does ____ start with?

Writing: letters, names, words

Social Skills Facilitated

Initiating interaction with peers and adults; responding to questions and requests from peers and adults

Negotiating with peers for toys and materials

Group cooperation: waiting for a turn in a group, taking a turn at the appropriate time

Cognitive Skills Facilitated

Problem-solving skills: how to write a *2*

Classification skills: things on a cruise ship

Sequencing skills: songs, stories

Narrative/story structure: adventure

Motor Skills Facilitated

Large motor: outdoor play activities—jumping, running, hopping, pedaling, climbing

Small motor: writing, drawing, gluing, fingerpainting

DRAMATIC PLAY **Boat/Cruise Ship**

Type of Activity: Central

Objectives
1. Learn new, and employ familiar, vocabulary
2. Learn new, and employ a variety of, syntactic constructions
3. Interact with peers
4. Sequence familiar routines
5. Expand conceptual knowledge of the world

Settings
- Ship (large cardboard box that has been unfolded to form a shell around the classroom's kitchen area)
- Kitchen
- Helm
- Cabins (mats)
- Dining area
- Gift store
- Shuffleboard area
- Sunbathing area
- Pool area
- Water

Props
- Tickets
- Gangplank
- Suitcases
- Mats
- Tables
- Pretend food
- Shuffleboard sticks and pieces
- Sunscreen
- Sunglasses
- Jewelry (for the gift store)
- Dishes
- Pots and pans
- Rudder
- Captain's hat

Roles
- Passengers
- Captain
- Purser
- Waiters and waitresses
- Gift shop salespeople
- Ship's doctor

General Description of Activity

Children can act out a variety of roles on a cruise ship, including the captain, the purser, waiters and waitresses, the gift store salespeople, and the cruise ship doctor. They can sleep in cabins, eat at tables arranged like in a restaurant, swim, play shuffleboard, sunbathe, and buy things at the gift store.

Verbal Productions

Level of linguistic complexity varies with the role or competency of the child playing the role.
- "He spotted a shark" or "Shark!"
- "I got an eight on the shuffleboard game" or "Eight"
- "He is swimming in the ocean" or "He swimming"
- "I am the captain. You must board now" or "Go now"
- "That's my suitcase" or "Mine"
- "She's turning the wheel fast" or "Fast"

Adult Facilitative Role

The adult is to facilitate role play and help expand language and literacy skills. Typical actions or strategies to use include

Playing a role: "I am the captain."

Asking an open question: "Which one are you buying?"

Expanding a child's utterance: "That's mine" to "That one is mine."

Using a cloze procedure: "Here is the table, and here are the _____ (chairs)."

Modeling a statement/structure (present progressive): "I am going to the gift store."

ART : **Easel Painting**

Objectives
1. Express creativity
2. Develop small motor skills (e.g., drawing, painting, cutting, pasting)
3. Practice turn-taking skills
4. Converse with peers and adults

Materials
- Smocks
- Easels
- Different colors of tempera
- Paint cups to hold the paint
- Large paintbrushes
- 9" × 12" or 12" × 18" paper
- Wooden rack or other area for drying

General Description of Activity

Set up two easels with a large sheet of paper clipped to each. Fill two to four cups with tempera paint and put a paintbrush in each cup. (It is helpful to have cup covers with holes in them for the brushes. As children dip the brush into the paint and pull it through the holes, some of the excess paint is removed. It is also helpful to put the easel over plastic or newspaper so that the drips will not stain the rug.)

Children put on their smocks, dip the brush into the paint, and paint shapes, objects, or anything else they want. Sometimes children will paint a picture and then experiment by painting other colors on top. Let the children experiment with the tempera for some projects. Sometimes you might have the children tell you about their painting, and you can label it for display. (Let the children decide if they want their paintings displayed.) Have a designated area for drying the pictures, such as a wooden clothes rack. Note: This is a large muscle activity, particularly appropriate for young children (3 years and up).

GROUP **How to Write a 2**

Objectives
1. Improve listening skills
2. Increase conceptual knowledge
3. Learn appropriate group-interaction skills
4. Practice turn-taking skills
5. Practice recognition and writing of numbers

Materials
- Number cards
- Chalkboards and chalk
- Paper and pencils (optional)
- Whiteboard and markers
- Number line (optional)

General Description of Activity

First, hold up a card with a *1* written on it. Repeat the *1* rhyme (see below) and have a few children practice on the whiteboard. It is good to practice the *1*, although most children can draw a straight line. Then hold up a card with the number *2* written on it. Trace the number with your finger and invite several children to come to the front of the group to trace the number, too. As the children trace, recite the jingle for the target number (*2*):

1: Start at the top, go down and you're done, that's the way to make a *1*.

2: Around and back on the railroad track, *2, 2, 2*.

3: Around the tree, around the tree, that's the way to make a *3*.

4: Down and over and down once more, that's the way to make a *4*.

5: Down around, make a hat on it, and look what you've found. (5)

6: Down around until it sticks, that's the way to make a *6*.

7: Over and down and it's not heaven, over and down makes a *7*.

8: Make an S and go back straight, that's the way to make an *8*.

9: A balloon and a line make *9*.

10: Draw a line and a circle with your pen, that's the way to make a *10*.

Group Participation

Distribute individual chalkboards and chalk (or paper and pencils) to the children, and have them practice writing the target number.

Variation 1

Whiteboards and markers may be easier for some children to use.

Variation 2

To introduce the number, use a number line and have the children count up to the target number on the line. One child could place the target number on the number line.

Summary/Transition Activity

Ask children to hold up their chalkboards and show the group their numbers.

WEEKLY PLANNING GUIDE

	Dramatic Play	Art	Group	Story	Song
Monday *Suggested Props and Materials*	Fall Cleaning *House and yard scenario, pretend lawnmowers, paint brushes, brooms, mops, rakes, "window" to be washed, pretend leaves*	Leaf Rubbings *Variety of real leaves, paper, crayons with paper covering removed, markers*	Leaf Classification *Variety of real leaves, mats (optional)*	*Red Leaf, Yellow Leaf*	"Five Little Leaves"
Tuesday *Suggested Props and Materials*	Fall Sports (Baseball) *Baseball diamond, plastic bat, baseball tee, plastic or Nerf balls, baseball mitts, ticket booth, spectator stand (folded gym mat with two rows of chairs), concession booth, pretend food, cash register*	Chalk Pictures with Liquid Starch *Chalk, paper, liquid starch (optional)*	Number Recognition *Two (or more) sets of cards with the numbers 1–10 written on them, 1–100 number chart, a 1–20 number line (optional)*	*Who's Counting*	"Take Me out to the Ballgame"
Wednesday *Suggested Props and Materials*	Harvest *Farm scenario, pumpkin patch scenario, pretend fruit trees, planting area (sand), blocks for fencing, play farm machinery, scarecrow, real or paper miniature pumpkins, Indian corn, and bowls to hold shelled corn or corn on stalks (optional)*	Tissue Paper Leaf Collage *Red, orange, yellow tissue paper; leaf outlines, glue, pencils*	Letter *H* *Alphabet chart, blackboard and chalk or poster paper and markers, pictures of objects (or objects themselves) with names that begin with H, picture dictionary*	*The Little Red Hen*	"Way Down Yonder in the Paw Paw Patch"
Thursday *Suggested Props and Materials*	State Fair *Fair scenario; animals in booths; "canned foods"; carnival rides; arena; ticket booth; cash register; blue, red, white ribbons*	Doghouse and Dog Prints *Doghouse, stamps, ink pads*	Act out a Story (*The Little Red Hen*) *Props for story (e.g., pretend wheat to plant, pretend wheat to grind, pretend oven to bake in, table and pretend bread)*	*Raccoons and Ripe Corn*	"Five Little Ducks"

NEWSLETTER

Vol. 1, No. 8

Date: _____

All About Fall

Monday

Today the children will be doing some fall cleaning. They will pretend to fix roofs, wash windows, mow lawns, rake leaves, and generally clean up. In art, children will make leaf rubbings. Our story today is *Red Leaf, Yellow Leaf.* During group time, they will classify some of the leaves they pick up during outside playtime. Our featured song is "Five Little Leaves."

Tuesday

Today we will focus on fall sports. Children will play baseball in dramatic play, acting as the players, the spectators, or the vendors. At the art table, they will make special chalk pictures by dipping their chalk in liquid starch and then drawing on paper. We will read the book *Who's Counting* during story and sing "Take Me out to the Ballgame" during music. Number recognition from 1–10 will be practiced at group time.

Wednesday

The children will focus on harvest time today. They will pretend to pick apples, go to the pumpkin patch, and harvest other fall crops. They might even set up a farmers' market. In art, they will make fall leaves from tissue paper. The story will be *The Little Red Hen.* The letter of the week is *H* for *harvest.* Our featured song is "Way Down Yonder in the Paw Paw Patch."

Thursday

The children will have fun at the "state fair" today. They will be the exhibitors, judges, carnival workers, or customers. In art, the children will make doghouse and dog prints. The featured story is *Raccoons and Ripe Corn.* During group time, they will act out their story from yesterday, *The Little Red Hen.* Our song of the day is "Five Little Ducks."

Monday

Dramatic Play	Art	Group	Story	Song
Fall Cleaning	Leaf Rubbings	Leaf Classification	*Red Leaf, Yellow Leaf*	"Five Little Leaves"

DAILY PLANNING GUIDE

Language and Literacy Skills Facilitated

Vocabulary: *fall, autumn, leaves, yard, fall cleaning, mowing the lawn, raking the leaves, painting the house, reseeding the lawn, washing the windows*

Verb phrase structures: *rak<u>ing</u> leaves, rake<u>s</u> leaves, rake<u>d</u> leaves, paint<u>s</u> the house, paint<u>ed</u> the house, clean<u>ed</u> the yard*

Adjective/object descriptions: *big leaf, red leaf, green leaf, yellow leaf, dirty windows, clean windows, big/little pile of leaves*

Question structures: *what, how, where, when, who, what if, why, how many, which one*

Pronouns: *I, you, he, she, we, they, my, your, him, her, his, our, their, me, us, them*

Prepositions: *in, on, under, over, near, beneath, next to, beside, around, inside, outside*

Sounds: /f/ <u>f</u>ix, of<u>f</u>; /s/ <u>s</u>it, talk<u>s</u>; /l/ <u>l</u>ittle, <u>l</u>eaf, ye<u>ll</u>ow, fa<u>ll</u>

Noting print has meaning: names on chairs and on cubbies, signs in dramatic play, words in books and on chalkboard

Noting sound–symbol associations: What sound does _____ start with?

Writing: letters, names, words

Social Skills Facilitated

Initiating interaction with peers and adults; responding to questions and requests from peers and adults

Negotiating with peers for toys and materials

Group cooperation: waiting for a turn in a group, taking a turn at the appropriate time

Cognitive Skills Facilitated

Problem-solving skills: how to clean or rake

Classification skills: different kinds of leaves

Sequencing skills: story, songs

Narrative/story structure: labeling

Motor Skills Facilitated

Large motor: outdoor play activities—jumping, running, hopping, pedaling, climbing

Small motor: writing, drawing, gluing

DRAMATIC PLAY **Fall Cleaning**

Type of Activity: Related

Objectives
1. Learn new, and employ familiar, vocabulary
2. Learn new, and employ a variety of, syntactic constructions
3. Interact with peers
4. Sequence familiar routines
5. Expand conceptual knowledge of the world

Settings
- House(s) with removable screens and roof (playhouse or a handmade construction from cardboard boxes)
- Household cupboards
- Play refrigerator
- Play stove and sink
- Extra room additions (cardboard added to extend house)

Props
- Window "screens"
- Cleaning supplies (e.g., mop, broom, dustpan, rags, vacuum cleaner)
- Shelves
- Pretend tools

Roles
- Mother
- Father
- Children
- Cleaning crew
- Roofer

General Description of Activity

Children act out fall cleaning, taking down or putting up window screens, washing windows, and fixing roofs. They might also straighten shelves and cupboards, fix walls, and put things back neatly. Note: Activity can also be done in spring as spring cleaning.

Verbal Productions

Level of linguistic complexity varies with the role or competency of the child playing the role.
- "Could I please use that mop when you're finished?" or "Mop, please"
- "These windows need to be washed" or "Window dirty"
- "We fixed the roof with new shingles" or "Fix roof"

Adult Facilitative Role

The adult is to facilitate role play and help expand language and literacy skills. Typical actions or strategies to use include

Playing a role: "I am washing the windows."

Modeling production of the /f/ sound: "You need to fix the fence."

Expanding a child's utterance: "That mine" to "That is my rake."

Asking open questions: "How do we fix the door?"

Using a cloze procedure: "This one is empty; that one is _____ (full)."

ART : **Leaf Rubbings**

Objectives
1. Express creativity
2. Develop small motor skills (e.g., drawing, painting, rubbing, cutting, pasting)
3. Practice turn-taking skills
4. Converse with peers and adults

Materials
- Newsprint or tracing paper
- Variety of leaves (freshly fallen leaves work best, but cardboard cutouts could also be used)
- Other cutouts
- Crayons with paper removed
- Container for crayons

General Description of Activity

Provide a variety of leaves. Have children place a leaf or several leaves under a piece of white paper, then rub a crayon (with paper covering removed) over the paper back and forth until the shape of the leaf appears. Children can use different colors of crayons and different arrangement of leaves under the paper to make a variety of pictures.

GROUP **Leaf Classification**

Objectives
1. Improve listening skills
2. Increase sequencing ability
3. Learn appropriate group-interaction skills
4. Practice turn-taking skills

Materials
- Different kinds of leaves (approximately 30)
- Five or six tubs or mats (optional)

General Description of Activity

Collect a bag or tub full of leaves (or have the children collect them while they are outside that day or the day before). Tell the children that they are going to sort the leaves. Pick up two leaves that vary on some feature (e.g., one is big and one is small, or one is pointy and one is smooth, or one is green and one is red). Put one of the leaves in a pile or tub and say something like "This one is big, so I am putting it here. This other one is small, so it goes here." Then pick up medium-sized green and red leaves and ask the children where these leaves should go. Explain that if they don't fit into the piles already established, a new pile can be made. Typically, children choose to make piles based on color.

Group Participation

Invite one or two children to the front of the group. Ask them to choose a leaf and to either place it in an already existing category or establish a new category. If they choose a new category, they have to tell why they need a new category and what that category is. Continue until all the children have had a turn.

Variation

Have children classify plastic or paper leaves instead of real ones.

Summary/Transition Activity

Review the categories established by having the children point to each one as you identify it (e.g., "Where are the big leaves?" "Where are the small leaves?" "Where are the green leaves?" "Where are the red leaves?").

Tuesday

Dramatic Play	Art	Group	Story	Song
Fall Sports (Baseball)	Chalk Pictures with Liquid Starch	Number Recognition	*Who's Counting*	"Take Me out to the Ballgame"

DAILY PLANNING GUIDE

Language and Literacy Skills Facilitated

Vocabulary: *baseball, ball, bat, bases, diamond, glove, concession stand, popcorn, peanuts, cotton candy, scores, runs, hit, pitcher, batter, home run*

Verb phrase structures: <u>hit</u> the ball, <u>swing</u> the bat, <u>run</u> the bases, <u>pitch</u> the ball

Adjective/object descriptions: *long bat, white bases, fast ball, first base glove, foul ball*

Question structures: *what, how, where, when, who, what if, why, how many, which one*

Pronouns: *I, you, he, she, we, they, my, your, him, her, his, our, their, me, us, them*

Prepositions: *in, on, under, over, near, beneath, next to, beside, around, inside, outside*

Sounds: /f/ <u>f</u>un, o<u>ff</u>; /s/ <u>s</u>it, talk<u>s</u>; /l/ <u>l</u>ittle, ba<u>ll</u>

Noting print has meaning: names on chairs and on cubbies, signs in dramatic play, words in books and on chalkboard

Noting sound–symbol associations: What sound does _____ start with?

Writing: letters, names, words

Social Skills Facilitated

Initiating interaction with peers and adults; responding to questions and requests from peers and adults

Negotiating with peers for toys and materials

Group cooperation: waiting for a turn in a group, taking a turn at the appropriate time

Cognitive Skills Facilitated

Problem-solving skills: how to play baseball

Classification skills: things used in baseball

Sequencing skills: story, songs, numbers

Narrative/Story Structure: informational

Motor Skills Facilitated

Large motor: outdoor play activities—jumping, running, hopping, swinging, catching, climbing

Small motor: writing, drawing, gluing

> DRAMATIC PLAY **Fall Sports (Baseball)**

Type of Activity: Central

Objectives
1. Learn new, and employ familiar, vocabulary
2. Learn new, and employ a variety, of syntactic constructions
3. Interact with peers
4. Sequence familiar routines
5. Expand conceptual knowledge of the world

Settings
- Taped-off diamond area with taped squares to indicate bases
- Bleacher area made of folded tumbling mat to form a riser with chairs, but on two levels (or two rows of chairs without the mat)
- Concession area
- Ticket sales area or area for announcers (optional)

Props
- Plastic bats
- Plastic Wiffle balls (balls with holes in them) or other indoor-use baseballs (some are soft and sponge-like)
- Baseball tee (to hold the baseball while children swing at it)
- Chairs and tumbling mat to make spectator area
- Concessions—pretend food (e.g., soda pop, popcorn, cotton candy, peanuts, hot dogs)
- Cash registers

Roles
- Batter
- Fielder
- Concession worker
- Spectators
- Ticket agents or announcers (optional)

General Description of Activity

Children act out a baseball game: Some are players on the field, some are spectators watching from the stands, and some work the concession area where people can buy drinks and popcorn and other food items. The scenario can be expanded by including ticket sellers or announcers, who give the play-by-play action of the players on the field. A diamond area can be taped off with little taped squares to indicate bases. The player swing plastic bats at a Wiffle ball on a baseball tee (if a baseball tee is not available, pitch the plastic Wiffle ball or other indoor use ball to the batter). Other children can play the outfield positions to field the balls. A tumbling mat can be folded over to form a riser so that chairs can be placed on two levels to form the spectator area. A small concession area can be set up using bookshelves to form a counter area as well as a space to put the concessions items (place the two bookcases in an L shape, with one part being the counter with the cash register and the other storing the food items).

Verbal Productions

Level of linguistic complexity varies with the role or competency of the child playing the role.
- "I want a turn to bat" or "My turn"
- "I can hit a home run" or "Hit ball"
- "I want some popcorn and some pop" or "Popcorn"

Adult Facilitative Role

The adult is to facilitate role play and help expand language and literacy skills. Typical actions or strategies to use include

Playing a role: "Look, he hit a home run."

Modeling a statement: "He has a baseball mitt on his hand. He uses it to catch the ball."

Redirecting a child to a peer: "Ask her for the bat and say, 'It's my turn to play.'"

Contrasting an error response with the correct response: "He <u>don't</u> give me the bat" to "He <u>didn't</u> give me the bat."

Providing a literacy model: "That sign says *peanuts,* and that one says *popcorn.*"

ART **Chalk Pictures with Liquid Starch**

Objectives
1. Express creativity
2. Develop small motor skills (e.g., drawing, painting, cutting, pasting)
3. Practice turn-taking skills
4. Converse with peers and adults

Materials
- Colored construction paper
- Chalk
- Liquid starch
- Flat dishes to hold starch

General Description of Activity

Provide colored construction paper and colored chalk. Have children dip one end of the chalk in liquid starch and then draw on the paper. The starch makes the colors more vibrant and ensures that the chalk does not rub off. Children can draw designs or pictures that follow the theme, or they can draw whatever they wish.

GROUP **Number Recognition**

Objectives
1. Improve listening skills
2. Increase conceptual knowledge
3. Learn appropriate group-interaction skills
4. Practice turn-taking skills

Materials
- Two (or more) sets of cards with the numbers *1–10* written on them
- *1–100* number chart
- A set of cards with numbers *1–100* written on them (optional)
- Box

General Description of Activity

Hold up a card with a number between *1* and *10* written on it. Ask the children to say the number as the card is displayed. Repeat. As the children identify each number, place the number card on the floor to form a number line.

Group Participation

Ask one child to pick a number card out of a box and place the card below the corresponding number on the number line. Continue with the other children until a second number line is created on the floor. This activity can be repeated with additional sets of number cards so that more children can participate in recognizing and labeling the numbers.

Variation

For children who know the numbers from *1* to *10*, higher numbers can be chosen and labeled on a *1–100* number chart.

Summary/Transition Activity

Have the group count as you pick up all the number cards in order.

Wednesday

Dramatic Play	Art	Group	Story	Song
Harvest	Tissue Paper Leaf Collage	Letter *H*	*The Little Red Hen*	"Way Down Yonder in the Paw Paw Patch"

DAILY PLANNING GUIDE

Language and Literacy Skills Facilitated

Vocabulary: *pumpkin patch, farm, dig, grow, seed, wagon, hay ride, apple cider, plow*

Verb phrase structures: <u>grow</u> *pumpkins,* <u>pick</u> *up pumpkins,* <u>plant</u> *seeds,* <u>harvest</u> *apples,* <u>make</u> *cider,* <u>make</u> *pies*

Adjective/object descriptions: *big/little pumpkin, round pumpkin, funny face*

Question structures: *what, how, where, when, who, what if, why, how many, which one*

Pronouns: *I, you, he, she, we, they, my, your, him, her, his, our, their, me, us, them*

Prepositions: *in, on, under, over, near, beneath, next to, beside, around, inside, outside*

Sounds: /f/ <u>f</u>ix, of<u>f</u>; /s/ <u>s</u>it, talk<u>s</u>; /l/ <u>l</u>ittle, bel<u>l</u>; /k/ <u>k</u>eep, <u>k</u>ick

Noting print has meaning: names on chairs and on cubbies, signs in dramatic play, words in books and on chalkboard

Noting sound–symbol associations: What sound does _____ start with?

Writing: letters, names, words

Social Skills Facilitated

Initiating interaction with peers and adults; responding to questions and requests from peers and adults

Negotiating with peers for toys and materials

Group cooperation: waiting for a turn in a group, taking a turn at the appropriate time

Cognitive Skills Facilitated

Problem-solving skills: how to decorate our pumpkin, finding pumpkins

Classification skills: big pumpkins, little pumpkins

Sequencing skills: story, songs

Narrative/story structure: adventure (classic)

Motor Skills Facilitated

Large motor: outdoor play activities—jumping, running, hopping, pedaling, climbing

Small motor: writing, drawing, gluing

DRAMATIC PLAY **Harvest**

Type of Activity: Related

Objectives
1. Learn new, and employ familiar, vocabulary
2. Learn new, and employ a variety of, syntactic constructions
3. Interact with peers
4. Sequence familiar routines
5. Expand conceptual knowledge of the world

Settings

- Farm house (child-sized house or dismantled cardboard boxes)
- Barn (toy barn or dismantled cardboard boxes)
- Pumpkin patch (marked by masking tape or pretend fencing) with paper or real miniature pumpkins
- Fruit trees (cardboard "tree" shapes with painted Ping-Pong balls attached with Velcro)
- Planting area (sand or soil in a refrigerator box cut to 4–6 inches deep)
- Cornfield area
- Farmers' market (optional)

Props

- Blocks for fencing
- Play farm machinery
- Scarecrow (optional)
- Cardboard tree (with removable painted Ping-Pong ball fruit)
- Paper or real miniature pumpkins
- Indian corn and bowls to hold shelled corn or corn on stalks
- Other fall produce (real or pretend)
- Counters or stalls for the farmers' market (optional)

Roles

- Farmers
- Machinery operators
- People to pick pumpkins and other fruit
- Corn shellers or pickers
- Farmers' market vendors (optional)
- Customers (optional)

General Description of Activity

Children pretend to harvest a variety of crops on a farm or in a garden. There may be a pumpkin patch and/or a fruit tree with fruit to be picked. If possible, use real corn stalks so that the children can harvest corn. (An alternative is to let the children shuck Indian corn into bowls.) Children can use small tractors and attachments (e.g., plow, combine) to plow their fields (large refrigerator box cut to 4–6 inches deep and filled with sand or soil). Another activity could be setting up a farmer's market, where the produce could be sold.

Verbal Productions

Level of linguistic complexity varies with the role or competency of the child playing the role.

- "It's my turn to drive the tractor" or "Drive tractor"
- "I plowed the field and then planted the corn," "I picked the apples," or "Apples"
- "He is picking the big pumpkin" or "Big pumpkin"

Adult Facilitative Role

The adult is to facilitate role play and help expand language and literacy skills. Typical actions or strategies to use include

Playing a role: "Who wants a ride in the hay wagon?"

Modeling beginning reading/writing: "Yes, the word *apple* starts with the letter *a*."

Contrasting present and past tense: "I am pick<u>ing</u> three apples" to "I pick<u>ed</u> three apples."

Modeling a statement: "We are selling tomatoes and potatoes at the farmers' market."

Identifying rhyming words: "Yes, the words *play, hay*, and *stay* rhyme."

ART **Tissue Paper Leaf Collage**

Objectives

1. Express creativity
2. Develop small motor skills (e.g., drawing, painting, cutting, pasting)

3. Practice turn-taking skills

4. Converse with peers and adults

Materials
- Precut construction paper leaves in a variety of sizes
- Paste or glue
- 1" tissue paper squares in fall colors
- Pencils or crayons

General Description of Activity

Children crush the 1" pieces of tissue paper and paste them onto a precut construction paper form. One way to crush the paper is to wrap it around the eraser end of a pencil (or one end of a crayon) and push it off onto glue or paste that is already on the form. Or children can just crumple the squares and then paste them on the paper. When the form is completely covered, the result is a three-dimensional picture, or a picture with texture. Note: This activity can be used at other times during the year with different colors of tissue paper. For example, in the spring, provide a variety of pastel color tissue paper and precut construction paper flowers.

GROUP **Letter *H***

Objectives
1. Improve listening skills
2. Increase knowledge of the alphabet and sounds
3. Learn appropriate group-interaction skills
4. Practice turn-taking skills

Materials
- Alphabet chart and other alphabet displays
- Blackboard and chalk or poster paper and markers
- Pictures of objects (or objects themselves) with names that begin with *H*
- Picture dictionary (or an alphabet video dictionary)

General Description of Activity

Write an upper- and a lowercase letter *H* on the blackboard (or on poster paper). Give several examples of words that begin with *H*, emphasizing the /h/ sound at the beginning of the words. You might hold up pictures of objects (or objects themselves) with names that begin with *H*. Direct the children's attention to the alphabet picture displays around the room.

Group Participation

Ask if anyone's name starts with *H* (e.g., Hannah, Harry). Have those children write the letter *H* on the blackboard (or on poster paper). Also have two or three other children write the letter *H* on the blackboard. Provide verbal guidance as children form the letter: "Start at the top, draw a line straight down, go the middle and draw a line to the right, start another line at the top and go straight down." If necessary, help children write the letter. Some of the other children can practice writing an *H* in the air with their fingers (or on individual chalkboards). Ask the children to think of words that begin with *H*. Write the words they offer on the blackboard, drawing quick sketches (when possible) of the suggested words. If a child suggests a word that does not begin with *H*, say, "No, that begins with ____," and say the two sounds so children can compare them. To help children who cannot think of any words, prompt them with pictures or objects representing *H* words. (Pictures or objects can be handed out at the beginning of the lesson or as the lesson proceeds.) Additional words can be sought in a picture dictionary if the group has difficulty arriving at words that begin with *H*.

Summary/Transition Activity

After about 10–15 words have been suggested, review the words, emphasizing the *H* sound.

Thursday

Dramatic Play	Art	Group	Story	Song
State Fair	Doghouse and Dog Prints	Act out a Story (*The Little Red Hen*)	*Raccoons and Ripe Corn*	"Five Little Ducks"

DAILY PLANNING GUIDE

Language and Literacy Skills Facilitated

Vocabulary: *arena, booths, canned goods display area, judges, ribbons, horses, cows, bridle, reins, carnival rides, cotton candy*

Verb phrase structures: *is riding, rode, judges, judged, eats/ ate cotton candy*

Adjective/object descriptions: *big/little animals, blue/red ribbons, fast/slow rides*

Question structures: *what, how, where, when, who, what if, why, how many, which one*

Pronouns: *I, you, he, she, we, they, my, your, him, her, his, our, their, me, us, them*

Prepositions: *in, on, under, over, near, beneath, next to, beside, around, inside, outside*

Sounds: /f/ *fell, off*; /k/ *kick, back*; /s/ *sit, jumps*

Noting print has meaning: names on chairs and on cubbies, signs in dramatic play, words in books and on chalkboard

Noting sound–symbol associations: What sound does _____ start with?

Writing: letters, names, words

Social Skills Facilitated

Initiating interaction with peers and adults; responding to questions and requests from peers and adults

Negotiating with peers for toys and materials

Group cooperation: waiting for a turn in a group, taking a turn at the appropriate time

Cognitive Skills Facilitated

Problem-solving skills: how to judge items, number recognition

Classification skills: animals at the fair

Sequencing skills: songs, story, art activity

Narrative/story structure: adventure

Motor Skills Facilitated

Large motor: outdoor play activities—jumping, running, hopping, pedaling, climbing

Small motor: writing, drawing, gluing, fingerpainting

DRAMATIC PLAY **State Fair**

Type of Activity: Related

Objectives
1. Learn new, and employ familiar, vocabulary
2. Learn new, and employ a variety, of syntactic constructions
3. Interact with peers
4. Sequence familiar routines
5. Expand conceptual knowledge of the world

Settings
- Food area
- Animal arena
- Carnival area
- Concession stand

Props
- Pretend canned foods and baked goods
- Variety of farm animals
- Ribbons
- Carnival rides and games (e.g., Sit 'N Spin, bean bag toss, trampoline, horseshoe throw)
- Concession stand with pretend food

Roles
- Judges
- People entering food or animals to be judged
- Carnival workers
- Concession workers and customers

General Description of Activity

Children take on roles at a state fair. There may be booths with foods that are to be judged and different kinds of animals that are led around a ring and judged. There may be a carnival with rides and game booths, and even a rodeo (optional). Tape off areas for the food judging, the animal judging, and the carnival (with concession stand). Ribbons can be awarded for 1st, 2nd, and 3rd place in the competitions. Also, there may be a biggest winner in a category (animal or food). Children can pretend to be the judges, the people in the competition, the carnival workers, or the visitors.

Verbal Productions

Level of linguistic complexity varies with the role or competency of the child playing the role.
- "My cookies are the best. They have a blue ribbon" or "Cookies"
- "I want to go on the ride" or "My turn"
- "That is the best one here" or "Best"

Adult Facilitative Role

The adult is to facilitate role play and help expand language and literacy skills. Typical actions or strategies to use include

Playing a role: "I am going to win a blue ribbon for my cake."

Modeling a statement: "Jim is the judge. He decides if my cake gets a ribbon."

Contrasting error and correct sound: "You say 'otay,' but I say 'okay.'"

Redirecting a child to a peer: "Ask Jacob to let you be the judge."

Asking open questions: "Which ride do you want to try?"

ART : **Doghouse and Dog Prints**

Objectives
1. Express creativity
2. Develop small motor skills (e.g., drawing, painting, cutting, pasting)
3. Practice turn-taking skills
4. Converse with peers and adults

Materials
- Paper
- Large paper squares to make a doghouse
- Paper triangles to form a roof
- Markers
- Paint
- Shallow dishes to hold paint
- Inkpads (optional)

General Description of Activity

Children paste squares and triangles on a piece of paper to make a doghouse. Then they make "dog prints" with tempera paint by dipping the tips of their fingers and thumb into the paint and pressing on the paper. (Ink pads could be used instead of paint.) The children can also draw dogs or other animals.

GROUP **Act out a Story (*The Little Red Hen*)**

Objectives
1. Improve listening skills
2. Increase sequencing ability
3. Increase knowledge of storytelling
4. Learn appropriate group-interaction skills
5. Practice turn-taking skills

Materials
- *The Little Red Hen*
- Props for the stories

General Description of Activity

Read or summarize a familiar story to children.

Group Participation

Assign children roles from the story (e.g., the little red hen, the other animals that did not help). As-sure the children who are not chosen the first time that everyone will have a turn and that they have the very important job of being a good listening audience. Narrate the story as the children act it out. They should say as many of the lines as they can, with prompts given when needed. Repeat the story with new actors until all the children have had a turn.

Summary/Transition Activity

Compliment children on their acting, and ask them what other stories they would like to act out an-other day.

WEEKLY PLANNING GUIDE

	Dramatic Play	Art	Group	Story	Song
Monday Suggested Props and Materials	School School scenario, school bus, area for assembly, calendar, name cards, art materials, books and puzzles, manipulative area, story area, alphabet cards, flannel board and flannel board stories, small blackboard, chalk	Popcorn Letters Popcorn and letter outlines, glue	Shapes— Triangles Various sizes/colors of triangle-shaped cutouts, several small and large square-shaped cutouts, several small and large circle-shaped cutouts, small chalkboard or paper (optional), chalk or markers (optional)	*Grover Goes to School*	"The Alphabet Song"
Tuesday Suggested Props and Materials	Laundromat Laundromat scenario, washing machines, dryer, ironing board, iron, folding area, clothes to wash, waiting area with magazines	Watercolor Paintings Watercolor paint, paper, markers	Oddity Match Several items that are exact matches (and some that are not),several items that are similar (and some that don't match), several items that are related, cardboard X (optional)	*A Pocket for Corduroy*	"Here We Go 'Round the Mulberry Bush"
Wednesday Suggested Props and Materials	Doctor's Office Doctor's office scenario, reception area, magazines, examining rooms, doctor kits, X-ray area with black paper X-rays, telephones, calendar	Doctor Kit Collages Cotton balls, Q-tips, tongue depressors, black paper in shape of a bag, glue	Emergency Information Emergency information (e.g., children's phone numbers and addresses), play telephones	*Jenny's in the Hospital*	"Five Little Monkeys"
Thursday Suggested Props and Materials	Fitness Center Fitness center scenario, treadmill, stationary bike, miniature trampo-line, giant Tinker Toys for barbells, reception area, sauna area, weightlifting area, phones, check-in desk, locker areas, paper and markers	Self-Portraits White construction paper, crayons, markers, watered-down tempera paint (optional)	Letter *I* Items/pictures that begin with I, sticky notes with lower- and uppercase letter I on them (optional), dictionary	*Bearobics*	"Teddy Bear, Teddy Bear, Turn Around"

NEWSLETTER

Vol. 1, No. 9

Date: _____

Places in the Community

Monday

Today the children will play school. They may be teachers or students or bus drivers during dramatic play. In art, the children will make popcorn letters. Today's story is *Grover Goes to School*. During group time, the children will learn about triangles. Our featured song is "The Alphabet Song."

Tuesday

The classroom becomes a Laundromat/dry cleaners today. Clothing will be washed, dried, and folded during dramatic play. The children will make water-color paintings in art. *A Pocket for Corduroy* will be the featured story. During group time, children will find the item that does not go with the others. Our song today is "Here We Go 'Round the Mulberry Bush."

Wednesday

The classroom will become a doctor's office today. The children will be doctors, nurses, and patients during dramatic play. They will make doctor's kit collages in art. The book of the day will be *Jenny's in the Hospital*. During group time, children will learn about what to do in an emergency. Song time will feature "Five Little Monkeys."

Thursday

Children will visit a fitness center today in the classroom. During dramatic play, they will exercise to stay fit and healthy. At the art table, they will make self-portraits. *Bearobics* will be read during storytime. During group time, we will focus on the letter *I*. We will finish our day by learning the chant "Teddy Bear, Teddy Bear, Turn Around."

Monday

Dramatic Play	Art	Group	Story	Song
School	Popcorn Letters	Shapes—Triangles	Grover Goes to School	"The Alphabet Song"

DAILY PLANNING GUIDE

Language and Literacy Skills Facilitated

Vocabulary: *school, bus, pencil, pen, paper, flashlight, check in, alphabet, sounds, cubes, shapes, numbers, paint*

Verb phrase structures: *is writing, reads the book, says the alphabet, goes to check in, drove the bus, painted a picture*

Adjective/object descriptions: *red, blue ____, big ____, little ____, pretty ____, dirty ____, fancy ____, nice ____, unusual ____*

Question structures: *what, how, where, when, who, what if, why, how many, which one*

Pronouns: *I, you, he, she, we, they, my, your, him, her, his, our, their, me, us, them*

Prepositions: *in, on, under, over, near, beneath, next to, beside, around, inside, outside*

Sounds: /s/ *say, pencil, bus;* /k/ *car, check in, look;* /l/ *look, flashlight, pencil, school*

Noting print has meaning: names on chairs and on cubbies, signs in dramatic play, words in books and on chalkboard

Noting sound–symbol associations: What sound does _____ start with?

Writing: letters, names, words

Social Skills Facilitated

Initiating interaction with peers and adults; responding to questions and requests from peers and adults

Negotiating with peers for toys and materials

Group cooperation: waiting for a turn in a group, taking a turn at the appropriate time

Cognitive Skills Facilitated

Problem-solving skills: how to be a teacher, how to write

Classification skills: things at school

Sequencing skills: songs, stories

Narrative/story structure: adventure

Motor Skills Facilitated

Large motor: outdoor play activities—jumping, running, hopping, pedaling, climbing

Small motor: writing, drawing, gluing, cutting

DRAMATIC PLAY **School**

Type of Activity: Central

Objectives
1. Learn new, and employ familiar, vocabulary
2. Learn new, and employ a variety of, syntactic constructions
3. Interact with peers
4. Sequence familiar routines
5. Expand conceptual knowledge of the world

Settings
- School area (circle outlined on floor with masking tape)
- Bus (playhouse with cardboard door that opens and closes and a box and dashboard in front to make the cab)
- Art area
- Quiet area (books and puzzles)

Props
- Name cards
- Alphabet cards
- Flannel board and flannel board stories
- Books
- Small blackboard
- Paper and pencils
- Art materials
- Flashlight (to use in check-in)

Roles
- Bus driver
- Children
- Teacher
- Staff members
- Principal
- School nurse
- Custodian
- Parents

General Description of Activity

Set up the school area in imitation of the classroom. Include name cards, alphabet cards, flannel board stories, books, writing materials, and so forth. Also have a school bus. The children can board the bus, be driven to school, disembark, be checked in (the children who are playing the roles of staff check the "children's" throats to see if they are too sick to be in school), and then play the roles of teachers, staff, and children. When school is over, they can return home by riding on the bus again.

Verbal Productions

Level of linguistic complexity varies with the role or competency of the child playing the role.
- "He wrote his name on the paper" or "Write name"
- "I am the bus driver. You need to sit down" or "Sit down"
- "I want to drive the bus. He has driven it for a long time" or "Drive bus"
- "What does this letter say?" or "What say?"

Adult Facilitative Role

The adult is to facilitate role play and help expand language and literacy skills. Typical actions or strategies to use include:

Playing a role: "I am going to work an alphabet puzzle. Do you want to help?"

Expanding a child's utterance: "He play with me" to "He plays with me here. We like to read stories."

Modeling phonological awareness: "Yes, 'car,' 'cat,' and 'cup' and all begin with the /k/ sound."

Redirecting a child to a peer: "Ask Sally if you can drive the bus. Say, 'Can I drive the bus now?'"

ART : **Popcorn Letters**

Objectives
1. Express creativity
2. Develop small motor skills (e.g., drawing, painting, cutting, pasting)
3. Practice turn-taking skills
4. Converse with peers and adults

Materials
- Various colors of construction paper (8½" × 11")
- Popped popcorn
- White glue

General Description of Activity

Have children choose a letter, perhaps the initial in their first name. Drizzle glue, or have children drizzle it, on a paper in the shape of the letter chosen. Children put popped popcorn on the glue line.

It might be fun to make a large chart of all 26 letters and let children cross off the letter they made until the whole class creates the entire alphabet. This makes a nice bulletin board display and gives children a chance to practice the alphabet.

GROUP **Shapes—Triangles**

Objectives

1. Improve listening skills
2. Increase conceptual knowledge
3. Learn appropriate group-interaction skills
4. Practice turn-taking

Materials

- Colored tape
- Various sizes and colors of triangle-shaped cutouts
- Several small and large square-shaped cutouts
- Several small and large circle-shaped cutouts
- Small chalkboard or paper (optional)
- Chalk or markers (optional)

General Description of Activity

Using colored tape, outline a large and a small triangle shape on the floor in front of the children, where large and small circles and squares are already outlined. Trace one of the triangle outlines on the floor, or a triangle cutout, noting that the triangle has three sides and three corners.

Group Participation

Ask different children to find the large or small triangle by standing on it or by putting the large or small triangle cutout on the appropriate outline. Vary the level of difficulty. For instance, you might ask one child to identify just the shape (e.g., triangle, square, or circle) and another child to find a shape of a specific size and color (e.g., "Find the large blue triangle"). The task can also be varied by having children place a hand on one shape and a foot on another. Ask most of the children to find or label triangles, but occasionally ask a child to identify a circle or square to review the previously taught shapes. If necessary, do this activity in smaller groups.

Variation

The children can also draw shapes (triangle, square, or circle) on small chalkboards or on paper.

Summary/Transition Activity

Review the shapes by pointing to or standing on them or by holding up one of the cutouts and having the children quickly label it in unison.

Tuesday

Dramatic Play	Art	Group	Story	Song
Laundromat	Watercolor Paintings	Oddity Match	*A Pocket for Corduroy*	"Here We Go 'Round the Mulberry Bush"

DAILY PLANNING GUIDE

Language and Literacy Skills Facilitated

Vocabulary: *clothes, Laundromat, washing machine, dryer, hangers, ironing board, iron*

Verb phrase structures: <u>is/are</u> wash<u>ing</u>, <u>was/were</u> dry<u>ing</u>, fold<u>ing</u>, fold<u>ed</u>, finish<u>ed</u>, rinse<u>s</u>, rinse<u>d</u>

Adjective/object descriptions: *wet/dry clothes, hot/cold water, dirty/clean clothes, small/large loads*

Question structures: *what, how, where, when, who, what if, why, how many, which one*

Pronouns: *I, you, he, she, we, they, my, your, him, her, his, our, their, me, us, them*

Prepositions: *in, on, under, over, near, beneath, next to, beside, around, inside, outside*

Sounds: /f/ *fold off*; /l/ *load, yellow, bell*; /s/ *soap, messy, mess*

Noting print has meaning: names on chairs and on cubbies, signs in dramatic play, words in books and on chalkboard

Noting sound–symbol associations: What sound does _____ start with?

Writing: letters, names, words

Social Skills Facilitated

Initiating interaction with peers and adults; responding to questions and requests from peers and adults

Negotiating with peers for toys and materials

Group cooperation: waiting for a turn in a group, taking a turn at the appropriate time

Cognitive Skills Facilitated

Problem-solving skills: sorting clothes

Classification skills: things at a Laundromat

Sequencing skills: story, songs

Narrative/story structure: adventure

Motor Skills Facilitated

Large motor: outdoor play activities—jumping, running, hopping, pedaling, climbing

Small motor: writing, drawing, gluing

DRAMATIC PLAY : **Laundromat**

Type of Activity: Central

Objectives
1. Learn new, and employ familiar, vocabulary
2. Learn new, and employ a variety of, syntactic constructions
3. Interact with peers
4. Sequence familiar routines
5. Expand conceptual knowledge of the world

Settings
- Laundromat
- Waiting area
- Dry cleaner (optional)
- Homes (optional)

Props
- Washing machines (made from cardboard boxes with buckets or tubs inside to hold the clothes and plastic cups with slits cut in the bottoms mounted on top for coin collection)
- Dryers (made from cardboard boxes with buckets or tubs inside to hold the clothes and plastic cups with slits cut in the bottoms mounted on top for coin collection)
- Clothes
- Quarters or tokens (poker chips)
- Sink
- Laundry baskets
- Empty soap boxes
- Pretend dryer sheets
- Folding tables
- Irons and ironing boards
- Hangers
- Pretend money
- Play cash register
- Receipts (to pick up dry cleaning)
- Soda pop machine
- Magazines in waiting area

Roles
- Customers
- Cashiers
- Owner of Laundromat
- Dry cleaners (optional)
- Custodian

General Description of Activity

Children pretend to take their laundry to the washers and dryers at the Laundromat. They can insert "quarters" (poker chips) in the slots to run the machines (see Props). A waiting area could be set up with a soda pop machine. The dramatic play could be expanded to include a dry cleaner, where clothes can be dropped off, cleaned and pressed, and then picked up.

Verbal Productions

Level of linguistic complexity varies with the role or competency of the child playing the role
- "I need some soap for my dirty clothes" or "Need soap"
- "He is folding all of the shirts first" or "Fold shirts"
- "It's my turn to put the money in" or "My turn"
- "She ironed all of the dresses" or "My turn to iron"
- "Please dry clean these clothes by tomorrow" or "Tomorrow"

Adult Facilitative Role

The adult is to facilitate role play and help expand language and literacy skills. Typical actions or strategies to use include
Playing a role: "I have a big load of clothes to wash. I will need more soap."
Expanding a child's utterance: "She washing" to "She is washing the clothes."
Modeling production of the /k/ sound: "You can keep the clothes in the basket."
Asking an open question: "How does the machine work?"
Contrasting two sounds: "Did you say 'shirt' or 'dirt'?"

ART **Watercolor Paintings**

Objectives
1. Express creativity
2. Develop small motor skills (e.g., drawing, painting, cutting, pasting)
3. Practice turn-taking skills
4. Converse with peers and adults

Materials
- Watercolor paints
- Brushes
- Water in tubs
- White construction paper

General Description of Activity

Place white construction paper, watercolor paint boxes, and brushes on the art table. Put tubs of water to clean the brushes above the paper. Children put on a smock, select a brush, wet it, and choose a paint color. They paint on the paper, rinsing the brush before selecting a new color. Children can paint a collage of colors, animals, people, scenery, and so on. You may want to stay close by so that children can talk about their paintings.

GROUP **Oddity Match**

Objectives
1. Improve listening skills
2. Increase sequencing ability
3. Learn appropriate group-interaction skills
4. Practice turn-taking skills

Materials
- Several items that are exact matches (and some that are not)
- Several items that are similar (and some that do not match)
- Several items that are related
- Cardboard X (optional)

General Description of Activity

Lay out four items. Three of the items should be identical and one should be different (e.g., three red cars and one doll). Ask the children to look for the item that does not belong with the others. Then point to the item that is different and say, "This one does not go with the others." Lay out another set, this time with three items that are not identical but are the same kind of item, and one that is different from the others (e.g., three different dolls, one boat). Ask one child to come to the front and find the one that is different (or that does not go with the others).

Group Participation

Continue to present three items that are the same and one that is different until each child has had a turn identifying the different item. Be sure to vary the placement of the different item so that the children do not think it is always the second item or the last item. The difficulty of the task can be varied depending on the children's abilities (some children may need exact matches, others can recognize relationships or that the items go together even though one is bigger than the other). The children also could put a cardboard X on top of the item that does not belong rather than say or point to the item. Note: You may want to do this activity after the lesson on same and different.

Variation

One way to vary the items is to put them is a 2 × 2 matrix instead of in a row. Another procedure would be to use related items instead of the same kind of items. For example, of the following items, coat, hat, fork, and mitten, the coat, hat, and mitten are the items that go together and the fork does not belong. Another variation is to use color or function as the identifying feature (e.g., all the red items go together and the blue item is the one that is different, or all the of writing instruments go together and the scissors are the item that is different).

Summary/Transition Activity

Lay out one more group of items and have the children, in unison, say which one does not go with the others.

Wednesday

Dramatic Play	Art	Group	Story	Song
Doctor's Office	Doctor Kit Collages	Emergency Information	*Jenny's in the Hospital*	"Five Little Monkeys"

DAILY PLANNING GUIDE

Language and Literacy Skills Facilitated

Vocabulary: *doctor, nurse, paramedic, ambulance, stethoscope, thermometer, fever, cast, X ray, oxygen, accident, vehicle, arm, leg, ankle, bandage, forehead, hospital*

Verb phrase structures: *is carry<u>ing</u> the stretcher, <u>drove</u> the ambulance, <u>gave</u> oxygen, <u>sets</u> the leg*

Adjective/object descriptions: *broken leg, big ambulance, loud siren*

Question structures: *what, how, where, when, who, what if, why, how many, which one*

Pronouns: *I, you, he, she, we, they, my, your, him, her, his, our, their, me, us, them*

Prepositions: *in, on, under, over, near, beneath, next to, beside, around, inside, outside*

Sounds: /k/ *<u>c</u>arry, do<u>c</u>tor, bro<u>ke</u>*; /s/ *<u>s</u>et, in<u>s</u>ide, u<u>s</u>, ambulan<u>ce</u>*

Noting print has meaning: names on chairs and on cubbies, signs in dramatic play, words in books and on chalkboard

Noting sound–symbol associations: What sound does _____ start with?

Writing: letters, names, words

Social Skills Facilitated

Initiating interaction with peers and adults; responding to questions and requests from peers and adults

Negotiating with peers for toys and materials

Group cooperation: waiting for a turn in a group, taking a turn at the appropriate time

Cognitive Skills Facilitated

Problem-solving skills: What does a doctor do?

Classification skills: things in an doctor's office, body parts

Sequencing skills: story, songs

Narrative/story structure: adventure

Motor Skills Facilitated

Large motor: outdoor play activities—jumping, running, hopping, pedaling, climbing

Small motor: writing, drawing, gluing, cutting

···· DRAMATIC PLAY **Doctor's Office** ····

Type of Activity: Central

Objectives
1. Learn new, and employ familiar, vocabulary
2. Learn new, and employ a variety of, syntactic constructions
3. Interact with peers
4. Sequence familiar routines
5. Expand conceptual knowledge of the world

Settings
- Several examination rooms
- Waiting room
- Patients' "homes"

Props
- Table with a telephone and appointment book
- Several tables or mats to represent examination rooms
- Doctor kits
- Bandages
- X-ray machine
- Telephone in area representing patients' "homes"

Roles
- Doctor
- Nurse
- Receptionist
- Patient
- Parent

General Description of Activity

Set up a doctor's office with several examination rooms and a waiting room. Patients call the receptionist and make appointments. When it is time for their appointments, they go into the examination room with the doctor. He or she examines them by looking into their mouth, ears, and eyes; checking reflexes; checking muscle tone; listening with the stethoscope; and so forth. A patient might have a broken bone that needs to be X-rayed, set in a cast, and wrapped with a bandage.

Verbal Productions

Level of linguistic complexity varies with the role or competency of the child playing the role.
- "Open your mouth, please" or "Open mouth"
- "Where does it hurt?" or "Hurt?"
- "I don't feel good. My tummy hurts" or "I sick"

Adult Facilitative Role

The adult is to facilitate role play and help expand language and literacy skills. Typical actions or strategies to use include

Playing a role: "You need to have an X-ray."

Recasting a child's utterance: "He break him arm" to "He broke his arm. He fell down."

Modeling a statement: "This is the stethoscope. I can hear your heartbeat with it."

Confirmatory feedback: "Yes, that is the biggest one."

ART **Doctor Kit Collages**

Objectives
1. Express creativity
2. Develop small motor skills (e.g., drawing, painting, cutting, pasting)
3. Practice turn-taking skills
4. Converse with peers and adults

Materials
- Glue or paste
- Black construction paper
- Q-tips
- Tongue depressors
- Cotton balls
- Bottles—shaped paper cutouts
- "Stethoscope" (yarn)

General Description of Activity

On half of a piece of black construction paper, children paste different medical items, such as Q-tips, tongue depressors, cotton balls, and so on. They fold the paper in half (with the collage on the inside) to make the doctor's kit. An adult can staple strips of black construction paper onto the bag for handles.

Variation

The black construction-paper cutouts could be cut with the handles included so that they resemble bags.

GROUP **Emergency Information**

Objectives
1. Improve listening skills
2. Increase conceptual knowledge
3. Learn appropriate group-interaction skills
4. Practice turn-taking skills

Materials
- Children's addresses and telephone numbers, written on index cards
- Play telephones

General Description of Activity

Ask the children what they need to know in case of an emergency. If the children do not seem to understand the word *emergency*, explain and give examples. After some brainstorming by the children, suggest that knowing their full name, address, and telephone number is important if they need to call for a police officer, an ambulance, or help from an emergency agency. Pretend to be an ambulance dispatcher and ask one or two children to say their full name, address, and telephone number. If some children do not know any of the information, tell them what it is and have them repeat it.

Group Participation

Have the children get together in groups of 5–10 children and one adult. Ask each child to say his or her full name, a parent's name, and his or her address. If the child knows the telephone number, he or she should say that, too. Have the children practice looking at the number that is listed on the program's telephone so that in an emergency they can read the numbers to the 911 operator.

You can extend this activity by having a pretend emergency in which one child calls 911 (on a play telephone, or at least one not in service) and tells what is happening, then tries to follow the instructions given by the "911 operator" (a staff member).

Summary/Transition Activity

End the activity by recombining into one group and doing the day's fingerplay:
"Five little monkeys jumping on the bed,
one fell off and hurt his head,
Mama called the doctor and the doctor said,
'No more monkeys jumping on the bed!'"

Thursday

Dramatic Play	Art	Group	Story	Song
Fitness Center	Self-Portraits	Letter *I*	*Bearobics*	"Teddy Bear, Teddy Bear, Turn Around"

DAILY PLANNING GUIDE

Language and Literacy Skills Facilitated

Vocabulary: *exercise, aerobics, trampoline, weights, bicycle, dance, run, jumping jacks, mats, workout, kick, stretch, hot tub, towels, sweatband*

Verb phrase structures: *is jumping, dances, jumped, runs, ran, lifts weights, rode the bicycle, who was riding? "I was"*

Adjective/object descriptions: *heavy/light weights, fast/slow dance, red face, sweaty shirt*

Question structures: *what, how, where, when, who, what if, why, how many, which one*

Pronouns: *I, you, he, she, we, they, my, your, him, her, his, our, their, me, us, them*

Prepositions: *in, on, under, over, near, beneath, next, beside, around, inside, outside*

Sounds: /z/ *zips, dances, runs, was*; /r/ *riding, their*; /k/ *kick, pick*; /f/ *five, off*; /g/ *go, dog*

Noting print has meaning: names on chairs and on cubbies, signs in dramatic play, words in books and on chalkboard

Noting sound–symbol associations: What sound does _____ start with?

Writing: letters, names, words

Social Skills Facilitated

Initiating interaction with peers and adults; responding to questions and requests from peers and adults.

Negotiating with peers for toys and materials

Group cooperation: waiting for a turn in a group, taking a turn at the appropriate time

Cognitive Skills Facilitated

Problem-solving skills: how to exercise

Classification skills: things that begin with *I*

Sequencing skills: songs, story

Narrative/story structure: adventure

Motor Skills Facilitated

Large motor: outdoor play activities—jumping, running, hopping, pedaling, climbing, stretching

Small motor: writing, drawing, gluing, fingerpainting

DRAMATIC PLAY **Fitness Center**

Type of Activity: Central

Objectives
1. Learn new, and employ familiar, vocabulary
2. Learn new, and employ a variety of, syntactic constructions
3. Interact with peers
4. Sequence familiar routines
5. Expand conceptual knowledge of the world

Settings
- Check-in counter
- Locker room
- Equipment area(s)
- Aerobic dancing area
- Pool
- Hot tub
- Sauna

Props
- Towels
- Stationary tricycles (mounted with front wheels off the floor so the front wheel is the only one that turns)
- Miniature trampoline
- Barbells (giant Tinker Toys or cardboard tubes)
- Other equipment, such as stepboards
- Wading pool or blue sheet (for pool or hot tub)
- Check-in counter with pretend computer
- Music (for aerobic dancing)
- Mirror (for aerobic dancing)
- Costumes (e.g., sneakers, leotards, headbands)

Roles
- Fitness center attendants
- Customers
- Aerobics instructors
- Pool attendants
- Receptionist

General Description of Activity

Children go to a fitness center to exercise. They can choose from many kinds of equipment, including stationary bikes and mini-trampolines. There should also be areas to do aerobics and jog. The center might have a hot tub, sauna, and swimming pool. The children can check in at the counter and then get on the equipment or do aerobic dancing. After exercising, they can go into the pool.

Verbal Productions

Level of linguistic complexity varies with the role or competency of the child playing the role.
- "I jumped for 2 minutes" or "Jump"
- "He is riding the bike" or "He rides the bike"
- "She lifted the barbells high" or "Lift it"
- "My mommy does aerobics, and I go with her" or "My mommy go"
- "You have had a long turn. I want to ride the bike" or "My turn"

Adult Facilitative Role

The adult is to facilitate role play and help expand language and literacy skills. Typical actions or strategies to use include

Playing a role: "I am on a treadmill. I can walk fast."

Recasting a child's utterance (present progressive to past tense): "Jimmy is jumping on the trampoline. Oh, he jumped off."

Expanding a child's utterance: "I lift it" to "Yes, you lifted the weights."

Redirecting a child to a peer: "Ask Allison for a turn on the exercise bike. Say, 'Can I have a turn, please?'"

Identifying rhyming words: "Yes, 'bike,' 'like,' and 'Mike' all rhyme."

ART **Self-Portraits**

Objectives
1. Express creativity
2. Develop small motor skills (e.g., drawing, painting, cutting, pasting)
3. Practice turn-taking skills
4. Converse with peers and adults

Materials
- Paper (white or colored)
- Crayons
- Markers
- Watered-down tempera paint (optional)

General Description of Activity

Provide the children with paper and a selection of crayons and/or markers. Let the children draw anything they want. Drawings could be of themselves, their family, their pets, different scenes, designs, rainbows, etc.

Children can turn their crayon drawings into "crayon washes" by painting over the pictures with a light coat of tempera paint (watered-down paint). The paint will not stick to the crayon but will fill in where there is no crayon marks to make a background of color.

GROUP **Letter *I***

Objectives

1. Improve listening skills
2. Increase knowledge of the alphabet and sounds
3. Learn appropriate group-interaction skills
4. Practice turn-taking skills

Materials

- Blackboard and chalk
- Pairs of pictures of objects (or objects themselves) whose names begin with *I*, such as *ice* and *igloo*, *iron* and *inch*
- Poster paper (optional)
- Sticky notes (optional)

General Description of Activity

Write an upper- and a lowercase letter *I* on the blackboard (or on poster paper). Tell the children that the letter *I* has several sounds. One of them sounds like the name of the letter, /aI/, as in the word *ice*. Another sound, /I/, is heard in the word *inch* or *igloo*. Ask if children can hear both sounds. Have them practice saying the long and short sounds of the letter *I*.

Group Participation

Invite two children to the front of the class. Give each a picture of an object (or the object itself) with a name that begins with *I*. One child's picture (or object) should begin with the long /aI/ sound and the other with the short /I/ sound. Ask the children to verbally label their pictures or objects for the class. Help them stress the long or short sound, as appropriate. Then have them place their pictures (or objects) in different piles, beginning a pile for each of the sounds. Invite two other children to the front to take a turn at naming *I* words and placing the pictures (or objects) in the correct pile. Continue until everyone has had a turn.

Summary/Transition Activity

Review the long and short vowels sounds of *I* by saying the sounds one last time and holding up representative pictures.

Optional Transitional Activity

Scatter several sticky notes with upper- and lowercase *I*s written on them around the room. Ask children to find an upper- or a lowercase *I* and give it to you or put it in their cubby.

WEEKLY PLANNING GUIDE

	Dramatic Play	Art	Group	Story	Song
Monday *Suggested Props and Materials*	Grocery Store *Grocery store scenario, baskets, carts, food items, shelves, cash register, pretend money*	Halloween Bags *Bags to decorate, cutouts or stamps to decorate bags*	Decorating Pumpkins *Big pumpkin, markers, stickers*	*It's Pumpkin Time*	"Did You Ever See a Pumpkin?"
Tuesday *Suggested Props and Materials*	Construction Worker *Construction worker scenario, playhouse cardboard box additions that can be taped to the toy house, blocks, play bricks, paper strips of various colors for roof or siding, glue, tools (e.g., plastic hammers, wrenches, saws, screwdrivers, screws, brushes), tool belts, pegs, play hard hats, masking tape, telephones*	Jack-o'-lanterns *Paper pumpkins; eyes, teeth, and nose shapes; glue; markers*	Letter *J* *Items/pictures that begin with letter J, dictionary, chalkboards, chalk*	*Trick or Treat, Little Critter*	"Three Little Witches"
Wednesday *Suggested Props and Materials*	Halloween House Decorating *Halloween house scenario; decorations for house; glue; spider webs, etc.; tissue and string to make ghosts, bats, and skeletons; party items (optional)*	Ghosts, Bats, and Skeletons *White tissue, 5-inch yarn strings, skeleton line drawings, black paper, bat outlines, ghost line drawings, construction paper, scissors, glue*	Bones in a Skeleton *Plastic skeleton (or picture of a skeleton), list of scientific names of bones (optional)*	*Halloween Day*	"Five Little Pumpkins"
Thursday *Suggested Props and Materials*	Halloween Parade *Costumes (for those who don't have them), parade route, trick-or-treat bags*	(No art) *Children dress in costumes and parade around the building.*	Trick-or-Treat Safety *List of safety rules, chalkboard and chalk, trick-or-treat bag*	*Trick or Treat Faces*	Review Halloween songs

NEWSLETTER

Vol. 1, No. 10

Date: _____

Halloween

Monday

In dramatic play, the children will pretend to go to the grocery store in preparation for our Halloween party. In art, the children will decorate Halloween bags to use in the parade on Thursday. The story is *It's Pumpkin Time*. During group time, the children will decorate a big pumpkin. We will be singing a variety of Halloween songs, including "Did You Ever See a Pumpkin?"

Tuesday

Today the children will be construction workers. They will construct the house that they will decorate tomorrow. In art, children will make paper jack-o'-lanterns. We will read *Trick or Treat, Little Critter* at storytime. For group time, we will focus on the letter *J* (for jack-o'-lantern). Our special song will be "Three Little Witches."

Wednesday

Today the children will decorate our Halloween House in dramatic play. They will put up decorations, and we will all have a Halloween party at our house. In art, the children will make things to decorate the house, such as ghosts, skeletons, and bats. Our story is *Halloween Day*. Children will learn about the bones in a skeleton today in group. "Five Little Pumpkins" will be featured in music, along with other Halloween songs.

Thursday

Today is the big day! The children will dress in their costumes after they get to school. Then they will parade around the building to show off their costumes. During storytime, the children will read *Trick or Treat Faces*. During group time, we will talk about trick-or-treat safety. Our songs for the day are a variety of Halloween songs.

Monday

Dramatic Play	Art	Group	Story	Song
Grocery Store	Halloween Bags	Decorating Pumpkins	*It's Pumpkin Time*	"Did You Ever See a Pumpkin?"

DAILY PLANNING GUIDE

Language and Literacy Skills Facilitated

Vocabulary: *groceries, cart, cereal, shop, checker, buy, sell, bag, sack, shelf, money, change*

Verb phrase structures: *eat<u>s</u>, <u>is</u> eat<u>ing</u>, <u>ate</u>, <u>has eaten</u>, push<u>es</u>, <u>is</u> push<u>ing</u>, push<u>ed</u>, buy<u>s</u>, <u>bought</u>, check<u>s</u>, <u>is</u> check<u>ing</u>, check<u>ed</u>*

Adjective/object descriptions: *big/little bag, full/empty shelf*

Question structures: *what, how, where, when, who, what if, why, how many, which one*

Pronouns: *I, you, he, she, we, they, my, your, her, his, our, their, me, us, them*

Prepositions: *in, on, under, over, near, beneath, next to, beside, around, inside, outside*

Sounds: /sh/ <u>sh</u>elf, pu<u>sh</u>; /k/ <u>c</u>art, sa<u>ck</u>; /s/ <u>s</u>ell, cart<u>s</u>

Noting print has meaning: names on chairs and on cubbies, signs in dramatic play, words in books and on chalkboard

Noting sound–symbol associations: What sound does _____ start with?

Writing: letters, names, words

Social Skills Facilitated

Initiating interaction with peers and adults; responding to questions and requests from peers and adults

Negotiating with peers for toys and materials

Group cooperation: waiting for a turn in a group, taking a turn at the appropriate time

Cognitive Skills Facilitated

Problem-solving skills: what to buy

Classification skills: fruits, vegetables, meats

Sequencing skills: songs, story

Narrative/story structure: labeling book

Motor Skills Facilitated

Large motor: outdoor play activities—jumping, running, hopping, pedaling, climbing

Small motor: writing, drawing, gluing

DRAMATIC PLAY **Grocery Store**

Type of Activity: Sequential

Objectives
1. Learn new, and employ familiar, vocabulary
2. Learn new, and employ a variety of, syntactic constructions
3. Interact with peers
4. Sequence familiar routines
5. Expand conceptual knowledge of the world

Settings
- Grocery store
- Shelves and aisles
- Check-out stand
- Customers' home

Props
- Shelves
- Canned goods and other food items
- Fruit and vegetable area
- Pumpkins
- Pretend cash register
- Pretend money
- Pretend credit cards
- Pretend coupons
- Shopping carts
- Grocery bags
- Pencil and paper for making lists
- Table for checkout area

Roles
- Shoppers
- Cashiers
- Stockers
- Baggers

General Description of Activity

The children pretend to go grocery shopping. They can make lists, take their "children" with them, choose the items on the list to put in their carts, pay, bag their groceries, and go home. Other children can be the grocery store workers. Some can keep the shelves stocked, and others can be checkers and baggers.

Verbal Productions

Level of linguistic complexity varies with the role or competency of the child playing the role.
- "Will that be all? Your total is $5" or "All? Five!"
- "Milk, please" or "Milk"
- "Do you have any cereal?" or "Want cereal"
- "How much does my pumpkin weigh?" or "Big pumpkin"

Adult Facilitative Role

The adult is to facilitate role play and help expand language and literacy skills. Typical actions or strategies to use include

Playing a role: "That will be $10 for your groceries."

Modeling correct production of /k/ sound: "The carrots cost $1, and the corn costs $1.50."

Modeling the reading of a sign: "That sign says *apples*, and this sign says *meat*."

Redirecting a child to a peer: "Ask Steven for the cart. Say, 'It is my turn now.'"

Contrasting error and correct sound of /s/ (focus contrast): "Did you say 'tip' or 'sip'?"

ART **Halloween Bags**

Objectives
1. Express creativity
2. Develop small motor skills (e.g., drawing, painting, cutting, pasting)
3. Practice turn-taking skills
4. Converse with peers and adults

Materials
- Brown grocery bags, one for each child
- Various Halloween cutouts
- Markers
- Stamps and stamp pads (optional)
- Stickers (optional)

General Description of Activity

Children decorate brown grocery bags with construction paper cutouts or stamps of Halloween items (e.g., ghosts, bats, skeletons, pumpkins). Stickers can also be used. The decorated bags are then taken on a trick-or-treat parade later in the week.

GROUP : **Decorating Pumpkins**

Objectives
1. Improve listening skills
2. Increase sequencing ability
3. Learn appropriate group-interaction skills
4. Practice turn-taking skills

Materials
- Large pumpkin
- Markers
- Carving tool (optional)

General Description of Activity

Place a large pumpkin (real one) in front of the children. Tell the children that they are going to decide how to decorate the pumpkin to make a face.

Group Participation

After some discussion with the children about what features and what shapes should be used, have one child come to the front to draw an eye on the pumpkin. Have another child draw the other eye. Other children can draw other features of the pumpkin face, such as hair, ears, nose, a mouth with funny teeth, and so on.

Variation

After the face is sketched out, carve the pumpkin into a jack-o'-lantern. Children can help scrape out the inside of the pumpkin. Save the seeds to roast later for a special Halloween treat.

Summary/Transition Activity

After the face is finished, review the features of the face. Ask the children if it is a scary or a friendly face.

Tuesday

Dramatic Play	Art	Group	Story	Song
Construction Worker	Jack-o'-lanterns	Letter *J*	*Trick or Treat, Little Critter*	"Three Little Witches"

DAILY PLANNING GUIDE

Language and Literacy Skills Facilitated

Vocabulary: *construction, build, building, hammer, nail, fix, make, work, hard hat, safety, paint*

Verb phrase structures: *is build<u>ing</u>, construct<u>ed</u>, <u>built</u>, hammer<u>ed</u>, Who <u>is</u> building? I <u>am</u>, mak<u>es</u>, carri<u>es</u>*

Adjective/object descriptions: *large/small _____, heavy/light _____, hard/soft material*

Question structures: *what, how, where, when, who, what if, why, how many, which one*

Pronouns: *I, you, he, she, we, they, my, your, her, his, our, their, me, us, them*

Prepositions: *in, on, under, over, near, beneath, next to, beside, around, inside, outside*

Sounds: /f/ <u>f</u>ix, <u>f</u>un, of<u>f</u>; /s/ <u>s</u>ize, walk<u>s</u>; /k/ <u>c</u>onstru<u>c</u>t, <u>c</u>an, ma<u>k</u>e

Noting print has meaning: names on chairs and on cubbies, signs in dramatic play, words in books and on chalkboard

Noting sound–symbol associations: What sound does _____ start with?

Writing: letters, names, words

Social Skills Facilitated

Initiating interaction with peers and adults; responding to questions and requests from peers and adults

Negotiating with peers for toys and materials

Group cooperation: waiting for a turn in a group, taking a turn at the appropriate time

Cognitive Skills Facilitated

Problem-solving skills: how to make a building

Classification skills: tools we use to construct things

Sequencing skills: songs, steps in building, stories

Narrative/story structure: adventure

Motor Skills Facilitated

Large motor: outdoor play activities—jumping, running, hopping, pedaling, climbing

Small motor: writing, drawing, gluing, pounding

DRAMATIC PLAY   Construction Worker

Type of Activity: Related

Objectives
1. Learn new, and employ familiar, vocabulary
2. Learn new, and employ a variety of, syntactic constructions
3. Interact with peers
4. Sequence familiar routines
5. Expand conceptual knowledge of the world

Settings
- Street (floor marked with masking tape) lined with houses made from a variety of materials (e.g., blocks, cardboard houses)

Props
- Playhouse
- Cardboard box additions that can be taped to the toy house
- LEGOs
- Blocks
- Play bricks
- Paper strips of various colors for roof or siding
- Glue
- Tools (e.g., plastic hammers, wrenches, saws, screwdrivers, screws)
- Tool belts
- Pegs for pounding (i.e., wooden clothespins that can be pounded into cardboard)
- Play hard hats
- Masking tape
- Telephones

Roles
- Carpenters
- Architects
- Homeowners
- Other construction workers

General Description of Activity

A construction/repair dramatic play involves putting together different materials to make buildings. A variety of materials can be used. One area can be set up for constructing buildings with LEGOs or other blocks. Another area can be designated for a new addition to the playhouse (using big boxes). A third area can utilize play bricks and boxes to make another house. The children can problem-solve how to construct houses or apartments by rearranging the boxes, bricks, and blocks. (Some of the houses could be doll size, while others could be big enough for the children to play in.)

Houses may also need to be repaired. The roof can be replaced by making "shingles" out of paper bag strips. The strips could be laid on top of cardboard. (Remind children to start at the outer edge and overlay the shingles so that "rain" will roll off the roof, not under the shingles.) The children can put new siding on a house by using strips of colored paper and glue, and wallpaper can be put on the inside of the houses.

Verbal Productions

Level of linguistic complexity varies with the role or competency of the child playing the role.
- "I'm building a big house" or "Me build house"
- "We need to make that side higher. Call the carpenter" or "Higher"
- "Look, I pounded the nail into the wall" or "Look"

Adult Facilitative Role

Playing a role: "I am painting the wall. You paint that side."

Modeling a statement/vocabulary: "That is a wrench. This is a screwdriver."

Expanding a child's utterance: "Joe help me" to "Joe helped me fix the window."

Using a cloze procedure: "Here is the paint; there are the paint _____ (brushes)."

Using event casting: "Billy is pounding the nails and Sally is fixing the door. Jane is putting shingles on the roof. Look, Mike is sanding the board."

ART **Jack-o'-Lanterns**

Objectives
1. Express creativity
2. Develop small motor skills (drawing, painting, cutting, pasting, etc.)
3. Practice turn-taking skills
4. Converse with peers and adults

Materials
- Construction-paper cutouts in the shape of pumpkins, various sizes (at least one per child)
- Construction-paper cutouts in various sizes and shapes (e.g., circles, triangles, rectangles, crescents)
- Containers for the cutouts (one per shape)

- Glue sticks
- Sheets of black construction paper
- Scissors
- Miniature pumpkins (optional—at least one per child)
- Black markers (optional)
- Shallow container (optional)

General Description of Activity

Each child makes a jack-o'-lantern out of a construction-paper cutout in the shape of a pumpkin by pasting on eyes, a nose, and a mouth. The shapes should be in separate containers so children can easily choose the shapes they want. The children can add other decorations, if they wish, by cutting out extra shapes.

Variation

Instead of separating the various cutout shapes, put all the cutouts in one shallow container so children must communicate to get the pieces they want. Another option is for each child to decorate a real miniature pumpkin using a black marker to indicate the eyes, a nose, a mouth, teeth, and so forth.

GROUP **Letter *J***

Objectives
1. Improve listening skills
2. Increase knowledge of the alphabet and sounds
3. Learn appropriate group-interaction skills
4. Practice turn-taking skills

Materials
- Alphabet chart and other alphabet displays
- Blackboard and chalk or poster paper and markers
- Pictures of objects (or objects themselves) with names that begin with *J*
- Picture dictionary (or an alphabet video dictionary)

General Description of Activity

Write an upper- and a lowercase letter *J* on the blackboard (or on poster paper). Give several examples of words that begin with *J*, emphasizing the /j/ sound at the beginning of the words. You might also hold up pictures of objects (or objects themselves) with names that begin with *J*. Direct the children's attention to the alphabet picture displays around the room. One featured word could be *jack-o'-lantern*.

Group Participation

Ask if anyone's name starts with *J* (e.g., Jessica, Jimmy, Jaquan), and have these children write the letter *J* on the blackboard (or poster paper). Also have two or three other children whose names do not begin with *J* write the letter *J* on the blackboard. Provide guidance as the children form the letter: "Start at the top, draw a line straight down, and make a curved line to the left." If necessary, help children write the letter. Some of the other children can practice writing *J* in the air with their fingers (or on individual chalkboards). Ask the children to think of words that begin with *J*. Write the words they offer on the blackboard, drawing quick sketches (when possible) of the suggested words. If a child suggests a word that does not begin with *J*, say, "No, that begins with ____," and say the two sounds so children can compare them. If children cannot think of any words, prompt them with pictures or objects representing *J* words. (Pictures or objects can be handed out at the beginning of the lesson or as the lesson proceeds.) Additional words can be sought in a picture dictionary if the group has difficulty arriving at words that begin with *J*.

Summary/Transition Activity

After about 10–15 words have been suggested, review the words, emphasizing the *J* sound.

Wednesday

Dramatic Play	Art	Group	Story	Song
Halloween House Decorating	Ghosts, Bats, and Skeletons	Bones in a Skeleton	*Halloween Day*	"Five Little Pumpkins"

DAILY PLANNING GUIDE

Language and Literacy Skills Facilitated

Vocabulary: *Halloween, house, dough, witches, broomstick, construct, cookie cutters, glue, paste, helper, fix*

Verb phrase structures: *builds the house, is building, built, fixes, was fixing, fixed, pastes the paper, pasted the paper*

Adjective/object descriptions: *black cat, black house, orange pumpkin*

Question structures: *what, how, where, when, who, what if, why, how many, which one*

Pronouns: *I, you, he, she, we, they, my, your, her, his, our, their, me, us, them*

Prepositions: *in, on, under, over, near, beneath, next to, beside, around, inside, outside*

Sounds: /ch/ *child, witches, witch*; /s/ *see, misses, cats*; /k/ *cat, make*; /r/ *run, carrot*

Noting print has meaning: names on chairs and on cubbies, signs in dramatic play, words in books and on chalkboard

Noting sound–symbol associations: What sound does _____ start with?

Writing: letters, names, words

Social Skills Facilitated

Initiating interaction with peers and adults; responding to questions and requests from peers and adults.

Negotiating with peers for toys and materials

Group cooperation: waiting for a turn in a group, taking a turn at the appropriate time

Cognitive Skills Facilitated

Problem-solving skills: how to build an extra room

Classification skills: Halloween things

Sequencing skills: songs, story

Narrative/story structure: adventure

Motor Skills Facilitated

Large motor: outdoor play activities—jumping, running, hopping, pedaling, climbing

Small motor: writing, drawing, gluing, molding clay

DRAMATIC PLAY **Halloween House Decorating**

Type of Activity: Central

Objectives
1. Learn new, and employ familiar, vocabulary
2. Learn new, and employ a variety of, syntactic constructions
3. Interact with peers
4. Sequence familiar routines
5. Expand conceptual knowledge of the world

Setting
- House with cardboard extensions or other big boxes
- Kitchen area/play house area

Props
- Decorations (e.g., bats, spiders, webs, pumpkins, witches, skeletons, ghosts)
- Tables and chairs
- Kitchen appliances
- Dishes and play food

Roles
- Decorators
- Family members
- Guests

General Description of Activity

The children decorate the house area with Halloween decorations. The area may be expanded by attaching a 3" × 10" piece of cardboard to the playhouse so children have more area to decorate. Decorations might consist of paper bats, Kleenex ghosts, cotton spider webs, or commercial decorations that are glued or otherwise attached to the cardboard. After the decorations are completed, children can have a party in their "haunted" house.

Verbal Productions

The level of linguistic complexity can vary with the role or competence of the child playing the role.
- "I have two ghosts and one bat. I'm gluing them here" or "My bats here"
- "That looks very scary" or "That scary"
- "I am wearing a ghost costume for Halloween" or "Me ghost"

Adult Facilitative Role

The adult is to facilitate role play and help expand language and literacy skills. Typical actions or strategies to use include

Playing a role: "Let's put the spider webs here. Our house is scary."

Expanding a child's utterance: "Put ghost here" to "Put the big ghost here and put the little ghost there."

Asking open questions: "What are you wearing for Halloween?"

ART **Ghosts, Bats, and Skeletons**

Objectives
1. Express creativity
2. Develop small motor skills (e.g., drawing, painting, cutting, pasting)
3. Practice turn-taking skills
4. Converse with peers and adults

Materials
- Box of white Kleenex
- 5" yarn strings
- Skeleton line drawings
- Black paper
- Ghost line drawings (optional)

General Description of Activity

Children make ghosts out of Kleenex by taking one Kleenex and crushing it into a ball. They cover this ball with another Kleenex. Tie a piece of yarn around the Kleenex for the children in such a way that the crushed ball forms the head of the ghost and the rest of the second Kleenex flows down from the head. The child then makes facial features (eyes, mouth, nose) using a black marker. They can use the ghosts to decorate the Halloween house. Some children may want to cut ghost shapes out of line drawings and paste these on the house. They can also make skeletons by cutting out line drawings of skeleton heads and pasting them onto black paper. The children add the other bones by using white chalk to draw ribs, arms, legs, etc. These pictures also can be used as house decorations.

Variation

Have children cut bats out of black paper and tape them to the Halloween house.

GROUP **Bones in a Skeleton**

Objectives
1. Improve listening skills
2. Increase conceptual knowledge
3. Learn appropriate group-interaction skills
4. To practice turn-taking skills

Materials
- Skeleton
- List of scientific names of bones (optional)

General Description of Activity

The children look at "Smiley" the skeleton or at a cardboard cutout of a skeleton. Tell the children that Smiley has a lot of bones and that they are going to take turns finding some of the bones. Ask one child to point to one of Smiley's toes and another child to locate one of Smiley's fingers.

Group Participation

One by one, the children find bones on their own bodies and then locate them on Smiley (e.g., ribs, hand bones, wrist bone, arm, leg, shoulder, head, jaw).

Variation

Some children might be interested in learning the scientific as well as common names of some of the bones (for example, *femur* is a leg bone; *radius* and *ulna* are arm bones, and *patella* is the kneecap).

Summary/Transition Activity

Review the bones the group has talked about by locating them on the skeleton.

Thursday

Dramatic Play	Art	Group	Story	Song
Halloween Parade	(No art)	Trick-or-Treat Safety	*Trick or Treat Faces*	Review Halloween songs

DAILY PLANNING GUIDE

Language and Literacy Skills Facilitated

Vocabulary: *trick-or-treat, Halloween, witches, ghosts, cats, costumes, candy, Halloween bag, fun, parade, masks, pretend, spider*

Verb phrase structures: *is wearing a mask, wore a costume, walks in a parade, walked, was walking, "Who has a costume?" I do*

Adjective/object descriptions: *scary mask, funny mask, long parade*

Question structures: *what, how, where, when, who, what if, why, how many, which one*

Pronouns: *I, you, he, she, we, they, my, your, him, her, his, our, their, me, us, them*

Prepositions: *in, on, under, over, near, beneath, next to, beside, around, inside, outside*

Sounds: /r/ *run, parade*; /s/ *see, costume, nice*; /f/ *fun, telephone, off*; /ch/ *child, witches, which*

Noting print has meaning: names on chairs and on cubbies, signs in dramatic play, words in books and on chalkboard

Noting sound–symbol associations: What sound does _____ start with?

Writing: letters, names, words

Social Skills Facilitated

Initiating interaction with peers and adults; responding to questions and requests from peers and adults

Negotiating with peers for toys and materials

Group cooperation: waiting for a turn in a group, taking a turn at the appropriate time

Cognitive Skills Facilitated

Problem-solving skills: where to go to trick-or-treat

Classification skills: Halloween goodies

Sequencing skills: story, video

Motor Skills Facilitated

Large motor: outdoor play activities—jumping, running, hopping, pedaling, climbing

Small motor: pouring juice

DRAMATIC PLAY **Halloween Parade**

Type of Activity: Central

Objectives
1. Learn new, and employ familiar, vocabulary
2. Learn new, and employ a variety of, syntactic constructions
3. Interact with peers
4. Sequence familiar routines
5. Expand conceptual knowledge of the world

Settings
- Halloween house
- Parade throughout the building or around the classroom

Props
- Children's costumes
- Decorated house
- Trick-or-treat bags (optional)
- Treats

Roles
- Different characters/creatures (e.g., ghosts, Superman, Spiderman, fairy princess)
- Hosts (party—optional)
- Guests (party—optional)

General Description of Activity

The children get dressed in their costumes (either ones they have brought from home or ones borrowed/made at school). They then get in a line and parade around the room or throughout the building so all can see their costumes. They may carry trick-or-treat bags and staff members may provide treats for the bag (optional). They may be asked to sing some Halloween songs. When children return to the classroom, they have a party in their Halloween house that they decorated earlier in the week.

Verbal Productions

Level of linguistic complexity can vary with the role or competence of the child playing the role.
- "I am Spiderman. I have a red cape" or "Spiderman"
- "I have a trick-or-treat bag at home" or "My bag"
- "We have a long parade with lots of scary people" or "Me scary"

Adult Facilitative Role

The adult is to facilitate role play and help expand language and literacy skills. Typical actions or strategies to use include

Playing a role: "We are lining up for our Halloween parade."

Modeling a statement: "Say, 'trick or treat.'"

Expanding a child's utterance: "He candy" to "Yes, he has a lot of candy."

Identifying rhyming words: Yes, the words *candy*, *sandy*, and *Mandy* all rhyme."

Contrasting error response with correct response (focus contrast): "You say 'tandy,' but I say 'candy.'"

GROUP **Trick-or-Treat Safety**

Objectives
1. Improve listening skills
2. Increase sequencing ability
3. Increase knowledge of story telling
4. Learn appropriate group-interaction skills
5. Practice turn-taking skills

Materials
- Chalkboard and chalk
- Trick-or-treat bag

General Description of Activity

Show the children a trick-or-treat bag (one the children have made or a commercial one). Tell the group that sometimes children dress up in costumes for Halloween and then go to different neighbors' houses to show the costumes. The neighbors often will give treats to the children for their trick-or-treat bags. The neighbors may ask the children for a "trick," which means that the children sing a song or do some other "trick" before they get their treat.

Tell the children that there are several things they should remember in order to be safe when going trick-or-treating. One thing is to only trick-or-treat at houses where the children know the people. Ask the children if there are other things they need to do to be safe.

Group Participation

Ask children to suggest some safety rules for trick-or-treating. Some of them might be

1. Take a flashlight, because it may be dark.
2. Wear light-colored clothing or reflector tape so that other people can see you.
3. Always go with an adult.
4. Be careful crossing streets.
5. Don't eat any of the treats until they have been examined by your parents.
6. Be careful that your costume allows you to walk safely.
7. If you wear a mask, be careful that you can easily see out of it.

If the children don't suggest some of these safety rules, make the suggestions yourself. You may also want to write down the rules generated (or make quick sketches).

Summary/Transition Activity

Review the safety rules by reading back the list.

November

Activities	Monday	Tuesday	Wednesday	Thursday
Week 11 — Things Big Kids Do				
Dramatic Play	Work on Cars	Newspaper Route	Fast-Food Job	Babysitting
Art	Shape Pictures	Newspaper Collage	Playdough	Fingerpainting
Group	Sound Patterns	Write a Class Newsletter	Letter *K*	Color Red
Story	*Red Light, Green Light*	*Curious George Rides a Bike*	*Froggy Eats Out*	*Just Me and My Little Sister*
Song	"Twinkle, Twinkle, Traffic Light"	"Extra, Extra, Read All About It"	"I Like to Eat Apples and Bananas"	"Rock-a-Bye Baby"
Week 12 — All About Animals				
Dramatic Play	Farm	Zoo	Pet Store	Rodeo
Art	Easel Painting	Animal Rubbings	Animal Stamps and Craft Stick Cages	Lace a Cowboy Boot
Group	Letter *L*	Zoo/Farm Animals Classification	How to Write a *3*	Act out a Story *(The Cow Who Went Oink)*
Story	*If You Give a Pig a Pancake*	*Zoo Song*	*Franklin Gets a Pet*	*The Cow Who Went Oink*
Song	"Old MacDonald Had a Farm"	"Five Little Monkeys"	"How Much Is that Doggy in the Window?"	"Shake Your Sillies Out"
Week 13 — Taking Care of Ourselves and Our World				
Dramatic Play	A Day in the Park	Utility Worker	Hospital/Paramedic	Sanitation Worker
Art	Pinecone Bird Feeders	String Painting	Create a Face	Trash Collage
Group	Color Patterns	Letter *M*	What Is Your Address?	Recycling (Classification)
Story	*Are You My Mother?*	*Katy and the Big Snow*	*Teddy Bear Cures a Cold*	*The Berenstain Bears Don't Pollute*
Song	"Raindrops and Lemondrops"	"It's a Small World"	"Head, Shoulders, Knees, and Toes"	"The Cleanup Song"
Week 14 — Homes— Thanksgiving Week				
Dramatic Play	Pilgrims	Native American Homes	Our Home Today	Thanksgiving Day— no school
Art	Food Collage	Cheerios Necklaces	Watercolor Paintings	
Group	Alphabet Grab Bag	Letter *N*	Thankfulness List	
Story	*Friendship's First Thanksgiving*	*The Legend of the Bluebonnet*	*Thanksgiving Today*	
Song	"London Bridge"	"A Turkey Is a Funny Bird"	"Five Little Turkeys"	
Week 15 — Adventure				
Dramatic Play	Pioneers	Space Exploration	Under-the-Sea Exploration	Jungle/Safari
Art	Playdough	Space Pictures	Crayon Washes	Coffee Filter/ Clothespin Butterflies
Group	Letter *O*	Things that Fly	Sorting Shells	Tapping out Syllables
Story	*And You Can Be the Cat*	*Big Silver Space Shuttle*	*Rainbow Fish to the Rescue*	*Peanut Butter Rhino*
Song	"She'll Be Coming 'Round the Mountain"	"Twinkle, Twinkle, Little Star"	"All the Little Fishies"	"Tarzan of the Apes"

WEEKLY PLANNING GUIDE

	Dramatic Play	Art	Group	Story	Song
Monday *Suggested Props and Materials*	Work on Cars *Gas station and car wash scenarios, appointment book and pencil or crayon, toy cash register, pretend money, hoses for pumps, car with hood, dashboard, tools, pretend battery, pretend computer, pretend cans for oil change, play telephones, hoses, sponges*	Shape Pictures *Paper circles, squares, triangles; colored construction paper; glue*	Sound Patterns *Drum, patterns, keyboard (optional)*	*Red Light, Green Light*	"Twinkle, Twinkle, Traffic Light"
Tuesday *Suggested Props and Materials*	Newspaper Route *Newspaper carrier scenario, at least two to three house areas with "porches," paper bag carrier bags, rubber bands, dispatch office*	Newspaper Collage *Comics, strips of paper to make comic strip, scissors to cut out comics, or sequence pictures*	Write a Class Newsletter *Poster paper with columns, marker*	*Curious George Rides a Bike*	"Extra, Extra, Read All About It"
Wednesday *Suggested Props and Materials*	Fast-Food Job *Fast-food restaurant scenario, counters, drink counter, hamburgers, french fries, other pretend food, cash register, play money*	Playdough *Smocks, playdough, rolling pins, cookie cutters, presses, wooden craft sticks*	Letter *K* *Objects or pictures of items beginning with K, chalkboard, chalk, sticky notes (optional)*	*Froggy Eats Out*	"I Like to Eat Apples and Bananas"
Thursday *Suggested Props and Materials*	Babysitting *Babysitter scenario, two house areas, dolls, cooking items, blankets, bottles, books, pretend TV*	Fingerpainting *Fingerpaint, smocks, fingerpaint paper*	Color Red *Red paper, variety of red objects, red tub, yellow tub, blue tub, four yellow objects, two blue objects*	*Just Me and My Little Sister*	"Rock-a-Bye Baby"

MY NOTES

NEWSLETTER

Vol. 1, No. 11

Date: _____

Things Big Kids Do

Monday

Teenagers like cars, and today the children will pretend to be mechanics and fix cars. In art, they will make shape pictures. Our story is *Red Light, Green Light*. During group time, children will identify and match sound patterns. Our featured song is "Twinkle, Twinkle, Traffic Light."

Tuesday

This is another great day to learn about jobs for big kids. Today the children will be newspaper carriers. They will roll newspapers and deliver them to their customers. In art, the children will create a newspaper collage. Our Tuesday story is *Curious George Rides a Bike*. During group time, we will write a class newsletter. Our song is the chant "Extra, Extra, Read All About It."

Wednesday

In dramatic play today, the children will be fast-food workers. They will cook food and sell it to hungry people. The food theme continues in art, where the children will make "food" items out of playdough. The story for Wednesday is *Froggy Eats Out*. Group time will be about the letter *K*. "I Like to Eat Apples and Bananas" is the featured song for today.

Thursday

What a fun day for the children! Today they will pretend to be babysitters during dramatic play and take care of babies and children. In art, they will fingerpaint. The story will be *Just Me and My Little Sister*. During group time, we will focus on the color red. Please have your child wear something red today. Our song for today is "Rock-a-Bye Baby."

Monday

Dramatic Play	Art	Group	Story	Song
Work on Cars	Shape Pictures	Sound Patterns	*Red Light, Green Light*	"Twinkle, Twinkle, Traffic Light"

DAILY PLANNING GUIDE

Language and Literacy Skills Facilitated

Vocabulary: *transportation, vehicle, car, track, garage, mechanic, truck, finish, battery, brakes, ignition, hose, tools, engine, wheels, shapes, rectangle, square, circle, triangle*

Verb phrase structures: *work<u>s</u>, is work<u>ing</u>, crash<u>ed</u> the car, push<u>ed</u> it, <u>was</u> rac<u>ing</u>, start<u>s</u>, stopp<u>ed</u>, fix<u>ed</u> the car*

Adjective/object descriptions: *broken part, dead battery, big/little*

Question structures: *what, how, where, when, who, what if, why, how many, which one*

Pronouns: *I, you, he, she, we, they, my, your, him, her, his, our, their, me, us, them*

Prepositions: *in, on, under, over, near, beneath, next to, beside, around, inside, outside*

Sounds: /r/ <u>r</u>ace, star<u>t</u>er, ca<u>r</u>; /s/ <u>s</u>ee, mi<u>ss</u>es, mi<u>ss</u>; /sh/ <u>sh</u>ape, fini<u>sh</u>; blends: <u>fl</u>ag, <u>tr</u>uck, <u>st</u>art

Noting print has meaning: names on chairs and on cubbies, signs in dramatic play, words in books and on chalkboard

Noting sound–symbol associations: What sound does _____ start with?

Writing: letters, names, words

Social Skills Facilitated

Initiating interaction with peers and adults; responding to questions and requests from peers and adults

Negotiating with peers for toys and materials

Group cooperation: waiting for a turn in a group, taking a turn at the appropriate time

Cognitive Skills Facilitated

Problem-solving skills: how to fix the cars

Classification skills: different sound patterns

Sequencing skills: song, art

Narrative/story structure: labeling

Motor Skills Facilitated

Large motor: outdoor play activities—jumping, running, hopping, pedaling, climbing

Small motor: writing, drawing, gluing

DRAMATIC PLAY **Work on Cars**

Type of Activity: Related

Objectives
1. Learn new, and employ familiar, vocabulary
2. Learn new, and employ a variety of, syntactic constructions
3. Interact with peers
4. Sequence familiar routines
5. Expand conceptual knowledge of the world

Settings	• Garage/repair shop • Car lift (cardboard blocks holding a plastic • Desk truck high enough for a child to slide under) • Cashier's station • Car wash (optional) • Gas pumps

Settings
- Garage/repair shop
- Desk
- Cashier's station
- Gas pumps
- Car lift (cardboard blocks holding a plastic truck high enough for a child to slide under)
- Car wash (optional)

Props
- Appointment book and pencil or crayon
- Toy cash register
- Pretend money
- Hoses for pumps
- Dashboard
- Car with hood, which can be made out of cardboard
- Tools
- Pretend battery
- Pretend computer
- Pretend cans for oil change
- Play telephones
- Hoses
- Sponges

Roles
- Mechanics
- Customers
- Receptionist
- Sales clerk
- Cashier

General Description of Activity

Children take their vehicle to a gas station or garage to be repaired, gassed up, or tuned up. The oil in the car may need to be changed or the battery recharged. Customers can call ahead and make appointments. In one area, a receptionist/cashier desk is arranged. Another area might have a wooden or cardboard facsimile of a car with a hood that opens so that the mechanics can work under the hood if needed. Also, blocks or a vehicle Erector Set may be placed in one area to build cars. An optional activity is to have a parts counter or store.

Verbal Productions

Level of linguistic complexity varies with the role or competency of the child playing the role.
- "May I please have the wrench?" or "Wrench, please"
- "Please start the car now" or "Start"
- "My car needs a new battery" or "Battery"

Adult Facilitative Role

The adult is to facilitate role play and help expand language and literacy skills. Typical actions or strategies to use include

Playing a role: "My car won't start. I think the battery is bad."

Modeling a statement/vocabulary: "The engine makes the car go."

Modeling correct production of /f/: "The car needs to be <u>f</u>ixed. Turn the engine o<u>ff</u>. It's <u>f</u>un to work on cars."

Recasting an utterance: (preset tense to future tense): "I am working on the car. I will work on it again tomorrow."

Using a cloze procedure: "The red light means *stop*, the green light means _____ *(go)*."

ART : **Shape Pictures**

Objectives
1. Express creativity
2. Develop small motor skills (e.g., drawing, painting, cutting, pasting)
3. Practice turn-taking skills
4. Converse with peers and adults

Materials
- White construction paper
- Construction paper cutouts in different shapes, colors, and sizes
- Paste or glue sticks
- Scissors (optional) for children to make own shapes
- Extra construction paper

General Description of Activity

Children can make a variety of pictures or designs by pasting different cutout shapes on paper. They may paste the shapes to form people, animals, houses, toys, designs, and so on.

GROUP ACTIVITY PLAN **Sound Patterns**

Objectives
1. Improve listening skills
2. Increase ability to recognize and sequence patterns
3. Learn appropriate group-interaction skills
4. Practice turn-taking skills

Materials
- Drum
- Keyboard (optional)

General Description of Activity

Place a drum in front of the children. Tap out a simple pattern while the children listen, then repeat the pattern while they listen again. Invite one child to come up to the front and try to make the same pattern. If necessary, give assistance.

Group Participation

Play a different pattern and have another child try to match it. Continue until all the children have had at least one turn. The patterns can vary from two short taps to complicated patterns involving a series of taps grouped in two or three sequences. For example, one pattern might be *tap-tap-pause-tap*. Another might be *tap-tap-tap-pause-tap-tap*. Other sample patterns include the following:

tap-tap (pause) *tap-tap*

tap-tap-tap (pause) *tap*

tap (pause) *tap-tap*

loud tap (pause) soft tap

two loud taps (pause) two soft taps

Variation

Set a rhythm on the keyboard and have the children clap to the rhythm.

Summary/Transition Activity

Play one more pattern and have the children clap the pattern, or play a rhythm from a song that will be sung during music time and have the children clap out that rhythm.

Tuesday

Dramatic Play	Art	Group	Story	Song
Newspaper Route	Newspaper Collage	Write a Class Newsletter	*Curious George Rides a Bike*	"Extra, Extra, Read All About It"

DAILY PLANNING GUIDE

Language and Literacy Skills Facilitated

Vocabulary: *newspaper carrier, bag, rubber band, porch, payment, list, newsprint, headline, advertisement, bundle*

Verb phrase structures: *delivers papers, is tossing on porch, collected payment, was folding papers, carried paper bag, wrote story*

Adjective/object descriptions: *heavy papers, light load, funny papers, white paper, black ink, big _____, little ____*

Question structures: *what, how, where, when, who, what if, why, how many, which one*

Pronouns: *I, you, he, she, we, they, my, your, him, her, his, our, their, me, us, them*

Prepositions: *in, on, under, over, near, beneath, next to, beside, around, inside, outside*

Sounds: /k/ *carry, ink;* /s/ *sit, beside, toss;* /r/ *road, car, paper*

Noting print has meaning: names on chairs and on cubbies, signs in dramatic play, words in books and on chalkboard

Noting sound–symbol associations: What sound does _____ start with?

Writing: letters, names, words

Social Skills Facilitated

Initiating interaction with peers and adults; responding to questions and requests from peers and adults

Negotiating with peers for toys and materials

Group cooperation: waiting for a turn in a group, taking a turn at the appropriate time

Cognitive Skills Facilitated

Problem-solving skills: how to fold a newspaper, what to write in a newsletter

Classification skills: things in a newspaper

Sequencing skills: story and song/chant

Narrative/story structure: adventure

Motor Skills Facilitated

Large motor: outdoor play activities—jumping, running, hopping, pedaling, climbing

Small motor: writing, drawing, gluing, folding

DRAMATIC PLAY : **Newspaper Route**

Type of Activity: Sequential

Objectives
1. Learn new, and employ familiar, vocabulary
2. Learn new, and employ a variety of, syntactic constructions
3. Interact with peers
4. Sequence familiar routines
5. Expand conceptual knowledge of the world

Settings
- Newspaper office
- Homes (Each home could be represented by a chair with a doll [or another child.] A mat placed in front of the chair could represent the porch.)
- Streets (area of floor marked with masking tape)

Props
- Bags (two grocery bags cut in half with straps attached so that there is a bag in front and a bag in back)
- Newspapers
- Rubber bands
- Route lists
- Homes (chairs with dolls or children seated in them and mats placed as the porches)
- Play money
- Play telephones
- Desk (for newspaper office)
- Paper and pencils

Roles
- Carriers
- Customers
- Office workers

General Description of Activity

The children pretend to be newspaper carriers by counting newspapers, folding them, securing them with rubber bands, putting them in their delivery bag, and then delivering them to homes. It is important that the newspapers be delivered on the porch or placed in front of the door at each house or apartment. Children might have to call the newspaper office to have more papers delivered and collect money from the subscribers. The carrier also goes to the newspaper office each month to pay the bill for the number of papers delivered.

Verbal Productions

Level of linguistic complexity varies with the role or competency of the child playing the role.
- "Here's your paper" or "Paper"
- "I need five more papers for Lawrence Street" or "More paper"
- "He's collecting money for the newspaper. You owe $10" or "Money, please"

Adult Facilitative Role

The adult is to facilitate role play and help expand language and literacy skills. Typical actions or strategies to use include

Playing a role: "I have to roll 10 papers for my paper route."

Using event casting: "You put the newspaper on the mat. Look, she is picking up the paper. You are being a good paper carrier. You put the paper on the front step."

Modeling correct pronunciation of /l/: "Look, I have the list. I need to collect the money. I deliver papers to 10 people."

Providing a literacy model: "That word says 'play.'"

Expanding a child's utterance: "I frow paper" to "I am throwing the newspaper" (model of correct sound production and expansion of correct verb structure).

ART **Newspaper Collage**

Objectives
1. Express creativity
2. Develop small motor skills (e.g., drawing, painting, cutting, pasting)
3. Practice turn-taking skills
4. Converse with peers and adults

Materials
- White paper
- Scissors
- Newspapers (including cartoons)
- Sequence stories (optional)

General Description of Activity

Lay out white paper on the art table. Children can cut letters, cartoons, or pictures from newspaper and paste them on the paper to make a collage.

Variation

Draw lines on the paper so children can paste their "articles" in columns. The children can also use the cartoon pictures to tell a story.

GROUP **Write a Class Newsletter**

Objectives

1. Improve listening skills
2. Increase knowledge about newsletters
3. Improve sequencing skills
4. Learn appropriate group-interaction skills
5. Practice turn-taking skills

Materials

- Poster paper with columns drawn on it
- Tape
- Blackboard or chart holder
- Markers and crayons

General Description of Activity

On the blackboard, tape a large piece of poster paper with columns drawn on it to resemble a newspaper. Tell the children that they are going to write a class newsletter to tell their parents what has been happening in the class. Have the children come up with a title for the newsletter (e.g., "LAPlines"), and write the title at the top along with the date. Then ask children for ideas about what to write.

Group Participation

Write down the children's ideas. Have children come up two or three at a time to sign the articles or to draw pictures. You could write two or three news stories and write/illustrate a couple of advertisements.

Variation

Add comic strips, drawn by the children or an adult, or use an already prepared picture.

Summary/Transition Activity

Reread all of the stories, pointing out the headlines, bylines, illustrations, and so forth.

Wednesday

Dramatic Play	Art	Group	Story	Song
Fast-Food Job	Playdough	Letter *K*	*Froggy Eats Out*	"I Like to Eat Apples and Bananas"

DAILY PLANNING GUIDE

Language Skills Facilitated

Vocabulary: *fast food, hamburger, french fries, soft drinks, shakes, wrappers, cartons, cook, cashier, customer, order, pizza parlor, pizza*

Verb phrase structures: *place<u>s</u> an order, buy<u>s</u> a hamburger, pay<u>s</u> money, <u>eat</u> out, <u>is</u> mak<u>ing</u> a burger, serv<u>ed</u> the customer, flipp<u>ed</u> a burger, choose<u>s</u> a drink, <u>are</u> mak<u>ing</u> pizzas*

Adjective/object descriptions: *large drink, small hamburger, paper hat, red cup*

Question structures: *what, how, where, when, who, what if, why, how many, which one*

Pronouns: *I, you, he, she, we, they, my, your, him, her, his, our, their, me, us, them*

Prepositions: *<u>in</u> the cash register, <u>on</u> the plate, <u>near</u> the stove (in, on, under, over, near, beneath, next to, beside, around, inside, outside)*

Noting print has meaning: names on chairs and on cubbies, signs in dramatic play, words in books and on chalkboard

Noting sound–symbol associations: What sound does _____ start with?

Writing: letters, names, words

Social Skills Facilitated

Initiating interaction with peers and adults; responding to questions and requests from peers and adults

Negotiating with peers for toys and materials

Group cooperation: waiting for a turn in a group, taking a turn at the appropriate time

Cognitive Skills Facilitated

Problem-solving skills: setting up a restaurant, remembering items

Classification skills: things in a fast-food restaurant

Sequencing skills: putting a hamburger together, words to song

Narrative/story structure: adventure

Motor Skills Facilitated

Large motor: outdoor play activities—jumping, running, hopping, pedaling, climbing

Small motor: writing, drawing, gluing

DRAMATIC PLAY   **Fast-Food Job**

Type of Activity: Central

Objectives
1. Learn new, and employ familiar, vocabulary
2. Learn new, and employ a variety of, syntactic constructions
3. Interact with peers
4. Sequence familiar routines
5. Expand conceptual knowledge of the world

Settings
- Counter (or facsimile)
- Kitchen
- Eating area (booths or tables and chairs)
- Drive-up window (optional)

Props
- Cash register(s)
- Pretend money
- Dishes (plastic or Styrofoam)
- Soda pop dispenser (box lid with pretend levers)
- Posted menu
- Variety of pretend food (e.g., hamburgers, french fries)
- Pretend "Kids' Meals" (small boxes with little toys and pretend food inside)
- Paper bags
- Trays
- Dolls
- Walkie-talkie for the drive-thru cashier
- Pretend cars

Roles
- Customers
- Cooks
- Cashiers
- Custodians
- Drive-thru cashier

General Description of Activity

Children act out eating and working at a fast-food restaurant. They may have customers order food at a counter from a posted list of items. Cashiers could ring up the food order on a cash register, then place the prepared food on a tray or in a bag. The customer would pay for the food and either consume it at a table or booth or take it somewhere else to eat it. The restaurant might serve hamburgers, hot dogs, chicken sandwiches, roast beef sandwiches, french fries, salads, pizza, and so forth. Drinks may include soda pop, milk, coffee, milkshakes, and so forth. The dishes and utensils could be made of plastic or Styrofoam. The customers could bus their own dishes.

Verbal Productions

Level of linguistic complexity varies with the role or competency of the child playing the role.
- "May I take your order?" or "Yes?"
- "I want a hamburger, french fries, and a Coke" or "Coke, please"
- "He is cooking the french fries now" or "Cooking now"

Adult Facilitative Role

The adult is to facilitate role play and help expand language and literacy skills. Typical actions or strategies to use include

Playing a role: "Do you want some french fries with your hamburger?"

Contrasting present and past tense (focus contrast): "He is paying for the food. He paid me $10."

Modeling a statement/vocabulary: "The cash register is on the counter. Put the money in the cash register."

Providing confirmatory feedback: "Yes, hamburger starts with 'h.'"

Recasting a child's utterance: "He flips a hamburger" to "Yes, he flipped it over" (third person singular to past tense).

ART **Playdough**

Objectives
1. Express creativity
2. Develop small motor skills (e.g., drawing, painting, cutting, pasting)
3. Practice turn-taking skills
4. Converse with peers and adults

Materials
- Smocks
- Playdough
- Rolling pins
- Cookie cutters
- Presses or molds
- Wooden craft sticks
- Rolling boards (optional)

General Description of Activity

Children wash their hands and put on smocks to explore playdough at the art table, using various presses, cutters, rolling pins, wooden craft sticks, and other tools. Children can make pretend food or any other objects by rolling, cutting, or making pressing motions. They can form animals or people by rolling a main body and then adding heads, arms, and legs. Yarn can be used for hair (if children want to take their creations home). When children are finished, they roll the dough into a ball, wash their hands, and take off and fold their smocks.

GROUP **Letter K**

Objectives
1. Improve listening skills
2. Increase knowledge of the alphabet and sounds
3. Learn appropriate group-interaction skills
4. Practice turn-taking skills

Materials
- Alphabet chart and other alphabet displays
- Blackboard and chalk or poster paper and markers
- Pictures of objects (or objects themselves) with names that begin with K
- Picture dictionary (or an alphabet video dictionary)

General Description of Activity

Write an upper- and a lowercase letter K on the blackboard (or on poster paper). Give several examples of words that begin with K, emphasizing the /k/ sound at the beginning of the words. You might hold up pictures of objects (or objects themselves) with names that begin with K. Direct the children's attention to the alphabet picture displays around the room.

Group Participation

Ask if anyone's name starts with K (e.g., Katie, Kenyon), and have those children write the letter K on the blackboard (or poster paper). Also ask two or three other children whose names do not begin with K to write the letter K on the blackboard. Provide verbal guidance as children form the letters: "Start at the top, draw a line straight down, go back to the middle of the straight line and draw a slant to the top, go back to the middle of the straight line and draw a slant to the bottom." If necessary, help children write the letter. Some of the other children can practice writing K in the air with their fingers (or on individual chalkboards). Then ask the children to think of words that begin with K. Write the words they offer on the blackboard, drawing quick sketches (when possible) of the suggested words. If a child suggests a word that does not begin with K, say, "No, that begins with ___," and say the two sounds so children can compare them. To help children who cannot think of any words, prompt them with pictures or objects representing K words. (Pictures or objects can be handed out at the beginning of the lesson or as the lesson proceeds.) Additional words can be sought in a picture dictionary if the group has difficulty arriving at words that begin with K.

Summary/Transition Activity

After about 10–15 words have been suggested, review the words, emphasizing the K sound.

Thursday

Dramatic Play	Art	Group	Story	Song
Babysitting	Fingerpainting	Color Red	*Just Me and My Little Sister*	"Rock-a-Bye Baby"

DAILY PLANNING GUIDE

Language and Literacy Skills Facilitated

Vocabulary: *sitter, babysitter, babies, bath, story, highchair, crib, spoon, knife, fork, play, cry, feed, bottle, diaper*

Verb phrase structures: <u>is</u> crying, cr<u>ies</u>, cr<u>ied</u>, <u>will</u> cry, play<u>s</u>, play<u>ed</u>, eat<u>s</u>, <u>ate</u>, <u>has eaten</u>, sleep<u>s</u>, <u>slept</u>

Adjective/object descriptions: *happy baby, crying baby, cute baby, hungry baby, wet baby, funny toy*

Question structures: *what, how, where, when, who, what if, why, how many, which one*

Pronouns: *I, you, he, she, we, they, my, your, him, her, his, our, their, me, us, them*

Prepositions: *in, on, under, over, near, beneath, next to, beside, around, inside, outside*

Sounds: /k/ <u>c</u>over, ba<u>ck</u>; /t/ <u>t</u>op, si<u>tt</u>er, sa<u>t</u>; /f/ <u>f</u>our, o<u>f</u>ten, o<u>ff</u>

Noting print has meaning: names on chairs and on cubbies, signs in dramatic play, words in books and on chalkboard

Noting sound–symbol associations: What sound does _____ start with?

Writing: letters, names, words

Social Skills Facilitated

Initiating interaction with peers and adults; responding to questions and requests from peers and adults

Negotiating with peers for toys and materials

Group cooperation: waiting for a turn in a group, taking a turn at the appropriate time

Cognitive Skills Facilitated

Problem-solving skills: how to take care of babies

Classification skills: things a baby needs

Sequencing skills: songs, story

Narrative/story structure: adventure

Motor Skills Facilitated

Large motor: outdoor play activities—jumping, running, hopping, pedaling, climbing

Small motor: writing, drawing, gluing, constructing

DRAMATIC PLAY: **Babysitting**

Type of Activity: Central

Objectives
1. Learn new, and employ familiar, vocabulary
2. Learn new, and employ a variety of, syntactic constructions
3. Interact with peers
4. Sequence familiar routines
5. Expand conceptual knowledge of the world

Settings
- House(s)
- Park (optional)

Props
- Play stove
- Play refrigerator
- Tables and chairs
- Highchairs
- Cupboards, dishes, utensils, and bottles
- Play food
- Beds, blankets, and pillows
- Dolls
- Dolls' clothes
- Books
- Baby carriage
- Play bathtub
- Washcloths and towels
- Pretend soap
- Bath toys (e.g., rubber duck)

Roles
- Babysitters
- Children
- Babies
- Parents

General Description of Activity

Children act as babysitters and take care of babies and children. They might feed and bathe the children, read them stories, play with them, take them for walks, put them to bed, and so forth.

Verbal Productions

Level of linguistic complexity varies with the role or competency of the child playing the role.
- "It's time for bed, now" or "Bed, now."
- "The baby needs a bottle. Please get it from the table" or "Bottle!"
- "First, I'll read you the story, and then you go to bed" or "Story, bed"

Adult Facilitative Role

The adult is to facilitate role play and help expand language and literacy skills. Typical actions or strategies to use include

Playing a role: "My baby is hungry. Please give me the bottle."

Contrasting two sounds (focus contrast): "Did you say 'key' or 'tea?'"

Expanding a child's utterance: "My baby cry" to "My baby cries."

Redirecting a child to a peer: "Ask Emily for a turn with the buggy. Say, 'May I have the buggy, please?'"

Asking an open question: "How should we dress the baby?"

ART **Fingerpainting**

Objectives
1. Express creativity
2. Develop small motor skills (e.g., drawing, painting, cutting, pasting)
3. Practice turn-taking skills
4. Converse with peers and adults

Materials
- Fingerpaints
- Fingerpaint paper
- Smocks
- Glitter (optional)

General Description of Activity

Put a dab of paint on each child's paper. The children can use their hands and fingers to smear the paint all over the paper, then draw and write in the paint with their fingers. The children can make abstract designs, make full hand prints, or use their fingers to draw pictures or write letters or numbers. Shaving cream can be used instead of paint and placed on a formboard rather than on paper. Fingerpainting is a good excuse to get messy and gooey. Some children love this; others may need some coaxing to get their fingers dirty.

Variation

For additional effect, mix glitter into the fingerpaint before the children create their designs.

GROUP **Color Red**

Objectives

1. Improve listening skills
2. Increase conceptual knowledge
3. Learn appropriate group-interaction skills
4. Practice turn-taking skills

Materials
- Red paper
- Variety of red objects
- Red tub
- Yellow tub
- Blue tub
- Four yellow objects
- Two blue objects

General Description of Activity

On the first Thursday of November, gather an assortment of red, blue, and yellow objects. At group time, hold up a piece of red construction paper and label the color as *red*. Ask the children to look around the room to locate other red objects. Have one child choose an object that is red from the pile of assorted objects and place it in the red tub (have a blue and yellow tub also available).

Group Participation

Have other children take turns choosing an item that is red and placing it in the red tub. Occasionally, ask a child to choose a blue item and place it in the blue tub or to choose a yellow item and place it in the yellow tub.

Variation

Some of the children may choose from different shades of the target color (e.g., choosing lighter red, fire-engine red, or different shades of yellow or blue).

Summary/Transition Activity

Because it is "red" day and all the children are wearing something red, dismiss the children one by one by asking them to point to the red color on their clothes.

Week 12
All About Animals

WEEKLY PLANNING GUIDE

	Dramatic Play	Art	Group	Story	Song
Monday *Suggested Props and Materials*	Farm *Farm scenario, cows, horses, barns, other farm animals, wagon, hats, tractor, sand or dirt for field (optional)*	Easel Painting *Easels, paper, tempera paint, brushes, smocks*	Letter *L* *Pictures and objects beginning with letter L*	*If You Give a Pig a Pancake*	"Old MacDonald Had a Farm"
Tuesday *Suggested Props and Materials*	Zoo *Zoo scenario, variety of zoo animals (bears, lion, tigers, giraffes), cages, train*	Animal Rubbings *Animal forms, paper, crayons with paper covering removed*	Zoo/Farm Animals Classification *Toy barn, toy fence, zoo mat, toy farm animals, toy zoo animals, pictures of farm and zoo animals (optional)*	*Zoo Song*	"Five Little Monkeys"
Wednesday *Suggested Props and Materials*	Pet Store *Pet store scenario, stuffed animals, birds, cages, pretend food, leashes, aquariums, fish, cash registers, pretend money*	Animal Stamps and Craft Stick Cages *Animal stamps, stamp pads, paper, wooden craft sticks, glue, markers, smocks*	How to Write a *3* *Cards with 3 written on them, chalkboards and chalk, number line, paper and pencils (optional)*	*Franklin Gets a Pet*	"How Much Is that Doggy in the Window?"
Thursday *Suggested Props and Materials*	Rodeo *Rodeo scenario, arena, spectator area, concession stand and pretend food, horses, cows, clown outfit, barrels for barrel racing, judges, judges' stand*	Lace a Cowboy Boot *Boot pictures with holes for lacing (out of cardstock), laces or yarn*	Act out a Story *(The Cow Who Went Oink)* *Story and props for the story*	*The Cow Who Went Oink*	"Shake Your Sillies Out"

MY NOTES

NEWSLETTER

Vol. 1, No. 12

Date: _____

All About Animals

Monday

The children will be farmers, pretending to take care of farm animals. They will make easel paintings in art. Our story is *If You Give a Pig a Pancake.* During group time, the children will learn about the letter *L* and words that begin with *L*. Today's song is "Old MacDonald Had a Farm."

Tuesday

The children will care for and visit the animals in the zoo today in dramatic play. They can be the zookeepers, the concession workers, or the visitors. Today's art activity is making animal rubbings. The children will hear a story called *Zoo Song.* During group time, the children will classify animals according to those who live at a zoo and those who live on a farm. "Five Little Monkeys" will be our featured song.

Wednesday

The classroom will become a pet store during dramatic play today. At the art table, the children will make animal stamp art. They might also make cages for their animals from craft sticks. The children will read *Franklin Gets a Pet.* During group time, the children will learn about writing the number *3*. One of our songs will be "How Much Is that Doggy in the Window?"

Thursday

Today the children will pretend to go to the rodeo and learn about animals they might find in a rodeo. The children can be spectators, vendors, or participants. In art, the children will lace a cowboy boot. Our story is *The Cow Who Went Oink,* which the children will act out at group time. The song for today is called "Shake Your Sillies Out."

Monday

Dramatic Play	Art	Group	Story	Song
Farm	Easel Painting	Letter *L*	*If You Give a Pig a Pancake*	"Old MacDonald Had a Farm"

DAILY PLANNING GUIDE

Language and Literacy Skills Facilitated

Vocabulary: *farm, barn, cow, horse, pig, goose, chicken, rabbit, feed, hay, fence, corral, milk, pail, silo, pen, tractor*

Verb phrase structures: *feeds, is feeding, fed the animals, milks, milked the cow, is bailing the hay, stacked the hay*

Adjective/object descriptions: *big/little _____, hungry _____, milking pail, white/brown/___ cow, yellow/____ chicken*

Question structures: *what, how, where, when, who, what if, why, how many, which one*

Pronouns: *I, you, he, she, we, they, my, your, him, her, his, our, their, me, us, them*

Prepositions: *in, on, under, over, near, beneath, next to, beside, around, inside, outside*

Sounds: /k/ cow, chicken, milk; /f/ farm, off; /m/ milk, hammer, them

Noting print has meaning: names on chairs and on cubbies, signs in dramatic play, words in books and on chalkboard

Noting sound–symbol associations: What sound does _____ start with?

Writing: letters, names, words

Social Skills Facilitated

Initiating interaction with peers and adults; responding to questions and requests from peers and adults

Negotiating with peers for toys and materials

Group cooperation: waiting for a turn in a group, taking a turn at the appropriate time

Cognitive Skills Facilitated

Problem-solving skills: things that start with *L*

Classification skills: animals on a farm

Sequencing skills: story, songs

Narrative/story structure: adventure, repetitive line

Motor Skills Facilitated

Large motor: outdoor play activities—jumping, running, hopping, pedaling, climbing,

Small motor: writing, drawing, cutting, pasting

DRAMATIC PLAY : **Farm**

Type of Activity: Central

Objectives
1. Learn new, and employ familiar, vocabulary
2. Learn new, and employ a variety of, syntactic constructions
3. Interact with peers
4. Sequence familiar routines
5. Expand conceptual knowledge of the world

Settings
- Farm house (child-sized house or dismantled cardboard boxes)
- Barn (child-sized house or dismantled cardboard boxes)
- Field (floor area marked with masking tape or pretend fences)
- Planting area (wading pool filled with sand or soil)

Props
- Pretend tractor
- Pretend machinery
- Cow to be milked (Latex gloves filled with milky water)
- Horses (yardsticks)
- Blocks for fencing
- Different farm animals (stuffed animals resembling horses, chickens, pigs)
- Hats
- Pretend seeds
- Scarecrow
- Trees (with removable Ping-Pong balls for fruit)

Roles
- Farmer(s)
- Farmer's helper(s)
- Different animals (the children pretend to be animals)
- Tractor operator
- Other machinery operators
- Milker (optional)
- Fruit pickers (optional)

General Description of Activity

Children act out the different roles and activities found on a farm. There may be animals to care for, such as cows, horses, pigs, and chickens. They may grow crops or run a dairy farm. Different types of activities can be designed around the farm theme. For example, if the focus is on animals, then a barn and corral areas are needed. If the focus is on growing food, then an area with soil in which to "plant" should be provided. For a focus on farm machinery, pretend tractors and other machinery should be available. A harvesting focus requires a variety of pretend crops. (Painted Ping-Pong balls can become apples to be harvested, particularly if Velcro is attached so the balls will stick to a cardboard tree.)

Verbal Productions

Level of linguistic complexity varies with the role or competency of the child playing the role.
- "It's my turn to feed the chickens" or "Feed chickens"
- "I plowed the field and then planted the corn" or "I plowed the field"
- "He is milking the cow" or "Milk cow"

Adult Facilitative Role

The adult is to facilitate role play and help expand language and literacy skills. Typical actions or strategies to use include

Playing a role: "I am feeding the hay to the cow. Do you want to help me?"

Using a cloze procedure: "This bucket is empty, and this bucket is _____ (full)."

Expanding a child's utterance: "Him big" to "He is a big horse." (This is a model of correct pronoun and expansion of verb form.)

Contrasting two location terms (focus contrast): "This chicken is on the nest. This chicken is between the nests."

Identifying rhyming words: "That's right. "Pig' and 'big' rhyme."

ART : **Easel Painting**

Objectives
1. Express creativity
2. Develop small motor skills (e.g., drawing, painting, cutting, pasting)
3. Practice turn-taking skills
4. Converse with peers and adults

Materials
- Smocks
- Easels
- Different colors of tempera
- Paint cups to hold the paint
- Large paintbrushes
- 9" × 12" or 12" × 18" paper
- Wooden rack or other area for drying

General Description of Activity

Set up two easel boards with a large piece of paper clipped to each. Set out 2–4 cups filled with tempera paint and a paintbrush in each cup. (It is helpful to have cup covers with holes in them for the brushes. As children dip the brushes into the paint and pull them through the hole, some of the excess paint is removed. It is also helpful to place the easel over plastic or newspaper so that the paint drips do not stain the floor.)

Children put on their smocks, dip the brush into the paint, and paint shapes, objects, or anything else they want. Sometimes children will paint a picture and then experiment by painting other colors on top. Let the children experiment with the tempera for some projects. Sometimes you might have the children tell you about their painting, and you can label it for display. (Let the children decide if they want their paintings displayed.) Have a designated area for drying the pictures, such as a wooden clothes rack.

GROUP **Letter _L_**

Objectives
1. Improve listening skills
2. Increase knowledge of the alphabet and sounds
3. Learn appropriate group-interaction skills
4. Practice turn-taking skills

Materials
- Alphabet chart and other alphabet displays
- Blackboard and chalk or poster paper and markers
- Pictures of objects (or objects themselves) with names that begin with _L_
- Picture dictionary (or an alphabet video dictionary)

General Description of Activity

Write an upper- and a lowercase letter _L_ on the blackboard (or on poster paper). Give several examples of words that begin with _L_, emphasizing the /l/ sound at the beginning of the words. You might hold up pictures of objects (or objects themselves) with names that begin with _L_. Direct the children's attention to the alphabet picture displays around the room.

Group Participation

Ask if anyone's name starts with _L_ (e.g., Laura, Liam, Lazaro), and have those children write the letter _L_ on the blackboard (or poster paper). Also have two or three other children whose names do not begin with L write the letter _L_ on the blackboard. Provide verbal guidance as children form the letter: "Start at the top, draw a line straight down, then draw a line to the right." If necessary, help children write the letter. Some of the other children can practice writing _L_ in the air with their fingers (or on individual chalkboards). Then ask the children to think of words that begin with _L_. Write the words they offer on the blackboard, drawing quick sketches (when possible) of the suggested words. If a child suggests a word that does not begin with _L_, say, "No, that begins with ___," and say the two sounds so children can compare them. To help children who cannot think of any words, prompt them with pictures or objects representing _L_ words. (Pictures or objects can be handed out at the beginning of the lesson or as the lesson proceeds.) Additional words can be sought in a picture dictionary if the group has difficulty arriving at words that begin with _L_.

Summary/Transition Activity

After about 10–15 words have been suggested, reviews the words, emphasizing the _L_ sound.

Tuesday

Dramatic Play	Art	Group	Story	Song
Zoo	Animal Rubbings	Zoo/Farm Animals Classification	Zoo Song	"Five Little Monkeys"

DAILY PLANNING GUIDE

Language and Literacy Skills Facilitated

Vocabulary: *zoo, elephant, giraffe, monkey, hippo, lion, tiger, roar, parrot, ticket booth, train, cage*

Verb phrase structures: *I am watching/watched _____, I see/saw _____, I am riding the train, he rides the train*

Adjective/object descriptions: *large/small elephant, loud monkey, soft fur, long/short train, long/short tail*

Question structures: *what, how, where, when, who, what if, why, how many, which one*

Pronouns: *I, you, he, she, we, they, my, your, him, her, his, our, their, me, us, them*

Prepositions: *in, on, under, over, near, beneath, next to, beside, around, inside, outside*

Sounds: */f/ fix, off; /s/ sit, talks; /l/ little, bell; /z/ zoo, zebra, bees*

Noting print has meaning: names on chairs and on cubbies, signs in dramatic play, words in books and on chalkboard

Noting sound–symbol associations: What sound does _____ start with?

Writing: letters, names, words

Social Skills Facilitated

Initiating interaction with peers and adults; responding to questions and requests from peers and adults

Negotiating with peers for toys and materials

Group cooperation: waiting for a turn in a group, taking a turn at the appropriate time

Cognitive Skills Facilitated

Problem-solving skills: which animal to make out of playdough, what animals do

Classification skills: animals in the zoo

Sequencing skills: story, songs

Narrative/story structure: adventure

Motor Skills Facilitated

Large motor: outdoor play activities—jumping, running, hopping, pedaling, climbing

Small motor: writing, drawing, gluing, squeezing, rolling

DRAMATIC PLAY **Zoo**

Type of Activity: Central

Objectives
1. Learn new, and employ familiar, vocabulary
2. Learn new, and employ a variety of, syntactic constructions
3. Interact with peers
4. Sequence familiar routines
5. Expand conceptual knowledge of the world

Settings
- Cages
- Defined spaces for animals
- Pond (blue sheet)
- Pool area (blue sheet)
- Ticket office
- Concession stand area
- Train (optional)

Props
- Cages
- Fencing
- Stuffed animals
- Tickets
- Pretend cash register
- Pretend money
- Pretend food for animals
- Dishes for animal food
- Pretend food for visitors
- Tickets
- Balloons
- Soda pop dispensers
- Broom and mop
- Doctor kit (optional)

Roles
- Zookeeper
- Animals
- Ticket vendor
- Visitors
- Concession stand vendors
- Veterinarian (optional)

General Description of Activity

Set up a zoo with a variety of animals in cages or defined spaces (e.g., field areas for large animals, pond for ducks, pool areas for bears or penguins) in the dramatic play area. Children who are visitors to the zoo can buy a ticket, look at the animals, and perhaps feed them. They might take a train ride through the zoo and buy a balloon or other memento. They can purchase food at the zoo or bring a picnic basket. Other children could be workers at the zoo, taking care of the animals by feeding them and cleaning their cages.

Verbal Productions

Level of linguistic complexity varies with the role or competency of the child playing the role.
- "How many tickets do you want?" or "How many?"
- "I need to have six tickets" or "Six"
- "This is an African elephant. He is bigger than the Indian elephant" or "Big elephant"
- "I'm feeding the tigers now" or "Feed tigers"

Adult Facilitative Role

The adult is to facilitate role play and help expand language and literacy skills. Typical actions or strategies to use include

Playing a role: "I have a ticket for the train. It goes by the monkey house."

Modeling a statement/vocabulary: "A baby elephant is called a calf."

Contrasting size terms (focus contrast): "The baby monkey is small, and the daddy monkey is large."

Modeling phonological awareness: "Lion and like both start with the letter *L*."

Prompting an imitation to a peer: "Go tell Jim you want to play. Say, 'Can I play, too?'"

ART **Animal Rubbings**

Objectives
1. Express creativity
2. Develop small motor skills (e.g., drawing, painting, cutting, pasting)
3. Practice turn-taking skills
4. Converse with peers and adults

Materials
- Newsprint
- Cardboard animal cutouts
- Other cutouts
- Crayons with paper removed
- Container to hold crayons

General Description of Activity

Cut outlines of different zoo animals from cardboard (or they may be purchased). Children place these cutouts under a sheet of newsprint and rub a crayon (laid flat on the paper) back and forth on the paper to slowly reveal the shape underneath the paper. A variety of other cutouts can be used to add to the picture.

GROUP **Zoo/Farm Animals Classification**

Objectives
1. Improve listening skills
2. Increase sequencing ability
3. Learn appropriate group-interaction skills
4. Practice turn-taking skills

Materials
- Toy barn
- Toy fence
- Zoo mat
- Toy farm animals
- Toy zoo animals
- Pictures of farm and and zoo animals (optional)

General Description of Activity

Set up a farm area (a toy barn with a toy fence) and a zoo area (a plastic or cardboard mat with zoo scenes drawn on it). Tell the children that they are going to put the farm animals by the barn and the zoo animals in the zoo. Ask one child to put a toy cow in the farm area and another child to place a toy elephant in the zoo area.

Group Participation

Distribute the different toy animals to the children. Have them come up one at a time to label their animal and decide whether it belongs on the farm or at the zoo. You can also ask children to think of other animals that are not among the toys and tell the group where those animals live.

Variation

If toy animals are not available, use pictures of animals.

Summary/Transition Activity

Review the classifications of farm and zoo, renaming a few of the animals in each classification.

		Wednesday		
Dramatic Play	**Art**	**Group**	**Story**	**Song**
Pet Store	Animal Stamps and Craft Stick Cages	How to Write a *3*	*Franklin Gets a Pet*	"How Much Is that Doggy in the Window?"

DAILY PLANNING GUIDE

Language and Literacy Skills Facilitated

Vocabulary: *dog, cats, birds, gerbils, Dalmatians, pets, rabbits, camera, ribbons, awards, phone, cash register, cages, podium*

Verb phrase structures: *take<u>s</u> a picture, <u>is</u> tak<u>ing</u> the pet home, <u>fed</u> the dog, <u>gave</u> a ribbon, pett<u>ed</u> the dog, walk<u>ed</u> the dog*

Adjective/object descriptions: *blue/red ribbon, first place, big/little _____, white/black _____, long/short leash*

Question structures: *what, how, where, when, who, what if, why, how many, which one*

Pronouns: *I, you, he, she, we, they, my, your, him, her, his, our, their, me, us, them*

Prepositions: *in, on, under, over, near, beneath, next to, beside, around, inside, outside*

Sounds: /k/ <u>c</u>atch, pa<u>ck</u>, tri<u>ck</u>; /f/ <u>f</u>ed, o<u>ff</u>; /r/ <u>r</u>abbit, fa<u>r</u>

Noting print has meaning: names on chairs and on cubbies, signs in dramatic play, words in books and on chalkboard

Noting sound–symbol associations: What sound does _____ start with?

Writing: letters, names, words

Social Skills Facilitated

Initiating interaction with peers and adults; responding to questions and requests from peers and adults

Negotiating with peers for toys and materials

Group cooperation: waiting for a turn in a group, taking a turn at the appropriate time

Cognitive Skills Facilitated

Problem-solving skills: how to take care of our pets

Classification skills: things at a pet show

Sequencing skills: story, songs, art activity

Narrative/story structure: adventure

Motor Skills Facilitated

Large motor: outdoor play activities—jumping, running, hopping, pedaling, climbing

Small motor: writing, drawing

DRAMATIC PLAY **Pet Store**

Type of Activity: Central

Objectives
1. Learn new, and employ familiar, vocabulary
2. Learn new, and employ a variety of, syntactic constructions
3. Interact with peers
4. Sequence familiar routines
5. Expand conceptual knowledge of the world

Settings	• Pet store	• Children's houses (child-sized houses or
	• Counter	dismantled cardboard boxes)

Props
- Stuffed animals
- Pretend cash register
- Play money
- Pretend credit cards
- Shelves of pretend pet products (e.g., food, leashes, collars, toys)
- Cages

- Aquariums
- Bowls for food and water
- Brushes for grooming
- Pet carriers
- Pretend cleaning supplies
- Owners' cars (optional)

Roles
- Clerks
- Cashier

- Customers
- Animals

General Description of Activity

Children buy pets at the pet store. The store should have a variety of pets (stuffed animals or children pretending to be the animals), such as dogs, cats, birds, hamsters, turtles, and fish, in appropriate containers and cages. A clerk can ring up sales on a cash register and be given money for the purchases. Pretend pet food, leashes, collars, and pet toys can also be sold at the pet store. Children can then take the pets to their houses. Children can also be workers in the store, caring for the pets by feeding and grooming them.

Verbal Productions

Level of linguistic complexity varies with the role or competency of the child playing the role.
- "How much is this doggy?" or "Buy doggy"
- "I need five pounds of cat food for Fuzzy" or "Cat food, please"
- "He is cleaning the dog's cage" or "Clean"
- "My turn to use the cash register" or "Mine"

Adult Facilitative Role

The adult is to facilate role play and help expand language and literacy skills. Typical actions or strategies to use include

Playing a role: "I have some cat food over here. It costs $5."

Providing a literacy model: "That sign says *pet toys*."

Modeling a statement/vocabulary: "That is a parrot."

Expanding a child's utterance: "That my cat" to "That is my cat."

Providing confirmatory feedback: "Yes, that is called a 'leash.'"

ART : Animal Stamps and Craft Stick Cages

Objectives
1. Express creativity
2. Develop small motor skills (e.g., drawing, painting, cutting, pasting)
3. Practice turn-taking skills
4. Converse with peers and adults

Materials
- Stamp pads (in different colors)
- Paper
- Animal or other rubber stamps

General Description of Activity

Lay out paper, ink pads, and stamps. Let the children make a variety of pictures of animals. They can draw cages around the animals or they can paste on wooden craft sticks to make the cages. Variation: Have the children stamp out animals on a mural and then draw a scene around them.

GROUP **How to Write a 3**

Objectives

1. Improve listening skills
2. Increase conceptual knowledge
3. Learn appropriate group-interaction skills
4. Practice turn-taking skills
5. Practice recognition and writing of numbers

Materials

- Number cards
- Chalkboards and chalk
- Paper and pencils (optional)
- Whiteboard and markers
- Number line (optional)

General Description of Activity

Hold up a card with the number 3 on it. Trace the number with your finger and invite several children to come to the front of the group to trace the number, too. As the children trace, recite the jingle for the target number (3):

1: Start at the top, go down and you're done, that's the way to make a *1*.

2: Around and back on the railroad track, *2, 2, 2*.

3: Around the tree, around the tree, that's the way to make a *3*.

4: Down and over and down once more, that's the way to make a *4*.

5: Down around, make a hat on it, and look what you've found. *(5)*

6: Down around until it sticks, that's the way to make a *6*.

7: Over and down and it's not heaven, over and down makes a *7*.

8: Make an S and go back straight, that's the way to make an *8*.

9: A balloon and a line make *9*.

10: Draw a line and a circle with your pen, that's the way to make a *10*.

Group Participation

Distribute individual chalkboards and chalk (or paper and pencils) to the children, and have them practice writing the target number.

Variation 1

Whiteboards and markers may be easier for some children to use.

Variation 2

To introduce the number, use a number line and have the children count up to the target number on the line. One child could place the target number on the number line.

Summary/Transition Activity

Ask children to hold up their chalkboards and show the group their numbers.

Thursday

Dramatic Play	Art	Group	Story	Song
Rodeo	Lace a Cowboy Boot	Act out a Story (The Cow Who Went Oink)	The Cow Who Went Oink	"Shake Your Sillies Out"

DAILY PLANNING GUIDE

Language and Literacy Skills Facilitated

Vocabulary: *rodeo, boots, cowboy, cowgirl, saddle, bridle, reins, rodeo clown, barrel, race, chute, horse, cow, calf, bull, riders*

Verb phrase structures: *is rid<u>ing</u>, <u>rode</u>, buck<u>s</u> off, buck<u>ed</u> off, jump<u>s</u>, is jump<u>ing</u>, jump<u>ed</u>, is fall<u>ing</u>, fell*

Adjective/object descriptions: *big/little ____, fast/slow race, bucking bronco, happy/sad clown*

Question structures: *what, how, where, when, who, what if, why, how many, which one*

Pronouns: *I, you, he, she, we, they, my, your, him, her, his, our, their, me, us, them*

Prepositions: *in, on, under, over, near, beneath, next to, beside, around, inside, outside*

Sounds: /f/ *<u>f</u>ell, o<u>ff</u>;* /k/ *<u>k</u>ick, ba<u>ck</u>;* /s/ *<u>s</u>it, jump<u>s</u>*

Noting print has meaning: names on chairs and on cubbies, signs in dramatic play, words in books and on chalkboard

Noting sound–symbol associations: What sound does _____ start with?

Writing: letters, names, words

Social Skills Facilitated

Initiating interaction with peers and adults; responding to questions and requests from peers and adults

Negotiating with peers for toys and materials

Group cooperation: waiting for a turn in a group, taking a turn at the appropriate time

Cognitive Skills Facilitated

Problem-solving skills: how to lace

Classification skills: animals at the rodeo

Sequencing skills: songs, story, art activity

Narrative/story structure: adventure

Motor Skills Facilitated

Large motor: outdoor play activities—jumping, running, hopping, pedaling, climbing

Small motor: writing, drawing, gluing, fingerpainting

DRAMATIC PLAY **Rodeo**

Type of Activity: Related

Objectives
1. Learn new, and employ familiar, vocabulary
2. Learn new, and employ a variety of, syntactic constructions
3. Interact with peers
4. Sequence familiar routines
5. Expand conceptual knowledge of the world

Settings
- Arena
- Chute with gate that opens
- Barrel race area
- Judges' stand
- Spectator area
- Concession stand area (optional)

Props
- Stick horses (stuffed paper bag horse stapled onto a yardstick)
- Reins
- Clown costume
- Barrels (upside-down wastebaskets)
- Dolls (representing riders)
- Stationary horse with saddle
- Cowboy boots, hats, and vests
- Timer
- Judges' stand
- Awards for winners
- Soda pop dispenser
- Pretend cash register
- Pretend money
- Pretend food

Roles
- Announcer
- Rodeo clown
- Barrel race riders
- Rodeo participants
- Horses
- Bulls
- Audience members
- Judges
- Concession stand workers

General Description of Activity

Children participate in a rodeo. There should be an arena where different types of cowboy activities take place. There could be an opening ceremony in which the participants ride around the ring on their horses. Then children could take part in the different events, such as a barrel racing, riding bucking broncos, and bull riding. A rodeo clown can help keep the bull or horses away from fallen riders. Judges decide whether a rider stayed on long enough to win. A barrel race could be set up using upside-down wastebaskets and stick horses. Children can pretend to be horses or bulls, with dolls as the riders. A separate area may feature a stationary horse set up for children to ride. Cowboy boots, hats, and vests should be available, and a concession stand could also be set up.

Verbal Productions

Level of linguistic complexity varies with the role or competency of the child playing the role.
- "He stayed on the whole time. He gets ten points" or "Ride long time"
- "I can go fast around the barrels" or "Fast"
- "He has had a long turn. It is my turn now" or "My turn"

Adult Facilitative Role

The adult is to facilitate role play and help expand language and literacy skills. Typical actions or strategies to use include

Playing a role: "I am watching barrel races. Do you want to sit with me?"

Modeling a statement/vocabulary: "The horses race around three barrels in a barrel race."

Recasting of a child's utterance: "I ride parade" to "Yes, you rode in the parade."

Contrasting two sounds: "Did you say 'dumps' or 'jumps?'"

Using a cloze procedure: "I have one horse, you have two _____ (horses)."

ART **Lace a Cowboy Boot**

Objectives
1. Express creativity
2. Develop small motor skills (e.g., drawing, painting, cutting, pasting)
3. Practice turn-taking skills
4. Converse with peers and adults

Materials
- Boot (out of card stock) with holes cut to pull yarn through, one per child
- Yarn with tips covered with tape
- Markers
- Lacing formboards (optional)

General Description of Activity

Children practice lacing and tying by lacing a paper boot or using lacing formboards. Children lace up the boot starting at the bottom with a piece of yarn. (The ends should be wrapped in tape to aid in going through the holes.) The children can then color the boot or draw designs on it.

GROUP **Act out a Story *(The Cow Who Went Oink)***

Objectives
1. Improve listening skills
2. Increase sequencing ability
3. Increase knowledge of storytelling
4. Learn appropriate group-interaction skills
5. Practice turn-taking skills

Materials
- *The Cow Who Went Oink*
- Props for the story

General Description of Activity

Read *The Cow Who Went Oink*, or summarize it if children are familiar with the story.

Group Participation

Assign children roles from the story. Assure the children who are not chosen the first time that everyone will have a turn and that they have the very important job of being a good listening audience. Narrate the story as the children act it out. They should say as many of the lines as they can, with prompts given when needed. Repeat the story with new actors until all the children have had a turn.

Summary/Transition Activity

Compliment the children's acting, and ask children what other stories they would like to act out another day.

	Dramatic Play	Art	Group	Story	Song
Monday *Suggested Props and Materials*	A Day in the Park *Park cleanup scenario, picnic items, music items, trash, trash cans, concession area, pretend food, cash register, play money*	Pinecone Bird Feeders *Pinecones, birdseed, peanut butter (or syrup), yarn*	Color Patterns *Variety of 1" colored cubes, cardboard to cover patterns (optional)*	*Are You My Mother?*	"Raindrops and Lemondrops"
Tuesday *Suggested Props and Materials*	Utility Worker *Utility workers scenario, housing area, office area, roads (marked with masking tape), trucks, cardboard tubes (gas pipes), throw rugs (to represent the ground), yarn or string, giant Tinker Toys (telephone poles), tools, tool belts, desk, telephones*	String Painting *Tempera paint, bowls, string, paper, smocks*	Letter *M* *Pictures and objects beginning with the letter M, alphabet chart, picture dictionary, sticky notes (optional), pencils*	*Katy and the Big Snow*	"It's a Small World"
Wednesday *Suggested Props and Materials*	Hospital/ Paramedic *Hospital scenario, ambulance, telephones, doctor kits, white coats or scrubs, bandages, gurney, beds (mats)*	Create a Face *Paper plates, eyes, noses, mouths, yarn, glue, markers*	What Is Your Address? *Index cards with children's addresses, telephones*	*Teddy Bear Cures a Cold*	"Head, Shoulders, Knees, and Toes"
Thursday *Suggested Props and Materials*	Sanitation Worker *House scenario (with trash baskets), sanitation truck (wheeled cart with large bags attached), wastebaskets, crunched-up garbage (newspaper), plastic containers, aluminum cans, desk, telephones, big box for trash to be dumped into for sorting*	Trash Collage *Paper, glue, variety of "trashables" (newspaper, Styrofoam pieces, paper scraps)*	Recycling (Classification) *Plastic bottles, newspapers, soda pop cans, cardboard, Styrofoam items, bins (one per type of item to be recycled)*	*The Berenstain Bears Don't Pollute*	"The Cleanup Song"

NEWSLETTER

Vol. 1, No. 13

Date: _____

Taking Care of Ourselves and Our World

Monday Today the children will have a pretend picnic and then clean up the park area. They also might enjoy a concert in the park. In art, they will make birdfeeders out of pinecones. At recess, they will hang them in the trees on the playground. Our story for today is *Are You My Mother?* At group time, children will match and extend different patterns made of different colored one-inch cubes. Some children may be asked to repeat a pattern from memory after they have seen it. Our featured song is "Raindrops and Lemondrops."

Tuesday Today the children will be utility workers laying telephone lines or gas lines, or homeowners who need service. They will make string paintings in art. Our story is *Katy and the Big Snow.* In group, the children will learn to make the letter *M* and learn all about words that start with the letter *M.* Today's song is "It's a Small World."

Wednesday The children will learn about being paramedics and working in a hospital today. They might pretend to be the person who is injured, the ambulance driver, the paramedic, or the doctor. They will have fun making faces out of paper plates in art. Our story is *Teddy Bear Cures a Cold.* At group time, the children will practice reciting their address in case anyone would have to call 911. Our featured song is "Head, Shoulders, Knees, and Toes."

Thursday The children will be sanitation workers, homeowners, or people who run the recycling center in dramatic play today. They will make a collage of "trashables" in art. Our story is *The Berenstain Bears Don't Pollute.* At group time, the children will sort different recyclable items, such as plastic, aluminum cans, newspaper, and so forth. Our song is "The Cleanup Song."

Monday

Dramatic Play	Art	Group	Story	Song
A Day in the Park	Pinecone Bird Feeders	Color Patterns	*Are You My Mother?*	"Raindrops and Lemondrops"

DAILY PLANNING GUIDE

Language and Literacy Skills Facilitated

Vocabulary: *music, drum, instruments, picnic, barbecue, parade, march, fun, lemonade, three-legged race*

Verb phrase structures: *barbecues hamburgers, made lemonade, cooks, cooked, is marching, marched, played an instrument*

Adjective/object descriptions: *loud/soft music, little/big drum, red, white and blue flag, spicy barbecue, sour lemonade*

Question structures: *what, how, where, when, who, what if, why, how many, which one*

Pronouns: *I, you, he, she, we, they, my, your, him, her, his, our, their, me, us, them*

Prepositions: *in, on, under, over, near, beneath, next to, beside, around, inside, outside*

Sounds: /l/ l*emonade, ba*ll; /r/ *r*ace, hambu*r*ger, ca*r*; /k/ *c*ar, par*k*; /f/ *f*un, o*ff*

Noting print has meaning: names on chairs and on cubbies, signs in dramatic play, words in books and on chalkboard

Noting sound–symbol associations: What sound does _____ start with?

Writing: letters, names, words

Social Skills Facilitated

Initiating interaction with peers and adults; responding to questions and requests from peers and adults

Negotiating with peers for toys and materials

Group cooperation: waiting for a turn in a group, taking a turn at the appropriate time

Cognitive Skills Facilitated

Problem-solving skills: how to sort into different kinds of recyclable materials

Classification skills: things that are newspaper, things that are plastic

Sequencing skills: songs, dramatic play (picnic)

Narrative/story structure: adventure

Motor Skills Facilitated

Large motor: outdoor play activities—jumping, running, hopping, pedaling, climbing

Small motor: writing, drawing, gluing, cutting

DRAMATIC PLAY **A Day in the Park**

Type of Activity: Related

Objectives
1. Learn new, and employ familiar, vocabulary
2. Learn new, and employ a variety of, syntactic constructions
3. Interact with peers
4. Sequence familiar routines
5. Expand conceptual knowledge of the world

November

Week 13
Taking Care
of Ourselves
and Our World

MONDAY

Settings	• A gazebo, or bandshell for the band (marked off with masking tape)	• Trash can area • Concession stands	• Picnic area
Props	• Trash cans • Trash paper bags • Music stand • Musical instruments • Microphones	• Baton (for the director) • Chairs for audience • Pretend food and picnic basket • Pretend cash register	• Pretend money • Lemonade (can have a real lemonade stand) • Stuffed dogs • Leashes
Roles	• Cleanup workers • Band members • Director	• Picnic goers • Audience members	• Concession stand workers

General Description of Activity

A day in the park might include an outdoor concert and an art show. The children can play musical instruments or sell their art. The children could also go on a picnic, walk their dogs, or buy pretend food at a concession stand. They can also take care of the park by cleaning it up.

Verbal Productions

Level of linguistic complexity varies with the role or competency of the child playing the role.

• "This is a number *4* plastic, put it in that pile" or "That's number *4*"

• "We recycle newspapers every Saturday" or "Save newspapers"

• "Bobby, pick up that piece of cardboard!" or "Save cardboard"

• "I like to eat fried chicken when I go to picnics" or "Eat fried chicken"

• "He played the music too loudly!" or "Too loud"

Adult Facilitative Role

The adult is to facilitate role play and help expand language and literacy skills. Typical actions or strategies to use include

Playing a role: "I am packing a picnic basket."

Modeling a statement/vocabulary: "I like to go on picnics. It is fun to eat at the park."

Expanding a child's utterances: "He play Frisbee" to "He plays Frisbee in the park."

Providing an event cast of action: "I am picking up some trash. Now I am throwing it in the trashcan. I want my park to look good. I am taking care of my park."

Providing phonological awareness: "The words *my* and *mom* both start with the letter *M*."

ART **Pinecone Bird Feeders**

Objectives	1. Express creativity 2. Develop small motor skills (e.g., drawing, painting, cutting, pasting) 3. Practice turn-taking skills 4. Converse with peers and adults
Materials	• Pinecones • String or colored yarn • Peanut butter (or syrup) • Birdseed • Box lids to put birdseed in for rolling

November

Week 13
Taking Care
of Ourselves
and Our World

MONDAY

General Description of Activity

Attach string or colored yarn to a pinecone by winding the yarn around the cone and then tying it together. Leave enough yarn to tie around a tree branch. Children smear peanut butter on the pinecone and roll it in birdseed. For easy transport home, place the pinecone in a small plastic bag. Some of the extra bird feeders can be attached to trees in the play yard.

GROUP Color Patterns

Objectives

1. Improve listening skills
2. Increase ability to recognize and sequence patterns on the basis of color
3. Learn appropriate group-interaction skills
4. Practice turn-taking skills

Materials

- 1" colored cubes
- Cardboard (optional)

General Description of Activity

Present a pattern of 1" colored cubes (e.g., red–yellow–red–yellow), and show the children how to continue the pattern by adding the appropriate blocks.

Variation

Have the children repeat the pattern by creating new rows of blocks that match your pattern (i.e., this becomes a matching activity).

Group Participation

On the floor, set out a block pattern appropriate for a particular child's level. Have the child come up (or have two children come for peer support and help) and repeat or extend the pattern. Some children can repeat a simple pattern (e.g., red–blue–red–blue); others will be able to do more complicated patterns (e.g., red–blue–blue, red–blue–blue, or red–blue–green–green, red–blue–green–green). Continue until all the children have had a turn.

Variation

For a greater challenge, make a pattern, cover it with a piece of cardboard, and have the child repeat the pattern from memory.

Summary/Transition Activity

Give each child a small pile of blocks to create a pattern. Children could then trade with a partner to see if they can copy each other's patterns. Collect the blocks and review colors.

Tuesday

Dramatic Play	Art	Group	Story	Song
Utility Worker	String Painting	Letter *M*	*Katy and the Big Snow*	"It's a Small World"

DAILY PLANNING GUIDE

Language and Literacy Skills Facilitated

Vocabulary: *utility, telephone worker, telephone wire, tools, wrench, screwdriver, hammer, splice, shovel, pipe, gasoline, construction*

Verb phrase structures: <u>lay</u> *the gas line,* <u>string</u> *telephone wire,* <u>pound</u> *the nails,* <u>splice</u> *the wire,* <u>fix</u> *the phone*

Adjective/object descriptions: *thin wire, thick wire, big pipe, little pipe, red wire, blue wire, heavy load, light load*

Question structures: *what, how, where, when, who, what if, why, how many, which one*

Pronouns: *I, you, he, she, we, they, my, your, him, her, his, our, their, me, us, them*

Prepositions: *in, on, under, over, near, beneath, next to, beside, around, inside, outside*

Noting print has meaning: names on chairs and on cubbies, signs in dramatic play, words in books and on chalkboard

Noting sound–symbol associations: What sound does _____ start with?

Writing: letters, names, words

Social Skills Facilitated

Initiating interaction with peers and adults; responding to questions and requests from peers and adults

Negotiating with peers for toys and materials

Group cooperation: waiting for a turn in a group, taking a turn at the appropriate time

Cognitive Skills Facilitated

Problem-solving skills: how to lay the gas line

Classification skills: different kinds of tools

Sequencing skills: story, song

Narrative/story structure: adventure

Motor Skills Facilitated

Large motor: outdoor play activities—jumping, running, hopping, pedaling, climbing

Small motor: writing, drawing, gluing

DRAMATIC PLAY **Utility Worker**

Type of Activity: Related

Objectives
1. Learn new, and employ familiar, vocabulary
2. Learn new, and employ a variety of, syntactic constructions
3. Interact with peers
4. Sequence familiar routines
5. Expand conceptual knowledge of the world

November

Week 13
Taking Care
of Ourselves
and Our World

TUESDAY

Settings
- New subdivision area
- Office area
- Roads (floor marked with masking tape)
- Truck

Props
- Cardboard tubes (gas pipes)
- Throw rug (to represent the ground)
- Yarn or string
- Giant Tinker Toys (telephone poles)
- Tools (e.g., hammer, pliers)
- Tool belts
- Utility truck (made from dismantled cardboard boxes)
- Play telephone
- Desk

Roles
- Various utility workers
- Customers
- Drivers
- Receptionist

General Description of Activity

If possible, have a utility worker visit the classroom and describe his or her job before you set up this dramatic play. Children can pretend to be a utility worker maintaining and repairing telephone lines, electric wires, or gas lines. One area of the classroom can be designated as a new subdivision, for which gas lines (cardboard tubes) need to be laid, telephone and electric wires need to be strung, and so forth. The tubes can be laid under a throw rug so that they seem to be underground. The wires can be strung between poles made of the giant Tinker Toys. Another area can be set up for a pretend emergency; the utility workers come out to make repairs. Another aspect of the activity could be an office area where the receptionist answers the telephones and then calls the workers to tell them where they should go.

Verbal Productions

Level of linguistic complexity varies with the role or competency of the child playing the role.
- "You need a new gas line here. Let me call the office for a truck," "You need gas line," or "New line"
- "The phone doesn't work" or "Phone broken"
- "He laid the new pipe" or "New pipe"

Adult Facilitative Role

The adult is to facilitate role play and help expand language and literacy skills. Typical actions or strategies to use include

Playing a role: "I am going to fix the telephone line. It is broken."

Modeling a statement/vocabulary: "I will use a wrench to loosen the bolt."

Identifying rhyming words: "Yes, the words *wire* and *fire* rhyme."

Asking an open question: "This is broken. How can we fix it?"

Expanding a child's utterance: "Twist wires" to "Oh, we need to twist the wires together."

ART **String Painting**

Objectives
1. Express creativity
2. Develop small motor skills (e.g., drawing, painting, cutting, pasting)
3. Practice turn-taking skills
4. Converse with peers and adults

Materials
- Strings for dipping in paint, approximately 20" long
- Tempera paint
- Cups to hold paint
- Construction paper

November

Week 13
Taking Care
of Ourselves
and Our World

TUESDAY

General Description of Activity

Children create pictures or designs by dipping string in tempera paint and then arranging the string on half of a sheet of construction paper. They can arrange the string on the paper in an "S" pattern, in a circle, or in any other pattern that allows one end of the string to protrude from the paper when it is folded. Children fold the paper in half and pull the end of the string. When the paper is unfolded, there will be mirror image designs on both sides of the fold. Two-color designs can be made by dipping a second string in a different paint color and arranging it on the paper, folding the paper, and pulling the string through. The paper can then be unfolded and allowed to dry.

Additional activity

Make frames for the designs.

GROUP **Letter *M***

Objectives

1. Improve listening skills
2. Increase knowledge of the alphabet and sounds
3. Learn appropriate group-interaction skills
4. Practice turn-taking skills

Materials

- Alphabet chart and other alphabet displays
- Blackboard and chalk or poster paper and markers
- Pictures of objects (or objects themselves) with names that begin with *M*
- Picture dictionary (or an alphabet video dictionary)

General Description of Activity

Write an upper- and a lowercase letter *M* on the blackboard (or on poster paper). Give several examples of words that begin with *M*, emphasizing the /m/ or "mmmm" sound at the beginning of the words. You might hold up pictures of objects (or objects themselves) with names that begin with *M*. Direct the children's attention to the alphabet picture displays around the room.

Group Participation

Ask if anyone's name starts with *M* (e.g., Marissa, Mark, Mia), and have those children write the letter *M* on the blackboard (or poster paper). Also have two or three other children whose names do not begin with *M* write the letter *M* on the blackboard. Provide verbal guidance as children form the letter: "Start at the top, draw a line straight down, go the top of the straight line and draw a slant down to the bottom, draw a slant up to the top, and draw a straight line down." If necessary, help children write the letter. Some of the other children can practice writing *M* in the air with their fingers (or on individual chalkboards). Ask the children to think of words that begin with *M*. Write the words they suggest on the blackboard, drawing quick sketches (when possible) of the suggested words. If a child suggests a word that does not begin with *M*, say, "No, that begins with ____," and say the two sounds so children can compare them. To help children who cannot think of any words, prompt them with pictures or objects representing *M* words. (Pictures or objects can be handed out at the beginning of the lesson or as the lesson proceeds.) Additional words can be sought in a picture dictionary if the group has difficulty arriving at words that begin with *M*.

Summary/Transition Activity

After about 10–15 words have been suggested, review the words, emphasizing the *M* sound.

Wednesday

Dramatic Play	Art	Group	Story	Song
Hospital/ Paramedic	Create a Face	What Is Your Address?	*Teddy Bear Cures a Cold*	"Head, Shoulders, Knees, and Toes"

DAILY PLANNING GUIDE

Language and Literacy Skills Facilitated

Vocabulary: *paramedic, ambulance, stethoscope, thermometer, fever, cast, X-ray, oxygen, accident, vehicle*

Verb phrase structures: *carry the stretcher, drive the ambulance, ride, examine, give oxygen, set the leg*

Adjective/object descriptions: *broken leg, white coats*

Question structures: *what, how, where, when, who, what if, why, how many, which one*

Pronouns: *I, you, he, she, we, they, my, your, him, her, his, our, their, me, us, them*

Prepositions: *in, on, under, over, near, beneath, next to, beside, around, inside, outside*

Noting print has meaning: names on chairs and on cubbies, signs in dramatic play, words in books and on chalkboard

Noting sound–symbol associations: What sound does _____ start with?

Writing: letters, names, words

Social Skills Facilitated

Initiating interaction with peers and adults; responding to questions and requests from peers and adults

Negotiating with peers for toys and materials

Group cooperation: waiting for a turn in a group, taking a turn at the appropriate time

Cognitive Skills Facilitated

Problem-solving skills: What does a paramedic do?

Classification skills: things in an ambulance, hospital

Sequencing skills: story, song

Narrative/story structure: Adventure

Motor Skills Facilitated

Large motor: outdoor play activities—jumping, running, hopping, pedaling, climbing

Small motor: writing, drawing, gluing

DRAMATIC PLAY **Hospital/Paramedic**

Type of Activity: Related

Objectives
1. Learn new, and employ familiar, vocabulary
2. Learn new, and employ a variety of, syntactic constructions
3. Interact with peers
4. Sequence familiar routines
5. Expand conceptual knowledge of the world

November

Week 13
Taking Care
of Ourselves
and Our World

WEDNESDAY

Settings
- Ambulance (a large box covered in white paper, with a dashboard and a smaller box to form the cab or house)
- Hospital emergency room
- Roads (floor marked with masking tape)

Props
- Ambulance
- Child-sized house
- Play telephones
- Doctor kits
- White coats
- Bandages
- Gurney
- Beds (mats)

Roles
- Dispatcher
- Paramedics
- Injured patients
- Ambulance driver
- Doctors
- Nurses
- Families of the patients

General Description of Activity

Children act out emergency assistance. They can be paramedics, who often ride in an ambulance and are the first to help after an accident or medical emergency. A pretend ambulance can be made from boxes or by using a child-sized house as the back of the ambulance and a box for the cab. Children can use doctor kits to treat the injured. A hospital can be set up so that the injured people can be taken there for further treatment by doctors.

Verbal Productions

Level of linguistic complexity varies with the role or competency of the child playing the role.
- "I hurt my elbow. I think my arm is broken" or "I'm hurt"
- "I'm a paramedic. We'll take you to the hospital in the ambulance" or "Take to hospital"

Adult Facilitative Role

The adult is to facilitate role play and help expand language and literacy skills. Typical actions or strategies to use include

Playing a role: "I am very sick. Please call an ambulance."

Modeling a statement/vocabulary: "The ambulance will take me to the hospital quickly."

Modeling future tense: "I will get to see a doctor at the hospital."

Expanding a child's utterance: "Broke leg" to "The doll has a broken leg."

Redirecting a child to a peer: "Johnny has the siren. Ask him for a turn. Say, 'May I have a turn, please?'"

ART : **Create a Face**

Objectives
1. Express creativity
2. Develop small motor skills (e.g., drawing, painting, cutting, pasting)
3. Practice turn-taking skills
4. Converse with peers and adults

Materials
- Paper plates or large cutout circles, one for each child
- Small cutouts in a variety of shapes
- Yarn
- Extra paper
- Scissors
- Glue

General Description of Activity

Children create a face using a paper plate or a construction-paper circle as a base. They can glue a variety of shapes onto the plate to make facial features, such as eyes, noses, mouths, and so forth. Place the shapes in separate containers so the children can easily choose the shapes they want.

November

Week 13
**Taking Care
of Ourselves
and Our World**

WEDNESDAY

Add other items, such as yarn for hair, extra paper, scissors, and markers, that children can use to add details to the faces. Label the different shapes and colors as the children glue them on the faces they are creating.

Variation

Instead of separating the various cutout shapes, place them all in one shallow container so that children must communicate to get the pieces they want.

GROUP : **What Is Your Address?**

Objectives
1. Improve listening skills
2. Increase conceptual knowledge
3. Learn appropriate group-interaction skills
4. Practice turn-taking skills

Materials
• Address cards with children's addresses

General Description of Activity

Tell the children that it is important for them to know their addresses. Addresses tell where they live, and without addresses people cannot send letters to them, and firefighters would not know where to come if there was a fire. Explain that an address has several parts. The first part is the house or apartment number, the second part is the name of the street, and the last part is the city (and state). Write a sample address on the board, pointing out each part.

Group Participation

Ask if anyone knows his or her address. Have those who do come to the front of the group and state their address. Give them a card with their address on it, and pass out address cards to the remaining children as well. Divide the class into smaller groups and have the other staff members help the children recite their address to their group.

Summary/Transition Activity

After all of the groups have practiced their addresses, have the children gather back in one large group and remind them of the different parts of an address. The children can take their index cards home and practice with their parents until they can recite their address.

Thursday

Dramatic Play	Art	Group	Story	Song
Sanitation Worker	Trash Collage	Recycling (Classification)	*The Berenstain Bears Don't Pollute*	"The Cleanup Song"

DAILY PLANNING GUIDE

Language and Literacy Skills Facilitated

Vocabulary: *trash, sanitation worker, garbage, recycle, plastic, cardboard, glass, newspaper, litter, cleanup*

Verb phrase structures: <u>are</u> pick<u>ing</u>/pick<u>ed</u> up trash, <u>throw</u> away, litter<u>ed</u>, clean<u>ed</u>, <u>is</u> clean<u>ing</u>, <u>are</u> recycl<u>ing</u>, recycl<u>ed</u>

Adjective/object descriptions: *big truck, dirty/clean yard, plastic bottle, glass bottle*

Question structures: *what, how, where, when, who, what if, why, how many, which one*

Pronouns: *I, you, he, she, we, they, my, your, him, her, his, our, their, me, us, them*

Prepositions: *in, on, under, over, near, beneath, next to, beside, around, inside, outside*

Sounds: /l/ <u>l</u>itter, be<u>ll</u>; /f/ <u>f</u>ix, of<u>f</u>; /k/ <u>c</u>an, pi<u>ck</u> up; /s/ <u>s</u>ee, bu<u>s</u>

Noting print has meaning: names on chairs and on cubbies, signs in dramatic play, words in books and on chalkboard

Noting sound–symbol associations: What sound does _____ start with?

Writing: letters, names, words

Social Skills Facilitated

Initiating interaction with peers and adults; responding to questions and requests from peers and adults

Negotiating with peers for toys and materials

Group cooperation: waiting for a turn in a group, taking a turn at the appropriate time

Cognitive Skills Facilitated

Problem-solving skills: what a sanitation worker does

Classification skills: things we recycle

Sequencing skills: story, song

Narrative/story structure: adventure

Motor Skills Facilitated

Large motor: outdoor play activities—jumping, running, hopping, pedaling, climbing

Small motor: writing, drawing, gluing

DRAMATIC PLAY : **Sanitation Worker**

Type of Activity: Central

Objectives
1. Learn new, and employ familiar, vocabulary
2. Learn new, and employ a variety of, syntactic constructions
3. Interact with peers
4. Sequence familiar routines
5. Expand conceptual knowledge of the world

November

Week 13
Taking Care
of Ourselves
and Our World

THURSDAY

Settings
- Sanitation truck (wheeled cart with large bags attached)
- Houses with wastebaskets
- Road (floor marked with masking tape)
- Recycling plant office
- Sorting area

Props
- Sanitation truck (wheeled cart with large bags attached)
- Wastebaskets
- Crunched-up "garbage" (newspaper)
- Plastic containers
- Aluminum cans
- Desks
- Telephones
- Boxes (for trash to be dumped into for sorting)

Roles
- Sanitation workers
- Homeowners
- Truck drivers
- Workers at recycling plant

General Description of Activity

Children pretend to be sanitation workers who are picking up garbage from houses and from parks. They can ride a sanitation truck made out of a cart with wheels. Large bags can be attached so that children can stop at a house, empty trash cans into the large bag, and then go on to the next house. If the cart is sturdy enough, some of the children can actually ride on it while others push it. When the large bag is full, the truck goes to the plant to drop off the garbage. Some of the garbage can be taken to a recycling plant, where it can be sorted by workers to be made into new things. (Be aware that this activity requires that someone refill the wastebaskets so the play can continue.)

Verbal Productions

Level of linguistic complexity varies with the role or competency of the child playing the role.
- "He picked up three trash cans. It's my turn" or "My turn"
- "I want to ride the cart. He has ridden it a long time" or "Ride long time"
- "We have three piles—one for cans, one for paper, and one for plastic" or "Three piles"

Adult Facilitative Role

The adult is to facilitate role play and help expand language and literacy skills. Typical actions or strategies to use include

Playing a role: "I am driving the truck. You ride in the back."

Modeling a statement/vocabulary: "The sanitation worker picks up the trash."

Asking an open question: "Where can we put the trash?"

Identifying rhyming words: "Do 'crash' and 'trash' rhyme?"

Expanding a child's utterance: "We can here" to "We put the cans here."

ART : **Trash Collage**

Objectives
1. Express creativity
2. Develop small motor skills (e.g., drawing, painting, cutting, pasting)
3. Practice turn-taking skills
4. Converse with peers and adults

Materials
- Construction paper
- Scissors
- "Trashable" items, including crumpled and torn paper, other scrap paper, Styrofoam, metal washers or clips (make sure metal parts are too big to swallow), and newspaper.
- Glue

November

Week 13
Taking Care
of Ourselves
and Our World

THURSDAY

General Description of Activity

Children paste a variety of "trashable" items to construction paper to make collages.

GROUP **Recycling (Classification)**

Objectives
1. Improve listening skills
2. Increase sequencing ability
3. Learn appropriate group-interaction skills
4. Practice turn-taking skills

Materials
- Plastic bottles
- Newspapers
- Soda pop cans
- Cardboard
- Styrofoam items
- Bins (one per type of item to be recycled)

General Description of Activity

Explain what the word *recycle* means. Tell the children that some items that are often thrown away can be reused, but they must be taken to special places to be specially processed. Place a pile of recyclable items in front of the children. Show them the different items, pointing out the recycle symbol where possible (i.e., on the plastic or Styrofoam items). Set up bins for separating plastic, cardboard, aluminum, newspaper, and Styrofoam items.

Group Participation

Give each child an opportunity to sort some "trash" into the recycling bins, checking the plastic and Styrofoam items for symbols indicating that they can be recycled. Help children find the recycle symbol on bottles and other items.

Variation

Divide the class into small groups and have each group look for a specific type of recyclable item.

Summary/Transition Activity

Verbally label each recycling bin that is set up in front of the class. Remind children that many trash items can be recycled by sorting them into bins and taking them to a recycling center (or having them picked up at their home).

WEEKLY PLANNING GUIDE

	Dramatic Play	Art	Group	Story	Song
Monday *Suggested Props and Materials*	Pilgrims *Pilgrim scenario, log houses (made from cardboard boxes—logs can be made from wrapping paper tubes), sandbox area for "planting," fishing area, boat area, boat, dishes, pots and pans, pretend food, blue sheet (lake), fish, fishing poles*	Food Collage *Magazine pictures of food, paper plates, glue, markers*	Alphabet Grab Bag *Alphabet letters, drawstring bag, alphabet chart*	*Friendship's First Thanksgiving*	"London Bridge"
Tuesday *Suggested Props and Materials*	Native American Homes *Native American scenario, two wickiups, fire area, pond area, fish, fishing poles, pretend food, brown paper sacks, feathers, headbands, horses, pottery dishes*	Cheerios Necklaces *Colored Cheerios, string or yarn, pieces of paper, straws cut up in small pieces*	Letter *N* *Pictures and objects beginning with N, alphabet chart*	*The Legend of the Bluebonnet*	"A Turkey Is a Funny Bird"
Wednesday *Suggested Props and Materials*	Our Home Today *House area, dishes, pretend food, tables, chairs, couch, beds, dolls, party decorations*	Watercolor Paintings *Watercolor paints, brushes, water in tubs, white construction paper*	Thankfulness List *Poster board or a large piece of paper, markers*	*Thanksgiving Today*	"Five Little Turkeys"
Thursday *Suggested Props and Materials*	Thanksgiving Day—No school				

MY NOTES

NEWSLETTER

Vol. 1, No. 14

Date: _____

Homes—Thanksgiving Week

Monday

Today the children will be Pilgrims, traveling by boat to a new world where they will set up new homes and plant crops for food. Their new friends, the Native Americans, will help them learn to live in a new land. The children will make a collage of their favorite foods during art. Our story will be *Friendship's First Thanksgiving.* At group time, the children will play Alphabet Grab Bag, in which they pull out a letter *(A–M)* and match it to the alphabet chart or identify it. We will sing the song "London Bridge" during music time.

Tuesday

Our Thanksgiving theme continues today as the children learn about Native Americans and their homes. They will dramatize the lives of the people who lived here before the Pilgrims arrived. They will make necklaces out of colored Cheerios. *The Legend of the Bluebonnet* is Tuesday's story. The children will focus on the letter *N* during group time. Music time will include "A Turkey Is a Funny Bird."

Wednesday

Today the children celebrate Thanksgiving in today's homes. They will pretend to be mommies, daddies, or children. They will fix a big dinner and have a Thanksgiving party. During art, the children will make watercolor paintings. Our story is *Thanksgiving Today.* During group time, we will make a list of things we are thankful for. We will recite the poem "Five Little Turkeys" during music time.

Thursday

Happy Thanksgiving, everyone.

Monday

Dramatic Play	Art	Group	Story	Song
Pilgrims	Food Collage	Alphabet Grab Bag	*Friendship's First Thanksgiving*	"London Bridge"

DAILY PLANNING GUIDE

Language and Literacy Skills Facilitated

Vocabulary: *Thanksgiving, thanks, grateful, trip, ocean, sail, Mayflower, pilgrim, hungry, log cabin, corn*

Verb phrase structures: <u>*is* sail*ing*</u>, <u>*was* sail*ing*</u>, *sail<u>ed</u>*, <u>*is* land*ing*</u>, *land<u>ed</u>*, *build<u>s</u> houses, buil<u>t</u> a house*

Adjective/object descriptions: *hungry people, long trip, yellow corn, big/little house*

Question structures: *what, how, where, when, who, what if, why, how many, which one*

Pronouns: *I, you, he, she, we, they, my, your, him, her, his, our, their, me, us, them*

Prepositions: *in, on, under, over, near, beneath, next to, beside, around, inside, outside*

Sounds: /p/ *p*ie, u*p*; /f/ *f*ar, o*ff*; /k/ *c*ame, pa*ck*

Noting print has meaning: names on chairs and on cubbies, signs in dramatic play, words in books and on chalkboard

Noting sound–symbol associations: What sound does _____ start with?

Writing: letters, names, words

Social Skills Facilitated

Initiating interaction with peers and adults; responding to questions and requests from peers and adults

Negotiating with peers for toys and materials

Group cooperation: waiting for a turn in a group, taking a turn at the appropriate time

Cognitive Skills Facilitated

Problem-solving skills: what to pack, how to sail, what to eat

Classification skills: things Pilgrims ate

Sequencing skills: story, songs

Narrative/story structure: adventure

Motor Skills Facilitated

Large motor: outdoor play activities—jumping, running, hopping, pedaling, climbing

Small motor: writing, drawing, gluing

DRAMATIC PLAY **Pilgrims**

Type of Activity: Central

Objectives
1. Learn new, and employ familiar, vocabulary
2. Learn new, and employ a variety of, syntactic constructions
3. Interact with peers
4. Sequence familiar routines
5. Expand conceptual knowledge of the world

November

Week 14
Homes—
Thanksgiving
Week

MONDAY

Settings
- Houses (made from cardboard boxes)
- Sandbox area for "planting"
- Fishing area
- Camps
- Boat area

Props:
- Boat (Mayflower)
- Houses (made from cardboard boxes)
- Dishes, pots, and pans
- Pretend food
- Blue sheet (for lake or river)
- Fishing poles (with magnets attached to catch fish)
- Fish (with paper clips attached)
- Sandbox for "planting"

Roles
- Mothers
- Fathers
- Children
- Sailors

General Description of Activity

Children pretend to be Pilgrims, who traveled by boat to the new world. They can build houses, plant corn, and go fishing for food. The children can work on the houses and in the fields. They can also have a big dinner to celebrate the harvest!

Verbal Productions

Level of linguistic complexity varies with the role or competency of the child playing the role.
- "I need five fish for supper. Go catch some" or "Catch fish, please"
- "He is building the house" or "Build house"
- "My turn to plant the corn" or "My turn now"

Adult Facilitative Role:

The adult is to facilitate role play and help expand language and literacy skills. Typical actions or strategies to use include

Playing a role: "I am a Pilgrim. I am going to the New World."

Modeling a statement/vocabulary: "The name of the boat is the Mayflower."

Expanding a child's utterances: "Big log cabin" to "He made a big log cabin."

Redirecting a child to a peer: "Ask John if you can help build another log cabin. Say, 'Can I help?'"

Modeling phonological awareness: "Yes, 'new,' 'nose,' and 'nice' all start with the letter N."

ART **Food Collage**

Objectives
1. Express creativity
2. Develop small motor skills (e.g., drawing, painting, cutting, pasting)
3. Practice turn-taking skills
4. Converse with peers and adults

Materials
- White paper plates or construction paper
- Scissors
- Magazines (with pictures of food)
- Newspapers (food ads)
- Glue

General Description of Activity

Children cut out pictures of food from magazines or newspapers advertisements, then glue these pictures on round white paper plates (or construction paper) to make a food collage. With assistance, older children could make a picture of the different food groups.

November

Week 14
Homes—
Thanksgiving
Week

MONDAY

GROUP **Alphabet Grab Bag**

Objectives
1. Improve listening skills
2. Improve knowledge of the alphabet and sounds
3. Learn appropriate group-interaction skills
4. Practice turn-taking skills

Materials
- Alphabet chart
- Drawstring bag
- Letters to be placed on the chart

General Description of Activity

Place an alphabet chart on the floor in front of the children. Put several letters into a drawstring bag. Draw out one letter and have the children label it. Place the letter on top of the same letter on the alphabet chart. Tell the children that next they will draw a letter out of the bag and find the letter on the chart.

Group Participation

Pass the bag around and have each child pull out a letter. Ask different children to come up and label their letter and place it on the chart. There may be several of the same letters depending on how many letters are being reviewed.

Variation

The children may provide the sound as well as the label of the letter. Or the child may only be asked to match the letter to the one on the chart, without identifying it.

Optional

Use a chart with uppercase letters and put only lowercase letters in the bag.

Summary/Transition Activity

Review the letters by having the children recite the alphabet as you point to each letter on the chart.

Tuesday

Dramatic Play	Art	Group	Story	Song
Native American Homes	Cheerios Necklaces	Letter *N*	*The Legend of the Bluebonnet*	"A Turkey Is a Funny Bird"

DAILY PLANNING GUIDE

Language and Literacy Skills Facilitated

Vocabulary: *Indian, wickiups, drums, headbands, hunting, fishing, corn, Thanksgiving, turkey, waddle, necklaces*

Verb phrase structures: *is hunting, hunts, hunted, works, was working, worked, runs, ran, eat, ate, was eating*

Adjective/object descriptions: *tall wikiup, loud drums, big/little fish*

Question structures: *what, how, where, when, who, what if, why, how many, which one*

Pronouns: *I, you, he, she, we, they, my, your, him, her, his, our, their, me, us, them*

Prepositions: *in, on, under, over, near, beneath, next to, beside, around, inside, outside*

Sounds: /k/ *can, turkey, work;* /s/ *sit, inside, works;* /r/ *ran, carrot, far*

Noting print has meaning: names on chairs and on cubbies, signs in dramatic play, words in books and on chalkboard

Noting sound–symbol associations: What sound does _____ start with?

Writing: letters, names, words

Social Skills Facilitated

Initiating interaction with peers and adults; responding to questions and requests from peers and adults

Negotiating with peers for toys and materials

Group cooperation: waiting for a turn in a group, taking a turn at the appropriate time

Cognitive Skills Facilitated

Problem-solving skills: how to build a wickiup

Classification skills: words that start with *N*

Sequencing skills: story, songs

Narrative/story structure: adventure

Motor Skills Facilitated

Large motor: outdoor play activities—jumping, running, hopping, pedaling, climbing

Small motor: writing, drawing, gluing, cutting

DRAMATIC PLAY: **Native American Homes**

Type of Activity: Central

Objectives
1. Learn new, and employ familiar, vocabulary
2. Learn new, and employ a variety of, syntactic constructions
3. Interact with peers
4. Sequence familiar routines
5. Expand conceptual knowledge of the world

November

Week 14
Homes—
Thanksgiving
Week

TUESDAY

Setting
- Two wickiups (e.g., tents covered with a dark sheet that makes the tent look rounded on top or boxes covered with straw placemats to simulate a wikiup)
- Fire area
- Pond area

Props
- Fish
- Fishing poles
- Pretend food (e.g., corn, carrots)
- Brown paper sacks (for clothes)
- Feathers
- Headbands
- Horses
- Pottery dishes

Roles
- Native American men
- Native American women
- Native American children
- Chief

General Description of Activity

The children learn about some of the homes and life of early plains Native Americans by pretending to live in a wickiup and to cook over a campfire. Children ride horses, looking for buffalos, and fish for food. They decorate their wickiup with drawings and wear clothes made of leather.

Verbal Productions

Level of linguistic complexity varies with the role or competency of the child playing the role.
- "I am riding my horse to look for buffalo" or "My horse"
- "I caught five fish" or "Fish"
- "My headband has two feathers" or "That mine"
- "I am going hunting in the woods" or "Hunt"

Adult Facilitative Role

The adult is to facilitate role play and help expand language and literacy skills. Typical actions or strategies to use include

Playing a role: "I am planting some corn. Do you want to help?"

Modeling a statement/vocabulary: "We are taking turkey and corn to feast with the pilgrims. A feast is a big dinner with friends."

Identifying rhyming words: "The words *corn, horn,* and *born* all rhyme."

Expanding a child's utterance: "He eat corn" to "He eats corn."

Asking open questions: "What should we take to the feast?"

ART **Cheerios Necklaces**

Objectives
1. Express creativity
2. Develop small motor skills (e.g., drawing, painting, cutting, pasting)
3. Practice turn-taking skills
4. Converse with peers and adults

Materials
- Different colors of Cheerios (with holes big enough for a string to go through)
- String or yarn (one end wrapped in tape to make threading easier)
- Pieces of paper
- Straws cut up in small pieces

General Description of Activity

Children make necklaces by stringing Cheerios. The Cheerios can be different colors. Children can also string small pieces of construction paper or straws cut to different lengths between the

Cheerios, if desired. Tie one Cheerio to one end of the string so the others will not fall off the string after they are strung.

November

Week 14
Homes—
Thanksgiving
Week

TUESDAY

GROUP **Letter *N***

Objectives
1. Improve listening skills
2. Increase knowledge of the alphabet
3. Learn appropriate group-interaction skills
4. Practice turn-taking skills

Materials
- Alphabet chart
- Poster paper and markers (optional)
- Blackboard and chalk
- Pictures of objects (or objects themselves) with names that begin with *N*
- Alphabet picture displays
- Picture dictionary
- Individual chalkboards (optional)
- Cards or sticky notes with *N* and *n* written on them (optional)
- Cards or sticky notes with previously learned letters written on them (optional)

General Description of Activity

Have two or three children come to the front of the group to sing the alphabet song. Point to the letters on the alphabet chart as the song is sung, then write an upper- and a lowercase *N* on the blackboard (or poster paper). Give several examples of words that begin with *N*, emphasizing the /n/ ("nnn") sound at the beginning of the words. You might hold up objects or pictures of objects whose names begin with *N*. Direct the children's attention to the alphabet picture displays around the room.

Group Participation

Ask if anyone's name starts with *N* (e.g., Nydia, Nathan, Natasha). Have those children write the letter *N* on the board. Also have two or three other children write the letter *N* on the blackboard. Provides verbal guidance as children form the letter: "Start at the top and draw a line straight down. Go back to the top and draw a slanted line from the first line to the bottom. Stay at the bottom and draw a straight line back up, even with the top." If necessary, help the children write the letter. Some of the children can practice writing *N* in the air with their fingers (or on individual chalkboards). Ask the children to think of words that begin with N. Write the words they offer on the blackboard and draws quick sketches (when possible) of the suggested words. If a child suggests a word that does not begin with *N*, say, "No, that begins with ____," and say the two sounds so children can compare them. To help children who cannot think of any words, prompt them with pictures or objects representing words that begin with *N*. (Pictures or objects can be handed out at the beginning of the lesson or as the lesson proceeds.) Additional words can be sought in a picture dictionary if the group has difficulty arriving at words that begin with *N*.

Summary/Transition Activity

After about 10–15 words have been suggested, review the words, emphasizing the "nnn" sound. You might also give the children cards or sticky notes with the upper- and lowercase *N* written on them as children identify the letter or the sound. The children can take the cards or notes home.

Variation

Scatter several sticky notes with either an upper- or lowercase *N* written on them around the room. Ask children, one at a time, to find the capital *N* or the lowercase *n*. Put out a few letters previously learned, too, so children have to discriminate between *N* and other letters.

Wednesday

Dramatic Play	Art	Group	Story	Song
Our Home Today	Watercolor Paintings	Thankfulness List	*Thanksgiving Today*	"Five Little Turkeys"

DAILY PLANNING GUIDE

Language and Literacy Skills Facilitated

Vocabulary: *cook, house, food, soup, stew, muffins, babies, wash, table, clean, button, zip, teeth, toothbrush, dentist*

Verb phrase structures: *is cooking, was cooking, cooks, cooked, fixes, fixed, makes, made, do you have ___?, eats, ate, has eaten, washes, washed*

Adjective/object descriptions: *good food, hot/cold food, sweet/tart fruit, green vegetables, red apple, yellow banana, dirty/clean baby*

Question structures: *what, how, where, when, who, what if, why, how many, which one*

Pronouns: *I, you, he, she, we, they, my, your, him, her, his, our, their, me, us, them*

Prepositions: *in, on, under, over, near, beneath, next to, beside, around, inside, outside*

Sounds: /k/ *cook, cooking, make;* /l/ *lick, Jell-o, yell;* /s/ *see, cooks;* /r/ *roof, carrot, bar*

Noting print has meaning: names on chairs and on cubbies, signs in dramatic play, words in books and on chalkboard

Noting sound–symbol associations: What sound does _____ start with?

Writing: letters, names, words

Social Skills Facilitated

Initiating interaction with peers and adults; responding to questions and requests from peers and adults

Negotiating with peers for toys and materials

Group cooperation: waiting for a turn in a group, taking a turn at the appropriate time

Cognitive Skills Facilitated

Problem-solving skills: how to brush teeth, zip jackets, button buttons

Classification skills: things we use to care for ourselves

Sequencing skills: story, songs

Narrative/story structure: rhyming, repetitive lines

Motor Skills Facilitated

Large motor: outdoor play activities—jumping, running, hopping, pedaling, climbing

Small motor: writing, drawing, gluing, squeezing, swirling

DRAMATIC PLAY **Our Home Today**

Type of Activity: Central Sequential Related

Objectives
1. Learn new, and employ familiar, vocabulary
2. Learn new, and employ a variety of, syntactic constructions
3. Interact with peers
4. Sequence familiar routines
5. Expand conceptual knowledge of the world

November

Week 14
Homes—
Thanksgiving
Week

WEDNESDAY

Settings	• Kitchen area • Bedrooms	• Dining rooms • Family rooms	• House (child-sized house or dismantled cardboard box—optional)
Props	• Play refrigerator • Cupboards • Play stove • Play sink • Dishes	• Pots and pans • Beds • Dolls • Pretend food • Baby bottles	• Mops and brooms • Pretend vacuum • Tablecloths (optional) • Thanksgiving party decorations
Roles	• Mothers • Fathers	• Babies and other children	• Party guests (optional)

General Description of Activity

The housekeeping center is where the children can set up a pretend house or apartment, including a kitchen. Here the children can clean the house, take care of their babies, cook food, set the table, make table decorations, and prepare for a Thanksgiving party.

Verbal Productions

Level of linguistic complexity varies with the role or competency of the child playing the role.

- "Clean the table" or "Clean"
- "Use the broom to sweep the floor" or "Sweep here"
- "I'll do it later" or "Okay"
- "The baby is hungry. Please get the bottle" or "Baby crying"

Adult Facilitative Role

The adult is to facilitate role play and help expand language and literacy skills. Typical actions or strategies to use include

Playing a role: "Let's have a turkey for Thanksgiving and some apple pie."

Expanding a child's utterance: "Jane set table for company" to "Jane is setting the table for company."

Redirecting a child to a peer: "Ask her to pass the pumpkin pie. Say, 'May I have some pie, please?'"

Providing confirmatory feedback: "Yes, the words *pie* and *cry* rhyme."

Using a cloze procedure: "This bowl is full, and this bowl is _____(empty)."

ART **Watercolor Paintings**

Objectives	1. Express creativity 2. Develop small motor skills (e.g., drawing, painting, cutting, pasting) 3. To practice turn-taking skills 4. Converse with peers and adults
Materials	• Watercolor paints • Water in tubs • Brushes • White construction paper

General Description of Activity

Lay out white construction paper, watercolor paint boxes, and brushes. Place tubs of water to clean the brushes above the paper. Children put on a smock, select a brush, wet it, and choose a paint color. The children can paint a collage of colors, animals, people, scenery, and so on. The children

November

Week 14

Homes—
Thanksgiving
Week

WEDNESDAY

should rinse their brush before selecting a new color. You may want to be close by so that children can talk about their paintings.

GROUP **Thankfulness List**

Objectives
1. Improve listening skills
2. Increase sequencing ability
3. Learn appropriate group-interaction skills
4. Practice turn-taking skills

Materials
• Large sheet of paper
• Markers

General Description of Activity

Briefly discuss Thanksgiving, what it means, and why we celebrate it. Then ask the children what they are thankful for. Make a list of what they say on a big sheet of poster-sized paper. Be sure to add your own thoughts, too.

Group Participation

Have the children draw or write down what they are thankful for on an individual sheet of paper.

Summary/Transition Activity

Review what the children (and adults) have written or drawn. Display the poster paper for parents and have children take home individual drawings or writings.

WEEKLY PLANNING GUIDE

	Dramatic Play	Art	Group	Story	Song
Monday *Suggested Props and Materials*	Pioneers *Pioneer scenario, wagons (made from cardboard boxes), stick horses, reins, cows, wild animals, dishes, pretend food, campfire sticks, pots and pans, blue sheet for river, cowboy hats, bonnet, sleeping bags, guitars*	Playdough *Playdough, smocks, rolling pins, cookie cutters, presses, wooden craft sticks*	Letter *O* *Pictures and objects of words that begin with letter O, alphabet chart, dictionary*	*And You Can Be the Cat*	"She'll Be Coming 'Round the Mountain"
Tuesday *Suggested Props and Materials*	Space Exploration *Space scenario, pretend rocket ship, helmets, backpacks, walking boards, "moon rocks," mini-trampoline, pretend television sets, microphones, headsets, pretend computers*	Space Pictures *Black paper, glitter paint, gold stars (optional), smocks*	Things that Fly *Items/pictures of things that fly (e.g., birds) and do not fly (e.g., cars), two containers*	*Big Silver Space Shuttle*	"Twinkle, Twinkle, Little Star"
Wednesday *Suggested Props and Materials*	Under-the-Sea Exploration *Under-the-sea scenario, pretend ship, steering wheel, ocean area, toy sea animals, coral reef, goggles, divers' helmets, fishing poles, fish, telescope, pretend radio*	Crayon Washes *Crayons, watered-down tempera paint, brushes, water, smocks*	Sorting Shells *Seashells of varying shape and color and texture, two or three containers or tubs*	*Rainbow Fish to the Rescue*	"All the Little Fishies"
Thursday *Suggested Props and Materials*	Jungle/Safari *Jungle scenario, pretend palm trees, paper chains for vines, variety of stuffed jungle animals, safari van, play cameras, jungle pictures, food for animals, tickets for safari van, pretend microphone for tour guide, safari hats, pretend money*	Coffee Filter/ Clothespin Butterflies *Wooden clothespins, coffee filters, markers, yarn (optional), tissue paper, pipe cleaners*	Tapping out Syllables *Drum, patterns*	*Peanut Butter Rhino*	"Tarzan of the Apes"

MY NOTES

NEWSLETTER

Vol. 1, No. 15

Date: _____

Adventure

Monday

Wagons ho! Pioneers who settled the west will be busy in the classroom during dramatic play. The children will drive wagons, ride horses, make camp, and even pan for gold. In art, the children will make playdough constructions. The story is *And You Can Be the Cat*. Children will focus on the letter *O* during group time. "She'll Be Coming 'Round the Mountain" will be one of the songs during music.

Tuesday

This day's dramatic play activity will be about space exploration. The children can be the astronauts in the shuttle, the astronauts visiting the moon, or the ground controllers. In art, the children will make space pictures with glitter paint. Our story today will be *The Big Silver Space Shuttle*. During group time, we will talk about things that fly. Our featured song is "Twinkle, Twinkle, Little Star."

Wednesday

Today the children will explore life under the sea. They will look for sea animals and for shells and coral reefs. They will also be fishing. Children will make a crayon wash picture in art. Our story today will be *Rainbow Fish to the Rescue*. During group time, children will sort seashells into several classifications: big, little, round, fan shaped, and others. Our featured song will be "All the Little Fishies."

Thursday

Today the children will go on a jungle adventure. They can be the safari guides, the van driver, the tourists, or the animals. In art, children will make coffee filter butterflies. *Peanut Butter Rhino* is our story for today. During group time, children will tap out the syllables in words, such as their names. Our featured song is "Tarzan of the Apes."

Monday

Dramatic Play	Art	Group	Story	Song
Pioneers	Playdough	Letter O	*And You Can Be the Cat*	"She'll Be Coming 'Round the Mountain"

DAILY PLANNING GUIDE

Language and Literacy Skills Facilitated

Vocabulary: *cowboys, pioneers, covered wagon, search, reins, land, campfire, explore, pitch camp, guitar, wheels, travel, horses*

Verb phrase structures: *is gathering wood, he searches, searched, played the guitar, built a fire, who is going? I am, who is lost? John is*

Adjective/object descriptions: *open spaces, big wagon, brave pioneer, covered wagon*

Question structures: *what, how, where, when, who, what if, why, how many, which one*

Pronouns: *I, you, he, she, we, they, my, your, him, her, his, our, their, me, us, them*

Prepositions: *in, on, under, over, near, beneath, next to, beside, around, inside, outside*

Sounds: /k/ *cowboy, milk;* /r/ *range, pioneer, star;* /f/ *find, food, off;* /l/ *land, yellow, wheel*

Noting print has meaning: names on chairs and on cubbies, signs in dramatic play, words in books and on chalkboard

Noting sound–symbol associations: What sound does _____ start with?

Writing: letters, names, words

Social Skills Facilitated

Initiating interaction with peers and adults; responding to questions and requests from peers and adults

Negotiating with peers for toys and materials

Group cooperation: waiting for a turn in a group, taking a turn at the appropriate time

Cognitive Skills Facilitated

Problem-solving skills: how to make a covered wagon

Classification skills: things a pioneer uses

Sequencing skills: songs, story

Narrative/story structure: adventure

Motor Skills Facilitated

Large motor: outdoor play activities—jumping, running, hopping, pedaling, climbing

Small motor: writing, drawing, gluing, painting

DRAMATIC PLAY **Pioneers**

Type of Activity: Central

Objectives
1. Learn new, and employ familiar, vocabulary
2. Learn new, and employ a variety of, syntactic constructions
3. Interact with peers
4. Sequence familiar routines
5. Expand conceptual knowledge of the world

General Description of Activity

Children explore pioneer life. They can ride in pretend wagons or on stick horses, or they can pretend to be the horses pulling the wagon. They can take care of their animals. They can wear cowboy hats and boots or bonnets and long dresses. They can catch fish and then cook them over their campfires. They can play guitars and sing around the campfire or in the wagons.

Settings	
• Wagons (made from cardboard boxes)	• Fishing area
	• Camps

Props

- Wagons (made from cardboard boxes)
- Stick horses
- Cows and other farm animals (made out of brown paper bags)
- Wild animals (stuffed animals)
- Reins
- Dishes
- Pretend food

- Blue sheet (for lake or river)
- Fishing poles (with magnets attached to catch fish)
- Fish (with paper clips attached)
- Pots and pans
- Cowboy hats and boots
- Bonnets and long dresses
- Sleeping bags
- Guitars

Roles

- Mothers
- Fathers
- Children

- Animals
- Wagon train leader

Verbal Productions

Level of linguistic complexity varies with the role or competency of the child playing the role.

- "How far is it to the next camp?" or "How far?"
- "I need five fish for supper. Go catch some" or "Catch fish, please"
- "He is driving the wagon" or "Drive wagon"
- "My turn to play the guitar" or "My turn now"

Adult Facilitative Role

The adult is to facilitate role play and help expand language and literacy skills. Typical actions or strategies to use include

Playing a role: "I am driving the covered wagon. We are going to California."

Modeling a statement/vocabulary: "A pioneer is one who travels to new places where few people have before. Some pioneers traveled to California hoping to discover gold."

Expanding a child's utterance: "Want gold" to "He wants to find some gold."

Contrasting two sounds: "Do you mean 'told' or 'sold?'"

Providing a literacy model: "That sign says *California or bust.*"

ART **Playdough**

Objectives

1. Express creativity
2. Develop small motor skills (e.g., drawing, painting, cutting, pasting)
3. Practice turn-taking skills
4. Converse with peers and adults

Materials

- Smocks
- Playdough
- Rolling pins
- Cookie cutters
- Cookie presses
- Wooden craft sticks
- Cutting boards

General Description of Activity

Children wash their hands and put on smocks to explore playdough on the art table, using various presses, cutters, rolling pins, wooden craft sticks, and other tools. Children can make pretend food or any other objects out of the dough by rolling, cutting, or making pressing motions. They can form animals or people by rolling a main body and then adding heads, arms, and legs. Yarn can be used for hair (if children want to take their creations home). When children are finished, they roll the dough into a ball, wash their hands, and take off and fold their smocks.

GROUP **Letter *O***

Objectives

1. Improve listening skills
2. Increase knowledge of the alphabet and sounds
3. Learn appropriate group-interaction skills
4. Practice turn-taking skills

Materials

- Blackboard and chalk
- Pairs of pictures of objects (or objects themselves) whose names begin with *O*, such as oboe and octopus
- Poster paper (optional)

General Description of Activity

Write an upper- and a lowercase letter *O* on the blackboard (or on poster paper). Tell the children, "*O* has several sounds. You hear one of them when the letter sounds like its name: /o/ (oh), as in the word *open*. Another sound is heard in the word *octopus*. Can you hear the /a/ sound?" Have the children practice saying the long and short *O* sounds.

Group Participation

Ask if anyone's name starts with *O* (e.g, Oliver, Owen), and have those children write the letter *O* on the blackboard. Also have two other children come up to the front. Give each a picture of an object (or the object itself) with a name that begins with *O*. One child's picture (or object) should begin with the long *O* sound and the other with the short *O* sound. The children verbally label their pictures or objects for the group. Help them elongate the long or short *O* sound, as appropriate. Have the children place their pictures (or objects) in different piles, beginning a pile for each of the *O* sounds. Invite two more children at a time to take a turn at naming *O* words and placing the pictures (or objects) in the correct piles.

Summary/Transition Activity

Review the long and short vowels sounds of *O* by saying the sounds one last time and holding up representative pictures.

Tuesday

Dramatic Play	Art	Group	Story	Song
Space Exploration	Space Pictures	Things that Fly	*Big Silver Space Shuttle*	"Twinkle, Twinkle, Little Star"

DAILY PLANNING GUIDE

Language Skills Facilitated

Vocabulary: *space, rocket ship, planet, gravity, adventure, spacesuit, astronaut, orbit, sun, moon, stars, blast off, oxygen*

Verb phrase structures: *count<u>ed</u> down, <u>are</u> count<u>ing</u>, travel<u>ing</u> in space, <u>saw</u> stars, blast<u>ing</u> off, pack<u>ed</u> food, us<u>ing</u> oxygen*

Adjective/object descriptions: *bright stars, fast ship, big planet, weird colors, little stars, black hole*

Question structures: *what, how, where, when, who, what if, why, how many, which one*

Pronouns: *I, you, he, she, we, they, my, your, him, her, his, our, their, me, us, them*

Prepositions: *in, on, under, over, near, beneath, next to, beside, around, inside, outside*

Sounds: /r/ <u>r</u>ocket, sta<u>r</u>; /s/ <u>s</u>pace, <u>s</u>un, fa<u>ce</u>; /l/ <u>l</u>ight, Je<u>ll</u>-o, be<u>ll</u>; /k/ <u>c</u>an, ro<u>ck</u>et, lo<u>ck</u>

Noting print has meaning: names on chairs and on cubbies, signs in dramatic play, words in books and on chalkboard

Noting sound–symbol associations: What sound does _____ start with?

Writing: letters, names, words

Social Skills Facilitated

Initiating interaction with peers and adults; responding to questions and requests from peers and adults

Negotiating with peers for toys and materials

Group cooperation: waiting for a turn in a group, taking a turn at the appropriate time

Cognitive Skills Facilitated

Problem-solving skills: how to get up in space

Classification skills: What things are in outer space?

Sequencing skills: countdown, story, songs

Narrative/story structure: adventure

Motor Skills Facilitated

Large motor: outdoor play activities—jumping, running, hopping, pedaling, climbing

Small motor: writing, drawing, gluing, fingerpainting

DRAMATIC PLAY **Space Exploration**

Type of Activity: Central

Objectives
1. Learn new, and employ familiar, vocabulary
2. Learn new, and employ a variety of, syntactic constructions
3. Interact with peers
4. Sequence familiar routines
5. Expand conceptual knowledge of the world

Settings
- Rocket ship (playhouse with chairs placed sideways on the floor so children can lie in them and look upward)
- Command center (with pretend television sets and computers)
- Moon

Props
- Rocket ship (playhouse with chairs placed sideways on the floor so children can lie in them and look upward)
- Helmets
- Backpacks
- Walking boards
- Moon rocks (crushed newspaper covered with gray duct tape)
- Miniature trampoline
- Television sets (shoeboxes with one side cut out and a picture pasted over the cutout area)
- Microphones (toilet paper rolls)
- Headsets
- Pretend computers
- Videotape about the space program
- Walkie-talkies
- Moon vehicle (optional)

Roles
- Astronauts
- Command center workers
- Technicians

General Description of Activity

Children pretend to be astronauts and go to the moon in a spacecraft. Once on the moon, they can find moon rocks, jump (on a miniature trampoline) to see how light they feel, and so forth. Some of the children can remain on earth at the command center and talk to the astronauts. Show a brief videotape on the space program to the children so they begin to understand about rocket ships, the need to wear special suits in space, and what the moon really looks like.

Verbal Productions

Level of linguistic complexity varies with the role or competency of the child playing the role.
- "She found a big moon rock" or "Big"
- "I can jump high. Watch me!" or "Look!"
- "He is landing the rocket ship" or "He landed it"
- "You can see the earth. It is blue." "I see the moon"

Adult Facilitative Role

The adult is to facilitate role play and help expand language and literacy skills. Typical actions or strategies to use include

Playing a role: "We are ready for take-off. Ten, nine, eight, seven, six, five, four, three, two, one, blast-off!"

Modeling a statement/vocabulary: "We are astronauts and our rocket ship is going to the moon."

Redirecting a child to a peer: "Ask Joseph for a turn on the toy Land Rover. Say, 'May I have a turn, please?'"

Identifying rhyming words: "Yes, the words *moon, soon,* and *noon* all rhyme."

Recasting a child's utterance (present progressive to third person singular): "He is jump<u>ing</u>" to "He jump<u>s</u> very high."

ART Space Pictures

Objectives
1. Express creativity
2. Develop small motor skills (e.g., drawing, painting, cutting, pasting)
3. Practice turn-taking skills
4. Converse with peers and adults

Materials
- Black construction paper
- Glitter paint in a variety of colors (Glitter paint can be made by adding glitter to tempera paint.)

General Description of Activity

The teacher gives each child a piece of black construction paper. The children paint a variety of pictures onto the black paper using glitter paint. They can paint planets, rocket ships, or stars on their paper. Silver and gold stickers may also be added to the pictures.

GROUP **Things that Fly**

Objectives
1. Improve listening skills
2. Increase conceptual knowledge
3. Learn appropriate group-interaction skills
4. Practice turn-taking skills

Materials
- Toys and objects that can fly (e.g., airplane, bird, helicopter, kite, paper airplane, glider)
- Toys and objects that cannot fly (car, doll, train, block, ball)
- Tubs labeled *fly* and *can't fly* (with picture labels of an airplane and a car)

General Description of Activity

Begin by "flying" a paper airplane and then talk about the characteristics of things that fly. Put the airplane in the container labeled *fly*.

Group Participation

Give each child an object that represents something that either flies or does not fly. Have children come to the front, one by one, and tell whether their object can fly or not. They can put the object in the box that corresponds with their correct decision.

Summary/Transition Activity

Have everyone stand up, pretend to fly, and then land on the ground.

Wednesday

Dramatic Play	Art	Group	Story	Song
Under-the-Sea Exploration	Crayon Washes	Sorting Shells	*Rainbow Fish to the Rescue*	"All the Little Fishies"

DAILY PLANNING GUIDE

Language and Literacy Skills Facilitated

Vocabulary: *whale, shark, fish, seaweed, diving, ocean, microscope, coral, shell, submarine, scuba dive*

Verb phrase structures: *go<u>ing</u> to the beach, fish<u>ing</u>, look<u>ing</u> for sea shells, <u>swam</u>*

Adjective/object descriptions: *big fish, soft sand, rough shell, deep water, bright sun*

Question structures: *what, how, where, when, who, what if, why, how many, which one*

Pronouns: *I, you, he, she, we, they, my, your, him, her, his, our, their, me, us, them*

Prepositions: *in, on, under, over, near, beneath, next to, beside, around, inside, outside*

Sounds: /sh/ <u>sh</u>ark, fi<u>sh</u>; /f/ <u>f</u>un, of<u>f</u>; /s/ <u>s</u>un, bu<u>s</u>

Noting print has meaning: names on chairs and on cubbies, signs in dramatic play, words in books and on chalkboard

Noting sound–symbol associations: What sound does _____ start with?

Writing: letters, names, words

Social Skills Facilitated

Initiating interaction with peers and adults; responding to questions and requests from peers and adults

Negotiating with peers for toys and materials

Group cooperation: waiting for a turn in a group, taking a turn at the appropriate time

Cognitive Skills Facilitated

Problem-solving skills: learning how to fish, searching for sea shells, story

Classification skills: sorting shells

Sequencing skills: story, songs

Motor Skills Facilitated

Large motor: outdoor play activities—jumping, running, hopping, spinning

Small motor: coloring, painting, searching for shells

DRAMATIC PLAY : **Under-the-Sea Exploration**

Type of Activity: Central

Objectives
1. Learn new, and employ familiar, vocabulary
2. Learn new, and employ a variety of, syntactic constructions
3. Interact with peers
4. Sequence familiar routines
5. Expand conceptual knowledge of the world

Settings
- Under the sea area
- Coral reef (cardboard box with an open top, wrapped in construction paper)
- Sand area
- Sea area with boat
- Fishing area (optional)

Props
- Goggles
- Swimming fins
- Seashells
- Fish
- Fishing poles
- Plastic sea animals
- Boat
- Plastic "fish" shower curtain
- Sandbox and sand
- Blue sheet or piece of large paper (for water)
- Sand toys
- Camera

Roles
- Divers
- Boat riders
- Sunbathers
- Fishermen and women
- People playing in the sand

General Description of Activity

Set up an under-the-sea environment by aligning bookshelves in straight lines, two on one side and two facing them, with a "fish" shower curtain (a curtain that is transparent with different fish on it) draped over all the bookshelves. The children can "swim" under the curtain amid shells and plastic fish on the shelves. In another area, set up a boat area or an area where divers can jump into the "water." A sand area might have seashells buried in the sand for children to find (instead of a sand table, use a large cardboard box 4' × 6' × 5" high, lined with plastic—the low sides will allow children to kneel outside the sand area while they play). Still another area can be set up for fishing. (If desired, use a water table.) Thus, children can pretend to be divers, boat riders, people fishing, or people enjoying the water or beach.

Verbal Productions

Level of linguistic complexity varies with the role or competency of the child playing the role.
- "I am diving under the water with my goggles" or "My goggles"
- "I found a big shell and a little shell" or "That my shell"
- "See all of the red coral" or "See coral"

Adult Facilitative Role

The adult is to facilitate role play and help expand language and literacy skills. Typical actions or strategies to use include

Playing a role: "I am looking for different kinds of fish. Oh, look, there is a dolphin."

Contrasting two sounds: "Do you mean 'fat' or 'pat?'"

Asking open questions: "How can we catch the fish?"

Modeling the reading of a sign: "That sign says *wait here*. We wait here for a ride in the boat."

Modeling correct production of /sh/ sound: "I see a <u>sh</u>ark and some fi<u>sh</u>. Let's see if we can take the <u>sh</u>ells back to the <u>sh</u>ip."

Expanding a child's utterance: "It's not here" to "You're right; it is not here. Let's look in the boat."

```
ART   Crayon Washes
```

Objectives
1. Express creativity
2. Develop small motor skills (e.g., drawing, painting, cutting, pasting)
3. Practice turn-taking skills
4. Converse with peers and adults

Materials
- Paper suitable for watercolors, such as manila paper or white construction paper
- Crayons
- Tempera paint (some full strength, some watered down)
- Rinse water
- Brushes
- Smocks

General Description of Activity

The children draw on their paper with vividly colored crayons, pressing hard so that the lines can be seen easily. They may want to make pictures of their families, pets, or houses, or of flowers, shapes, or something related to the daily or weekly theme. After the drawings are completed, the children paint over their pictures with watered-down tempera paint. The paint will not stick to the crayon but will fill in a background color. Children can also paint frames around the pictures with full-strength tempera paint of the same, or a contrasting, color from that used in the wash.

Variation

For holidays, children might draw images associated with the holiday and do the wash in paint of a holiday color. For example, at Halloween, they could draw pumpkins, cats, bats, and so forth and then use watered-down orange tempera paint for the wash.

GROUP **Sorting Shells**

Objectives
1. Improve listening skills
2. Increase identification skills
3. Increase vocabulary skills
4. Increase comparative skills
5. Practice turn-taking skills
6. Learn appropriate group-interaction skills

Materials
- Shells of varying sizes, shapes, colors, and textures

General Description of Activity

Present several kinds of shells. Include large, small, rough, and smooth shells, along with some of different colors and shapes. Place some of the fan-shaped shells in one pile and some cone-shaped ones in another to show the children one way of sorting the shells.

Group Participation

Give each child a shell. Ask children to examine their shells and decide if they go in any of the categories already determined or if a new category is needed. As each child places a shell in a pile (or starts a new one), ask the child to explain why the shell belongs in that pile. Children may decide to sort shells based on size, shape, color, texture, or some other characteristic.

Summary/ Transition Activity

Review the different categories created by the children.

Thursday

Dramatic Play	Art	Group	Story	Song
Jungle/Safari	Coffee Filter/ Clothespin Butterflies	Tapping out Syllables	*Peanut Butter Rhino*	"Tarzan of the Apes"

DAILY PLANNING GUIDE

Language and Literacy Skills Facilitated

Vocabulary: *jungle, elephant, rhino, giraffe, tiger, lion, monkey, ape, rainforest, snakes, vines, palm trees, safari, camera*

Verb phrase structures: *walk in the jungle, photograph the ____, find the snake, see the ____, cross the river*

Adjective/object descriptions: *big ____, little ____, large ____, small ____, yellow lion, spotted leopard, striped tiger*

Question structures: *what, how, where, when, who, what if, why, how many, which one*

Pronouns: *I, you, he, she, we, they, my, your, him, her, his, our, their, me, us, them*

Prepositions: *in, on, under, over, near, beneath, next to, beside, around, inside, outside*

Sounds: /g/ *go, tiger, log;* /k/ *camera, monkey, snake;* /f/ *find, often, off*

Noting print has meaning: names on chairs and on cubbies, signs in dramatic play, words in books and on chalkboard

Noting sound–symbol associations: What sound does ____ start with?

Writing: letters, names, words

Social Skills Facilitated

Initiating interaction with peers and adults; responding to questions and requests from peers and adults

Negotiating with peers for toys and materials

Group cooperation: waiting for a turn in a group, taking a turn at the appropriate time

Cognitive Skills Facilitated

Problem-solving skills: things in a jungle

Classification skills: jungle animals

Sequencing skills: songs, story

Narrative/story structure: adventure

Motor Skills Facilitated

Large motor: outdoor play activities—jumping, running, hopping, pedaling, climbing

Small motor: writing, drawing, painting

DRAMATIC PLAY **Jungle/Safari**

Type of Activity: Central

Objectives
1. Learn new, and employ familiar, vocabulary
2. Learn new, and employ a variety of, syntactic constructions
3. Interact with peers
4. Sequence familiar routines
5. Expand conceptual knowledge of the world

Settings
- Jungle (pretend palm trees and paper chain vines hung around the dramatic play area)
- Safari van (a cardboard box in front of child-sized house to make a cab area for driver)
- River or pond (marked with tape or a blue sheet)
- Amusement park (optional)

Props
- Pretend palm trees (made from two pieces of tagboard stapled together over a pretend stop sign or use a large piece of cardboard to form the trunk)
- Paper chains
- Variety of stuffed jungle animals
- Safari van (a cardboard box in front of child-sized house)
- Play cameras
- Jungle pictures
- Food for animals
- Tickets for the safari van ride
- Pretend microphone for the tour guide
- Tour guide hat
- Pretend money
- Bridge over the river
- Concession stand (optional)
- Pretend rides for the amusement park (optional)

Roles
- Van driver
- Tour guide
- Passengers
- Animals
- Amusement park workers

General Description of Activity

Set up a mock jungle with palm trees, vines, and a river, along with stuffed animals to inhabit it. Create a safari van to take children on tours. They can take pictures of the animals, pretend to be the animals, or be the tour guides and tell tourists all about the animals they see. An extension of this activity is to make the jungle part of an amusement park scenario. Some of the children can be the workers at "Jungleland" and take tickets or feed the animals.

Verbal Productions

Level of linguistic complexity varies with the role or competency of the child playing the role.
- "On the left, you see the big elephant, and on the right, the tiger" or "See tiger"
- "I want a ticket to ride on the van," "I want a ride," or "Ticket"
- "There is a baby elephant and a mommy one" or "Baby"
- "I am the driver" or "It's my turn to drive"

Adult Facilitative Role

The adult is to facilitate role play and help expand language and literacy skills. Typical actions or strategies to use include

Playing a role: "I am driving the safari bus. Look out the window to see the lions."

Contrasting two location terms: "That monkey is in the tree. The other monkey is under the tree."

Modeling a statement/vocabulary: "The jungle has very thick vines."

Recasting a child's utterance (present progressive to irregular past tense): "She is taking a picture" to "She took three pictures of the elephant."

Identifying rhyming words: "Yes, the words *green, seen,* and *mean* all rhyme."

ART : **Coffee Filter/Clothespin Butterflies**

Objectives
1. Express creativity
2. Develop small motor skills (e.g., drawing, painting, cutting, pasting)
3. Practice turn-taking skills
4. Converse with peers and adults

Materials
- Wooden clothespins with slot (at least one per child)
- Coffee filters
- Markers
- Yarn (optional)
- Tissue paper
- Pipe cleaners

General Description of Activity

Give children a clothespin and coffee filter to make a butterfly. Children draw designs on the coffee filter, then slide it into the wooden slot of a clothespin to form the butterfly's wings. Children can also draw faces on the clothespins and make antennae out of pipe cleaners.

Variation

Instead of having children make designs on the filters, have them use a variety of colored tissue paper for the butterflies' wings.

GROUP : **Tapping out Syllables**

Objectives
1. Improve listening skills
2. Increase sequencing ability
3. Learn appropriate group-interaction skills
4. Practice turn-taking skills

Materials
- Drum

General Description of Activity

Place a drum in front of the children. Explain that there are "beats" in words, called *syllables*. Tell children that you are going to make as many taps on the drum as there are syllables in your name. Say your name while tapping on the drum the appropriate number of times, one beat per syllable. Repeat this task once while the children listen again. Have one child come up to try the task using his or her own name. Assist the child if necessary.

Group Participation

Call up one child at a time and have the child tap out the number of syllables in his or her name. Continue until each child has had at least one turn.

Variation

If a drum is unavailable, have the children clap out the number of syllables in their name. You might also give the children other words to tap out, such as *rabbit, dinosaur,* or *caterpillar*.

Summary/Transition Activity

Remind children that the "beats" in words are called syllables and that these syllables are important because they help us divide up words.

December

MONTHLY PLANNING GUIDE

Activities	Monday	Tuesday	Wednesday	Thursday
Week 16 Occupations				
Dramatic Play	Mechanic	Police Officer	Grocery Store	Scientist
Art	Chalk Drawings	Badges	Vegetable Prints	Cornstarch and Water (Goop)
Group	Empty/Full	Letter *P*	How to Write a *4*	Ice Cube Melt
Story	*Working Hard with the Mighty Loader*	*Play It Safe*	*Don't Forget the Oatmeal!*	*I Was Walking Down the Road*
Song	"Johnny Works with One Hammer"	"One, Two, Bubble Gum Chew"	"On Top of Spaghetti"	"Raindrops and Lemondrops"
Week 17 Seasons				
Dramatic Play	Fall (Cleanup)	Winter (Snow)	Spring (Garden)	Summer (Beach)
Art	Marble Painting	Snowmen	Egg Carton Caterpillars	Sand Pictures
Group	Letter *Q*	Classifying Seasonal Clothing	Flannel Board Story	Loud/Soft
Story	*Apples and Pumpkins*	*Snow Day*	*Big Sarah's Little Boots*	*A House for Hermit Crab*
Song	"Building Song"	"Jingle Bells"	"Little Ducky Duddle"	"All the Little Fishies"
Week 18 Hobbies				
Dramatic Play	Craft Fair	Fishing/Picnic	Car Racing	Movie/Puppet Show
Art	Painted Rocks	Tissue Paper Fish	Vehicle Rubbings	Drawings
Group	Letter *R*	How to Write a *5*	Seatbelt Safety	Oddity Match
Story	*What Rhymes with Snake?*	*Brown Bear, Brown Bear, What Do You See?*	*Go, Dog. Go!*	*The Gingerbread Man*
Song	"Where Is Thumbkin?"	"Five Little Fishies"	"Twinkle, Twinkle, Traffic Light"	"If You're Happy and You Know It"
Week 19 At the Mall				
Dramatic Play	Department Store	Pizza Parlor	Pet Store	Toy Store
Art	Catalog Collage	Crayon Wash Pizzas	Easel Painting	Teddy Bear Pictures
Group	Letter *S*	Follow/Give Directions	What Does _____ Eat?	Act out a Story (*Corduroy*)
Story	*At the Mall*	*Bread, Bread, Bread*	*Scallywag*	*Corduroy*
Song	"Something in My Pocket"	"I Wish I Were a Pepperoni Pizza"	"I Have a Little Turtle"	"Going on a Bear Hunt"
Week 20 The Elements				
Dramatic Play	Camping (Fire)	Garden (Earth)	Boat (Water)	Rocket Ship (Air)
Art	Red Fingerpaint	Playdough	Watercolor Painting	Paper Airplanes
Group	Shapes—Rectangle	Letter *T*	Float or Sink?	Counting and Writing Numbers *1–5*
Story	*Who Said Red?*	*The Giving Tree*	*Boats*	*Goodnight Moon*
Song	"A-Camping We Will Go"	"The Alphabet Song"	"Five Little Speckled Frogs"	"The Rocket Song"

WEEKLY PLANNING GUIDE

	Dramatic Play	Art	Group	Story	Song
Monday *Suggested Props and Materials*	Mechanic *Gas station scenario, cashier station, car wash (optional), mechanic's tools, tracks, riding cars, gas pumps, taped road*	Chalk Drawings *Colored construction paper, chalk, liquid starch, flat dishes to hold starch*	Empty/Full *Several containers of varying shapes, sizes, and materials; variety of objects (e.g., toys, plastic food, blocks); water*	*Working Hard with the Mighty Loader*	"Johnny Works with One Hammer"
Tuesday *Suggested Props and Materials*	Police Officer *Police station scenario, roads, motorcycles, tickets, pretend driver's licenses, traffic signs, pencils, telephone, steering wheels (paper plates) or cars, seatbelts, walkie-talkies*	Badges *Cardboard cut in the shape of badges, glue (or paste), scrap pieces of paper, pieces of string, foil (enough to cover the badges), masking tape, pre-drawn badges to color (optional), scissors (optional), crayons or markers (optional)*	Letter *P* *Pictures and objects of words beginning with P, dictionary, alphabet chart*	*Play It Safe*	"One, Two, Bubble Gum Chew"
Wednesday *Suggested Props and Materials*	Grocery Store *Grocery store scenario; shelves; pretend food, including pretend can goods, fruits, vegetables; cash register; play money; bags; coupons; shopping carts*	Vegetable Prints *Cut-up vegetables (peppers, celery, potatoes, carrots, etc.), tempera paint, containers, paper*	How to Write a *4* *Chalkboard, chalk, cards with the target number on it, paper and pencils*	*Don't Forget the Oatmeal!*	"On Top of Spaghetti"
Thursday *Suggested Props and Materials*	Scientist *Science lab scenario, sand table, sifters, jars, plastic bugs, microscopes, magnifying glasses, pictures of birds*	Cornstarch and Water (Goop) *Cornstarch, water, containers, smocks*	Ice Cube Melt *20 ice cubes with small plastic rings or other toys inside (toys can be omitted), 20 baby food jars, chart paper or blackboard, markers or chalk*	*I Was Walking Down the Road*	"Raindrops and Lemondrops"

MY NOTES

NEWSLETTER

Vol. 1, No. 16

Date: _____

Occupations

Monday

We will focus on what a mechanic does today. The children can pretend to be mechanics, gas station attendants, or customers. In art, they will make chalk drawings using liquid starch as a fixative. We will read the story *Working Hard with the Mighty Loader*. During group time, children will learn about the concepts *empty* and *full*. Our featured song is "Johnny Works with One Hammer."

Tuesday

A police officer is today's featured occupation. We will have a police station set up in the classroom and officers who watch out for "speeders." The children can be the officers, citizens who need help, or people who are "speeding" when driving. In art, they will make their own police badges. Our story is *Play It Safe*. During group time, children will learn about the letter *P*, including what sound it makes and words that start with it. Our song today is "One, Two, Bubble Gum Chew."

Wednesday

Today we focus on the grocery clerk's job. The classroom will be set up like a grocery store. The children can pretend to be the clerks, stockers, customers, or managers. In art, the children will make vegetable prints using real vegetables. Our story is *Don't Forget the Oatmeal!* We will practice writing the number *4* during group time. Our featured song is "On Top of Spaghetti."

Thursday

Today the children are scientists. They will wear lab coats and look for insects and other items in the sand. They will use magnifying glasses, microscopes, and other scientific equipment. In art, they will make cornstarch constructions (goop). The story of the day is *I Was Walking Down the Road*. We will do an experiment with ice cubes during group time (the experiment will start at circle time). Our special song of the day is "Raindrops and Lemondrops."

Monday

Dramatic Play	Art	Group	Story	Song
Mechanic	Chalk Drawings	Empty/Full	*Working Hard with the Mighty Loader*	"Johnny Works with One Hammer"

DAILY PLANNING GUIDE

Language and Literacy Skills Facilitated

Vocabulary: *transportation, vehicle, car, track, garage, mechanic, truck, finish, battery, brakes, ignition, hose, tools, engine, wheels, shapes, rectangle, square, circle, triangle*

Verb phrase structures: *work<u>s</u>, is work<u>ing</u>, crash<u>ed</u> the car, push<u>ed</u> it, <u>was</u> rac<u>ing</u>, start<u>s</u>, stopp<u>ed</u>, fix<u>ed</u> the car*

Adjective/object descriptions: *broken part, dead battery, big/little* _____

Question structures: *what, how, where, when, who, what if, why, how many, which one*

Pronouns: *I, you, he, she, we, they, my, your, him, her, his, our, their, me, us, them*

Prepositions: *in, on, under, over, near, beneath, next to, beside, around, inside, outside*

Sounds: /r/ <u>r</u>ace, star<u>t</u>er, ca<u>r</u>; /s/ <u>s</u>ee, mi<u>ss</u>es, mi<u>ss</u>; /sh/ <u>sh</u>ape, fini<u>sh</u>

Noting print has meaning: names on chairs and on cubbies, signs in dramatic play, words in books and on chalkboard

Noting sound–symbol associations: What sound does _____ start with?

Writing: letters, names, words

Social Skills Facilitated

Initiating interaction with peers and adults; responding to questions and requests from peers and adults

Negotiating with peers for toys and materials

Group cooperation: waiting for a turn in a group, taking a turn at the appropriate time

Cognitive Skills Facilitated

Problem-solving skills: how to fix the cars

Classification skills: kinds of tools

Sequencing skills: song, art, sound patterns

Narrative/story structure: adventure

Motor Skills Facilitated

Large motor: outdoor play activities—jumping, running, hopping, pedaling, climbing

Small motor: writing, drawing, gluing

DRAMATIC PLAY **Mechanic**

Type of Activity: Related

Objectives
1. Learn new, and employ familiar, vocabulary
2. Learn new, and employ a variety of, syntactic constructions
3. Interact with peers
4. Sequence familiar routines
5. Expand conceptual knowledge of the world

Settings
- Garage/repair shop
- Desk
- Cashier's station
- Gas pumps
- Car lift (cardboard blocks holding a plastic truck high enough for a child to slide under)
- Parts counter or store (optional)

Props
- Appointment book and pencil or crayon
- Toy cash register
- Pretend money
- Hoses for pumps
- Pretend battery
- Car with hood, which can be made out of cardboard
- Dashboard
- Tools
- Pretend computer
- Pretend cans for oil change
- Play telephones
- Pretend parts to sell (optional)

Roles
- Mechanics
- Customers
- Receptionist
- Sales clerk
- Cashier

General Description of Activity

Children take their vehicles to a gas station or garage to be repaired, gassed up, or tuned up. The oil in the car may need to be changed or the battery recharged. Customers can call ahead and make appointments. In one area, a receptionist/cashier desk is arranged. Another area might have a wooden or cardboard facsimile of a car with a hood that opens so the mechanics can work under the hood if needed. Also, blocks or a vehicle Erector Set may be placed in one area to build cars. An optional activity is to have a parts counter or store.

Verbal Productions

Level of linguistic complexity varies with the role or competency of the child playing the role.
- "May I please have the wrench?" or "Wrench, please"
- "Please start the car now" or "Start"
- "My car needs a new battery" or "Battery"

Adult Facilitative Role

The adult is to facilitate role play and help expand language and literacy skills. Typical actions or strategies to use include

Playing a role: "My car needs an oil change. Can you help me?"

Modeling a statement/vocabulary: "The battery wire was not connected. The battery gives power to the car. I fixed the wire."

Contrasting location terms: "This screw goes on the front of the car. It holds the bumper on. The screws go underneath the car. The screws hold the axle on."

Expanding a child's utterance: "That $10" to "That will be $10, please."

Contrasting two sounds: "Did you say 'tar' or car?'"

ART **Chalk Drawings**

Objectives
1. Express creativity
2. Develop small motor skills (e.g., drawing, painting, cutting, pasting)
3. Practice turn-taking skills
4. Converse with peers and adults

Materials
- Colored construction paper
- Chalk
- Liquid starch
- Flat dishes to hold starch

General Description of Activity

Provide colored construction paper and colored chalk. Have children dip one end of the chalk in liquid starch and then draw on the paper. The starch makes the colors more vibrant and ensures that they do not rub off. Children can draw designs or pictures that follow the theme, or they can draw whatever they wish.

GROUP **Empty/Full**

Objectives

1. Improve listening skills
2. Increase conceptual knowledge
3. Learn appropriate group-interaction skills
4. Practice turn-taking skills

Materials

- Several containers of varying shapes, sizes, and materials
- A variety of objects (e.g., toys, plastic food, blocks)
- Water

General Description of Activity

Hold up two containers, one filled with small objects and one empty. Verbally label each container (e.g., "This one is full of LEGO blocks; this one is empty—nothing's there"). Ask one child to come to the front of the group and identify the full container.

Group Participation

Place two other containers in front of the children, one full of water and one empty. As you point to each container, have the group, in chorus, label the containers as full or empty. Then place an empty cup and a full cup in front of the children. Ask one child to point to the empty cup. Continue presenting two containers and asking a child to point to the full or empty one.

Variation

Ask children to pour water (or objects) into empty containers to make them full containers.

Summary/Transition Activity

In chorus, the whole group again labels two containers—one as empty and one as full.

Tuesday

Dramatic Play	Art	Group	Story	Song
Police Officer	Badges	Letter *P*	*Play It Safe*	"One, Two, Bubble Gum Chew"

DAILY PLANNING GUIDE

Language and Literacy Skills Facilitated

Vocabulary: *police officer, ticket, speed limit, seatbelts, street, safety rules, motorcycle, handcuffs, one-way street*

Verb phrase structures: <u>drive</u> safely, <u>ride</u> motorcycle, <u>write</u> ticket, <u>put</u> on belt, <u>drive</u> car

Adjective/object descriptions: big ____, small ____, red ____, blue ____, purple ____

Question structures: *what, how, where, when, who, what if, why, how many, which one*

Pronouns: *I, you, he, she, we, they, my, your, him, her, his, our, their, me, us, them*

Prepositions: *in, on, under, over, near, beneath, next to, beside, around, inside, outside*

Sounds: /s/ <u>s</u>afe, <u>s</u>eatbelt; /m/ <u>m</u>otorcycle, <u>m</u>icrophone

Noting print has meaning: names on chairs and on cubbies, signs in dramatic play, words in books and on chalkboard

Noting sound–symbol associations: What sound does _____ start with?

Writing: letters, names, words

Social Skills Facilitated

Initiating interaction with peers and adults; responding to questions and requests from peers and adults

Negotiating with peers for toys and materials

Group cooperation: waiting for a turn in a group, taking a turn at the appropriate time

Cognitive Skills Facilitated

Problem-solving skills: safety rules

Classification skills: traffic signs

Sequencing skills: songs, story, art activity

Narrative/story structure: informational

Motor Skills Facilitated

Large motor: outdoor play activities—jumping, running, hopping, pedaling, climbing

Small motor: writing, drawing, gluing, painting

DRAMATIC PLAY **Police Officer**

Type of Activity: Central

Objectives
1. Learn new, and employ familiar, vocabulary
2. Learn new, and employ a variety of, syntactic constructions
3. Interact with peers
4. Sequence familiar routines
5. Expand conceptual knowledge of the world

Settings
- Dispatch office
- Roads (floor marked by masking tape)
- Shopping areas
- Police station

Props
- Motorcycles (two paper plates together and affixed on each end of a yardstick)
- Tickets
- Pretend driver's licenses
- Pencils
- Traffic signs
- Play telephones
- Steering wheels (paper plates)
- Seatbelts (men's ties or string loosely tied around chairs)
- Microphones (for dispatch office)
- Walkie-talkies

Roles
- Police officers
- Police chief
- Dispatcher
- Parents
- Children
- Motorcycle riders
- Store clerks

General Description of Activity

The children enact different police officer scenarios. For example, police officers on motorcycles can stop those who speed or do not wear their seatbelts. They can help someone whose car has broken down. Other officers can help children who get separated from their parents in the shopping area and need help. The police station can be set up as a place to bring the "lost" children and a place to pay "tickets."

Verbal Productions

Level of linguistic complexity varies with the role or competency of the child playing the role.
- "Where is your mommy?" or "Where Mommy?"
- "I don't know. I'm lost" or "I lost"
- "I've lost my child. Please help me" or "Help me"
- "You ran the stop sign, and I must give you a ticket" or "Too fast"
- "I did not see the sign" or "Not see!"

Adult Facilitative Role

The adult is to facilitate role play and help expand language and literacy skills. Typical actions or strategies to use include

Playing a role: "You are driving too fast. Here is a ticket."

Expanding a child's utterance: "She lost. She want Mommy" to "Oh, she is lost and wants her Mommy. I will help her."

Modeling the reading of a sign: "That sign says *stop*."

Modeling phonological awareness: "The words *police, pop, put, pat,* and *pick* all start with the letter *P*."

Using a cloze procedure: "This red light means stop, and the green light means _____."

ART **Badges**

Objectives
1. Express creativity
2. Develop small motor skills (e.g., drawing, painting, cutting, pasting)
3. Practice turn-taking skills
4. Converse with peers and adults

Materials
- Cardboard cut in the shape of badges
- Glue (or paste)
- Scrap pieces of paper
- Pieces of string
- Foil (enough to cover the badges)
- Masking tape
- Predrawn badges to color (optional)
- Scissors (optional)
- Crayons or markers (optional)

General Description of Activity

The children glue pieces of paper and bits of string onto cardboard pre-cut in the shape of a badge. The paper and string give the badges texture. They then cover the "badge" with foil. Attach children's badges to their clothing with masking tape. An alternative is to have the children color pre-designed badges, cut them out, and glue them onto the cardboard cut in the shape of a badge.

GROUP **Letter *P***

Objectives
1. Improve listening skills
2. Increase knowledge of the alphabet and sounds
3. Learn appropriate group interaction skills
4. Practice turn-taking skills

Materials
- Alphabet chart and other alphabet displays
- Blackboard and chalk or poster paper and markers
- Pictures of objects (or objects themselves) with names that begin with *P*
- Picture dictionary (or an alphabet video dictionary)

General Description of Activity

The teacher writes an upper and lowercase letter *P* on the blackboard (or on poster paper) and gives several examples of words that begin with *P*, emphasizing the /p/ sound at the beginning of the words. The teacher can note that the word police is one word that starts with a /p/ sound. (The teacher may also hold up objects or pictures of objects that begin with the letter *P*.) The teacher then directs the children's attention to the alphabet picture displays around the room.

Group Participation

The teacher asks if anyone's name starts with *P* (e.g., Pam, Peter). Those children write the letter *P* on the blackboard or poster paper. Two or three other children are given the opportunity to write the letter *P* on the blackboard. If necessary, the staff members can help the children write the letter. The teacher provides ongoing commentary when the letter is being written (e.g., "Start at the top and draw a line straight down. Go back to the top of the straight line and draw a half circle that ends in the middle of the straight line."). Some of the other children can practice writing the letter *P* in the air with their fingers (or use individual chalkboards). The teacher then asks the children to think of words that begin with the letter *P*. The teacher writes these words on the blackboard, drawing quick sketches when possible of the suggested words. If a child suggests a word that does not begin with the letter *P*, he or she is told, "No, that words begins with _____." Pictures or objects representing words that begin with the letter *P* can be provided as prompts for children who do not know any words so that they can participate. (Cards can be handed out at the beginning of the lesson or as the lesson proceeds.) Additional words can be sought in a picture dictionary if the class has difficulty arriving at words that begin with the letter *P*.

Summary/Transition Activity

After about 10–15 words have been suggested, the teacher reviews the words, emphasizing the /p/ sound.

Wednesday

Dramatic Play	Art	Group	Story	Song
Grocery Store	Vegetable Prints	How to Write a 4	*Don't Forget the Oatmeal!*	"On Top of Spaghetti"

DAILY PLANNING GUIDE

Language and Literacy Skills Facilitated

Vocabulary: *groceries, cart, cereal, shop, checker, buy, sell, bag, sack, shelf, money, change*

Verb phrase structures: *eats, is eating, ate, has eaten, pushes, is pushing, pushed, buys, bought, checks, is checking, checked*

Adjective/object descriptions: *big/little bag, full/empty shelf*

Question structures: *what, how, where, when, who, what if, why, how many, which one*

Pronouns: *I, you, he, she, we, they, my, your, him, her, his, our, their, me, us, them*

Prepositions: *in, on, under, over, near, beneath, next to, beside, around, inside, outside*

Sounds: /sh/ *shelf, push;* /k/ *cart, sack;* /s/ *sell, carts*

Noting print has meaning: names on chairs and on cubbies, signs in dramatic play, words in books and on chalkboard

Noting sound–symbol associations: What sound does _____ start with?

Writing: letters, names, words

Social Skills Facilitated

Initiating interaction with peers and adults; responding to questions and requests from peers and adults

Negotiating with peers for toys and materials

Group cooperation: waiting for a turn in a group, taking a turn at the appropriate time

Cognitive Skills Facilitated

Problem-solving skills: what to buy

Classification skills: fruits, vegetables, meats

Sequencing skills: songs, story

Narrative/story structure: adventure

Motor Skills Facilitated

Large motor: outdoor play activities—jumping, running, hopping, pedaling, climbing

Small motor: writing, drawing, gluing

DRAMATIC PLAY **Grocery Store**

Type of Activity: Sequential

Objectives
1. Learn new, and employ familiar, vocabulary
2. Learn new, and employ a variety of, syntactic constructions
3. Interact with peers
4. Sequence familiar routines
5. Expand conceptual knowledge of the world

Settings
- Grocery store
- Shelves and aisles
- Check-out stand
- Customers' homes

Props
- Shelves
- Canned goods and other food items
- Fruit and vegetable area
- Pretend cash register
- Pretend money
- Pretend credit cards
- Pretend coupons
- Shopping carts
- Grocery bags
- Pencil and paper for making lists
- Table for checkout area

Roles
- Shoppers
- Cashiers
- Stockers
- Baggers

General Description of Activity

The children pretend to go grocery shopping. They can make lists, take their "children" with them, choose the items on the list to put in their carts, pay, bag their groceries, and go home. Other children can be the grocery store workers. Some keep the shelves stocked, and others are checkers and baggers.

Verbal Productions

Level of linguistic complexity varies with the role or competency of the child playing the role.
- "Will that be all? Your total is $5" or "All? Five!"
- "Milk, please" or "Milk"
- "Do you have any cereal?" or "Want cereal"

Adult Facilitative Role

The adult is to facilitate role play and help expand language and literacy skills. Typical actions or strategies to use include

Playing a role: "I am buying some meat and some fruit for my supper."

Contrasting error and correcting structure: "The apple fall down" to "The apple fell down."

Asking open questions: "What should I buy for dinner?"

Identifying rhyming words: "Do the words *can* and *man* rhyme?"

Providing confirmatory feedback: "That sign says *cake*."

ART **Vegetable Prints**

Objectives
1. Express creativity
2. Develop small motor skills (e.g., drawing, painting, cutting, pasting)
3. Practice turn-taking skills
4. Converse with peers and adults

Materials
- Assortment of vegetables, sliced (e.g., peppers, carrots, broccoli, cauliflower, celery)
- Tempera paint
- Shallow container (e.g., meat tray)
- Light-colored construction paper
- Smocks

General Description of Activity

Pour small amounts of tempera paint into shallow containers, such as Styrofoam meat trays. Children touch the vegetable piece to the paint and then press it on their paper, making a print of the vegetable's shape. The more choice of vegetables and colors, the more creative and colorful the prints will turn out.

GROUP **How to Write a 4**

Objectives
1. Improve listening skills
2. Increase conceptual knowledge
3. Learn appropriate group-interaction skills
4. Practice turn-taking skills
5. Practice recognition and writing of numbers

Materials
- Number cards
- Chalkboards and chalk
- Paper and pencils (optional)
- Whiteboard and marker

General Description of Activity

Hold up a card with the number *4* on it. Trace the number with your finger and invite several children to come to the front of the group to trace the number, too. As the children trace, recite the jingle for the target number *(4)*:

1: Start at the top, go down and you're done, that's the way to make a *1*.

2: Around and back on the railroad track, *2, 2, 2*.

3: Around the tree, around the tree, that's the way to make a *3*.

4: Down and over and down once more, that's the way to make a *4*.

5: Down around, make a hat on it, and look what you've found. *(5)*

6: Down around until it sticks, that's the way to make a *6*.

7: Over and down and it's not heaven, over and down makes a *7*.

8: Make an S and go back straight, that's the way to make an *8*.

9: A balloon and a line make *9*.

10: Draw a line and a circle with your pen, that's the way to make a *10*.

Group Participation

Distribute individual chalkboards and chalk (or paper and pencils) to the children, and have them practice writing the target number.

Variation 1

Whiteboards and markers may be easier for some children to use.

Variation 2

To introduce the number, use a number line and have the children count up to the target number on the line. One child could place the target number on the number line.

Summary/Transition Activity

Ask children to hold up their chalkboards and show the group their numbers.

Thursday

Dramatic Play	Art	Group	Story	Song
Scientist	Cornstarch and Water (Goop)	Ice Cube Melt	*I Was Walking Down the Road*	"Raindrops and Lemondrops"

DAILY PLANNING GUIDE

Language and Literacy Skills Facilitated

Vocabulary: *insect, bug, ant, spider, ladybug, sand, butterfly, caterpillar, microscope, magnifying glass, dig, magnets*

Verb phrase structures: *look<u>s</u>, <u>is</u> look<u>ing</u>, look<u>ed</u>, find/found, <u>were</u> digging, dug, is fly<u>ing</u>, flew*

Adjective/object descriptions: *big/little _____, tiny _____, flying insect, stinging bee*

Question structures: *what, how, where, when, who, what if, why, how many, which one*

Pronouns: *I, you, he, she, we, they, my, your, him, her, his, our, their, me, us, them*

Prepositions: *in, on, under, over, near, beneath, next to, beside, around, inside, outside*

Sounds: /k/ *catch, look;* /s/ *see, glass;* /f/ *find, if*

Noting print has meaning: names on chairs and on cubbies, signs in dramatic play, words in books and on chalkboard

Noting sound–symbol associations: What sound does _____ start with?

Writing: letters, names, words

Social Skills Facilitated

Initiating interaction with peers and adults; responding to questions and requests from peers and adults

Negotiating with peers for toys and materials

Group cooperation: waiting for a turn in a group, taking a turn at the appropriate time

Cognitive Skills Facilitated

Problem-solving skills: how to mix colors

Classification skills: things that dissolve

Sequencing skills: story, song

Narrative/story structure: repetitive line story

Motor Skills Facilitated

Large motor: outdoor play activities—jumping, running, hopping, pedaling, climbing

Small motor: writing, drawing, painting, stirring

DRAMATIC PLAY **Scientist**

Type of Activity: Related

Objectives
1. Learn new, and employ familiar, vocabulary
2. Learn new, and employ a variety of, syntactic constructions
3. Interact with peers
4. Sequence familiar routines
5. Expand conceptual knowledge of the world

Settings
- Sand table or wading pool filled with sand
- Science laboratory

Props
- Sand table or wading pool filled with sand
- Plastic insects
- Shovels and pails
- Play microscope
- Slides
- Magnifying glasses
- Pretend binoculars (or two toilet paper rolls taped together)
- Pictures of birds

Roles
- Laboratory scientists
- Field scientists
- Bird watchers

General Description of Activity

The children can pretend to be scientists, finding all kinds of insects, worms, and birds. The sand table or wading pool can be set up with pretend worms, ants, and other insects buried in the sand. Other children can look at the bugs under microscopes or through magnifying glasses, or use binoculars to locate birds.

Verbal Productions

Level of linguistic complexity varies with the role or competency of the child playing the role.
- "He found a big bug" or "Big bug"
- "This is a microscope. I can see the bug" or "See bug"
- "She is digging in the sand" or "She found an ant"
- "The slide looks funny" or "Funny?"

Adult Facilitative Role

The adult is to facilitate role play and help expand language and literacy skills. Typical actions or strategies to use include

Playing a role: "I am looking for some bugs. I found one. Let's look at it under the microscope."

Redirecting a child to a peer: "Ask Sonya for a turn at the microscope. Say, 'May I have a turn, please?'"

Using a cloze procedure: "Here is one bug. Here are three _____" (bugs).

Recasting a child's utterance (present tense to past tense): He look<u>s</u> for the big fly" to "Yes, he look<u>ed</u> very hard and he found it."

Identifying rhyming words: "Yes, the words *bug, rug,* and *mug* all rhyme."

ART : **Cornstarch and Water (Goop)**

Objectives
1. Express creativity
2. Develop small motor skills (e.g., drawing, painting, cutting, pasting)
3. Practice turn-taking skills
4. Converse with peers and adults

Materials
- Cornstarch (1 or 2 1 lb boxes per container)
- Water (2–2½ cups of water per box)
- Containers (plastic tubs)

General Description of Activity

Provide several containers of a cornstarch and water mixture for children to experiment with. Containers should be big enough for two hands, and it is more fun for children and facilitates more language if the containers accommodate at least four hands. This mixture is very interesting in that it feels hard in the container and children can make a ball of it in their fist, but as it sits in their hand it melts and drips out. This is an experimentation, a discovery activity. (The mixture washes off of hands quite easily.)

GROUP **Ice Cube Melt**

Objectives
1. Improve listening skills
2. Increase conceptual knowledge
3. Learn appropriate group-interaction skills
4. Practice turn-taking skills

Materials
- Ice cubes with small plastic rings or other toys inside (toys can be omitted), at least one per child
- Baby food jars, one per child
- Chart paper or blackboard
- Markers or chalk

General Description of Activity

Early in the day, show children ice cubes that have been frozen with a toy inside. Have them touch the cubes to see how they feel (cold). Give each child an ice cube to put in a baby food jar. Then have them put the jars in their cubbies. During group time, ask children to bring their jar with the ice cube in it to the group area. Ask how the ice cube had felt when they first put it in the jars (e.g., cold, wet, hard) and what shape the cube was.

Group Participation

Ask the children if the ice cube looks the same as it did earlier. Why not? Have the children discuss what has happened to their ice cube (it has melted). Why can they now touch the toy inside that they could not touch earlier? Discuss the different states of water.

Variation

Write the children's comments on the blackboard or on chart paper to make an experience story or "science" report.

Summary/Transition Activity

Have each child empty the water out of the jar into a tub and put the toy in his or her cubby.

WEEKLY PLANNING GUIDE

	Dramatic Play	Art	Group	Story	Song
Monday *Suggested Props and Materials*	Fall (Cleanup) *Fall scenario, house(s) with removable screens and roof (child-sized toys or handmade constructions from cardboard boxes), extra room additions (cardboard added to extend house), cupboards, dishes, kitchen scenario, window "screens," cleaning supplies and other tools, shingles, lawn mower, (dry) paintbrushes*	Marble Painting *Paint dishes filled with different colors of tempera paint, several marbles, five or six Pringles cans (tube-shaped containers); paper cut to fit inside the can without overlapping the edges, smocks*	Letter Q *Alphabet chart and other alphabet displays, blackboard and chalk, pictures of objects (or objects themselves) with names that begin with Q, picture dictionary*	*Apples and Pumpkins*	"Building Song"
Tuesday *Suggested Props and Materials*	Winter (Snow) *Winter scenario, igloo (cardboard bricks wrapped in white paper), ice pond (plastic area rug), campfire, newspaper (crumpled for "snowballs"), fishing pole, fish, white pillowcases (to make a snowman), pretend hot chocolate, cups*	Snowmen *Paper; small, medium, and large white circles; scraps of paper; scraps of cloth; markers; white chalks; glue sticks*	Classifying Seasonal Clothing *Variety of clothing representing the four seasons, four tubs*	*Snow Day*	"Jingle Bells"
Wednesday *Suggested Props and Materials*	Spring (Garden) *Spring scenario, two or three large boxes cut about 4–6" deep, sand, garden tools, hats, gloves, pretend plants, pails, pretend seeds, garden store scenario (optional), cash register, pretend money (optional)*	Egg Carton Caterpillars *Egg cartons cut into four segments, pipe cleaners, markers*	Flannel Board Story *Flannel board, flannel board story*	*Big Sarah's Little Boots*	"Little Ducky Duddle"
Thursday *Suggested Props and Materials*	Summer (Beach) *Beach scenario, sandbox, blue sheet for water, pails and shovels, seashells, boats, lifeguard chair, megaphone, towels, beach balls, pretend sunscreen, concession area, pretend food, drinks*	Sand Pictures *Sand, glue, papers*	Loud/Soft *Drum, triangle, other instruments*	*A House for Hermit Crab*	"All the Little Fishies"

NEWSLETTER

Vol. 1, No. 17

Date: _____

Seasons

Monday

Today the children will focus on the fall season and fixing up/cleaning the house area. They may fix the roof, wash the windows, mow the lawn, and do other chores. In art, they will make marble paintings. Our story is *Apples and Pumpkins*. Our group activity involves learning about the letter *Q*. We might even make a paper quilt. Our featured song is the "Building Song."

Tuesday

Today the featured season is winter, so the children will have some winter fun. They might pretend to go ice skating or ice fishing or build an igloo or a snowman. In art, they will make paper snowmen. Our story is *Snow Day*. During group time, the children will classify clothes people wear in winter or summer (or even fall and spring). Our special song is "Jingle Bells."

Wednesday

Spring will be in the air today as the children work in the garden, planting flowers and other seeds. They might even have to go to the garden store to get supplies and some advice from the store owner. In art, they will make caterpillars out of egg cartons. Our story is *Big Sarah's Little Boots*. During group time, we will have a flannel board story, and the children will practice retelling the story. Our song is "Little Ducky Duddle."

Thursday

We will pretend it is summer today and go to the beach. The children can pretend to be the swimmers, the lifeguard, or the concession stand workers. In art, they will make sand pictures. The children will classify sounds as loud or soft during group time. Our story today is *A House for Hermit Crab*. Our featured song is "All the Little Fishies."

Monday

Dramatic Play	Art	Group	Story	Song
Fall (Cleanup)	Marble Painting	Letter Q	*Apples and Pumpkins*	"Building Song"

DAILY PLANNING GUIDE

Language and Literacy Skills Facilitated

Vocabulary: *fall, autumn, leaves, yard, fall cleaning, mowing the lawn, raking the leaves, painting the house, reseeding the lawn, washing the windows, roof, shingles, tools*

Verb phrase structures: *rak<u>ing</u> leaves, rake<u>s</u> leaves, rake<u>d</u> leaves, paint<u>s</u> the house, paint<u>ed</u> the house, clean<u>ed</u> the yard*

Adjective/object descriptions: *big leaf, red leaf, green leaf, yellow leaf, dirty/clean windows, big/little pile of leaves*

Question structures: *what, how, where, when, who, what if, why, how many, which one*

Pronouns: *I, you, he, she, we, they, my, your, her, his, our, their, me, us, them*

Prepositions: *in, on, under, over, near, beneath, next to, beside, around, inside, outside*

Sounds: /f/ *fix, off*; /s/ *sit, talks*; /l/ *little, leaf, yellow, fall*

Noting print has meaning: names on chairs and on cubbies, signs in dramatic play, words in books and on chalkboard

Noting sound–symbol associations: What sound does _____ start with?

Writing: letters, names, words

Social Skills Facilitated

Initiating interaction with peers and adults; responding to questions and requests from peers and adults

Negotiating with peers for toys and materials

Group cooperation: waiting for a turn in a group, taking a turn at the appropriate time

Cognitive Skills Facilitated

Problem solving skills: how to clean or rake

Classification skills: different kinds of leaves

Sequencing skills: story, songs

Narrative/story structure: labeling

Motor Skills Facilitated

Large motor: outdoor play activities—jumping, running, hopping, pedaling, climbing

Small motor: writing, drawing, gluing

DRAMATIC PLAY **Fall (Cleanup)**

Type of Activity: Related

Objectives
1. Learn new, and employ familiar, vocabulary
2. Learn new, and employ a variety of, syntactic constructions
3. Interact with peers
4. Sequence familiar routines
5. Expand conceptual knowledge of the world

Settings
- House(s) with removable screens and roof (child-sized house or handmade constructions from cardboard boxes)
- Household cupboards
- Play refrigerator
- Play stove and sink
- Extra room additions (cardboard added to extend house)

Props
- Window "screens" (cardboard frame with plastic mesh or clear plastic inserts for screens)
- Cleaning supplies (e.g., mop, broom, dustpan, rags, vacuum cleaner)
- Shelves
- Pretend tools

Roles
- Mother
- Cleaning crew
- Father
- Roofer
- Children

General Description of Activity

Children act out the rites of fall (could also be done in spring) cleaning, such as taking down or putting up window screens, washing windows, and fixing roofs. Children could straighten shelves and cupboards, make small repairs, and put things back neatly. They could also rake leaves.

Verbal Productions

Level of linguistic complexity varies with the role or competency of the child playing the role.
- "Could I please use that mop when you're finished?" or "Mop, please"
- "These windows need to be washed" or "Window dirty"
- "We fixed the roof with new shingles" or "Fix roof"

Adult Facilitative Role

The adult is to facilitate role play and help expand language and literacy skills. Typical actions or strategies to use include

Playing a role: "I am raking the leaves. Then I will wash the windows."

Asking open questions: "How do you fix this?"

Contrasting two adjectives: "This is the yellow leaf, and that is the red leaf."

Providing an event cast of a child's action: "You are fixing the roof. The shingle was broken. Now it is fixed. Now you are putting another shingle on the roof."

Redirecting a child to a peer: "I don't have the mop. Ask Johnny for a turn. Say, 'Can I have a turn, please?'"

ART **Marble Painting**

Objectives
1. Express creativity
2. Develop small motor skills (e.g., drawing, painting, cutting, pasting)
3. Practice turn-taking skills
4. Converse with peers and adults

Materials
- Four or five paint dishes filled with different colors of tempera paint
- Four or five marbles (one for each paint dish)
- Five or six potato chip cans
- Paper cut to fit inside the can without overlapping the edges
- Paint smocks

General Description of Activity

Put several colors of tempera paint into dishes, one dish for each color of paint, and place a marble in the paint. Place, or have children place, a rolled-up piece of paper into a potato chip can (or other long cylinder can). Have children pick up one marble that is covered in paint and place it into the can. The child then puts the plastic lid on the can and shakes or rotates the can so that the marble "paints" the paper inside the can. The child takes the marble out and puts it back into the paint dish, then chooses another marble (from a different paint color) and shakes the can again. After three or four colors, remove, or have children remove, the paper to see the design. The paper can be placed on newspaper until the paint is dry.

GROUP **Letter *Q***

Objectives

1. Improve listening skills
2. Increase knowledge of the alphabet and sounds
3. Learn appropriate group-interaction skills
4. Practice turn-taking skills

Materials

- Alphabet chart and other alphabet displays
- Blackboard and chalk
- Pictures of objects (or objects themselves) with names that begin with *Q*
- Picture dictionary
- Poster paper marked off in squares (optional)
- Glue (optional)

General Description of Activity

Write an upper- and a lowercase letter *Q* on the blackboard (or on poster paper).Give several examples of words that begin with *Q*, emphasizing the /kw/ or "kwuh" sound at the beginning of the words. You might hold up pictures of objects (or objects themselves) with names that begin with *Q*. Direct the children's attention to the alphabet picture displays around the room.

Group Participation

Ask if anyone's name starts with *Q* (e.g., Quentin), and have those children write the letter *Q* on the blackboard (or poster paper). Also have two or three other children write the letter *Q* on the blackboard. Provide verbal guidance as children form the letter: "Draw a circle. Go to the bottom right of the circle and draw a slant." If necessary, help children write the letter. Some of the other children can practice writing *Q* in the air with their fingers (or on individual chalkboards). Ask the children to think of words that begin with *Q*. Write the words they offer on the blackboard, drawing quick sketches (when possible) of the suggested words. If a child suggests a word that does not begin with *Q*, say, "No, that begins with ____," and say both sounds so children can compare them. To help children who cannot think of any words, prompt them with pictures or objects representing *Q* words. (Pictures or objects can be handed out at the beginning of the lesson or as the lesson proceeds.) Additional words can be sought in a picture dictionary if the group has difficulty arriving at words that begin with *Q*.

Variation

Display a large piece of paper with block squares drawn on it to represent a quilt. Have the children paste pictures of *Q* words in the square blocks.

Summary/Transition Activity

After about 10–15 words have been suggested, review the words, emphasizing the *Q* sound.

Tuesday

Dramatic Play	Art	Group	Story	Song
Winter (Snow)	Snowmen	Classifying Seasonal Clothing	*Snow Day*	"Jingle Bells"

DAILY PLANNING GUIDE

Language and Literacy Skills Facilitated

Vocabulary: *snow, snowflake, winter, snowball fight, snow fort, snowball, season, ice, slick, slide, shovel*

Verb phrase structures: <u>are</u> shovel<u>ing</u>, <u>was</u> shovel<u>ing</u>, throw<u>s</u> snowballs, <u>threw</u> snowballs, <u>were</u> building a snow fort, <u>built</u> a snow fort, hit<u>s</u> the fort, <u>was</u> hitting the wall

Adjective/object descriptions: *cold snow, heavy coat, warm mittens*

Question structures: *what, how, where, when, who, what if, why, how many, which one*

Pronouns: *I, you, he, she, we, they, my, your, him, her, his, our, their, me, us, them*

Prepositions: *in, on, under, over, near, beneath, next to, beside, around, inside, outside*

Sounds: /s/ <u>s</u>eason, <u>s</u>ee, mi<u>ss</u>es, fort<u>s</u>; /l/ <u>l</u>ike, ye<u>ll</u>ow, ye<u>ll</u>; /f/ <u>f</u>ort, <u>f</u>un, o<u>ff</u>, i<u>f</u>

Noting print has meaning: names on chairs and on cubbies, signs in dramatic play, words in books and on chalkboard

Noting sound–symbol associations: What sound does _____ start with?

Writing: letters, names, words

Social Skills Facilitated

Initiating interaction with peers and adults; responding to questions and requests from peers and adults

Negotiating with peers for toys and materials

Group cooperation: waiting for a turn in a group, taking a turn at the appropriate time

Cognitive Skills Facilitated

Problem solving skills: how to make a snowflake

Classification skills: winter things

Sequencing skills: story, songs, and fingerplays

Narrative/story structure: adventure

Motor Skills Facilitated

Large motor: outdoor play activities—jumping, running, hopping, pedaling, climbing

Small motor: writing, drawing, gluing, painting, folding

DRAMATIC PLAY **Winter (Snow)**

Type of Activity: Related

Objectives

1. Learn new, and employ familiar, vocabulary
2. Learn new, and employ a variety of, syntactic constructions
3. Interact with peers
4. Sequence familiar routines
5. Expand conceptual knowledge of the world

Settings
- Igloo
- Ice pond
- Snowy field
- Ice fishing area
- Campfire

Props
- Cardboard bricks wrapped in white paper (for building igloo)
- Newspaper (crumpled for "snowballs" and made into confetti for "snow")
- White bricks or blocks covered with white paper (pillows)
- Ice pond (large piece of plastic)
- Fishing poles (with magnets attached to catch fish)
- Fish (with paper clips attached)
- Ice fishing area (box covered with foil—the children break the foil to begin fishing)
- Campfire (sticks or blocks and red cellophane paper)
- Pillowcase (to stuff to make a snowman)
- Cups
- Thermos of hot chocolate

Roles
- Children
- Mothers
- Fathers
- Ice skaters
- Ice fishermen and women
- Skiers

General Description of Activity

Fun winter activities include skating, skiing, building snow forts, and so forth. Children can make an igloo out of cardboard bricks that have been wrapped in white paper. They can also make snowballs out of crushed newspapers. Newspaper confetti can be shaped into snow banks in which to jump. White pillowcases can be stuffed with newspaper "snow" to make snowmen. The children can pretend to ice skate by taking off their shoes and sliding on a large piece of plastic. They can build campfires to get warm and to make hot chocolate. They could also go ice fishing.

Verbal Productions

Level of linguistic complexity varies with the role or competency of the child playing the role.
- "How many times did you fall?" or "How many?"
- "I need to have new skates" or "Two"
- "This is the biggest snowman" or "Big snowman"
- "Here's your hot chocolate" or "Hot"

Adult Facilitative Role

The adult is to facilitate role play and help expand language and literacy skills. Typical actions or strategies to use include

Playing a role: "I am going ice fishing. It's fun to put my pole through the hole. I hope I catch a fish."

Expanding a child's utterance: "I skate" to "I'm skating, too. It's fun."

Modeling a statement/vocabulary: "I am making an igloo. An igloo is a house made of bricks of ice. I am using pretend ice blocks."

Contrasting two locations/adjective terms: "The small block goes on top of the wall. The large block goes beside the wall."

Modeling the reading of a sign: "The sign says *fishing permitted.*"

ART **Snowmen**

Objectives
1. Express creativity
2. Develop small motor skills (e.g., drawing, painting, cutting, pasting)
3. Practice turn-taking skills
4. Converse with peers and adults

Materials:
- Small, medium, and large white circles, one of each for each child
- Scraps of construction paper
- Scraps of cloth
- Black markers
- White chalk
- Glue sticks

General Description of Activity

Children make snowmen by pasting three circles of different sizes on blue construction paper. They can add details by pasting pieces of cloth or paper. They can also add facial features with black markers and snow or snowflakes with white chalk.

GROUP **Classifying Seasonal Clothing**

Objectives
1. Improve listening skills
2. Increase knowledge of seasons
3. Increase awareness of why people wear certain clothes
4. Learn appropriate group-interaction skills
5. To practice turn-taking skills

Materials
- Heavy coats, mittens, snow caps
- Light jacket, sweaters
- Raincoats
- Long- and short-sleeved shirts
- Swimming suits
- Long pants, shorts
- Skirts, dresses (some wool, some lightweight cotton)
- Tank tops
- Baseball caps
- *Fall, Winter, Spring, Summer* labels

General Description of Activity

Hold up four articles of clothing, one that represents each of the four seasons. Place each piece of clothing on the floor in front of the children, and place the label that indicates the corresponding season above each article to set up the categories.

Group Participation

Hold up a winter coat and have one child put it in the *winter* pile. Hold up a swimming suit and have another child put it in the *summer* pile. Hold up a light jacket, noting that it could go in either the *spring* or *fall* pile. Then hand out four items of clothing to four different children. The children come to the front of the group, one at a time, to place their item in the appropriate pile. Continue the activity until everyone has had a turn. You might vary the difficulty of the task for different children. For instance, ask some of the children to explain why a particular item belongs in a particular category. Children who find it difficult to choose from four categories could choose from only two.

Variation

Have the children dress dolls in the clothes appropriate for a particular season instead of putting the clothes in a pile.

Summary/Transition Activity

Ask the children to name, in unison, the four seasons as you indicate each pile of clothing representing what is typically worn during each season.

Wednesday

Dramatic Play	Art	Group	Story	Song
Spring (Garden)	Egg Carton Caterpillars	Flannel Board Story	*Big Sarah's Little Boots*	"Little Ducky Duddle"

DAILY PLANNING GUIDE

Language and Literacy Skills Facilitated

Vocabulary: *garden, grow, flowers, digging, planting, watering, planting, working, bugs, insects, hoe, weeds, seeds, shovel*

Verb phrase structures: *is/are* plant*ing*, plant*ed*, will plant, plant*s*, digs, dug, grow*s*, grew, waters, water*ed*, *is* work*ing*, work*ed*

Adjective/object descriptions: *little seed, big hole, yellow flower, dirty shovel, hard work*

Question structures: *what, how, where, when, who, what if, why, how many, which one*

Pronouns: *I, you, he, she, we, they, my, your, him, her, his, our, their, me, us, them*

Prepositions: *in, on, under, over, near, beneath, next to, beside, around, inside, outside*

Sounds: /k/ come, work; /l/ like, yellow, fall; /s/ seed, miss

Noting print has meaning: names on chairs and on cubbies, signs in dramatic play, words in books and on chalkboard

Noting sound–symbol associations: What sound does _____ start with?

Writing: letters, names, words

Social Skills Facilitated

Initiating interaction with peers and adults; responding to questions and requests from peers and adults

Negotiating with peers for toys and materials

Group cooperation: waiting for a turn in a group, taking a turn at the appropriate time

Cognitive Skills Facilitated

Problem solving skills: what to grow in a garden

Classification skills: things in spring

Sequencing skills: songs, stories

Narrative/story structure: adventure

Motor Skills Facilitated

Large motor: outdoor play activities—jumping, running, hopping, pedaling, climbing

Small motor: writing, drawing, gluing

DRAMATIC PLAY **Spring (Garden)**

Type of Activity: Central

Objectives
1. Learn new, and employ familiar, vocabulary
2. Learn new, and employ a variety of, syntactic constructions
3. Interact with peers
4. Sequence familiar routines
5. Expand conceptual knowledge of the world

Settings
- Two or three garden areas
- Seed and gardening store (optional)
- Market (optional)

Props
- Two or three large boxes cut about 4–6" deep
- Sand or soil
- Child-sized garden tools
- Gardening clothes (e.g., hats, gloves)
- Seeds or other small objects (e.g., lima beans, LEGOs)
- Plants (e.g., pretend flowers, vegetables)
- Pails
- Watering can
- Counter (optional)
- Pretend cash register (optional)
- Pretend money (optional)

Roles
- Gardeners
- Store clerks (optional)
- Garden produce sellers (optional)
- Customers (optional)

General Description of Activity

Children work in a pretend garden, digging, planting seeds, and growing flowers or vegetables. Two or three large boxes (e.g., a refrigerator box) cut about 4–6" deep and filled with sand or soil make a good garden. The children can use child-sized gardening tools to prepare the sand or soil. Lima beans or other small objects (e.g., LEGOs) make good "seeds." A seed and gardening store or a market for selling garden produce can be added to the play activity. (Be aware that the activity will need to be restarted after the plants have "grown" and have been "harvested.")

Verbal Productions

Level of linguistic complexity varies with the role or competency of the child playing the role.
- "Do you have any flower seeds?" or "Seeds, please"
- "Do you have any shovels or pails?" or "Diggers?"
- "He is digging a big hole" or "Dig hole"
- "I want a large, round, orange pumpkin" or "Big pumpkin, please"

Adult Facilitative Role

The adult is to facilitate role play and help expand language and literacy skills. Typical actions or strategies to use include

Playing a role: "I am planting a garden. I am going to grow flowers and some vegetables. Do you want to help me?"

Using a cloze procedure: "This is a big flower and this is a _____ (little) flower."

Recasting present tense with past tense irregular: "He digs in the garden" to "He dug a big hole."

Contrasting two sounds: "Did you say 'flower' or 'power?'"

Modeling the reading of a sign: "That sign says roses."

ART : **Egg Carton Caterpillars**

Objectives
1. Express creativity
2. Develop small motor skills (e.g., drawing, painting, cutting, pasting)
3. Practice turn-taking skills
4. Converse with peers and adults

Materials
- Various colors of Styrofoam or cardboard egg cartons, one for each child
- Hole punch
- Various colors of pipe cleaners cut to lengths of 2–3"
- Crayons
- Markers
- Paper scraps
- Glue

General Description of Activity

The children will make caterpillars out of Styrofoam or cardboard egg cartons. Cut the egg section of the cartons into strips of two to four humps ahead of time. Have each child choose a caterpillar and decorate it with crayons or markers or by gluing on different colors or textures of paper. Pipe cleaners make great antennae, and children may even want to add some pipe cleaner legs to their caterpillar. If the children have trouble poking the pipe cleaners through the Styrofoam, use a hole punch first. Then, have children push the pipe cleaner through, bend it around, and twist it around itself to hold it on. Remind them to draw or glue on a face!

GROUP | **Flannel Board Story**

Objectives
1. Improve listening skills
2. Increase conceptual knowledge
3. Learn appropriate group-interaction skills
4. Practice turn-taking skills

Materials
- Flannel board
- Flannel board story pieces

General Description of Activity

Set up the flannel board and lay out the felt pieces for the story. Tell the story, placing the appropriate pieces on the board as the story develops.

Group Participation

After telling the story, give the felt pieces to several children and have one child come up to retell the story. As the storyteller tells the story, the child with the appropriate felt piece places it on the flannel board.

Variation

Have children act out the story after the teacher tells it using the flannel board.

Summary/Transition Activity

Review the story by having some of the children take down the felt pieces as the story is told once again.

Thursday

Dramatic Play	Art	Group	Story	Song
Summer (Beach)	Sand Pictures	Loud/Soft	*A House for Hermit Crab*	"All the Little Fishies"

DAILY PLANNING GUIDE

Language and Literacy Skills Facilitated

Vocabulary: *water, summer, swim, fish, shark, shrimp, octopus, crab, sunshine, dive, splash, sand, shell, dig, beach*

Verb phrase structures: *swims, is/are/was/were swimming, diving, splashing, splashed, swam, has swum, dove, who is swimming? I am*

Adjective/object descriptions: *sunny day, hot day, cold water, funny fish, pink shrimp, mean octopus, hungry shark*

Question structures: *what, how, where, when, who, what if, why, how many, which one*

Pronouns: *I, you, he, she, we, they, my, your, him, her, his, our, their, me, us, them*

Prepositions: *in, on, under, over, near, beneath, next to, beside, around, inside, outside*

Sounds: /s/ *sit, sing, miss;* /s-blends/ *swim, splash, stand;* /r/ *run, row, narrow, our;* /k/ *catch, come, octopus, back*

Noting print has meaning: names on chairs and on cubbies, signs in dramatic play, words in books and on chalkboard

Noting sound–symbol associations: What sound does _____ start with?

Writing: letters, names, words

Social Skills Facilitated

Initiating interaction with peers and adults; responding to questions and requests from peers and adults.

Negotiating with peers for toys and materials

Group cooperation: waiting for a turn in a group, taking a turn at the appropriate time

Cognitive Skills Facilitated

Problem solving skills: how to make sand pictures

Classification skills: things at a beach

Sequencing skills: story, songs, fingerplays

Narrative/story structure: adventure

Motor Skills Facilitated

Large motor: outdoor play activities—jumping, running, hopping, pedaling, climbing

Small motor: writing, drawing, gluing, painting

DRAMATIC PLAY **Summer (Beach)**

Type of Activity: Central

Objectives
1. Learn new, and employ familiar, vocabulary
2. Learn new, and employ a variety of, syntactic constructions
3. Interact with peers
4. Sequence familiar routines
5. Expand conceptual knowledge of the world

Settings
- Blue sheet (or other demarcation) to represent a lake, or filled water table
- Small plastic pools filled with sand
- Volleyball area with a taped line to represent the net
- Concession stand(s) or boardwalk
- Lifeguard stand

Props
- Pails and shovels
- Seashells
- Boats (boxes or rubber rafts)
- Lifejackets (plastic painting smocks worn backward)
- Fishing poles (with magnets attached to catch fish)
- Fish (with paper clips attached)
- Surf boards (pieces of sturdy cardboard)
- Megaphone (for lifeguard)
- Towels
- Pretend sunscreen
- Balloons (for use as volleyballs)
- Pretend food
- Pretend soda fountain (box lid with levers)
- Dishes
- Cash registers

Roles
- Sand diggers
- Sunbathers
- Surfers
- Beach vendors
- Customers
- Volleyball players
- Lifeguards
- Boat riders/fishermen and women

General Description of Activity

A day at the beach usually involves playing with sand near the water. Fill small plastic pools with sand, and bury some seashells in the sand so that children can dig for them. Other activities might include playing sand volleyball, laying out on towels to get a tan, and riding in and/or fishing from boats. You could also set up a concession stand area or boardwalk. Children could surf on pretend surfboards made from cardboard.

Verbal Productions

Level of linguistic complexity varies with the role or competency of the child playing the role.
- "Hit the balloon to me" or "Hit it"
- "I found a pretty shell" or "My shell"
- "He is riding the surfboard and he didn't fall" or "Ride"
- "There's a shark! Get out!" or "Shark!"
- "She wants the shovel now" or "Her turn"
- "He will get an ice cream cone, and I will have a Coke" or "Cone"

Adult Facilitative Role

The adult is to facilitate role play and help expand language and literacy skills. Typical actions or strategies to use include

Playing a role: "I am going to the beach. I think I will play in the sand."

Modeling a statement/vocabulary: "It's summertime. It gets hot at the beach in the summer."

Contrasting two adjectives: "This fish is small, but this shark is large."

Identifying rhyming words: "The words *beach, reach,* and *teach* all rhyme."

Providing confirmatory feedback: "You're right. We dug in the sand."

ART : **Sand Pictures**

Objectives
1. Express creativity
2. Develop small motor skills (e.g., drawing, painting, cutting, pasting)
3. Practice turn-taking skills
4. Converse with peers and adults

Materials
- Paper
- Sand
- Glue
- Paper plates (optional)
- Fish cutouts (optional)
- Seaweed (green construction paper or green yarn)
- Blue plastic wrap (optional)

General Description of Activity

Children can drip glue in a pattern on their paper and then sprinkle sand (or glitter) over the glue to make a picture.

Variation

Have children glue sand to the bottom of a paper plate. They can then glue different items that might be found under the water, such as fish, sharks, and seaweed, on the plate above the sand. Wrap the whole plate in blue plastic wrap to represent the water (this gives an aquarium effect). You may need to tape the plastic wrap to the bottom of the plate.

GROUP **Loud/Soft**

Objectives
1. Improve listening skills
2. Increase conceptual knowledge
3. Learn appropriate group-interaction skills
4. Practice turn-taking skills

Materials
- Drum
- Triangle (optional)
- Other instruments (optional)

General Description of Activity

Place a drum in the middle of the floor. Hit it hard so the sound is *loud*, then hit it softly so the sound is *soft*. Label each sound. Hit a triangle (musical instrument) softly, then loudly. Again, label each sound.

Group Participation

Invite several children to hit the drum (or triangle or other instrument) either hard or softly. Each time, the other children decide whether the sound is loud or soft. Then ask a child to speak softly (or loudly). The class decides if the child's voice was loud or soft. Tell the group to yell when you raise your hand high and whisper when you lower your hand.

Summary/Transition Activity

Review the terms *loud* and *soft*. Sing a familiar song, such as "The Alphabet Song," and have children sing loudly when you raise your hand and softly when you lower it.

WEEKLY PLANNING GUIDE

	Dramatic Play	Art	Group	Story	Song
Monday *Suggested Props and Materials*	Craft Fair *Craft fair scenario, booths for the different craft exhibits, beads or macaroni and yarn, marbles, box lids, construction paper for folding fans and for paper weaving, paint, paintbrushes, paper, concession stand, pretend food, cash registers, money*	Painted Rocks *Rocks, tempera paint (at least three colors), brushes, newspaper*	Letter *R* *Pictures and objects beginning with the letter R, alphabet chart, picture dictionary*	*What Rhymes with Snake?*	"Where is Thumbkin?"
Tuesday *Suggested Props and Materials*	Fishing/Picnic *Lake and picnic area scenario, blue sheet (for water), fish, fishing poles, picnic basket, dishes, pretend food, campfire*	Tissue Paper Fish *Cut-up tissue paper, paper or pre-cut forms, glue, pencils*	How to Write a 5 *Chalkboards and chalk (or white boards), index card with 5 on it*	*Brown Bear, Brown Bear, What Do You See?*	"Five Little Fishies"
Wednesday *Suggested Props and Materials*	Car Racing *Car racing scenario, track area, pit area, spectator area, cars, tracks, flags, pretend stopwatch, pretend concession stand, pretend food, cash register, tools*	Vehicle Rubbings *Paper, vehicle cutouts, crayons with paper covering removed*	Seatbelt Safety *Chair with man's tie (seatbelt), variety of "vehicles" with "seat belts"*	*Go, Dog. Go!*	"Twinkle, Twinkle, Traffic Light"
Thursday *Suggested Props and Materials*	Movie/ Puppet Show *Movies/puppet show scenario, ticket booth, concession stand, spectator seats, stage or puppet area, tickets, cash register, food items, TV monitor/VCR, movie, puppets*	Drawings *Paper; colored pencils, markers, or crayons*	Oddity Match *Several items that are exact matches, several items that are similar, some that do not match, and several items that are related; cardboard X (optional)*	*The Gingerbread Man*	"If You're Happy and You Know It"

NEWSLETTER

Vol. 1, No. 18

Date: _____

Hobbies

Monday Today the children will have a craft fair. They will make and "sell" their wares in dramatic play (necklaces, weavings, paintings, etc). They may even have a picnic in the park along with attending the fair. They will paint rocks in art. The featured story is *What Rhymes with Snake?* During group time, children will learn about the letter *R*. Our song will be "Where is Thumbkin?"

Tuesday Today our hobby is going to the lake to fish and have a picnic. The children can be the fishermen, the picnickers, or the concessions workers. In art, they will make colorful tissue paper fish. Our story is *Brown Bear, Brown Bear, What Do You See?* During group time, we will learn about the number *5*. We will count up to five and we will practice writing the number *5*. Our featured song is "Five Little Fishies."

Wednesday Today the featured hobby is cars and car racing. The children will pretend to be mechanics, drivers, spectators, and even concession stand workers. In art, they will make vehicle rubbings. Our story is *Go, Dog. Go!* During group time, we will focus on seatbelt safety. Our featured song is "Twinkle, Twinkle, Traffic Light."

Thursday Today our hobbies are movies and puppet shows. We will have a movie theater and puppet show scenario. In art, children will make drawings. Our story is *The Gingerbread Man*. The children will classify objects that match during group time. Our song is "If You're Happy and You Know It."

Monday

Dramatic Play	Art	Group	Story	Song
Craft Fair	Painted Rocks	Letter *R*	*What Rhymes with Snake?*	"Where is Thumbkin?"

DAILY PLANNING GUIDE

Language and Literacy Skills Facilitated

Vocabulary: *beads, marbles, paper weaving, paper strip, easel, drawings, crafts, necklace, macaroni, painting, selling*

Verb phrase structures: *is paint<u>ing</u>, paint<u>ed</u> , <u>are</u> fold<u>ing</u>, fold<u>ed</u>, weav<u>es</u>, <u>wove</u>, <u>has woven</u>, Who's ready? I <u>am</u>*

Adjective/object descriptions: _____ *beads (e.g., blue, green), narrow/wide strip, long/short necklace*

Question structures: *what, how, where, when, who, what if, why, how many, which one*

Pronouns: *I, you, he, she, we, they, my, your, him, her, his, our, their, me, us, them*

Prepositions: *in, on, under, over, near, beneath, next to, beside, around, inside, outside*

Sounds: /g/ <u>g</u>o, do<u>g</u>; /m/ <u>m</u>ake, co<u>m</u>e; /s/ <u>s</u>ee, ni<u>ce</u>

Noting print has meaning: names on chairs and on cubbies, signs in dramatic play, words in books and on chalkboard

Noting sound–symbol associations: What sound does _____ start with?

Writing: letters, names, words

Social Skills Facilitated

Initiating interaction with peers and adults; responding to questions and requests from peers and adults

Negotiating with peers for toys and materials

Group cooperation: waiting for a turn in a group, taking a turn at the appropriate time

Cognitive Skills Facilitated

Problem-solving skills: how to make necklaces

Classification skills: things that are crafts

Sequencing skills: story, songs

Narrative/story structure: adventure

Motor Skills Facilitated

Large motor: outdoor play activities—jumping, running, hopping, pedaling, climbing

Small motor: writing, drawing, gluing, weaving, painting

DRAMATIC PLAY **Craft Fair**

Type of Activity: Related

Objectives
1. Learn new, and employ familiar, vocabulary
2. Learn new, and employ a variety of, syntactic constructions
3. Interact with peers
4. Sequence familiar routines
5. Expand conceptual knowledge of the world

Settings
- Booths for the different craft exhibits
- Concession stands

Props
- Beads or macaroni and strings
- Marbles, box lids, and paint
- Construction paper (for folding fans)
- Construction paper strips (for paper weaving)
- Paint, paintbrushes, and paper
- Cups
- Pretend soda pop dispenser
- Pretend cotton candy or popcorn
- Play cash registers

Roles
- Craftspeople
- Customers (dolls may be included for children)
- Concession stand workers
- Band members (optional)

General Description of Activity

Set up a variety of activities for an arts and crafts fair so children can make and sell their crafts. They can string beads and/or macaroni for necklaces, fold paper into paper fans, weave with paper, paint pictures, do marble painting (i.e., dip marbles in paint and roll them back and forth on paper that has been placed in a shoebox lid), draw pictures, make stencils, and so forth. Other children can be customers—some of whom may make purchases while others merely browse. Concession stands may be available as well. Pretend cash registers are needed to make change. A band may play as well.

Verbal Productions

Level of linguistic complexity varies with the role or competency of the child playing the role.
- "Look! Please buy my special necklace. I worked hard to make it," "Look!" or "Buy this?"
- "I am making a ____" or "I made a ____"
- "What are you making?" or "What doing?"

Adult Facilitative Role

The adult is to facilitate role play and help expand language and literacy skills. Typical actions or strategies to use include

Playing a role: "I am making a necklace with yarn and colored macaroni. Sometimes I add pieces of paper between the macaroni."

Contrasting error and correct usage of pronouns: "Her have red paint" to "You mean, she has the red paint."

Redirecting a child to a peer: "Ask Billy for the glue. Say, 'Billy, please pass the glue.'"

Modeling the reading of a sign: "The sign on the booth says *necklaces for sale*."

ART **Painted Rocks**

Objectives
1. Express creativity
2. Develop small motor skills (e.g., drawing, painting, cutting, pasting)
3. Practice turn-taking skills
4. Converse with peers and adults

Materials
- Small rocks, approximately 2" × 2" (one for each child)
- Tempera paint (at least three colors)
- Brushes
- Newspaper (to protect drying surfaces)

General Description of Activity

The children use tempera paint and brushes to paint on small rocks. Smooth rounded rocks are preferable, but others can be used. Set the rocks on newspaper to dry. The children may want to make them as presents for their parents to use as paperweights.

GROUP **Letter *R***

Objectives

1. Improve listening skills
2. Increase knowledge of the alphabet *(R)*
3. Learn appropriate group-interaction skills
4. Practice turn-taking skills

Materials

- Alphabet chart and other alphabet displays
- Blackboard and chalk or poster paper and markers
- Pictures of objects (or objects themselves) with names that begin with *R*
- Picture dictionary (or an alphabet video dictionary)

General Description of Activity

Write an upper- and a lowercase letter *R* on the blackboard (or on poster paper). Give several examples of words that begin with *R*, emphasizing the /r/ or "rrr" sound at the beginning of the words. You might hold up pictures of objects (or objects themselves) with names that begin with *R*. Direct the children's attention to the alphabet picture displays around the room.

Group Participation

Ask if anyone's name starts with *R* (e.g., Ryan, Ramon, Reece). Those children write the letter *R* on the board. Also have two or three other children write the letter *R* on the blackboard. Provide verbal guidance as children form the letter: "Start at the top and draw a straight line down. Go back to the top and draw a half circle, ending at the middle of the straight line. Now, draw a slanting line from the half circle to the bottom." If necessary, help the children write the letter. Some of the other children can practice writing *R* in the air with their fingers (or on individual chalkboards). Ask the children to think of words that begin with *R*. Write the words they suggest on the blackboard and draw quick sketches (when possible) of the suggested words. If a child suggests a word that does not begin with *R*, say, "No, that begins with ____," and say both sounds so children can compare them. To help children who cannot think of any words, prompt them with pictures of objects (or objects themselves) representing words that begin with *R*. (Pictures or objects can be handed out at the beginning of the lesson or as the lesson proceeds.) Additional words can be sought in a picture dictionary if the group has difficulty arriving at words that begin with *R*.

Variation

Lead an activity in which the children discriminate between words that begin with *R* and other words that rhyme with the *R* words (e.g., *r*ed, bed, led; *r*ope, soap; *r*attle, battle; *r*un, fun, sun, bun).

Summary/Transition Activity

After about 10–15 words have been suggested, review the words, emphasizing the *R* sound.

Tuesday

Dramatic Play	Art	Group	Story	Song
Fishing/Picnic	Tissue Paper Fish	How to Write a 5	Brown Bear, Brown Bear, What Do You See?	"Five Little Fishies"

DAILY PLANNING GUIDE

Language and Literacy Skills Facilitated

Vocabulary: *fishing, fish, pole, tissue paper, sink, float, picnic, pool, worms, bait, bubble, tackle box*

Verb phrase structures: *is fish<u>ing</u>, fish<u>es</u>, fish<u>ed</u>; <u>are</u> past<u>ing</u>, past<u>es</u>, past<u>ed</u>; catch<u>es</u>, <u>caught</u>; Who <u>is</u> fish<u>ing</u>? I <u>am</u>*

Adjective/object descriptions: *fishing pole, big/little fish, hard, wet, long/short picnic*

Question structures: *what, how, where, when, who, what if, why, how many, which one*

Pronouns: *I, you, he, she, we, they, my, your, him, her, his, our, their, me, us, them*

Prepositions: *in, on, under, over, near, beneath, next to, beside, around, inside, outside*

Sounds: /sh/ <u>sh</u>ip, fi<u>sh</u>ing, fi<u>sh</u>; /s/ <u>s</u>ea, mi<u>ss</u>es, mi<u>ss</u>; /f/ <u>f</u>un, <u>f</u>i<u>sh</u>, o<u>f</u>ten, o<u>ff</u>

Noting print has meaning: names on chairs and on cubbies, signs in dramatic play, words in books and on chalkboard

Noting sound–symbol associations: What sound does _____ start with?

Writing: letters, names, words

Social Skills Facilitated

Initiating interaction with peers and adults; responding to questions and requests from peers and adults

Negotiating with peers for toys and materials

Group cooperation: waiting for a turn in a group, taking a turn at the appropriate time

Cognitive Skills Facilitated

Problem-solving skills: how to catch a fish, how to write the number 5

Classification skills: finding five items versus four or three or two items

Sequencing skills: story, songs

Narrative/story structure: rhyming

Motor Skills Facilitated

Large motor: outdoor play activities—jumping, running, hopping, pedaling, climbing, fishing

Small motor: writing, drawing, gluing

DRAMATIC PLAY **Fishing/Picnic**

Type of Activity: Central

Objectives

1. Learn new, and employ familiar, vocabulary
2. Learn new, and employ a variety of, syntactic constructions
3. Interact with peers
4. Sequence familiar routines
5. Expand conceptual knowledge of the world

Settings
- Park
- Lake (blue sheet or a wading pool)
- Bait shop (optional)
- Boat (child-sized boat or dismantled cardboard box—optional)

Props
- Fishing poles (with magnets attached to catch fish)
- Fish (with paper clips attached)
- Pretend bait
- Pretend cash register (optional—at the bait shop)
- Picnic baskets
- Pretend money (optional—to buy the bait)
- Pretend food
- Blankets
- Dishes
- Grill and blocks for campfire
- Trash can

Roles
- Fishermen and women
- Park ranger
- Children
- Bait shop clerk

General Description of Activity

Children can pack their fishing equipment and a picnic basket and go to a lakeside park. There they can fish, cook what they catch, and eat their picnic lunch. When they are finished, they can clean up, pack up their supplies, and go home. (Be aware that the lake will need to be restocked and the picnic basket repacked so that the activity can continue.)

Verbal Productions

Level of linguistic complexity varies with the role or competency of the child playing the role.
- "I caught a big fish" or "Big fish"
- "I like to go fishing with my dad. We go to the lake" or "Like fishing"
- "He has my pole. It is my turn" or "Mine"
- "We fished all day and caught twenty fish" or "Lots of fish"

Adult Facilitative Role

The adult is to facilitate role play and help expand language and literacy skills. Typical actions or strategies to use include

Playing a role: "I am going fishing today. I need to bring my fishing pole to the lake."

Modeling the reading of a sign: "That sign says, 'Worms for Sale.'"

Expanding a child's utterance: "We fish now" to "Yes, we are fishing now. I hope we can catch a fish for dinner."

Identifying rhyming words: "Yes, the words *lake, bake,* and *cake* all rhyme."

Modeling a statement/vocabulary: "When we go on a picnic, we bring food to eat while we are outside."

ART : **Tissue Paper Fish**

Objectives
1. Express creativity
2. Develop small motor skills (e.g., drawing, painting, cutting, pasting)
3. Practice turn-taking skills
4. Converse with peers and adults

Materials
- Precut forms in shape of fish (or other shapes)
- Paste or glue
- 1" tissue paper squares (several colors)
- Pencils or crayons

General Description of Activity

Children crush the 1" pieces of tissue paper and paste them onto a precut construction paper fish. One way to crush the paper is to wrap it around the eraser end of a pencil (or one end of a crayon) and push it off onto glue or paste that is already on the form. Or children can just crumple the squares and then paste them on the paper. When the fish is completely covered, the result is a three-dimensional picture, or a picture with texture.

GROUP **How to Write a 5**

Objectives

1. Improve listening skills
2. Increase conceptual knowledge
3. Learn appropriate group-interaction skills
4. Practice turn-taking skills
5. Practice recognition and writing of numbers

Materials

- Number cards
- Chalkboards and chalk
- Paper and pencils (optional)
- Whiteboard and markers
- Number line (optional)

General Description of Activity

Hold up a card with the number 5 on it. Trace the number with your finger and invite several children to come to the front of the group to trace the number, too. As the children trace, recite the jingle for the target number (5):

1: Start at the top, go down and you're done, that's the way to make a 1.

2: Around and back on the railroad track, 2, 2, 2.

3: Around the tree, around the tree, that's the way to make a 3.

4: Down and over and down once more, that's the way to make a 4.

5: Down around, make a hat on it, and look what you've found. (5)

6: Down around until it sticks, that's the way to make a 6.

7: Over and down and it's not heaven, over and down makes a 7.

8: Make an S and go back straight, that's the way to make an 8.

9: A balloon and a line make 9.

10: Draw a line and a circle with your pen, that's the way to make a 10.

Group Participation

Distribute individual chalkboards and chalk (or paper and pencils) to the children, and have them practice writing the target number.

Variation

Whiteboards and markers may easier for some children to use.

Summary/Transition Activity

Have children hold up their chalkboards and show the group their numbers.

Wednesday

Dramatic Play	Art	Group	Story	Song
Car Racing	Vehicle Rubbings	Seatbelt Safety	*Go, Dog. Go!*	"Twinkle, Twinkle, Traffic Light"

DAILY PLANNING GUIDE

Language and Literacy Skills Facilitated

Vocabulary: *transportation, vehicle, car, track, ramp, garage, truck, win, lose, flag, start, finish, wheels, square*

Verb phrase structures: *goes fast, wins the race, crashed the car, pushed it, was racing, starts, stopped, won, were losing*

Adjective/object descriptions: *race car, fast/slow ____, big/little ___, yellow flag, checkered flag*

Question structures: *what, how, where, when, who, what if, why, how many, which one*

Pronouns: *I, you, he, she, we, they, my, your, him, her, his, our, their, me, us, them*

Prepositions: *in, on, under, over, near, beneath, next to, beside, around, inside, outside*

Sounds: /r/ *race, starter, car;* /s/ *see, misses, race;* /f/ *fast, off;* /sh/ *shape, finish;* blends: *flag, truck, start*

Noting print has meaning: names on chairs and on cubbies, signs in dramatic play, words in books and on chalkboard

Noting sound–symbol associations: What sound does _____ start with?

Writing: letters, names, words

Social Skills Facilitated

Initiating interaction with peers and adults; responding to questions and requests from peers and adults

Negotiating with peers for toys and materials

Group cooperation: waiting for a turn in a group, taking a turn at the appropriate time

Cognitive Skills Facilitated

Problem-solving skills: how to set up the tracks

Classification skills: vehicles/non-vehicles

Sequencing skills: song, racing the cars, art

Narrative/story structure: rhyming

Motor Skills Facilitated

Large motor: outdoor play activities—jumping, running, hopping, pedaling, climbing

Small motor: writing, drawing, gluing, rubbing

DRAMATIC PLAY **Car Racing**

Type of Activity: Sequential

Objectives
1. Learn new, and employ familiar, vocabulary
2. Learn new, and employ a variety of, syntactic constructions
3. Interact with peers
4. Sequence familiar routines
5. Expand conceptual knowledge of the world

Settings
- Three or four different track areas (one with two tracks elevated on one end and other tracks that form circles or ovals)
- Garage or pit area
- Spectator area
- Portable slide elevated on one end (optional—another track)
- Concession stand (optional)

Props
- Assortment of toy cars
- Tracks
- Electric tracks (optional)
- Checkered flag
- Play stopwatch
- Chairs for spectators
- Tools (e.g., wrench, screwdriver, pretend batteries)
- Pretend drink machine
- Cups
- Pretend cotton candy (optional)

Roles
- Drivers
- Mechanics
- Timers or judges
- Spectators
- Concession stand workers

General Description of Activity

Arrange several tracks for the toy cars to race on, an area for the cars to be worked on, and an area for spectators. Children play the roles of drivers, mechanics, timers, or spectators. The drivers race the cars by releasing two cars simultaneously and watching as they race down the tracks, which are elevated on one end. (Electric tracks could also be used, particularly for children with physical disabilities so they could press the switches.) The activity could be expanded to include concession stands.

Verbal Productions

Level of linguistic complexity varies with the role or competency of the child playing the role.
- "Get your cars ready" or "Ready"
- "Your car needs a new engine" or "New car"
- "That car went very fast" or "Fast car"
- "I fixed it" or "Fix"

Adult Facilitative Role

The adult is to facilitate role play and help expand language and literacy skills. Typical actions or strategies to use include

Playing a role: "I am going to put two cars at the top of the track. Watch what happens when I let them go."

Using a cloze procedure: "That car was fast but this car is _____(faster)."

Expanding a child's utterance: "Want car" to "I want that car, please."

Using event casting: "I am hungry. I am going to the concession stand to get a hot dog. Then I will come back and watch the car races."

Modeling the reading of a sign: "That sign says *hot dogs $1*."

Contrasting two sounds: "Did you say 'sit' or 'fit?'"

ART : **Vehicle Rubbings**

Objectives
1. Express creativity
2. Develop small motor skills (e.g., drawing, painting, rubbing, cutting, pasting)
3. Practice turn-taking skills
4. Converse with peers and adults

Materials
- Newsprint or tracing paper
- Variety of cutouts
- Crayons with paper removed
- Container to hold crayons

- Brick wall, sidewalk, and other interesting textures for outdoor rubbings (optional)

General Description of Activity

Cut a variety of vehicle outlines out of cardboard. Have the children place one or more under a piece of paper. Holding a crayon (with the paper covering removed) or a piece of chalk on one side, they rub over the paper back and forth until the shape of the object appears on their paper. Children can use different-colored crayons and different arrangements of objects under the paper to make a variety of pictures.

Variation

Tape large pieces of paper to a brick wall for children to make crayon rubbings. A sidewalk or manhole cover would also produce interesting rubbings.

GROUP : **Seatbelt Safety**

Objectives
1. Improve listening skills
2. Increase conceptual knowledge
3. Learn appropriate group-interaction skills
4. Practice turn-taking skills

Materials
- Neckties (pretend seatbelts)
- Toy car
- Toy tractor
- Toy airplane
- Toy boat

General Description of Activity

Tell the children that when they ride in cars (or airplanes), they should wear their seatbelts. Have children put on pretend seatbelts (children do the motion of fastening a seatbelt) and pretend to drive to the park.

Group Participation

Place a toy car, tractor, airplane, and boat in front of the children. Have a chair representing a particular vehicle behind each toy. Be sure to have pretend seatbelts for the car and airplane. Have children come up and pretend to ride in the different vehicles. Ask the children which vehicles have seatbelts, and make sure the children riding those vehicles have put on the seatbelts.

Summary/Transition Activity

Lead a discussion of why seatbelts should be worn.

Thursday

Dramatic Play	Art	Group	Story	Song
Movie/Puppet Show	Drawings	Oddity Match	*The Gingerbread Man*	"If You're Happy and You Know It"

DAILY PLANNING GUIDE

Language and Literacy Skills Facilitated

Vocabulary: *movie, film, picture show, screen, ticket, watch, puppet, Oscar, Miss Piggy, dog, cat, popcorn, soft drink, actor, actress, costume, props*

Verb phrase structures: *act like a dog, watch the film, act in the show, put on costumes*

Adjective/object descriptions: *good picture, pink piggy, noisy/quiet show, funny/sad puppet*

Question structures: *what, how, where, when, who, what if, why, how many, which one*

Pronouns: *I, you, he, she, we, they, my, your, him, her, his, our, their, me, us, them*

Prepositions: *in, on, under, over, near, beneath, next to, beside, around, inside, outside*

Sounds: /f/ *fix, off;* /s/ *sit, talks;* /l/ *little, bell*

Noting print has meaning: names on chairs and on cubbies, signs in dramatic play, words in books and on chalkboard

Noting sound–symbol associations: What sound does _____ start with?

Writing: letters, names, words

Social Skills Facilitated

Initiating interaction with peers and adults; responding to questions and requests from peers and adults

Negotiating with peers for toys and materials

Group cooperation: waiting for a turn in a group, taking a turn at the appropriate time

Cognitive Skills Facilitated

Problem-solving skills: What does not go with the others?

Classification skills: things at a movie

Sequencing skills: story, songs

Narrative/story structure: adventure (classic tale)

Motor Skills Facilitated

Large motor: outdoor play activities—jumping, running, hopping, pedaling, climbing

Small motor: writing, drawing, gluing

DRAMATIC PLAY **Movie/Puppet Show**

Type of Activity: Central

Objectives

1. Learn new, and employ familiar, vocabulary
2. Learn new, and employ a variety of, syntactic constructions
3. Interact with peers
4. Sequence familiar routines
5. Expand conceptual knowledge of the world

Settings
- Ticket booth
- Concession stand
- Stage or puppet area
- Spectator seats

Props
- Tickets
- Cash register
- Puppets
- Chairs and mat for making risers
- TV monitor/VCR and movie
- Food items (e.g., pretend popcorn, candy, and soft drinks)

Roles
- Cashier
- Ticket taker
- Customers
- Concession workers
- Puppeteers

General Description of Activity

Set up a movie theater with a ticket booth area, a spectator section, a concession area, and a stage. The children can purchase tickets, buy their popcorn and other food, find their seats, and prepare to watch a movie or puppet show. It is helpful if the spectator area is raised (this can be accomplished by folding over a tumbling mat and putting chairs on one level and a second row on a higher level). Set up a TV monitor and a short film for the children to watch. You could also add a puppet area—a shelf with a blanket thrown over it so that the children can use hand puppets on the shelf and hide behind the shelf while they are doing the puppet actions.

Verbal Productions

Level of linguistic complexity varies with the role or competency of the child playing the role.
- "I need tickets for three adults and two children, please" or "Tickets, please"
- "I'll be Big Bird, you be Elmo" or "Big Bird"
- "Do you want popcorn and a coke?" or "Popcorn?"
- "I watched that at my birthday party" or "Watch at party"

Adult Facilitative Role

The adult is to facilitate role play and help expand language and literacy skills. Typical actions or strategies to use include

Playing a role: "I like to go to the movies."

Expanding a child's utterance: "Buy ticket" to "Yes, he is buying the tickets."

Modeling the reading of a sign: "The sign says 'Puppet Show.'"

Modeling phonological awareness: "Yes, 'puppet,' 'puppy,' and 'Polly' all start with the letter *P*."

Redirecting a child to a peer: "Ask Mike for a turn. Say, 'May I have a turn, please?'"

ART **Drawings**

Objectives
1. Express creativity
2. Develop small motor skills (e.g., drawing, painting, cutting, pasting)
3. Practice turn-taking skills
4. Converse with peers and adults

Materials
- Paper (white or colored)
- Crayons
- Markers
- Watered-down tempera paint (optional)

General Description of Activity

Provide the children with paper and a selection of pencils, crayons, and/or markers. Let the children draw anything they want. Drawings could be of themselves, their family, their pets, different scenes, designs, rainbows, etc.

Children can turn their crayon drawings into crayon washes by painting over the pictures with a light coat of tempera paint (watered-down paint). The paint will not stick to the crayon but will fill in where there are no crayon marks to make a background of color.

GROUP **Oddity Match**

Objectives
1. Improve listening skills
2. To increase sequencing ability
3. Learn appropriate group-interaction skills
4. To practice turn-taking

Materials
- Several items that are exact matches (and some that are not)
- Several items that are similar (and some that do not match)
- Several items that are related
- Cardboard X (optional)

General Description of Activity

Lay out four items. Three of the items should be identical and one should be different (e.g., three red cars and one doll). Ask the children to look for the item that does not belong with the others. Then point to the item that is different and say, "This one does not go with the others." Lay out another set, this time with three items that are not identical but are the same kind of item, and one that is different from the others (e.g., three different dolls, one boat). Ask one child to come to the front and find the one that is different (or that does not go with the others).

Group Participation

Continue to present three items that are the same and one that is different until each child has had a turn identifying the different item. Be sure to vary the placement of the different item so that the children do not think it is always the second item or the last item. The difficulty of the task can be varied depending on the children's abilities (some children may need exact matches; others can recognize relationships or that the items go together even though one is bigger than the other). The children also could put a cardboard X on top of the item that does not belong rather than say or point to the item. Note: You may want to do this activity after the lesson on same and different.

Variation

One way to vary the items is to put them is a 2 × 2 matrix instead of in a row. Another procedure would be to use related items instead of the same kind of items. For example, of the following items, coat, hat, fork, and mitten, the coat, hat, and mitten are the items that go together and the fork does not belong. Another variation is to use color or function as the identifying feature (e.g., all the red items go together and the blue item is the one that is different, or all the writing instruments go together and the scissors are the item that is different).

Summary/Transition Activity

Lay out one more group of items and have the children, in unison, say which one does not go with the others.

WEEKLY PLANNING GUIDE

	Dramatic Play	Art	Group	Story	Song
Monday *Suggested Props and Materials*	Department Store *Department store scenario, counters and racks, shelves, dressing rooms, clothes, hangers, purses, mirror, pretend cash register, shoes, pretend money, pretend credit cards*	Catalog Collage *Construction paper, scissors, catalogs*	Letter S *Pictures and objects beginning with the letter S, alphabet chart, picture dictionary*	*At the Mall*	"Something in My Pocket"
Tuesday *Suggested Props and Materials*	Pizza Parlor *Pizza parlor scenario, menus, pizza oven, pizza ingredients, dishes, cups, soda pop dispenser, utensils, tables, chairs, dishes and cups, cash register, pretend money*	Crayon Wash Pizzas *Paper, crayons, watered-down red tempera paint*	Follow/Give Directions *Two sets of plastic food items (e.g., buns, hamburger patty, lettuce, pickle, cheese, etc.), mat, two sets of small objects (e.g., blocks, cars, dolls, etc.), barrier (optional)*	*Bread, Bread, Bread*	"I Wish I Were a Pepperoni Pizza"
Wednesday *Suggested Props and Materials*	Pet Store *Pet store scenario, counter, stuffed animals, cash register, play money, cages, shelves, pretend pet food, pet carriers, pretend cleaning supplies, fish, aquariums*	Easel Painting *Easels, tempera paint, paintbrushes, smocks, drying rack*	What Does _____ Eat? My First Book of Nature: How Living Things Grow *(Kuhn)*	*Scallywag*	"I Have a Little Turtle"
Thursday *Suggested Props and Materials*	Toy Store *Toy store scenario, cash register, pretend money, counter, shelves, various toys, wrapping paper, tape, ribbons, scissors*	Teddy Bear Pictures *Teddy bear outlines, glue, Cheerios*	Act out a Story *(Corduroy)* *Props for story*	*Corduroy*	"Going on a Bear Hunt"

MY NOTES

NEWSLETTER

Vol. 1, No. 19

Date: _____

At the Mall

Monday

The classroom will become a department store today. The children can be the customers, the clerks, or the managers. The children can try on clothes and shoes and buy an assortment of items. In art, they can make a catalog collage. Our story today is *At the Mall*. During group time, the children will learn about the letter *S*. Our song is "Something in My Pocket."

Tuesday

Today the children will visit the pizza parlor while at the mall. They can be the pizza cooks, the customers, or the clean-up crew. In art, the children will make pizza pictures with crayons and red tempera paint. Our story is *Bread, Bread, Bread*. The children will practice following and giving directions to one another during group time. Our featured song is "I Wish I Were a Pepperoni Pizza."

Wednesday

Today the classroom becomes a pet store. The children can be the pets, the pet owners, the pet store owner, or clerks. In art, the children will do easel painting with tempera paint. Our book today is *Scallawag*. During group time, children will discover what different animals eat as we read the book by Dwight Kuhn called *My First Book of Nature*.

Thursday

The classroom will be a toy store today. The children can be the clerks, the customers, or the ones who wrap the presents. In art, the children will make teddy bear pictures. Our story is *Corduroy*. During group time, the children will act out *Corduroy*. This story is about a bear at the toy store that gets lost in the mall. Our featured song is "Going on a Bear Hunt."

Monday

Dramatic Play	Art	Group	Story	Song
Department Store	Catalog Collage	Letter *S*	*At the Mall*	"Something in My Pocket"

DAILY PLANNING GUIDE

Language and Literacy Skills Facilitated

Vocabulary: *shopping, mall, department store, sales clerks, cash register, money, clothes, shoes, pants, dress, hangers*

Verb phrase structures: *shop<u>s</u>, <u>is</u> shopp<u>ing</u>, shopp<u>ed</u>, pay<u>s</u>, <u>paid</u>, tr<u>ies</u> on, tr<u>ied</u> on*

Adjective/object descriptions: *big/small ____, pretty ____, too tight, too big*

Question structures: *what, how, where, when, who, what if, why, how many, which one*

Pronouns: *I, you, he, she, we, they, my, your, him, her, his, our, their, me, us, them*

Prepositions: *in, on, under, over, near, beneath, next to, beside, around, inside, outside*

Sounds: /f/ <u>f</u>ind, o<u>ff</u>; /k/ <u>c</u>ash, ja<u>ck</u>et, sa<u>ck</u>; /l/ <u>l</u>ittle, ma<u>ll</u>

Noting print has meaning: names on chairs and on cubbies, signs in dramatic play, words in books and on chalkboard

Noting sound–symbol associations: What sound does _____ start with?

Writing: letters, names, words

Social Skills Facilitated

Initiating interaction with peers and adults; responding to questions and requests from peers and adults

Negotiating with peers for toys and materials

Group cooperation: waiting for a turn in a group, taking a turn at the appropriate time

Cognitive Skills Facilitated

Problem-solving skills: how to make a fabric collage, what to buy

Classification skills: words that begin with *S*

Sequencing skills: song, story, buying things at a store

Narrative structure: adventure

Motor Skills Facilitated

Large motor: outdoor play activities—jumping, running, hopping, pedaling, climbing

Small motor: writing, drawing, gluing

DRAMATIC PLAY **Department Store**

Type of Activity: Central

Objectives
1. Learn new, and employ familiar, vocabulary
2. Learn new, and employ a variety of, syntactic constructions
3. Interact with peers
4. Sequence familiar routines
5. Expand conceptual knowledge of the world

Settings
- Department store
- Counters and racks
- Check-out area
- Shelves and other display areas
- Dressing rooms
- Elevator (optional)

Props
- Clothes, including shoes, belts, and ties
- Hangers
- Pretend money
- Pretend credit cards
- Pretend cash register
- Purses
- Mirror

Roles
- Clerks
- Custodians
- Customers (dolls may be included for children)
- Cashiers

General Description of Activity

Children shop at a department store, choosing from a variety of items, including clothes. They can try on the clothes and purchase them. Store clerks can help the customers in purchasing the clothes and in hanging up clothes that are tried on but not purchased. Cashiers can take the customers' money or credit cards.

Verbal Productions

Level of linguistic complexity varies with the role or competency of the child playing the role.
- "This dress is too big. I need a smaller size" or "Too big"
- "He is working at the cash register now" or "He there"
- "She has had a long turn. I want a turn now" or "My turn"

Adult Facilitative Role

The adult is to facilitate role play and help expand language and literacy skills. Typical actions or strategies to use include

Playing a role: "I am going to buy some new clothes for my son. He needs a new shirt."

Expanding a child's utterance: "Him big" to "He is very big."

Modeling the reading of the sign: "That sign says *furniture for sale*."

Contrasting two different verb structures (present tense to irregular past tense): "I am buying the chair. I already bought the table."

Providing event casts of child's actions: "John is trying on some shirts. The shirt is too big. He tries on another shirt. Now this shirt fits. John goes to pay for the shirt."

ART : Catalog Collage

Objectives
1. Express creativity
2. Develop small motor skills (e.g., drawing, painting, cutting, pasting)
3. Practice turn-taking skills
4. Converse with peers and adults

Materials
- Construction paper
- Scissors
- Glue
- Catalogs

General Description of Activity

Children cut out pictures of clothes and other items from a catalog, then glue them on construction paper. Children can choose from a variety of pictures.

GROUP **Letter S**

Objectives
1. Improve listening skills
2. Increase knowledge of the alphabet and sounds
3. Learn appropriate group interaction skills
4. Practice turn-taking skills

Materials
- Alphabet chart and other alphabet displays
- Blackboard and chalk or poster paper and markers
- Pictures of objects (or objects themselves) with names that begin with S
- Picture dictionary (or an alphabet video dictionary)

General Description of Activity

Write an upper- and a lowercase letter S on the blackboard (or on poster paper). Give several examples of words that begin with S, emphasizing the /s/ or "sss" sound at the beginning of the words. You might hold up pictures of objects (or objects themselves) with names that begin with S. Direct the children's attention to the alphabet picture displays around the room.

Group Participation

Asks if anyone's name starts with S (e.g., Simone, Scott), and have those children write the letter S on the blackboard (or poster paper). Also have two or three other children write the letter S on the blackboard. Provide verbal guidance as children form the letter: "Make a curved line like a C, and then make the line turn to the left." If necessary, help children write the letter. Some of the other children can practice writing S in the air with their fingers (or on individual chalkboards). Ask the children to think of words that begin with S. Write the words they offer on the blackboard, drawing quick sketches (when possible) of the suggested words. If a child suggests a word that does not begin with S, say, "No, that begins with ___," and say both sounds so children can compare them. To help children who cannot think of any words, prompt them with pictures or objects representing S words. (Pictures or objects can be handed out at the beginning of the lesson or as the lesson proceeds.) Additional words can be sought in a picture dictionary if the group has difficulty arriving at words that begin with S.

Summary/Transition Activity

After about 10–15 words have been suggested, review the words, emphasizing the S sound.

Tuesday

Dramatic Play	Art	Group	Story	Song
Pizza Parlor	Crayon Wash Pizzas	Follow/Give Directions	*Bread, Bread, Bread*	"I Wish I Were a Pepperoni Pizza"

DAILY PLANNING GUIDE

Language and Literacy Skills Facilitated

Vocabulary: *soft drinks, pizzas, spaghetti, shakes, wrappers, boxes, cook, cashier, customer, order, pizza parlor, pizza delivery*

Verb phrase structures: *places an order, buys a pizza, pays money, eat out, is making a pizza, served the customer, served a pizza, chooses a drink, are making pizzas*

Adjective/object descriptions: *large drink, small pizza, paper hat, red cup*

Question structures: *what, how, where, when, who, what if, why, how many, which one*

Pronouns: *I, you, he, she, we, they, my, your, him, her, his, our, their, me, us, them*

Prepositions: *in the cash register, on the plate, near the stove, in the oven (in, on, under, over, near, beneath, next to, beside, around, inside, outside)*

Sounds: /p/ *pizza, plate, paper hat;* /c/ *cook, cashier, customer*

Noting print has meaning: names on chairs and on cubbies, signs in dramatic play, words in books and on chalkboard

Noting sound–symbol associations: What sound does _____ start with?

Writing: letters, names, words

Social Skills Facilitated

Initiating interaction with peers and adults; responding to questions and requests from peers and adults

Negotiating with peers for toys and materials

Group cooperation: waiting for a turn in a group, taking a turn at the appropriate time

Cognitive Skills Facilitated

Problem-solving skills: setting up a restaurant, remembering items, giving directions

Classification skills: things that go on pizza

Sequencing skills: putting a pizza together, words to song

Narrative/story structure: information

Motor Skills Facilitated

Large motor: outdoor play activities—jumping, running, hopping, pedaling, climbing

Small motor: writing, drawing, gluing

DRAMATIC PLAY : **Pizza Parlor**

Type of Activity: Central

Objectives
1. Learn new, and employ familiar, vocabulary
2. Learn new, and employ a variety of, syntactic constructions
3. Interact with peers
4. Sequence familiar routines
5. Expand conceptual knowledge of the world

Settings
- Restaurant kitchen
- Dining area
- Counter
- Carry-out window
- Salad bar (optional)

Props
- Tables and chairs
- Menus
- Pretend pizzas (plastic facsimiles or cardboard circles for crusts; variety of cutouts for toppings, such as pepperoni, green peppers, and mushrooms; pieces of yellow yarn for cheese)
- Dishes and cups
- Trays
- Pretend soda pop dispenser
- Pretend cash register
- Pretend money
- Order form and pencils
- Delivery van (optional)
- Roads (marked with masking tape—optional)
- English muffins, real pizza toppings, and microwave oven (optional)

Roles
- Customers
- Waiters and waitresses
- Cashier
- Cooks
- Delivery van driver (optional)

General Description of Activity

Children run a pizza parlor. The waiter or waitress seats the guests and gives them menus. The guests order their pizzas, with various toppings, and possibly other items, such as spaghetti or bread sticks. Children who are the cooks must construct the pizzas, which are then taken to the customers by the waiter or waitress. A pizza delivery van can also be used to deliver pizzas to homes. Note: Real pizzas can be made at snack time by using English muffins as the crust. The children can add different toppings and cook the pizzas in a microwave oven.

Verbal Productions

Level of linguistic complexity varies with the role or competency of the child playing the role.
- "We have two kinds of pizza, pepperoni and cheese. Which do you want?" or "Which one?"
- "Cheese?" or "More pizza"
- "You ate my pizza" or "My pizza!"
- "You bought two pizzas and I bought one" or "One pizza"

Adult Facilitative Role

The adult is to facilitate role play and help expand language and literacy skills. Typical actions or strategies to use include

Playing a role: "I want to order a large cheese pizza."

Asking an open question: "What do you want on your pizza?"

Modeling the reading of a sign: "The sign says *Please wait to be seated*."

Expanding a child's utterance: "Make pizza?" to "Do you want me to make a pizza?"

Contrasting location terms: "The pizza is in the oven" to "This pizza is on the table."

ART **Crayon Wash Pizzas**

Objectives
1. Express creativity
2. Develop small motor skills (e.g., drawing, painting, cutting, pasting)
3. Practice turn-taking skills
4. Converse with peers and adults

Materials
- Paper (white)
- Crayons
- Smocks
- Watered-down red tempera paint

General Description of Activity

Provide the children with paper and a selection of crayons. Have the children draw a pizza shape, then mushrooms and other toppings with the crayons. After they have put the "toppings" on the pizza, have them paint over the pizza with watered-down red paint. The red paint becomes the tomato sauce. It will not stick to the crayon but will fill in where there are no crayon marks, giving a background of color.

GROUP : **Follow/Give Directions**

Objectives

1. Improve listening skills
2. Increase conceptual knowledge
3. Learn appropriate group interaction skills
4. Practice turn-taking skills

Materials

- Two sets of plastic food items (e.g., buns, hamburger patty, lettuce, pickle, cheese)
- Mat
- Two sets of small objects (e.g., blocks, cars, dolls), optional
- Barrier (optional)

General Description of Activity

Lay out the plastic food items and put them together into a sandwich while the children watch. When you're finished, ask the children to tell what you did, step by step (e.g., first, the bun was opened, then the hamburger was placed on the bun, then the cheese went on top of the hamburger).

Group Participation

Have two children come to the front of the group. Have one child make a sandwich using one set of the ingredients. Ask this child to give the second child directions on how to make the same sandwich with the second set of ingredients. You might place a barrier between the two children to make following and giving directions more difficult. Have the rest of the group decide whether the directions were followed. Have two more children try the task. A final task would be for a child to give you directions for making a sandwich, with the other children judging whether you followed the directions correctly.

Variation

Arrange a pattern using colored blocks or small toys on a mat. Have one child tell another child how to make the same pattern on a second mat. Again, a barrier could be used so that the two children cannot see what the other is doing.

Summary/Transition Activity

Makes one last pattern, reviewing the important items to remember in giving directions.

Wednesday

Dramatic Play	Art	Group	Story	Song
Pet Store	Easel Painting	What Does _____ Eat?	*Scallywag*	"I Have a Little Turtle"

DAILY PLANNING GUIDE

Language and Literacy Skills Facilitated

Vocabulary: *dog, cats, birds, gerbils, Dalmatians, pets, rabbits, camera, ribbons, awards, phone, cash register, cages, podium*

Verb phrase structures: *take<u>s</u> a picture, <u>is</u> tak<u>ing</u> the pet home, <u>fed</u> the dog, <u>gave</u> a ribbon, pett<u>ed</u> the dog, walk<u>ed</u> the dog*

Adjective/object descriptions: *blue/red ribbon, first place, big/little _____, white/black _____, long/short leash*

Question structures: *what, how, where, when, who, what if, why, how many, which one*

Pronouns: *I, you, he, she, we, they, my, your, him, her, his, our, their, me, us, them*

Prepositions: *in, on, under, over, near, beneath, next to, beside, around, inside, outside*

Sounds: /k/ <u>c</u>atch, pa<u>ck</u>, tri<u>ck</u>; /f/ <u>f</u>ed, of<u>f</u>; /r/ <u>r</u>abbit, fa<u>r</u>

Noting print has meaning: names on chairs and on cubbies, signs in dramatic play, words in books and on chalkboard

Noting sound–symbol associations: What sound does _____ start with?

Writing: letters, names, words

Social Skills Facilitated

Initiating interaction with peers and adults; responding to questions and requests from peers and adults

Negotiating with peers for toys and materials

Group cooperation: waiting for a turn in a group, taking a turn at the appropriate time

Cognitive Skills Facilitated

Problem-solving skills: how to take care of pets

Classification skills: things at a pet show

Sequencing skills: story, songs, art activity

Narrative/story structure: adventure

Motor Skills Facilitated

Large motor: outdoor play activities—jumping, running, hopping, pedaling, climbing

Small motor: writing, drawing, constructing with playdough

DRAMATIC PLAY **Pet Store**

Type of Activity: Central

Objectives
1. Learn new, and employ familiar, vocabulary
2. Learn new, and employ a variety of, syntactic constructions
3. Interact with peers
4. Sequence familiar routines
5. Expand conceptual knowledge of the world

Settings
- Children's houses (child-sized houses or dismantled cardboard boxes)
- Pet store
- Counter

Props
- Stuffed animals
- Pretend cash register
- Play money
- Pretend credit cards
- Shelves of pretend pet products (e.g., food, leashes, collars, toys)
- Cages
- Aquariums
- Bowls for food and water
- Brushes for grooming
- Pet carriers
- Pretend cleaning supplies
- Owners' cars (optional)

Roles
- Clerks
- Cashier
- Customers
- Animals

General Description of Activity

Children buy pets at the pet store. The store should have a variety of pets (stuffed animals or children pretending to be the animals), such as dogs, cats, birds, hamsters, turtles, and fish, in appropriate containers and cages. A clerk can ring up sales on a cash register and be given money for the purchases. Pretend pet food, leashes, collars, and pet toys can also be sold at the pet store. Children can then take the pets to their houses. Children can also be workers in the store, caring for the pets by feeding and grooming them.

Verbal Productions

Level of linguistic complexity varies with the role or competency of the child playing the role.
- "How much is this doggy?" or "Buy doggy"
- "I need five pounds of cat food for Fuzzy" or "Cat food, please"
- "He is cleaning the dog's cage" or "Clean"
- "My turn to use the cash register" or "Mine"

Adult Facilitative Role

The adult is to facilitate role play and help expand language and literacy skills. Typical actions or strategies to use include

Playing a role: "I want to buy a new leash for my puppy."

Expanding a child's utterance: "Buy kitty" to "I want to buy the kitty."

Identifying rhyming words: "Yes, the words *cat, bat, hat,* and *mat* all rhyme."

Recasting a child's utterance (present tense to future tense): I need some cat food today. Later I will need some dog food."

Modeling phonological awareness: "The words *pet, puppy,* and *pal* all start with the /p/ sound."

ART **Easel Painting**

Objectives
1. Express creativity
2. Develop small motor skills (e.g., drawing, painting, cutting, pasting)
3. Practice turn-taking skills
4. Converse with peers and adults

Materials
- Smocks
- Easels
- Different colors of tempera paint
- Cups to hold the paint
- Large paintbrushes
- 9" × 12" or 12" × 18" paper
- Wooden rack or other area for drying

General Description of Activity

Set up two easel boards with a large piece of paper clipped to each. Set out 2–4 cups filled with tempera paint and a paintbrush in each cup. (It is helpful to have cup covers with holes in them for the brushes. As children dip the brushes into the paint and pull them through the hole, some of the excess paint is removed. It is also helpful to place the easel over plastic or newspaper so that the paint drips do not stain the floor.)

Children put on their smocks, dip the brush into the paint, and paint shapes, objects, or anything else they want. Sometimes children will paint a picture and then experiment by painting other colors on top. Let the children experiment with the tempera for some projects. Sometimes you might have the children tell you about their painting, and you can label it for display. (Let the children decide if they want their paintings displayed.) Have a designated area for drying the pictures, such as a wooden clothes rack.

Note

This is a large muscle activity, particularly appropriate for young children (3 years and up).

GROUP **What Does _____ Eat?**

Objectives
1. Improve listening skills
2. Increase conceptual knowledge
3. Learn appropriate group interaction skills
4. Practice turn-taking skills

Materials
- *My First Book of Nature: How Living Things Grow* by Dwight Kuhn

General Description of Activity

Discuss the kinds of food people eat. Tell the children that they are going to look at a book called *My First Book of Nature: How Living Things Grow* (Kuhn, 1993), which tells what different animals eat. Open the book and show the group a picture of a bird. Point out that the mother bird is feeding her babies worms.

Group Participation

Before you show the picture of each animal, ask the children to guess what the animal eats. Then show the picture of the animal. For example, you might begin by asking the children, "What do kittens eat?" When the children guess milk, show them the picture of the kittens drinking milk. Continue with the other animals shown in the book.

Variation

At the end of the book, discuss what animals not pictured in the book might eat.

Summary/Transition Activity

Review that some animals eat grass, some milk, some fish, and so forth.

Thursday

Dramatic Play	Art	Group	Story	Song
Toy Store	Teddy Bear Pictures	Act out a Story *(Corduroy)*	*Corduroy*	"Going on a Bear Hunt"

DAILY PLANNING GUIDE

Language and Literacy Skills Facilitated

Vocabulary: *toys, teddy bears, dolls, cars, trucks, blocks, shop, puzzles, toy store, clerk, check-out, cashier, shelf, mall*

Verb phrase structures: *is selling, sells, sold, drops, dropped, buys, bought, plays, played, will play, who is going shopping? we are*

Adjective/object descriptions: *big/little ____, large/small ____, soft teddy bear, funny/sad bear*

Question structures: *what, how, where, when, who, what if, why, how many, which one*

Pronouns: *I, you, he, she, we, they, my, your, him, her, his, our, their, me, us, them*

Prepositions: *in, on, under, over, near, beneath, next to, beside, around, inside, outside*

Sounds: /l/ *likes, yellow, sell;* /k/ *keep, ticket, pick;* /f/ *find, puffy, off*

Noting print has meaning: names on chairs and on cubbies, signs in dramatic play, words in books and on chalkboard

Noting sound–symbol associations: What sound does _____ start with?

Writing: letters, names, words

Social Skills Facilitated

Initiating interaction with peers and adults; responding to questions and requests from peers and adults

Negotiating with peers for toys and materials

Group cooperation: waiting for a turn in a group, taking a turn at the appropriate time

Cognitive Skills Facilitated

Problem-solving skills: what to buy, how to wrap a present

Classification skills: what is in a toy store

Sequencing skills: story, song, dramatic play

Narrative/story structure: adventure

Motor Skills Facilitated

Large motor: outdoor play activities—jumping, running, hopping, pedaling, climbing

Small motor: writing, drawing, gluing, wrapping, taping

DRAMATIC PLAY **Toy Store**

Type of Activity: Central

Objectives
1. Learn new, and employ familiar, vocabulary
2. Learn new, and employ a variety of, syntactic constructions
3. Interact with peers
4. Sequence familiar routines
5. Expand conceptual knowledge of the world

Settings
- Shelving area for toys
- Table for gift wrapping
- Counter area

Props
- Toys
- Little cars
- Stuffed animals
- Blocks
- Puzzles
- Trucks
- Books
- Cash registers
- Pretend money
- Bags
- Paper for gift wrapping
- Scissors
- Tape
- Ribbons

Roles
- Shoppers
- Clerks
- People to do the gift wrapping
- Cashier

General Description of Activity

Set up a toy store area with a variety of toys different shelves and tables. Add a counter area where toys can be purchased and perhaps also a gift-wrap area. Some of the children can be the shoppers, some the clerks or cashier. Still other children can be the ones to gift-wrap the items.

Verbal Productions

Level of linguistic complexity varies with the role or competency of the child playing the role.
- "I want to buy the big brown bear" or "Buy bear"
- "May I help you find something?" or "Help you?"
- "I want this big truck wrapped, please" or "Wrap, please"

Adult Facilitative Role

The adult is to facilitate role play and help expand language and literacy skills. Typical actions or strategies to use include

Playing a role: "I want to buy a present for my little girl. She wants a new doll."

Asking open questions: "How do you put this puzzle together?"

Contrasting error response with the correct sound: "You said 'tat,' but I think you meant 'eat.'"

Modeling statement/vocabulary: "A clerk is the person who works for the store and helps you find things."

ART **Teddy Bear Pictures**

Objectives
1. Express creativity
2. Develop small motor skills (e.g., drawing, painting, cutting, pasting)
3. Practice turn-taking skills
4. Converse with peers and adults

Materials
- Teddy bear outlines drawn on paper, one for each child
- Markers
- Scraps of fabric
- Cheerios
- Glue

General Description of Activity

Children use the materials listed to fill in their teddy bear outline. For example, they might draw a face on their teddy bear with markers and fill in the bear by gluing the fabric scraps on it, coloring it, or outlining it with Cheerios.

GROUP **Act out a Story** *(Corduroy)*

Objectives
1. Improve listening skills
2. Increase sequencing ability
3. Increase knowledge of storytelling
4. Learn appropriate group interaction skills
5. Practice turn-taking skills

Materials
- *Corduroy*
- Props for the story

General Description of Activity

Read a familiar story to the children or quickly summarize it.

Group Participation

Assign roles from the story. Assure the children not chosen the first time that everyone will have a turn and that they have the very important job of being a good listening audience. Narrate the story as the children act it out. They should say as many of the lines as they can, with prompts given when needed. Repeat with new actors until all the children have had a turn.

Summary/Transition Activity

Compliment the children's acting, and ask children what other stories they would like to act out another day.

WEEKLY PLANNING GUIDE

	Dramatic Play	Art	Group	Story	Song
Monday *Suggested Props and Materials*	Camping (Fire) *Campground scenario, campfire, sleeping bags, tents, pretend food, picnic food, fish, fishing poles, blue sheet (water)*	Red Fingerpaint *Fingerpaint, fingerpaint paper*	Shapes—Rectangles *Various sizes/colors of rectangle-shaped cut-outs; several small and large circle-, square-, triangle-shaped cutouts; individual chalkboards or paper (optional); chalk or markers (optional)*	*Who Said Red?*	"A-Camping We Will Go"
Tuesday *Suggested Props and Materials*	Garden (Earth) *Garden scenario, garden store, sandbox, sand, pail, shovels, hoe, tractors, seeds, items to buy, plants*	Playdough *Brown playdough, smocks, cookie cutters, rolling pins*	Letter *T* *Pictures and objects of words beginning with the letter T, alphabet chart, picture dictionary*	*The Giving Tree*	"The Alphabet Song"
Wednesday *Suggested Props and Materials*	Boat (Water) *Boat scenario, water table, water pool, toy boats, toy people, various rubber sea animals, boats, fishing poles, fish, wooden boat*	Watercolor Painting *Watercolor paints, brushes, containers for water, paper*	Float or Sink? *Container filled with water, objects that float (e.g., boats, corks, plastic spoon), objects that sink (e.g., screw, metal spoon, penny)*	*Boats*	"Five Little Speckled Frogs"
Thursday *Suggested Props and Materials*	Rocket Ship (Air) *Rocket ship scenario, helmets, backpacks, walking boards, moon rocks, miniature trampoline, micro-phones, headsets, pretend computers, walkie-talkies*	Paper Airplanes *Paper, markers, paper clips*	Counting and Writing Numbers 1–5 *Index cards with 1, 2, 3, 4, and 5 written on them; counting items (e.g., counting puppies, small blocks); white-board (or chalkboard), whiteboard markers (or chalk)*	*Goodnight Moon*	"The Rocket Song"

MY NOTES

NEWSLETTER

Vol. 1, No. 20

Date: _____

The Elements

Monday

Today's element is fire. The children will pretend to be camping with a campfire. They can sleep in their sleeping bags and cook the fish they catch. In art, they will play with red fingerpaint. Our story is *Who Said Red?* During group time, the children will learn about rectangles. Our song is "A-Camping We Will Go."

Tuesday

Earth is the element today. We will investigate earth by having a garden scenario in dramatic play. Children will pretend to hoe, plant seeds, and harvest fruits and vegetables. There might also be a garden store where they can "buy" garden items. The children will play with brown playdough in art. Our story is *The Giving Tree*. During group time, children will learn about words that begin with letter *T*. Our song is "The Alphabet Song."

Wednesday

Today children will learn about the element water. They will have water play in dramatic play, where they can pour water from one container to another. They will also have fun with boats and a variety of sea animals. In art, children will paint with water and watercolors. Our story is *Boats*. During group time, children will guess which items will sink and which items will float. Our song is "Five Little Speckled Frogs."

Thursday

Today's element is air. The children will learn about air by traveling in a pretend rocket ship. The children can be astronauts or the scientist at command central. They will make and fly paper airplanes in art. Our story is *Goodnight Moon*. We will review how to write the numbers *1–5* during group time. Our featured song is "The Rocket Song."

Monday

Dramatic Play	Art	Group	Story	Song
Camping (Fire)	Red Fingerpaint	Shapes—Rectangle	*Who Said Red?*	"A-Camping We Will Go"

DAILY PLANNING GUIDE

Language and Literacy Skills Facilitated

Vocabulary: *tent, campfire, stick, marshmallow, backpack, sleeping bag, hike, bear, deer, animals, trees, mountains, trail*

Verb phrase structures: *roasts marshmallows, is roasting hot dogs, roasted marshmallows, sleeps in a tent, is sleeping, slept in a tent, hikes, hiked, lights a fire, lit a fire*

Adjective/object descriptions: *big ____, little ____, hot ____, sleepy ____, hungry ____, yellow ____, blue ____*

Question structures: *what, how, where, when, who, what if, why, how many, which one*

Pronouns: *I, you, he, she, we, they, my, your, him, her, his, our, their, me, us, them*

Prepositions: *in, on, under, over, near, beneath, next to, beside, around, inside, outside*

Sounds: /k/ cook; /l/ light, yellow, ball; /z/ zipper, balls; /r/ roast, bear; /f/ fire, off

Noting print has meaning: names on chairs and on cubbies, signs in dramatic play, words in books and on chalkboard

Noting sound–symbol associations: What sound does _____ start with?

Writing: letters, names, words

Social Skills Facilitated

Initiating interaction with peers and adults; responding to questions and requests from peers and adults

Negotiating with peers for toys and materials

Group cooperation: waiting for a turn in a group, taking a turn at the appropriate time

Cognitive Skills Facilitated

Problem-solving skills: how to follow a map, how to read directions

Classification skills: things we take on a camping trip

Sequencing skills: songs and stories

Narrative/story structure: rhyming story

Motor Skills Facilitated

Large motor: outdoor play activities—jumping, running, hopping, pedaling, climbing

Small motor: writing, drawing, gluing, painting

DRAMATIC PLAY **Camping (Fire)**

Type of Activity: Central

Objectives
1. Learn new, and employ familiar, vocabulary
2. Learn new, and employ a variety of, syntactic constructions
3. Interact with peers
4. Sequence familiar routines
5. Expand conceptual knowledge of the world

Settings	• Campground • Lake • Mountains	• Hiking area • Ranger station

Props	• Tent(s)
	• Sleeping bags
	• Campfire (wooden blocks)
	• Grill
	• Picnic items (e.g., basket,
	  food, paper plates, utensils)
	• Pretend marshmallows
	  (e.g., cotton balls on sticks)
		• Boats
		• Fishing poles (with magnets
		  attached to catch the fish)
		• Fish (with paper clips attached)
		• Backpacks
		• Maps
		• Pretend forest animals
		  (e.g., bears, raccoons, rabbits)

Roles	• Campers (family members) • Fishermen and women	• Hikers • Ranger

General Description of Activity

Children act out camping trips and activities. Children might choose to camp at a lake, in the mountains, or in a camping area. They might sleep in tents or under the stars in sleeping bags. They could cook their food over a wood fire or pack a lunch and go hiking or fishing. The class might establish a ranger station so families can get maps that show them where to camp.

Verbal Productions

Level of linguistic complexity varies with the role or competency of the child playing the role.

- "I am packing a lunch for the picnic" or "Picnic"
- "Let's unroll our sleeping bags" or "Let's sleep"
- "Fix the tent, please" or "My turn, please"
- "John is walking too fast" or "Too fast"
- "You missed the trail" or "Missed it"

Adult Facilitative Role

The adult is to facilitate role play and help expand language and literacy skills. Typical actions or strategies to use include

Playing a role: "I am going to cook my hot dogs over the campfire."

Expanding a child's utterance: "He my tent" to "He is in your tent. Now he is in my tent."

Modeling a statement/vocabulary: "Let's put our sleeping bags in the tent so they are ready when we want to go to sleep."

Contrasting two adjectives: "The fire is hot, and the water is cold."

Redirecting a child to a peer: "Ask Sou Young for a turn making the campfire. Say, 'May I have a turn, please?'"

ART : **Red Fingerpaint**

Objectives	1. Express creativity 2. Develop small motor skills (e.g., drawing, painting, cutting, pasting) 3. Practice turn-taking skills 4. Converse with peers and adults

Materials	• Red fingerpaint • Fingerpaint paper	• Smocks • Glitter (optional)

General Description of Activity

Put a dab of paint on each child's paper. The children can use their hands and fingers to smear the paint all over the paper, then draw and write in the paint with their fingers. The children can make abstract designs, make full hand prints, or use their fingers to draw pictures or write letters or numbers. Shaving cream can be used instead of paint and placed on a formboard rather than on paper. Fingerpainting is also a good excuse to get messy and gooey. Some children love this; others may need some coaxing to get their fingers dirty.

Variation

For additional effect, mix glitter into the fingerpaint before the children create their designs.

GROUP **Shapes–Rectangle**

Objectives
1. Improve listening skills
2. Increase conceptual knowledge
3. Learn appropriate group-interaction skills
4. Practice turn-taking skills

Materials
- Colored tape
- Various sizes and colors of rectangle-shaped cutouts
- Several small and large circle-, square-, and triangle-shaped cutouts
- Small chalkboard or paper; chalk or markers (optional)

General Description of Activity

Using colored tape, outline a large and a small rectangle shape on the floor in front of the children, where large and small circles, squares, and triangles are already outlined. Trace one of the triangle outlines on the floor, or a triangle cutout, noting that the rectangle has four sides and four corners like a square. However, rectangles typically have two sides that are long and two that are short. Ask a child to stand on the large or small rectangle and to repeat that it is a rectangle because it has four corners and two sides that are long and two that are short.

Group Participation

Ask different children to find the large or small rectangle by standing on it or by putting a large or small rectangle cutout on the appropriate outline. Vary the level of difficulty. You might ask one child simply to identify a shape (e.g., rectangle, triangle, square, or circle) and another child to find a shape of a specific size and color (e.g., "Find a large orange rectangle"). The task can also be varied by having children place a hand on one shape and a foot on another. Ask most of the children to find or label rectangles, but occasionally ask a child to identify a circle, square, or triangle to review the previously taught shapes. If necessary, do this activity in smaller groups.

Variation

The children can also draw shapes (rectangle, triangle, square, or circle) on small chalkboards or on paper. Other common shapes can be taught in a similar manner (e.g., diamond, heart, oval).

Summary/Transition Activity

Review the shapes by pointing to or standing on them or by holding up a shape cutout and having the children quickly label it in unison.

Tuesday

Dramatic Play	Art	Group	Story	Song
Garden (Earth)	Playdough	Letter *T*	*The Giving Tree*	"The Alphabet Song"

DAILY PLANNING GUIDE

Language and Literacy Skills Facilitated

Vocabulary: *garden, grow, flowers, digging, planting, watering, working, bugs, insects, hoe, weeds, seeds, shovel*

Verb phrase structures: *is/are planting, planted, will plant, plants, digs, dug, grows, grew, waters, watered, is working, worked*

Adjective/object descriptions: *little seed, big hole, yellow flower, dirty shovel, hard work*

Question structures: *what, how, where, when, who, what if, why, how many, which one*

Pronouns: *I, you, he, she, we, they, my, your, him, her, his, our, their, me, us, them*

Prepositions: *in, on, under, over, near, beneath, next to, beside, around, inside, outside*

Sounds: /k/ *come, work;* /l/ *like, yellow, fall;* /s/ *seed, miss*

Noting print has meaning: names on chairs and on cubbies, signs in dramatic play, words in books and on chalkboard

Noting sound–symbol associations: What sound does _____ start with?

Writing: letters, names, words

Social Skills Facilitated

Initiating interaction with peers and adults; responding to questions and requests from peers and adults

Negotiating with peers for toys and materials

Group cooperation: waiting for a turn in a group, taking a turn at the appropriate time

Cognitive Skills Facilitated

Problem-solving skills: how to make items out of playdough

Classification skills: things that begin with *T*

Sequencing skills: songs, stories

Narrative/story structure: adventure

Motor Skills Facilitated

Large motor: outdoor play activities—jumping, running, hopping, pedaling, climbing

Small motor: writing, drawing, gluing

DRAMATIC PLAY **Garden (Earth)**

Type of Activity: Central

Objectives
1. Learn new, and employ familiar, vocabulary
2. Learn new, and employ a variety of, syntactic constructions
3. Interact with peers
4. Sequence familiar routines
5. Expand conceptual knowledge of the world

Settings
- Two or three garden areas
- Market (optional)
- Seed and gardening store (optional)

Props
- Two or three large boxes cut about 4–6" deep
- Sand or soil
- Child-sized garden tools
- Gardening clothes (e.g., hats, gloves)
- Seeds or other small objects (e.g., lima beans, LEGOs)
- Plants (e.g., pretend flowers, pretend vegetables)
- Pails
- Watering can
- Counter (optional)
- Pretend cash register (optional)
- Pretend money (optional)

Roles
- Gardeners
- Store clerks (optional)
- Garden produce sellers (optional)
- Customers (optional)
- Toy tractors with variety of attachments

General Description of Activity

Children work in a pretend garden, digging, planting seeds, and growing flowers or vegetables. Two or three large boxes (e.g., a refrigerator box) cut about 4–6" deep and filled with sand or soil make a good garden. The children can use child-sized gardening tools to prepare the sand or soil. Lima beans or other small objects (e.g., LEGOs) make good "seeds." A seed and gardening store or a market for selling garden produce can be added to the play activity. (Be aware that the activity will need to be restarted after the plants have "grown" and have been "harvested.")

Verbal Productions

Level of linguistic complexity varies with the role or competency of the child playing the role.
- "Do you have any flower seeds?" or "Seeds, please"
- "Do you have any shovels or pails?" or "Diggers?"
- "He is digging a big hole" or "Dig hole"
- "I want a large, round, orange pumpkin" or "Big pumpkin, please"

Adult Facilitative Role

The adult is to facilitate role play and help expand language and literacy skills. Typical actions or strategies to use include

Playing a role: "I am growing flowers in my garden."

Using a cloze procedure: "This flower is red, and this flower is _____ (yellow)."

Asking an open question: "What should we plant in our garden?"

Expanding a child's utterance: "He need help" to "He needs help with the tractor."

ART **Playdough**

Objectives
1. Express creativity
2. Develop small motor skills (e.g., drawing, painting, cutting, pasting)
3. Practice turn-taking skills
4. Converse with peers and adults

Materials
- Smocks
- Playdough
- Rolling pins
- Cookie cutters
- Presses
- Flat wooden sticks
- Rolling boards

General Description of Activity

Children wash their hands and put on smocks to explore playdough on the art table, using various presses, cutters, rolling pins, wooden craft sticks, and other tools. Children can make pretend food or any other objects out of the dough by rolling, cutting, or making pressing motions. They can form animals or people by rolling a main body and then adding heads, arms, and legs. Yarn can be used for hair (if children want to take their creations home). When children are finished, they roll the dough into a ball, wash their hands, and take off and fold their smocks.

GROUP **Letter *T***

Objectives

1. Improve listening skills
2. Increase knowledge of the alphabet and sounds
3. Learn appropriate group-interaction skills
4. Practice turn-taking skills

Materials

- Alphabet chart and other alphabet displays
- Blackboard and chalk or poster paper and markers
- Pictures of objects (or objects themselves) with names that begin with *T*
- Picture dictionary (or an alphabet video dictionary)

General Description of Activity

Write an upper- and a lowercase letter *T* on the blackboard (or on poster paper). Give several examples of words that begin with *T*, emphasizing the /t/ sound at the beginning of the words. You might hold up pictures of objects (or objects themselves) with names that begin with *T*. Direct the children's attention to the alphabet picture displays around the room.

Group Participation

Ask if anyone's name starts with *T* (e.g., Tanesha, Tim). Have those children write the letter *T* on the blackboard (or poster paper). Also have two or three other children write the letter *T* on the blackboard. Provide verbal guidance as children form the letter: "Draw a line straight down. Go back to the top and draw a line straight across." If necessary, help children write the letter. Some of the other children can practice writing a *T* in the air with their fingers (or on individual chalkboards). Ask the children to think of words that begin with *T*. Write the words they offer on the blackboard, drawing quick sketches (when possible) of the suggested words. If a child suggests a word that does not begin with *T*, say, "No, that begins with _____," and say both sounds so children can compare them. To help children who cannot think of any words, prompt them with pictures or objects representing *T* words. (Pictures or objects can be handed out at the beginning of the lesson or as the lesson proceeds.) Additional words can be sought in a picture dictionary if the group has difficulty arriving at words that begin with *T*.

Summary/Transition Activity

After about 10–15 words have been suggested, reviews the words, emphasizing the *T* sound.

Wednesday

Dramatic Play	Art	Group	Story	Song
Boat (Water)	Watercolor Painting	Float or Sink?	*Boats*	"Five Little Speckled Frogs"

DAILY PLANNING GUIDE

Language and Literacy Skills Facilitated

Vocabulary: *water, splash, drip, fish, walrus, water pump, shell, shark, net, sink, float, boat, sailboat*

Verb phrase structures: *is splashing, was splashing; sails, is sailing, sailed; rides, rode; swims, swam*

Adjective/object descriptions: *wet/dry ___; fast/slow ___; big/little ___*

Question structures: *what, how, where, when, who, what if, why, how many, which one*

Pronouns: *I, you, he, she, we, they, my, your, him, her, his, our, their, me, us, them*

Prepositions: *in, on, under, over, near, beneath, next to, beside, around, inside, outside*

Sounds: */s/ sink, swim, sit, pass, eats; /f/ fish, off, float; /k/ keep, sink*

Noting print has meaning: names on chairs and on cubbies, signs in dramatic play, words in books and on chalkboard

Noting sound–symbol associations: What sound does _____ start with?

Writing: letters, names, words

Social Skills Facilitated

Initiating interaction with peers and adults; responding to questions and requests from peers and adults

Negotiating with peers for toys and materials

Group cooperation: waiting for a turn in a group, taking a turn at the appropriate time

Cognitive Skills Facilitated

Problem-solving skills: What things sink? What things float?

Classification skills: things that sink or float

Sequencing skills: story, song

Narrative/story structure: labeling story

Motor Skills Facilitated

Large motor: outdoor play activities—jumping, running, hopping, pedaling, climbing

Small motor: writing, drawing, gluing, painting

DRAMATIC PLAY **Boat (Water)**

Type of Activity: Central

Objectives
1. Learn new, and employ familiar, vocabulary
2. Learn new, and employ a variety of, syntactic constructions
3. Interact with peers
4. Sequence familiar routines
5. Expand conceptual knowledge of the world

Settings
- Water table filled with water
- Wading pool filled with water
- Boat facsimile
- Fishing area (blue cloth or a taped-off area)

Props
- Toy boats
- Toy people
- Various rubber sea animals (e.g., seals, whales, sharks, fish)
- Wooden or cardboard boat and submarine
- Paper fish (with paper clips attached)
- Fishing poles (with magnets attached to catch the fish)
- Pails
- Pretend grill (to cook the fish)
- Picnic items (e.g., basket, food, paper plates, utensils)
- Blue satin sheet (optional)

Roles
- Fishermen and women
- Captain of the boat
- Operator(s) of the toy boats, toy people, and toy animals

General Description of Activity

Children learn that boats are used on the water to travel from one place to another and that people often fish from boats. Toy boats, toy people, and toy sea animals can be used in the water table to represent boats on an ocean. A fishing boat area can be set up so that children can catch "fish." The activity could be extended by having a picnic and "cooking" the fish.

Verbal Productions

Level of linguistic complexity varies with the role or competency of the child playing the role
- "I caught a fish" or "Fish"
- "My boat can float with all these people in it" or "My boat"
- "I'm the captain. You sit here" or "You sit"
- "It's sinking" or "Sink"

Adult Facilitative Role

The adult is to facilitate role play and help expand language and literacy skills. Typical actions or strategies to use include

Playing a role: "I like to pour water in the water pump."

Contrasting two verb structures (present tense with past tense): "The fish swims fast" to "That fish swims very fast."

Identifying rhyming words: "The words *fast, last,* and *cast* all rhyme."

Modeling production of the /k/ sound: "Look, I caught a fish. I can keep in the bucket."

Providing a contrast between error and correct sound: "She 'dot' a fish?" to "Oh, you mean she caught a fish."

ART **Watercolor Painting**

Objectives
1. Express creativity
2. Develop small motor skills (e.g., drawing, painting, cutting, pasting)
3. Practice turn-taking skills
4. Converse with peers and adults

Materials
- Watercolor paints
- Brushes
- Water in tubs
- White construction paper

General Description of Activity

Lay out white construction paper, watercolor paint boxes, and brushes on the art table. Place tubs of water to clean the brushes above the paper. The children put on smocks and sit down in front of the paper, paint box, and water tub. Each child selects a brush, wets it, and chooses the paint color. The children paint on the paper, rinsing the brush before selecting a new color. Children can paint a collage of colors, animals, people, scenery, and so on. You may want to be close by so children can talk about their paintings.

GROUP **Float or Sink?**

Objectives
1. Improve listening skills
2. Increase conceptual knowledge
3. Learn appropriate group-interaction skills
4. Practice turn-taking skills

Materials
- A clear plastic container filled with water
- Objects that will float (e.g., boats, corks, plastic spoon)
- Objects that will sink (e.g., screw, metal spoon, penny)

General Description of Activity

Fill a clear plastic container with water and float a boat on the water. Say, "The boat is floating." Then place a penny in the water and have everyone watch as it sinks. Have a child come to the front of the group and identify the object that floats.

Group Participation

Have the children come one at a time to the front and choose an object. Each child predicts whether the object will sink or float. Have the child put the object in the water, and ask the class to judge whether the child was correct. Repeat until all the children have had a turn.

Variation

Pass around a plastic spoon and a metal spoon so children can feel the difference in weight. Then have one child demonstrate which spoon floats and which sinks.

Summary/Transition Activity

Have the children try to explain why an object will float or sink. Demonstrate that some things that are big float and some things that are small sink. The children should note that the reason an object floats depends on the material the object is made out of rather than its size.

Thursday

Dramatic Play	Art	Group	Story	Song
Rocket Ship (Air)	Paper Airplanes	Counting and Writing Numbers 1–5	*Goodnight Moon*	"The Rocket Song"

DAILY PLANNING GUIDE

Language and Literacy Skills Facilitated

Vocabulary: *space, rocket ship, planet, gravity, adventure, spacesuit, astronaut, orbit, sun, moon, stars, blast off, oxygen*

Verb phrase structures: *count<u>ed</u> down, <u>are</u> count<u>ing</u>, travel<u>ing</u> in space, <u>saw</u> stars, blast<u>ing</u> off, pack<u>ed</u> food, us<u>ing</u> oxygen*

Adjective/object descriptions: *bright stars, fast ship, big planet, weird colors, little stars, black hole*

Question structures: *what, how, where, when, who, what if, why, how many, which one*

Pronouns: *I, you, he, she, we, they, my, your, him, her, his, our, their, me, us, them*

Prepositions: *in, on, under, over, near, beneath, next to, beside, around, inside, outside*

Sounds: /r/ <u>r</u>ocket, sta<u>r</u>; /s/ <u>s</u>pace, <u>s</u>un, fa<u>c</u>e; /l/ <u>l</u>ight, Je<u>ll</u>-o, be<u>ll</u>; /k/ <u>c</u>an, ro<u>ck</u>et, lo<u>ck</u>

Noting print has meaning: names on chairs and on cubbies, signs in dramatic play, words in books and on chalkboard

Noting sound–symbol associations: What sound does _____ start with?

Writing: letters, names, words

Social Skills Facilitated

Initiating interaction with peers and adults; responding to questions and requests from peers and adults

Negotiating with peers for toys and materials

Group cooperation: waiting for a turn in a group, taking a turn at the appropriate time

Cognitive Skills Facilitated

Problem-solving skills: how to get up in space

Classification skills: What things are in outer space?

Sequencing skills: countdown, story, songs

Narrative/story structure: labeling story, rhyming

Motor Skills Facilitated

Large motor: outdoor play activities—jumping, running, hopping, pedaling, climbing

Small motor: writing, drawing, gluing, fingerpainting

DRAMATIC PLAY **Rocket Ship (Air)**

Type of Activity: Central

Objectives

1. Learn new, and employ familiar, vocabulary
2. Learn new, and employ a variety of, syntactic constructions
3. Interact with peers
4. Sequence familiar routines
5. Expand conceptual knowledge of the world

Settings
- Rocket ship (child-sized house with chairs placed sideways on the floor so the children lie in them and look upward)
- Command center (with pretend television sets and computers)
- Moon

Props
- Rocket ship (child-sized house with chairs placed sideways on the floor so the children lie in them and look upward)
- Helmets
- Backpacks
- Walking boards
- Moon rocks
- Miniature trampoline
- Television sets (shoeboxes with one side cut out and a picture pasted over the cutout area)
- Microphones (toilet paper rolls)
- Headsets
- Pretend computers
- Videotape about the space program
- Walkie-talkies
- Moon vehicle (optional)

Roles
- Astronauts
- Technicians
- Command center workers

General Description of Activity

The children can pretend to be astronauts and go to the moon in a spacecraft. Once on the moon, they can find moon rocks, jump (on a miniature trampoline) to see how light they feel, and so forth. Some of the children can remain on earth at the command center and talk to the astronauts. Show a brief videotape on the space program to the children so that they begin to understand about rocket ships, the need to wear special suits in space, and what the moon really looks like.

Verbal Productions

Level of linguistic complexity varies with the role or competency of the child playing the role.
- "She found a big moon rock" or "Big"
- "I can jump high. Watch me!" or "Look!"
- "He is landing the rocket ship" or "He landed it"
- "You can see the earth. It is blue." "I see the moon"

Adult Facilitative Role

The adult is to facilitate role play and help expand language and literacy skills. Typical actions or strategies to use include

Playing a role: "Did you see the rocket ship? It is going to take off soon."

Asking an open question: "This is broken. How can we fix it?"

Modeling a statement/vocabulary: "An astronaut has to wear a special suit and helmet because there is not much air (oxygen) in space. We need air to breathe."

Event casting: "You are putting on the helmet and getting into the rocket ship. You are ready for take-off."

Expanding a child's utterances: "That mine" to "That is mine. May I have it, please?"

ART : **Paper Airplanes**

Objectives
1. Express creativity
2. Develop small motor skills (e.g., drawing, painting, cutting, folding)
3. Practice turn-taking skills
4. Converse with peers and adults

Materials
- 8" × 10" paper (or other size)
- Paper clips
- Markers
- Crayons
- Stickers

General Description of Activity

Children decorate a piece of paper to make into a paper airplane with markers, crayons, and/or stickers. The paper is then folded to make an airplane. First, fold the paper in half lengthwise. Then fold a top edge down until it is even with the folded bottom to form a triangle shape. Turn the paper over and fold the other side the same way so that one third of the paper is slanted and ends in a point. Clip a paper clip to the point of the triangle (the nose of the airplane) to hold the plane together and to provide appropriate weight so the airplane will fly. Fold the rest of the top edge even with the bottom fold. Make a crease. Let go of the paper so it sticks out to make a wing. Turn the paper over and fold the other side in the same way. The paper airplane is ready to fly. (Other paper folding can be done to form other styles of airplanes).

GROUP : Counting and Writing Numbers *1–5*

Objectives

1. Improve listening skills
2. Recognize knowledge of the alphabet and sounds.
3. Learn appropriate group-interaction skills
4. Practice turn-taking skills

Materials

- Index cards with *1, 2, 3, 4,* and *5* written on them (one number per card)
- Counting items (e.g., counting puppies, small blocks)
- Whiteboard (or chalkboard)
- Whiteboard markers (or chalk)

General Description of Activity

Place the numbered index cards in front of the children. Identify each number, then write the numbers on the whiteboard. Remind the children how to write each one, using the jingle for the appropriate number:

1: Start at the top, go down and you're done, that's the way to make a *1.*

2: Around and back on the railroad track, *2, 2, 2.*

3: Around the tree, around the tree, that's the way to make a *3.*

4: Down and over and down once more, that's the way to make a *4.*

5: Down around, make a hat on it, and look what you've found. *(5)*

6: Down around until it sticks, that's the way to make a *6.*

7: Over and down and it's not heaven, over and down makes a *7.*

8: Make an *S* and go back straight, that's the way to make an *8.*

9: A balloon and a line make *9.*

10: Draw a line and a circle with your pen, that's the way to make a *10.*

Group Participation

Ask one child to point to a number (for example, *3*). Ask another child to place three items below the index card with the *3* on it. Finally, have a third child demonstrate on the whiteboard (or chalkboard) how to write a *3*. Provide support as needed. Continue until all the children have had a turn and the numbers *1–5* have been covered.

Summary/Transition Activity

Quickly point to different number cards and have the children, as a group, label the number indicated.

January

	Activities	Monday	Tuesday	Wednesday	Thursday
Week 21 Places in the Community	Dramatic Play	Laundromat	Hospital	Bakery	Library
	Art	Watercolor Painting	Chalk Skeletons	Food Collage	Family Portrait
	Group	Sock Classification	Body Parts (Skeleton)	Mixing Primary Colors	Letter *U*
	Story	*A Pocket for Corduroy*	*Going to the Hospital*	*If You Give a Mouse a Cookie*	*Goodnight Moon*
	Song	"Mary Wore a Red Dress"	"Head, Shoulders, Knees, and Toes"	"Do You Know the Muffin Man?"	"The Alphabet Song"
Week 22 Seasons	Dramatic Play	Winter Fun	Spring (Baseball)	Summer (Beach)	Fall Festival
	Art	Make Snowflakes	Baseball Outlines	Watercolor Painting	Leaf Rubbings
	Group	How to Write a *6*	Shapes—Diamond	Letter *V*	Review the Seasons
	Story	*Snow Day*	*This Is Baseball*	*Commotion in the Ocean*	*The Apple Pie Tree*
	Song	"The Snowman and the Bunny" (fingerplay)	"Take Me out to the Ball Game"	"All the Little Fishies"	"Five Little Leaves"
Week 23 Places Animals Live	Dramatic Play	Zoo	Pet Store	Forest	Farm
	Art	Playdough Animals	Paper Bag Puppets	Cereal Art	Farm Mural
	Group	Sound Sequencing	Caring for Pets	Letter *W*	Classifying Animals (Zoo/Farm)
	Story	*Corduroy At The Zoo*	*How Much Is That Doggy in the Window?*	*Going on a Bear Hunt*	*Inside a Barn in the Country*
	Song	"Going to the Zoo"	"How Much Is That Doggy in the Window?"	"Going on a Bear Hunt" (fingerplay)	"Old MacDonald Had a Farm"
Week 24 Homes Across the Ages	Dramatic Play	Castle	Pioneer	Today's Houses	Space Station
	Art	Crowns	Craft Stick Constructions	Draw a House	Glitter Space Pictures
	Group	Act out a Story (*The Princess and the Pea*)	Hard/Soft	Emergency Information	Letter *X*
	Story	*The Princess and the Pea*	*And You Can Be The Cat*	*A House Is a House for Me*	*Big Silver Space Shuttle*
	Song	"The Grand Old Duke of York"	"She'll Be Coming 'Round the Mountain"	"Two Little Houses" (fingerplay)	"Twinkle, Twinkle, Little Star"

WEEKLY PLANNING GUIDE

	Dramatic Play	Art	Group	Story	Song
Monday *Suggested Props and Materials*	Laundromat *Laundromat scenario, pretend washers, dryers, ironing boards, iron, baskets, clothes*	Watercolor Painting *Watercolor paints, paper, smocks*	Sock Classification *Socks of different sizes and colors*	*A Pocket for Corduroy*	"Mary Wore a Red Dress"
Tuesday *Suggested Props and Materials*	Hospital *Hospital scenario, waiting room, examining rooms, doctor kits, ambulance*	Chalk Skeletons *Chalk, black construction paper*	Body Parts (Skeleton) *Paper skeleton (or doll) for labeling body parts, pictures of body parts (optional)*	*Going to the Hospital*	"Head, Shoulders, Knees, and Toes"
Wednesday *Suggested Props and Materials*	Bakery *Bakery scenario, flour, containers, sifter, measuring cups, display area, pretend bakery items*	Food Collage *Magazines with food pictures, scissors, glue, paper*	Mixing Primary Colors *Food coloring (red, blue, yellow), six glass jars for mixing colors, stirring stick or spoon*	*If You Give a Mouse a Cookie*	"Do You Know the Muffin Man?"
Thursday *Suggested Props and Materials*	Library *Library scenario, books, bookshelves, desk, check-out procedure, computer, index cards, reading area*	Family Portrait *Paper, pencils or markers*	Letter *U* *Objects and pictures starting with letter U, paper or slates, pencils, chalk*	*Goodnight Moon*	"The Alphabet Song"

MY NOTES

NEWSLETTER

Vol. 1, No. 21

Date: _____

Places in the Community

Monday

Today the classroom becomes a Laundromat. The children will pretend to wash, dry, iron, and fold their clothes. The children can be the customers, the owner, or the people who clean up/repair the machines. In art, the children will make watercolor paintings. Our story is *A Pocket for Corduroy*. During group time, children will sort socks by size, color, and other characteristics. Our featured song is "Mary Wore a Red Dress."

Tuesday

Today the children will pretend to be at a hospital. They can be the doctors, nurses, patients, or the ambulance drivers. In art, the children will make pretend X-rays with white chalk drawings on black paper. *Going to the Hospital* will be read at storytime. During group time, children will label different body parts on a skeleton or doll. In music, the children will sing "Head, Shoulders, Knees, and Toes."

Wednesday

The classroom becomes a bakery today. The children will be busy using dough and making and selling delicious food in dramatic play. The art project will be a food collage. Our story is *If You Give a Mouse a Cookie*. During group time, children will learn that purple, orange, and green (secondary colors) are made by mixing red, blue, and yellow (primary colors). During music, our featured song is "Do You Know the Muffin Man?"

Thursday

Today the children will go to the library in dramatic play. They will sort books, check books out, be the librarian, or listen to taped stories in the reading area. In art, the children will draw a picture of their families. Our featured story is *Goodnight Moon*. During group time, we will focus on the letter *U*. Our song of the day is "The Alphabet Song."

Monday

Dramatic Play	Art	Group	Story	Song
Laundromat	Watercolor Painting	Sock Classification	*A Pocket for Corduroy*	"Mary Wore a Red Dress"

DAILY PLANNING GUIDE

Language and Literacy Skills Facilitated

Vocabulary: *clothes, Laundromat, washing machine, dryer, hangers, ironing board, iron*

Verb phrase structures: <u>is/are</u> wash<u>ing</u>, <u>was/were</u> dry<u>ing</u>, fold<u>ing</u>, fold<u>ed</u>, finish<u>ed</u>, rinse<u>s</u>, rins<u>ed</u>

Adjective/object descriptions: *wet/dry clothes, hot/cold water, dirty/clean clothes, small/large loads*

Question structures: *what, how, where, when, who, what if, why, how many, which one*

Pronouns: *I, you, he, she, we, they, my, your, him, her, his, our, their, me, us, them*

Prepositions: *in, on, under, over, near, beneath, next to, beside, around, inside, outside*

Sounds: /f/ <u>f</u>old, o<u>ff</u>; /l/ <u>l</u>oad, ye<u>ll</u>ow, be<u>ll</u>; /s/ <u>s</u>oap, me<u>ss</u>y, me<u>ss</u>

Noting print has meaning: names on chairs and on cubbies, signs in dramatic play, words in books and on chalkboard

Noting sound–symbol associations: What sound does _____ start with?

Writing: letters, names, words

Social Skills Facilitated

Initiating interaction with peers and adults; responding to questions and requests from peers and adults

Negotiating with peers for toys and materials

Group cooperation: waiting for a turn in a group, taking a turn at the appropriate time

Cognitive Skills Facilitated

Problem-solving skills: sorting clothes

Classification skills: things at a Laundromat

Sequencing skills: story, songs

Narrative/story structure: adventure

Motor Skills Facilitated

Large motor: outdoor play activities—jumping, running, hopping, pedaling, climbing

Small motor: writing, drawing, gluing

DRAMATIC PLAY **Laundromat**

Type of Activity: Central

Objectives

1. Learn new, and employ familiar, vocabulary
2. Learn new, and employ a variety of, syntactic constructions
3. Interact with peers
4. Sequence familiar routines
5. Expand conceptual knowledge of the world

Settings
- Laundromat
- Waiting area
- Dry cleaner
- Homes (optional)

Props
- Washing machines (made from cardboard boxes with buckets or tubs inside to hold the clothes and plastic cups with slits cut in the bottoms, mounted on top for coin collection)
- Dryers (made from cardboard boxes with buckets or tubs inside to hold the clothes and plastic cups with slits cut in the bottoms, mounted on top for coin collection)
- Clothes
- Quarters or tokens (poker chips)
- Sink
- Laundry baskets
- Empty soap boxes
- Pretend dryer sheets
- Folding tables
- Irons and ironing boards
- Hangers
- Pretend money
- Play cash register
- Receipts (to pick up dry cleaning)
- Soda pop machine
- Magazines in waiting area

Roles
- Customers
- Cashiers
- Owner of Laundromat
- Dry cleaners (optional)
- Custodian

General Description of Activity

Children pretend to take their laundry to the washers and dryers at the Laundromat. They can insert "quarters" (poker chips) in the slots to run the machines (see Props). A waiting area could be set up with a soda pop machine. The dramatic play could be expanded to include a dry cleaner, where clothes can be dropped off, cleaned and pressed, and then picked up.

Verbal Productions

Level of linguistic complexity varies with the role or competency of the child playing the role.

- "I need some soap for my dirty clothes" or "Need soap"
- "He is folding all of the shirts first" or "Fold shirts"
- "It's my turn to put the money in" or "My turn"
- "She ironed all of the dresses" or "My turn to iron"
- "Please dry clean these clothes by tomorrow" or "Tomorrow"

Adult Facilitative Role

The adult is to facilitate role play and help expand language and literacy skills. Typical actions or strategies to use include

Playing a role: "I am putting soap in the washing machine. My clothes are very dirty."

Modeling a statement/vocabulary: "A Laundromat is a place where people can do their laundry if they don't have a washing machine in their home."

Expanding a child's utterance: "He use cart" to "Yes, he is using the cart."

Contrasting two adjectives: "These clothes are clean, and those clothes are dirty."

ART : **Watercolor Painting**

Objectives
1. Express creativity
2. Develop small motor skills (e.g., drawing, painting, cutting, pasting)
3. Practice turn-taking skills
4. Converse with peers and adults

Materials
- Watercolor paints
- Brushes
- Water in tubs
- White construction paper

General Description of Activity

Place white construction paper, watercolor paint boxes, and brushes on the art table. Put tubs of water to clean the brushes above the paper. Children put on a smock, select a brush, wet it, and choose a paint color. They paint on the paper, rinsing the brush before selecting a new color. Children can paint a collage of colors, animals, people, scenery, and so on. You may want to stay close by so that children can talk about their paintings.

GROUP **Sock Classification**

Objectives
1. Improve listening skills
2. Increase sequencing ability
3. Learn appropriate group-interaction skills
4. Practice turn-taking skills

Materials
- 20 different kinds of socks (at least four different colors and two to three sizes)
- 10 matched pairs of socks (optional)

General Description of Activity

Put about 20 different socks in front of the children and tell them they are going to sort the socks. First they will sort them by color. Pick up a red sock and put it in a pile. Then pick up a white sock and put it in another pile. Have one child come to the front of the group and choose a red or white sock to put in one of the two established piles.

Group Participation

Have other children come up to sort the socks, making additional piles as needed. After the socks are sorted by color, ask the children if they can be sorted any other way. If necessary, put one big sock in a pile, labeling it "the big pile," and put one small sock in another pile, labeling it "the small pile." Have the children come up one by one to sort the socks into large and small categories.

Variation

The children could also put the socks into pairs and then match according to color or size.

Summary/Transition Activity

Review the different ways the socks were sorted. Note that the socks could be sorted other ways (e.g., those that are girls' socks, those that are boys' socks).

Tuesday

Dramatic Play	Art	Group	Story	Song
Hospital	Chalk Skeletons	Body Parts (Skeleton)	*Going to the Hospital*	"Head, Shoulders, Knees, and Toes"

DAILY PLANNING GUIDE

Language and Literacy Skills Facilitated

Vocabulary: *doctor, nurse, paramedic, ambulance, stethoscope, thermometer, fever, cast, X-ray, oxygen, accident, vehicle, arm, leg, ankle, bandage, forehead, hospital*

Verb phrase structures: *is carrying the stretcher, drove the ambulance, rides, examines, gave oxygen, sets the leg*

Adjective/object descriptions: *broken leg, big ambulance, loud siren*

Question structures: *what, how, where, when, who, what if, why, how many, which one*

Pronouns: *I, you, he, she, we, they, my, your, him, her, his, our, their, me, us, them*

Prepositions: *in, on, under, over, near, beneath, next to, beside, around, inside, outside*

Sounds: /k/ *carry, doctor, broke*; /s/ *set, inside, us, ambulance*

Noting print has meaning: names on chairs and on cubbies, signs in dramatic play, words in books and on chalkboard

Noting sound–symbol associations: What sound does _____ start with?

Writing: letters, names, words

Social Skills Facilitated

Initiating interaction with peers and adults; responding to questions and requests from peers and adults

Negotiating with peers for toys and materials

Group cooperation: waiting for a turn in a group, taking a turn at the appropriate time

Cognitive Skills Facilitated

Problem-solving skills: What does a doctor do?

Classification skills: things in an doctor's office, body parts

Sequencing skills: story and songs

Narrative/story structure: labeling

Motor Skills Facilitated

Large motor: outdoor play activities—jumping, running, hopping, pedaling, climbing

Small motor: writing, drawing, gluing, cutting

DRAMATIC PLAY **Hospital**

Type of Activity: Related

Objectives
1. Learn new, and employ familiar, vocabulary
2. Learn new, and employ a variety of, syntactic constructions
3. Interact with peers
4. Sequence familiar routines
5. Expand conceptual knowledge of the world

Settings

- Reception area
- Emergency examination rooms
- Patient rooms

Props

- Waiting room chairs
- Magazines for waiting area
- Table with a telephone and appointment book

- Several tables or mats for emergency examination rooms
- Doctor kits
- Mats to represent patient rooms

- Telephones for patient rooms
- Trays for patient food (optional)
- Pretend food items (optional)
- X-ray machine

Roles

- Doctors
- X-ray technician

- Nurses
- Receptionist

- Patients
- Parents

General Description of Activity:

Set up a hospital setting with an emergency room as well as several patient rooms and nurses' stations. Patients might arrive at the hospital in an ambulance and go to the emergency room. After filling out paperwork, the patient could be seen by the doctor and then sent home or admitted. The doctor can examine the patient by looking into his or her mouth, ears, and eyes; checking reflexes; checking muscle tone, listening to the patient's heart and lungs with the stethoscope, etc. A patient might have a broken bone that needs to be X-rayed and set in a cast or bandage. The nurse can help the patient get settled in bed and come when the patient presses a call button. The patient also can be served food in bed.

Verbal Productions

Level of linguistic complexity varies with the role or competency of the child playing the role.

- "Open your mouth, please" or "Open mouth"
- "Where does it hurt?" or "Hurt?"
- "He is looking in my mouth" or "He looks in my mouth to see if I have a sore throat"
- "He is checking my muscles" or "He checked my muscles"

Adult Facilitative Role

The adult is to facilitate role play and help expand language and literacy skills. Typical actions or strategies to use include

Playing a role: "This is an emergency. Please call 911 for an ambulance."

Providing an event casting: "James is listening to the baby's heart. The baby is very sick. James is giving the baby a shot. The baby is crying very loud. James is putting the baby in the ambulance."

Recasting a child's utterance (present progressive to past tense): "That baby is crying" to "Yes, that baby cried all day. He is sick."

Identifying rhyming words: "The words *shot, hot, got*, and *lot* all rhyme."

Helping children read and write: "You need to sign your name here."

ART : **Chalk Skeletons**

Objectives

1. Express creativity
2. Develop small motor skills (e.g., drawing, painting, cutting, pasting)
3. Practice turn-taking skills
4. Converse with peers and adults

Materials

- Black construction paper
- White chalk
- Other chalk

- Chalk fixative (sprayed on to keep pictures from smudging)

374

General Description of Activity

Give children pieces of black construction paper on which to draw with white chalk. Some of the children might like to draw X-ray pictures by making line drawings of skeleton-like people. Some of the X-ray pictures could be of "broken" arms and then could be incorporated into the dramatic play. (The artists could be the "radiologists.") Other children might want to draw general pictures that have nothing to do with the X-ray activity.

GROUP **Body Parts (Skeleton)**

Objectives
1. Improve listening skills
2. Increase conceptual knowledge
3. Learn appropriate group-interaction skills
4. Practice turn-taking skills

Materials
- Doll
- Paper skeleton
- List of body parts
- Riddles about body parts

General Description of Activity

Hold up a doll or a paper skeleton and tell the children that they are going to take turns finding and labeling different parts of a body. Have one child point to the doll's or skeleton's arm.

Group Participation

Ask other children to find the doll's _____ (e.g., wrist, toes, head, eyes). Point to a body part on the doll (or on a child) and have another child label it. If using a skeleton is used, focus on the names of the different bones.

Variation

Play a guessing game. For instance, say, "I'm thinking of a body part that you use to point with. What is it?" The children can take turns guessing the riddle or can point to the answer on the doll. The guessing game could be embedded within the activity to provide a more difficult task for some children who find the original requests too easy.

Summary/Transition Activity

Hold up the doll again. Quickly have the children say the label as you point to the doll's hair, eyes, arm, hand, leg, and toes.

Wednesday

Dramatic Play	Art	Group	Story	Song
Bakery	Food Collage	Mixing Primary Colors	*If You Give a Mouse a Cookie*	"Do You Know the Muffin Man?"

DAILY PLANNING GUIDE

Language and Literacy Skills Facilitated

Vocabulary: *doughnuts, cookies, bread, eat, bake, dough, rolls, pies, chocolate, nuts, rolling pin, oven*

Verb phrase structures: <u>is</u>/<u>are</u> bak<u>ing</u>, bak<u>ed</u>, cook<u>ed</u>, roll<u>ed</u>, roll<u>s</u>, <u>was</u>/<u>were</u> mak<u>ing</u>

Adjective/object descriptions: *fancy/plain cookies, big/little, gooey, chocolate chip cookies*

Question structures: *what, how, where, when, who, what if, why, how many, which one*

Pronouns: *I, you, he, she, we, they, my, your, him, her, his, our, their, me, us, them*

Prepositions: *in, on, under, over, near, beneath, next to, beside, around, inside, outside*

Sounds: /k/ <u>c</u>a<u>k</u>e, ba<u>k</u>ing; /s/ <u>s</u>ift, walk<u>s</u>; /f/ <u>f</u>inds, o<u>ff</u>

Noting print has meaning: names on chairs and on cubbies, signs in dramatic play, words in books and on chalkboard

Noting sound–symbol associations: What sound does _____ start with?

Writing: letters, names, words

Social Skills Facilitated

Initiating interaction with peers and adults; responding to questions and requests from peers and adults

Negotiating with peers for toys and materials

Group cooperation: waiting for a turn in a group, taking a turn at the appropriate time

Cognitive Skills Facilitated

Problem-solving skills: how to run a bakery

Classification skills: things in a bakery

Sequencing skills: story and songs

Narrative/story structure: repetitive line story

Motor Skills Facilitated

Large motor: outdoor play activities—jumping, running, hopping, pedaling, climbing

Small motor: writing, drawing, gluing

....
DRAMATIC PLAY **Bakery**
....

Type of Activity: Central

Objectives
1. Learn new, and employ familiar, vocabulary
2. Learn new, and employ a variety of, syntactic constructions
3. Interact with peers
4. Sequence familiar routines
5. Expand conceptual knowledge of the world

Settings
- Stove, oven (kitchen area)
- Sand/water table filled with flour, or flour in tubs
- Counter area with display case (bookshelves)
- Eating area with tables and chairs

Props
- Pretend food (e.g., cookies, cakes, breads, pies)
- Flour (two 5-lb. bags or as needed)
- Sifters, measuring cups, measuring spoons, baking tins
- Cash register and money
- Dishes
- Aprons, chef hats (optional)

Roles
- Bakers
- Cashiers
- Customers
- Custodians

General Description of Activity

Children operate a bakery, making and offering for sale food items such as doughnuts, breads, and cookies. They can pretend to make the food items using a pretend stove and oven and then display them in a display case. Other children can act as customers to buy the food. The bakery might have an eating area and sell additional items, such as sandwiches.

As most bakery items are made from flour, one area can be set up so that the children can sift real flour and use measuring cups. This area might be similar to a sand/water table area, with flour replacing the sand. The flour could be placed in dish tubs and then in the empty sand/water table so that the flour is less likely to spill on the floor.

Children could also make real cookies in a separate area by decorating premade cookie dough and having an adult bake the cookies in a toaster oven (not in the classroom). Children can eat the cookies at snack time.

Verbal Productions

Level of linguistic complexity varies with the role or competency of the child playing the role.
- "I want to buy a doughnut and two cookies" or "Want cookie"
- "The flour feels soft, but it is making my nose itch" or "Flour soft"
- "Look, the flour is coming out of the sifter" or "Flour out"

Adult Facilitative Role

The adult is to facilitate role play and help expand language and literacy skills. Typical actions or strategies to use include

Playing a role: "I want to buy a pie."

Using a cloze procedure: "A brownie is square, and a doughnut is _____(round/circle)."

Expanding a child's utterance: "He like it" to "Yes, he likes it."

Modeling a statement/vocabulary: "The flour feels soft. I like to sift through it."

Modeling phonological awareness: "Yes, the words *doughnut, doll, dig*, and *dinosaur* all start with the /d/ sound."

Helping a child make signs for the bakery: "Write the word *doughnuts* or *cookies* or *pies*."

ART **Food Collage**

Objectives
1. Express creativity
2. Develop small motor skills (e.g., drawing, painting, cutting, pasting)
3. Practice turn-taking skills
4. Converse with peers and adults

Materials
- White paper plates or construction paper
- Scissors
- Magazines (with pictures of food)
- Newspapers (food ads)
- Glue

General Description of Activity

Have children cut out pictures of food from magazines or newspapers advertisements, then glue them onto round white paper plates (or construction paper) to make a food collage. Help older children make a picture of the different food groups.

GROUP **Mixing Primary Colors**

Objectives
1. Improve listening skills
2. Increase sequencing ability
3. Learn appropriate group-interaction skills
4. Practice turn-taking skills

Materials
- Six baby food jars (three filled with water)
- Food coloring (red, yellow, blue)
- Wooden craft sticks for stirring

General Description of Activity

Place six baby food jars, three filled with water, in front of you so the children can see them. Put a few drops of blue food coloring in one of the jars and ask children to name the color of the water. Put yellow food coloring in the second jar and red food coloring in the third jar. Have the children name the colors. Tell the children that these are the primary colors. Tell the children that they are going to make other colors from these colors.

Group Participation

Ask what the children think will happen if you mix the blue and yellow colors. After some children have responded, invite one child to the front of the group to put some of the blue water in one of the empty jars. Have another child put some of the yellow water in the same jar. Stir the water in the new jar with a wooden craft stick, and ask the children to name the new color (green). Ask another child to put blue water in the fifth jar. Then have another child put some red water in the fifth jar. After you stir the water, ask the children to name the color (purple). For the last jar, ask a child to put red water in the jar. Ask another child to put yellow water in the same jar. After you mix the two colors, have the children name the new color (orange).

Variation

Use tempera paint instead of food coloring and mix on paper.

Summary/Transition Activity

Have the children label all the new colors. Tell the children that these are the secondary colors. They are called that because they are made up of the primary colors. Have the children label all six colors.

Thursday

Dramatic Play	Art	Group	Story	Song
Library	Family Portrait	Letter *U*	*Goodnight Moon*	"The Alphabet Song"

DAILY PLANNING GUIDE

Language and Literacy Skills Facilitated

Vocabulary: *library, picture books, index, letters, magazines, check out, counter*

Verb phrase structures: <u>check</u> *out books,* <u>look</u> *at books,* <u>read</u> *books,* <u>paste</u> *pictures*

Adjective/object descriptions: *big _____, little _____, library book, library card, torn _____*

Question structures: *what, how, where, when, who, what if, why, how many, which one*

Pronouns: *I, you, he, she, we, they, my, your, him, her, his, our, their, me, us, them*

Prepositions: *in, on, under, over, near, beneath, next to, beside, around, inside, outside*

Sounds: /l/ <u>l</u>*ibrary,* <u>l</u>*etters;* /k/ <u>c</u>*ard,* <u>c</u>*atalog,* <u>c</u>*ounter*

Noting print has meaning: names on chairs and on cubbies, signs in dramatic play, words in books and on chalkboard

Noting sound–symbol associations: What sound does _____ start with?

Writing: letters, names, words

Social Skills Facilitated

Initiating interaction with peers and adults; responding to questions and requests from peers and adults

Negotiating with peers for toys and materials

Group cooperation: waiting for a turn in a group, taking a turn at the appropriate time

Cognitive Skills Facilitated

Problem-solving skills: how to draw a picture of people

Classification skills: categorizing books

Sequencing skills: songs, alphabet

Narrative/story structure: labeling

Motor Skills Facilitated

Large motor: outdoor play activities—jumping, running, hopping, pedaling, climbing

Small motor: writing, drawing, gluing

DRAMATIC PLAY **Library**

Type of Activity: Sequential

Objectives
1. Learn new, and employ familiar, vocabulary
2. Learn new, and employ a variety of, syntactic constructions
3. Interact with peers
4. Sequence familiar routines
5. Expand conceptual knowledge of the world

Settings
- Library with shelves for books, magazines, and videotapes
- Counter for checking out books
- Box for checked-in materials
- Reading room
- Office

379

Props
- Books
- Magazines
- Videotapes
- Rubber stamps and inkpads
- Card catalog (index card file)

- Index cards with pictures of the book covers
- Pretend computer
- Alphabet cards and other alphabet games

Roles
- Librarian
- Mothers
- Fathers
- Children (dolls or other children)

- Stacker (who puts returned materials back on the shelves)
- Sorter (who sorts card catalog entries)

General Description of Activity

Children can visit a library in this dramatic play. Here they can read books and magazines; look up items in a card catalog; and borrow books, magazines, and videotapes. The children can choose books, go to the counter, and check them out by having another child stamp a card with the picture of the book cover on it. Another child can put the card back in the book when it is returned. Children can sit in the reading room and look at books and magazines. Other children can put name cards in alphabetical order (or pretend to do this). (Be aware that the books will need to be stacked back on the shelves in order to have the play activity continue.)

Verbal Productions

Level of linguistic complexity varies with the role or competency of the child playing the role.
- "Do you want this book?" or "Book?"
- "Please find this book for me" or "That one"
- "This is a book on elephants" or "Elephants"
- "Stamp my card, please" or "Stamp, please"
- "He checked out a book about cars" or "My book"
- "This is the letter *C*" or "*C*"

Adult Facilitative Role

The adult is to facilitate role play and help expand language and literacy skills. Typical actions or strategies to use include

Playing a role: "Do you want to check this book out?"

Redirecting a child to a peer: "Ask Maura for that book on cars. Say, 'Do you have a book on cars?'"

Contrasting error and correct usage of pronouns and third person singular: "Him want that book" to "He wants that book."

Modeling the reading and writing of words: "The sign says to check out books here."

ART : **Family Portrait**

Objectives
1. Express creativity
2. Develop small motor skills (e.g., drawing, painting, cutting, pasting)
3. Practice turn-taking skills
4. Converse with peers and adults

Materials
- Paper (white or colored)
- Crayons
- Markers
- Watered-down tempera paint (optional)

General Description of Activity

Provide the children with paper and a selection of crayons and/or markers. Let the children draw anything they want. Drawings could be of themselves, their family, their pets, different scenes, designs, rainbows, and so on. Children can turn their drawings into crayon washes by painting over the pictures with a light coat of tempera paint (watered-down paint). The paint will not stick to the crayon but will fill in where there are no crayon marks to make a background of color.

GROUP **Letter _U_**

Objectives
1. Improve listening skills
2. Increase knowledge of the alphabet
3. Learn appropriate group-interaction skills
4. Practice turn-taking skills

Materials
- Alphabet chart and other alphabet displays
- Blackboard and chalk or poster paper and markers
- Pictures of objects (or objects themselves) with names that begin with _U_
- Picture dictionary (or an alphabet video dictionary)

General Description of Activity

Write an upper- and a lowercase letter _U_ on the blackboard (or on poster paper) and give several examples of words that begin with _U_. Emphasize the short /u/ or "uh" sound at the beginning of the words. Tell the children that _U_ is a vowel and has several other sounds. One of the other sounds is the long _U_ sound, like "oo" as in cute. You might hold up pictures of objects (or objects themselves) with names that begin with _U_. Direct the children's attention to the alphabet picture displays around the room.

Group Participation

Ask if anyone's name starts with _U_ (e.g., Ulrich), and have those children write the letter _U_ on the blackboard (or poster paper). Also have two or three other children write the letter _U_ on the blackboard. Provide verbal guidance as children form the letter. If necessary, help children write the letter. Some of the other children can practice writing _U_ in the air with their fingers (or on individual chalkboards). Then ask the children to think of words that begin with _U_. Write the words they offer on the blackboard, drawing quick sketches (when possible) of the suggested words. If a child suggests a word that does not begin with _U_, say, "No, that begins with ___," and say the two sounds so children can compare them. To help children who cannot think of any words, prompt them with pictures or objects representing words that start with _U_. (Pictures or objects can be handed out at the beginning of the lesson or as the lesson proceeds.) Additional words can be sought in a picture dictionary if the group has difficulty arriving at words that begin with _U_.

Summary/Transition Activity

After about 10–15 words have been suggested, review the words, emphasizing the _U_ sound.

··
WEEKLY PLANNING GUIDE
··

	Dramatic Play	Art	Group	Story	Song
Monday *Suggested Props and Materials*	Winter Fun *Winter scenario, cardboard bricks wrapped in white paper, newspaper, ice pond, fishing poles, fish, ice fishing area, campfire, pillowcase, cups, pretend thermos of hot chocolate*	Make Snowflakes *Folded square sheets of white paper in a variety of sizes; scissors; markers or crayons; glitter (optional); glue, glue sticks, or paste (optional); Q-tips and blue paper*	How to Write a *6* *Whiteboard or chalkboard and chalk, number cards 1–6, variety of objects for counting, paper and pencils or slates and chalk*	*Snow Day*	"The Snowman and the Bunny" (fingerplay)
Tuesday *Suggested Props and Materials*	Spring (Baseball) *Spring scenario, masking tape outline of a baseball diamond, Nerf ball, T-ball stand, soft bat, gloves (optional), large mat for bleachers (optional), chairs, tables for ticket and concession stands, pretend cash register, pretend money, tickets, pretend food (e.g., hot dogs, popcorn), cups, pretend soda dispenser*	Baseball Outlines *White construction paper with baseball outline, Cheerios or other items to use to outline the ball, glue*	Shapes—Diamond *Various sets of shapes (circle, square, triangle, rectangles, diamond); taped shape outlines; whiteboard or chalkboard; chalk; and small chalkboards (optional)*	*This Is Baseball*	"Take Me out to the Ball Game"
Wednesday *Suggested Props and Materials*	Summer (Beach) *Summer scenario, water area (blue sheet), sand area, shells, barbecue, food, megaphone (for lifeguard), towels, pretend sunscreen*	Watercolor Painting *Watercolor paint, brushes, paper, water*	Letter *V* *Objects and pictures representing letter V*	*Commotion in the Ocean*	"All the Little Fishies"
Thursday *Suggested Props and Materials*	Fall Festival *Summer scenario, strips of yellow paper (for hay), scarecrow, flannel shirts, bandanas, pumpkins (optional), pretend farm animals (e.g., horses, cows, chickens), musical instruments or CD with children's music, masking tape to mark off dancing area, wagon*	Leaf Rubbings *Leaf cutouts, chalk or crayons, paper*	Review the Seasons *Large piece of paper or chalkboard, markers or chalk, pictures representing activities done during the different seasons*	*The Apple Pie Tree*	"Five Little Leaves"

NEWSLETTER

Vol. 1, No. 22

Date: _____

Seasons

Monday

Dramatic play will feature winter fun with ice skating (on plastic), building snow forts, and making newspaper snowballs as the children learn about things to do during the winter. Children will make snowflakes out of cotton swabs at the art table and listen to *Snow Day* during storytime. The number *6* will be discussed at group time. We will finish our day by singing "The Snowman and the Bunny."

Tuesday

We will celebrate spring by going to a baseball game set up in the classroom today. The children will outline a baseball shape using Cheerios. *This Is Baseball* is our story for the day. We will learn about the diamond shape during group time. Our song for the day is "Take Me out to the Ballgame."

Wednesday

We will celebrate summer by going to the beach. Children can play on the shore, enjoy water sports, and have a picnic. They will make watercolor paintings at the art table. We will read *Commotion in the Ocean* at storytime. We will learn about letter *V* during group time. "All the Little Fishies" is our song for today.

Thursday

The leaves begin to fall today as we learn about autumn. We will have a fall festival with square dancing, hay rides, and scarecrows. In art, the children will make leaf rubbings. The story will be *The Apple Pie Tree*. During group time, children will review what they learned about seasons this week by finishing sentences like these: "In winter we . . ., In spring, we . . ." We will sing "Five Little Leaves" during music.

Monday

Dramatic Play	Art	Group	Story	Song
Winter Fun	Make Snowflakes	How to Write a 6	*Snow Day*	"The Snowman and the Bunny" (fingerplay)

DAILY PLANNING GUIDE

Language and Literacy Skills Facilitated

Vocabulary: *snow, snowflake, winter, snowball fight, snow fort, snowball, season, ice, slick, slide, shovel*

Verb phrase structures: <u>are</u> shovel<u>ing</u>, <u>was</u> shovel<u>ing</u>, throw<u>s</u> snowballs, <u>threw</u> snowballs, <u>were</u> build<u>ing</u> a snow fort, <u>built</u> a snow fort, hit<u>s</u> the fort, <u>was</u> hitting the wall

Adjective/object descriptions: *cold snow, heavy coat, warm mittens*

Question structures: *what, how, where, when, who, what if, why, how many, which one*

Pronouns: *I, you, he, she, we, they, my, your, him, her, his, our, their, me, us, them*

Prepositions: *in, on, under, over, near, beneath, next to, beside, around, inside, outside*

Sounds: /s/ *<u>s</u>eason, <u>s</u>now, mi<u>ss</u>es, fort<u>s</u>*; /l/ *<u>l</u>ike, ye<u>ll</u>ow, <u>y</u>ell*; /f/ *<u>f</u>ort, <u>f</u>un, of<u>f</u>, i<u>f</u>*

Noting print has meaning: names on chairs and on cubbies, signs in dramatic play, words in books and on chalkboard

Noting sound–symbol associations: What sound does _____ start with?

Writing: letters, names, words

Social Skills Facilitated

Initiating interaction with peers and adults; responding to questions and requests from peers and adults

Negotiating with peers for toys and materials

Group cooperation: waiting for a turn in a group, taking a turn at the appropriate time

Cognitive Skills Facilitated

Problem-solving skills: how to make a snowflake

Classification skills: winter things

Sequencing skills: story, songs, and fingerplays

Narrative/story structure: adventure

Motor Skills Facilitated

Large motor: outdoor play activities—jumping, running, hopping, pedaling, climbing

Small motor: writing, drawing, gluing, painting, folding

DRAMATIC PLAY : **Winter Fun**

Type of Activity: Related

Objectives
1. Learn new, and employ familiar, vocabulary
2. Learn new, and employ a variety of, syntactic constructions
3. Interact with peers
4. Sequence familiar routines
5. Expand conceptual knowledge of the world

Settings
- Plastic sheet for skating area
- Snow fort building area/snowball throwing area
- Bobsled area
- "Campfire" area (optional)

Props
- Music from CD or tape player (optional for skating activity)
- Cardboard bricks wrapped in white paper
- Newspaper
- Toy people or other small dolls
- Plastic saucers or plastic dishes
- Incline board (or slide)
- Dishes or cups and pretend campfire

Roles
- Ice skaters
- Bobsled racers
- Fort builder
- Hot chocolate drinkers

General Description of Activity

The children participate in recreational and sporting activities that are typically done in the winter, such as ice skating, building igloos/snow forts, throwing snowballs, bobsledding, and drinking hot chocolate. For ice skating, tape down a sheet of plastic onto the floor and let the children slide around with their socks on. Wrap play bricks in white paper to assemble igloos and snow forts. Newspaper can be wadded up into soft "snowballs." Children can have miniature or doll bobsled races by placing small dolls on small plastic saucers or dishes and sliding them down an incline made up of a board or small slide.

Verbal Productions

Level of linguistic complexity varies with the role or competency of the child playing the role.
- "Let's have a race" or "Wanna race"
- "I'm skating faster than you are" or "Skate fast"
- "Do you want to have some hot chocolate?" or "Drink?"
- "He's throwing snowballs" or "Throw ball"

Adult Facilitative Role

The adult is to facilitate role play and help expand language and literacy skills. Typical actions or strategies to use include

Playing a role: "I am going ice skating. Would you like to come, too?"

Modeling the reading of the sign: "That sign says *skates for rent*."

Modeling confirmatory feedback: "That's right. The words *snow* and *blow* rhyme."

Providing an event casting: "I am making a snowman. I make a big ball out of newspaper and make a smaller ball on top. Finally I make the snowman's head. I have to tape them together. I think I will put a red scarf around my snowman's neck. Here is a hat to put on top."

Redirecting a child to a peer: "Ask Billy for a turn. Say, 'May I have a turn, please?'"

Contrasting two prepositions: "The snowman is between the trees. That snowman is on the house."

ART : Make Snowflakes

Objectives
1. Express creativity
2. Develop small motor skills (e.g., drawing, painting, cutting, pasting)
3. Practice turn-taking skills
4. Converse with peers and adults

Materials
- Different sizes of white paper
- Scissors
- Markers
- Colored construction paper (optional)
- Glue sticks (optional)
- Cotton swabs (optional)

General Description of Activity

Children make snowflakes by folding white paper into fourths, then folding each fourth into thirds to form a triangle. Have them cut or tear holes in the paper. They can unfold the snowflakes and color or decorate them if desired. Snowflakes may also be pasted onto other construction paper. Use different sizes of paper for different sizes of snowflakes.

Variation

Have children glue cotton swabs on a blue or black piece of paper to form snowflakes.

GROUP **How to Write a 6**

Objectives

1. Improve listening skills
2. Increase conceptual knowledge
3. Learn appropriate group-interaction skills
4. Practice turn-taking skills
5. Practice recognition and writing of numbers

Materials

- Number cards
- Counting objects
- Chalkboards and chalk
- Whiteboard and markers
- Other number cards
- Paper and pencils (optional)

General Description of Activity

Hold up a card with the number 6 on it. Trace the number with your finger and invite several children to come to the front of the group to trace the number, too. As the children trace, recite the jingle for the target number (6):

1: Start at the top, go down and you're done, that's the way to make a *1.*

2: Around and back on the railroad track, *2, 2, 2.*

3: Around the tree, around the tree, that's the way to make a *3.*

4: Down and over and down once more, that's the way to make a *4.*

5: Down around, make a hat on it, and look what you've found. (*5*)

6: Down around until it sticks, that's the way to make a *6.*

7: Over and down and it's not heaven, over and down makes a *7.*

8: Make an S and go back straight, that's the way to make an *8.*

9: A balloon and a line make *9.*

10: Draw a line and a circle with your pen, that's the way to make a *10.*

Group Participation

Have different children place the correct number of counting objects under the numeral card. Distribute individual chalkboards and chalk (or paper and pencils or whiteboards and markers) to the children. Have the children practice writing the target number(s) and/or drawing the appropriate quantity (e.g., *3* and three circles).

Summary/Transition Activity

Ask children to hold up their chalkboards and show one another their numbers.

Tuesday

Dramatic Play	Art	Group	Story	Song
Spring (Baseball)	Baseball Outlines	Shapes—Diamond	*This Is Baseball*	"Take Me out to the Ball Game"

DAILY PLANNING GUIDE

Language and Literacy Skills Facilitated

Vocabulary: *baseball, ball, bat, bases, diamond, glove, concession stand, popcorn, peanuts, cotton candy, scores, runs, hit, pitcher, batter, home run*

Verb phrase structures: <u>hit</u> the ball, <u>swing</u> the bat, <u>run</u> the bases, <u>pitch</u> the ball

Adjective/object descriptions: *long bat, white bases, fast ball, first base glove, foul ball*

Question structures: *what, how, where, when, who, what if, why, how many, which one*

Pronouns: *I, you, he, she, we, they, my, your, him, her, his, our, their, me, us, them*

Prepositions: *in, on, under, over, near, beneath, next to, beside, around, inside, outside*

Sounds: /f/ <u>f</u>un, o<u>ff</u>; /s/ <u>s</u>it, talk<u>s</u>; /l/ <u>l</u>ittle, bal<u>l</u>

Noting print has meaning: names on chairs and on cubbies, signs in dramatic play, words in books and on chalkboard

Noting sound–symbol associations: What sound does _____ start with?

Writing: letters, names, words

Social Skills Facilitated

Initiating interaction with peers and adults; responding to questions and requests from peers and adults

Negotiating with peers for toys and materials

Group cooperation: waiting for a turn in a group, taking a turn at the appropriate time

Cognitive Skills Facilitated

Problem-solving skills: how to hit the ball

Classification skills: things that are the same or different

Sequencing skills: story, songs

Motor Skills Facilitated

Large motor: outdoor play activities—jumping, running, hopping, swinging, catching, climbing

Small motor: writing, drawing, gluing

DRAMATIC PLAY **Spring (Baseball)**

Type of Activity: Central

Objectives
1. Learn new, and employ familiar, vocabulary
2. Learn new, and employ a variety of, syntactic constructions
3. Interact with peers
4. Sequence familiar routines
5. Expand conceptual knowledge of the world

Settings
- Taped-off diamond area with taped squares to indicate bases
- Bleacher area made of folded tumbling mat to form a riser with chairs, but on two levels (or two rows of chairs without the mat)
- Concession area
- Ticket sales area or area for announcers (optional)

Props
- Plastic bats
- Plastic Wiffle balls (balls with holes in them) or other indoor-use baseballs (some are soft and sponge-like)
- Baseball tee (to hold the baseball while children to swing at)
- Chairs and tumbling mat to make spectator area
- Concessions—pretend food (e.g., soda pop, popcorn, cotton candy, peanuts, hot dogs, etc.)
- Cash registers

Roles
- Batter
- Fielder
- Concession worker
- Spectators
- Ticket agents or announcers (optional)

General Description of Activity

Children act out a baseball game: Some are players on the field, some are spectators watching from the stands, and some work the concession area where people can buy drinks and popcorn and other food items. The scenario can be expanded by including ticket sellers or announcers, who give the play-by-play action of the players on the field. A diamond area can be taped off with little taped squares to indicate bases. The player swing plastic bats at a Wiffle ball on a baseball tee (if a baseball tee is not available, pitch the plastic Wiffle ball or other indoor use ball to the batter). Other children can play the outfield positions to field the balls. A tumbling mat can be folded over to form a riser so that chairs can be placed on two levels to form the spectator area. A small concession area can be set up using bookshelves to form a counter area as well as a space to put the concessions items (place the two bookcases in an L shape, with one part being the counter with the cash register and the other storing the food items).

Verbal Productions

Level of linguistic complexity varies with the role or competency of the child playing the role.
- "I want a turn to bat" or "My turn"
- "I can hit a home run" or "Hit ball"
- "I want some popcorn and some pop" or "Popcorn"

Adult Facilitative Role

The adult is to facilitate role play and help expand language and literacy skills. Typical actions or strategies to use include

Playing a role: "I am going to watch the ballgame. Look, he hit the ball."

Expanding a child's utterance: "Them playing" to "They are playing ball."

Modeling the correct pronunciation of the /s/ sound: "Did you see the silly face?"

Contrasting two sounds: "Did you mean to say 'hit' or 'sit?'"

Modeling the reading of signs: "That sign says *hot dogs* and this sign says *peanuts*."

ART **Baseball Outlines**

Objectives
1. Express creativity
2. Develop small motor skills (e.g., drawing, painting, cutting, pasting)
3. Practice turn-taking skills
4. Converse with peers and adults

Materials
- Cheerios or other small items
- Glue
- Baseball outlines

General Description of Activity

Before the children arrive, draw a baseball about 3" in size. Have the children outline the baseball (including the stitches) by gluing string or small items such as Cheerios on the lines. Children may also make other pictures with the Cheerios, either following lines or free form.

Variation

The children could draw shapes themselves and glue or paste the Cheerios on the lines.

GROUP **Shapes—Diamond**

Objectives
1. Improve listening skills
2. Increase conceptual knowledge
3. Learn appropriate group-interaction skills
4. Practice turn-taking skills

Materials
- Colored tape
- Various sizes and colors of diamond-shaped cutouts
- Several small and large circle-, square-, triangle-, and rectangle-shaped cutouts
- Small chalkboard or paper; chalk or markers (optional)

General Description of Activity

Using colored tape, outline a large and a small diamond shape on the floor in front of the children, where large and small circles, squares, triangles, and rectangles are already outlined. Trace one of the triangle outlines on the floor, or trace a triangle cutout, noting that the diamond could be made if two triangles are place one upside down and the other right side up (use equilateral triangles). Note that a diamond has four sides and four corners, like a square. But the diamond's corners are not the same; two have angles that are narrow and two have angles that are wide. Ask one child to stand on a large or small diamond and to label it as a diamond.

Group Participation

Ask different children to identify the large or small diamond by standing on it or by putting a large or small cutout on the appropriate outline. Vary the level of difficulty. For example, you might ask one child simply to identify a shape you name (e.g., rectangle, triangle, square, or diamond) and another to find a shape that is a specific size and color (e.g., "Find a large, orange diamond"). The task can also be varied by having children place a hand on one shape and a foot on another. Have most of the children find and/or label diamonds, but occasionally ask a child to identify some of the other shapes (circle, square, triangle, rectangle) to provide a review of the previously taught shapes. Do this activity in smaller groups, if necessary.

Variation

Have children draw shapes (diamond, rectangle, triangle, square, or circle) on small chalkboards or on paper. Other common shapes can be taught in a similar manner (e.g., heart, oval, etc.)

Summary/Transition Activity

Review the shapes by pointing to or standing on them or by holding up a shape cutout and having the children quickly label it in unison.

Wednesday

Dramatic Play	Art	Group	Story	Song
Summer (Beach)	Watercolor Painting	Letter *V*	*Commotion in the Ocean*	"All the Little Fishies"

DAILY PLANNING GUIDE

Language and Literacy Skills Facilitated

Vocabulary: *water, summer, swim, fish, shark, shrimp, octopus, crab, sunshine, dive, splash, sand, shell, dig, beach*

Verb phrase structures: *swim<u>s</u>, <u>is</u>/<u>are</u>/<u>was</u>/<u>were</u> swimm<u>ing</u>, div<u>ing</u>, splash<u>ing</u>, splash<u>ed</u>, <u>swam, has swum, dove, who is swimming? I am</u>*

Adjective/object descriptions: *sunny day, hot day, cold water, funny fish, pink shrimp, mean octopus, hungry shark*

Question structures: *what, how, where, when, who, what if, why, how many, which one*

Pronouns: *I, you, he, she, we, they, my, your, him, her, his, our, their, me, us, them*

Prepositions: *in, on, under, over, near, beneath, next to, beside, around, inside, outside*

Sounds: /s/ <u>s</u>it, <u>s</u>ing, mi<u>ss</u>; /s-blends/ <u>sw</u>im, <u>spl</u>ash, <u>st</u>and; /r/ <u>r</u>un, <u>r</u>ow, na<u>rr</u>ow, ou<u>r</u>; /k/ <u>c</u>atch, <u>c</u>ome, o<u>c</u>topus, ba<u>ck</u>

Noting print has meaning: names on chairs and on cubbies, signs in dramatic play, words in books and on chalkboard

Noting sound–symbol associations: What sound does _____ start with?

Writing: letters, names, words

Social Skills Facilitated

Initiating interaction with peers and adults; responding to questions and requests from peers and adults
Negotiating with peers for toys and materials

Group cooperation: waiting for a turn in a group, taking a turn at the appropriate time

Cognitive Skills Facilitated

Problem-solving skills: how to catch a fish
Classification skills: things at a beach
Sequencing skills: story, songs, fingerplays
Narrative/story structure: rhyming

Motor Skills Facilitated

Large motor: outdoor play activities—jumping, running, hopping, pedaling, climbing
Small motor: writing, drawing, gluing, painting

DRAMATIC PLAY **Summer (Beach)**

Type of Activity: Related

Objectives
1. Learn new, and employ familiar, vocabulary
2. Learn new, and employ a variety of, syntactic constructions
3. Interact with peers
4. Sequence familiar routines
5. Expand conceptual knowledge of the world

Settings	• Blue sheet (or other demarcation) to represent a lake, or filled water table	• Volleyball area with a taped line to represent the net
	• Small plastic pools filled with sand	• Concession stand(s) or boardwalk
		• Lifeguard stand

Props	• Pails and shovels	• Megaphone (for lifeguard)
	• Seashells	• Towels
	• Boats (boxes or rubber rafts)	• Pretend sunscreen
	• Lifejackets (plastic painting smocks worn backward)	• Balloons (for use as volleyballs)
	• Fishing poles (with magnets attached to catch fish)	• Pretend food
	• Fish (with paper clips attached)	• Pretend soda fountain (box lid with levers)
	• Surfboards (pieces of sturdy cardboard)	• Dishes
		• Cash registers

Roles	• Sand diggers	• Customers
	• Sunbathers	• Volleyball players
	• Surfers	• Lifeguards
	• Beach vendors	• Boat riders/fishermen and women

General Description of Activity

A day at the beach usually involves playing with sand near the water. Fill small plastic pools with sand, and bury some seashells in the sand so children can dig for them. Other activities might include playing sand volleyball, laying out on towels to get a tan, and riding in and/or fishing from boats. You could also set up a concession stand area or boardwalk. Children could surf on pretend surfboards made from cardboard.

Verbal Productions

Level of linguistic complexity varies with the role or competency of the child playing the role.
- "Hit the balloon to me" or "Hit it"
- "I found a pretty shell" or "My shell"
- "He is riding the surfboard, and he didn't fall" or "Ride"
- "There's a shark! Get out!" or "Shark!"
- "She wants the shovel now" or "Her turn"
- "He will get an ice cream cone, and I will have a Coke" or "Cone"

Adult Facilitative Role

The adult is to facilitate role play and help expand language and literacy skills. Typical actions or strategies to use include

Playing a role: "I am going to have a picnic at the beach. I am packing a big lunch."

Asking open questions: "What should we put in our picnic basket?"

Modeling production of the /k/ sound: "I can keep the cookies in the cookie tin."

Redirecting a child to a peer: "Ask Jennifer for the ball. Say, 'May I have a turn, please?'"

ART **Watercolor Painting**

Objectives	1. Express creativity
	2. Develop small motor skills (e.g., drawing, painting, cutting, pasting)
	3. Practice turn-taking skills
	4. Converse with peers and adults

Materials
- Watercolor paints
- Brushes (small)
- Paper (white works well with watercolors)
- Water to rinse brushes

General Description of Activity

Watercolor painting is a wonderful, creative experience. You might need to remind the children to rinse their brush between colors, but other than that let them paint whatever they like. Stay close by to talk about their picture. You might want to suggest some picture ideas around the theme of the day. For example, children might want to paint the park or the band they're listening to for "art in the park day." They might want to paint an animal for "vet" day, a family for "moving day," or a beach scene if they are at the "beach."

GROUP **Letter *V***

Objectives
1. Improve listening skills
2. Increase knowledge of the alphabet and sounds
3. Learn appropriate group-interaction skills
4. Practice turn-taking skills

Materials
- Alphabet chart and other alphabet displays
- Blackboard and chalk or poster paper and markers
- Pictures of objects (or objects themselves) with names that begin with V
- Picture dictionary (or an alphabet video dictionary)

General Description of Activity

Write an upper- and a lowercase letter V on the blackboard (or on poster paper). Give several examples of words that begin with *V*, emphasizing the /v/ or "vvv" sound at the beginning of the words. You might hold up pictures of objects (or objects themselves) with names that begin with *V*. Direct the children's attention to the alphabet picture displays around the room.

Group Participation

Ask if anyone's name starts with *V* (e.g., Vince, Victoria). Have those children write the letter *V* on the blackboard (or poster paper). Also have two or three other children write the letter *V* on the blackboard. Provide verbal guidance as children form the letter: "Start at the top. Draw a slant down to the right. Stay at the bottom and draw a slant up to the right until it's even with the first slant." If necessary, help children write the letter. Some of the other children can practice writing a *V* in the air with their fingers (or on individual chalkboards). Ask the children to think of words that begin with *V*. Write the words they offer on the blackboard, drawing quick sketches (when possible) of the suggested words. If a child suggests a word that does not begin with *V*, say, "No, that begins with ____," and say both sounds so children can compare them. To help children who cannot think of any words, prompt them with pictures or objects representing *V*. (Pictures or objects can be handed out at the beginning of the lesson or as the lesson proceeds.) Additional words can be sought in a picture dictionary if the group has difficulty arriving at words that begin with *V*.

Summary/Transition Activity

After about 10–15 words have been suggested, review the words, emphasizing the *V* sound.

Thursday

Dramatic Play	Art	Group	Story	Song
Fall Festival	Leaf Rubbings	Review the Seasons	*The Apple Pie Tree*	"Five Little Leaves"

DAILY PLANNING GUIDE

Language and Literacy Skills Facilitated

Vocabulary: *square dance, fall, seasons, leaves, hay, hay wagon, barn, paint, autumn, outside, chilly, music, guitar*

Verb phrase structures: *is danc<u>ing</u>, danc<u>es</u>, <u>was</u> danc<u>ing</u>, danc<u>ed</u>, clean<u>s</u>, clean<u>ed</u> up, paint<u>s</u>, paint<u>ed</u>, who paint<u>ed</u> the house? I <u>did</u>, Who <u>can</u> dance? I <u>can</u>*

Adjective/object descriptions: *red ___, yellow ____, orange ____, fast/slow dance, heavy/light load*

Question structures: *what, how, where, when, who, what if, why, how many, which one*

Pronouns: *I, you, he, she, we, they, my, your, him, her, his, our, their, me, us, them*

Prepositions: *in, on, under, over, near, beneath, next to, beside, around, inside, outside*

Sounds: */r/ <u>r</u>un, <u>r</u>ubbings, ove<u>r</u>, unde<u>r</u>; /s/ <u>s</u>ee, out<u>s</u>ide, paint<u>s</u>; /l/ <u>l</u>ook, ye<u>ll</u>ow, fa<u>ll</u>*

Noting print has meaning: names on chairs and on cubbies, signs in dramatic play, words in books and on chalkboard

Noting sound–symbol associations: What sound does _____ start with?

Writing: letters, names, words

Social Skills Facilitated

Initiating interaction with peers and adults; responding to questions and requests from peers and adults

Negotiating with peers for toys and materials

Group cooperation: waiting for a turn in a group, taking a turn at the appropriate time

Cognitive Skills Facilitated

Problem-solving skills: how to dance, how to play music

Classification skills: seasonal clothes (What do we wear in fall?)

Sequencing skills: songs, seasons, fingerplays

Narrative/story structure: expository

Motor Skills Facilitated

Large motor: outdoor play activities—jumping, running, hopping, pedaling, climbing, raking

Small motor: writing, drawing, gluing, rubbings

DRAMATIC PLAY **Fall Festival**

Type of Activity: Related

Objectives
1. Learn new, and employ familiar, vocabulary
2. Learn new, and employ a variety of, syntactic constructions
3. Interact with peers
4. Sequence familiar routines
5. Expand conceptual knowledge of the world

Settings
- Barn
- Square dance area
- Pumpkin patch and/or apple orchard
- Horseback riding area
- Stand to sell pumpkins, apples, and drinks

Props
- Horses/other farm animals
- Wagon with shredded yellow paper to represent hay
- Bales of hay (cardboard blocks covered with yellow paper)
- Pumpkin patch (with paper pumpkins)
- Apple orchard (mock tree with paper apples, or Ping-Pong balls painted red and stuck with Velcro onto a cardboard tree)
- Music for square dance (taped or CDs)
- Pillows to be stuffed to represent a scarecrow

Roles
- Farmer
- Guests
- Hay rack riders
- Vendors

General Description of Activity

The children can celebrate a fall harvest festival by going to a farm. Set up a square dance area, and make hay rides (using a wagon) available. The children can also pick pumpkins and apples and sell them at a stand. They can stuff a scarecrow. Horseback rides can also be available.

Verbal Productions

Level of linguistic complexity varies with the role or competency of the child playing the role.
- "My turn" or "I want to ride the horse"
- "My pumpkin" or "How much is that big pumpkin?"
- "Dancing" or "I'm dancing fast."
- "I want to ride on the hay wagon" or "I ride"

Adult Facilitative Role

The adult is to facilitate role play and help expand language and literacy skills. Typical actions or strategies to use include

Playing a role: "I am going on a hay ride. Do you want to come along?"

Providing a cloze procedure: "These leaves are in a pile. Those leaves still need to be _____(raked)."

Modeling a statement/vocabulary: "During the fall, many trees lose their leaves."

Recasting present tense with present progressive: "He plays the guitar" to "Yes, he is playing the guitar."

Identifying rhyming words: "Yes, the words *ball, fall*, and *call* all rhyme."

ART **Leaf Rubbings**

Objectives
1. Express creativity
2. Develop small motor skills (e.g., drawing, painting, cutting, pasting)
3. Practice turn-taking skills
4. Converse with peers and adults

Materials
- Newsprint or tracing paper
- Variety of leaves (freshly fallen leaves work best, but cardboard cutouts in the shape of leaves could also be used)
- Other cutouts
- Crayons with paper removed
- Container to hold crayons

General Description of Activity

Provide a variety of leaves. Have children place a leaf or several leaves under a piece of white paper, then rub a crayon (with paper covering removed) over the paper back and forth until the shape of the leaf appears. Children can use different colors of crayons and different arrangement of leaves under the paper to make a variety of pictures.

GROUP **Review the Seasons**

Objectives
1. Improve listening skills
2. Increase sequencing ability
3. Increase knowledge of storytelling
4. Learn appropriate group-interaction skills
5. Practice turn-taking skills

Materials
- Book about seasons
- Four tubs with season labels
- 20 pictures of activities representing the seasons, five for each season
- Season dice (optional)

General Description of Activity

Hold up a book about seasons that has pictures representing each one (e.g., *Seasons* by Sarah Leslie, illustrated by Aurelius Battaglia, 1977). Other books or appropriate pictures can be used. Label each season. Place four tubs in front of the children, each labeled with the name of a season. Choose one of the pictures depicting a season and say, "In winter we can go ice skating." Show the children the picture of children ice skating, and then put the picture in the *Winter* tub.

Group Participation

Have one child come to the front of the group and choose a picture to describe. The child says something like "In spring, we can plant flowers," then shows the picture of children planting flowers. The child then places the picture in the *Spring* tub. Have other children take turns choosing a picture, describing the activities represented by the picture, and putting the picture in the appropriate tub.

Variation 1

Assign groups of children a particular tub. One group makes all the statements about winter, another group makes all the statements about spring, and so forth.

Variation 2

Have the different seasons represented on a box, similar to a die, and have the children throw the die to see which season they are to describe.

Summary/Transition Activity

Review the seasons by holding up a picture and having the children, in chorus, say the name of the season depicted.

WEEKLY PLANNING GUIDE

	Dramatic Play	Art	Group	Story	Song
Monday *Suggested Props and Materials*	Zoo *Zoo scenario, cages or designated zoo area (simulate a fenced-off area) stuffed animals, pretend food (e.g., bananas, apples, shredded paper, LEGOs for peanuts), dishes, train (optional), ticket stand, concession stand*	Playdough Animals *Playdough, animal cookie cutters, rollers*	Sound Sequencing *Drum*	*Corduroy at the Zoo*	"Going to the Zoo"
Tuesday *Suggested Props and Materials*	Pet Store *Pet store scenario, cages (arranged on shelves in an aisle format), variety of stuffed animals, pretend aquarium, fish, pretend food (may be in boxes), leashes, cat and dog toys, counter, cash register, house*	Paper Bag Puppets *Brown and/or white paper bags; construction paper cutouts for eyes, noses, ears, and tails as appropriate for a particular animal (e.g., cat, dog, or rabbit); glue*	Caring for Pets *Cat or dog food, water and water dish, leashes, chart with items that are needed in taking care of a pet (e.g., food, water, place to sleep, exercise)*	*How Much Is that Doggy in the Window?*	"How Much Is that Doggy in the Window?"
Wednesday *Suggested Props and Materials*	Forest *Camping scenario, one or two play tents, pretend sleeping bags, backpacks or picnic baskets, picnic table or tablecloth for picnic, campfire area, dishes, pretend food (e.g., cotton ball marsh-mallows on chopsticks, corn on the cob), variety of forest animals, pretend trees, blue sheet or blue paper to represent a river or lake, fish, hiking area or ranger station (optional)*	Cereal Art *Cheerios, glue, bear (or other animal) outline*	Letter *W* *Capital and lowercase letter W, items or pictures that start with W (e.g., wildcat, walrus, walk)*	*Going on a Bear Hunt*	"Going on a Bear Hunt" (fingerplay)
Thursday *Suggested Props and Materials*	Farm *Farm scenario, barn area, field, chicken coop with nest and eggs, variety of stuffed or plastic farm animals (including stick riding horses), pretend food, hay (shredded yellow paper or paper-covered pillows), hay wagon*	Farm Mural *Large paper, markers, cutout animals or barn (optional), glue*	Classifying Animals (Zoo/Farm) *Toy barn, fence, zoo mat, variety of zoo and farm animals or pictures (or could use two tubs-one labeled farm, one labeled zoo)*	*Inside a Barn in the Country*	"Old McDonald Had a Farm"

NEWSLETTER

Vol. 1, No. 23

Date: _____

Places Animals Live

Monday
The children will care for and visit the animals in the zoo today in dramatic play. They can be the zookeepers, the concession workers, or the customers. Monday's art activity is making animals out of playdough. The children will hear the story *Corduroy at the Zoo*. During group time, the children will sequence sounds by making different patterns on a drum. "Going to the Zoo" will be our featured song.

Tuesday
The classroom will become a pet store during dramatic play. The children will make paper bag puppets for art and read *How Much Is that Doggy in the Window* at storytime. During group time, children will learn about caring for animals. Our Tuesday songs will include "How Much Is that Doggy in the Window?"

Wednesday
Today will feature animals that live in the forest. The children will pretend to explore the forest and will camp there while they look for animals during dramatic play. At art, children will make cereal art. *Going on a Bear Hunt* will be the story. During group time, the children will focus on the letter *W*. Music will include the chant and fingerplay "Going on a Bear Hunt."

Thursday
The children will pretend to be farmers and will be taking care of farm animals. They will make a farm mural in art. Our story is *Inside a Barn in the Country*. During group time, the children will classify animals according to those who live at a zoo and those who live on a farm. Today's song is "Old MacDonald Had a Farm."

Monday

Dramatic Play	Art	Group	Story	Song
Zoo	Playdough Animals	Sound Sequencing	*Corduroy at the Zoo*	"Going to the Zoo"

DAILY PLANNING GUIDE

Language and Literacy Skills Facilitated

Vocabulary: *zoo, elephant, giraffe, monkey, hippo, lion, tiger, roar, parrot, ticket booth, train, cage*

Verb phrase structures: *I am watching/I watched ____, I see/saw ____, I am riding the train, he rides the train*

Adjective/object descriptions: *large/small elephant, loud monkey, soft fur, long/short train, long/short tail*

Question structures: *what, how, where, when, who, what if, why, how many, which one*

Pronouns: *I, you, he, she, we, they, my, your, him, her, his, our, their, me, us, them*

Prepositions: *in, on, under, over, near, beneath, next to, beside, around, inside, outside*

Sounds: */f/ fix, off; /s/ sit, talks; /l/ little, bell; /z/ zoo, zebra, bees*

Noting print has meaning: names on chairs and on cubbies, signs in dramatic play, words in books and on chalkboard

Noting sound–symbol associations: What sound does _____ start with?

Writing: letters, names, words

Social Skills Facilitated

Initiating interaction with peers and adults; responding to questions and requests from peers and adults

Negotiating with peers for toys and materials

Group cooperation: waiting for a turn in a group, taking a turn at the appropriate time

Cognitive Skills Facilitated

Problem-solving skills: what animal to make out of playdough, what animals do

Classification skills: animals in the zoo

Sequencing skills: story, songs

Narrative/story structure: adventure

Motor Skills Facilitated

Large motor: outdoor play activities—jumping, running, hopping, pedaling, climbing

Small motor: writing, drawing, gluing, squeezing, rolling

DRAMATIC PLAY **Zoo**

Type of Activity: Central

Objectives
1. Learn new, and employ familiar, vocabulary
2. Learn new, and employ a variety of, syntactic constructions
3. Interact with peers
4. Sequence familiar routines
5. Expand conceptual knowledge of the world

Settings
- Cages
- Defined spaces for animals
- Pond (blue sheet)
- Pool area (blue sheet)
- Ticket office
- Concession stand area
- Train (optional)

Props
- Cages
- Fencing
- Stuffed animals
- Tickets
- Pretend cash register
- Pretend money
- Pretend food for animals
- Dishes for animal food
- Pretend food for visitors
- Tickets
- Balloons
- Soda pop dispensers
- Broom and mop
- Doctor kit (optional)

Roles
- Zookeeper
- Animals
- Ticket vendor
- Visitors
- Concession stand vendors
- Veterinarian (optional)

General Description of Activity

Set up a zoo with a variety of animals in cages or defined spaces (e.g., field areas for large animals, pond for ducks, pool areas for bears or penguins) in the dramatic play area. Children who are visitors to the zoo can buy a ticket, look at the animals, and perhaps feed them. They might take a train ride through the zoo and buy a balloon or other memento. They can purchase food at the zoo or bring a picnic basket. Other children could be workers at the zoo, taking care of the animals by feeding them and cleaning their cages.

Verbal Productions

Level of linguistic complexity varies with the role or competency of the child playing the role.
- "How many tickets do you want?" or "How many?"
- "I need to have six tickets" or "Six"
- "This is an African elephant. He is bigger than the Indian elephant" or "Big elephant"
- "I'm feeding the tigers now" or "Feed tigers"

Adult Facilitative Role

The adult is to facilitate role play and help expand language and literacy skills. Typical actions or strategies to use include

Playing a role: "I am going to see the monkeys. I like to go to the zoo to see the different animals."

Contrasting error response with correct response (focus contrast): "He have a horn" to "Oh, you mean he has a horn."

Modeling phonological awareness: "The words *rhino, rabbit,* and *run* all start with the /r/ sound."

Modeling the reading of a sign: "That sign says *lion*."

Redirecting a child to a peer: "Ask Mohammed for a turn on the train. Say, 'May I get on now, please?'"

ART **Playdough Animals**

Objectives
1. Express creativity
2. Develop small motor skills (e.g., drawing, painting, cutting, pasting)
3. Practice turn-taking skills
4. Converse with peers and adults

Materials
- Smocks
- Playdough
- Rolling pins
- Cookie cutters
- Presses
- Wooden craft sticks
- Rolling boards

General Description of Activity

Children wash their hands and put on smocks to explore playdough on the art table, using various presses, cutters, rolling pins, wooden craft sticks, and other tools. Children can make pretend food or any other objects out of the dough by rolling, cutting, or making pressing motions. They can form animals or people by rolling a main body and then adding heads, arms, and legs. Yarn can be used for hair (if children want to take their creations home). When children are finished, they roll the dough into a ball, wash their hands, and take off and fold their smocks.

GROUP **Sound Sequencing**

Objectives

1. Improve listening skills
2. Increase ability to recognize and sequence patterns
3. Learn appropriate group-interaction skills
4. Practice turn-taking skills

Materials

- Drum
- Keyboard (optional)

General Description of Activity

Place a drum in front of the children. Tap out a simple pattern while the children listen, then repeat the pattern while they listen again. Invite one child to come up to the front of the group and try to make the same pattern. If necessary, give assistance.

Group Participation

Play a different pattern and have another child try to match it. Continue this until all the children have had at least one turn. The patterns can vary from two short taps to complicated patterns involving a series of taps grouped in two or three sequences. For example, one pattern might be tap-tap (pause) tap. Another might be tap-tap-tap (pause) tap-tap. Other sample patterns include the following:

tap-tap (pause) *tap-tap*

tap-tap-tap (pause) *tap*

tap (pause) *tap-tap*

loud tap (pause), soft tap

two loud taps (pause), two soft taps

Variation

Set a rhythm on a keyboard and have the children clap to the rhythm.

Summary/Transition Activity

Play one more pattern and have the children clap the pattern, or play a rhythm from a song that is to be sung during music time and have the children clap out that rhythm.

Tuesday

Dramatic Play	Art	Group	Story	Song
Pet Store	Paper Bag Puppets	Caring for Pets	*How Much Is That Doggy in the Window?*	"How Much is That Doggy in the Window?"

DAILY PLANNING GUIDE

Language and Literacy Skills Facilitated

Vocabulary: *dog, cats, birds, gerbils, Dalmatians, pets, rabbits, camera, ribbons, awards, phone, cash register, cages, podium*

Verb phrase structures: *take<u>s</u> a picture, <u>is</u> tak<u>ing</u> the pet home, <u>fed</u> the dog, <u>gave</u> a ribbon, pet<u>ted</u> the dog, walk<u>ed</u> the dog*

Adjective/object descriptions: *blue/red ribbon, first place, big/little _____, white/black _____, long/short leash*

Question structures: *what, how, where, when, who, what if, why, how many, which one*

Pronouns: *I, you, he, she, we, they, my, your, him, her, his, our, their, me, us, them*

Prepositions: *in, on, under, over, near, beneath, next to, beside, around, inside, outside*

Sounds: /k/ <u>c</u>atch, pa<u>ck</u>, tri<u>ck</u>; /f/ <u>f</u>ed, of<u>f</u>; /r/ <u>r</u>abbit, fa<u>r</u>

Noting print has meaning: names on chairs and on cubbies, signs in dramatic play, words in books and on chalkboard

Noting sound–symbol associations: What sound does _____ start with?

Writing: letters, names, words

Social Skills Facilitated

Initiating interaction with peers and adults; responding to questions and requests from peers and adults

Negotiating with peers for toys and materials

Group cooperation: waiting for a turn in a group, taking a turn at the appropriate time

Cognitive Skills Facilitated

Problem-solving skills: how to take care of our pets

Classification skills: things at a pet show

Sequencing skills: story, songs, art activity

Narrative/story structure: adventure

Motor Skills Facilitated

Large motor: outdoor play activities—jumping, running, hopping, pedaling, climbing

Small motor: writing, drawing

DRAMATIC PLAY **Pet Store**

Type of Activity: Central

Objectives
1. Learn new, and employ familiar, vocabulary
2. Learn new, and employ a variety of, syntactic constructions
3. Interact with peers
4. Sequence familiar routines
5. Expand conceptual knowledge of the world

Settings
- Pet store
- Counter
- Children's houses (child-sized houses or dismantled cardboard boxes)

Props
- Stuffed animals
- Pretend cash register
- Play money
- Pretend credit cards
- Shelves of pretend pet products (e.g., food, leashes, collars, toys)
- Cages
- Aquariums
- Bowls for food and water
- Brushes for grooming
- Pet carriers
- Pretend cleaning supplies
- Owners' cars (optional)

Roles
- Clerks
- Cashier
- Customers
- Animals

General Description of Activity

Children buy pets at the pet store. The store should have a variety of pets (stuffed animals or children pretending to be the animals), such as dogs, cats, birds, hamsters, turtles, and fish, in appropriate containers and cages. A clerk can ring up sales on a cash register and be given money for the purchases. Pretend pet food, leashes, collars, and pet toys can also be sold at the pet store. Children can then take the pets to their houses. Children can also be workers in the store, caring for the pets by feeding and grooming them.

Verbal Productions

Level of linguistic complexity varies with the role or competency of the child playing the role.
- "How much is this doggy?" or "Buy doggy"
- "I need five pounds of cat food for Fuzzy" or "Cat food, please"
- "He is cleaning the dog's cage" or "Clean"
- "My turn to use the cash register" or "Mine"

Adult Facilitative Role

The adult is to facilitate role play and help expand language and literacy skills. Typical actions or strategies to use include

Playing a role: "I want to buy a new leash for my puppy. Do you think the red one is nice?"

Expanding a child's utterance: "Buy food" to "I want to buy food."

Identifying rhyming words: "The words *cat, hat,* and *mat* all rhyme."

Contrasting two sounds: "Did you say 'vet' or 'bet?'"

Using a cloze procedure: "This dog is big, and this dog is _____ (little)."

Helping a child read a sign: "That sign says *dog food*."

ART **Paper Bag Puppets**

Objectives
1. Express creativity
2. Develop small motor skills (e.g., drawing, painting, cutting, pasting)
3. Practice turn-taking skills
4. Converse with peers and adults

Materials
- Paper bags, one for each child
- Construction paper
- Construction cutouts (e.g., circles, triangles, squares)
- Scissors
- Glue or paste

General Description of Activity

Children make paper bag puppets by decorating small brown paper bags. The puppet might be a pet or other creature. The base fold of the paper bag will be the face so that when the child's hand is placed inside the bag, the fold can be used to open and close the mouth. Children may glue red construction paper inside the fold to represent the tongue. Other construction paper cutouts can be used for facial features, such as ears, a nose, and a mouth, or children can use markers to draw in the facial features. Yarn can be used for fur. When the puppets are finished, the children can stick their hands into the bag and make their puppets "talk."

GROUP **Caring for Pets**

Objectives

1. Improve listening skills
2. Increase conceptual knowledge
3. Learn appropriate group-interaction skills
4. Practice turn-taking skills

Materials

- Water dish
- Pet food (can have both cat and dog food)
- Food dish
- Leash and collar

- Cage or dog houses
- Bird cage (optional)
- Aquarium (optional)
- Fish food (optional)

General Description of Activity

Place water dishes, food dishes, collars, leashes, and cages in front of the children. Ask the children who uses these items. After they have responded (e.g., "dogs," "cats," "pets"), tell them that they are going to talk about taking care of a pet.

Group Participation

Hold up a food dish and have one child come to the front to put some cat or dog food in it. Remind the children that animals need food. You might ask, "Why do animals need food?" or "What food do you feed your pet?" Ask what else pets need, and have another child fill a water dish. Discuss different places that pets sleep and their need for some kind of shelter. Also talk about what to do if a pet gets sick or needs shots and how a pet gets exercise. Continue to ask the children about their pets' needs (e.g., love, attention) until each child has had a chance to speak.

Variation

Discuss caring for other kinds of pets, such as fish, hamsters, or birds. For example, a fish would need an aquarium, a hamster would need a maze, a bird would need a cage, and so forth.

Summary/Transition Activity

Review the items a pet needs. As each is mentioned, point to it.

Wednesday

Dramatic Play	Art	Group	Story	Song
Forest	Cereal Art	Letter *W*	*Going on a Bear Hunt*	"Going on a Bear Hunt" (fingerplay)

DAILY PLANNING GUIDE

Language and Literacy Skills Facilitated

Vocabulary: *tent, campfire, stick, marshmallow, backpack, sleeping bag, hike, bear, deer, animals, trees, mountains, trail*

Verb phrase structures: *roasts marshmallows, is roasting hot dogs, roasted marshmallows, sleeps in a tent, is sleeping, slept in a tent, hikes, hiked, lights a fire, lit a fire*

Adjective/object descriptions: *big ____, little ____, hot ____, sleepy ___, hungry ____, yellow ____, blue ____*

Question structures: *what, how, where, when, who, what if, why, how many, which one*

Pronouns: *I, you, he, she, we, they, my, your, him, her, his, our, their, me, us, them*

Prepositions: *in, on, under, over, near, beneath, next to, beside, around, inside, outside*

Sounds: /k/ *cook*; /l/ *light, yellow, ball*; /z/ *zipper, balls*; /r/ *roast, bear*; /f/ *fire, off*

Noting print has meaning: names on chairs and on cubbies, signs in dramatic play, words in books and on chalkboard

Noting sound–symbol associations: What sound does _____ start with?

Writing: letters, names, words

Social Skills Facilitated

Initiating interaction with peers and adults; responding to questions and requests from peers and adults

Negotiating with peers for toys and materials

Group cooperation: waiting for a turn in a group, taking a turn at the appropriate time

Cognitive Skills Facilitated

Problem-solving skills: what food to cook over the fire, how to go fishing

Classification skills: things we take on a camping trip

Sequencing skills: songs, stories

Narrative/story structure: adventure with choral repetition of each story line

Motor Skills Facilitated

Large motor: outdoor play activities—jumping, running, hopping, pedaling, climbing

Small motor: writing, drawing, gluing, painting

.... DRAMATIC PLAY **Forest** ....

Type of Activity: Central

Objectives
1. Learn new, and employ familiar, vocabulary
2. Learn new, and employ a variety of, syntactic constructions
3. Interact with peers
4. Sequence familiar routines
5. Expand conceptual knowledge of the world

Settings
- Campground
- Lake
- Mountains
- Hiking area
- Ranger station
- Bear cave
- Trees

Props
- Tent(s)
- Sleeping bags
- Campfire (wooden blocks)
- Grill
- Picnic items (e.g., basket, food, paper plates, utensils)
- Marshmallows (cotton balls on sticks)
- Boats
- Fishing poles (with magnets attached to catch the fish)
- Fish (with paper clips attached)
- Backpacks
- Maps
- Pretend forest animals (e.g., bears, raccoons, rabbits, squirrels)
- Trees

Roles
- Campers (family members)
- Fishermen and women
- Hikers
- Ranger
- Forest animals (children can pretend to be the animals)

General Description of Activity

Children act out camping trips and activities in the forest. They might sleep in tents or under the stars in sleeping bags. They could cook their food over a wood fire or pack a lunch and go hiking or fishing. The class might establish a ranger station so families can get maps that show them where to camp. To reinforce the theme this week, emphasize the forest animals children might see on a hike. You might have a pretend bear cave with stuffed bears in it.

Verbal Productions

Level of linguistic complexity varies with the role or competency of the child playing the role.
- "I am packing a lunch for the picnic" or "Picnic"
- "Let's unroll our sleeping bags" or "Let's sleep"
- "Fix the tent, please" or "My turn, please"
- "John is walking too fast" or "Too fast"
- "You missed the trail" or "Missed it"
- " I see the bear [animal]" or "See"

Adult Facilitative Role

The adult is to facilitate role play and help expand language and literacy skills. Typical actions or strategies to use include

Playing a role: "We are hiking in the woods. Maybe we will see some animals."

Modeling a structure (present progressive): "She is setting up the tent."

Using an open question: "What kind of animal do you think we will see?"

Providing confirmatory feedback: "That's right. It is a brown bear behind the tree."

Modeling the /w/ sound: "Wait for me. I am going to get some water. We need water to make waffles for breakfast."

ART **Cereal Art**

Objectives
1. Express creativity
2. Develop small motor skills (e.g., drawing, painting, cutting, pasting)
3. Practice turn-taking skills
4. Converse with peers and adults

Materials
- Cheerios
- Glue
- Outline of bear on paper, one for each child
- Other animal outlines (optional)

General Description of Activity

Have the children outline the bear shapes by gluing or pasting Cheerios on the lines. Children may also make other pictures with the Cheerios by either following lines or arranging them free form.

Variation

Have children draw their own shapes and then glue or paste the Cheerios on the lines.

GROUP **Letter *W***

Objectives
1. Improve listening skills
2. Increase knowledge of the alphabet and sounds
3. Learn appropriate group-interaction skills
4. Practice turn-taking skills

Materials
- Alphabet chart and other alphabet displays
- Blackboard and chalk or poster paper and markers
- Pictures of objects (or objects themselves) with names that begin with *W*
- Picture dictionary (or an alphabet video dictionary)

General Description of Activity

Write an upper- and a lowercase letter *W* on the blackboard (or on poster paper). Give several examples of words that begin with *W*, emphasizing the /w/ sound at the beginning of the words. You might hold up pictures of objects (or objects themselves) with names that begin with *W*. Direct the children's attention to the alphabet picture displays around the room.

Group Participation

Ask if anyone's name starts with *W* (e.g., Winnie, William), and have those children write the letter *W* on the blackboard (or poster paper). Also have two or three other children write the letter *W* on the blackboard. Provide verbal guidance as children form the letter: "Start at the top, draw a slant down to the right, a slant up from the first slant, another slant down, and another slant up." If necessary, help children write the letter. Some of the other children can practice writing *W* in the air with their fingers (or on individual chalkboards). Ask the children to think of words that begin with *W*. Write the words they offer on the blackboard, drawing quick sketches (when possible) of the suggested words. If a child suggests a word that does not begin with *W*, say, "No, that begins with ___," and say both sounds so children can compare them. To help children who cannot think of any words, prompt them with pictures or objects representing *W* words. (Pictures or objects can be handed out at the beginning of the lesson or as the lesson proceeds.) Additional words can be sought in a picture dictionary if the group has difficulty arriving at words that begin with *W*.

Summary/Transition Activity:

After about 10–15 words have been suggested, review the words, emphasizing the /w/ sound.

Thursday

Dramatic Play	Art	Group	Story	Song
Farm	Farm Mural	Classifying Animals (Zoo/Farm)	*Inside a Barn in the Country*	"Old MacDonald Had a Farm"

DAILY PLANNING GUIDE

Language and Literacy Skills Facilitated

Vocabulary: *farm, barn, cow, horse, pig, goose, chicken, rabbit, feed, hay, fence, corral, milk, pail, silo, pen, tractor*

Verb phrase structures: *feeds, is feeding, fed the animals, milks, milked the cow, is bailing the hay, stacked the hay*

Adjective/object descriptions: *big/little _____, hungry _____, milking pail, white/brown/____ cow; yellow/____ chicken*

Question structures: *what, how, where, when, who, what if, why, how many, which one*

Pronouns: *I, you, he, she, we, they, my, your, him, her, his, our, their, me, us, them*

Prepositions: *in, on, under, over, near, beneath, next to, beside, around, inside, outside*

Sounds: /k/ *cow, chicken, milk;* /f/ *farm, off;* /m/ *milk, hammer, them*

Noting print has meaning: names on chairs and on cubbies, signs in dramatic play, words in books and on chalkboard

Noting sound–symbol associations: What sound does _____ start with?

Writing: letters, names, words

Social Skills Facilitated

Initiating interaction with peers and adults; responding to questions and requests from peers and adults. Negotiating with peers for toys and materials

Group cooperation: waiting for a turn in a group, taking a turn at the appropriate time

Cognitive Skills Facilitated

Problem-solving skills: how to milk a cow

Classification skills: animals on a farm

Sequencing skills: story, song

Narrative/story structure: repetitive line

Motor Skills Facilitated

Large motor: outdoor play activities—jumping, running, hopping, pedaling, climbing

Small motor: writing, drawing, cutting, pasting

DRAMATIC PLAY **Farm**

Type of Activity: Central

Objectives
1. Learn new, and employ familiar, vocabulary
2. Learn new, and employ a variety of, syntactic constructions
3. Interact with peers
4. Sequence familiar routines
5. Expand conceptual knowledge of the world

Settings

- Farm house (child-sized house or dismantled cardboard boxes)
- Barn (child-sized house or dismantled cardboard boxes)
- Field (floor area marked with masking tape or pretend fences)
- Planting area (a wading pool filled with sand or soil)

Props

- Pretend tractor
- Pretend machinery
- "Cow" to be milked (latex gloves filled with milky water)
- Horses (yardsticks)
- Blocks for fences
- Farm animals (stuffed animals, toy animals)

- Hats
- Pretend seeds
- Scarecrow
- Cardboard trees (with painted, removable Ping-Pong balls for fruit)

Roles

- Farmer(s)
- Farmer's helper(s)
- Animals (the children pretend to be animals)

- Tractor operator
- Other machinery operation
- Milker (optional)
- Fruit pickers (optional)

General Description of Activity

Children can care for the animals found on a farm, such as cows, horses, pigs, and chickens. They can also act out other farm activities, such as growing and harvesting crops and running tractors and other machinery. Emphasize the animal theme by having a barn and corral areas.

Verbal Productions

Level of linguistic complexity varies with the role or competency of the child playing the role.

- "It's my turn to feed the chickens" or "Feed chickens"
- "I plowed the field and then planted the corn" or "I plowed the field"
- "He is milking the cow" or "Milk cow"

Adult Facilitative Role

The adult is to facilitate role play and help expand language and literacy skills. Typical actions or strategies to use include

Playing a role: "We need to go and feed the chickens."

Modeling a statement/vocabulary: "The chickens lay eggs in the nest. We can gather them and put them in our basket."

Contrasting error and structure (past tense error): "The egg falled and breaked" to "The egg fell and broke."

Expanding a child's utterance: "Want feed horse" to "I want to feed the horse."

Using a cloze procedure: "This basket is full, and this basket is _____(empty)."

ART **Farm Mural**

Objectives

1. Express creativity
2. Develop small motor skills (e.g., drawing, painting, cutting, pasting)
3. Practice turn-taking skills
4. Converse with peers and adults

Materials

- Large sheet of paper (e.g., 3', 8')
- Masking tape (optional)
- Plastic or newsprint to protect the floor
- Smocks
- Tempera paint

- Paint cups
- Paintbrushes
- Crayons or markers (optional)
- Small bowls of water to rinse brushes
- Appropriate pictures to be pasted

General Description of Activity

Tape a large piece of paper to a wall, or lay it on the floor on top of plastic or newsprint. The children don smocks and paint pictures or designs on the paper using tempera paint. The children may choose to draw with crayons or markers instead of using tempera paint, or they may paste previously produced pictures on the mural. For example, a farm mural might include precut drawings of a house, barn, fields, horses, cows, sheep, chickens, and so forth. Drawing a horizontal line first might be helpful in placing the pictures.

Variation

If painting scenery for a program or for a dramatic play theme, outline the objects on the mural and have the children fill them in with paint. For example, you might outline a house or tree, and the children can add the colors to the outline.

GROUP : **Classifying Animals (Zoo/Farm)**

Objectives
1. Improve listening skills
2. Increase sequencing ability
3. Learn appropriate group-interaction skills
4. Practice turn-taking skills

Materials
- Toy barn
- Toy fence
- Zoo mat
- Toy farm animals
- Toy zoo animals
- Pictures of farm and zoo animals (optional)

General Description of Activity

Create a farm area (a toy barn with a toy fence) and a zoo area (a plastic or cardboard mat with zoo scenes drawn on it). Tell the children that they are going to put the farm animals by the barn and the zoo animals in the zoo. Ask one child to put a toy cow in the farm area and another child to put a toy elephant in the zoo area.

Group Participation

Distribute several different toy animals to the children. Have children come up to the front one at a time to label their animal and decide whether it belongs in the zoo or on the farm. Ask the children to name some animals not represented as toys and tell where they live.

Variation

If toy animals are not available, use pictures of animals instead.

Summary/Transition Activity

Review the classifications of farm and zoo, and rename a few of the animals in each classification.

WEEKLY PLANNING GUIDE

	Dramatic Play	Art	Group	Story	Song
Monday *Suggested Props and Materials*	Castle *Castle scenario, moat, two thrones, crowns, other headdresses, scepters, shields, stick horses, area for dancing, CD player or tape recorder, CD or music tape, fancy clothes, cave with dragon (optional)*	Crowns *2"–3" strips of construction paper (approximately 28"–30" long) with the top edge cut in a zigzag manner, glue, glitter*	Act out a Story (*The Princess and the Pea*) *Castle door, several mats, LEGO (for the pea), crowns, costumes if desired*	*The Princess and the Pea*	"The Grand Old Duke of York"
Tuesday *Suggested Props and Materials*	Pioneer *Pioneer scenario, pretend wagon (e.g., a child-sized house turned on side with blanket hanging down, plus small bench in front for the driver), reins, stick horses, sleeping bags, campfire equipment, dishes, long dresses, cowboy hats, bonnets, cows, "river" area, fishing poles, fish*	Craft Stick Constructions *Paper, wooden craft sticks, glue, markers*	Hard/Soft *Hard and soft objects, plastic tub, and pillow*	*And You Can Be the Cat*	"She'll Be Coming 'Round the Mountain"
Wednesday *Suggested Props and Materials*	Today's Houses *Housekeeping area, stove, refrigerator, sink and table, other rooms such as a family room or bedrooms, pretend food, pots and pans, silverware, dishes, dolls, doll beds, brooms, brushes, rags, bath tubs for washing babies, TV, couch, telephones*	Draw a House *Paper, crayons, (watered-down tempera paint for crayon washes)*	Emergency Information *Children's addresses and telephone numbers written on index cards, play telephones*	*A House Is a House for Me*	"Two Little Houses" (fingerplay)
Thursday *Suggested Props and Materials*	Space Station *Space station scenario, rocket ship, moon area, space station, command central, space suits and helmets, moon area (trampoline to represent walking with less gravity), command area with computer and other equipment (walkie-talkies), cooking and sleeping areas for space station*	Glitter Space Pictures *Black paper, glitter paint, brushes*	Letter *X* *Items and pictures that begin with X, picture dictionary, alphabet chart and other alphabet displays, blackboard, chalk, whiteboards and markers, or poster paper and markers*	*Big Silver Space Shuttle*	"Twinkle, Twinkle, Little Star"

NEWSLETTER

Vol. 1, No. 24

Date: _____

Homes Across the Ages

Monday

Today the children will have a castle set up for dramatic play. They will be kings and queens and knights who look for dragons. In art, the children will make their own crowns. *The Princess and the Pea* is the story. During group time, the children will act out the story. "The Grand Old Duke of York" will be one of the songs we sing in music.

Tuesday

Wagons Ho! Pioneers who settled the West will be busy in the classroom during dramatic play. The children will drive wagons, ride horses, make camp, and even pan for gold. In art, the children will make craft stick constructions. The story is *And You Can Be the Cat*. They will classify things that are hard and things that are soft at group. "She'll Be Coming 'Round the Mountain" will be one of the songs during music.

Wednesday

The children will talk about and play house today in the dramatic play area. They will take care of babies, prepare food, and maybe watch TV! In art, the children will draw houses. At storytime, we will read *A House Is a House for Me*. During group time, children will learn about emergency information and how and when to call 911. "Two Little Houses" will be included in music time today.

Thursday

This day's dramatic play activity will be about homes of the future. Will we live in a space station someday? In art, the children will make glitter space pictures. The story will be *Big Silver Space Shuttle*. Group time will focus on the letter *X*. One of the songs in music will be "Twinkle, Twinkle, Little Star."

Monday

Dramatic Play	Art	Group	Story	Song
Castle	Crowns	Act out a Story (*The Princess and the Pea*)	*The Princess and the Pea*	"The Grand Old Duke of York"

DAILY PLANNING GUIDE

Language and Literacy Skills Facilitated

Vocabulary: *castle, knight, prince, princess, king, queen, moat, drawbridge, palace, dragon, Cinderella, ball, scepter, crown*

Verb phrase structures: *is king/queen, works at the castle, has a crown, is riding a horse, rode a horse*

Adjective/object descriptions: *large castle, small princess, filmy scarf, jeweled crown, pretty dress*

Question structures: *what, how, where, when, who, what if, why, how many, which one*

Pronouns: *I, you, he, she, we, they, my, your, him, her, his, our, their, me, us, them*

Prepositions: *in, on, under, over, near, beneath, next to, beside, around, inside, outside*

Sounds: /k/ *castle, cook;* /l/ *little, ball;* /f/ *fight, off*

Noting print has meaning: names on chairs and on cubbies, signs in dramatic play, words in books and on chalkboard

Noting sound–symbol associations: What sound does _____ start with?

Writing: letters, names, words

Social Skills Facilitated

Initiating interaction with peers and adults; responding to questions and requests from peers and adults

Negotiating with peers for toys and materials

Group cooperation: waiting for a turn in a group, taking a turn at the appropriate time

Cognitive Skills Facilitated

Problem-solving skills: how to act out the story/how to take turns

Classification skills: things in a castle

Sequencing skills: alphabet, songs, story

Narrative/story structure: fairy tale

Motor Skills Facilitated

Large motor: outdoor play activities—jumping, running, hopping, pedaling, climbing

Small motor: writing, drawing, gluing, squeezing, rolling

DRAMATIC PLAY : **Castle**

Type of Activity: Central

Objectives
1. Learn new, and employ familiar, vocabulary
2. Learn new, and employ a variety of, syntactic constructions
3. Interact with peers
4. Sequence familiar routines
5. Expand conceptual knowledge of the world

Settings
- Castles and drawbridge (child-sized house with cardboard bridge that can be raised and lowered over the moat)
- Ballroom
- Roads (floor area marked with masking tape)
- Throne room

Props
- Torn clothes
- Fancy clothes
- Jewelry
- Crowns
- Scepters
- Horses
- Carriages (stick horses and a box)
- Thrones
- Slippers (for Cinderella)
- Music

Roles
- Cinderella
- Stepmother
- Stepsisters
- Fairy godmother
- King
- Queen
- Prince
- Carriage drivers
- Knights
- Ball attendants

General Description of Activity

This dramatic play can center on the story of Cinderella or be a more generic activity about kings, queens, princes, and princesses. Set up one or two castles. The children can dress up in fancy clothes and jewelry, wear crowns and hold scepters, go to a ball, ride on horses or in a carriage, sit on thrones, and so forth.

Verbal Productions

Level of linguistic complexity varies with the role or competency of the child playing the role.
- "I don't have a dress. I can't go" or "No dress. Can't go"
- "May I have this dance?" or "Dance?"
- "Lower the drawbridge. We want in" or "Want in"
- "We danced a long time. It was fun" or "Dance. Fun"

Adult Facilitative Role

The adult is to facilitate role play and help expand language and literacy skills. Typical actions or strategies to use include

Playing a role: "I want to be a princess and go to a dance."

Event casting of an adult's utterance: "I am putting on my shield. Now I will get my horse. Now I am looking for a dragon. I didn't find a dragon so I came home to my castle."

Modeling of vocabulary: "The moat surrounds the castle and is filled with water. You have to use the bridge to get across the moat."

Recasting a child's utterance (present tense to present progressive): "They dance" to "Yes, they are dancing."

Identifying rhyming words: "Yes, the words *round, sound,* and *found* all rhyme."

ART : **Crowns**

Objectives
1. Express creativity
2. Develop small motor skills (e.g., drawing, painting, cutting, pasting)
3. Practice turn-taking skills
4. Converse with peers and adults

Materials

- 2"–3" strips of construction paper, approximately 28"–30" long, with points cut on the top edge in a zigzag manner (to simulate a crown)
- Glue
- Glitter
- Shallow box lids
- Staplers
- Tape
- Markers (optional)

General Description of Activity

Give children a strip of construction paper to make into a crown. They use white glue to outline the points on the top edge of the crowns, then sprinkle glitter over the glue. To prevent glitter from getting everywhere, have children put the crowns in a shallow box lid before they sprinkle the glitter. They can lift out the crown and shake it slightly so that the excess glitter falls back into the box lid. Let the crowns dry, then staple the ends together so that each child's crown fits snugly. You can put tape over the staples so they do not scratch the children's head.

Variation

The children can also decorate the crowns with markers.

GROUP **Act out a Story (*The Princess and the Pea*)**

Objectives

1. Improve listening skills
2. Increase sequencing ability
3. Increase knowledge of story telling
4. Learn appropriate group-interaction skills
5. Practice turn-taking skills

Materials

- *The Princess and the Pea*
- Props for the story (e.g., mats, a "pea," a castle area, costumes if desired)

General Description of Activity

Read *The Princess and the Pea* to the group, or quickly summarize it if children are familiar with it.

Group Participation

Assign children roles from the story. Assure the children not chosen the first time that everyone will have a turn and that they have the very important job of being a good listening audience. Narrate the story as the children act it out. They should say as many of the lines as they can, with prompts given when needed. Repeat the story with new actors until all the children have had a turn.

Summary/Transition Activity

Compliment the children's acting, and ask children what other stories they would like to act out another day.

Tuesday

Dramatic Play	Art	Group	Story	Song
Pioneer	Craft Stick Constructions	Hard/Soft	*And You Can Be the Cat*	"She'll Be Coming 'Round the Mountain"

DAILY PLANNING GUIDE

Language and Literacy Skills Facilitated

Vocabulary: *cowboys, pioneers, covered wagon, search, reins, land, campfire, explore, pitch camp, guitar, wheels, travel, horses*

Verb phrase structures: *is gathering wood, he searches, searched, played the guitar, built a fire, who is going? I am, who is lost? John is*

Adjective/object descriptions: *open spaces, big wagon, brave pioneer, covered wagon*

Question structures: *what, how, where, when, who, what if, why, how many, which one*

Pronouns: *I, you, he, she, we, they, my, your, him, her, his, our, their, me, us, them*

Prepositions: *in, on, under, over, near, beneath, next to, beside, around, inside, outside*

Sounds: /k/ *cowboy, milk;* /r/ *range, pioneer, star;* /f/ *find, food, off;* /l/ *land, yellow, wheel*

Noting print has meaning: names on chairs and on cubbies, signs in dramatic play, words in books and on chalkboard

Noting sound–symbol associations: What sound does _____ start with?

Writing: letters, names, words

Social Skills Facilitated

Initiating interaction with peers and adults; responding to questions and requests from peers and adults

Negotiating with peers for toys and materials

Group cooperation: waiting for a turn in a group, taking a turn at the appropriate time

Cognitive Skills Facilitated

Problem-solving skills: how to make a covered wagon

Classification skills: things a pioneer uses

Sequencing skills: songs, story

Narrative/story structure: adventure

Motor Skills Facilitated

Large motor: outdoor play activities—jumping, running, hopping, pedaling, climbing

Small motor: writing, drawing, gluing, painting

DRAMATIC PLAY **Pioneer**

Type of Activity: Central

Objectives
1. Learn new and employ familiar vocabulary
2. Learn new and employ a variety of syntactic constructions
3. Interact with peers
4. Sequence familiar routines
5. Expand conceptual knowledge of the world

Settings
- Wagons (made from cardboard boxes)
- Fishing area
- Camps

Props
- Wagons (made from cardboard boxes)
- Stick horses
- Cows and other farm animals
- Wild animals
- Reins
- Dishes, pots, and pans
- Pretend food
- Blue sheet (for lake or river)

- Fishing poles (with magnets attached to catch fish)
- Fish (with paper clips attached)
- Cowboy hats and boots
- Bonnets and long dresses
- Sleeping bags
- Guitars

Roles
- Mothers
- Fathers
- Children

- Animals
- Wagon train leader

General Description of Activity

Children explore pioneer life. They can ride in pretend wagons or on stick horses, or they can pretend to be the horses pulling the wagon. They can take care of their animals. They can wear cowboy hats and boots or bonnets and long dresses. They can catch fish and then cook it over their campfires. They can play guitars and sing around the campfire or in the wagons.

Verbal Productions

Level of linguistic complexity varies with the role or competency of the child playing the role.
- "How far is it to the next camp?" or "How far?"
- "I need five fish for supper. Go catch some" or "Catch fish, please"
- "He is driving the wagon" or "Drive wagon"
- "My turn to play the guitar" or "My turn now"

Adult Facilitative Role

The adult is to facilitate role play and help expand language and literacy skills. Typical actions or strategies to use include

Playing a role: "I am driving the wagon. You can sit next to me."

Contrasting two sounds: "Did you say 'cold' or 'told?'"

Expanding a child's utterance and providing corrective feedback: "Build fire" to "I will build a fire. I am cold."

Redirecting a child to a peer: "I am not driving the wagon. Go ask Mary for a turn. Say, 'May I have a turn, please?'"

Modeling the reading of a sign: "That sign says *California or bust*."

ART Craft Stick Constructions

Objectives
1. Express creativity
2. Develop small motor skills (e.g., drawing, painting, cutting, pasting)
3. Practice turn-taking skills
4. Converse with peers and adults

Materials
- Large and small wooden craft sticks
- Glue
- Markers
- Yarn

- Paper of various sizes and colors (small pieces and 12" × 14" in case children want to glue their sticks on the paper)
- Scissors

General Description of Activity

Lay out an assortment of large and small wooden craft sticks. Let the children glue them together to form a variety of constructions. They can make triangle shapes, log cabins, people or animals, or whatever they like. Provide other items, such as yarn, markers, and construction paper, for the children to use in their constructions.

GROUP **Hard/Soft**

Objectives
1. Improve listening skills
2. Increase sequencing ability
3. Increase knowledge of storytelling
4. Learn appropriate group-interaction skills
5. Practice turn-taking skills

Materials
- Plastic tub
- Pillow
- 10 pairs of items that are either soft or hard (e.g., puppet, plastic doll, soft cap, hard hat)

General Description of Activity

Place a plastic tub upside down in front of the children and put a pillow next to it. Tap the bottom of the tub, noting that the tub is hard. Then press down on the pillow and note that the pillow is soft and that your hand can "sink" into the pillow but not the tub. Hold up a plastic cup and a marshmallow, and have one child come to the front and decide whether the cup is hard or soft. The child should put the cup on top of the tub to start a "hard" pile. Ask another child to put the marshmallow on the pillow because it is soft. Tell the children that you have some other hard and soft items and that they are going to help you sort them.

Group Participation

Hold up other items that are either hard or soft. For each one, ask a child to put it on the tub if it is hard and on the pillow if it is soft. Ask the children to explain why they put the items where they did (e.g., "I put it there because it is *soft*" or "Because it is *hard*"). Continue with several item pairs.

Summary/Transition Activity

Have the children, in chorus, indicate whether the items are hard or soft as you point to the plastic tub and the items on it and then to the pillow with the soft items.

Wednesday

Dramatic Play	Art	Group	Story	Song
Today's Houses	Draw a House	Emergency Information	*A House Is a House for Me*	"Two Little Houses"

DAILY PLANNING GUIDE

Language and Literacy Skills Facilitated

Vocabulary: *cook, house, food, soup, stew, muffins, babies, wash, table, clean, buttons, address, phone number, 911*

Verb phrase structures: *is cooking, was cooking, cooks, cooked, fixes, fixed, makes, made, do you have ___?, eats, ate, has eaten, calls, is calling, called 911, washes, washed*

Adjective/object descriptions: *good food, hot/cold food, sweet/tart fruit, green vegetables, red apple, yellow banana, dirty/clean baby*

Question structures: *what, how, where, when, who, what if, why, how many, which one*

Pronouns: *I, you, he, she, we, they, my, your, him, her, his, our, their, me, us, them*

Prepositions: *in, on, under, over, near, beneath, next to, beside, around, inside, outside*

Sounds: /k/ *cook, cooking, make*; /l/ *lick, Jell-o, yell*; /s/ *see, cooks*; /r/ *roof, carrot, bar*

Noting print has meaning: names on chairs and on cubbies, signs in dramatic play, words in books and on chalkboard

Noting sound–symbol associations: What sound does _____ start with?

Writing: letters, names, words

Social Skills Facilitated

Initiating interaction with peers and adults; responding to questions and requests from peers and adults

Negotiating with peers for toys and materials

Group cooperation: waiting for a turn in a group, taking a turn at the appropriate time

Cognitive Skills Facilitated

Problem-solving skills: when to use emergency information (911), how to draw a house

Classification skills: emergency information/nonemergency information

Sequencing skills: story, emergency information (911 or phone number)

Narrative/story structure: rhyming, repetitive lines

Motor Skills Facilitated

Large motor: outdoor play activities—jumping, running, hopping, pedaling, climbing

Small motor: writing, drawing, gluing, squeezing, swirling

DRAMATIC PLAY : **Today's Houses**

Type of Activity: Central

Objectives
1. Learn new, and employ familiar, vocabulary
2. Learn new, and employ a variety of, syntactic constructions
3. Interact with peers
4. Sequence familiar routines
5. Expand conceptual knowledge of the world

Settings	• Kitchen area	• Family rooms
	• Bedrooms	• House (Playskool house or
	• Dining rooms	dismantled cardboard box—optional)

Props	• Play refrigerator	• Dolls
	• Cupboards	• Pretend food
	• Play stove	• Baby bottles
	• Play sink	• Mops and brooms
	• Dishes	• Pretend vacuum
	• Pots and pans	• Tablecloths (optional)
	• Beds	• Party decorations (optional)

Roles	• Mothers	• Babies and children
	• Fathers	• Party guests (optional)

General Description of Activity

In the housekeeping center, set up a pretend house or apartment, including a kitchen. Here the children can clean the house, take care of babies, cook food, set the table, make table decorations, and prepare for a party.

Verbal Productions

Level of linguistic complexity varies with the role or competency of the child playing the role.

- "Clean the table" or "Clean"
- "Use the broom to sweep the floor" or "Sweep here"
- "I'll do it later" or "Okay"
- "The baby is hungry. Please get the bottle" or "Baby crying"
- "Do you want some more food?" or "Food?"
- "I'm glad you came" or "Hi, come in"

Adult Facilitative Role

The adult is to facilitate role play and help expand language and literacy skills. Typical actions or strategies to use include

Playing a role: "I am cooking some dinner. Do you want to feed the babies?"

Modeling a structure (irregular past tense): "I fed the chicken. Then they went out to play."

Providing confirmatory feedback: "You're right. The word *house* does start with the /h/ sound."

Providing a focus contrast: "The red cup is on the table, and the blue cup is in the cupboard."

Asking an open question: "How do we play this game?"

ART **Draw a House**

Objectives	1. Express creativity
	2. Develop small motor skills (e.g., drawing, painting, cutting, pasting)
	3. Practice turn-taking skills
	4. Converse with peers and adults

Materials	• Paper (white or colored)
	• Crayons
	• Markers
	• Watered-down tempera paint (optional)

General Description of Activity

Provide the children with paper and a selection of crayons and/or markers. They might be interested in drawing a house, perhaps one of those the class has studied this week. However, let the children draw anything they want. For example, drawings could be of themselves, their family, their pets, different scenes, their house, designs, or rainbows. The children can turn their crayon drawings into crayon washes by painting over the pictures with a light coat of tempera paint (watered-down paint). The paint will not stick to the crayon but will fill in where there are no crayon marks to make a background of color.

GROUP **Emergency Information**

Objectives

1. Improve listening skills
2. Increase conceptual knowledge
3. Learn appropriate group-interaction skills
4. Practice turn-taking skills

Materials

- Children's addresses and telephone numbers written on index cards
- Play telephones

General Description of Activity

Ask the children what they need to know in case of an emergency. If the children do not seem to understand the word *emergency*, explain and give examples. After some brainstorming by the children, suggest that knowing their full name, address, and telephone number is important if they need to call for a police officer, an ambulance, or help from an emergency agency. Pretend to be an ambulance dispatcher and ask one or two children to say their full name, address, and telephone number. If some children do not know any of the information, tell them what it is and have them repeat it.

Group Participation

Have the children get together in groups of 5–10 children and one adult. Ask each child to say his or her full name, a parent's name, and his or her address. If the child knows the telephone number, he or she should say that, too. Have the children practice looking at the number that is listed on the program's telephone so that in an emergency they can read the numbers to the 911 operator.

You can extend this activity by having a pretend emergency in which one child calls 911 (on a play telephone, or at least one not in service) and tells what is happening, then tries to follow the instructions given by the "911 operator" (a staff member).

Summary/Transition Activity

End the activity by recombining into one group and doing the following fingerplay. Start at five monkeys jumping and repeat until there is one monkey jumping.

"Five little monkeys jumping on the bed,

One fell off and hurt his head.

Mama called the doctor and the doctor said,

No more monkeys jumping on the bed!"

Thursday

Dramatic Play	Art	Group	Story	Song
Space Station	Glitter Space Pictures	Letter *X*	*Big Silver Space Shuttle*	"Twinkle, Twinkle, Little Star"

DAILY PLANNING GUIDE

Language and Literacy Skills Facilitated

Vocabulary: *space, rocket ship, planet, gravity, adventure, spacesuit, astronaut, orbit, sun, moon, stars, blast off, oxygen*

Verb phrase structures: *counted down, are counting, traveling in space, saw stars, blasting off, packed food, using oxygen*

Adjective/object descriptions: *bright stars, fast ship, big planet, weird colors, little stars, black hole*

Question structures: *what, how, where, when, who, what if, why, how many, which one*

Pronouns: *I, you, he, she, we, they, my, your, him, her, his, our, their, me, us, them*

Prepositions: *in, on, under, over, near, beneath, next to, beside, around, inside, outside*

Sounds: /r/ *rocket, star;* /s/ *space, sun, face;* /l/ *light, Jell-o, bell;* /k/ *can, rocket, lock*

Noting print has meaning: names on chairs and on cubbies, signs in dramatic play, words in books and on chalkboard

Noting sound–symbol associations: What sound does _____ start with?

Writing: letters, names, words

Social Skills Facilitated

Initiating interaction with peers and adults; responding to questions and requests from peers and adults

Negotiating with peers for toys and materials

Group cooperation: waiting for a turn in a group, taking a turn at the appropriate time

Cognitive Skills Facilitated

Problem-solving skills: how to get up in space

Classification skills: What things are in outer space?

Sequencing skills: countdown, story, songs

Narrative/story structure: adventure/labeling

Motor Skills Facilitated

Large motor: outdoor play activities—jumping, running, hopping, pedaling, climbing

Small motor: writing, drawing, gluing

DRAMATIC PLAY : **Space Station**

Type of Activity: Central

Objectives
1. Learn new, and employ familiar, vocabulary
2. Learn new, and employ a variety of, syntactic constructions
3. Interact with peers
4. Sequence familiar routines
5. Expand conceptual knowledge of the world

Setting
- Rocket ship
- Moon area
- Space station
- Command central

Props
- Rocket ship
- Space suits and helmets
- Moon area (trampoline to represent walking with less gravity)
- Command area with computer and other equipment (walkie-talkies)
- Cooking and sleeping areas for space station

Roles
- Astronauts
- Control tower personnel
- Engineer/repair personnel

General Description of Activity

The children participate in a variety of space exploration activities, such as riding in a spaceship, living on a space station, landing on the moon, doing a variety of experiments, and repairing the space ship.

Verbal Productions

Level of linguistic complexity varies with the role or competency of the child playing the role.
- "I am the astronaut that drives the rocket" or "Astronaut"
- "I am walking on the moon" or "Moon"
- "It is my turn to be the engineer" or "My turn"

Adult Facilitative Role

The adult is to facilitate role play and help expand language and literacy skills. Typical actions or strategies to use include

Playing a role: "I am an astronaut. I am going to the space station."

Modeling a statement/vocabulary: "A space station is a big man-made house that is in space. The astronauts can live there, but they have to use a rocket ship to go there and also when they come back to earth."

Modeling the reading of a sign: "The sign says *space station*."

Expanding a child's utterance: "Space walk too" to "I am going on the space walk, too. We must wear a space suit."

Identifying rhyming words: "The words *space, race, face*, and *case* all rhyme."

ART **Glitter Space Pictures**

Objectives
1. Express creativity
2. Develop small motor skills (e.g., drawing, painting, cutting, pasting)
3. Practice turn-taking skills
4. To converse with peers and adults

Materials
- Black construction paper
- Variety of colors of glitter paint (glitter paint can be purchased or made by adding glitter to tempera paint)
- Self-stick stars, gold or silver (optional)

General Description of Activity

Give the children a piece of black (or other dark-colored) construction paper. The children paint a variety of pictures on the paper using glitter paint. They can paint planets, rocket ships, or stars on their paper. Silver or gold self-stick stars may be added to the pictures.

GROUP **Letter X**

Objectives
1. Improve listening skills
2. Increase knowledge of the alphabet and sounds
3. Learn appropriate group-interaction skills
4. Practice turn-taking

Materials
- Alphabet chart and other alphabet displays
- Blackboard and chalk or poster paper and markers
- Pictures of objects (or objects themselves) with names that begin with X
- Picture dictionary (or an alphabet video dictionary)

General Description of Activity

Write an upper- and a lowercase letter X on the blackboard (or on poster paper). Give several examples of words that begin with X, emphasizing the "eks" sound at the beginning of the words. Tell children that sometimes the letter X makes a "zzzz" sound. You might hold up pictures of objects (or objects themselves) with names that begin with X. Direct the children's attention to the alphabet picture displays around the room.

Group Participation

Ask if anyone's name starts with X (e.g., Xavier), and have those children write the letter X on the blackboard (or poster paper). Also have two or three other children write the letter X on the blackboard. Provide verbal guidance as children form the letter: "Draw a line slanted to the right. Go back to the top and draw a line slanted to the left." If necessary, help children write the letter. Some of the other children can practice writing X in the air with their fingers (or on individual chalkboards). Ask the children to think of words that begin with X. Write the words they suggest on the blackboard, drawing quick sketches (when possible) of the suggested words. If a child suggests a word that does not begin with X, say, "No, that begins with ____," and say the different sounds so children can compare. To help children who cannot think of any words, prompt them with pictures or objects representing X words. (Pictures or objects can be handed out at the beginning of the lesson or as the lesson proceeds.) Additional words can be sought in a picture dictionary if the group has difficulty arriving at words that begin with X.

Summary/Transition Activity

After about 10–15 words have been suggested, review the words, emphasizing the X sounds.

February

MONTHLY PLANNING GUIDE

Activities	Monday	Tuesday	Wednesday	Thursday
Week 25 Occupations				
Dramatic Play	Mechanic	Doctor	Construction Worker	Teacher
Art	Vehicles of Different Shapes	Doctor's Kit Collage	Cornstarch and Water (Goop)	Easel Painting
Group	Review Shapes	Number 7	Color Purple	Letter Y
Story	*What's Under Your Hood, Orson?*	*Germs Make Me Sick*	*Building a House*	*Chicka Chicka Boom Boom*
Song	"The Wheels on the Bus"	"Baby Bear's Chicken Pox"	"Johnny Works with One Hammer"	"The Alphabet Song"
Week 26 Friendship/Valentine's Day				
Dramatic Play	Pretend Birthday Party	Amusement Park	Pizza Parlor	Post Office
Art	Drawing Friends	Fingerpainting	Valentine Bags	Valentine Cards for Parents
Group	Color Patterns	Act out a Story (*Hiccups For Elephant*)	Counting and Writing Numbers 1–5	Letter Z
Story	*The Jolly Postman*	*Hiccups For Elephant*	*Will You Be My Valentine?*	*A Letter to Amy*
Song	"Mary Wore Her Red Dress"	"Mickey Mouse Club"	"I Wish I Were a Pepperoni Pizza"	"Name Game Song"
Week 27 Weekend Chores				
Dramatic Play	Washing the Car	Babysitting	Grocery Shopping	House Cleaning
Art	Vehicle Rubbings	Faces	Vegetable Prints	Chalk Pictures with Liquid Starch
Group	Many/Few	Act out a Story (*Little Tiger's Big Surprise*)	Focus on Vowels	Recycling
Story	*Cars! Cars! Cars!*	*Little Tiger's Big Surprise*	*Don't Forget the Oatmeal!*	*The Relatives Came*
Song	"Twinkle, Twinkle, Traffic Light"	"Rock-a-Bye Baby"	"I Like to Eat Apples and Bananas"	"This Is the Way We Wash Our Clothes"
Week 28 Exploring				
Dramatic Play	Archaeology/Paleontology	Under the Sea	Science Investigations	Space
Art	Dinosaur Mural	Aquariums	Gak	Clothespin Creations
Group	Pattern Sequencing—Dinosaur Footprints	Sorting Shells	Identifying *A, B,* and *C*	Things that Fly
Story	*Dinosaur Roar!*	*What's Under the Ocean?*	*The Mystery of Magnets*	*Ten Black Dots*
Song	"Five Crazy Dinosaurs" (fingerplay)	"All the Little Fishies"	"Raindrops and Lemondrops"	"The Rocket Song"

	Dramatic Play	Art	Group	Story	Song
Monday *Suggested Props and Materials*	Mechanic *Mechanic scenario: pretend car with dashboard, hood, battery, pistons (could use LEGOs or other manipulatives to make engines, Bristle Blocks and pipe cleaners to make sparkplugs, etc.); variety of tools; gas pump; riding cars; road; take-apart cars (optional)*	Vehicles of Different Shapes *Paper shapes to make the car body, wheels, etc.; markers*	Review Shapes *Variety of shapes in different sizes, whiteboard marker, individual slate boards and chalk (optional)*	*What's Under Your Hood, Orson?*	"The Wheels on the Bus"
Tuesday *Suggested Props and Materials*	Doctor *Doctor scenario, table with a telephone and appointment book, several tables or mats for examination rooms, doctor kits, X-ray area (black paper and chalk), waiting area with magazines*	Doctor's Kit Collage *Black construction paper, glue or paste, Q-tips, tongue depressors, cotton balls, cutouts in shape of bottles, stethoscope (yarn)*	Number 7 *Cards with the number 7, chalkboards and chalk, paper and pencils (optional)*	*Germs Make Me Sick*	"Baby Bear's Chicken Pox"
Wednesday *Suggested Props and Materials*	Construction Worker *Construction scenario, cardboard boxes for houses, hole puncher, clothespin pegs (nails), hammers, saws, screwdrivers and other tools, paint-brushes, tape, hard hats, etc.*	Cornstarch and Water (Goop) *One to two boxes of cornstarch, 2–2½ cups of water per box*	Color Purple *Purple construction paper mats; other colored construction paper; variety of purple objects; variety of red, yellow, blue, orange objects*	*Building a House*	"Johnny Works with One Hammer"
Thursday *Suggested Props and Materials*	Teacher *Teacher scenario, alphabet cards, paper and pencils, books, flannel board and flannel board stories, puzzles, circle area, table area, manipulative area, pretend bus*	Easel Painting *Easels, tempera paint, paint cups, brushes, smocks*	Letter Y *Alphabet chart, blackboard and chalk, pictures of objects (or objects themselves) with names that begin with Y, picture dictionary*	*Chicka Chicka Boom Boom*	"The Alphabet Song"

NEWSLETTER

Vol. 1, No. 25

Date: _____

Occupations

Monday Today is all about cars. The children will be at the mechanic, fixing cars, putting gas in the cars, taking customers' money at the cash register, and changing tires. They will make vehicles out of shapes in art. *What's Under Your Hood, Orson?* is the story of the day. During group time, we will review the names of different shapes (squares, circle, triangles, and rectangles). Music will include the song "The Wheels on the Bus."

Tuesday The doctor is today's dramatic play theme. The children will take care of people who are sick or injured. The art activity will be making a doctor's kit collage. *Germs Make Me Sick* will be read at storytime. During group time, we will focus on the number 7. In music, the children will sing "Baby Bear's Chicken Pox."

Wednesday The children will spend their day working at a construction site. In dramatic play, they will use hammers, saws, and other tools to experience what it is like to be a builder. Art time will focus on making cornstarch and water constructions (goop). *Building a House* is the story for the day. During group time, we will talk about colors, with a focus on purple. Please have your child wear something purple today. "Johnny Works with One Hammer" will be our special music activity.

Thursday Today the children will play teacher. The children may be teachers, students, or bus drivers during dramatic play. In art, the children will do easel paintings. Today's story is *Chicka Chicka Boom Boom*. During group time, the children will focus on the letter Y. Our featured song is "The Alphabet Song."

Monday

Dramatic Play	Art	Group	Story	Song
Mechanic	Vehicles of Different Shapes	Review Shapes	*What's Under Your Hood, Orson?*	"The Wheels on the Bus"

DAILY PLANNING GUIDE

Language and Literacy Skills Facilitated

Vocabulary: *transportation, vehicle, car, track, garage, mechanic, truck, finish, battery, brakes, ignition, hose, tools, engine, wheels, shapes, rectangle, square, circle, triangle*

Verb phrase structures: *work<u>s</u>, is work<u>ing</u>, crash<u>ed</u> the car, push<u>ed</u> it, was racing, starts, stopp<u>ed</u>, fix<u>ed</u> the car*

Adjective/object descriptions: *broken part, dead battery, big/little*

Question structures: *what, how, where, when, who, what if, why, how many, which one*

Pronouns: *I, you, he, she, we, they, my, your, him, her, his, our, their, me, us, them*

Prepositions: *in, on, under, over, near, beneath, next to, beside, around, inside, outside*

Sounds: /r/ <u>r</u>ace, star<u>ter</u>, <u>car</u>; /s/ <u>s</u>ee, mi<u>ss</u>es, mi<u>ss</u>; /sh/ <u>sh</u>ape, fini<u>sh</u>, blends: <u>fl</u>ag, <u>tr</u>uck, <u>st</u>art

Noting print has meaning: names on chairs and on cubbies, signs in dramatic play, words in books and on chalkboard

Noting sound–symbol associations: What sound does _____ start with?

Writing: letters, names, words

Social Skills Facilitated

Initiating interaction with peers and adults; responding to questions and requests from peers and adults

Negotiating with peers for toys and materials

Group cooperation: waiting for a turn in a group, taking a turn at the appropriate time

Cognitive Skills Facilitated

Problem-solving skills: how to fix the cars

Classification skills: tools to use in fixing cars

Sequencing skills: song, art

Narrative/story structure: adventure

Motor Skills Facilitated

Large motor: outdoor play activities—jumping, running, hopping, pedaling, climbing

Small motor: writing, drawing, gluing

DRAMATIC PLAY **Mechanic**

Type of Activity: Central

Objectives
1. Learn new, and employ, familiar vocabulary
2. Learn new, and employ a variety of, syntactic constructions
3. Interact with peers
4. Sequence familiar routines
5. Expand conceptual knowledge of the world

Settings
- Garage/repair shop
- Desk
- Cashier's station
- Gas pumps
- Car lift (cardboard blocks holding a plastic truck high enough for a child to slide under)
- Parts counter or store (optional)

Props
- Appointment book and pencil or crayon
- Toy cash register
- Pretend money
- Hoses for pumps
- Car with hood, which can be made out of cardboard
- Dashboard

- Tools
- Pretend battery
- Pretend computer
- Pretend cans for oil change
- Play telephones
- Pretend parts to sell (optional)

Roles
- Mechanics
- Customers
- Receptionist

- Sales clerk
- Cashier

General Description of Activity

Children take their vehicles to a gas station or garage to be repaired, filled up with gas, or tuned up. The oil in the car may need to be changed or the battery recharged. Customers can call ahead and make appointments. In one area, a receptionist/cashier desk is arranged. Another area might have a wooden or cardboard facsimile of a car with a hood that opens so that the mechanics can work under the hood if needed. Also, blocks or a vehicle Erector Set may be placed in one area to build cars. An optional activity is to have a parts counter or store.

Verbal Productions

Level of linguistic complexity varies with the role or competency of the child playing the role.
- "May I please have the wrench?" or "Wrench, please"
- "Please start the car now" or "Start"
- "My car needs a new battery" or "Battery"

Adult Facilitative Role

The adult is to facilitate role play and help expand language and literacy skills. Typical actions or strategies to use include

Playing a role: "I think you have brake problems. I will have to fix your brakes."

Modeling the reading of a sign: "That sign says *pay here*."

Modeling correct production of the /l/ sound: "<u>L</u>ook, you wi<u>ll</u> like this <u>l</u>ittle car."

Modeling a focus contrast (size): "That is the little screw. Here is the big screw."

Modeling a structure (regular past tense): "I fixed that car. I used the big screw."

ART : **Vehicles of Different Shapes**

Objectives
1. Express creativity
2. Develop small motor skills (e.g., drawing, painting, cutting, pasting)
3. Practice turn-taking skills
4. Converse with peers and adults

Materials
- Glue sticks
- White construction paper
- Large and small colored construction paper cutouts: circles, squares, triangles, and rectangles

General Description of Activity

Have children glue the shapes onto white paper in the form of a truck or other vehicle.

GROUP **Review Shapes**

Objectives
1. Improve listening skills
2. Increase sequencing ability
3. Learn appropriate group-interaction skills
4. Practice turn-taking skills

Materials
- Colored tape to make shape outlines
- Variety of shapes out of construction paper
- Small chalkboards and chalk

General Description of Activity

From previous activities, circle, square, triangle, rectangle, and diamond shapes should already be taped on the floor. Point to the different outlines on the floor and label each one (e.g., circle, square, triangle, rectangle, diamond). Ask a child to name his or her favorite shape. Stand in the outlined area of the shape named (e.g., if the child chooses the circle, stand in the circle area).

Group Participation

Ask different children to stand on a particular shape. Vary the difficulty of the requests by asking some children to find only the shape and others to find a shape of a particular size (large or small). Color can be included in the requests as well if tape of different colors was used to make the outlines (e.g., "Find the big red square"). The task can be made more challenging by having children place a hand in one shape area and a foot in another. It may be necessary to have children do this activity in smaller groups.

Variation

Give children individual whiteboards (or chalkboards) and ask them to draw the various shapes. You might also give children cutout shapes and ask them to place them inside the matching shapes on the floor.

Summary/Transition Activity

Review the shape labels by pointing to or standing in the outlined area as you identify them.

Note

Prior to this activity, children should have had lessons on circles, squares, triangles, rectangles, and diamonds.

Tuesday

Dramatic Play	Art	Group	Story	Song
Doctor	Doctor's Kit Collage	Number 7	*Germs Make Me Sick*	"Baby Bear's Chicken Pox"

DAILY PLANNING GUIDE

Language and Literacy Skills Facilitated

Vocabulary: *doctor, nurse, paramedic, ambulance, stethoscope, thermometer, fever, cast, X-ray, oxygen, accident, vehicle, arm, leg, ankle, bandage, forehead, hospital*

Verb phrase structures: <u>is</u> carry<u>ing</u> the stretcher, drove the ambulance, rides, examines, gave oxygen, sets the leg, listens to my heart, gave medicine

Adjective/object descriptions: *broken leg, big ambulance, loud siren*

Question structures: *what, how, where, when, who, what if, why, how many, which one*

Pronouns: *I, you, he, she, we, they, my, your, him, her, his, our, their, me, us, them*

Prepositions: *in, on, under, over, near, beneath, next to, beside, around, inside, outside*

Sounds: /k/ <u>c</u>arry, do<u>c</u>tor, bro<u>ke</u>; /s/ <u>s</u>et, in<u>s</u>ide, u<u>s</u>, ambulan<u>ce</u>

Noting print has meaning: names on chairs and on cubbies, signs in dramatic play, words in books and on chalkboard

Noting sound–symbol associations: What sound does _____ start with?

Writing: letters, names, words

Social Skills Facilitated

Initiating interaction with peers and adults; responding to questions and requests from peers and adults

Negotiating with peers for toys and materials

Group cooperation: waiting for a turn in a group, taking a turn at the appropriate time

Cognitive Skills Facilitated

Problem-solving skills: What does a doctor do?

Classification skills: things in a doctor's office, body parts

Sequencing skills: story, songs

Narrative/story structure: labeling

Motor Skills Facilitated

Large motor: outdoor play activities—jumping, running, hopping, pedaling, climbing

Small motor: writing, drawing, gluing, cutting

DRAMATIC PLAY **Doctor**

Type of Activity: Central

Objectives
1. Learn new, and employ familiar, vocabulary
2. Learn new, and employ a variety of, syntactic constructions
3. Interact with peers
4. Sequence familiar routines
5. Expand conceptual knowledge of the world

Settings
- Several examination rooms
- Waiting room
- Patients' "homes"

Props
- Table with a telephone and appointment book
- Several tables or mats to represent examination rooms
- Doctor kits
- Bandages
- X-ray machine
- Telephone in area representing patients' "homes"

Roles
- Doctor
- Nurse
- Receptionist
- Patient
- Parent

General Description of Activity

A doctor's office with several examination rooms and a waiting room is set up. Children who are patients call the receptionist and make an appointment. When it is time for their appointment, they go into the examination room. A nurse might take their temperature and their weight and ask what is wrong with them. Then the doctor examines the patients by looking into the mouth, ears, and eyes; checking reflexes; checking muscle tone; listening with the stethoscope; and so forth. A patient might have a broken bone that needs to be X-rayed, set in a cast, and wrapped with a bandage.

Verbal Productions

Level of linguistic complexity varies with the role or competency of the child playing the role.
- "Open your mouth, please" or "Open mouth"
- "Where does it hurt?" or "Hurt?"
- "I don't feel good. My tummy hurts" or "I'm sick"

Adult Facilitative Role

The adult is to facilitate role play and help expand language and literacy skills. Typical actions or strategies to use include

Playing a role: "I will take your temperature. Then I will listen to your heart."

Event casting a child's actions: "You are getting out the stethoscope. Now you are listening to the baby's heartbeat. Now you are giving the baby a shot."

Expanding a child's utterance and providing corrective feedback: "Him hurt" to "He is hurt. He needs a Band-Aid."

Modeling the reading and writing of words: "That says *appointment*. You can make an appointment for Sally."

Redirecting a child to a peer: "Ask Jim for a turn. Say, 'Can I use the stethoscope, please?'"

ART **Doctor's Kit Collage**

Objectives
1. Express creativity
2. Develop small motor skills (e.g., drawing, painting, cutting, pasting)
3. Practice turn-taking skills
4. Converse with peers and adults

Materials
- Glue or paste
- Black construction paper
- Cotton swabs
- Tongue depressors
- Cotton balls
- Bottles—shaped paper cutouts
- "Stethoscope" (yarn)

General Description of Activity

On half of a piece of black construction paper, children paste different medical items, such as cotton swabs, tongue depressors, and cotton balls. They fold the paper in half (with the collage on the inside) to make the doctor's kit. An adult can staple strips of black construction paper onto the bag for handles.

Variation

The black construction-paper cutouts could be cut with the handles included so that they resemble bags.

GROUP **Number 7**

Objectives
1. Improve listening skills
2. Increase conceptual knowledge
3. Learn appropriate group-interaction skills
4. Practice turn-taking skills
5. Practice recognition and writing of numbers

Materials
- Number cards
- Chalkboards and chalk
- Paper and pencils (optional)
- Whiteboard and markers

General Description of Activity

Hold up a card with the number 7 on it. Trace the number with your finger, and invite several children to come to the front of the group to trace the number, too. As they trace, recite the jingle for the target number (7):

1: Start at the top, go down and you're done, that's the way to make a *1*.

2: Around and back on the railroad track, *2, 2, 2*.

3: Around the tree, around the tree, that's the way to make a *3*.

4: Down and over and down once more, that's the way to make a *4*.

5: Down around, make a hat on it, and look what you've found (*5*).

6: Down around until it sticks, that's the way to make a *6*.

7: Over and down and it's not heaven, over and down makes a *7*.

8: Make an S and go back straight, that's the way to make an *8*.

9: A balloon and a line make *9*.

10. Draw a line and a circle with your pen, that's the way to make a *10*.

Group Participation

Distribute individual chalkboards and chalk (or paper and pencils) to the children, and have them practice writing the target number(s).

Variation

Whiteboards and markers may easier for some children to use.

Summary/Transition Activity

Have the children hold up their chalkboards and show one another their numbers.

Wednesday

Dramatic Play	Art	Group	Story	Song
Construction Worker	Cornstarch and Water (Goop)	Color Purple	*Building a House*	"Johnny Works with One Hammer"

DAILY PLANNING GUIDE

Language and Literacy Skills Facilitated

Vocabulary: *construction, build, building, hammer, nail, fix, make, work, hardhat, safety, paint, shingle, roof, saw, screw, screwdrivers*

Verb phrase structures: *is build*<u>*ing*</u>*, construct*<u>*ed*</u>*,* <u>*built*</u>*, hammer*<u>*ed*</u>*, Who* <u>*is*</u> *building? I* <u>*am*</u>*, mak*<u>*es*</u>*, carri*<u>*es*</u>

Adjective/object descriptions: *large/small ____, heavy/light ____, hard/soft material*

Question structures: *what, how, where, when, who, what if, why, how many, which one*

Pronouns: *I, you, he, she, we, they, my, your, him, her, his, our, their, me, us, them*

Prepositions: *in, on, under, over, near, beneath, next to, beside, around, inside, outside*

Sounds: /f/ <u>*f*</u>*ix,* <u>*f*</u>*un, of*<u>*f*</u>*;* /s/ <u>*s*</u>*ize, walk*<u>*s*</u>*;* /k/ <u>*c*</u>*onstruct,* <u>*c*</u>*an, ma*<u>*k*</u>*e*

Noting print has meaning: names on chairs and on cubbies, signs in dramatic play, words in books and on chalkboard

Noting sound–symbol associations: What sound does _____ start with?

Writing: letters, names, words

Social Skills Facilitated

Initiating interaction with peers and adults; responding to questions and requests from peers and adults

Negotiating with peers for toys and materials

Group cooperation: waiting for a turn in a group, taking a turn at the appropriate time

Cognitive Skills Facilitated

Problem-solving skills: how to make a building

Classification skills: tools for constructing things

Sequencing skills: songs, steps in building, stories

Narrative/story structure: labeling

Motor Skills Facilitated

Large motor: outdoor play activities—jumping, running, hopping, pedaling, climbing

Small motor: writing, drawing, gluing, pounding

DRAMATIC PLAY **Construction Worker**

Type of Activity: Related

Objectives
1. Learn new, and employ familiar, vocabulary
2. Learn new, and employ a variety of, syntactic constructions
3. Interact with peers
4. Sequence familiar routines
5. Expand conceptual knowledge of the world

Settings
- Street (floor area marked with masking tape) lined with houses made from a variety of materials (e.g., blocks, cardboard)

Props
- Playhouse
- Cardboard box additions that can be taped to the playhouse
- LEGOs
- Blocks
- Play bricks
- Paper strips of various colors for roof or siding
- Glue

- Tools (e.g., plastic hammers, wrenches, saws, screwdrivers, screws)
- Tool belts
- Pegs for pounding (wooden clothespins that can be pounded into cardboard)
- Play hardhats
- Masking tape
- Telephones

Roles
- Carpenters
- Architects

- Homeowners
- Other construction workers

General Description of Activity

Children participate in a construction/repair dramatic play involving putting together different materials to make buildings. A variety of materials can be used. One area can be set up for constructing buildings with LEGOs or other blocks. Another area can be designated for a new addition to the playhouse (using big boxes). A third area can utilize play bricks and boxes to make another house. The children can problem-solve how to construct houses or apartments by rearranging the boxes, bricks, and blocks. (Some of the houses could be doll-size; others could be big enough for the children to play in).

Houses may also need to be repaired. Children can replace a roof by making "shingles" out of paper bag strips. The strips could be laid on top of cardboard. (You might suggest that children start at the outer edge and overlay the shingles so "rain" will roll off the roof and not under the shingles.) The children can put new siding on a house by using strips of colored paper and glue, and they could even put up wallpaper on the inside of a house.

Verbal Productions

Level of linguistic complexity varies with the role or competency of the child playing the role.
- "I'm building a big house" or "Me build house"
- "We need to make that side higher. Call the carpenter" or "Higher"
- "Look, I pounded the nail into the wall" or "Look"

Adult Facilitative Role

The adult is to facilitate role play and help expand language and literacy skills. Typical actions or strategies to use include

Playing a role: "I am going to paint the wall. It is going to be pretty when I am finished."

Contrasting two sounds: "Did you says 'tall' or 'call?'"

Asking an open question: "How do we make a window?"

Recasting a child's utterance (past progressive to past tense): "He was working on the house" to "Yes, he worked on the house for a long time."

Contrasting location terms: "The paint can is in font of the door, and the paint brush is behind the door."

ART : **Cornstarch and Water (Goop)**

Objectives
1. Express creativity
2. Develop small motor skills (e.g., drawing, painting, cutting, pasting)
3. Practice turn-taking skills
4. Converse with peers and adults

Materials

- Smocks
- Water (2–2½ cups per box of cornstarch)
- Cornstarch (one or two boxes)
- Containers or tubs
- Spoons

General Description of Activity

Provide several containers of a cornstarch and water mixture for children to experiment with. Containers should be big enough for two hands, and it is more fun for children and facilitates more language if the containers accommodate at least four hands. This mixture is very interesting in that it feels hard in the container and children can make a ball of it in their fist, but as it sits in their hand it melts and drips out. This is experimentation. (The mixture washes off from hands quite easily.)

GROUP **Color Purple**

Objectives

1. Improve listening skills
2. Increase conceptual knowledge
3. Learn appropriate group-interaction skills
4. Practice turn-taking skills

Materials

- Red, blue, yellow, orange, and purple construction paper, one sheet of each (use as mats)
- Several purple objects
- Two yellow objects
- Two blue objects
- Two red objects
- Two orange objects

General Description of Activity

On the first Thursday of February, gather an assortment of red, blue, yellow, and purple objects. At group time, hold up a purple piece of construction paper and label the color as purple. Remind the children that purple is a combination of blue and red. Ask the children to look around the room to locate other purple objects. Have one child choose an object that is purple from the pile of assorted objects and place it on the purple paper (have red, blue, yellow, and orange paper mats also available).

Group Participation

Have other children take turns choosing an item that is purple and placing it on the purple paper mat. Occasionally, ask a child to find an item of a different color and place it on the mat of that color.

Variation

Some of the children may choose from different shades of the target color (e.g., choosing light purple or deep purple or from different shades of the other colors).

Summary/Transition Activity

Because it is "purple" day and all the children are wearing something purple, dismiss the children one by one by asking them to point to the purple color on their clothes.

Thursday

Dramatic Play	Art	Group	Story	Song
Teacher	Easel Painting	Letter Y	*Chicka Chicka Boom Boom*	"The Alphabet Song"

DAILY PLANNING GUIDE

Language and Literacy Skills Facilitated

Vocabulary: *school, bus, pencil, pen, paper, flashlight, check-in, alphabet, sounds, cubes, shapes, numbers, paint*

Verb phrase structures: *is writing, reads the book, says the alphabet, goes to check-in, drove the bus, painted a picture*

Adjective/object descriptions: *red, blue ____, big ____, little ____, pretty ____, dirty ____, fancy ____, nice ____, unusual ____*

Question structures: *what, how, where, when, who, what if, why, how many, which one*

Pronouns: *I, you, he, she, we, they, my, your, him, her, his, our, their, me, us, them*

Prepositions: *in, on, under, over, near, beneath, next to, beside, around, inside, outside*

Sounds: */s/ say, pencil, bus; /k/ car, check-in, look; /l/ look, flashlight, pencil, school*

Noting print has meaning: names on chairs and on cubbies, signs in dramatic play, words in books and on chalkboard

Noting sound–symbol associations: What sound does ____ start with?

Writing: letters, names, words

Social Skills Facilitated

Initiating interaction with peers and adults; responding to questions and requests from peers and adults

Negotiating with peers for toys and materials

Group cooperation: waiting for a turn in a group, taking a turn at the appropriate time

Cognitive Skills Facilitated

Problem-solving skills: what words start with *Y*, how to make a *Y*

Classification skills: objects that do and do not begin with *Y*

Sequencing skills: songs, stories

Narrative/story structure: labeling and rhyming

Motor Skills Facilitated

Large motor: outdoor play activities—jumping, running, hopping, pedaling, climbing

Small motor: writing, drawing, gluing, cutting

DRAMATIC PLAY **Teacher**

Type of Activity: Related

Objectives
1. Learn new, and employ familiar, vocabulary
2. Learn new, and employ a variety of, syntactic constructions
3. Interact with peers
4. Sequence familiar routines
5. Expand conceptual knowledge of the world

Settings
- School area (circle outlined on floor with masking tape)
- Bus (playhouse with cardboard door that opens and closes and a box and dashboard in front to make the cab)
- Art area
- Quiet area (books and puzzles)

Props
- Name cards
- Alphabet cards
- Flannel board and flannel board stories
- Books
- Small blackboard
- Paper and pencils
- Art materials
- Flashlight (to use for check-in)

Roles
- Bus driver
- Children
- Teacher
- Staff members
- Principal
- School nurse
- Custodian
- Parents

General Description of Activity

Set up the school area in imitation of the classroom. Including name cards, alphabet cards, flannel board stories, books, writing materials, and so forth. Also have a school bus. The children can board the bus, be driven to school, disembark, be checked in (the children who are playing the roles of staff check the "children's" throats to see if they are too sick to be in school), and then play the roles of teachers, staff, and children. When school is over, they can return home by riding on the bus again.

Verbal Productions

Level of linguistic complexity varies with the role or competency of the child playing the role
- "He wrote his name on the paper" or "Write name"
- "I am the bus driver. You need to sit down" or "Sit down"
- "I want to drive the bus. He has driven it for a long time" or "Drive bus"
- "What does this letter say?" or "What say?"

Adult Facilitative Role

The adult is to facilitate role play and help expand language and literacy skills. Typical actions or strategies to use include

Playing a role: "Children, please sit in a circle. It is time for the story."

Modeling the reading of words: "The title of the story is *The Little Red Hen*. That word is *little* and that word is *red*."

Redirecting a child to a peer: "Ask Jacob where the ABC puzzle is. Say, 'Do you know where the ABC puzzle is?'"

Identifying rhyming words: "You're right. The words *more, floor, door*, and *tore* all rhyme."

Using a cloze procedure: "Here is one pencil. Here are five _____" (pencils).

ART **Easel Painting**

Objectives
1. Express creativity
2. Develop small motor skills (e.g., drawing, painting, cutting, pasting)
3. Practice turn-taking skills
4. Converse with peers and adults

Materials
- Smocks
- Easels
- Different colors of tempera paint
- Cups to hold the paint
- Large paint brushes
- 9" × 12" or 12" × 18" paper
- Wooden rack or other area for drying

General Description of Activity

Set up two easel boards with a large piece of paper clipped to each. Set out two to four cups filled with tempera paint and a paintbrush in each cup. (It is helpful to have cup covers with holes in them for the brushes. As children dip the brushes into the paint and pull them through the hole, some of the excess paint is removed. It is also helpful to place the easel over plastic or newspaper so that the paint drips do not stain the floor.)

Children put on their smocks, dip the brush into the paint, and paint shapes, objects, or anything else they want. Sometimes children will paint a picture and then experiment by painting other colors on top. Let the children experiment with the tempera for some projects. Sometimes you might have the children tell you about their painting, and you can label it for display. (Let the children decide if they want their paintings displayed.) Have a designated area for drying the pictures, such as a wooden clothes rack.

GROUP **Letter *Y***

Objectives
1. Improve listening skills
2. Increase knowledge of the alphabet and sounds
3. Learn appropriate group-interaction skills
4. Practice turn-taking skills

Materials
- Alphabet chart and other alphabet displays
- Blackboard and chalk or poster paper and markers
- Pictures of objects (or objects themselves) with names that begin with *Y*
- Picture dictionary (or an alphabet video dictionary)

General Description of Activity

Write an upper- and lowercase letter *Y* on the blackboard (or on poster paper). Give several examples of words that begin with *Y*, emphasizing the /y/ sound at the beginning of the words. You might hold up pictures of objects (or objects themselves) with names that begin with *Y*. Direct the children's attention to the alphabet picture displays around the room.

Group Participation

Ask if anyone's name starts with *Y* (e.g., Yolanda, Ying). Have those children write the letter *Y* on the blackboard (or poster paper). Also have two or three other children write the letter *Y* on the blackboard. Provide verbal guidance as children form the letter: "Start at the top and draw a little slant to the right. Start at the top again and draw another little slant to the left until the slants make a point. Draw a line down from the point." If necessary, help children write the letter. Some of the other children can practice writing *Y* in the air with their fingers (or on individual chalkboards). Ask the children to think of words that begin with *Y*. Write the words they offer on the blackboard, drawing quick sketches (when possible) of the suggested words. If a child suggests a word that does not begin with *Y*, say, "No, that begins with ___," and say both sounds so children can compare them. To help children who cannot think of any words, prompt them with pictures or objects representing *Y* words. (Pictures or objects can be handed out at the beginning of the lesson or as the lesson proceeds.) Additional words can be sought in a picture dictionary if the group has difficulty arriving at words that begin with *Y*.

Summary/Transition Activity

After about 10–15 words have been suggested, review the words, emphasizing the /y/ sound.

WEEKLY PLANNING GUIDE

	Dramatic Play	Art	Group	Story	Song
Monday *Suggested Props and Materials*	Pretend Birthday Party *Birthday party scenario, toys to be wrapped, pretend birthday cake and candles, Ring Toss, Pin the Tail on the Donkey game, Candy Land, other games, balloons and streamers*	Drawing Friends *Paper (white or colored), crayons, markers, watered-down tempera paint (optional)*	Color Patterns *1" colored cubes, mat, cardboard shield (optional)*	*The Jolly Postman*	"Mary Wore Her Red Dress"
Tuesday *Suggested Props and Materials*	Amusement Park *Amusement park scenario, clown bean bag toss, miniature trampoline, ball target, roller coaster, concession stand, cash register, tickets*	Fingerpainting *Fingerpaints, fingerpaint paper, smocks, glitter (optional)*	Act out a Story (*Hiccups for Elephant*) *Props for the story (e.g., water, spoon, banana, costumes [optional])*	*Hiccups for Elephant*	"Mickey Mouse Club"
Wednesday *Suggested Props and Materials*	Pizza Parlor *Pizza parlor scenario, restaurant and kitchen areas, menus, tableware and dishes, cash register, pretend pizza and toppings*	Valentine Bags *White bags, construction paper hearts of various sizes, doilies, glue*	Counting and Writing Numbers 1–5 *Index cards with 1, 2, 3, 4, and 5 written on them; counting items; whiteboard (or chalkboard); markers (or chalk)*	*Will You Be My Valentine?*	"I Wish I Were a Pepperoni Pizza"
Thursday *Suggested Props and Materials*	Post Office *Post office scenario, post office counter, envelopes, mailing "stamps," ink stamps and ink, scale, boxes, areas to sort mail, delivery bags, mailbox, home areas for delivery (optional)*	Valentine Cards for Parents *40 folded pink construction papers with 8 1/2" × 11" sheets of paper stapled inside to form a card; 50–60 construction paper valentines of various sizes; doilies; glue; card with words Happy Valentine's Day, Mom and Dad*	Letter *Z* *Pictures of objects (or objects themselves) with names that begin with Z, alphabet chart, blackboards and chalk, picture dictionary*	*A Letter to Amy*	"Name Game Song"

NEWSLETTER

Vol. 1, No. 26

Date: _____

Friendship/Valentine's Day

Monday
Today the children will hold a pretend birthday party during dramatic play. They will play party games, eat cake and ice cream, and wrap and give gifts. In art, the children will make drawings of their friends. Monday's story is *The Jolly Postman*. During group time, the children will learn to match color patterns. Our song is "Mary Wore Her Red Dress."

Tuesday
"Amusement park" is the theme today for dramatic play. The children will ride on exciting rides and pretend to buy and eat snack foods. At the art center, they will make fingerpaintings. The story is *Hiccups for Elephant*. During group time, the children will act out this story. The "Mickey Mouse Club" song will be a featured song during music.

Wednesday
The children will have fun with their friends today by pretending to go to a pizza parlor. Some of the children will work in the pizza parlor, and others will be the customers. During art time, children will make their Valentine bags. They will read *Will You Be My Valentine?* Group time will be learning about counting and writing numbers 1–5. "I Wish I Were a Pepperoni Pizza" will be a featured song.

Thursday
A post office will be the setup in dramatic play today. Important letters and valentines will be delivered by our post office workers. In art, the children will make valentines for their parents. The story is *A Letter to Amy*. The letter *Z* will be the focus of our group activity. During music, we will sing the "Name Game Song."

	Monday			
Dramatic Play	**Art**	**Group**	**Story**	**Song**
Pretend Birthday Party	Drawing Friends	Color Patterns	*The Jolly Postman*	"Mary Wore Her Red Dress"

DAILY PLANNING GUIDE

Language and Literacy Skills Facilitated

Vocabulary: *party, presents, birthday, cake, candles, wrapping paper, ribbons, games, pin the tail on the donkey*

Verb phrase structures: *open<u>s</u> a present, open<u>ed</u> a present, <u>is</u> open<u>ing</u>, like<u>s</u>/ like<u>d</u> the cake*

Adjective/object descriptions: *big/little present, pretty bow, white/chocolate cake, nice present*

Question structures: *what, how, where, when, who, what if, why, how many, which one*

Pronouns: *I, you, he, she, we, they, my, your, him, her, his, our, their, me, us, them*

Prepositions: *in, on, under, over, near, beneath, next to, beside, around, inside, outside*

Sounds: /f/ *fix, off;* /s/ *sit, talks;* /l/ *little, bell*

Noting print has meaning: names on chairs and on cubbies, signs in dramatic play, words in books and on chalkboard

Noting sound–symbol associations: What sound does _____ start with?

Writing: letters, names, words

Social Skills Facilitated

Initiating interaction with peers and adults; responding to questions and requests from peers and adults

Negotiating with peers for toys and materials

Group cooperation: waiting for a turn in a group, taking a turn at the appropriate time

Cognitive Skills Facilitated

Problem-solving skills: how to wrap a present, how to match or continue patterns

Classification skills: things that are the same color

Sequencing skills: story, songs

Narrative/story structure: adventure

Motor Skills Facilitated

Large motor: outdoor play activities—jumping, running, hopping, pedaling, climbing

Small motor: writing, drawing, gluing

DRAMATIC PLAY **Pretend Birthday Party**

Type of Activity: Central

Objectives
1. Learn new, and employ familiar, vocabulary
2. Learn new, and employ a variety of, syntactic constructions
3. Interact with peers
4. Sequence familiar routines
5. Expand conceptual knowledge of the world

Settings
- Housekeeping area set up with tables for gifts and food
- Several game areas

Props
- Variety of toys to be wrapped (children can wrap the toys over and over)
- Pretend birthday cake and candles (not to be lit)
- Ring Toss, Pin the Tail on the Donkey, Candy Land, or other games
- Balloons and streamers

Roles
- Birthday child
- Guests
- Parents
- Clown

General Description of Activity

One child is selected to be the birthday child. (The children can take turns). The dramatic play area may be decorated with streamers and/or balloons. The rest of the children bring birthday presents and play a variety of games. Some of the games could include Pin the Tail on the Donkey, Ring Toss, or Candy Land. There might be a cake or special treats for the guests, and a clown who entertains them. Encourage children to write names on pretend presents and read them.

Verbal Productions

Level of linguistic complexity varies with the role or competency of the child playing the role.
- "It's my birthday, and I am now 5 years old" or "It's my birthday"
- "Blow out all of the candles" or "Blow"
- "I want some more chocolate cake, please" or "Cake"

Adult Facilitative Role

The adult is to facilitate role play and help expand language and literacy skills. Typical actions or strategies to use include

Playing a role: "I like to go to birthday parties. I am bringing a present."

Providing a literacy model: "That card says *Alice*. The present is for her."

Expanding a child's utterance and providing corrective feedback: "Her want that toy" to "Yes, she wants that toy. It's new toy."

Modeling a statement/vocabulary: "There are four candles on the cake because Susie is 4 years old."

Modeling future tense: "Now she will blow out the candles."

ART : **Drawing Friends**

Objectives
1. Express creativity
2. Develop small motor skills (e.g., drawing, painting, cutting, pasting)
3. Practice turn-taking skills
4. Converse with peers and adults

Materials
- Paper (white or colored)
- Crayons
- Markers
- Watered-down tempera paint (optional)

General Description of Activity

Provide the children with paper and a selection of crayons and/or markers, and let them draw a picture of their friends. The teacher can encourage the children to draw pictures of their friends, but they can be allowed to draw other things. Children can turn their crayon drawings into crayon washes by painting over the pictures with a light coat of tempera paint (watered-down paint). The paint will not stick to the crayon but will fill in where there are no crayon marks to make a background of color.

GROUP **Color Patterns**

Objectives
1. Improve listening skills
2. Increase ability to recognize and sequence patterns on the basis of color
3. Learn appropriate group-interaction skills
4. Practice turn-taking skills

Materials
- 1" colored cubes
- Cardboard (optional)

General Description of Activity

Present a pattern of 1" colored cubes (e.g., red-yellow-red-yellow), and show the children how to continue the pattern by adding the appropriate blocks.

Variation

Have the children repeat the pattern by creating new rows of blocks that match your pattern (i.e., this becomes a matching activity).

Group Participation

On the floor, set out a block pattern appropriate for a particular child's level. Have the child come up (or have two children come together for peer support and help), and repeat or extend the pattern. Some children can repeat a simple pattern (e.g., *red-blue-red-blue*); others will be able to do more complicated patterns (e.g., *red-blue-blue, red-blue-blue* or *red-blue-green-green, red-blue-green-green*). Continue until all the children have had a turn.

Variation

For a greater challenge, make a pattern, cover it with a piece of cardboard, and have the child repeat the pattern from memory.

Summary/Transition Activity

Give each child a small pile of blocks to create a pattern. Children could then trade with a partner to see if they can copy each other's patterns. Collect the blocks and review colors.

Tuesday

Dramatic Play	Art	Group	Story	Song
Amusement Park	Fingerpainting	Act out a Story (*Hiccups for Elephant*)	*Hiccups for Elephant*	"Mickey Mouse Club"

DAILY PLANNING GUIDE

Language and Literacy Skills Facilitated

Vocabulary: *tickets, amusement park, hot dogs, hamburgers, Ring Toss, Mickey Mouse, Sit 'N Spin, merry-go-round, target*

Verb phrase structures: *rides/ is riding the Sit 'N Spin, rode the merry-go-round, spins around, eats/ is eating hot dogs, throws/threw the ball at the target, is buying/ bought tickets, draws/drew, writes/ wrote*

Adjective/object descriptions: *big ___, little ____, large ___, small ___, fast ___, slow ___, red ___, blue ____, yellow ___*

Question structures: *what, how, where, when, who, what if, why, how many, which one*

Pronouns: *I, you, he, she, we, they, my, your, him, her, his, our, their, me, us, them*

Prepositions: *in, on, under, over, near, beneath, next to, beside, around, inside, outside*

Sounds: */t/ ticket, target; /m/ mouse, merry-go-round*

Noting print has meaning: names on chairs and on cubbies, signs in dramatic play, words in books and on chalkboard

Noting sound–symbol associations: What sound does _____ start with?

Writing: letters, names, words

Social Skills Facilitated

Initiating interaction with peers and adults; responding to questions and requests from peers and adults

Negotiating with peers for toys and materials

Group cooperation: waiting for a turn in a group, taking a turn at the appropriate time

Cognitive Skills Facilitated

Problem-solving skills: how to act out the story

Classification skills: things in a amusement park

Sequencing skills: story, songs

Narrative/story structure: adventure

Motor Skills Facilitated

Large motor: outdoor play activities—jumping, running, hopping, pedaling, climbing

Small motor: writing, drawing, gluing, painting

DRAMATIC PLAY **Amusement Park**

Type of Activity: Central

Objectives
1. Learn new, and employ familiar, vocabulary
2. Learn new, and employ a variety of, syntactic constructions
3. Interact with peers
4. Sequence familiar routines
5. Expand conceptual knowledge of the world

Settings
- Various rides (e.g., Sit 'N Spin, miniature trampolines)
- Ticket office
- Concession areas

Props
- Tickets
- Bowling ball and pins
- Bean Bag Toss
- Pretend roller coaster (made from several boxes lined up like a train that children can pretend is a roller coaster)
- Target board and balls with Velcro adhesive so they stick to the target
- Pretend food (e.g., hot dogs, sodas, ice cream, cotton candy)
- Two cash registers
- Pretend money

Roles
- Customers
- Park workers (to run the games and the rides)
- Ticket sellers
- Concession stand workers

General Description of Activity

An amusement park has several rides and other activities in which the children can participate. In this dramatic play, the children may circulate among activities. There might be concession stands where they can purchase food items, such as hot dogs, or they might bring a picnic to the park. The park might have a train for transportation from one area to another.

Verbal Productions

Level of linguistic complexity varies with the role or competency of the child playing the role.
- "I want a ride on the roller coaster, please" or "Want ride"
- "She needs a ticket" or "Ticket?"
- "It's his turn" or "Turn, please"

Adult Facilitative Role

The adult is to facilitate role play and help expand language and literacy skills. Typical actions or strategies to use include

Playing a role: "I am going to buy a ticket to ride on the rocking boat."

Expanding a child's utterance and providing corrective feedback: "Me horsie" to "Say, I want to ride the horsie.'"

Modeling the reading of a sign: "That sign says *wait here*."

Contrasting two location terms (focus contrast): "That bean bag went into the hole. This bean bag is on the ground."

Recasting a child's utterance: "That baby is crying" to "That baby cried because she wanted her turn on the ride."

ART : Fingerpainting

Objectives
1. Express creativity
2. Develop small motor skills (e.g., drawing, painting, cutting, pasting)
3. To practice turn-taking skills
4. To converse with peers and adults

Materials
- Fingerpaints
- Fingerpaint paper
- Smocks
- Glitter (optional)

General Description of Activity

Put a dab of paint on each child's paper. The children can use their hands and fingers to smear the paint all over the paper, then draw and write in the paint with their fingers. The children can make abstract designs, make full hand prints, or use their fingers to draw pictures or write letters or numbers. Shaving cream can be used instead of paint and placed on a formboard rather than on paper. Children can also use fingerpaint to decorate their Valentine bags. Fingerpainting is a good excuse to get messy and gooey. Some children love this; others may need some coaxing to get their fingers dirty.

Variation

For additional effect, mix glitter into the fingerpaint before the children create their designs.

GROUP **Act out a Story (*Hiccups for Elephant*)**

Objectives

1. Improve listening skills
2. Increase sequencing ability
3. Increase knowledge of story telling
4. Learn appropriate group-interaction skills
5. Practice turn-taking skills

Materials

- *Hiccups for Elephant*
- Props (e.g., water, spoon, banana)

General Description of Activity

Read *Hiccups for Elephant* or another familiar story to children, or summarize it.

Group Participation

Assign children roles from the story. Assure the children not chosen the first time that everyone will have a turn and that they have the very important job of being a good listening audience. Narrate the story as the children act it out. They should say as many of the lines as they can, with prompts given when needed. Repeat with new actors until all the children have had a turn.

Variation

Have a child do the narration, or have children retell the story as you put up flannel board figures for it.

Summary/Transition Activity

Compliment the children's acting, and ask children what other stories they would like to act out another day.

Wednesday

Dramatic Play	Art	Group	Story	Song
Pizza Parlor	Valentine Bags	Counting and Writing Numbers 1–5	*Will You Be My Valentine?*	"I Wish I Were a Pepperoni Pizza"

DAILY PLANNING GUIDE

Language and Literacy Skills Facilitated

Vocabulary: *soft drinks, pizza, spaghetti, shakes, wrappers, boxes, cook, cashier, customer, order, pizza parlor, pizza delivery*

Verb phrase structures: *places an order, buys a pizza, pays money, eat out, is making a pizza, served the customer, served a pizza, chooses a drink, are making pizzas*

Adjective/object descriptions: *large drink, small pizza, paper hat, red cup*

Question structures: *what, how, where, when, who, what if, why, how many, which one*

Pronouns: *I, you, he, she, we, they, my, your, him, her, his, our, their, me, us, them*

Prepositions: *in, on, under, over, near, beneath, next to, beside, around, inside, outside*

Sounds: */p/ pizza parlor, pays; /m/ money, make, menu*

Noting print has meaning: names on chairs and on cubbies, signs in dramatic play, words in books and on chalkboard

Noting sound–symbol associations: What sound does _____ start with?

Writing: letters, names, words

Social Skills Facilitated

Initiating interaction with peers and adults; responding to questions and requests from peers and adults

Negotiating with peers for toys and materials

Group cooperation: waiting for a turn in a group, taking a turn at the appropriate time

Cognitive Skills Facilitated

Problem-solving skills: setting up a restaurant, remembering items

Classification skills: matching number to numerals

Sequencing skills: putting a pizza together, words to song

Narrative/story structure: adventure

Motor Skills Facilitated

Large motor: outdoor play activities—jumping, running, hopping, pedaling, climbing

Small motor: writing, drawing, gluing

DRAMATIC PLAY **Pizza Parlor**

Type of Activity: Central

Objectives

1. Learn new, and employ familiar, vocabulary
2. Learn new, and employ a variety of, syntactic constructions
3. Interact with peers
4. Sequence familiar routines
5. Expand conceptual knowledge of the world

Settings	• Dining area	• Counter	• Restaurant kitchen

Props
- Menus
- Dishes and cups
- Tables and chairs
- Trays
- Pretend soda pop dispenser
- Pretend cash register
- Pretend money
- Order form and pencils

- Delivery van (optional)
- Roads (floor area marked with masking tape—optional)
- English muffins, real pizza toppings, and microwave oven (optional)
- Carry-out window
- Salad bar (optional)

- Pretend pizzas (Children can make pizzas by putting a cardboard circle for the crust on a table and adding toppings using a variety of construction paper cutouts that represent pepperoni, green peppers, mushrooms, or other items. Yellow yarn can be used to represent cheese.)

Roles
- Customers
- Cashier

- Delivery van driver (optional)

- Cooks
- Waiters and waitresses

General Description of Activity

Children run a pizza parlor. The waiter or waitress seats the guests and gives them menus. The guests order their pizzas, with various toppings, and possibly other items, such as spaghetti or bread sticks. Children who are the cooks must construct the pizzas, which are then taken to the customers by the waiter or waitress. A pizza delivery van can also be used to deliver pizzas to homes. Note: Real pizzas can be made at snack time by using English muffins as the crust. The children can add different toppings and cook the pizzas in a microwave oven.

Verbal Productions

Level of linguistic complexity varies with the role or competency of the child playing the role.
- "We have two kinds of pizza, pepperoni and cheese. Which do you want?" or "Which one?"
- "Cheese?" or "More pizza"
- "You ate my pizza" or "My pizza!"
- "You bought two pizzas, and I bought one" or "One pizza"

Adult Facilitative Role

The adult is to facilitate role play and help expand language and literacy skills. Typical actions or strategies to use include

Playing a role: "I am going to order a hamburger and a cheese pizza. What kind of pizza do you want?"

Modeling a statement/vocabulary: "Pizza is like a round, flat pie with meat and cheese on it. Sometimes it just has cheese on it."

Redirecting a child to a peer: "Ask John if he wants some pizza. Say, 'Do you want some pizza?'"

Modeling the reading of a sign: "The sign says *cheese pizza*—$2."

Providing a contrast between error and correct sound: "You said you <u>took</u> the pizza. You meant that you will <u>cook</u> the pizza."

ART **Valentine Bags**

Objectives
1. Express creativity
2. Develop small motor skills (e.g., drawing, painting, cutting, pasting)
3. Practice turn-taking skills
4. Converse with peers and adults

Materials
- White paper bags
- Markers
- Cutout hearts of various sizes and colors (red, white, pink, purple), several per child
- Doilies
- Glue

General Description of Activity

Write each child's name (or have the child write it) on a white bag. Have children glue hearts of various sizes and doilies on the bag. These bags will be used for collecting children's Valentines.

GROUP **Counting and Writing Numbers *1–5***

Objectives
1. Improve listening skills
2. Recognize knowledge of the alphabet and sounds.
3. Learn appropriate group-interaction skills
4. Practice turn-taking skills

Materials
- Index cards with *1, 2, 3, 4,* and *5* written on them (one number per card)
- Counting items (e.g., counting dogs, small blocks)
- Whiteboard (or chalkboard)
- Whiteboard markers (or chalk)

General Description of Activity

Place the numbered index cards in front of the children. Identify each number and write the numbers on the whiteboard. Remind the children how to write each one, using the jingle for the appropriate number:

1: Start at the top, go down and you're done, that's the way to make a *1.*

2: Around and back on the railroad track, *2, 2, 2.*

3: Around the tree, around the tree, that's the way to make a *3.*

4: Down and over and down once more, that's the way to make a *4.*

5: Down around, make a hat on it, and look what you've found. (*5*)

6: Down around until it sticks, that's the way to make a *6.*

7: Over and down and it's not heaven, over and down makes a *7.*

8: Make an S and go back straight, that's the way to make an *8.*

9: A balloon and a line make *9.*

10: Draw a line and a circle with your pen, that's the way to make a *10.*

Group Participation

Ask one child to point to a number (e.g., *4*). Ask another child to place four items below the index card with the *4* on it. Finally, have a third child demonstrate on the whiteboard (or chalkboard) how to write a *4.* Provide support as needed. Continue until all the children have had a turn and the numbers *1–5* have been covered.

Summary/Transition Activity

Quickly point to different number cards and have the children, as a group, label the number indicated.

Thursday

Dramatic Play	Art	Group	Story	Song
Post Office	Valentine Cards for Parents	Letter *Z*	*A Letter to Amy*	"Name Game Song"

DAILY PLANNING GUIDE

Language and Literacy Skills Facilitated

Vocabulary: *valentines, hearts, office, mail, letter, typewriter, computer, bills, tape, paper clip, stapler, three-hole punch, file, envelope, file cabinet, secretary, telephone, paste, folder, glue, copier, adding machine*

Verb phrase structures: *sorts, is/was typing, types, typed, Who's typing? I am, punching, punches, punched, is/was calling, calls, called*

Adjective/object descriptions: *fast/slow typing, big/little _____, two-hole/three-hole punch*

Question structures: *what, how, where, when, who, what if, why, how many, which one*

Pronouns: *I, you, he, she, we, they, my, your, him, her, his, our, their, me, us, them*

Prepositions: *in, on, under, over, near, beneath, next to, beside, around, inside, outside*

Sounds: /t/ *type, computer, letter, at;* /k/ *call, ticket, back;* /l/ *lick, calling, bill*

Noting print has meaning: names on chairs and on cubbies, signs in dramatic play, words in books and on chalkboard

Noting sound–symbol associations: What sound does _____ start with?

Writing: letters, names, words

Social Skills Facilitated

Initiating interaction with peers and adults; responding to questions and requests from peers and adults

Negotiating with peers for toys and materials

Group cooperation: waiting for a turn in a group, taking a turn at the appropriate time

Cognitive Skills Facilitated

Problem-solving skills: What does a post office worker do?

Classification skills: items found at a post office

Sequencing skills: story, songs, alphabet

Motor Skills Facilitated

Large motor: outdoor play activities—jumping, running, hopping, pedaling, climbing

Small motor: sorting, writing, drawing, gluing, stapling, painting

---

DRAMATIC PLAY **Post Office**

Type of Activity: Related

Objectives
1. Learn new, and employ familiar, vocabulary
2. Learn new, and employ a variety of, syntactic constructions
3. Interact with peers
4. Sequence familiar routines
5. Expand conceptual knowledge of the world

Settings

- Counter
- Houses (with mailboxes)
- Mail box(es) at post office
- Sorting area

Props

- Paper and pencils
- Envelopes
- Pretend computer or typewriter
- Mailing stamps (stickers)
- Inkpad and stamp
- Scale

- Boxes
- Delivery bags
- Play cash register
- Play money
- Houses with mailboxes
- Mail truck

Roles

- Post office workers
- Mail carriers
- Customers
- Mail recipients

General Description of Activity

Children operate a post office, sorting, weighing, and mailing letters and packages; canceling stamps; and helping customers. The customers can bring envelopes and packages to mail, or they can buy stamps. The mail carriers can deliver the mail to homes and business.

Children can also use this time to deliver their Valentines to one another that they brought from home. They can put them in their Valentine bags (made in art the previous day).

Verbal Productions

Level of linguistic complexity varies with the role or competency of the child playing the role.

- "I need a stamp, please" or "Stamp, please"
- "That weighs two pounds, so you need to pay me $5" or "That will be $5"
- "Do you want to mail this letter?" or "Here's your mail"

Adult Facilitative Role

The adult is to facilitate role play and help expand language and literacy skills. Typical actions or strategies to use include

Playing a role: "I made a Valentine for my mom. I am going to mail it at the post office."

Event casting of an adult's actions: "I am putting the Valentines in everybody's Valentine bag. Here is Mike's bag. Here's Mary's bag. Watch while I put the Valentines in the bags."

Modeling phonological awareness: "That is right. The words *letter, like*, and *Lily* all start with the letter *L*."

Providing confirmatory feedback: "Yes, that says *Maddie*."

Contrasting error and correct usage of pronouns and third person singular irregular form: "Her have a Valentine" to "She has a Valentine."

ART : **Valentine Cards for Parents**

Objectives

1. Express creativity
2. Develop small motor skills (e.g., drawing, painting, cutting, pasting)
3. Practice turn-taking skills
4. Converse with peers and adults

Materials
- Precut heart shapes in all sizes and variety of colors (e.g., pink, red, white, purple), several per child
- Folded white paper to make a card
- Markers
- Glitter
- Doilies
- Glue
- Scissors
- Folded paper with half-heart shape drawn (encircling the fold) for children to cut their own hearts
- Word cards showing words (e.g., *Mom, Dad, love*) for children to copy

General Description of Activity

Have children glue the heart cutouts on the folded piece of white paper to make a card for their parents (or other family members, if they wish). They can also decorate the card with glitter, doilies, and drawings. Children can cut out their own heart shapes if they wish by cutting on the half-heart shape on the folded paper.

GROUP **Letter *Z***

Objectives
1. Improve listening skills
2. Increase knowledge of the alphabet and sounds
3. Learn appropriate group-interaction skills
4. Practice turn-taking skills

Materials
- Alphabet chart and other alphabet displays
- Blackboard and chalk or poster paper and markers
- Pictures of objects (or objects themselves) with names that begin with *Z*
- Picture dictionary (or an alphabet video dictionary)

General Description of Activity

Write an upper- and a lowercase letter *Z* on the blackboard (or on poster paper). Give several examples of words that begin with *Z*, emphasizing the /z/ or "zzz" sound at the beginning of the words. You might hold up pictures of objects (or objects themselves) with names that begin with *Z*. Direct the children's attention to the alphabet picture displays around the room.

Group Participation

Ask if anyone's name starts with *Z* (e.g., Zoe, Zachary). Have those children write the letter *Z* on the blackboard (or poster paper). Also have two or three other children write the letter *Z* on the blackboard. Provide verbal guidance as children form the letter: "Start at the top and draw a line to the right. Draw a slant down to the left. Then draw another line to the right." If necessary, help children write the letter. Some of the other children can practice writing *Z* in the air with their fingers (or on individual chalkboards). Ask the children to think of words that begin with *Z*. Write the words they offer on the blackboard, drawing quick sketches (when possible) of the suggested words. If a child suggests a word that does not begin with *Z*, say, "No, that begins with ___," and say both sounds so children can compare them. To help children who cannot think of any words, prompt them with pictures or objects representing *Z* words. (Pictures or objects can be handed out at the beginning of the lesson or as the lesson proceeds.) Additional words can be sought in a picture dictionary if the group has difficulty arriving at words that begin with *Z*.

Summary/Transition Activity

After about 10–15 words have been suggested, review the words, emphasizing the *Z* sound.

WEEKLY PLANNING GUIDE

	Dramatic Play	Art	Group	Story	Song
Monday *Suggested Props and Materials*	Washing the Car *Car wash scenario, car wash made of boxes and crêpe paper, hose area, cardboard tubes for hoses, cardboard cars or plastic riding cars, cashier, gas pumps, masking tape (to designate a road)*	Vehicle Rubbings *Paper, cardboard vehicle cutouts, crayons with paper removed, container to hold crayons*	Many/Few *10–12 different sets of items (e.g., small blocks, balls, cars, dolls, paper, pencils) with at least 8–12 items in each set, two tubs or mats to place items on*	*Cars! Cars! Cars!*	"Twinkle, Twinkle, Traffic Light"
Tuesday *Suggested Props and Materials*	Babysitting *Babysitting scenario, playhouse set up with stoves, sink, refrigerator, highchair, baby beds, clothes, blankets, dishes, books, bottle, and pretend park (optional)*	Faces *Paper or paper plates for face; construction paper eyes, noses, mouth; fabric scraps; tissue paper; glue; markers; yarn*	Act out a Story *(Little Tiger's Big Surprise)* *Story props (toy animals, sheet for water)*	*Little Tiger's Big Surprise*	"Rock-a-Bye Baby"
Wednesday *Suggested Props and Materials*	Grocery Shopping *Grocery shopping scenario, grocery shelves set up with food containers, pretend food, checkout stand with play cash registers, shopping carts, grocery bags*	Vegetable Prints *Tempera paint, cut-up vegetables, paper*	Focus on Vowels *Two sets of vowel cards containing both upper- and lowercase letters, pictures of items beginning with long and short vowels (e.g., ape, alligator, eel, elephant, ice cream, igloo, oatmeal, octopus, ukulele, umbrella)*	*Don't Forget the Oatmeal!*	"I Like to Eat Apples and Bananas"
Thursday *Suggested Props and Materials*	House Cleaning *House cleaning scenario; housekeeping area set up with a stove, refrigerator, sink, and table; pretend food; pots and pans; silverware; dishes; dolls; doll beds; brooms; brushes; rags*	Chalk Pictures with Liquid Starch *Colored construction paper, chalk, liquid starch, flat dishes to hold the starch*	Recycling *Plastic bottles, newspapers, soda pop cans, cardboard, Styrofoam items, and bins (one per type of item to be recycled)*	*The Relatives Came*	"This Is the Way We Wash Our Clothes"

NEWSLETTER

Vol. 1, No. 27

Date: _____

Weekend Chores

Monday The children will start their weekend chores by visiting the car wash during dramatic play. They will do vehicle rubbings in art. The story for the day will be *Cars! Cars! Cars!* During group time, they will learn about the concepts of *many* and *few*. "Twinkle, Twinkle, Traffic Light" will be sung during music.

Tuesday The children will be babysitters during dramatic play and take care of babies and children. The children can pretend to be the babysitter, the children, or the babies. In art, they will make different faces by drawing and by gluing paper and yarn to make different features. The story will be *Little Tiger's Big Surprise*. During group time, the children will act out the story. "Rock-a-Bye Baby" will be our featured song of the day.

Wednesday The children go to the grocery store today. Some will buy the groceries; others will be workers. There will be shelves to stock and people to help during dramatic play. Printing on paper with vegetables dipped in paint will keep children interested during art time. They will read *Don't Forget the Oatmeal* at storytime. Group time will focus on the vowel sounds. Wednesday's featured song is "I Like to Eat Apples and Bananas."

Thursday Today the children will be busy cleaning house during dramatic play. In art, they will make a chalk drawing by dipping the chalk in liquid starch and then drawing a picture. The story of the day is *The Relatives Came*. During group time, the children will talk about recycling. Music will feature "This Is the Way We Wash Our Clothes."

Monday

Dramatic Play	Art	Group	Story	Song
Washing the Car	Vehicle Rubbings	Many/Few	*Cars! Cars! Car!*	"Twinkle, Twinkle, Traffic Light"

DAILY PLANNING GUIDE

Language and Literacy Skills Facilitated

Vocabulary: *car, truck, car wash, mechanic, tune-up, oil change, car wax, hood, bumper, windshield, sponge, drying cloth*

Verb phrase structures: *wash<u>es</u>, <u>is</u> wash<u>ing</u>, wash<u>ed</u>, wax<u>es</u>, wax<u>ed</u>, polish<u>es</u>, <u>is</u> polish<u>ing</u>, polish<u>ed</u>, <u>will</u> polish, who wash<u>ed</u> the car? I <u>did</u>*

Adjective/object descriptions: *wet car, soapy car, shiny car, large car, small car, medium-sized car, dirty/clean*

Question structures: *what, how, where, when, who, what if, why, how many, which one*

Pronouns: *I, you, he, she, we, they, my, your, him, her, his, our, their, me, us, them*

Prepositions: *in, on, under, over, near, beneath, next to, beside, around, inside, outside*

Sounds: /k/ <u>c</u>ar, me<u>ch</u>anic, lo<u>ck</u>; /f/ <u>f</u>ix, o<u>ft</u>en, o<u>ff</u>; /l/ <u>l</u>ittle, ye<u>ll</u>ow, be<u>ll</u>; /s/ <u>s</u>it, me<u>ss</u>y, hi<u>s</u>

Noting print has meaning: names on chairs and on cubbies, signs in dramatic play, words in books and on chalkboard

Noting sound–symbol associations: What sound does _____ start with?

Writing: letters, names, words

Social Skills Facilitated

Initiating interaction with peers and adults; responding to questions and requests from peers and adults

Negotiating with peers for toys and materials

Group cooperation: waiting for a turn in a group, taking a turn at the appropriate time

Cognitive Skills Facilitated

Problem-solving skills: how to take care of cars

Classification skills: many items versus few items

Sequencing skills: story, songs, art activity

Narrative/story structure: labeling story

Motor Skills Facilitated

Large motor: outdoor play activities—jumping, running, hopping, pedaling, climbing

Small motor: writing, drawing, gluing, washing

DRAMATIC PLAY **Washing the Car**

Type of Activity: Central

Objectives
1. Learn new, and employ familiar, vocabulary
2. Learn new, and employ a variety of, syntactic constructions
3. Interact with peers
4. Sequence familiar routines
5. Expand conceptual knowledge of the world

Settings
- Car wash (a large open box with crêpe paper streamers hanging from the opening so the cars can be driven through the box to get washed)
- Hand car wash with hose
- Road (floor area marked by masking tape)
- Office
- Gas station (optional)
- Car dealership (optional)

Props
- Cars (medium-size boxes with the tops and bottoms cut off and paper wheels attached to the sides) or real child-sized plastic cars
- Sponges
- Hoses (cardboard tubes)
- Pretend vacuum
- Pretend air pump
- Pretend soap
- Cash registers
- Play money
- Gas pumps (optional for gas station)
- Toy cars (optional for car dealership)
- Masking tape (to mark the road)

Roles
- Car wash attendants
- Drivers
- Customers
- Cashier
- Gas station attendant (optional for gas station)
- Salespersons (optional for car dealership)

General Description of Activity

Children take their cars to the car wash to get them washed. Cars can be made from boxes with both the tops and bottoms cut off and paper wheels attached to the sides. Children can drive the cars by holding on to both sides of the box. There might be an automatic car wash, where the car is driven through and washed by machines, and an area where customers use a hose to wash their cars by hand. The car wash set-up can be part of a gas station scenario, or it can be an individual dramatic play setting. It might also be part of a car dealership dramatic play, where the workers must keep the new cars clean.

Verbal Productions

Level of linguistic complexity varies with the role or competency of the child playing the role.
- "I want my car washed" or "Wash car"
- "My car sure is dirty" or "Dirty"
- "This car is next in line" or "Next"
- "It costs $5 to go through" or "$5, please"
- "She needs a new car" or "Need a car"

Adult Facilitative Role

The adult is to facilitate role play and help expand language and literacy skills. Typical actions or strategies to use include

Playing a role: "We are having a car wash. We get to wash and wax our cars. First, let's drive through our car wash. Then we will wax our cars and maybe have a car show."

Modeling the /sh/ sound: "We <u>sh</u>ould find a new bru<u>sh</u>. I want to <u>sh</u>ow you how to wa<u>sh</u> the car."

Expanding a child's utterance: "Wash car" to "We can wash the car now."

Redirecting a child to a peer: "Ask Hannah for a turn. Say, 'Can I have a turn, please?'"

Helping a child make signs for the car wash: "The sign says *car wash*."

ART : **Vehicle Rubbings**

Objectives
1. Express creativity
2. Develop small motor skills (e.g., drawing, painting, cutting, pasting)
3. To practice turn-taking skills
4. To converse with peers and adults

Materials
- Newsprint
- Cardboard vehicle cutouts
- Other cutouts
- Crayons with paper removed
- Container to hold crayons

General Description of Activity

Cut a variety of vehicle outlines out of cardboard. Have the children place one or more under a piece of paper. Holding a crayon (with the paper covering removed) or a piece of chalk on one side, they rub over the paper back and forth until the shape of the object appears on their paper. Children can use several colors and different arrangements of objects under the paper to make a variety of pictures.

GROUP **Many/Few**

Objectives
1. Improve listening skills
2. Increase sequencing ability
3. Learn appropriate group-interaction skills
4. Practice turn-taking skills

Materials
- 10–12 different sets of items (e.g., small blocks, balls, cars, dolls, paper, pencils) with at least 8–12 items in each set
- Two tubs or mats

General Description of Activity

Place two mats (or tubs) in front of the children. On one mat, place a couple of 1" blocks (or other items). On the other mat, place five or six of the same blocks. Label each group, saying, "This mat has a few blocks, and this mat has many blocks." Put 3–4 blocks on a mat and 10–12 on the other mat. Again, label the two groups as one having a few blocks and one having many blocks. Tell the children that few and many are not exact numbers. However, few refers to the group that has the smaller number of items.

Group Participation

Put a variety of items in tubs or on mats and ask one child to find the group that has a few items. Ask another child to find the one that has many items. Continue with different groupings of items, sometimes asking the whole class to point to the correct group and other times having the class label, in chorus, the *few* group or the *many* group.

Summary/Transition Activity

Have children label one last group of few/many items in chorus.

Tuesday

Dramatic Play	Art	Group	Story	Song
Babysitting	Faces	Act out a Story (*Little Tiger's Big Surprise*)	*Little Tiger's Big Surprise*	"Rock-a-Bye Baby"

DAILY PLANNING GUIDE

Language and Literacy Skills Facilitated

Vocabulary: *sitter, babysitter, babies, bath, story, highchair, crib, spoon, knife, fork, play, cry, feed, bottle, diaper*

Verb phrase structures: *is* crying, c*ries*, c*ried*, *will* cry, play*s*, play*ed*, eats, *ate*, *has eaten*, sleeps, *slept*

Adjective/object descriptions: *happy baby, crying baby, cute baby, hungry baby, wet baby, funny toy*

Question structures: *what, how, where, when, who, what if, why, how many, which one*

Pronouns: *I, you, he, she, we, they, my, your, him, her, his, our, their, me, us, them*

Prepositions: *in, on, under, over, near, beneath, next to, beside, around, inside, outside*

Sounds: /k/ *cover, back*; /t/ *top, sitter, sat*; /f/ *four, often, off*

Noting print has meaning: names on chairs and on cubbies, signs in dramatic play, words in books and on chalkboard

Noting sound–symbol associations: What sound does _____ start with?

Writing: letters, names, words

Social Skills Facilitated

Initiating interaction with peers and adults; responding to questions and requests from peers and adults

Negotiating with peers for toys and materials

Group cooperation: waiting for a turn in a group, taking a turn at the appropriate time

Cognitive Skills Facilitated

Problem-solving skills: how to take care of babies, how to act out

Classification skills: things used to take care of babies

Sequencing skills: songs, story

Narrative/story structure: adventure

Motor Skills Facilitated

Large motor: outdoor play activities—jumping, running, hopping, pedaling, climbing

Small motor: writing, drawing, gluing, constructing

DRAMATIC PLAY **Babysitting**

Type of Activity: Central

Objectives
1. Learn new, and employ familiar, vocabulary
2. Learn new, and employ a variety of, syntactic constructions
3. Interact with peers
4. Sequence familiar routines
5. Expand conceptual knowledge of the world

Settings
- House(s)
- Park (optional)

Props
- Play stove
- Play refrigerator
- Tables and chairs
- Highchairs
- Cupboards, dishes, utensils, and bottles
- Pretend food
- Beds, blankets, and pillows

- Dolls
- Dolls' clothes
- Books
- Baby stroller
- Play bathtub
- Washcloths and towels
- Pretend soap
- Bath toys (e.g., rubber duck, toy boat)

Roles
- Babysitters
- Children

- Babies
- Parents

General Description of Activity

Children pretend to be babysitters taking care of babies and children. They might feed and bathe the children, read them stories, play with them, take them for walks, and put them to bed.

Verbal Productions

Level of linguistic complexity varies with the role or competency of the child playing the role.
- "It's time for bed" or "Bed, now"
- "The baby needs a bottle. Please get it from the table" or "Bottle!"
- "First, I'll read you the story, and then you go to bed" or "Story, bed"

Adult Facilitative Role

The adult is to facilitate role play and help expand language and literacy skills. Typical actions or strategies to use include

Playing a role: "I am taking care of the baby. I get to feed the baby and then rock it to sleep. The baby sleeps in a crib. A crib is a little bed."

Identifying rhyming words: "Yes, the words *bed, red, Fred*, and *fed* all rhyme."

Expanding a child's utterance: "Rock baby" to "Rock the little baby."

Providing confirmatory feedback: "Yes, that is a red blanket."

Contrasting two verb structures (present tense with past tense): "The baby kisses Mommy" to "The baby kissed Mommy yesterday, too."

ART **Faces**

Objectives
1. Express creativity
2. Develop small motor skills (e.g., drawing, painting, cutting, pasting)
3. To practice turn-taking skills
4. To converse with peers and adults

Materials
- Paper plates or large circle cutouts, one for each child
- Small cutouts in a variety of colors
- Yarn
- Other paper
- Scissors
- Glue

General Description of Activity

Children create a face using a paper plate or a construction-paper circle as a base. They can glue a variety of shapes onto the plate to make facial features, such as eyes, noses, mouths, and so forth. Place the shapes in separate containers so the children can easily choose the shapes they want. Add other items, such as yarn for hair, extra paper, scissors, and markers that children can use to add details to the faces. Label the different shapes and colors as the children glue them on the faces they are creating.

Variation

Instead of separating the various cutout shapes, place them all in one shallow container so that children must communicate to get the pieces they want.

GROUP **Act out a Story (*Little Tiger's Big Surprise*)**

Objectives
1. Improve listening skills
2. Increase sequencing ability
3. Increase knowledge of storytelling
4. Learn appropriate group-interaction skills
5. Practice turn-taking skills

Materials
- *Little Tiger's Big Surprise*
- Props for the story

General Description of Activity

Read the story to the children, or summarize it if they are familiar with it.

Group Participation

Assign children roles from the story. Assure the children not chosen the first time that everyone will have a turn and that they have the very important job of being a good listening audience. Narrate the story as the children act it out. They should say as many of the lines as they can, with prompts given when needed. Repeat with new actors until all the children have had a turn.

Summary/Transition Activity

Compliment the children's acting, and ask children what other stories they would like to act out another day.

Wednesday

Dramatic Play	Art	Group	Story	Song
Grocery Shopping	Vegetable Prints	Focus on Vowels	*Don't Forget the Oatmeal!*	"I Like to Eat Apples and Bananas"

DAILY PLANNING GUIDE

Language and Literacy Skills Facilitated

Vocabulary: *groceries, cart, cereal, shop, checker, buy, sell, bag, sack, shelf, money, change*

Verb phrase structures: *eats, is eating, ate, has eaten, pushes, is pushing, pushed, buys, bought, checks, is checking, checked*

Adjective/object descriptions: *big/little bag, full/empty shelf*

Question structures: *what, how, where, when, who, what if, why, how many, which one*

Pronouns: *I, you, he, she, we, they, my, your, him, her, his, our, their, me, us, them*

Prepositions: *in, on, under, over, near, beneath, next to, beside, around, inside, outside*

Sounds: /sh/ *shelf, push;* /k/ *cart, sack;* /s/ *sell, carts*

Noting print has meaning: names on chairs and on cubbies, signs in dramatic play, words in books and on chalkboard

Noting sound–symbol associations: What sound does _____ start with?

Writing: letters, names, words

Social Skills Facilitated

Initiating interaction with peers and adults; responding to questions and requests from peers and adults

Negotiating with peers for toys and materials

Group cooperation: waiting for a turn in a group, taking a turn at the appropriate time

Cognitive Skills Facilitated

Problem-solving skills: what to buy

Classification skills: fruits, vegetables, meats

Sequencing skills: songs, story

Narrative/story structure: adventure

Motor Skills Facilitated

Large motor: outdoor play activities—jumping, running, hopping, pedaling, climbing

Small motor: writing, drawing, gluing

DRAMATIC PLAY **Grocery Shopping**

Type of Activity: Sequential

Objectives
1. Learn new, and employ familiar, vocabulary
2. Learn new, and employ a variety of, syntactic constructions
3. Interact with peers
4. Sequence familiar routines
5. Expand conceptual knowledge of the world

Settings
- Grocery store
- Shelves and aisles
- Check-out stand
- Customers' homes

Props
- Shelves
- Canned goods and other food items
- Fruit and vegetable area
- Pretend cash register
- Pretend money
- Pretend credit cards
- Pretend coupons
- Shopping carts
- Grocery bags
- Pencil and paper for making lists
- Table for checkout area

Roles
- Shoppers
- Cashiers
- Stockers
- Baggers

General Description of Activity

The children pretend to be grocery shopping. They can make lists, take their "children" with them, choose the items on the list to put in their carts, pay, bag their groceries, and go home to put their items away. Other children can be the grocery store workers. Some keep the shelves stocked, and others are checkers and baggers.

Verbal Productions

- "Will that be all? Your total is $5" or "All? $5!"
- "Milk, please" or "Milk"
- "Do you have any cereal?" or "Want cereal"

Adult Facilitative Role

The adult is to facilitate role play and help expand language and literacy skills. Typical actions or strategies to use include

Playing a role: "I am going to buy the groceries. I get to push the shopping cart."

Expanding a child's utterance: "Buy milk" to "I am going to buy the milk."

Providing confirmatory feedback: "Yes, that is an apple."

ART **Vegetable Prints**

Objectives
1. Express creativity
2. Develop small motor skills (e.g., drawing, painting, cutting, pasting)
3. Practice turn-taking skills
4. Converse with peers and adults

Materials
- Assortment of vegetables, sliced (e.g., peppers, carrots, broccoli, cauliflower, celery)
- Tempera paint
- Shallow container (e.g., meat tray)
- Light-colored construction paper
- Smocks

General Description of Activity

Pour small amounts of tempera paint into shallow containers, such as Styrofoam meat trays. Children touch the vegetable piece to the paint and then press it on their paper, making a print of the vegetable's shape. The more choice of vegetables and colors, the more creative and colorful the prints will turn out.

GROUP **Focus on Vowels**

Objectives
1. Improve listening skills
2. Increase knowledge of the alphabet and sounds
3. Learn appropriate group-interaction skills
4. Practice turn-taking skills

Materials
- Two sets of vowel charts containing both upper- and lowercase letters (One set has pictures representing the long vowel sounds and one set with pictures representing the short vowel sounds.)
- Children's name cards that begin with vowels
- Pictures of items beginning with long and short vowels (e.g., ape, alligator, eel, elephant, ice cream, igloo, oatmeal, octopus, ukulele, umbrella)

General Description of Activity

Places two sets of vowel charts in front of the children in a vertical orientation. Remind the children that each vowel has at least two sounds (some vowels have other sounds, too, but the focus is on the long and short vowels). First, the vowels "say their name." This is the *long vowel sound*. Point to the first set of vowel cards and have children repeat the labeling of the vowels. Note any child's name that begins with a long vowel sound, and have that child place his or her name card by the appropriate vowel (e.g., Amy for *A*, Ethan for *E*, Ivan for *I*, Owen for *O*, and so forth).

Next, tell the children that the other sounds the vowels make are called the *short vowel sounds*. Say each of the short vowel sounds in turn as you point to the letters in the right column. Note any child's name that begins with a short vowel sound (e.g., Angelique for *A*, Emily for *E*, Indira for *I*, Oliver for *O*, Ulrich for *U*), and have that child place his or her name card by the appropriate letter.

Group Participation

Ask different children to label a picture beginning with a vowel sound and decide if it begins with the long or short sound of the vowel. The child then places the picture beside the appropriate vowel. Point to the correct place if the children are having difficulty deciding. (The purpose of the lesson is to recognize that vowels have at least two sounds, not to test whether the children can identify the correct sound.)

Summary/Transition Activity

After the children have placed the picture cards, review the vowel sounds by having the children say the long sounds together (a, e, i, o, u) and then the short vowel sounds (a, e, i, o, u) as you point to each vowel. Note: You can mount the vowel chart and key words so you and the children can refer to the chart in later activities.

Thursday

Dramatic Play	Art	Group	Story	Song
House Cleaning	Chalk Pictures with Liquid Starch	Recycling	*The Relatives Came*	"This Is the Way We Wash Our Clothes"

DAILY PLANNING GUIDE

Language and Literacy Skills Facilitated

Vocabulary: *clean, dust, vacuum, sweep, broom, cook, house, food, soup, stew, muffins, babies, wash, table*

Verb phrase structures: <u>is</u> clean<u>ing</u>, <u>was</u> dust<u>ing</u>, vacuum<u>ed</u>, <u>is</u> cook<u>ing</u>, <u>was</u> cook<u>ing</u>, cook<u>s</u>, cook<u>ed</u>, fix<u>es</u>, fix<u>ed</u>, make<u>s</u>, <u>made</u>, <u>do</u> you <u>have</u> ___?, eat<u>s</u>, <u>ate</u>, <u>has eaten</u>, wash<u>es</u>, wash<u>ed</u>

Adjective/object descriptions: *clean/dirty, dusty, good food, hot/cold food, red apple, yellow banana, dirty/clean baby*

Question structures: *what, how, where, when, who, what if, why, how many, which one*

Pronouns: *I, you, he, she, we, they, my, your, him, her, his, our, their, me, us, them*

Prepositions: *in, on, under, over, near, beneath, next to, beside, around, inside, outside*

Sounds: /k/ <u>c</u>oo<u>k</u>, <u>c</u>ooking, ma<u>k</u>e; /l/ <u>l</u>ick, Je<u>ll</u>-o, ye<u>ll</u>; /s/ <u>s</u>ee, cook<u>s</u>; /r/ <u>r</u>oof, ca<u>rr</u>ot, ba<u>r</u>

Noting print has meaning: names on chairs and on cubbies, signs in dramatic play, words in books and on chalkboard

Noting sound–symbol associations: What sound does _____ start with?

Writing: letters, names, words

Social Skills Facilitated

Initiating interaction with peers and adults; responding to questions and requests from peers and adults

Negotiating with peers for toys and materials

Group cooperation: waiting for a turn in a group, taking a turn at the appropriate time

Cognitive Skills Facilitated

Problem-solving skills: how to clean, dust, vacuum, cook

Classification skills: things we use to care for ourselves

Sequencing skills: story, songs

Narrative/story structure: rhyming, repetitive lines

Motor Skills Facilitated

Large motor: outdoor play activities—jumping, running, hopping, pedaling, climbing

Small motor: writing, drawing, gluing, squeezing, swirling, sweeping

---

DRAMATIC PLAY **House Cleaning**

Type of Activity: Central

Objectives
1. Learn new, and employ familiar, vocabulary
2. Learn new, and employ a variety of, syntactic constructions
3. Interact with peers
4. Sequence familiar routines
5. Expand conceptual knowledge of the world

Settings

- Kitchen area
- Bedrooms
- Dining rooms
- Family rooms
- House (playhouse or dismantled cardboard box—optional)

Props

- Play refrigerator
- Cupboards
- Play stove and sink
- Play washer and dryer
- Dishes
- Pots and pans
- Beds
- Dolls
- Pretend food
- Baby bottles
- Mops and brooms, dust cloths
- Pretend vacuum cleaners
- Cleaning supplies (empty or water-filled squirt bottles)

Roles

- Mothers
- Fathers
- Babies and other children

General Description of Activity

Children clean the housekeeping area by dusting, vacuuming, sweeping, and spraying. They can also do other chores, such as wash the dishes, make the beds, and do the laundry.

Verbal Productions

Level of linguistic complexity varies with the role or competency of the child playing the role.

- "Clean the table" or "Clean"
- "Use the broom to sweep the floor" or "Sweep here"
- "I'll do it later" or "Okay"
- "I'm washing the dishes" or "Wash dishes"
- "Do you want some more food?" or "Food?"
- "I'm vacuuming the rug" or "Clean rug"

Adult Facilitative Role

The adult is to facilitate role play and help expand language and literacy skills. Typical actions or strategies to use include

Playing a role: "It is the weekend and time to clean and vacuum the house."

Asking an open question: "What should we clean next?"

Recasting a child's utterance (past tense error and possessive pronoun error): "She wash him car yesterday" to "She washed his car yesterday."

Contrasting two verb structures (present tense with past tense): "He cleans the house" to "He cleaned the house yesterday."

ART Chalk Pictures with Liquid Starch

Objectives

1. Express creativity
2. Develop small motor skills (e.g., drawing, painting, cutting, pasting)
3. Practice turn-taking skills
4. Converse with peers and adults

Materials

- Colored construction paper
- Chalk
- Liquid starch
- Flat dishes to hold the starch

General Description of Activity

Provide colored construction paper and colored chalk. Have children dip one end of the chalk in liquid starch and then draw on the paper. The starch makes the colors more vibrant and ensures that the chalk does not rub off. Children can draw designs or pictures that follow the theme, or they can draw whatever they wish.

GROUP Recycling

Objectives
1. Improve listening skills
2. Increase sequencing ability
3. Learn appropriate group-interaction skills
4. Practice turn-taking skills

Materials
- Plastic bottles
- Newspapers
- Soda pop cans
- Cardboard
- Styrofoam items
- Bins (one per type of item to be recycled)

General Description of Activity

Explain what the word *recycle* means. Tell the children that some items that are often thrown away can be reused, but they must be taken to special places to be specially processed. Place a pile of recyclable items in front of the children. Show them the different items, pointing out the recycle symbol where possible (i.e., on the plastic or Styrofoam items). Set up bins for separating plastic, cardboard, aluminum, newspaper, and Styrofoam items.

Group Participation

Give each child an opportunity to sort some "trash" into the recycling bins, checking the plastic and Styrofoam items for symbols indicating that they can be recycled. Help children find the recycle symbol on bottles and other items.

Variation

Divide the class into small groups and have each group look for a specific type of recyclable item.

Summary/Transition Activity

Verbally label each recycling bin that is set up in front of the class. Remind children that many trash items can be recycled by sorting them into bins and taking them to a recycling center (or having them picked up at their home).

WEEKLY PLANNING GUIDE

	Dramatic Play	Art	Group	Story	Song
Monday *Suggested Props and Materials*	Archaeology/ Paleontology *Archaeology/paleontology scenario, large box cut about 4–6" inches deep, sand, toy dinosaurs and dinosaur bones, pails, shovels, sifting pans, tent, explorers' hats (optional), mats or sleeping bags, campfire, grill, pot and pans, pretend food, dishes, table, chairs, microscope, telephone, pretend computer*	Dinosaur Mural *Large sheet of paper, masking tape (optional), plastic or newsprint to place on the floor, smocks, tempera paint, paint cups, paintbrushes*	Pattern Sequencing—Dinosaur Footprints *Construction paper cutouts in the shape of dinosaur footprints of various sizes and colors*	*Dinosaur Roar!*	"Five Crazy Dinosaurs" (fingerplay)
Tuesday *Suggested Props and Materials*	Under the Sea *Under-the-sea scenario, pretend ship, steering wheel, ocean area, toy sea animals, coral reef (may be made from a cardboard box with an open top wrapped in construction paper), fishing poles, fish, telescope, pretend radio*	Aquariums *Paper plates, glue, sand, fish and shark cutouts, seashells, green construction paper or yarn, blue plastic wrap*	Sorting Shells *Seashells of varying shape and color and texture, two or three containers or tubs*	*What's Under the Ocean?*	"All the Little Fishies"
Wednesday *Suggested Props and Materials*	Science Investigations *Science investigation scenario, sand table or wading pool filled with sand, plastic insects, shovels and pails, play microscope, slides, magnifying glasses, pretend binoculars (or two toilet paper rolls taped together), pictures of birds*	Gak *Smocks, white glue, liquid starch, several containers or tubs, spoons (optional)*	Identifying *A, B,* and *C* *Index cards (or magnetic letters) with upper- and lowercase A, B, C written upon them (one letter per card)*	*The Mystery of Magnets*	"Raindrops and Lemondrops"
Thursday *Suggested Props and Materials*	Space *Space scenario, pretend rocket ship, helmets, backpacks, walking boards, "moon rocks," miniature trampoline, pretend television sets, microphones, headsets, pretend computers*	Clothespin Creations *Wooden clothespins, fabric scraps, glue, yarn, pipe cleaners*	Things that Fly *Items/pictures representing things that fly (e.g., birds) and do not fly (e.g., cars), two containers*	*Ten Black Dots*	"The Rocket Song"

NEWSLETTER

Vol. 1, No. 28

Date: _____

Exploring

Monday

The children will start the week by being archaeologists or paleontologists. They will go on a dig for dinosaur bones, camp at the dig and sift through the sand for finds. In art, they will make a dinosaur mural. Our story is *Dinosaur Roar!* During group time, children will follow pattern sequences involving dinosaur footprints. Our featured fingerplay is "Five Crazy Dinosaurs."

Tuesday

Today the children will explore things under the sea. They will look for sea animals, shells, and different coral reefs. They will also go fishing. Our book today is *What's Under the Ocean?* During group time, children will sort seashells into several classifications, like *big*, *little*, *round*, and *fan shaped*. Our featured song is "All the Little Fishies."

Wednesday

Today the children will be scientists. They will explore the properties of water and look at items with the microscope. They also might do some experiments with magnets. In art we will have fun exploring "gak," a mixture of white glue and liquid starch. Our story is *The Mystery of Magnets*. During group time, children will identify upper- and lowercase letters, focusing on *A*, *B*, and *C* today. The children might even practice writing the letters. Our song today is "Raindrops and Lemondrops."

Thursday

This day's dramatic play activity will be about space exploration. The children can pretend to be astronauts in the shuttle, astronauts visiting the moon, or ground controllers. In art, the children will make astronauts or robots out of wooden clothespins. Our story today will be *Ten Black Dots*. During group time, we will talk about things that fly. Our featured song is "The Rocket Song."

		Monday		
Dramatic Play	**Art**	**Group**	**Story**	**Song**
Archaeology/ Paleontology	Dinosaur Mural	Pattern Sequencing— Dinosaur Footprints	*Dinosaur Roar!*	"Five Crazy Dinosaurs" (fingerplay)

DAILY PLANNING GUIDE

Language and Literacy Skills Facilitated

Vocabulary: *archaeologist, dinosaur, bones, dig, scientist, sand, sifting, computer, analyze, museum*

Verb phrase structures: *dig/dug in the sand, sift/sifted the sand, examine/examined the bones*

Adjective/object descriptions: *large/small bones, sandy soil, many/few bones*

Question structures: *what, how, where, when, who, what if, why, how many, which one*

Pronouns: *I, you, he, she, we, they, my, your, him, her, his, our, their, me, us, them*

Prepositions: *in, on, under, over, near, beneath, next to, beside, around, inside, outside*

Sounds: /f/ *fix, off;* /s/ *sit, talks;* /l/ *little, bell*

Noting print has meaning: names on chairs and on cubbies, signs in dramatic play, words in books and on chalkboard

Noting sound–symbol associations: What sound does _____ start with?

Writing: letters, names, words

Social Skills Facilitated

Initiating interaction with peers and adults; responding to questions and requests from peers and adults

Negotiating with peers for toys and materials

Group cooperation: waiting for a turn in a group, taking a turn at the appropriate time

Cognitive Skills Facilitated

Problem-solving skills: how to dig for bones, putting a dinosaur together

Classification skills: large and small bones

Sequencing skills: story, songs

Narrative/story structure: adventure

Motor Skills Facilitated

Large motor: outdoor play activities—jumping, running, hopping, pedaling, climbing

Small motor: writing, drawing, gluing

DRAMATIC PLAY **Archaeology/Paleontology**

Type of Activity: Related

Objectives
1. Learn new, and employ familiar, vocabulary
2. Learn new, and employ a variety of, syntactic constructions
3. Interact with peers
4. Sequence familiar routines
5. Expand conceptual knowledge of the world

Settings
• Sand area for the dig
• Camping area
• Lab area

Props
• Sand
• Dinosaurs
• Bones
• Shells or other items to be found
• Microscopes for lab
• Slides (if possible)
• Pretend computer (can use just keyboard)

• Paper
• Pens
• Lab coats
• Tent
• Sleeping bags
• Firewood (Lincoln Logs)
• Cooking utensils

Roles
• Scientists
• Workers

• People at the camp

General Description of Activity

The children pretend to go on an archaeological dig. Have a sand area set up, with pretend dinosaur bones and other items buried in the sand. There can also be a lab area for looking at different finds and a camping area for the workers to live in. The children can be the workers at the dig, the scientists looking the items under the microscope, and people who are living at the camp.

Verbal Productions

Level of linguistic complexity varies with the role or competency of the child playing the role.
• "Look, I found a Stegosaurus bone" or "Bone"
• "I can put the slide under the microscope" or "See slide"
• "Let's fix our sleeping bags" or "Sleeping bags here"

Adult Facilitative Role

The adult is to facilitate role play and help expand language and literacy skills. Typical actions or strategies to use include

Playing a role: "We are on a dig. We are looking for dinosaur bones or maybe some pottery."

Modeling a structure (irregular past tense): "We dug in the sand."

Expanding a child's utterance: "Dig in sand" to "We can dig in the sand with the shovel."

Identifying rhyming words: "Yes, the words *pot, lot, got*, and *hot* all rhyme."

Providing confirmatory feedback: "Yes, that is a leg bone from a dinosaur."

ART : **Dinosaur Mural**

Objectives
1. Express creativity
2. Develop small motor skills (e.g., drawing, painting, cutting, pasting)
3. To practice turn-taking skills
4. To converse with peers and adults

Materials
• Large sheet of paper (e.g., 3' × 8')
• Masking tape (optional)
• Plastic or newsprint to protect the floor
• Smocks
• Tempera paint
• Paint cups
• Paintbrushes
• Crayons or markers (optional)
• Small bowls of water to rinse brushes
• Pictures of dinosaurs

General Description of Activity

Tape a large piece of paper to a wall, or lay it on the floor on top of plastic or newsprint. The children don smocks and paint pictures or designs on the paper using tempera paint. The children may choose to draw with crayons or markers instead of using tempera paint, or they may glue previously produced pictures on the mural. For a dinosaur mural, the children might fill in a predrawn jungle scene with paint or markers and then draw or glue pictures representing different dinosaurs.

Variation

If painting scenery for a program or for a dramatic play, outline the objects on the mural and have children fill them in with paint. For example, you might outline a lake or a tree, and the children can add the colors to the outline.

GROUP | **Pattern Sequencing—Dinosaur Footprints**

Objectives
1. Improve listening skills
2. Increase sequencing ability
3. Learn appropriate group-interaction skills
4. Practice turn-taking skills

Materials
- Dinosaur footprint cutouts, large and small, variety of colors
- Cardboard (optional)

General Description of Activity

Present a pattern of dinosaur footprint cutouts, such as *big red–little blue–big red–little blue*, and show the children how to continue the pattern by adding the appropriate footprint cutouts.

Variation

Have the children repeat the pattern by creating new rows of footprints that match your pattern (i.e., this becomes a matching activity). For a greater challenge, make a pattern, cover it with a piece of cardboard, and have a child repeat the pattern from memory.

Group Participation

On the floor, set out a pattern appropriate for a particular child's level. Have the child come up (or have two children come for peer support and help), and repeat or extend the pattern. Some children repeat a simple pattern (e.g., *little yellow-big green-little yellow-big green*), while others will be able to do more complicated patterns (e.g., *big red-little blue-little blue-big red-little blue-little blue, big yellow-little green-little red-little red-big yellow-little green-little red-little red*). Continue until all the children have had a turn.

Summary/Transition Activity

Give each child a few dinosaur footprints to create a pattern. Children could then trade with a partner to see if they can copy each other's patterns. Collect the cutouts and review the sizes and colors.

Tuesday

Dramatic Play	Art	Group	Story	Song
Under the Sea	Aquariums	Sorting Shells	*What's Under the Ocean?*	"All the Little Fishies"

DAILY PLANNING GUIDE

Language and Literacy Skills Facilitated

Vocabulary: *whale, shark, fish, seaweed, diving, ocean, microscope, coral, shell, submarine, scuba dive*

Verb phrase structures: *go<u>ing</u> to the beach, fish<u>ing</u>, look<u>ing</u> for sea shells, <u>swam</u>*

Adjective/object descriptions: *big fish, soft sand, rough shell, deep water, bright sun*

Question structures: *what, how, where, when, who, what if, why, how many, which one*

Pronouns: *I, you, he, she, we, they, my, your, him, her, his, our, their, me, us, them*

Prepositions: *in, on, under, over, near, beneath, next to, beside, around, inside, outside*

Sounds: /sh/ *<u>sh</u>ark, fi<u>sh</u>;* /f/ *<u>f</u>un, of<u>f</u>;* /s/ *<u>s</u>un, bu<u>s</u>*

Noting print has meaning: names on chairs and on cubbies, signs in dramatic play, words in books and on chalkboard

Noting sound–symbol associations: What sound does _____ start with?

Writing: letters, names, words

Social Skills Facilitated

Initiating interaction with peers and adults; responding to questions and requests from peers and adults

Negotiating with peers for toys and materials

Group cooperation: waiting for a turn in a group, taking a turn at the appropriate time

Cognitive Skills Facilitated

Problem-solving skills: learning how to fish, searching for seashells

Classification skills: shell sorting

Sequencing skills: stories, songs

Motor Skills Facilitated

Large motor: outdoor play activities—jumping, running, hopping, spinning

Small motor: coloring, painting, searching for shells

DRAMATIC PLAY **Under the Sea**

Type of Activity: Related

Objectives
1. Learn new and employ familiar vocabulary
2. Learn new and employ a variety of syntactic constructions
3. Interact with peers
4. Sequence familiar routines
5. Expand conceptual knowledge of the world

Settings
- Under-the-sea area
- Coral area
- Sand area
- Sea area with boat
- Fishing area (optional)

Props
- Goggles
- Swimming fins
- Boat
- Seashells
- Fish
- Fishing poles
- Plastic sea animals
- Plastic "fish" shower curtain
- Sandbox and sand
- Blue sheet or large piece of paper (for water)
- Sand toys
- Camera

Roles
- Divers
- Boat riders
- Fishermen and women
- People sunbathing
- People playing in the sand

General Description of Activity

Set up an under-the-sea environment by aligning bookshelves in straight lines, two on one side and two facing them, with a "fish" shower curtain (a curtain that is transparent with different fish on it) draped over all the bookshelves. The children can "swim" under the curtain amid shells and plastic fish on the shelves. In another area, set up a boat area or an area where divers can jump into the "water." A sand area might have sea shells buried in the sand for children to find (instead of a sand table, use a large cardboard box 4' × 6' × 5" high, lined with plastic—the low sides will allow children to kneel outside the sand area while they play). Still another area can be set up for fishing. (If desired, use a water table.) Thus, children can pretend to be divers, boat riders, people fishing, or people enjoying the water or beach.

Verbal Productions

Level of linguistic complexity varies with the role or competency of the child playing the role.
- "I am diving under the water with my goggles" or "My goggles"
- "I found a big shell and a little shell" or "That my shell"
- "See all of the red coral" or "See coral"

Adult Facilitative Role

The adult is to facilitate role play and help expand language and literacy skills. Typical actions or strategies to use include

Playing a role: "I am a diver looking for new kinds of fish and coral. The coral is sharp."

Modeling a statement/vocabulary: "Divers have to wear a mask and an oxygen tank so they can breathe underwater. Divers usually wear special rubber suits so they don't get cold in the water."

Event casting a child's actions: "You are diving into the water. Now you are swimming under the sea. Be careful of the coral; you are very close to it. Oh, you see a dolphin."

Contrasting present and irregular past tense: "We swim in the water" to "Yesterday, we swam in the water."

ART Aquariums

Objectives
1. Express creativity
2. Develop small motor skills (e.g., drawing, painting, cutting, pasting)
3. Practice turn-taking skills
4. Converse with peers and adults

Materials
- Glue
- Paper plates
- Wooden craft sticks or cotton swabs
- Sand
- Fish and shark cutouts
- Seashells
- Green construction paper or yarn
- Blue plastic wrap

General Description of Activity

Children smear glue on the bottom half of a paper plate using a wooden craft stick or a cotton swab. They then sprinkle sand over the glue to represent the bottom of the ocean. On the top half of the plate, above the sand, children can glue on items that are found under the sea, such as fish cutouts, shark cutouts, seashells, and seaweed (green construction paper or yarn). Wrap the plate in blue plastic wrap and tape it to the back of the plate to represent the water and to create an aquarium effect.

GROUP : **Sorting Shells**

Objectives
1. Improve listening skills
2. Increase identification skills
3. Increase vocabulary skills
4. Increase comparative skills
5. Practice turn-taking skills
6. Learn appropriate group-interaction skills

Materials
- Shells of varying sizes and textures
- Additional objects that are rough, smooth, small, or large

General Description of Activity

Present several different kinds of shells, including ones that are large, small, rough, and smooth.

Group Participation

Give each child a shell. Have children examine their shells as you explain the differences between large and small and rough and smooth. Have each child come to the front, individually, and say whether his or her shell is rough or smooth. Ask each child to place the shell in the large or small bucket, depending on its size. Give assistance as needed.

Summary/Transition Activity

Review the sizes of the shells and the textures. Introduce other objects that are rough, smooth, large, or small.

Wednesday

Dramatic Play	Art	Group	Story	Song
Science Investigations	Gak	Identifying *A, B,* and *C*	*The Mystery of Magnets*	"Raindrops and Lemondrops"

DAILY PLANNING GUIDE

Language and Literacy Skills Facilitated

Vocabulary: *scientist, water, eyedropper, wax paper, primary colors, microscope, magnifying glass, straw, sponge, dissolve*

Verb phrase structures: <u>is</u> mix<u>ing</u>, mix<u>ed</u> water, <u>is</u> dissolv<u>ing</u>, dissolv<u>ed</u>, dissolve<u>s</u>, <u>is</u> blow<u>ing</u>, bl<u>ew</u>, <u>has</u> bl<u>own</u>, <u>was</u> focus<u>ing</u>, focus<u>ed</u>

Adjective/object descriptions: *red/blue/yellow water; green/orange/ purple water; green droplets, big/little droplets*

Question structures: *what, how, where, when, who, what if, why, how many, which one*

Pronouns: *I, you, he, she, we, they, my, your, him, her, his, our, their, me, us, them*

Prepositions: *in, on, under, over, near, beneath, next to, beside, around, inside, outside*

Sounds: /s/ <u>s</u>ee, <u>s</u>cienti<u>s</u>t, di<u>ss</u>olve, look<u>s</u>; /f/ <u>f</u>ind, <u>f</u>ocus, o<u>ff</u>; /k/ <u>c</u>ome, bu<u>ck</u>et, ba<u>ck</u>

Noting print has meaning: names on chairs and on cubbies, signs in dramatic play, words in books and on chalkboard

Noting sound–symbol associations: What sound does _____ start with?

Writing: letters, names, words

Social Skills Facilitated

Initiating interaction with peers and adults; responding to questions and requests from peers and adults

Negotiating with peers for toys and materials

Group cooperation: waiting for a turn in a group, taking a turn at the appropriate time

Cognitive Skills Facilitated

Problem-solving skills: how to mix colors

Classification skills: things that dissolve

Sequencing skills: story, song

Narrative/story structure: expository

Motor Skills Facilitated

Large motor: outdoor play activities—jumping, running, hopping, pedaling, climbing

Small motor: writing, drawing, painting, stirring

DRAMATIC PLAY **Science Investigations**

Type of Activity: Related

Objectives
1. Learn new, and employ familiar, vocabulary
2. Learn new, and employ a variety of, syntactic constructions
3. Interact with peers
4. Sequence familiar routines
5. Expand conceptual knowledge of the world

Settings
- Colored-water mixing lab
- Droplet-cutting laboratory area
- Sponge area
- Microscope laboratory area
- Magnet area
- Balloon area (optional)
- Fan area (optional)
- Paper-airplane design area (optional)
- Other science laboratory areas

Props
- Bowls of colored water
- Mixing bowls
- Eyedroppers
- Water
- Wax paper
- Plastic strips
- Magnifying glasses
- Containers of water and sponges
- Microscope
- Slides
- Magnets
- Metal objects
- Nonmetal objects
- Balloons
- Pinwheels
- Fans
- Paper airplanes

Roles
- Scientists at the microscope laboratory
- Scientists finding germs in slides
- Scientists conducting other experiments

General Description of Activity

Children pretend to be scientists investigating water. Set up a variety of experiments with water in the dramatic play area, such as mixing water of different colors and dripping water on a variety of absorbent textures. The children can put drops of water on wax paper, divide the droplets using a plastic chip, and then blow the droplets back together until they form a large droplet. The children can also look at the droplets with a magnifying glass. Another activity could be transferring water from one container to another with sponges or using a microscope to look at slides of water droplets.

You could also set up an area for children to investigate magnetism. Other science experiments might involve investigations of air. Children can inflate balloons, use fans to blow a variety of objects, make paper airplanes, and so forth.

Verbal Productions

Level of linguistic complexity varies with the role or competency of the child playing the role.
- "He mixed red and yellow and got orange" or "Orange"
- "This is a microscope. I can see the bug" or "See bug"
- "She is blowing the bubbles" or "See the big bubble"
- "I can blow the bubbles back together" or "Blow back"

Adult Facilitative Role

The adult is to facilitate role play and help expand language and literacy skills. Typical actions or strategies to use include

Playing a role: "I am a scientist working in my lab. I am looking at water under the microscope."

Expanding a child's model: "Look in" to "I want to look in the microscope."

Event casting an adult's utterance: "I am mixing yellow water with red water. Look, the water is now orange."

Providing a literacy model: "That sign says *magnet*."

ART **Gak**

Objectives
1. Express creativity
2. Develop small motor skills (e.g., drawing, painting, cutting, pasting)
3. Practice turn-taking skills
4. Converse with peers and adults

Materials

- Smocks
- White glue (enough for each child to have ¼ cup)
- Liquid starch (enough for each child to have ¼ cup)
- Two ¼ cup measuring cups (one for each ingredient)
- Six containers big enough to mix the two ingredients by hand (or three larger containers)
- Food coloring (optional)

General Description of Activity

Gak is made with white glue and liquid starch. For each child, pour ¼ cup white glue into a container, then add ¼ cup liquid starch. Have the child mix the two ingredients together with his or her hands. After mixing, the mixture will be smooth and rubbery, and the child can play with the gak similar to playdough. (More liquid starch may need to be added to make the gak smooth.) Containers should be big enough for a child to get two hands in, and it's more fun and facilitates more language if the containers will hold at least four hands. If a larger container is used, several children can mix the ingredients together (multiply the per-child amount if more than one child is making the gak). Have plastic bags for children to put the gak in so that they can take home their "science" experiment.

Variation

For visual appeal, you can add food coloring to the glue before the liquid starch is added; keep in mind, however, that the mixture might stain clothing.

GROUP **Identifying *A*, *B*, and *C***

Objectives

1. Improve listening skills
2. Improve knowledge of the alphabet and sounds
3. Learn appropriate group-interaction skills
4. Practice turn-taking skills

Materials

- Target alphabet letters (or use magnetic letters)
- Alphabet chart
- Individual chalkboards and chalk or paper and pencils or markers (optional)

General Description of Activity

This is the first of a series of lessons on the letters of the alphabet. Each week, a group activity will focus on two or three letters.

Lay the letters *A*, *B*, and *C* on the floor in front of the children (or magnetic letters could be used with a large magnetic board in front of the class). Have the children, in chorus, say the letters as you point to each one. Have one child come to the front and point to a specific letter.

Group Participation

Ask different children to point to specific letters, helping them as necessary. Vary the difficulty by having children identify letters in order or out of order, or by having some match a letter card to the letters on the floor instead of pointing to a designated letter. You can also ask them to match lowercase letters to uppercase letters. Children can also point to a letter and have the class label it.

Summary/Transition Activity

Say the whole alphabet with the children as you point to an alphabet chart. Then have everyone say the target alphabet letters (*A*, *B*, *C*) as you point to each letter in turn. An alternative activity is to have the children practice writing the three target letters.

Thursday

Dramatic Play	Art	Group	Story	Song
Space	Clothespin Creations	Things that Fly	*Ten Black Dots*	"The Rocket Song"

DAILY PLANNING GUIDE

Language and Literacy Skills Facilitated

Vocabulary: *space, rocket ship, planet, gravity, adventure, spacesuit, astronaut, orbit, sun, moon, stars, blast off, oxygen*

Verb phrase structures: *count<u>ed</u> down, <u>are</u> count<u>ing</u>, travel<u>ing</u> in space, <u>saw</u> stars, blast<u>ing</u> off, pack<u>ed</u> food, <u>us</u><u>ing</u> oxygen*

Adjective/object descriptions: *bright stars, fast ship, big planet, weird colors, little stars, black hole*

Question structures: *what, how, where, when, who, what if, why, how many, which one*

Pronouns: *I, you, he, she, we, they, my, your, him, her, his, our, their, me, us, them*

Prepositions: *in, on, under, over, near, beneath, next to, beside, around, inside, outside*

Sounds: /r/ <u>r</u>ocket, sta<u>r</u>; /s/ <u>s</u>pace, <u>s</u>un, fa<u>ce</u>; /l/ <u>l</u>ight, Je<u>ll</u>-o, be<u>ll</u>; /k/ <u>c</u>an, ro<u>ck</u>et, lo<u>ck</u>

Noting print has meaning: names on chairs and on cubbies, signs in dramatic play, words in books and on chalkboard

Noting sound–symbol associations: What sound does _____ start with?

Writing: letters, names, words

Social Skills Facilitated

Initiating interaction with peers and adults; responding to questions and requests from peers and adults

Negotiating with peers for toys and materials

Group cooperation: waiting for a turn in a group, taking a turn at the appropriate time

Cognitive Skills Facilitated

Problem-solving skills: how to get up in space

Classification skills: What things are in outer space?

Sequencing skills: countdown, story, songs

Narrative/story structure: adventure

Motor Skills Facilitated

Large motor: outdoor play activities—jumping, running, hopping, pedaling, climbing

Small motor: writing, drawing, gluing, fingerpainting

- -
DRAMATIC PLAY **Space**
- -

Type of Activity: Central

Objectives
1. Learn new, and employ familiar, vocabulary
2. Learn new, and employ a variety of, syntactic constructions
3. Interact with peers
4. Sequence familiar routines
5. Expand conceptual knowledge of the world

Settings
- Rocket ship (playhouse with chairs placed sideways on the floor so children can lie in them and look upward)
- Command center (with pretend television sets and computers)
- Moon

Props
- Rocket ship (playhouse with chairs placed sideways on the floor so children can lie in them and look upward)
- Helmets
- Backpacks
- Walking boards or balance beams
- Moon rocks (crushed newspaper balls covered with silver duct tape or rubber rocks)
- Miniature trampoline
- Television sets (shoeboxes with one side cut out and a picture pasted over the cutout area)
- Microphones (toilet paper rolls)
- Headsets
- Pretend computers
- Videotape about the space program
- Walkie-talkies
- Moon vehicle (optional)

Roles
- Astronauts
- Command center workers
- Technicians

General Description of Activity

Children pretend to be astronauts and go to the moon in a spacecraft. Once on the moon, they can find moon rocks, jump (on a miniature trampoline) to see how light they are, and so forth. Some of the children can remain on earth at the command center and talk to the astronauts. Show a brief videotape on the space program to the children so that they begin to understand about rocket ships, the need to wear special suits in space, and what the moon really looks like.

Verbal Productions

Level of linguistic complexity varies with the role or competency of the child playing the role.
- "She found a big moon rock" or "Big"
- "I can jump high. Watch me!" or "Look!"
- "He is landing the rocket ship" or "He landed it"
- "You can see the earth. It is blue" "I see the moon"

Adult Facilitative Role

The adult is to facilitate role play and help expand language and literacy skills. Typical actions or strategies to use include

Playing a role: "I am in outer space on a science mission. We are going to explore the moon."

Using a cloze procedure: "Five, four, three, two, one, _____(blast-off)"

Recasting a child's utterance: "He wants to drive the land rover" to "He wanted to drive the land rover the last time we played this game."

Modeling correct production of /s/ blends: "We are in space. I want to slide down the chute. I have to go slow, or I will have to stop."

Identifying rhyming words: "The words *space, race, face,* and *lace* all rhyme."

ART **Clothespin Creations**

Objectives
1. Express creativity
2. Develop small motor skills (e.g., drawing, painting, cutting, pasting)
3. Practice turn-taking skills
4. Converse with peers and adults

Materials
- Wooden clothespins with slot (at least one per child)
- Scraps of fabric of a variety of colors or designs
- Small pieces of aluminum foil
- Glue
- Markers
- Yarn

General Description of Activity

Give each child a wooden clothespin to turn into a toy doll, robot, or astronaut. Children can glue on scraps of fabric and yarn for their creations and draw faces with markers. Pieces of foil can be added for robots and astronauts.

GROUP **Things that Fly**

Objectives
1. Improve listening skills
2. Increase conceptual knowledge
3. Learn appropriate group-interaction skills
4. Practice turn-taking skills

Materials
- Toys and objects that can fly (e.g., airplane, bird, helicopter, kite, paper airplane, glider)
- Toys and objects that cannot fly (e.g., car, doll, train, block, ball)
- Tubs labeled *fly* and *can't fly*

General Description of Activity

Begin by flying a paper airplane, and then talk about the characteristics of things that fly. Put the airplane in a container labeled *fly*.

Group Participation

Give each child an object that represents something that either flies or does not fly. Have children come to the front, one by one, and decide whether their object can fly or not. Have the children put the object in the box that corresponds with their correct decision.

Summary/Transition Activity

Have everyone stand up and pretend to fly, then land on the ground.

March

Activities	Monday	Tuesday	Wednesday	Thursday
Week 29 Family Fun				
Dramatic Play	Movie Theater	Camping	School Fair	Beach
Art	Draw a Picture	Pinecone Bird Feeder	Macaroni Necklace	Coffee Filter Painting
Group	Act out a Story (*Goldilocks and the Three Bears*)	Identifying *D, E,* and *F*	How to Write an *8*	Color Green
Story	*Goldilocks and the Three Bears*	*Arthur Goes To Camp*	*Who Took the Cookies from the Cookie Jar?*	*Rainbow Fish to the Rescue*
Song	"If You're Happy and You Know It"	"There's Something in My Pocket"	"One, Two, Buckle My Shoe"	"All the Little Fishies" and "Ocean Shell" (fingerplay)
Week 30 Spring				
Dramatic Play	Spring Cleaning	Gardening	Baseball	Building a House
Art	Texture Rubbings	Crushed Tissue Paper Flowers	Watercolor Paintings	Wallpaper Collage
Group	How to Write a *9*	Identifying *G, H,* and *I*	Flannel Board Story Retelling	Act out a Story (*The Three Little Pigs*)
Story	*The Berenstain Bears and the Messy Room*	*The Garden In Our Yard*	*Just My Friend and Me*	*The Three Little Pigs*
Song	"The Itsy, Bitsy Spider"	"Raindrops and Lemondrops"	"Take Me out to the Ballgame"	"Johnny Works with One Hammer"
Week 31 Taking Care of Ourselves				
Dramatic Play	Grocery Store (Healthy Food)	Fitness Center	Health Screening (Clinic)	Beauty Salon/Barber Shop
Art	Food Collage	Playdough	Self-Portraits	Shaving Cream Fingerpainting
Group	Food Pyramid	Identifying *J, K,* and *L*	Focus on Rhyming Words	Rough/Smooth
Story	*Just Shopping with Mom*	*Bearobics*	*Going to the Doctor*	*All by Myself*
Song	"On Top of Spaghetti"	"Head, Shoulders, Knees, and Toes"	"Brush Your Teeth"	"The Alphabet Song"
Week 32 Vacations				
Dramatic Play	Airplane	Motel	Amusement Park	Cruise Ship
Art	Fold/Decorate Paper Airplanes	Post Cards	Watercolor Paintings	Tissue Paper Fish
Group	How to Write a *10*	Identifying *M, N,* and *O*	Act out a Story (*Anansi and the Moss-Covered Rock*)	Sound Sequencing
Story	*The Trip*	*Emma's Vacation*	*Anansi and the Moss-Covered Rock*	*Out of the Ocean*
Song	"I'm a Little Airplane"	"Going to Kentucky"	"It's a Small World"	"Row, Row, Row Your Boat"

```
.......................................
:          WEEKLY PLANNING GUIDE        :
.......................................
```

	Dramatic Play	Art	Group	Story	Song
Monday *Suggested Props and Materials*	Movie Theater *Movie theater scenario, booth area, tickets, cash register, chairs and mat for making risers (i.e., a stair step so that chairs can be placed at different heights and levels), food items (e.g., pretend popcorn, pretend candy, pretend soft drinks), TV monitor/VCR and movie, puppets*	Draw a Picture *Construction paper (white or colored), crayons, markers, watered-down tempera paint (optional)*	Act out a Story (*Goldilocks and the Three Bears*) *Book, props for the story, costumes*	*Goldilocks and the Three Bears*	"If You're Happy and You Know It"
Tuesday *Suggested Props and Materials*	Camping *Camping scenario, tent or tents, boats, mats for sleeping bags, backpacks, grill, wooden blocks for fire wood, wooden craft stick matches, cotton balls (pretend marshmallows) on chopsticks for roasting over the fire, pretend food, stuffed bears and other animals, trees made of paper*	Pinecone Bird Feeder *Pinecones, peanut butter or margarine, plastic knives, birdseed, container for seed, string*	Identifying *D, E,* and *F* *D, E, F alphabet cards, alphabet chart, individual chalkboards and chalk or paper and pencils or markers (optional)*	*Arthur Goes to Camp*	"There's Something in My Pocket"
Wednesday *Suggested Props and Materials*	School Fair *School fair scenario, booths, tickets, balls and/or beanbags, rings and bottles or stakes, fish and fishing poles (paper fish have numbers on them to match prizes on shelf), plastic ducks (with numbers written on the bottom to match prizes on the shelf)*	Macaroni Necklace *Different kinds of macaroni (with holes big enough for string to go through), string or yarn (wrap one end in tape to make threading easier), pieces of paper, straws (cut up in 1" pieces)*	How to Write an 8 *Card with 8 on it, chalkboards and chalk, paper and pencils or whiteboard and markers (optional)*	*Who Took the Cookies from the Cookie Jar?*	"One, Two, Buckle My Shoe"
Thursday *Suggested Props and Materials*	Beach *Beach scenario, area for laying on towels, wading pool filled with sand, concession with pretend food, cash register, volleyball area, balloons (for volleyball)*	Coffee Filter Painting *Watercolor paints, brushes, coffee filters, containers of water for rinsing brushes, smocks*	Color Green *Variety of green items; construction paper mats (green, orange, purple, red, blue, yellow); a few purple, orange, red, blue, and yellow items*	*Rainbow Fish to the Rescue*	"All the Little Fishies" and "Ocean Shell" (fingerplay)

NEWSLETTER

Vol. 1, No. 29

Date: _____

Family Fun

Monday The children will enjoy their favorite movies and movie snacks at the movie theater today. During dramatic play, they will be theater workers and customers. At the art table, they will make drawings. We will read *Goldilocks and the Three Bears* during storytime and act out the story during group time. We will end the day by singing "If You're Happy and You Know It."

Tuesday Today's fun will be going camping. The children will pitch tents, hike in the woods, and go fishing during dramatic play. They will make pinecone bird feeders in art. Our featured story is *Arthur Goes to Camp*. During group time, children will learn about the letters *D*, *E*, and *F*. We will sing "There's Something in My Pocket."

Wednesday We will enjoy a pretend school fair today. During dramatic play, children will play carnival games and sell and eat carnival food. At the art table, they will make macaroni necklaces. *Who Took the Cookies From the Cookie Jar?* will be read during storytime. During group time, they will learn about the number *8*. We will finish our day by singing "One, Two, Buckle My Shoe."

Thursday The children will enjoy the beach during dramatic play today. They might swim, play in the sand, or play volleyball. At the art table, children will paint designs on coffee filters. We will read *Rainbow Fish to the Rescue* during storytime. During group time, the children will review the color green. Please have your child wear something green today. We will sing "All the Little Fishies" and do the "Ocean Shell" fingerplay during music.

Monday

Dramatic Play	Art	Group	Story	Song
Movie Theater	Draw a Picture	Act out a Story (*Goldilocks and the Three Bears*)	*Goldilocks and the Three Bears*	"If You're Happy and You Know It"

DAILY PLANNING GUIDE

Language and Literacy Skills Facilitated

Vocabulary: *movie, film, picture show, screen, ticket, watch, puppet, Oscar, Miss Piggy, dog, cat, popcorn, soft drink, actor, actress, costume, props*

Verb phrase structures: <u>act</u> *like a* ___, <u>watch</u> *the film,* <u>act</u> *in the show,* <u>put</u> *on costumes*

Adjective/object descriptions: *good picture, pink piggy, noisy/quiet show, funny/sad puppet*

Question structures: *what, how, where, when, who, what if, why, how many, which one*

Pronouns: *I, you, he, she, we, they, my, your, him, her, his, our, their, me, us, them*

Prepositions: *in, on, under, over, near, beneath, next to, beside, around, inside, outside*

Sounds: /f/ <u>f</u>ix, o<u>ff</u>; /s/ <u>s</u>it, talk<u>s</u>; /l/ <u>l</u>ittle, be<u>ll</u>

Noting print has meaning: names on chairs and on cubbies, signs in dramatic play, words in books and on chalkboard

Noting sound–symbol associations: What sound does _____ start with?

Writing: letters, names, words

Social Skills Facilitated

Initiating interaction with peers and adults; responding to questions and requests from peers and adults

Negotiating with peers for toys and materials

Group cooperation: waiting for a turn in a group, taking a turn at the appropriate time

Cognitive Skills Facilitated

Problem-solving skills: what to draw

Classification skills: things at a movie theater

Sequencing skills: story, songs

Narrative/story structure: classic fairy tale

Motor Skills Facilitated

Large motor: outdoor play activities—jumping, running, hopping, pedaling, climbing

Small motor: writing, drawing, gluing

DRAMATIC PLAY **Movie Theater**

Type of Activity: Central

Objectives
1. Learn new, and employ familiar, vocabulary
2. Learn new, and employ a variety of, syntactic constructions
3. Interact with peers
4. Sequence familiar routines
5. Expand conceptual knowledge of the world

Settings
- Ticket booth
- Concession stand
- Spectator seats
- Stage or puppet area

Props
- Tickets
- Cash register
- Chairs and mat for making risers
- Food items (e.g., pretend popcorn, candy, soft drinks)
- TV monitor/VCR and movie
- Puppets

Roles
- Cashier
- Ticket taker
- Customers
- Concession workers
- Puppeteers

General Description of Activity

Set up a movie theater with a ticket booth area, a spectator section, a concession area, and a stage. The children can purchase tickets, buy their popcorn and other food, find their seats, and prepare to watch a movie or puppet show. It is helpful if the spectator area is raised (this can be accomplished by folding over a tumbling mat and putting chairs on one level and a second row on a higher level). Set up a TV monitor and a short film for the children to watch. You could also add a puppet area—a shelf with a blanket thrown over it so that the children can use hand puppets on the shelf and hide behind the shelf while they are doing the puppet actions.

Verbal Productions

Level of linguistic complexity varies with the role or competency of the child playing the role.
- "I need tickets for three adults and two children, please" or "Tickets, please"
- "I'll be Big Bird. You be Elmo" or "Big Bird"
- "Do you want popcorn and a coke?" or "Popcorn?"
- "I watched that at my birthday party" or "Watch at party"

Adult Facilitative Role

The adult is to facilitate role play and help expand language and literacy skills. Typical actions or strategies to use include

Playing a role: "I am selling tickets to the movie. How many tickets do you want?"

Recasting a child's utterance: "She wants to see the new movie about the horse" to "She wanted to see the same movie last week."

Contrasting two sounds: "Did you say 'care' or 'tear?'"

Providing a literacy model: The sign says *tickets here*."

Redirecting a child to a peer: "Ask Johnny if he will move over. Say, 'Move over, please!'"

ART **Draw a Picture**

Objectives
1. Express creativity
2. Develop small motor skills (e.g., drawing, painting, cutting, pasting)
3. Practice turn-taking skills
4. Converse with peers and adults

Materials
- Paper (white or colored)
- Crayons
- Markers
- Watered-down tempera paint (optional)

General Description of Activity

Provide the children with paper and a selection of crayons and/or markers. Let the children draw anything they want. Drawings could be of themselves, their family, their pets, different scenes, designs, rainbows, or of other things. Children can turn their crayon drawings into crayon washes by painting over the pictures with a light coat of tempera paint (watered-down paint). The paint does not stick to the crayon but will fill in where there are no crayon marks to make a background of color.

GROUP Act out a Story (*Goldilocks and the Three Bears*)

Objectives
1. Improve listening skills
2. Increase sequencing ability
3. Increase knowledge of storytelling
4. Learn appropriate group-interaction skills
5. Practice turn-taking skills

Materials
Goldilocks and the Three Bears
Props for the story

General Description of Activity

Read *Goldilocks and the Three Bears* to the children, or summarize it if they are familiar with it.

Group Participation

Assign children roles from the story. Assure the children not chosen the first time that everyone will have a turn and that they have the very important job of being a good listening audience. Narrate the story as the children act it out. They should say as many of the lines as they can, with prompts given when needed. Repeat with new actors until all of the children have had a turn.

Summary/Transition Activity

Compliment the children's acting, and ask children what other stories they would like to act out.

Tuesday

Dramatic Play	Art	Group	Story	Song
Camping	Pinecone Bird Feeder	Identifying *D, E,* and *F*	*Arthur Goes to Camp*	"There's Something in My Pocket"

DAILY PLANNING GUIDE

Language and Literacy Skills Facilitated

Vocabulary: *tent, campfire, stick, marshmallow, backpack, sleeping bag, hike, bear, deer, animals, trees, mountains, trail*

Verb phrase structures: *roasts marshmallows, is roasting hot dogs, roasted marshmallows, sleeps in a tent, is sleeping, slept in a tent, hikes, hiked, lights a fire, lit a fire*

Adjective/object descriptions: *big ____, little ____, hot ____, sleepy ___, hungry ____, yellow ____, blue ____*

Question structures: *what, how, where, when, who, what if, why, how many, which one*

Pronouns: *I, you, he, she, we, they, my, your, him, her, his, our, their, me, us, them*

Prepositions: *in, on, under, over, near, beneath, next to, beside, around, inside, outside*

Sounds: /k/ cook; /l/ light, yellow, ball; /z/ zipper, balls; /r/ roast, bear; /f/ fire, off

Noting print has meaning: names on chairs and on cubbies, signs in dramatic play, words in books and on chalkboard

Noting sound–symbol associations: What sound does _____ start with?

Writing: letters, names, words

Social Skills Facilitated

Initiating interaction with peers and adults; responding to questions and requests from peers and adults

Negotiating with peers for toys and materials

Group cooperation: waiting for a turn in a group, taking a turn at the appropriate time

Cognitive Skills Facilitated

Problem-solving skills: putting peanut butter or margarine on the pinecone, identifying letters

Classification skills: things we take on a camping trip

Sequencing skills: songs, stories, alphabet letters

Narrative/story structure: adventure

Motor Skills Facilitated

Large motor: outdoor play activities—jumping, running, hopping, pedaling, climbing

Small motor: writing, drawing, gluing, painting

DRAMATIC PLAY **Camping**

Type of Activity: Central

Objectives
1. Learn new, and employ familiar, vocabulary
2. Learn new, and employ a variety of, syntactic constructions
3. Interact with peers
4. Sequence familiar routines
5. Expand conceptual knowledge of the world

Settings
- Campground
- Lake
- Mountains
- Hiking area
- Ranger station

Props
- Tent(s)
- Sleeping bags
- Campfire (wooden blocks)
- Grill
- Picnic items (e.g., basket, food, paper plates, utensils)
- Marshmallows (cotton balls on sticks)
- Boats
- Fishing poles (with magnets attached to catch the fish)
- Fish (with paper clips attached)
- Backpacks
- Maps
- Pretend forest animals (e.g., bears, raccoons, rabbits)

Roles
- Campers (family members)
- Fishermen and women
- Hikers
- Ranger

General Description of Activity

Children act out camping trips and activities. Children might choose to camp at a lake, in the mountains, or in a camping area. They might sleep in tents or under the stars in sleeping bags. They could cook their food over a wood fire or pack a lunch and go hiking or fishing. The class might establish a ranger station so families can get maps that show them where to camp.

Verbal Productions

Level of linguistic complexity varies with the role or competency of the child playing the role.
- "I am packing a lunch for the picnic" or "Picnic"
- "Let's unroll our sleeping bags" or "Let's sleep"
- "Fix the tent, please" or "My turn, please"
- "John is walking too fast" or "Too fast"
- "You missed the trail" or "Missed it"

Adult Facilitative Role

The adult is to facilitate role play and help expand language and literacy skills. Typical actions or strategies to use include

Playing a role: "I am going to sleep in this tent."

Asking an open question: "Where should we make the campfire?"

Contrasting error response with correct structure (focus contrast): "She do not help" to "Oh, you mean she did not help."

Modeling a statement/vocabulary: "When you camp you often sleep in a tent and cook your food over a campfire. Sometimes you go hiking or fishing when you are camping."

Using a cloze procedure: "This tent is big, and this tent is _____ (little)."

ART **Pinecone Bird Feeder**

Objectives
1. Express creativity
2. Develop small motor skills (e.g., drawing, painting, cutting, pasting)
3. Practice turn-taking skills
4. Converse with peers and adults

Materials
- Pinecones
- String or colored yarn
- Peanut butter (or margarine)
- Birdseed
- Box lids to put birdseed in for rolling

General Description of Activity

Attach string or colored yarn to a pinecone. Children, with a teacher's help, smear peanut butter or margarine on the pinecone and roll it in birdseed. For easy transport home, place the pinecone in a small plastic bag. Some of the extra bird feeders can be attached to trees in the play yard.

GROUP **Identifying *D*, *E*, and *F***

Objectives
1. Improve listening skills
2. Improve knowledge of the alphabet and sounds
3. Learn appropriate group-interaction skills
4. Practice turn-taking skills

Materials
- Target alphabet letters on cards or on one large card with all three letters written on it
- Alphabet chart
- Individual chalkboards and chalk or paper and pencils or markers (optional)

General Description of Activity

Lay the letters *D, E,* and *F* in front of the children. Have the children, in chorus, say the letters as you point to each one. Have one child come to the front and point to a specific letter.

Group Participation

Ask different children to point to specific letters, helping them as necessary. Vary the difficulty by having children identify letters in order or out of order, or by having some match a letter card to the letters on the floor instead of pointing to a designated letter. You can also ask them to match lower-case letters to uppercase letters. Children can also point to a letter and have the class label it.

Summary/Transition Activity

Say the whole alphabet with the children as you point to an alphabet chart. Then have everyone say the target alphabet letters (*D, E, F*) as you point to each letter in turn. An alternative activity is to have the children practice writing the three target letters.

Wednesday

Dramatic Play	Art	Group	Story	Song
School Fair	Macaroni Necklace	How to Write an 8	*Who Took the Cookies from the Cookie Jar?*	"One, Two, Buckle My Shoe"

DAILY PLANNING GUIDE

Language and Literacy Skills Facilitated

Vocabulary: *tickets, booths, Ring Toss, fishing pole, duck pond, beanbags, prize*

Verb phrase structures: *tosses, tossed the ring, wins/won the prize, throws/ threw the beanbag, buys/bought the ticket*

Adjective/object descriptions: *big/little beanbag, red/blue ring, large/small duck*

Question structures: *what, how, where, when, who, what if, why, how many, which one*

Pronouns: *I, you, he, she, we, they, my, your, him, her, his, our, their, me, us, them*

Prepositions: *in, on, under, over, near, beneath, next to, beside, around, inside, outside*

Sounds: /f/ *fix, off;* /s/ *sit, talks;* /l/ *little, bell*

Noting print has meaning: names on chairs and on cubbies, signs in dramatic play, words in books and on chalkboard

Noting sound–symbol associations: What sound does _____ start with?

Writing: letters, names, words

Social Skills Facilitated

Initiating interaction with peers and adults; responding to questions and requests from peers and adults

Negotiating with peers for toys and materials

Group cooperation: waiting for a turn in a group, taking a turn at the appropriate time

Cognitive Skills Facilitated

Problem-solving skills: how to win a prize, how to write an 8

Classification skills: things at a fair

Sequencing skills: story, songs

Narrative/story structure: repetitive line

Motor Skills Facilitated

Large motor: outdoor play activities—jumping, running, hopping, pedaling, climbing

Small motor: writing, drawing, gluing

DRAMATIC PLAY **School Fair**

Type of Activity: Related

Objectives
1. Learn new, and employ familiar, vocabulary
2. Learn new, and employ a variety of, syntactic constructions
3. Interact with peers
4. Sequence familiar routines
5. Expand conceptual knowledge of the world

March

Week 29
Family Fun

WEDNESDAY

Setting
- Ticket sale area
- Basketball throw and/or bean bag throw
- Ring toss
- Fishing area
- Duck pond (plastic ducks floating in shallow water)

Props
- Tickets
- Balls and/or beanbags
- Rings and bottles or stakes
- Fish and fishing poles (paper fish have numbers on them to match prizes on shelf)
- Plastic ducks (with numbers written on the bottom to match prizes on the shelf)

Roles
- Ticket sellers
- Ticket takers who run the games
- Game players

General Description of Activity

Set up a variety of games that might be played at a school fair, such as a basketball throw, a ring toss, a "go fishing" game, a choose-a-duck-out-of-water game, and a beanbag throw. Some of the children can sell tickets to play the games, some can run the games and hand out prizes, and some can be the players.

Verbal Productions

- "I want to play this game. How many tickets does it take?" or "Play game"
- "You can have three balls to throw" or "Three balls"
- "He is waiting for the next turn" or "His turn"

Adult Facilitative Role

Playing a role: "Do you want to buy a ticket?"

Expanding a child's utterance: "Throw it" to "Yes, he throws it in the hole."

Modeling phonological awareness: "Yes, the words *dog, David*, and *dish* all start with the letter *D*."

Event casting an adult's actions: "I am running the bean bag throw. I am giving Jane three bags to throw at the clown. I better get out of her way so that she can throw the bean bags at the clown."

Providing a literacy model: "The sign says *bean bag throw*."

ART **Macaroni Necklace**

Objectives
1. Express creativity
2. Develop small motor skills (e.g., drawing, painting, cutting, pasting)
3. Practice turn-taking skills
4. Converse with peers and adults

Materials
- Different kinds of macaroni (with holes big enough for a string to go through)
- String or yarn (with one end wrapped in tape to make threading easier)
- Pieces of paper
- Straws (cut up in 1" pieces)

General Description of Activity

Necklaces can be made by stringing different kinds of macaroni. The macaroni can be dyed different colors. Small pieces of construction paper or straws cut to different lengths can be strung between the macaroni pieces. Tie one piece of macaroni to one end of the string so that the others will not fall off the string after they are strung.

GROUP **How to Write an 8**

Objectives
1. Improve listening skills
2. Increase conceptual knowledge
3. Learn appropriate group-interaction skills
4. Practice turn-taking skills
5. Practice recognition and writing of numbers

Materials
- Number cards
- Chalkboards and chalk
- Paper and pencils (optional)
- Whiteboard and markers (optional)

General Description of Activity

Hold up a card with the number 8 written on it. Trace the number with your finger, and invite several children to come to the front of the group to trace the number, too. As the children trace, recite the jingle for the target number (8):

1: Start at the top, go down and you're done, that's the way to make a *1*.

2: Around and back on the railroad track, *2, 2, 2*.

3: Around the tree, around the tree, that's the way to make a *3*.

4: Down and over and down once more, that's the way to make a *4*.

5: Down around, make a hat on it, and look what you've found. (*5*)

6: Down around until it sticks, that's the way to make a *6*.

7: Over and down and it's not heaven, over and down makes a *7*.

8: Make an S and go back straight, that's the way to make an *8*.

9: A balloon and a line make *9*.

10: Draw a line and a circle with your pen, that's the way to make a *10*.

Group Participation

Distribute individual chalkboards and chalk (or paper and pencils) to the children, and have them practice writing the target number.

Variation 1

Whiteboards and markers may be easier for some children to use.

Variation 2

To introduce the number, use a number line and have the children count up to the target number on the line. One child could place the target number on the number line.

Summary/Transition Activity

Ask children to hold up their chalkboards and show the group their numbers.

Thursday

Dramatic Play	Art	Group	Story	Song
Beach	Coffee Filter Painting	Color Green	*Rainbow Fish to the Rescue*	"All the Little Fishies" and "Ocean Shell" (fingerplay)

DAILY PLANNING GUIDE

Language and Literacy Skills Facilitated

Vocabulary: *water, summer, swim, fish, shark, shrimp, octopus, crab, sunshine, dive, splash, sand, shell, dig, beach*

Verb phrase structures: *swims, is/are/was/were swimming, diving, splashing, splashed, swam, has swum, who is swimming? I am*

Adjective/object descriptions: *sunny day, hot day, cold water, funny fish, pink shrimp, mean octopus, hungry shark*

Question structures: *what, how, where, when, who, what if, why, how many, which one*

Pronouns: *I, you, he, she, we, they, my, your, him, her, his, our, their, me, us, them*

Prepositions: *in, on, under, over, near, beneath, next to, beside, around, inside, outside*

Sounds: /s/ *sit, sing, miss;* /r/ *run, row, narrow, our;* /k/ *catch, come, octopus, back*

Noting print has meaning: names on chairs and on cubbies, signs in dramatic play, words in books and on chalkboard

Noting sound–symbol associations: What sound does _____ start with?

Writing: letters, names, words

Social Skills Facilitated

Initiating interaction with peers and adults; responding to questions and requests from peers and adults

Negotiating with peers for toys and materials

Group cooperation: waiting for a turn in a group, taking a turn at the appropriate time

Cognitive Skills Facilitated

Problem-solving skills: what to do at the beach

Classification skills: things at a beach

Sequencing skills: story, songs, fingerplays

Narrative/story structure: adventure

Motor Skills Facilitated

Large motor: outdoor play activities—jumping, running, hopping, pedaling, climbing

Small motor: writing, drawing, gluing, painting

DRAMATIC PLAY : **Beach**

Type of Activity: Related

Objectives
1. Learn new, and employ familiar, vocabulary
2. Learn new, and employ a variety of, syntactic constructions
3. Interact with peers
4. Sequence familiar routines
5. Expand conceptual knowledge of the world

Settings

- Blue sheet (or other demarcation) to represent a lake, or filled water table
- Small plastic pools filled with sand
- Volleyball area with a taped line to represent the net
- Concession stand(s) or boardwalk
- Lifeguard stand

Props

- Pails and shovels
- Seashells
- Boats (boxes or rubber rafts)
- Life jackets (plastic painting smocks worn backward)
- Fishing poles (with magnets attached to catch fish)
- Fish (with paper clips attached)
- Surfboards (pieces of sturdy cardboard)

- Megaphone (for lifeguard)
- Towels
- Pretend sunscreen
- Balloons (for use as volleyballs)
- Pretend food
- Pretend soda fountain (box lid with levers)
- Dishes
- Cash registers

Roles

- Sand diggers
- Sunbathers
- Surfers
- Beach vendors

- Customers
- Volleyball players
- Lifeguards
- Boat riders/fishermen and women

General Description of Activity

A day at the beach usually involves playing with sand near the water. Fill small plastic pools with sand, and bury some seashells in the sand so children can dig for them. Other activities might include playing sand volleyball, laying out on towels to get a tan, and riding in and/or fishing from boats. You could also set up a concession stand area or boardwalk. Children could surf on pretend surfboards made from cardboard.

Verbal Productions

Level of linguistic complexity varies with the role or competency of the child playing the role.
- "Hit the balloon to me" or "Hit it"
- "I found a pretty shell" or "My shell"
- "He is riding the surfboard and he didn't fall" or "Ride"
- "There's a shark! Get out!" or "Shark!"
- "She wants the shovel now" or "Her turn"
- "He will get an ice cream cone, and I will have a coke" or "Cone"

Adult Facilitative Role

The adult is to facilitate role play and help expand language and literacy skills. Typical actions or strategies to use include

Playing a role: "I am going to play balloon volleyball. Do you want to play, too?"

Recasting a structure: "The balloon is going high" to "The balloon goes very high."

Identifying rhyming words: "The words *high, my, lie,* and *sky* all rhyme."

Providing confirmatory feedback: "You're right. The word *fall* does start with the letter *f*."

Contrasting present and irregular past tense: "The doll falls out of the stroller when you don't strap her in" to "The doll fell on the floor yesterday."

ART : **Coffee Filter Painting**

Objectives

1. Express creativity
2. Develop small motor skills (e.g., drawing, painting, cutting, pasting)
3. Practice turn-taking skills
4. Converse with peers and adults

Materials
- Watercolor paints
- Brushes
- Coffee filters
- Containers of water for rinsing brushes
- Smocks
- Green construction paper (optional)
- Scissors
- Glue Sticks (optional)
- Bulletin board (optional)

General Description of Activity

Children paint with watercolors on flattened coffee filters. The porous paper allows the paint to run, creating interesting designs.

Variation 1

Fold the coffee filter and have children paint on one side of it. When it is opened, the colors will have formed a design throughout the filter.

Variation 2

Have children glue the coffee filter paintings to paper stems created from green construction paper to make flowers. Display the flowers on a large bulletin board for a "flower garden."

GROUP **Color Green**

Objectives
1. Improve listening skills
2. Increase conceptual knowledge
3. Learn appropriate group-interaction skills
4. Practice turn-taking skills

Materials
- Red, blue, yellow, orange, purple, and green construction paper, one sheet of each (use as mats)
- Several green objects
- Two purple objects
- Two orange objects
- Two yellow objects
- Two blue objects
- Two red objects

General Description of Activity

Gather an assortment of objects that are blue, red, and yellow, green, purple, and orange. At group time, hold up a piece of green construction paper, labeling the color as green. Place the paper in a tub marked with a green label. Have the children look around the room to find other items that are green. When they see an object, they can raise their hand to announce what it is. One child can then choose a green object from the pile of assorted objects and place it in the green tub.

Group Participation

Other children take turns choosing an item that is green and placing it in the green tub.

Variation

Use objects of various shades of green. Some children might discriminate between light green and dark green; for those who don't, ask them just to find a green item.

Summary/Transition Activity

Because it is "green" day and all the children are wearing something green, dismiss the children one by one by asking them to point to the green color on their clothes.

	Dramatic Play	Art	Group	Story	Song
Monday *Suggested Props and Materials*	Spring Cleaning *Spring cleaning scenario in housekeeping area, dishes, pretend food, dolls, mops, brooms, vacuum cleaners, spray bottles and rags, windows, lawnmowers*	Texture Rubbings *Paper (newsprint if possible), crayons with paper removed, textured cutouts, textured wallpaper (optional)*	How to Write a *9* *Card with 9 on it, chalkboard and chalk, paper and pencils*	*The Berenstain Bears and the Messy Room*	"The Itsy, Bitsy Spider"
Tuesday *Suggested Props and Materials*	Gardening *Gardening scenario, sand, sandbox, pretend vegetables, pretend flowers, pretend seeds, tractors, rakes, hoes, trowels, stove, dishes*	Crushed Tissue Paper Flowers *Flower outline, small pieces of colored tissue paper, pencils, glue*	Identifying *G, H,* and *I* *Letter cards G, H, and I; alphabet chart; individual chalkboard and chalk (optional)*	*The Garden in Our Yard*	"Raindrops and Lemondrops"
Wednesday *Suggested Props and Materials*	Baseball *Baseball scenario, baseball tee, plastic baseball bat, plastic (or Nerf) balls, bases, concession area, cups, pretend drink dispenser, pretend food, spectator area, (chairs placed on a folded gym mat to form risers)*	Watercolor Paintings *Watercolor paints, paintbrushes, cups, water, smocks*	Flannel Board Story Retelling *Flannel board story, flannel board*	*Just My Friend and Me*	"Take Me out to the Ballgame"
Thursday *Suggested Props and Materials*	Building a House *House building scenario, playhouse, clothespin pegs, plastic tools, (e.g., hammer, saws, wrench), paintbrushes, pretend paint cans*	Wallpaper Collage *Wallpaper samples, glue, paper, scissors, markers or crayons*	Act out a Story (*The Three Little Pigs*) *Books, props for story, costumes (optional)*	*The Three Little Pigs*	"Johnny Works with One Hammer"

NEWSLETTER

Vol. 1, No. 30

Date: _____

Spring

Monday Today in dramatic play, the children will do some spring cleaning in the house area. They will vacuum, wash windows, wash clothes, and mow the yard. In art, they will do some crayon texture rubbings. *The Berenstain Bears and the Messy Room* is today's story. During group time, the children will learn how to write a *9*. Music time will include "The Itsy Bitsy Spider."

Tuesday Tuesday's dramatic play will be all about gardening. The children will plant seeds in the garden, hoe, and rake. They will make crushed tissue paper flower pictures in art. Our story today is *The Garden in Our Yard*. The children will practice identifying *G*, *H*, and *I* during group time. Our song for the day is "Raindrops and Lemondrops."

Wednesday Today we will focus on baseball in dramatic play. Children can be the players, the spectators, or the vendors. At the art table, they will make watercolor paintings. We will read the book *Just My Friend and Me*. During group time, we will retell stories using the flannel board. We will sing "Take Me out to the Ballgame" during music.

Thursday The children will spend their day working at a construction site. In dramatic play, they will use hammers, saws, and other tools to build a house. The art activity will be making wallpaper collages. *The Three Little Pigs* is the story today. During group time, we will act out the story *The Three Little Pigs*. "Johnny Works with One Hammer" will be our song.

Dramatic Play	Art	Group	Story	Song
Spring Cleaning	Texture Rubbings	How to Write a *9*	*The Berenstain Bears and the Messy Room*	"The Itsy, Bitsy Spider"

DAILY PLANNING GUIDE

Language and Literacy Skills Facilitated

Vocabulary: *seasons, spring, rain, flowers, kites, sorting, chameleon, clean, fix-up, rainbow, rain cloud*

Verb phrase structures: *clean<u>s</u>, <u>is</u>/<u>are</u>/<u>was</u>/<u>were</u> clean<u>ing</u>, clean<u>ed</u> the house, w<u>ill</u>/<u>would</u>/<u>can</u>/<u>could</u> scrub the floor, fix<u>es</u>, fix<u>ed</u>, he <u>does</u> it, she <u>has</u> it*

Adjective/object descriptions: *pretty flowers, beautiful rainbow, big kites, little kites, dirty/clean*

Question structures: *what, how, where, when, who, what if, why, how many, which one*

Pronouns: *I, you, he, she, we, they, my, your, him, her, his, our, their, me, us, them*

Prepositions: *in, on, under, over, near, beneath, next to, beside, around, inside, outside*

Sounds: /k/ <u>c</u>an, boo<u>k</u>, <u>c</u>lean; /sh/ <u>sh</u>eet, di<u>sh</u>es, wi<u>sh</u>; /r/ <u>r</u>ub, <u>r</u>un, na<u>rr</u>ow, ma<u>r</u>; /l/ <u>l</u>ook, ye<u>ll</u>ow, fa<u>ll</u>, c<u>l</u>ean

Noting print has meaning: names on chairs and on cubbies, signs in dramatic play, words in books and on chalkboard

Noting sound–symbol associations: What sound does _____ start with?

Writing: letters, names, words

Social Skills Facilitated

Initiating interaction with peers and adults; responding to questions and requests from peers and adults

Negotiating with peers for toys and materials

Group cooperation: waiting for a turn in a group, taking a turn at the appropriate time

Cognitive Skills Facilitated

Problem-solving skills: what to clean, how to fix ____

Classification skills: item groupings that make nine

Sequencing skills: songs, stories

Narrative/story structure: adventure

Motor Skills Facilitated

Large motor: outdoor play activities—jumping, running, hopping, pedaling, climbing

Small motor: writing, drawing, gluing, cutting

DRAMATIC PLAY **Spring Cleaning**

Type of Activity: Related

Objectives
1. Learn new, and employ familiar, vocabulary
2. Learn new, and employ a variety of, syntactic constructions
3. Interact with peers
4. Sequence familiar routines
5. Expand conceptual knowledge of the world

Settings
- House(s) with removable screens and roof (playhouse or a handmade construction from cardboard boxes)
- Household cupboards
- Play refrigerator
- Play stove and sink
- Extra room additions (cardboard added to extend house)

Props
- Window "screens" (strips of cardstock crossed to make a frame, with plastic netting to form the screen)
- Cleaning supplies (e.g., mop, broom, dustpan, rags, vacuum cleaner)
- Shelves
- Pretend tools

Roles
- Mother
- Father
- Children
- Cleaning crew
- Roofer

General Description of Activity

Children act out spring cleaning, taking down or putting up window screens, washing windows, and fixing roofs. They might also straighten shelves and cupboards, fix walls, and put things back neatly.

Verbal Productions

Level of linguistic complexity varies with the role or competency of the child playing the role.
- "Could I please use that mop when you're finished?" or "Mop, please"
- "These windows need to be washed" or "Window dirty"
- "We fixed the roof with new shingles" or "Fix roof"

Adult Facilitative Role

The adult is to facilitate role play and help expand language and literacy skills. Typical actions or strategies to use include

Playing a role: "I have a mop. I am cleaning the floor."

Contrasting two prepositions: "The plate is on the table. The napkin is under the table."

Expanding a child's utterance: "Wash window" to "Yes, you are washing the windows."

Using a cloze procedure: "This window is open, and this window is _____(closed)."

Modeling the reading of a sign: "This sign says *soap*."

ART **Texture Rubbings**

Objectives
1. Express creativity
2. Develop small motor skills (e.g., drawing, painting, cutting, pasting)
3. Practice turn-taking skills
4. Converse with peers and adults

Materials
- Newsprint or tracing paper
- Variety of cardboard cutouts (e.g., squares, triangles, houses, trees, flowers)
- Crayons with paper removed
- Container to hold crayons
- Textured wallpaper samples (optional)

General Description of Activity

Have the children place one or more cardboard cutouts under a piece of paper. Holding a crayon (with the paper covering removed) or a piece of chalk on one side, they rub over the paper back and forth until the shape of the object appears on their paper. Children can use several colors and different arrangements of objects under the paper to make a variety of pictures.

Variation

Place textured wallpaper pieces under the newsprint or tracing paper to make the rubbings.

GROUP **How to Write a 9**

Objectives
1. Improve listening skills
2. Increase conceptual knowledge
3. Learn appropriate group-interaction skills
4. Practice turn-taking skills
5. Practice recognition and writing of numbers

Materials
- Number cards
- Chalkboards and chalk
- Paper and pencils (optional)
- Whiteboard and markers (optional)

General Description of Activity

Hold up a card with the number *9* written on it. Trace the number with your finger and invite several children to come to the front of the group to trace the number, too. As the children trace, recite the jingle for the target number (*9*):

1: Start at the top, go down and you're done, that's the way to make a *1*.

2: Around and back on the railroad track, *2, 2, 2.*

3: Around the tree, around the tree, that's the way to make a *3*.

4: Down and over and down once more, that's the way to make a *4*.

5: Down around, make a hat on it, and look what you've found. (*5*)

6: Down around until it sticks, that's the way to make a *6*.

7: Over and down and it's not heaven, over and down makes a *7*.

8: Make an S and go back straight, that's the way to make an *8*.

9: A balloon and a line make *9*.

10: Draw a line and a circle with your pen, that's the way to make a *10*.

Group Participation

Distribute individual chalkboards and chalk (or paper and pencils) to the children and have them practice writing the target number.

Variation 1

Whiteboards and markers may be easier for some children to use.

Variation 2

To introduce the number, use a number line and have the children count up to the target number on the line. One child could place the target number on the number line.

Summary/Transition Activity

Ask children to hold up their chalkboards and show the group their numbers.

Tuesday

Dramatic Play	Art	Group	Story	Song
Gardening	Crushed Tissue Paper Flowers	Identifying *G, H,* and *I*	*The Garden in Our Yard*	"Raindrops and Lemondrops"

DAILY PLANNING GUIDE

Language and Literacy Skills Facilitated

Vocabulary: *garden, grow, flowers, digging, planting, watering, working, bugs, insects, hoe, weeds, seeds, shovel*

Verb phrase structures: *is/are* plant*ing*, plant*ed*, *will* plant, plant*s*, dig*s*, dug, grow*s*, grew, water*s*, water*ed*, *is* work*ing*, work*ed*

Adjective/object descriptions: *little seed, big hole, yellow flower, dirty shovel, hard work*

Question structures: *what, how, where, when, who, what if, why, how many, which one*

Pronouns: *I, you, he, she, we, they, my, your, him, her, his, our, their, me, us, them*

Prepositions: *in, on, under, over, near, beneath, next to, beside, around, inside, outside*

Sounds: /k/ *come, work;* /l/ *like, yellow, fall;* /s/ *seed, miss*

Noting print has meaning: names on chairs and on cubbies, signs in dramatic play, words in books and on chalkboard

Noting sound–symbol associations: What sound does _____ start with?

Writing: letters, names, words

Social Skills Facilitated

Initiating interaction with peers and adults; responding to questions and requests from peers and adults

Negotiating with peers for toys and materials

Group cooperation: waiting for a turn in a group, taking a turn at the appropriate time

Cognitive Skills Facilitated

Problem-solving skills: how to crush the tissue paper to make three-dimensional pictures

Classification skills: things in a garden

Sequencing skills: songs, stories

Narrative/story structure: labeling story

Motor Skills Facilitated

Large motor: outdoor play activities—jumping, running, hopping, pedaling, climbing

Small motor: writing, drawing, gluing

DRAMATIC PLAY **Gardening**

Type of Activity: Central

Objectives
1. Learn new, and employ familiar, vocabulary
2. Learn new, and employ a variety of, syntactic constructions
3. Interact with peers
4. Sequence familiar routines
5. Expand conceptual knowledge of the world

Settings
- Two or three garden areas
- Seed and gardening store (optional)
- Market (optional)

Props
- Two or three large boxes cut about 4"–6" deep
- Sand or soil
- Child-sized garden tools
- Gardening clothes (e.g., hats, gloves)
- Seeds or other small objects (e.g., lima beans, LEGOs)
- Plants (e.g., pretend flowers, vegetables)
- Pails
- Watering can
- Counter (optional)
- Pretend cash register (optional)
- Pretend money (optional)

Roles
- Gardeners
- Store clerks (optional)
- Garden produce sellers (optional)
- Customers (optional)

General Description of Activity

Children work in a pretend garden, digging, planting seeds, and growing flowers or vegetables. Two or three large boxes (e.g., a refrigerator box) cut about 4"–6" deep and filled with sand or soil make a good garden. The children can use child-sized gardening tools to prepare the sand or soil. Lima beans or other small objects (e.g., LEGOs) make good "seeds." A seed and gardening store or a market for selling garden produce can be added to the play activity. (Be aware that the activity will need to be restarted after the plants have "grown" and have been "harvested.")

Verbal Productions

Level of linguistic complexity varies with the role or competency of the child playing the role.
- "Do you have any flower seeds?" or "Seeds, please"
- "Do you have any shovels or pails?" or "Diggers?"
- "He is digging a big hole" or "Dig hole"
- "I want a large, round, orange pumpkin" or "Big pumpkin, please"

Adult Facilitative Role

The adult is to facilitate role play and help expand language and literacy skills. Typical actions or strategies to use include

Playing a role: "I like to plant flowers in my garden."

Providing a contrast between error and correct sound: "You said the word *power*, but you meant the word *flower*."

Expanding a child's utterance: "She plant blue flower" to "She planted a blue flower."

Redirecting a child to a peer: "Ask Lizzie for a turn with the rake. Say, 'May I have a turn, please?'"

Providing a literacy model: "The package says *sunflowers* on it."

ART **Crushed Tissue Paper Flowers**

Objectives
1. Express creativity
2. Develop small motor skills (e.g., drawing, painting, cutting, pasting)
3. To practice turn-taking skills
4. To converse with peers and adults

Materials
- Precut construction paper forms (e.g., flowers, fish)
- Glue or paste
- 1" tissue paper squares in pastel colors
- Pencils or crayons

General Description of Activity

Children crush the 1" pieces of tissue paper and paste them onto a precut construction paper form. One way to crush the paper is to wrap it around the eraser end of a pencil (or one end of a crayon) and push it off onto glue or paste that is already on the form. Or, children can just crumple the squares and then paste them on the paper. When the form is completely covered, the result is a three-dimensional picture, or a picture with texture.

GROUP   **Identifying *G*, *H*, and *I***

Objectives
1. Improve listening skills
2. Increase knowledge of the alphabet and sounds
3. Learn appropriate group-interaction skills
4. Practice turn-taking skills

Materials
- Target alphabet letters on cards or all on one card strip
- Alphabet chart
- Individual chalkboards and chalk or paper and pencils or markers (optional)

General Description of Activity

Lay the letters *G*, *H*, and *I* in front of the children. Have the children, in chorus, say the letters as you point to each one. Have one child come to the front and point to a specific letter.

Group Participation

Ask different children to point to specific letters, helping them as necessary. Vary the difficulty by having children identify letters in order or out of order, or by having some match a letter card to the letters on the floor instead of pointing to a designated letter. You can also ask them to match lower-case letters to uppercase letters. Children can also point to a letter and have the class label it.

Summary/Transition Activity

Say the whole alphabet with the children as you point to an alphabet chart. Then have everyone say the target alphabet letters (*G*, *H*, *I*) as you point to each letter in turn. An alternative activity is to have the children practice writing the three target letters.

Wednesday

Dramatic Play	Art	Group	Story	Song
Baseball	Watercolor Paintings	Flannel Board Story Retelling	*Just My Friend and Me*	"Take Me out to the Ballgame"

DAILY PLANNING GUIDE

Language and Literacy Skills Facilitated

Vocabulary: *baseball, ball, bat, bases, diamond, glove, concession stand, popcorn, peanuts, cotton candy, scores, runs, hit, pitcher, batter, home run*

Verb phrase structures: <u>hit</u> *the ball,* <u>swing</u> *the bat,* <u>run</u> *the bases,* <u>pitch</u> *the ball*

Adjective/object descriptions: *long bat, white bases, fast ball, first base, glove, foul ball*

Question structures: *what, how, where, when, who, what if, why, how many, which one*

Pronouns: *I, you, he, she, we, they, my, your, him, her, his, our, their, me, us, them*

Prepositions: *in, on, under, over, near, beneath, next to, beside, around, inside, outside*

Sounds: /f/ <u>f</u>un, o<u>ff</u>; /s/ <u>s</u>it, talk<u>s</u>; /l/ <u>l</u>ittle, ba<u>ll</u>

Noting print has meaning: names on chairs and on cubbies, signs in dramatic play, words in books and on chalkboard

Noting sound–symbol associations: What sound does _____ start with?

Writing: letters, names, words

Social Skills Facilitated

Initiating interaction with peers and adults; responding to questions and requests from peers and adults

Negotiating with peers for toys and materials

Group cooperation: waiting for a turn in a group, taking a turn at the appropriate time

Cognitive Skills Facilitated

Problem-solving skills: how to hit a ball, how to retell a story

Classification skills: things in baseball

Sequencing skills: story, songs

Narrative/story structure: adventure

Motor Skills Facilitated

Large motor: outdoor play activities—jumping, running, hopping, swinging, catching, climbing

Small motor: writing, drawing, gluing

> DRAMATIC PLAY : **Baseball**

Type of Activity: Central

Objectives
1. Learn new, and employ familiar, vocabulary
2. Learn new, and employ a variety of, syntactic constructions
3. Interact with peers
4. Sequence familiar routines
5. Expand conceptual knowledge of the world

Settings
- Taped-off diamond area with taped squares to indicate bases
- Bleacher area made of folded tumbling mat to form a riser with chairs, but on two levels (or two rows of chairs without the mat)
- Concession area
- Ticket sales area or area for announcers (optional)

Props
- Plastic bats
- Plastic Wiffle balls (balls with holes in them) or other indoor-use baseballs (some are soft and sponge-like)
- Baseball tee (to hold the baseball while children swing at it)
- Chairs and tumbling mat to make spectator area
- Concessions—pretend food (such as soda pop, popcorn, cotton candy, peanuts, and hot dogs)
- Cash registers

Roles
- Batter
- Fielder
- Concession worker
- Spectators
- Ticket agents or announcers (optional)

General Description of Activity

Children act out a baseball game: Some are players on the field, some are spectators watching from the stands, and some work at the concession area where people can buy drinks and popcorn and other food items. The scenario can be expanded by including ticket sellers or announcers, who give the play-by-play action of the players on the field. A diamond area can be taped off with little taped squares to indicate bases. The players swing plastic bats at a Wiffle ball on a baseball tee (if a baseball tee is not available, pitch the plastic Wiffle ball or other indoor use ball to the batter). Other children can play the outfield positions to field the balls. A tumbling mat can be folded over to form a riser so that chairs can be placed on two levels to form the spectator area. A small concession area can be set up using bookshelves to form a counter area as well as a space to put the concessions items (place the two bookcases in an L shape, with one part being the counter with the cash register and the other storing the food items).

Verbal Productions

Level of linguistic complexity can vary with the role or competence of the child playing the role.
- "I want a turn to bat" or "My turn"
- "I can hit a home run" or "Hit ball"
- "I want some popcorn and some pop" or "Popcorn"

Adult Facilitative Role

The adult is to facilitate role play and help expand language and literacy skills. Typical actions or strategies to use include

Playing a role: "I want to watch the game, so I am going to sit here. Do you want to join me?"

Recasting present progressive and past tense: "He is hitting the ball" to "He hit the ball hard."

Event casting of an adult's actions: "I am going to hit the ball with the foam bat. Oops, I missed the ball."

Modeling the /s/ sound: "Sally sits by the little girl Sue."

Expanding a child's utterance: "Jim popcorn" to "Yes, Jim has a box of pretend popcorn."

ART **Watercolor Paintings**

Objectives
1. Express creativity
2. Develop small motor skills (e.g., drawing, painting, cutting, pasting)
3. Practice turn-taking skills
4. Converse with peers and adults

Materials
- Watercolor paints
- Brushes
- Water in tubs
- White construction paper
- Smocks

General Description of Activity

Lay out white construction paper, watercolor paint boxes, and brushes on the art table. Place tubs of water to clean the brushes above the paper. The children put on smocks and sit down in front of the paper, paint box, and water tub. Each child selects a brush, wets it, and chooses the paint color. The children paint on the paper, rinsing the brush before selecting a new color. Children can paint a collage of colors, animals, people, scenery, and so on. You may want to be close by so children can talk about their paintings.

GROUP **Flannel Board Story Retelling**

Objectives
1. Improve listening skills
2. Increase conceptual knowledge
3. Learn appropriate group-interaction skills
4. Practice turn-taking skills

Materials
- Flannel board
- Flannel board story pieces

General Description of Activity

Set up the flannel board and lay out the felt pieces for the story. Tell the story, placing the appropriate pieces on the board as the story develops.

Group Participation

After telling the story, give the felt pieces to several children and have one child come up to retell the story. As the storyteller tells the story, the child with the appropriate felt piece places it on the flannel board.

Variation

Have children act out the story after they tell it using the flannel board.

Summary/Transition Activity

Review the story by having some of the children take down the felt pieces as the story is told once again.

Thursday

Dramatic Play	Art	Group	Story	Song
Building a House	Wallpaper Collage	Act out a Story (*The Three Little Pigs*)	*The Three Little Pigs*	"Johnny Works with One Hammer"

DAILY PLANNING GUIDE

Language and Literacy Skills Facilitated

Vocabulary: *construction, build, building, hammer, nail, fix, make, work, hardhat, safety, paint, wrench, saw*

Verb phrase structures: *is* build*ing*, construct*ed*, built, hammer*ed*, Who *is* build*ing*? I *am*, mak*es*, carri*es*

Adjective/object descriptions: *large/small ___, heavy/light _____, hard/soft material*

Question structures: *what, how, where, when, who, what if, why, how many, which one*

Pronouns: *I, you, he, she, we, they, my, your, him, her, his, our, their, me, us, them*

Prepositions: *in, on, under, over, near, beneath, next to, beside, around, inside, outside*

Sounds: /f/ *fix, fun, off;* /s/ *size, walks;* /k/ *construct, can, make*

Noting print has meaning: names on chairs and on cubbies, signs in dramatic play, words in books and on chalkboard

Noting sound–symbol associations: What sound does _____ start with?

Writing: letters, names, words

Social Skills Facilitated

Initiating interaction with peers and adults; responding to questions and requests from peers and adults

Negotiating with peers for toys and materials

Group cooperation: waiting for a turn in a group, taking a turn at the appropriate time

Cognitive Skills Facilitated

Problem-solving skills: how to make a building

Classification skills: tools we use to construct things

Sequencing Skills: songs, steps in building, stories

Narrative/story structure: classic adventure

Motor Skills Facilitated

Large motor: outdoor play activities—jumping, running, hopping, pedaling, climbing

Small motor: writing, drawing, gluing, pounding

DRAMATIC PLAY **Building a House**

Type of Activity: Related

Objectives
1. Learn new, and employ familiar, vocabulary
2. Learn new, and employ a variety of, syntactic constructions
3. Interact with peers
4. Sequence familiar routines
5. Expand conceptual knowledge of the world

509

Settings

- Street (floor area marked with masking tape) lined with houses made from a variety of materials (e.g., blocks, cardboard)

Props

- Playhouse
- Cardboard box additions that can be taped to the playhouse
- LEGOs
- Blocks
- Play bricks
- Paper strips of various colors for roof or siding
- Glue

- Tools (e.g., plastic hammers, wrenches, saws, screwdrivers, screws)
- Tool belts
- Pegs for pounding (wooden clothespins that can be pounded into cardboard)
- Play hardhats
- Masking tape
- Telephones

Roles

- Carpenters
- Architects

- Homeowners
- Other construction workers

General Description of Activity

Children participate in a construction/repair dramatic play involving putting together different materials to make buildings. A variety of materials can be used. One area can be set up for constructing buildings with LEGOs or other blocks. Another area can be designated for a new addition to the playhouse (using big boxes). A third area can utilize play bricks and boxes to make another house. The children can problem-solve how to construct houses or apartments by rearranging the boxes, bricks, and blocks. (Some of the houses could be doll-size; others could be big enough for the children to play in).

Houses may also need to be repaired. Children can replace a roof by making "shingles" out of paper bag strips. The strips could be laid on top of cardboard. (You might suggest that children start at the outer edge and overlay the shingles so "rain" will roll off the roof and not under the shingles.) The children can put new siding on a house by using strips of colored paper and glue, and they could even put up wallpaper on the inside of a house.

Verbal Productions

Level of linguistic complexity varies with the role or competency of the child playing the role.

- "I'm building a big house" or "Me build house"
- "We need to make that side higher. Call the carpenter" or "Higher"
- "Look, I pounded the nail into the wall" or "Look"

Adult Facilitative Role

The adult is to facilitate role play and help expand language and literacy skills. Typical actions or strategies to use include

Playing a role: "I am pounding a nail in the wall."

Using a cloze procedure: "This wall is high, and this wall is _____(low)."

Recasting a child's utterance: "We pound the nail" to "Yes, we pounded the nail all the way in."

Providing a literacy model: "The sign on the paint can says *white*."

Redirecting a child to a peer: "Ask Billy for a turn with the screwdriver. Say, 'May I have a turn, please?'"

ART **Wallpaper Collage**

Objectives

1. Express creativity
2. Develop small motor skills (e.g., drawing, painting, cutting, pasting)
3. Practice turn-taking skills
4. Converse with peers and adults

Materials
- Construction paper
- Scissors
- Wallpaper sample books
- Glue

General Description of Activity

Have children cut out shapes from different kinds of wallpaper and glue them on construction paper. The children can describe their pictures, and the teacher can write down their descriptions.

GROUP **Act out a Story (*The Three Little Pigs*)**

Objectives
1. Improve listening skills
2. Increase sequencing ability
3. Increase knowledge of storytelling
4. Practice turn-taking skills

Materials
- Book(s)
- Props for the story, including cut-up yellow paper for straw or a straw mat
- Sticks
- Bricks (made of cardboard)
- Pink tee shirts for costumes (optional)

General Description of Activity

The children are reminded of the story *The Three Little Pigs* as a staff member reads it or quickly summarizes it. The children act out the story of *The Three Little Pigs*.

Group Participation

Children are assigned roles from the story. There is the mama pig, the three little pigs, and the big bad wolf. The children not chosen for roles the first time are assured that everyone will have a turn and that they have the very important job of being a good listening audience. The teacher can narrate the story as the children act it out. They should say as many of the lines as they can, with prompts given as needed. The story is repeated with new actors until all the children have had turns.

Summary/Transition Activity

After everyone has had a turn, the children can talk about other stories that they would like to act out another day. The teacher should compliment the children's acting.

WEEKLY PLANNING GUIDE

	Dramatic Play	Art	Group	Story	Song
Monday *Suggested Props and Materials*	Grocery Store (Healthy Food) *Grocery store scenario, counters and shelves, canned goods and other food items, fruit and vegetable area, pretend cash register, pretend money, pretend credit cards, pretend coupons, shopping carts, grocery bags, pencil and paper for making lists, table for checkout area*	Food Collage *White paper plates or construction paper, scissors, magazines (with pictures of food), newspapers (food ads)*	Food Pyramid *Poster board food pyramid with pictures representing the food groups (breads and cereals on the bottom, then vegetables and fruits, then dairy and meat, and finally at the top, sweets), pictures to match the ones on the pyramid or facsimile plastic food items*	*Just Shopping with Mom*	"On Top of Spaghetti"
Tuesday *Suggested Props and Materials*	Fitness Center *Fitness center scenario, towels, stationary tricycles, miniature trampoline, barbells, stepboards, pretend treadmill, check-in counter, music for aerobics*	Playdough *Playdough, rollers, cookie cutters, plastic knives*	Identifying *J, K,* and *L* *Alphabet chart, alphabet cards J, K, and L, chalk and chalkboards (or white boards), or paper and markers*	*Bearobics*	"Head, Shoulders, Knees, and Toes"
Wednesday *Suggested Props and Materials*	Health Screening (Clinic) *Health screening scenario, doctor's office with area for vision and hearing testing, scale, area for measuring height, reception area, phones, appointment books*	Self-Portraits *Paper, crayons or markers, (watered down tempera paint for crayon washes [optional])*	Focus on Rhyming Words *At least 10 pairs of words (or objects) that rhyme. Have some word cards that do not rhyme*	*Going to the Doctor*	"Brush Your Teeth"
Thursday *Suggested Props and Materials*	Beauty Salon/Barber Shop *Beauty salon/barber shop scenario, sink area, smocks, pretend shampoo, pretend hair dryers (combs with children's names on them [optional]), manicurists' table and equipment, water (for polish) paint brushes, shaving cream and plastic "razors"*	Shaving Cream Fingerpainting *Shaving cream, formboards (to hold shaving cream), smocks*	Rough/Smooth *Items that are smooth or rough, feeling bag (optional), two tubs*	*All by Myself*	"The Alphabet Song"

NEWSLETTER

Vol. 1, No. 31

Date: _____

Taking Care of Ourselves

Monday
Today the children will be grocery store workers and customers. They will learn how to take care of their bodies by choosing good foods. The children will make a food collage out of pictures of food. We will read *Just Shopping with Mom* at storytime. Group time will focus on learning about the Food Pyramid and what kinds of food we should eat. The song of the day is "On Top of Spaghetti."

Tuesday
Today is fitness center day, and the children will be working out by running, doing aerobics, and lifting weights. In art, they will make playdough figures. Our story will be *Bearobics*. During group time, the children will review the letters and sounds of *J*, *K*, and *L*. The special music number for today will be "Head, Shoulders, Knees, and Toes."

Wednesday
Today the children take care of themselves by having a check-up at the health clinic in dramatic play. They can be patients seeking medical help or they can be the doctors and nurses, audiologists, or vision specialists. The children will make self-portraits during art. Our story is *Going to the Doctor*. During group time, the children will learn about rhyming. Our song is "Brush Your Teeth."

Thursday
The classroom will be full of beautiful people today as the dramatic play theme is beauty salon/barber shop. The children will pretend to be customers making appointments and having their hair washed and styled, or they will be the salon workers. During art, the children will fingerpaint with shaving cream. *All By Myself* is the story. For group time, the children will classify items that are rough or smooth. Our featured song is "The Alphabet Song."

Monday

Dramatic Play	Art	Group	Story	Song
Grocery Store (Healthy Food)	Food Collage	Food Pyramid	*Just Shopping with Mom*	"On Top of Spaghetti"

DAILY PLANNING GUIDE

Language and Literacy Skills Facilitated

Vocabulary: *groceries, cart, cereal, shop, checker, buy, sell, bag, sack, shelf, money, change*

Verb phrase structures: *eats, is eating, ate, has eaten, pushes, is pushing, pushed, buys, bought, checks, is checking, checked*

Adjective/object descriptions: *big/little bag, full/empty shelf*

Question structures: *what, how, where, when, who, what if, why, how many, which one*

Pronouns: *I, you, he, she, we, they, my, your, him, her, his, our, their, me, us, them*

Prepositions: *in, on, under, over, near, beneath, next to, beside, around, inside, outside*

Sounds: /sh/ *shelf, push;* /k/ *cart, sack;* /s/ *sell, carts*

Noting print has meaning: names on chairs and on cubbies, signs in dramatic play, words in books and on chalkboard

Noting sound–symbol associations: What sound does _____ start with?

Writing: letters, names, words

Social Skills Facilitated

Initiating interaction with peers and adults; responding to questions and requests from peers and adults

Negotiating with peers for toys and materials

Group cooperation: waiting for a turn in a group, taking a turn at the appropriate time

Cognitive Skills Facilitated

Problem-solving skills: what to buy

Classification skills: fruits, vegetables, meats

Sequencing skills: songs, story

Narrative/story structure: adventure

Motor Skills Facilitated

Large motor: outdoor play activities—jumping, running, hopping, pedaling, climbing

Small motor: writing, drawing, gluing

DRAMATIC PLAY **Grocery Store (Healthy Food)**

Type of Activity: Sequential

Objectives
1. Learn new, and employ familiar, vocabulary
2. Learn new, and employ a variety of, syntactic constructions
3. Interact with peers
4. Sequence familiar routines
5. Expand conceptual knowledge of the world

Settings
- Grocery store
- Shelves and aisles
- Check-out stand
- Customers' homes

Props
- Shelves
- Canned goods and other food items
- Fruit and vegetable area
- Pretend cash register
- Pretend money
- Pretend credit cards
- Pretend coupons
- Shopping carts
- Grocery bags
- Pencil and paper for making lists
- Table for checkout area

Roles
- Shoppers
- Cashiers
- Stockers
- Baggers

General Description of Activity

The children pretend to be grocery shopping. They can make lists, take their "children" with them, choose the items on the list to put in their carts, pay, bag their groceries, and go home. Other children can be the grocery store workers. Some can keep the shelves stocked; others can be checkers and baggers.

Verbal Productions

Level of linguistic complexity varies with the role or competency of the child playing the role.

- "Will that be all? Your total is $5" or "All? $5!"
- "Milk, please" or "Milk"
- "Do you have any cereal?" or "Want cereal"

Adult Facilitative Role

The adult is to facilitate role play and help expand language and literacy skills. Typical actions or strategies to use include

Playing a role: "I am going to buy several things at the grocery store."

Asking an open question: "What things should I buy?"

Identifying rhyming words: "The words *jam, lamb*, and *Sam* all rhyme."

Eventing casting of a child's actions: "You are pushing the cart. Now you are putting the meat in the cart. You also have apples in your cart."

Expanding a child's utterances and providing corrective feedback: "Her get bananas" to "Yes, she can get the bananas."

ART : **Food Collage**

Objectives
1. Express creativity
2. Develop small motor skills (e.g., drawing, painting, cutting, pasting)
3. Practice turn-taking skills
4. Converse with peers and adults

Materials
- White paper plates or construction paper
- Scissors
- Magazines (with pictures of food)
- Newspapers (food ads)

General Description of Activity

Children cut out pictures of food from magazines or newspaper advertisements. The children then paste these pictures on round white paper plates (or construction paper) to make a food collage. Children can choose from a variety of food pictures. Assist older children in making a picture of the different food groups.

GROUP **Food Pyramid**

Objectives
1. Improve listening skills
2. Improve sequencing ability
3. Learn appropriate group-interaction skills
4. Practice turn-taking skills

Materials
- Poster board food pyramid with pictures representing the food groups (grains—breads and cereals—on the bottom, then vegetables and fruits, then dairy and meat, and sweets at the top)
- Several play food items, representing each of the respective food groups
- Pictures of food (optional)

General Description of Activity

Place a poster board representation of the food pyramid on the floor in the front of the children. Explain that the foods we eat fall into different groups or categories. Label each food group while pointing to a picture representation of it on the food pyramid (e.g., meats, breads, fruits and vegetables). Tell the children that they are going to help decide which groups certain foods belong to. Hold up a toy apple and say, "I have an apple. An apple is a fruit. The apple goes with the fruits and vegetables." Then place the apple in the fruits and vegetables section of the food pyramid.

Group Participation

Give each child a play food item (or a picture of food). Have children come to the front of the group, one at a time, to tell what type of food he or she has and to decide into which section of the food pyramid the food should be placed. If the child puts it in the wrong section, remove the food and place it in the appropriate section, explaining why the item goes in that particular category.

Variation

Rather than give each child an item, have the children choose their own items from an assortment.

Summary/Transition Activity

Have the children label, as a group, the items in each food group.

Tuesday

Dramatic Play	Art	Group	Story	Song
Fitness Center	Playdough	Identifying *J, K,* and *L*	*Bearobics*	"Head, Shoulders, Knees, and Toes"

DAILY PLANNING GUIDE

Language and Literacy Skills Facilitated

Vocabulary: *exercise, aerobics, trampoline, weights, bicycle, dance, run, jumping jacks, mats, workout, kick, stretch, hot tub, towels, sweatband*

Verb phrase structures: *is jumping, dances, jumped, runs, ran, lifts weights, rode the bicycle, Who was riding? "I was"*

Adjective/object descriptions: *heavy/light weights, fast/slow dance, red face, sweaty shirt*

Question structures: *what, how, where, when, who, what if, why, how many, which one*

Pronouns: *I, you, he, she, we, they, my, your, him, her, his, our, their, me, us, them*

Prepositions: *in, on, under, over, near, beneath, next, beside, around, inside, outside*

Sounds: /z/ *zips, dances, runs, was;* /r/ *riding, their;* /k/ *kick, pick;* /f/ *five, off;* /g/ *go, dog*

Noting print has meaning: names on chairs and on cubbies, signs in dramatic play, words in books and on chalkboard

Noting sound–symbol associations: What sound does _____ start with?

Writing: letters, names, words

Social Skills Facilitated

Initiating interaction with peers and adults; responding to questions and requests from peers and adults

Negotiating with peers for toys and materials

Group cooperation: waiting for a turn in a group, taking a turn at the appropriate time

Cognitive Skills Facilitated

Problem-solving skills: how to exercise

Classification skills: words that begin with *J, K,* or *L*

Sequencing skills: songs, story

Narrative/story structure: adventure

Motor Skills Facilitated

Large motor: outdoor play activities—jumping, running, hopping, pedaling, climbing, stretching

Small motor: writing, drawing, gluing, squeezing

···· DRAMATIC PLAY **Fitness Center** ····

Type of Activity: Central

Objectives
1. Learn new, and employ familiar, vocabulary
2. Learn new, and employ a variety of, syntactic constructions
3. Interact with peers
4. Sequence familiar routines
5. Expand conceptual knowledge of the world

Settings
- Check-in counter
- Locker room
- Equipment area(s)
- Aerobic dancing area
- Pool
- Hot tub
- Sauna

Props
- Towels
- Stationary tricycles (mounted with front wheels off the floor so the front wheel is the only one to turn)
- Miniature trampoline
- Barbells (giant Tinker Toys or cardboard tubes)
- Other equipment, such as stepboards
- Wading pool or blue sheet (pool or hot tub)
- Check-in counter with pretend computer
- Music (for aerobic dancing)
- Mirror (for aerobic dancing)
- Costumes (e.g., sneakers, leotards, headbands)

Roles
- Fitness center attendants
- Customers
- Aerobics instructors
- Pool attendants
- Receptionist

General Description of Activity

Children go to a fitness center to exercise. They can choose from many kinds of equipment, including stationary bikes and miniature trampolines. There should also be areas to perform aerobics and jog. The center might have a hot tub, sauna, and swimming pool. The children can check in at the counter and then get on the equipment or do aerobic dancing. After exercising, they can go into the pool.

Verbal Productions

Level of linguistic complexity varies with the role or competency of the child playing the role.
- "I jumped for 2 minutes" or "Jump"
- "He is riding the bike" or "He rides the bike"
- "She lifted the barbells high" or "Lift it"
- "My mommy does aerobics, and I go with her" or "My mommy go"
- "You have had a long turn. I want to ride the bike" or "My turn"

Adult Facilitative Role

The adult is to facilitate role play and help expand language and literacy skills. Typical actions or strategies to use include

Playing a role: "I am jumping on the trampoline. I will jump five times, and then I will get off."

Modeling correct production of the /l/ sound: "I like to lift weights. I like the little ones."

Using a cloze procedure: "This weight is heavy, and this weight is _____(light)."

Recasting present and past tense: "I do five sit-ups" to "I did five sit-ups."

Event casting a child's actions: "You are jumping on the trampoline. Now you jumped off. You are good at jumping."

ART **Playdough**

Objectives
1. Express creativity
2. Develop small motor skills (e.g., drawing, painting, cutting, rolling)
3. Practice turn-taking skills
4. Converse with peers and adults

Materials
- Smocks
- Craft dough or playdough
- Rolling pins
- Cookie cutters
- Cookie presses
- Wooden craft sticks
- Rolling boards/ cutting boards
- Yarn

General Description of Activity

Children wash their hands and put on smocks to explore playdough on the art table, using various presses, cutters, rolling pins, wooden craft sticks, and other tools. Children can make pretend food or any other objects out of the dough by rolling, cutting, or making pressing motions. They can form animals or people by rolling a main body and then adding heads, arms, and legs. Yarn can be used for hair (if children want to take their creations home). When children are finished, they roll the dough into a ball, wash their hands, and take off and fold their smocks. If craft dough is used, the children can use a cookie cutter to cut out hearts, flowers, animals, or other shapes. They can press a hole in the dough and let the shape dry. When dry, children can thread a piece of yarn through the hole and wear the shape as a necklace.

GROUP **Identifying *J*, *K*, and *L***

Objectives
1. Improve listening skills
2. Increase knowledge of the alphabet and sounds
3. Learn appropriate group-interaction skills
4. Practice turn-taking skills

Materials
- Target alphabet letters on cards
- Alphabet chart
- Paper and pencils or markers (optional)
- Chalkboards, chalk (optional)

General Description of Activity

Lay the letters *J*, *K*, and *L* in front of the children. Have the children, in chorus, say the letters as you point to each one. Have one child come to the front and point to a specific letter.

Group Participation

Ask different children to point to specific letters, helping them as necessary. Vary the difficulty by having children identify letters in order or out of order, or by having some match a letter card to the letters on the floor instead of pointing to a designated letter. You can also ask them to match lower-case letters to uppercase letters. Children can also point to a letter and have the class label it.

Summary/Transition Activity

Say the whole alphabet with the children as you point to an alphabet chart. Then have everyone say the target alphabet letters (*J, K, L*) as you point to each letter in turn. An alternative activity is to have the children practice writing the three target letters.

Wednesday

Dramatic Play	Art	Group	Story	Song
Health Screening (Clinic)	Self-Portraits	Focus on Rhyming Words	*Going to the Doctor*	"Brush Your Teeth"

DAILY PLANNING GUIDE

Language and Literacy Skills Facilitated

Vocabulary: *nurse, doctor, eye doctor, shot, scale, measure, weigh, chart, appointment, stethoscope, sick, well*

Verb phrase structures: *is weighing, weighs, weighed, gets a shot, got a shot*

Adjective/object descriptions: *heavy/light ____, big, little ____, sick/well ____*

Question structures: *what, how, where, when, who, what if, why, how many, which one*

Pronouns: *I, you, he, she, we, they, my, your, him, her, his, our, their, me, us, them*

Prepositions: *in, on, under, over, near, beneath, next to, beside, around, inside, outside*

Sounds: /k/ *cut, back*; /sh/ *shot*; /s/ *sick, sit*

Noting print has meaning: names on chairs and on cubbies, signs in dramatic play, words in books and on chalkboard

Noting sound–symbol associations: What sound does _____ start with?

Writing: letters, names, words

Social Skills Facilitated

Initiating interaction with peers and adults; responding to questions and requests from peers and adults

Negotiating with peers for toys and materials

Group cooperation: waiting for a turn in a group, taking a turn at the appropriate time

Cognitive Skills Facilitated

Problem-solving skills: how to weigh

Classification skills: things found in a health clinic

Sequencing skills: songs, stories

Narrative/story structure: adventure

Motor Skills Facilitated

Large motor: outdoor play activities—jumping, running, hopping, pedaling, climbing

Small motor: writing, drawing, gluing

DRAMATIC PLAY **Health Screening (Clinic)**

Type of Activity: Central

Objectives
1. Learn new, and employ familiar, vocabulary
2. Learn new, and employ a variety of, syntactic constructions
3. Interact with peers
4. Sequence familiar routines
5. Expand conceptual knowledge of the world

Settings	• Waiting room	• Examination rooms	• Patients' "homes"

Props
- Waiting room chairs
- Magazines and toys for waiting room
- Table with a play telephone, appointment book, and pencil or crayon
- Several tables or mats to represent examination rooms

- Doctor kits
- Eye chart
- Pretend audiometer (box with knobs and earphones attached)
- X-ray machine and chalk drawings
- Patients' "homes," including play telephones

Roles
- Doctors
- Nurses
- Ophthalmologist
- Audiologist

- X-ray technician
- Receptionist
- Patients
- Parents

General Description of Activity

Children operate a health clinic consisting of a waiting room and several examination rooms where a variety of health professionals (e.g., doctors, nurses, ophthalmologists, audiologists) see patients. People call the receptionist and make appointments to be examined. The doctor or nurse examines the patient (a doll or another child) by looking into the mouth, ears, and eyes; checking reflexes and muscle tone; listening with the stethoscope; and so forth. Eyesight is tested by having the patient read an eye chart. Pretend hearing tests can be done. A patient might have a broken bone that needs to be X-rayed, set in a cast, and/or wrapped with a bandage.

Verbal Productions

Level of linguistic complexity varies with the role or competency of the child playing the role.
- "Open your mouth, please" or "Open mouth"
- "Where does it hurt?" or "Hurt?"
- "I can see all of the letters" or "See letters"
- "I don't feel good. My tummy hurts" or "I sick"
- "Raise your hand when you hear the beep" or "Raise hand"

Adult Facilitative Role

The adult is to facilitate role play and help expand language and literacy skills. Typical actions or strategies to use include

Playing a role: "I am checking the eyes today to see if everyone can see okay."

Modeling phonological awareness: "Yes, the words *jump*, *Jim*, and *Julie* all start with *J*."

Modeling the reading and writing of words: "I am signing the appointment book. I wrote the word *Jenny*. It starts with a *J*."

ART **Self-Portraits**

Objectives
1. Express creativity
2. Develop small motor skills (e.g., drawing, painting, cutting, pasting)
3. Practice turn-taking skills
4. Converse with peers and adults

Materials
- Paper (white or colored)
- Crayons
- Markers
- Watered-down tempera paint (optional)

General Description of Activity

Provide the children with paper and a selection of crayons and/or markers. Let the children draw a picture of themselves. Drawings could be also be of their family and their pets. They can turn their crayon drawings into crayon washes by painting over the pictures with a light coat of tempera paint (watered-down paint). The paint will not stick to the crayon but will fill in where there are no crayon marks to make a background of color.

GROUP **Focus on Rhyming Words**

Objectives
1. Improve listening skills
2. Increase knowledge about counting and grouping into sets
3. Learn appropriate group-interaction skills
4. Practice turn-taking skills

Materials
• Several pairs of objects that rhyme (e.g., *cat* and *hat*, *fish* and *dish*)

General Description of Activity

Tell the children that sometimes words sound the same at the end, and when they do, those words rhyme with each other. Ask the children to stand up. Tell them, "We are going to play a rhyming game today. I will say some words, and you will point to the parts of your body that rhyme with the words." Say a word that rhymes with a body part, such as *rose*. If the children do not point to their nose, say, "I said the word *rose*. *Rose* rhymes with *nose*. You should point to your nose." Then point to your own nose and ask the children to point to theirs. Then say, "Let's try some more rhymes. Listen, and be ready to point to the part of your body that rhymes with the word I say." (Pictures could be used to cue the children.)

Group Participation

Proceed through a list of words that rhyme with body parts (e.g., *bye, see, care, band*), and ask the children to find the body part(s) that rhymes with each word. Give assistance, if necessary.

After saying several words that rhyme with body parts, pick up two objects (e.g., a toy cat, a hat) and tell the children, "Now I am going to say some more words to you, and you see if you can tell me if they rhyme with each other. How about _____ and _____?" Proceed through several different pairs of objects, some of which rhyme and some of which do not. If the children are correct in saying that a particular set of words rhyme, say, "You're right. _____ and _____ rhyme with each other." If the children are incorrect, say, "No. _____ and _____ do not rhyme with each other. They do not sound like they end the same way."

Variation

Write the rhyming words on the chalkboard to show children that the endings are the same.

Summary/Transition Activity

Ask the children to think of other words that rhyme with each other (for instance, words from songs or nursery rhymes they know).

Thursday

Dramatic Play	Art	Group	Story	Song
Beauty Salon/ Barber Shop	Shaving Cream Fingerpainting	Rough/Smooth	*All by Myself*	"The Alphabet Song"

DAILY PLANNING GUIDE

Language and Literacy Skills Facilitated

Vocabulary: *comb, brush, hair, wash, cut, set, curl, dry, blow-dry, fix, shave, shaving cream, emery board, customer, appointment*

Verb phrase structures: *curls her hair, is curling, curled; dries, is drying, dried, will dry; cuts, is cutting, cut*

Adjective/object descriptions: *soft/hard ____, wet/dry hair, cold/hot ____, long/short hair, rough/smooth ____*

Question structures: *what, how, where, when, who, what if, why, how many, which one*

Pronouns: *I, you, he, she, we, they, my, your, him, her, his, our, their, me, us, them*

Prepositions: *in, on, under, over, near, beneath, next to, beside, around, inside, outside*

Sounds: /k/ *cut, back*; /s/ *set, cuts*; /sh/ *shave, brush*; /l/ *long, curl*

Noting print has meaning: names on chairs and on cubbies, signs in dramatic play, words in books and on chalkboard

Noting sound–symbol associations: What sound does _____ start with?

Writing: letters, names, words

Social Skills Facilitated

Initiating interaction with peers and adults; responding to questions and requests from peers and adults

Negotiating with peers for toys and materials

Group cooperation: waiting for a turn in a group, taking a turn at the appropriate time

Cognitive Skills Facilitated

Problem-solving skills: how to fix hair

Classification skills: things found in a beauty shop

Sequencing skills: songs, stories

Narrative/story structure: adventure

Motor Skills Facilitated

Large motor: outdoor play activities—jumping, running, hopping, pedaling, climbing

Small motor: writing, drawing, gluing

DRAMATIC PLAY **Beauty Salon/Barber Shop**

Type of Activity: Central

Objectives
1. Learn new, and employ familiar, vocabulary
2. Learn new, and employ a variety of, syntactic constructions
3. Interact with peers
4. Sequence familiar routines
5. Expand conceptual knowledge of the world

Settings
- Salon chair (use a highchair for dolls to sit in)
- Chairs (for children)
- Sink to "wash" hair
- Reception area with telephone, appointment book, and pencil or crayon
- Barber chair
- Manicurist table

Props
- Curlers and clips (put children's names on the curlers and clips so that they use only theirs, and disinfect at the end of the play)
- Combs (put children's names on the combs so that they use only theirs, and disinfect at the end of play)
- Mirrors
- Fingernail polish bottles (filled with water)
- Pretend shampoo and conditioner
- Pretend hair spray
- Pretend hair dryer (made out of two toilet paper rolls and a cottage cheese container, with a twisted pipe cleaner to represent the cord)
- Plastic chips (razors)
- Shaving cream
- Smocks (typically used when the children paint)
- Pretend nail polish remover
- Nail files
- Towels
- Toy cash register
- Pretend money

Roles
- Customers
- Receptionist
- Beautician
- Barber
- Manicurist

General Description of Activity

Children play beauty/barber shop and get their hair shampooed, cut, dried, and styled. They also might get a manicure (beauty salon) or a shave (barber shop). Children can use their fingers in a cutting motion to pretend to cut hair.

Verbal Productions

Level of linguistic complexity varies with the role or competency of the child playing the role.
- "I'm washing her hair" or "Wash hair"
- "Do you want your hair to be cut?" or "Cut?"
- "Your hair is wet" or "Wet"
- "Cut my hair, please" or "Cut hair"
- "He is shaving" or "He shaved"

Adult Facilitative Role

The adult is to facilitate role play and help expand language and literacy skills. Typical actions or strategies to use include

Playing a role: "I think I will get my nails polished at the beauty parlor."

Expanding a child's utterance: "Curl Jane hair" to "Yes, you are curling Jane's hair."

Asking an open question: "How should I fix the doll's hair?"

Identifying rhyming words: "The words *hair, chair*, and *bear* all rhyme."

Redirecting a child to a peer: "Ask Kris for a turn with the hair dryer. Say, 'May I have a turn, please?'"

ART **Shaving Cream Fingerpainting**

Objectives
1. Express creativity
2. Develop small motor skills (e.g., drawing, painting, cutting, pasting)
3. Practice turn-taking skills
4. Converse with peers and adults

Materials
- Shaving cream
- Formboards
- Wooden craft sticks
- Other tools for "drawing" in the cream

General Description of Activity

Put a dab of shaving cream on each child's formboard. The children can use their hands and fingers to smear the cream all over the board, then use their fingers to draw and write in the shaving cream. The children can also make abstract designs, make full handprints, or use their fingers to practice writing letters or numbers. Fingerpainting is a good excuse to get messy and gooey. Some children love this; others may need some coaxing to get their fingers dirty.

GROUP **Rough/Smooth**

Objectives
1. Improve listening skills
2. Increase conceptual knowledge
3. Learn appropriate group-interaction skills
4. Practice turn-taking skills

Materials
- Two tubs or containers
- Several items that are rough
- Several items that are smooth
- Carpet squares for "rough" mats (optional)
- Cardstock or other smooth paper for "smooth" mats (optional)

General Description of Activity

Place two tubs in front of the children. Hold up a rough object (e.g., a piece of sandpaper) and label it (e.g., "The sandpaper is rough and bumpy"). Then put this object into one of the tubs. Hold up a smooth object (e.g., a puzzle piece) and label it (e.g., "The puzzle piece is smooth"). Place the smooth object into the other tub. Tell the children that they are going to help sort some rough and smooth objects into the correct piles.

Group Participation

Distribute several different items to the children. Have children come one by one to the front, label their item, and decide into which tub the object goes. Ask each child why he or she put the item there (e.g., "I put it there because it is a rough [or smooth] _____"). Continue until each child has had a chance to participate.

Variation

Divide the class into groups of two or three children. Give each group a variety of smooth and rough objects and have the children work together to sort the items into the two categories. Offer mats for sorting the different objects (a rough carpet square could be used for the rough objects and finger-paint paper could be used for smooth objects).

Summary/Transition Activity

Review the items in each tub, starting with the rough objects and moving on to the smooth items.

March

Week 32
Vacations

WEEKLY PLANNING GUIDE

	Dramatic Play	Art	Group	Story	Song
Monday Suggested Props and Materials	Airplane *Airplane scenario, pilot area, seats, seatbelts, carts, suitcases, ticket area*	Fold/Decorate Paper Airplanes *Paper, markers, paper clip*	How to Write a *10* *Card with number 10 on it, number line, counting objects, chalkboards and chalk (or white-boards and markers)*	*The Trip*	"I'm a Little Airplane"
Tuesday Suggested Props and Materials	Motel *Motel scenario, check-in counter, rooms, housecleaning equipment, pool*	Post Cards *Index cards (3" × 5" or 4" × 6"), glue, pictures, markers, chalkboard with message*	Identifying *M, N,* and *O* *Upper- and lowercase letters M, N, and O and pictures and words beginning with these letters; chalkboards (individual) and chalk or paper and markers or whiteboards and markers*	*Emma's Vacation*	"Going to Kentucky"
Wednesday Suggested Props and Materials	Amusement Park *Amusement park scenario, ticket booth, tickets, different rides or games (e.g., Ring Toss, beanbag throw, fishing)*	Watercolor Paintings *Watercolor paints, water, paper, brushes*	Act out a Story *(Anansi and the Moss-Covered Rock)*	*Anansi and the Moss-Covered Rock*	"It's a Small World"
Thursday Suggested Props and Materials	Cruise Ship *Cruise ship scenario, captain's area, eating area, sleeping area, gift store, swimming area*	Tissue Paper Fish *Cut-up tissue paper, fish outline or cutout, glue*	Sound Sequencing *Drum, sound patterns for children to clap or tap out on the drum*	*Out of the Ocean*	"Row, Row, Row Your Boat"

MY NOTES

NEWSLETTER

Vol. 1, No. 32

Date: _____

Vacations

Monday

All aboard for an airplane ride! The children will work on the plane and be passengers during dramatic play. They will make and decorate paper airplanes at the art center. *The Trip* is the story for Monday. During group time, the children will learn about the number *10*. The theme song for music will be "I'm a Little Airplane."

Tuesday

The children continue their vacation theme today by staying in a motel. They will help guests check in or be guests during dramatic play. Art time will feature post cards. During storytime, the children will read *Emma's Vacation*. During group time, the children will learn about the letters and sounds of *M*, *N*, and *O*. The Tuesday song is "Going to Kentucky."

Wednesday

The theme today for dramatic play is amusement park. The children will ride on exciting rides and eat snack foods. At the art center, the children will paint with watercolors. The story is *Anansi and the Moss-Covered Rock*. During group time, the children will act out the story. "It's a Small World" will be a featured song during music.

Thursday

The children will be walking up the gangplank to get on the cruise ship during dramatic play. They will enjoy shipboard activities and good food. In art, the children will make tissue paper fish. Our story for the day is *Out of the Ocean*. During group time, the children will imitate a sequence of sound patterns. "Row, Row, Row Your Boat" will be sung during music.

Monday

Dramatic Play	Art	Group	Story	Song
Airplane	Fold/Decorate Paper Airplanes	How to Write a *10*	*The Trip*	"I'm a Little Airplane"

DAILY PLANNING GUIDE

Language and Literacy Skills Facilitated

Vocabulary: *transportation, airplane, pilot, flight attendant, baggage, suitcase, take-off, landing, seat belt, security check, ticket, seat, passenger, beverage, cockpit*

Verb phrase structures: <u>fasten</u> *your seatbelt, land<u>s</u> the plane, <u>is</u> land<u>ing</u>, land<u>ed</u>, <u>flew</u> the plane, serv<u>ed</u> food, check<u>ed</u> baggage, Who <u>is</u> going on the plane? I <u>am</u>* (uncontractible auxiliary verb), *I<u>'m</u> flying* (contractible auxiliary)

Adjective/object descriptions: *large plane, small plane, big suitcase, little bag, carry-on bag, blue ___, red _____, purple ____*

Question structures: *what, how, where, when, who, what if, why, how many, which one*

Pronouns: *I, you, he, she, we, they, my, your, him, her, his, our, their, me, us, them*

Prepositions: *in, on, under, over, near, beneath, next to, beside, around, inside, outside*

Sounds: /l/ *<u>l</u>ands, pi<u>l</u>ot, fi<u>ll</u>;* /r/ *<u>r</u>ide, ca<u>r</u>;* /s/ *<u>s</u>it, talk<u>s</u>;* /k/ *<u>c</u>arry, ti<u>ck</u>et, pa<u>ck</u>;* /f/ *<u>f</u>ive, of<u>f</u>*

Noting print has meaning: names on chairs and on cubbies, signs in dramatic play, words in books and on chalkboard

Noting sound–symbol associations: What sound does _____ start with?

Writing: letters, names, words

Social Skills Facilitated

Initiating interaction with peers and adults; responding to questions and requests from peers and adults

Negotiating with peers for toys and materials

Group cooperation: waiting for a turn in a group, taking a turn at the appropriate time

Cognitive Skills Facilitated

Problem-solving skills: how to fold paper to make an airplane

Classification skills: things to pack

Sequencing skills: songs, stories

Narrative/story structure: adventure

Motor Skills Facilitated

Large motor: outdoor play activities—jumping, running, hopping, pedaling, climbing

Small motor: writing, drawing, gluing, folding

DRAMATIC PLAY **Airplane**

Type of Activity: Central

Objectives
1. Learn new, and employ familiar, vocabulary
2. Learn new, and employ a variety of, syntactic constructions
3. Interact with peers
4. Sequence familiar routines
5. Expand conceptual knowledge of the world

Settings
- Airport
- Ticket office or counter
- Airplane facsimile (chairs arranged in rows behind a "cab," where a play dashboard is set up)
- Kitchen
- Cockpit
- Baggage claim area (optional)
- Metal detector (optional)

Props
- Tickets
- Chairs with seatbelts (men's ties can be used for seatbelts)
- Dashboard
- Luggage
- Food and drinks
- Trays
- Carts
- Dolls
- Pretend money
- Dishes

Roles
- Pilot and co-pilot
- Flight attendants
- Passengers
- Clerks at the ticket counter
- Security people

General Description of Activity

Children take a pretend airplane trip, including purchasing a ticket, checking baggage at the counter, going through a security check, and finding a seat on the airplane. They must store their carry-on luggage under a seat and fasten their seatbelts before take-off. Food and beverages can be served by children acting as flight attendants. Upon arrival, the passengers can claim their baggage in the baggage area.

Verbal Productions

Level of linguistic complexity varies with the role or competency of the child playing the role.
- "We're coming in for a landing, so fasten your seatbelts" or "Plane's landing"
- "Do you want a drink?" or "Drink, please"
- "May I see your ticket?" or "Ticket?"

Adult Facilitative Role

The adult is to facilitate role play and help expand language and literacy skills. Typical actions or strategies to use include

Playing a role: "I am going to visit my grandmother. She lives far away, so I will go on an airplane."

Modeling phonological awareness: "The words *no, nice, neat*, and *Nick* all start with the letter *N*."

Expanding a child's utterance: "Big plane" to "Yes, that is a big plane."

Providing a literacy model: "The ticket says *Boston* because that's where I'm flying."

ART : Fold/Decorate Paper Airplanes

Objectives
1. Express creativity
2. Develop small motor skills (e.g., drawing, painting, cutting, folding)
3. Practice turn-taking skills
4. Converse with peers and adults

Materials
- 8" × 10" paper
- Paper clips
- Markers
- Crayons
- Stickers

General Description of Activity

A paper airplane is made by first decorating the paper. Drawings or different colors can be used. The 8" × 10" sheet of paper (any size paper can be used) is then folded to make an airplane. A paper clip is used on the "nose" of the airplane to hold the plane together and to provide appropriate weight so the airplane will fly.

To make the airplane, fold the paper in half lengthwise. Then fold a top edge down until it is even with the folded bottom to form a triangle shape. Turn paper over and fold the other side the same way so that one third of the paper is slanted and ending in a point. Clip a paper clip to the point of the triangle. Fold the rest of the top edge even with the bottom fold. Make a crease. Let go of the paper so it sticks out to make a wing. Turn the paper over and fold the other side in the same way. The paper airplane is then ready to fly. (Other paper folding can be done to form other styles of airplanes.)

GROUP **How to Write a *10***

Objectives
1. Improve listening skills
2. Increase conceptual knowledge
3. Learn appropriate group-interaction skills
4. Practice turn-taking skills
5. Practice recognition and writing of numbers

Materials
- Number cards
- Chalkboards and chalk
- Paper and pencils (optional)
- Whiteboard and markers
- Number line (optional)

General Description of Activity

Hold up a card with the number *10* written on it. Trace the number with your finger and invite several children to come to the front of the group to trace the number, too. As the children trace, recite the jingle for the target number (*10*):

1: Start at the top, go down and you're done, that's the way to make a *1*.

2: Around and back on the railroad track, *2, 2, 2.*

3: Around the tree, around the tree, that's the way to make a *3*.

4: Down and over and down once more, that's the way to make a *4*.

5: Down around, make a hat on it, and look what you've found. (*5*)

6: Down around until it sticks, that's the way to make a *6*.

7: Over and down and it's not heaven, over and down makes a *7*.

8: Make an S and go back straight, that's the way to make an *8*.

9: A balloon and a line make *9*.

10: Draw a line and a circle with your pen, that's the way to make a *10*.

Group Participation

Distribute individual chalkboards and chalk (or paper and pencils) to the children, and have them practice writing the target number.

Variation 1

Whiteboards and markers may be easier for some children to use.

Variation 2

To introduce the number, use a number line and have the children count up to the target number on the line. One child could place the target number on the number line.

Summary/Transition Activity

Ask children to hold up their chalkboards and show the group their numbers.

Tuesday

Dramatic Play	Art	Group	Story	Song
Motel	Post Cards	Identifying *M, N,* and *O*	*Emma's Vacation*	"Going to Kentucky"

DAILY PLANNING GUIDE

Language and Literacy Skills Facilitated

Vocabulary: *motel, beds, check in, check out, key, clerk, maid, room service, suitcase, swimming suit, travel*

Verb phrase structures: *traveled, is checking in, checking out, checked out, is cleaning rooms, are making beds, swimming in the pool, packed*

Adjective/object descriptions: *room key, big ____, little ___, red ____, blue ____*

Question structures: *what, how, where, when, who, what if, why, how many, which one*

Pronouns: *I, you, he, she, we, they, my, your, him, her, his, our, their, me, us, them*

Prepositions: *in, on, under, over, near, beneath, next to, beside, around, inside, outside*

Sounds: /l/ *light, delight, pool;* /f/ *find, off*

Noting print has meaning: names on chairs and on cubbies, signs in dramatic play, words in books and on chalkboard

Noting sound–symbol associations: What sound does _____ start with?

Writing: letters, names, words

Social Skills Facilitated

Initiating interaction with peers and adults; responding to questions and requests from peers and adults

Negotiating with peers for toys and materials

Group cooperation: waiting for a turn in a group, taking a turn at the appropriate time

Cognitive Skills Facilitated

Problem-solving skills: how to make a post card

Classification skills: things in a motel

Sequencing skills: dramatic play (travel, check in, stay, check out)

Narrative/story structure: adventure

Motor Skills Facilitated

Large motor: outdoor play activities—jumping, running, hopping, pedaling, climbing

Small motor: writing, drawing, gluing

DRAMATIC PLAY **Motel**

Type of Activity: Central

Objectives
1. Learn new, and employ familiar, vocabulary
2. Learn new, and employ a variety of, syntactic constructions
3. Interact with peers
4. Sequence familiar routines
5. Expand conceptual knowledge of the world

Settings

- Check-in desk
- Different rooms with mats for beds
- Bathroom areas
- Pool
- Restaurant (optional)

Props

- Beds and pillows
- Play telephones
- Television sets (shoeboxes with a side cut out and a picture pasted over the cutout area)
- Registration book
- Pretend cash register
- Pretend money
- Pretend credit cards
- Keys
- Dolls (for babies)
- Towels
- Toothbrushes
- Brooms and mops
- Restaurant tables
- Play dishes
- Pretend food
- Suitcases
- Clothes
- Blue sheet or wading pool (the "pool")

Roles

- Clerks
- Customers
- Maids
- Room service attendants
- Lifeguard
- Waiters and waitresses (optional)
- Cooks (optional)

General Description of Activity

Children pretend they are staying at a motel while on a trip. Their rooms might have beds, television sets, and telephones. There might be a pool available and also a restaurant attached to the motel. Children can check in, go to their rooms, unpack their clothes, go out to eat (or order room service), come back to their rooms, go swimming in the pool, make telephone calls, and then sleep. They can then awake, check out, and continue their trip. They might want to stay for several days in the motel!

Verbal Productions

Level of linguistic complexity varies with the role or competency of the child playing the role.

- "May I have a room, please?" or "Room?"
- "I'm going to call for tickets" or "I calling"
- "She cleaned this room yesterday" or "Clean room"
- "Do you want your room cleaned now?" or "Clean now"
- "No, I'm sleeping" or "No, sleep"

Adult Facilitative Role

The adult is to facilitate role play and help expand language and literacy skills. Typical actions or strategies to use include

Playing a role: "I will check you in. You can write your name here."

Providing a literacy model: "Yes, the word *Mary* is spelled M-A-R-Y."

Contrasting two location terms: "That pillow is on the bed. This pillow is beside the bed. It fell off."

Providing an event casting of an adult's actions: "I am making the bed. Then I will dust the dresser."

Expanding a child's utterance: "My bed" to "That is your bed."

ART **Post Cards**

Objectives

1. Express creativity
2. Develop small motor skills (e.g., drawing, painting, cutting, pasting)
3. Practice turn-taking skills
4. Converse with peers and adults

Materials
- Scissors
- A variety of magazines, particularly travel magazines or those with scenery
- Glue or paste
- Index cards (3" × 5" or 4" × 6")
- Markers or crayons
- Chalkboard and chalk or a word chart with words for children to copy

General Description of Activity

Children cut out pictures from magazines and glue them on one side of an index card. They then "write" messages to their family and friends on the other side of their cards. It is helpful to have messages such as *Dear Mom and Dad, I am having fun,* and *Love,* written on a chalkboard (or a chart) for the children to copy.

GROUP **Identifying *M*, *N*, and *O***

Objectives
1. Improve listening skills
2. Increase knowledge of the alphabet and sounds
3. Learn appropriate group-interaction skills
4. Practice turn-taking skills

Materials
- Target alphabet letters on cards
- Alphabet chart
- Paper and pencils or markers (optional)
- Chalkboards, chalk (optional)

General Description of Activity

Lay the letters *M*, *N*, and *O* in front of the children. Have the children, in chorus, say the letters as you point to each one. Have one child come to the front and point to a specific letter.

Group Participation

Ask different children to point to specific letters, helping them as necessary. Vary the difficulty by having children identify letters in order or out of order, or by having some match a letter card to the letters on the floor instead of pointing to a designated letter. You can also ask them to match lowercase letters to uppercase letters. Children can also point to a letter and have the class label it.

Summary/Transition Activity

Say the whole alphabet with the children as you point to an alphabet chart. Then have everyone say the target alphabet letters (*M*, *N*, *O*) as you point to each letter in turn. An alternative activity is to have the children practice writing the three target letters.

Wednesday

Dramatic Play	Art	Group	Story	Song
Amusement Park	Watercolor Paintings	Act out a Story (*Anansi and the Moss-Covered Rock*)	*Anansi and the Moss-Covered Rock*	"It's a Small World"

DAILY PLANNING GUIDE

Language and Literacy Skills Facilitated

Vocabulary: ticket, amusement park, hot dogs, hamburgers, Ring Toss, mural, whirlie, target

Verb phrase structures: <u>ride</u> the whirlie, <u>spin</u> around, <u>eat</u> hot dogs, <u>throw</u> the ball at the target, <u>buy</u> tickets, <u>draw</u>, <u>write</u>

Adjective/object descriptions: big ___, little ____, large ___, small ___, fast ___, slow ___, red ___, blue ____, yellow ___

Question structures: what, how, where, when, who, what if, why, how many, which one

Pronouns: I, you, he, she, we, they, my, your, him, her, his, our, their, me, us, them

Prepositions: in, on, under, over, near, beneath, next to, beside, around, inside, outside

Noting print has meaning: names on chairs and on cubbies, signs in dramatic play, words in books and on chalkboard

Noting sound–symbol associations: What sound does _____ start with?

Writing: letters, names, words

Social Skills Facilitated

Initiating interaction with peers and adults; responding to questions and requests from peers and adults

Negotiating with peers for toys and materials

Group cooperation: waiting for a turn in a group, taking a turn at the appropriate time

Cognitive Skills Facilitated

Problem-solving skills: how to act out the story, what to say

Classification skills: things in a amusement park

Sequencing skills: acting out the story, songs

Narrative/story structure: adventure

Motor Skills Facilitated

Large motor: outdoor play activities—jumping, running, hopping, pedaling, climbing

Small motor: writing, drawing, gluing, painting

> DRAMATIC PLAY **Amusement Park**

Type of Activity: Central

Objectives
1. Learn new, and employ familiar, vocabulary
2. Learn new, and employ a variety of, syntactic constructions
3. Interact with peers
4. Sequence familiar routines
5. Expand conceptual knowledge of the world

Settings
- Various rides (e.g., Sit 'N Spin, miniature trampolines)
- Ticket office
- Concession areas
- Game area

Props
- Tickets
- Bowling ball and pins
- Bean Bag Toss
- Pretend roller coaster (made from boxes lined up in a row)
- Target board and balls with Velcro adhesive so they stick to the target
- Pretend food (e.g., hot dogs, sodas, ice cream, cotton candy)
- Two cash registers
- Pretend money

Roles
- Customers
- Park workers (to run the games and the rides)
- Ticket sellers
- Concession stand workers

General Description of Activity

An amusement park has several rides and other activities in which the children can participate. In this dramatic play, the children may circulate among activities. There might be concession stands where they can purchase food items, such as hot dogs, or they might bring a picnic to the park. The park might have a train for transportation from one area to another.

Verbal Productions

Level of linguistic complexity varies with the role or competency of the child playing the role.
- "I want a ride on the roller coaster, please" or "Want ride"
- "She needs a ticket" or "Ticket?"
- "It's his turn" or "Turn, please"

Adult Facilitative Role

The adult is to facilitate role play and help expand language and literacy skills. Typical actions or strategies to use include

Playing a role: "I am selling cotton candy at the amusement park. Do you want some?"

Contrasting error sound with correct production: "You asked, 'What did it tost?' but I think you meant, 'What did it cost?'"

Using a cloze procedure: "This box is big, and this box is _____ (little)."

Redirecting a child to a peer: "Ask Maria for a turn on the cash register. Say, 'Can I have a turn, please?'"

Expanding a child's utterance: "John spinning" to "Yes, John is spinning fast."

ART : **Watercolor Paintings**

Objectives
1. Express creativity
2. Develop small motor skills (e.g., drawing, painting, cutting, pasting)
3. Practice turn-taking skills
4. Converse with peers and adults

Materials
- Watercolor paints
- Brushes
- Water in tubs
- White construction paper

General Description of Activity

Lay out white construction paper, watercolor paint boxes, and brushes on the art table. Place tubs of water to clean the brushes above the paper. The children put on smocks and sit down in front of the paper, paint box, and water tub. Each child selects a brush, wets it, and chooses the paint color. The children paint on the paper, rinsing the brush before selecting a new color. Children can paint a collage of colors, animals, people, scenery, and so on. You may want to be close by so children can talk about their paintings.

GROUP **Act out a Story (*Anansi and the Moss-Covered Rock*)**

Objectives
1. Improve listening skills
2. To increase sequencing ability
3. Increase knowledge of storytelling
4. Learn appropriate group-interaction skills
5. Practice turn-taking skills

Materials
- *Anansi and the Moss-Covered Rock*
- Props for the story

General Description of Activity

Read *Anansi and the Moss-Covered Rock*, or summarize it if children are familiar with it.

Group Participation

Assign children roles from the story. Assure the children not chosen the first time that everyone will have a turn and that they have the very important job of being a good listening audience. Narrate the story as the children act it out. They should say as many of the lines as they can, with prompts given when needed. Repeat with new actors until all the children have had a turn.

Summary/Transition Activity

Compliment the children's acting, and ask children what other stories they would like to act out another day.

Thursday

Dramatic Play	Art	Group	Story	Song
Cruise Ship	Tissue Paper Fish	Sound Sequencing	Out of the Ocean	"Row, Row, Row Your Boat"

DAILY PLANNING GUIDE

Language and Literacy Skills Facilitated

Vocabulary: *sink, float, water, fish, boat, liner, rowboat, cruise, shark, sea, ocean, waves, swim*

Verb phrase structures: *is fishing, catches, floated, swam, has a fish, has gone sailing, rode in a boat, Who is going fishing? I am* (uncontractible auxiliary), *Who is the biggest? I am* (uncontractible copula)

Adjective/object descriptions: *big ____, little ____, high water, low water, tiny ____, green ____, blue ____*

Question structures: *what, how, where, when, who, what if, why, how many, which one*

Pronouns: *I, you, he, she, we, they, my, your, him, her, his, our, their, me, us, them*

Prepositions: *in, on, under, over, near, beneath, next to, beside, around, inside, outside*

Sounds: /f/ *fish*; /s/ *sail, boats*; /l/ *little, pail*; /r/ *rowboat, far*; /k/ *catch, sink* /sh/ *ship, fish*

Noting print has meaning: names on chairs and on cubbies, signs in dramatic play, words in books and on chalkboard

Noting sound–symbol associations: What sound does ____ start with?

Writing: letters, names, words

Social Skills Facilitated

Initiating interaction with peers and adults; responding to questions and requests from peers and adults

Negotiating with peers for toys and materials

Group cooperation: waiting for a turn in a group, taking a turn at the appropriate time

Cognitive Skills Facilitated

Problem-solving skills: how to make a crushed paper fish, how to make sound patterns

Classification skills: things on a cruise ship

Sequencing skills: songs, stories, sound patterns

Narrative/story structure: adventure

Motor Skills Facilitated

Large motor: outdoor play activities—jumping, running, hopping, pedaling, climbing

Small motor: writing, drawing, gluing, fingerpainting

DRAMATIC PLAY **Cruise Ship**

Type of Activity: Central

Objectives
1. Learn new, and employ familiar, vocabulary
2. Learn new, and employ a variety of, syntactic constructions
3. Interact with peers
4. Sequence familiar routines
5. Expand conceptual knowledge of the world

Settings
- Ship (large cardboard box that has been unfolded to form a shell around the classroom's kitchen area)
- Kitchen
- Helm
- Cabins (mats)
- Dining area
- Gift store
- Shuffleboard area
- Sunbathing area
- Pool area
- Water

Props
- Tickets
- Gangplank
- Suitcases
- Mats
- Tables
- Pretend food
- Shuffleboard sticks and pieces
- Sunscreen
- Sunglasses
- Jewelry (for the gift store)
- Dishes
- Pots and pans
- Rudder
- Captain's hat

Roles
- Passengers
- Captain
- Purser
- Waiters and waitresses
- Gift shop salespeople
- Ship's doctor

General Description of Activity

Children can act out a variety of roles on a cruise ship, including the captain, the purser, waiters and waitresses, the gift store salespeople, and the cruise ship doctor. They can sleep in cabins, eat at tables arranged like in a restaurant, swim, play shuffleboard, sunbathe, and buy things at the gift store.

Verbal Productions

Level of linguistic complexity varies with the role or competency of the child playing the role.
- "He spotted a shark" or "Shark!"
- "I got an eight on the shuffleboard game" or "Eight"
- "He is swimming in the ocean" or "He swimming"
- "I am the captain. You must board now" or "Go now"
- "That's my suitcase" or "Mine"
- "She is turning the wheel fast" or "Fast"

Adult Facilitative Role

The adult is to facilitate role play and help expand language and literacy skills. Typical actions or strategies to use include

Playing a role: "I want to play shuffleboard."

Modeling the correct production of the /sh/ sound: "This <u>sh</u>ip is big. We <u>sh</u>ould be safe."

Identifying rhyming words: "The words *dine, fine,* and *line* all rhyme."

Contrasting error and correct structures: "Her like swimming" to "Yes, she likes swimming a lot."

Modeling the reading of a sign: "The sign says *gift store.*"

ART : Tissue Paper Fish

Objectives
1. Express creativity
2. Develop small motor skills (e.g., drawing, painting, cutting, pasting)
3. Practice turn-taking skills
4. Converse with peers and adults

Materials
- Precut construction-paper fish shapes (also boat or other theme-related shapes)
- Glue or paste
- 1" tissue paper squares in several colors
- Pencils or crayons

General Description of Activity

Children crush the 1" pieces of tissue paper and paste them onto a pre-cut construction paper form. One way to crush the paper is to wrap it around the eraser end of a pencil (or one end of a crayon) and push it off onto glue or paste that is already on the form. Or, children can just crumple the squares and then paste them on the paper. When the form is completely covered, the result is a three-dimensional picture, or a picture with texture.

GROUP **Sound Sequencing**

Objectives
1. Improve listening skills
2. Increase ability to recognize and sequence patterns
3. Learn appropriate group-interaction skills
4. Practice turn-taking skills

Materials
- Drum
- Keyboard (optional)
- Markers
- Whiteboard

General Description of Activity

A drum is placed in front of the children. The teacher taps out a simple pattern while the children listen. The teacher then repeats the pattern while they listen again. One child is invited to come up to the front of the class and try to make the same pattern. (The child can be helped if necessary so that the sound pattern matches the teacher's.)

Group Participation

A different pattern is played, and another child tries to match it. This continues until all the children have had at least one turn. The patterns can vary from two short taps to complicated patterns involving a series of taps grouped in two or three sequences. For example, one pattern might be *tap-tap*-pause-*tap*. Another might be *tap-tap-tap*-pause-*tap-tap*. Other sample patterns include the following:

tap-tap (pause) *tap-tap*

tap-tap-tap (pause) *tap*

tap (pause) *tap-tap*

loud tap (pause) *soft tap*

two loud taps (pause) *two soft taps*

Variation

A keyboard can be used to set a rhythm and the children could clap to the rhythm.

Summary/Transition Activity

The teacher plays one more pattern and has the children clap the pattern, or the teacher can play a rhythm from a song that is to be sung during music time and have the children clap out that rhythm.

April

Activities	Monday	Tuesday	Wednesday	Thursday
Week 33 — Places Around the World				
Dramatic Play	China (Chinese Restaurant)	Egypt (Pyramids and Archaeology)	France Castle	Mexico (Fiesta and Market)
Art	Dragon Masks	Cheerios Art: Outline a Pyramid	Castle Mural	Make Tambourines
Group	Oddity Match	Pattern Matching with Shapes	Identifying *P, Q,* and *R*	Writing Class Letters
Story	*A Visit to China*	*Who Built the Pyramids?*	*Cinderella*	*This Is the Way We Eat Our Lunch*
Song	"I'm a Little Teapot"	"Sally the Camel"	"Are You Sleeping?"	"It's a Small World"
Week 34 — The Elements				
Dramatic Play	Water—Water Play	Fire—Firefighter	Air—Outdoor Sports	Earth—Gardening
Art	Watercolor Painting	Playdough Constructions	Make a Kite	Sand Pictures
Group	Identifying *S, T,* and *U*	Fire Safety Rules	Act out a Story (*Chicken Little*)	Planting Seeds
Story	*Fish Is Fish*	*Fire Truck*	*Chicken Little*	*Growing Vegetable Soup*
Song	"All the Little Fishies"	"Hurry, Hurry, Drive the Fire Truck"	"The Wind Came out To Play" (fingerplay)	"Way Down Yonder in the Paw Paw Patch"
Week 35 — Hobbies				
Dramatic Play	Craft Fair	Car Racing	Baking	All About Pets
Art	Macaroni Necklaces	Car Track Painting	Gingerbread Men	Paper Bag Puppets
Group	Act Out a Story (*The Wide-Mouth Frog*)	Identifying *V, W,* and *X*	Tap out Syllables	Classify Pets and Zoo Animals
Story	*The Wide-Mouth Frog*	*Play It Safe*	*Mr. Cookie Baker*	*Franklin Wants a Pet*
Song	"Going to Kentucky"	"Twinkle, Twinkle, Traffic Light"	"Do You Know the Muffin Man?"	"How Much Is that Doggy in the Window?"
Week 36 — Community Helpers				
Dramatic Play	Doctor	Teacher	Sanitation Engineer	Police Officer
Art	Chalk Drawings	Easel Paintings	Trash Collage	Badges
Group	Review Writing Numbers 1–10	Identifying *Y* and *Z*	Word Deletion	What Is Your Address?
Story	*Little Rabbit Goes to the Doctor*	*Who Took the Cookies from the Cookie Jar?*	*Dear Garbage Man*	*Edward Hurts His Knee*
Song	"Baby Bear Has Chicken Pox"	"The Alphabet Song"	"Hokey Pokey"	"Red Light, Red Light, What Do You Say?"

WEEKLY PLANNING GUIDE

	Dramatic Play	Art	Group	Story	Song
Monday *Suggested Props and Materials*	China (Chinese Restaurant) *Restaurant scenario, kitchen area, dining area, cash register, chopsticks, menus, dishes, pretend food, pretend money*	Dragon Masks *Dragon mask outline, scissors, construction paper cutouts, glitter, glue or paste, crayons or markers, large wooden craft sticks*	Oddity Match *Several items that are exact matches (and some that are not), several items that are similar (and some that don't match), several items that are related, cardboard X (optional)*	*A Visit to China*	"I'm a Little Teapot"
Tuesday *Suggested Props and Materials*	Egypt (Pyramids and Archaeology) *Pyramid/archaeological scenario, dig area (sand in sandbox with small items to be buried), sifters, microscope, pyramid (tent with cardboard covering), pretend camel*	Cheerios Art: Outline a Pyramid *Cheerios, pyramid outlines, glue*	Pattern Matching with Shapes *Variety of shape cutouts*	*Who Built the Pyramids?*	"Sally the Camel"
Wednesday *Suggested Props and Materials*	France Castle *Castle scenario, moat, ballroom, crowns, thrones, shields, horses*	Castle Mural *Mural paper, markers, glue, different picture cutouts*	Identifying *P, Q,* and *R* *Target alphabet letters on cards, alphabet chart, paper and pencils or markers (optional); individual chalkboard and chalk (optional)*	*Cinderella*	"Are You Sleeping?"
Thursday *Suggested Props and Materials*	Mexico (Fiesta and Market) *Marketplace scenario, various Mexican items (e.g., sombrero, serape, pottery, beads), pretend food, fiesta area with maracas, drums, tape recorder and tape of Mexican music*	Make Tambourines *Two paper plates, markers, Cheerios, stapler*	Writing Class Letters *Set of at least 10 rhyming word cards, objects whose names rhyme*	*This Is the Way We Eat Our Lunch*	"It's A Small World"

MY NOTES

NEWSLETTER

Vol. 1, No. 33

Date: _____

Places Around the World

Monday
An Asian restaurant comes to the classroom today. The children will pretend to be wait staff, cooks, customers, and hosts during dramatic play. They will be making dragon masks in art. Our featured story is *A Visit to China*. During group time, children will choose the object that does not belong with the others in a group. Our song is "I'm a Little Teapot."

Tuesday
The children will be going on an archaeological dig in Egypt. They may be scientists who find artifacts or tourists who visit the pyramids or ride on camels. In art, children will outline a pyramid shape with Cheerios. *Who Built the Pyramids?* is the story for today. The children will match, recall, or extend patterns involving a variety of shapes at group. Music time will include "Sally the Camel."

Wednesday
Today we will visit France and focus on castles. The children might pretend to be the king, queen, prince, or princess, or the knights and ladies in waiting in the France Castle. They will make a castle mural in art. Our story is *Cinderella*. During group time, children will practice identifying the letters *P*, *Q*, and *R*. Our song for the day is "Are You Sleeping?"

Thursday
There will be a marketplace in dramatic play today when we visit Mexico. The children will be vendors and customers enjoying fiesta music, dancing, and tortilla making. The children will make tambourines in art. The story for the day is *This Is the Way We Eat Our Lunch*. During group time, we will write a class letter reviewing the week. Our song is "It's a Small World."

Monday

Dramatic Play	Art	Group	Story	Song
China (Chinese Restaurant)	Dragon Masks	Oddity Match	*A Visit to China*	"I'm a Little Teapot"

DAILY PLANNING GUIDE

Language and Literacy Skills Facilitated

Vocabulary: *rice, chopsticks, wonton soup, food, chow mein, tea, soft drinks, egg rolls, cook, cashier, customer, order, fortune cookies*

Verb phrase structures: *place<u>s</u> an order, buy<u>s</u> a dinner, pay<u>s</u> money, <u>eat</u> out, <u>is mak<u>ing</u></u> an egg roll, serv<u>ed</u> the customer, choose<u>s</u> a drink, <u>are mak<u>ing</u></u> egg rolls*

Adjective/object descriptions: *large drink, small dish of rice, paper hat, red cup, fortune cookie*

Question structures: *what, how, where, when, who, what if, why, how many, which one*

Pronouns: *I, you, he, she, we, they, my, your, him, her, his, our, their, me, us, them*

Prepositions: *in, on, under, over, near, beneath, next to, beside, around, inside, outside*

Sounds: */r/ <u>r</u>ice, egg <u>r</u>olls, <u>r</u>ed cup; /p/ <u>p</u>aper, <u>p</u>late, <u>p</u>laces, <u>p</u>ays*

Noting print has meaning: names on chairs and on cubbies, signs in dramatic play, words in books and on chalkboard

Noting sound–symbol associations: What sound does _____ start with?

Writing: letters, names, words

Social Skills Facilitated

Initiating interaction with peers and adults; responding to questions and requests from peers and adults

Negotiating with peers for toys and materials

Group cooperation: waiting for a turn in a group, taking a turn at the appropriate time

Cognitive Skills Facilitated

Problem-solving skills: setting up a restaurant, remembering items

Classification skills: Chinese food items

Sequencing skills: story, words to song

Narrative/story structure: expository (informational)

Motor Skills Facilitated

Large motor: outdoor play activities—jumping, running, hopping, pedaling, climbing

Small motor: writing, drawing, gluing

DRAMATIC PLAY : China (Chinese Restaurant)

Type of Activity: Central

Objectives
1. Learn new, and employ familiar, vocabulary
2. Learn new, and employ a variety of, syntactic constructions
3. Interact with peers
4. Sequence familiar routines
5. Expand conceptual knowledge of the world

Setting
- Restaurant kitchen
- Buffet area
- Cashier area
- Tables and chairs
- Great Wall of China mural (optional)

Props
- Play food
- Chopsticks
- Menus (written in Chinese, if possible)
- Placemats with Chinese horoscope pictures (if possible)
- Dishes
- Silverware
- Cash register

Roles
- Waiters
- Customers
- Cashier
- Cooks

General Description of Activity

Set up a Chinese restaurant with a kitchen area, a buffet area, and tables and chairs. The children who are customers are seated at the table by wait staff and told to go through the buffet (with a variety of play food items) or to order from the menu. Include chopsticks at each place setting. You might display a mural (drawn on cardboard) representing the Great Wall of China, with blocks or steps behind it where children can "walk."

Verbal Productions

Level of linguistic complexity varies with the role or competency of the child playing the role.
- "I want wonton soup" or "Soup"
- "Do you want a menu or the buffet?" or "Buffet?"
- "Can I have some chopsticks?" or "My sticks?"
- "It is my turn now, please" or "My turn"

Adult Facilitative Role

The adult is to facilitate role play and help expand language and literacy skills. Typical actions or strategies to use include

Playing a role: "I have trouble eating with chopsticks."

Expanding a child's utterance: "Eat egg rolls" to "I like to eat egg rolls, too!"

Modeling correct production of /ch/ sound: "You can choose this Chinese soup but you can't use chopsticks to eat it."

Contrasting error and correct pronoun usage: "Him eat egg roll" to "He eats the egg roll. He likes the egg roll."

Providing a literacy model: "The menu says *egg drop soup*."

ART **Dragon Masks**

Objectives
1. Express creativity
2. Develop small motor skills (e.g., drawing, painting, cutting, pasting)
3. Practice turn-taking skills
4. Converse with peers and adults

Materials
- Pieces of construction paper cut in the shape of a dragon's head (with eyeholes cut out)
- Glitter (optional)
- Glue
- Crayons or markers
- Large wooden craft sticks

General Description of Activity

Give children a precut construction paper mask in the shape of a dragon's head. The children may use glitter, markers, or crayons to decorate the mask. On the back of the mask, at the bottom, have children glue a large wooden craft stick to use as a handhold.

GROUP **Oddity Match**

Objectives
1. Improve listening skills
2. Improve sequencing ability
3. Learn appropriate group-interaction skills
4. Practice turn-taking skills

Materials
- Several items that are exact matches (and some that are not)
- Several items that are similar (and some that don't match)
- Cardboard X (optional)

General Description of Activity

Lay out four items. Three of the items should be identical and one should be different (e.g., three red cars and one doll). Ask the children to look for the item that does not belong with the others. Then point to the item that is different and say, "This one does not go with the others." Lay out another set, this time with three items that are not identical but are the same kind of item, and one that is different from the others (e.g., three different dolls, one boat). Ask one child to come to the front and find the one that is different (or that does not go with the others).

Group Participation

Continue to present three items that are the same and one that is different until each child has had a turn identifying the different item. Be sure to vary the placement of the different item so that the children do not think it is always the second item or the last item. The difficulty of the task can be varied depending on the children's abilities. (Some children may need exact matches; others can recognize relationships or that the items go together even though one is bigger than the other.) The children also could put a cardboard X on top of the item that does not belong rather than say or point to the item.

Variation

One way to vary the items is to put them in a 2×2 matrix instead of in a row. Another procedure would be to use related items instead of the same kind of items. For example, of the following items, coat, hat, fork, and mitten, the coat, hat, and mitten are the items that go together and the fork does not belong. Another variation is to use color or function as the identifying feature (e.g., all the red items go together and the blue item is the one that is different, or all the of writing instruments go together and the scissors is the item that is different).

Summary/Transition Activity

Lay out one more group of items and have the children, in unison, say which one does not go with the others.

Tuesday

Dramatic Play	Art	Group	Story	Song
Egypt (Pyramids and Archaeology)	Cheerios Art: Outline a Pyramid	Pattern Matching with Shapes	*Who Built the Pyramids?*	"Sally the Camel"

DAILY PLANNING GUIDE

Language and Literacy Skills Facilitated

Vocabulary: *sand, pyramids, bazaar, necklace, food, camel, Egypt, map, hieroglyphics*

Verb phrase structures: *buil<u>ds</u> a pyramid, <u>ride</u>/<u>rode</u>/<u>riding</u> a camel*

Adjective/object descriptions: *long necklace, big pyramids, big/little camel, hot sand*

Question structures: *what, how, where, when, who, what if, why, how many, which one*

Pronouns: *I, you, he, she, we, they, my, your, him, her, his, our, their, me, us, them*

Prepositions: *in, on, under, over, near, beneath, next to, beside, around, inside, outside*

Sounds: /f/ *<u>f</u>ix, o<u>ff</u>;* /s/ *<u>s</u>it, talk<u>s</u>;* /l/ *<u>l</u>ittle, be<u>ll</u>*

Noting print has meaning: names on chairs and on cubbies, signs in dramatic play, words in books and on chalkboard

Noting sound–symbol associations: What sound does _____ start with?

Writing: letters, names, words

Social Skills Facilitated

Initiating interaction with peers and adults; responding to questions and requests from peers and adults

Negotiating with peers for toys and materials

Group cooperation: waiting for a turn in a group, taking a turn at the appropriate time

Cognitive Skills Facilitated

Problem-solving skills: pyramid shapes

Classification skills: things an archaeologist finds

Sequencing skills: story, songs, shape patterns

Narrative/story structure: expository (informational)

Motor Skills Facilitated

Large motor: outdoor play activities—jumping, running, hopping, pedaling, climbing

Small motor: writing, drawing, gluing

DRAMATIC PLAY **Egypt (Pyramids and Archaeology)**

Type of Activity: Related

Objectives
1. Learn new, and employ familiar, vocabulary
2. Learn new, and employ a variety of, syntactic constructions
3. Interact with peers
4. Sequence familiar routines
5. Expand conceptual knowledge of the world

Setting
- Sand area
- Artifact examination area
- Pyramid area
- Camel ride area

Props
- Pyramid (tent)
- Shovels, sifting materials
- Microscope and magnifying glasses
- Small objects to dig for and discover
- Pretend camel and sign for rides

Roles
- Camel driver
- Camel riders
- Archaeologists
- Pyramid writers/readers of hieroglyphics

General Description of Activity

The Egyptian pyramids have been the site for many archaeological digs. Set up a dig area using a large cardboard box (at least 4' × 6' and at least 5" in height) and fill it with sand. Also have an area for examining the finds. To represent a pyramid, erect a tent and cut paper or cardboard in triangles to attach to each side. The children can draw "hieroglyphics" on the paper or cardboard. An area for camel rides can also be set up. Children can choose to be archaeologists, the people drawing hiero-glyphics, or the ones providing or taking the camel rides.

Verbal Productions

Level of linguistic complexity varies with the role or competency of the child playing the role.
- "Look at the piece of pottery I found" or "Look!"
- "I am drawing a man and a camel" or "I draw"
- "Can I have a ride on your camel, please?" or "My turn" or "Ride?"

Adult Facilitative Role

The adult is to facilitate role play and help expand language and literacy skills. Typical actions or strategies to use include

Playing a role: "I want to ride a camel and see the pyramids."

Modeling a statement/vocabulary: "The pyramids look like big triangle buildings. They were built a long time ago in Egypt."

Recasting present tense with present progressive: "He rides the camel very well. He is riding the camel to go see the pyramids."

Modeling the reading of a sign: "The sign says camel rides."

Expanding a child's utterance: "Go dig" to "Yes, let's go dig. We can use the shovel and the sifters."

ART : **Cheerios Art: Outline a Pyramid**

Objectives
1. Express creativity
2. Develop small motor skills (e.g., drawing, painting, cutting, pasting)
3. Practice turn-taking skills
4. Converse with peers and adults

Materials
- Cheerios
- Glue or paste
- Outline of pyramid drawn on paper, one for each child

General Description of Activity

Have the children glue or paste Cheerios on the lines of the pyramid. Children may make other pictures with the Cheerios by either following lines or arranging them free-form.

Variation

Have children draw their own shapes and then glue or paste the Cheerios on the lines.

GROUP **Pattern Matching with Shapes**

Objectives
1. Improve listening skills
2. Increase ability to recognize and sequence patterns on the basis of color
3. Learn appropriate group-interaction skills
4. Practice turn-taking skills

Materials
- At least 20 different shape cutouts (circles, squares, triangles, rectangles) from construction paper or cardstock (different sizes and colors can be used)
- Cardboard (optional)

General Description of Activity

Present a pattern of different shape cutouts (e.g., *two triangles-one circle-two triangles-one circle*). Show the children how to continue the pattern by adding the appropriate cutout shapes.

Variation

Have the children repeat the pattern by creating new rows of shapes that match your pattern (i.e., this becomes a matching activity).

Group Participation

On the floor, set out a block pattern appropriate for a particular child's level. Have the child come up (or have two children come together for peer support and help), and repeat or extend the pattern. Some children can repeat a simple pattern (e.g., *circle-square-circle-square*); others will be able to do more complicated patterns in which they have to attend to color as well as shape (e.g., *red circle-two blue squares, red circle-two blue squares*). Other features, such as size, could be incorporated into the pattern instead of color. Continue the activity until all the children have had a turn.

Variation

For a greater challenge, make a pattern, cover it with a piece of cardboard, and have a child repeat the pattern from memory.

Summary/Transition Activity

Give each child a small pile of shapes to create a pattern. Children could then trade with a partner to see if they can copy each other's patterns. Finish the activity by saying the names of the shapes as you collect them.

Wednesday

Dramatic Play	Art	Group	Story	Song
France Castle	Castle Mural	Identifying *P, Q,* and *R*	*Cinderella*	"Are You Sleeping?"

DAILY PLANNING GUIDE

Language and Literacy Skills Facilitated

Vocabulary: *castle, knight, prince, princess, king, queen, moat, drawbridge, palace, dragon, Cinderella, ball, scepter, crown*

Verb phrase structures: *is king/queen, work*s *at the castle,* has *a crown,* is *riding a horse,* rode *a horse*

Adjective/object descriptions: *large castle, small princess, filmy scarf, jeweled crown, pretty dress*

Question structures: *what, how, where, when, who, what if, why, how many, which one*

Pronouns: *I, you, he, she, we, they, my, your, him, her, his, our, their, me, us, them*

Prepositions: *in, on, under, over, near, beneath, next to, beside, around, inside, outside*

Sounds: /k/ *c*astle, *c*oo*k*; /l/ *l*ittle, bal*l*; /f/ *f*ight, of*f*

Noting print has meaning: names on chairs and on cubbies, signs in dramatic play, words in books and on chalkboard

Noting sound–symbol associations: What sound does _____ start with?

Writing: letters, names, words

Social Skills Facilitated

Initiating interaction with peers and adults; responding to questions and requests from peers and adults

Negotiating with peers for toys and materials

Group cooperation: waiting for a turn in a group, taking a turn at the appropriate time

Cognitive Skills Facilitated

Problem-solving skills: what to put on the mural

Classification skills: things in a castle

Sequencing skills: alphabet, songs, story

Narrative/story structure: classic fairy tale

Motor Skills Facilitated

Large motor: outdoor play activities—jumping, running, hopping, pedaling, climbing

Small motor: writing, drawing, gluing, squeezing, rolling

DRAMATIC PLAY **France Castle**

Type of Activity: Central

Objectives
1. Learn new, and employ familiar, vocabulary
2. Learn new, and employ a variety of, syntactic constructions
3. Interact with peers
4. Sequence familiar routines
5. Expand conceptual knowledge of the world

Settings	• Castle (including a moat and drawbridge)	• Jewelry
	• Ballroom	• Thrones
	• Throne area	• Slippers
	• Props	• Scepters
	• Crowns	• Horses/carriages
	• Fancy clothes	

Roles	• Cinderella	• Queen
	• Stepmother	• Prince
	• Stepsisters	• Knight
	• King	

General Description of Activity

The story of Cinderella may be enacted, or a more generic dramatic play activity involving kings, queens, princes, princesses, and knights may be done. In any case, one or two castles are needed. The children can dress up in fancy clothes, wear crowns, go to a ball, ride horses, ride in a carriage, and sit on a throne.

Verbal Productions

Level of linguistic complexity varies with the role or competency of the child playing the role.

- "I don't have dress. I can't go" or "No dress, no go"
- "May I have this dance?" or "Dance?"
- "Lower the drawbridge. We want in" or "In"
- "We danced a long time. It was fun" or "Fun"

Adult Facilitative Role:

The adult is to facilitate role play and help expand language and literacy skills. Typical actions or strategies to use include

Playing a role: "Do you think there will be a dance at the castle?"

Expanding a child's utterance: "I want princess" to "I want to be a princess, too."

Modeling a statement/vocabulary: "When the drawbridge is down, we can go to the castle. The drawbridge is a bridge over the moat. It can go up and down."

Modeling phonological awareness: "The words *castle, catch, couch,* and *comb* all start with the /k/ sound."

ART : **Castle Mural**

Objectives	1. Express creativity
	2. Develop small motor skills (e.g., drawing, painting, cutting, pasting)
	3. Practice turn-taking skills
	4. Converse with peers and adults

Materials	• Large sheet of paper
	• Masking tape (optional)
	• Plastic or newsprint to place on the floor
	• Smocks
	• Tempera paint
	• Paint cups
	• Paintbrushes
	• Crayons or markers (optional)
	• Small bowls of water to rinse brushes
	• Appropriate pictures to be pasted
	• Glue

General Description of Activity

A large piece of paper is taped to a wall or placed on the floor on top of plastic or newsprint. The children put on smocks and paint pictures or designs on the floor using the tempera paint. The children may choose to draw with crayons or markers instead of the tempera paint. Children may also paste previously produced pictures on the mural instead of drawing them. For example, a castle mural would consist of a drawing of a castle with horses, knights, princes, princesses, kings, and queens. Pictures representing these people or objects could be glued to the mural. Drawing a horizontal line first might be helpful in placing the pictures.

Variation

If painting scenery for a program or dramatic play, the children can paint the objects previously outlined by the staff members. For example, the teacher might outline a house or a tree and the children can add colors to the outline.

GROUP **Identifying *P*, *Q*, and *R***

Objectives

1. Improve listening skills
2. Increase knowledge of the alphabet and sounds.
3. Learn appropriate group-interaction skills
4. Practice turn-taking skills

Materials

- Target alphabet letters on cards
- Alphabet chart
- Paper and pencils or markers (optional)
- Chalkboard, chalk (optional)

General Description of Activity

Lay the letters *P*, *Q*, and *R* in front of the children. Have the children, in chorus, say the letters as you point to each one. Have one child come to the front and point to a specific letter.

Group Participation

Ask different children to point to specific letters, helping them as necessary. Vary the difficulty by having children identify letters in order or out of order, or by having some match a letter card to the letters on the floor instead of pointing to a designated letter. You can also ask them to match lowercase letters to uppercase letters. Children can also point to a letter and have the class label it.

Summary/Transition Activity

Say the whole alphabet with the children as you point to an alphabet chart. Then have everyone say the target alphabet letters (*P, Q, R*) as you point to each letter in turn. An alternative activity is to have the children practice writing the three target letters.

Thursday

Dramatic Play	Art	Group	Story	Song
Mexico (Fiesta and Market)	Make Tambourines	Writing Class Letters	*This Is the Way We Eat Our Lunch*	"It's a Small World"

DAILY PLANNING GUIDE

Language and Literacy Skills Facilitated

Vocabulary: *fiesta, market, sombrero, serape, sell, buy, peso, fruit, vegetables, pottery*

Verb phrase structures: <u>buy</u> bananas, <u>sell</u> serapes, <u>dance</u> the cucaracha

Adjective/object descriptions: *red sombrero, fat piñata, busy market, decorated bowl*

Question structures: *what, how, where, when, who, what if, why, how many, which one*

Pronouns: *I, you, he, she, we, they, my, your, him, her, his, our, their, me, us, them*

Prepositions: *in, on, under, over, near, beneath, next to, beside, around, inside, outside*

Sounds: /f/ <u>f</u>ix, o<u>ff</u>; /s/ <u>s</u>it, talk<u>s</u>; /l/ <u>l</u>ittle, bel<u>l</u>

Noting print has meaning: names on chairs and on cubbies, signs in dramatic play, words in books and on chalkboard

Noting sound–symbol associations: What sound does _____ start with?

Writing: letters, names, words

Social Skills Facilitated

Initiating interaction with peers and adults; responding to questions and requests from peers and adults

Negotiating with peers for toys and materials

Group cooperation: waiting for a turn in a group, taking a turn at the appropriate time

Cognitive Skills Facilitated

Problem-solving skills: what to sell at the market

Classification skills: things from Mexico

Sequencing skills: story, songs

Narrative/story structure: expository (informational)

Motor Skills Facilitated

Large motor: outdoor play activities—jumping, running, hopping, pedaling, climbing

Small motor: writing, drawing, gluing, painting

DRAMATIC PLAY **Mexico (Fiesta and Market)**

Type of Activity: Related

Objectives
1. Learn new, and employ familiar, vocabulary
2. Learn new, and employ a variety of, syntactic constructions
3. Interact with peers
4. Sequence familiar routines
5. Expand conceptual knowledge of the world

Settings
- Different areas for selling wares (maybe five to six types of wares, such as pretend food, clothes, purses, dishes, jewelry, and blankets)
- Fiesta area with a place for singing and dancing
- Area for making wares (optional)

Props

- Different types of wares (pretend food, clothes [serape, hats, etc.], baskets, purses, dishes, jewelry, blankets)
- Cash registers
- Pretend money
- CD player and Spanish music CD
- Musical instruments (e.g., maracas, tambourines, guitars)
- Playdough (optional)
- Construction paper strips for weaving (optional)

Roles

- Sellers of wares
- Customers
- Dancers
- Singers
- Potters or weavers (optional)

General Description of Activity

Set up an open-air market with a variety of wares, typical of many places in Mexico. The children can pretend to be the customers or the sellers of a variety of wares. Also, set up a fiesta area where children can sing and dance using guitars and maracas. Children might even make some of the wares to be sold, such as playdough "pottery" or placemats woven from construction paper.

Verbal Productions

Level of linguistic complexity varies with the role or competency of the child playing the role.

- "Do you want to buy my beautiful basket?" or "Buy this?"
- "I am playing the guitar" or "Play"
- "He played with the guitar. Now it is my turn" or "My turn"
- "It costs 30 pesos, but you can have it for 20 pesos" or "Money"

Adult Facilitative Role

The adult is to facilitate role play and help expand language and literacy skills. Typical actions or strategies to use include

Playing a role: "I am selling some pottery. Would you like to buy a piece?"

Contrasting two adjectives (focus contrast): "This vase is large, but this vase is small. I think I will buy the small vase."

Modeling a statement/vocabulary: "I am going to play the maracas at the fiesta. They make noise when you shake them."

Recasting present progressive with past tense irregular form: "Today, I am buying the necklace. Yesterday I bought the ring."

Providing confirmatory feedback: "The words *fiesta*, *five*, and *fix* all rhyme."

ART : **Make Tambourines**

Objectives

1. Express creativity
2. Develop small motor skills (e.g., drawing, painting, cutting, pasting)
3. Practice turn-taking skills
4. Converse with peers and adults

Materials

- Paper plates (at least two per child)
- Dry beans or other small items (e.g., Cheerios)
- Small containers to hold the beans
- Markers or crayons
- Stapler
- Tape (optional)

General Description of Activity

Give each child two paper plates to use to create a tambourine. Have children decorate the bottom side of each plate with markers or crayons; the bottom of each plate will form the outer portions of the tambourine. After children finish decorating the plate, have them place a few dry beans or other small items (e.g., Cheerios) on the inside of one of the plates. They turn the other plate over, so that its bottom is facing upward, and put it on top of the first one. They then staple or tape the plates together along the rims (with assistance, if necessary).

GROUP **Writing Class Letters**

Objectives
1. Improve listening skills
2. Increase knowledge about counting and grouping into sets
3. Learn appropriate group-interaction skills
4. Practice turn-taking skills

Materials
- Poster paper
- Tape
- Blackboard or chart holder
- Markers
- Crayons

General Description of Activity

A large piece of poster paper is taped to the blackboard. The teacher tells the children that they are going to write a class letter to tell their parents what has been happening this week in school. *Dear Parents* is written at the top. The children are asked for ideas about what to write. The teacher reminds the children of all the activities that have occurred in the past week.

Group Participation

The teacher writes down the children's comments. Then the children come up to sign their names. The paper is then hung on a bulletin board for all to enjoy.

Variation

Children could add drawings of the various activities or pictures could be pasted to the letter. Pictures from magazines could also be used.

Summary/Transition Activity

The teacher rereads the letter.

WEEKLY PLANNING GUIDE

	Dramatic Play	Art	Group	Story	Song
Monday *Suggested Props and Materials*	Water—Water Play *Water table, wading pool, smocks, toy boats, toy people, water pumps, rubber and plastic water toys (e.g., fish, seal, walrus, worms), sponges, cups, drainers*	Watercolor Painting *Watercolor paints, brushes, paper, paint cups, water, smocks*	Identifying *S, T,* and *U* *Alphabet letters S, T, and U; alphabet chart; paper and pencils or markers (optional); or chalkboard and chalk*	*Fish Is Fish*	"All the Little Fishies"
Tuesday *Suggested Props and Materials*	Fire—Firefighter *Firefighter scenario, fire engine (made from boxes with cardboard tubes for hoses), pretend fire hydrants, mats, hats, and other uniform, telephones, pretend sirens (e.g., flashlights with siren), pole (optional)*	Playdough Constructions *Playdough, rolling pins, cookie cutters, presses, wooden craft sticks*	Fire Safety Rules *Pictures of children crawling and touching a door; pictures of children stopping, dropping, and rolling to put out a fire on their clothing; play telephones*	*Fire Truck*	"Hurry, Hurry, Drive the Fire Truck"
Wednesday *Suggested Props and Materials*	Air—Outdoor Sports *Outdoor sports scenario, plastic bat and ball, bases, mitts, volleyball, pretend net, soccer ball, soccer goal (big box), hopscotch diagram, beanbags for markers*	Make a Kite *Wooden craft sticks (two for each kite), paper cut in diamond shape, markers, crayons, stickers, yarn*	Act out a Story (*Chicken Little*) *Story and props*	*Chicken Little*	"The Wind Came out to Play" (fingerplay)
Thursday *Suggested Props and Materials*	Earth— Gardening *Gardening scenario, large boxes filled with sand or soil, child-sized garden tools, hats, gloves, small objects to plant (e.g., LEGOs), pretend plants, pails, counter and cash register (optional), garden items to sell (optional)*	Sand Pictures *Sand, paper, box lids, glue, glitter (optional)*	Planting Seeds *5-oz. paper cups or baby food jars, lima bean seeds, soil*	*Growing Vegetable Soup*	"Way Down Yonder in the Paw Paw Patch"

NEWSLETTER

Vol. 1, No. 34

Date: _____

The Elements

Monday

Today children will learn about the element water. During dramatic play, they can pour water from one container to another and have fun with boats and a variety of sea animals. At art, children will use water and watercolor paints to make some paintings. Our story is *Fish Is Fish*. We will focus on the letters *S*, *T*, and *U* at group time. We will have fun identifying these letters, reviewing their sounds, and writing them. Our song is "All the Little Fishies."

Tuesday

Today's element is fire. The children will pretend to be firefighters in dramatic play. Some children can be dispatchers, others the firefighters, and still others the family members in the house on fire. In art, children will make hoses out of play-dough and other items. Our story is *Fire Truck*. During group time, children will learn about fire safety rules and practice "stop, drop, and roll." They will also practice calling 911 for help. Our song is "Hurry, Hurry, Drive the Fire Truck."

Wednesday

Today's element is air. Children will learn about air in different balls and will play baseball, soccer, and volleyball when they go outside. They can also fly the kites they make in art. Our story is *Chicken Little*. We will act out the story at group time. Our featured fingerplay is "The Wind Came out to Play."

Thursday

Earth is the element today. Children will investigate the earth by having a garden scenario in dramatic play today. They will pretend to hoe, plant seeds, and harvest fruits and vegetables. We also might have a garden store where children can buy garden items. They will make sand pictures at art. Our story is *Growing Vegetable Soup*. At group, the children will plant seeds (lima beans) to take home. Our song is "Way Down Yonder in the Paw Paw Patch."

Monday

Dramatic Play	Art	Group	Story	Song
Water—Water Play	Watercolor Painting	Identifying *S, T,* and *U*	*Fish Is Fish*	"All the Little Fishies"

DAILY PLANNING GUIDE

Language and Literacy Skills Facilitated

Vocabulary: *water, splash, drip, fish, walrus, water pump, shell, shark, net, sink, float, boat, sailboat*

Verb phrase structures: *is splashing, was splashing; sails, is sailing, sailed; rides, rode; swims, swam*

Adjective/object descriptions: *wet/dry ___, fast/slow ___, big/little ___*

Question structures: *what, how, where, when, who, what if, why, how many, which one*

Pronouns: *I, you, he, she, we, they, my, your, him, her, his, our, their, me, us, them*

Prepositions: *in, on, under, over, near, beneath, next to, beside, around, inside, outside*

Sounds: /s/ sink, swim, sit, pass, eats; /f/ fish, off, float; /k/ keep, sink

Noting print has meaning: names on chairs and on cubbies, signs in dramatic play, words in books and on chalkboard

Noting sound–symbol associations: What sound does _____ start with?

Writing: letters, names, words

Social Skills Facilitated

Initiating interaction with peers and adults; responding to questions and requests from peers and adults

Negotiating with peers for toys and materials

Group cooperation: waiting for a turn in a group, taking a turn at the appropriate time

Cognitive Skills Facilitated

Problem-solving skills: What things sink? What things float?

Classification skills: things that sink or float

Sequencing skills: story, song

Narrative/story structure: labeling story

Motor Skills Facilitated

Large motor: outdoor play activities—jumping, running, hopping, pedaling, climbing

Small motor: writing, drawing, gluing, painting

DRAMATIC PLAY **Water—Water Play**

Type of Activity: Central

Objectives
1. Learn new, and employ familiar, vocabulary
2. Learn new, and employ a variety of, syntactic constructions
3. Interact with peers
4. Sequence familiar routines
5. Expand conceptual knowledge of the world

Settings
- Water table
- Wading pool

Props
- Smocks
- Toy boats
- Toy people
- Water pump
- Rubber and plastic water toys (e.g., fish, seal, walrus, worms)
- Sponges
- Cups
- Drainers

Roles
- Scientists
- Laboratory technicians

General Description of Activity

The children experiment with objects of various textures as they play in the water table and a wading pool. There should be water toys that are rough (e.g., play swordfish, walrus), smooth (e.g., toy boats), sticky (e.g., play worms, small fish used as pretend bait), soft (e.g., blow-up toys), and hard (e.g., water pump). In another area with tubs of water and sponges, children can see how a sponge feels with and without water in it.

Verbal Productions

Level of linguistic complexity varies with the role or competency of the child playing the role.
- "This fish feels squishy" or "Fish soft"
- "Look, if you take the air out, the boat sinks," "Look, sink," or "Boat sink"
- "You splashed me" or "Splash"
- "I did not mean to—sorry" or "Sorry"

Adult Facilitative Role

The adult is to facilitate role play and help expand language and literacy skills. Typical actions or strategies to use include

Playing a role: "I like to pour the water from one cup to another."

Recasting present tense with regular past tense: "It drips" to "It dripped on the floor."

Identifying rhyming words: "The words *bubble, double*, and *trouble* all rhyme."

Event casting of an adult's action: "I am pumping the water. I push the pump handle up and down, and the water comes out of the spout."

ART **Watercolor Painting**

Objectives
1. Express creativity
2. Develop small motor skills (e.g., drawing, painting, cutting, pasting)
3. Practice turn-taking skills
4. Converse with peers and adults

Materials
- Watercolor paints
- Brushes
- Tubs of water
- White construction paper

General Description of Activity

Lay out white construction paper, watercolor paint boxes, and brushes on the art table. Place tubs of water to clean the brushes above the paper. The children put on smocks and sit down in front of the paper, paint box, and water tub. Each child selects a brush, wets it, and chooses the paint color. The children paint on the paper, rinsing the brush before selecting a new color. Children can paint a collage of colors, animals, people, scenery, and so on. You may want to be close by so children can talk about their paintings.

GROUP **Identifying S, T, and U**

Objectives
1. Improve listening skills
2. Increase knowledge of the alphabet and sounds
3. Learn appropriate group-interaction skills
4. Practice turn-taking skills

Materials
- Target alphabet letters
- Alphabet chart
- Paper and pencils or markers (optional)
- Chalkboard, chalk (optional)

General Description of Activity

Lay the letters S, T, and U in front of the children. Have the children, in chorus, say the letters as you point to each one. Have one child come to the front and point to a specific letter.

Group Participation

Ask different children to point to specific letters, helping them as necessary. Vary the difficulty by having children identify letters in order or out of order, or by having some match a letter card to the letters on the floor instead of pointing to a designated letter. You can also ask them to match lower-case letters to uppercase letters. Children can also point to a letter and have the class label it.

Summary/Transition Activity

Say the whole alphabet with the children as you point to an alphabet chart. Then have everyone say the target alphabet letters (S, T, U) as you point to each letter in turn. An alternative activity is to have the children practice writing the three target letters.

Dramatic Play	Art	Group	Story	Song
Fire—Firefighter	Playdough Constructions	Fire Safety Rules	*Fire Truck*	"Hurry, Hurry, Drive the Fire Truck"

Tuesday

DAILY PLANNING GUIDE

Language and Literacy Skills Facilitated

Vocabulary: *fire, firefighter, hose, fire engine, ladder truck, siren, pole, uniform, protective clothing, face mask, oxygen, flames, smoke, fire hydrant, ashes, dispatch officer*

Verb phrase structures: *put out the fire, ride in the truck, turn on siren, honk horn, turn on hose, douse fire, dispatch the truck*

Adjective/object descriptions: *hot fire, cold ashes, red truck, green truck, loud siren, gray smoke, black smoke*

Question structures: *what, how, where, when, who, what if, why, how many, which one*

Pronouns: *I, you, he, she, we, they, my, your, him, her, his, our, their, me, us, them*

Prepositions: *in, on, under, over, near, beneath, next to, beside, around, inside, outside*

Sounds: /f/ <u>f</u>ire, <u>f</u>irefighter, <u>f</u>ire engine, <u>f</u>ire truck; /h/ <u>h</u>ose, <u>h</u>ydrant, <u>h</u>onk

Noting print has meaning: names on chairs and on cubbies, signs in dramatic play, words in books and on chalkboard

Noting sound–symbol associations: What sound does _____ start with?

Writing: letters, names, words

Social Skills Facilitated

Initiating interaction with peers and adults; responding to questions and requests from peers and adults

Negotiating with peers for toys and materials

Group cooperation: waiting for a turn in a group, taking a turn at the appropriate time

Cognitive Skills Facilitated

Problem-solving skills: safety rules, how/when to call 911

Classification skills: What's in a fire truck?

Sequencing skills: songs, fingerplays

Narrative/story structure: labeling story

Motor Skills Facilitated

Large motor: outdoor play activities—jumping, running, hopping, pedaling, climbing

Small motor: writing, drawing, gluing

DRAMATIC PLAY **Fire—Firefighter**

Type of Activity: Sequential

Objectives
1. Learn new, and employ familiar, vocabulary
2. Learn new, and employ a variety of, syntactic constructions
3. Interact with peers
4. Sequence familiar routines
5. Expand conceptual knowledge of the world

Settings
- Fire station
- Dispatch office
- Houses (made from dismantled cardboard boxes)
- Roads (floor area marked with masking tape)

Props
- Fire engine (made from boxes with cardboard tubes for hoses)
- Pretend fire hydrants
- Mats for beds
- Pole (optional)
- Hats and other uniform paraphernalia (rubber painting smocks can be used for fireproof jackets)
- Pretend telephones
- Microphones (toilet paper rolls)
- Sirens (flashlights with siren)

Roles
- Firefighters
- Fire chief
- Fire engine driver
- Homeowners
- Dispatch officers

General Description of Activity

Children play firefighter by staying at a fire station, sliding down a pole when there is an alarm, getting in the fire engine, arriving at the fire, and putting it out. A siren may be used to warn traffic to get out of the way so the firefighters can get to the fire. After putting out a fire, children can go back to the fire station can put their equipment away. (If possible, have real firefighters come to the classroom to talk about their jobs and show children their equipment.)

Verbal Productions

Level of linguistic complexity varies with the role or competency of the child playing the role.
- "I'm the fire chief" or "Chief"
- "My house is on fire. Come to 124 Lawrence Street" or "Fire! Come!"
- "It's my turn to drive the truck" or "Turn, please"
- "We are sleeping at the fire station in case there is a fire" or "Sleeping here"

Adult Facilitative Role

The adult is to facilitate role play and help expand language and literacy skills. Typical actions or strategies to use include

Playing a role: "We have to hurry. That house is on fire."

Contrasting error response with correct response (focus contrast): "Her have hose" to "Oh, you mean she has the hose."

Modeling a statement/vocabulary: "The siren tells people to get out of the way of the fire truck. It is very loud."

Modeling correct production of the /f/ sound: "That first fire truck is going very fast."

Redirecting a child to a peer: "I don't have the hose. Ask Jimmy. Say, 'Do you have the hose?'"

ART **Playdough Constructions**

Objectives
1. Express creativity
2. Develop small motor skills (e.g., drawing, painting, cutting, pasting)
3. Practice turn-taking skills
4. Converse with peers and adults

Materials
- Smocks
- Playdough
- Rolling pins
- Cookie cutters
- Cookie presses
- Wooden craft sticks
- Rolling boards (optional)

General Description of Activity

Children wash their hands and put on smocks to explore playdough on the art table, using various presses, cutters, rolling pins, wooden craft sticks, and other tools. Children can make fire hoses, pretend food, or any other objects out of the dough by rolling, cutting, or making pressing motions. They can form animals or people by rolling a main body and then adding heads, arms, and legs. Yarn can be used for hair (if children want to take their creations home). When children are finished, they roll the dough into a ball, wash their hands, and take off and fold their smocks.

GROUP Fire Safety Rules

Objectives
1. Improve listening skills
2. Increase conceptual knowledge
3. Learn appropriate group-interaction skills
4. Practice turn-taking skills

Materials
- Pictures of children crawling and touching a door
- Pictures of children stopping, dropping, and rolling to put out a fire on their clothing
- Play telephones

General Description of Activity

Ask the children what they should do if the fire alarm at the preschool center sounds. Discuss what they should do if their house catches on fire. Facilitate a conversation about crawling on the floor and touching doors to see if they are hot before opening them. You might show pictures of children following this procedure. Also discuss calling 911 and giving their names and addresses to the dispatcher.

Group Participation

Have some of the children practice crawling and touching a door before opening it. Ask the group what the children should do if the door is hot. In addition, talk about having a place for family members to gather outside if the family's house catches on fire. Explain that this helps everyone know where each person is. Have some children practice calling 911 on play telephones.

Finally, have the children discuss what to do if their clothing catches on fire. Some children could demonstrate the "stop, drop, and roll" technique (i.e., the children *stop* moving, *drop* to the ground, and *roll* over and over to put out the fire on their clothes). Show pictures of children doing the stop, drop, and roll technique.

Variation

Plan and carry out a real fire drill. Make sure children understand what will happen and what they are to do.

Summary/Transition Activity

Review what to do in case of a fire at school or at home and if children's clothing catches on fire.

Wednesday

Dramatic Play	Art	Group	Story	Song
Air—Outdoor Sports	Make a Kite	Act out a Story (*Chicken Little*)	*Chicken Little*	"The Wind Came out to Play"

Language and Literacy Skills Facilitated

Vocabulary: *soccer ball, baseball, bat, run, kick, hit, pitch, swing, score, net, jump, catcher, pitcher, goalie, balloon*

Verb phrase structures: <u>*is*</u> *swing<u>ing</u> the bat, hit<u>s</u> the ball, kick<u>s</u> the ball, kick<u>ed</u> the ball, <u>threw</u> the ball, Who hit the ball? I <u>did</u>, Who<u>'s</u> next? I <u>am</u>*

Adjective/object descriptions: *big ___, little ____, orange bat, white and black soccer ball*

Question structures: *what, how, where, when, who, what if, why, how many, which one*

Pronouns: *I, you, he, she, we, they, my, your, him, her, his, our, their, me, us, them*

Prepositions: *in, on, under, over, near, beneath, next to, beside, around, inside, outside*

Sounds: /l/ <u>l</u>ook, bal<u>l</u>; /s/ <u>s</u>occer, hit<u>s</u>; /r/ <u>r</u>un, batte<u>r</u>

Noting print has meaning: names on chairs and on cubbies, signs in dramatic play, words in books and on chalkboard

Noting sound–symbol associations: What sound does _____ start with?

Writing: letters, names, words

Social Skills Facilitated

Initiating interaction with peers and adults; responding to questions and requests from peers and adults

Negotiating with peers for toys and materials

Group cooperation: waiting for a turn in a group, taking a turn at the appropriate time

Cognitive Skills Facilitated

Problem-solving skills: how to play soccer, how to play baseball

Classification skills: kinds of balls, features of balls

Sequencing skills: stories, songs, game rules

Narrative/story structure: adventure, classic tale

Motor Skills Facilitated

Large motor: outdoor play activities—jumping, running, hopping, pedaling, climbing, catching

Small motor: writing, drawing, rubbing

DRAMATIC PLAY **Air—Outdoor Sports**

Objectives
1. Learn new, and employ familiar, vocabulary
2. Learn new, and employ a variety of, syntactic constructions
3. Interact with peers
4. Sequence familiar routines
5. Expand conceptual knowledge of the world

Settings
- Baseball diamond
- Soccer field
- Grassy area
- Sidewalk with hopscotch diagram

Props
- Plastic bat and ball
- Base at first on baseball diamond
- Mitts
- Rubber (soccer) ball
- Large box (for a soccer goal)
- Hopscotch diagram or chalk to make one on the sidewalk or playground
- Volleyball and pretend net
- Kite flyers

Roles
- Batters
- Catchers
- Fielders
- Umpire
- Referee
- Soccer players
- Hopscotch players

General Description of Activity

This dramatic play focuses on being out in the air with some outdoor sports, such as baseball and soccer. (Some of the children likely have older brothers and sisters who play on summer teams.) Set up a temporary baseball diamond with only one base at first. Pitch a plastic ball to a child, who attempts to hit it with the bat. Assist with swinging as necessary. If the child hits the ball, he or she runs to first base. Other children chase the ball and throw it back to the pitcher. An alternative way is to have the children hit the baseball off of a baseball tee.

Other children can play soccer by kicking the ball back and forth and trying to make a goal by kicking it into a large box or net. Others might fly a kite that they made. Still other children can play hopscotch-hopping or jumping into and out of marked area. A hopscotch diagram can be made on the sidewalk, or it can be marked by laying yardsticks in the shape of rectangles on the grassy area.

Verbal Productions

Level of linguistic complexity varies with the role or competency of the child playing the role.

- "She hit the ball hard" or "Hard"
- "I can hop. Watch me!" or "Look!"
- "He is kicking the soccer ball in the goal" or "He kicked it"
- "You hit a home run" or "I missed it"
- "Try again" or "Again"
- "This is fun" or "Fun"

Adult Facilitative Role

The adult is to facilitate role play and help expand language and literacy skills. Typical actions or strategies to use include

Playing a role: "I like to play soccer. I like to kick the ball into the net."

Modeling the production of the /s/ sound: "You can swing the bat. No sliding into first base. Don't forget to stop and stay on the base."

Event casting of a child's actions: "You are standing at the home base. Now you are ready to swing the bat. Here comes the ball. You hit it! Now you are running fast to first base."

Expanding a child's utterance and providing correcting feedback: "Him turn" to "It is his turn at the hopscotch game."

Modeling a statement/vocabulary: "Many of the balls have air in them. This ball is a beach ball."

ART **Make a Kite**

Objectives
1. Express creativity
2. Develop small motor skills (e.g., constructing, pasting, drawing, cutting)
3. Practice turn-taking skills
4. Converse with peers and adults

Materials
- Wooden craft sticks, two for each kite
- Paper cut in diamond shape to fit on the craft-stick kite frame, one for each kite
- Markers or crayons
- Stickers (optional, for decoration)
- Yarn
- Small scraps of paper

General Description of Activity

Children glue two wooden craft sticks together in the form of a cross. They then paste the diamond-shaped paper to the wooden craft sticks. They can decorate the paper, add yarn to make a tail for the kite, and glue small bits of paper to the tail for decoration. They attach another piece of yarn or string to the kite frame. The kites are now ready to fly.

GROUP : Act out a Story (*Chicken Little*)

Objectives
1. Improve listening skills
2. Improve sequencing ability
3. Increase knowledge of storytelling
4. Learn appropriate group-interaction skills
5. Practice turn-taking skills

Materials
- *Chicken Little*
- Props for the story

General Description of Activity

Read *Chicken Little*, or summarize it if children are familiar with the story.

Group Participation

Assign children roles from the story. Assure the children not chosen the first time that everyone will have a turn and that they have the very important job of being a good listening audience. Narrate the story as the children act it out. They should say as many of the lines as they can, with prompts given when needed. Repeat with new actors until all the children have had a turn.

Summary/Transition Activity

Compliment the children's acting, and ask children what other stories they would like to act out another day.

Thursday

Dramatic Play	Art	Group	Story	Song
Earth—Gardening	Sand Pictures	Planting Seeds	*Growing Vegetable Soup*	"Way Down Yonder in the Paw Paw Patch"

DAILY PLANNING GUIDE

Language and Literacy Skills Facilitated

Vocabulary: *garden, grow, flowers, digging, planting, watering, working, bugs, insects, hoe, weeds, seeds, shovel*

Verb phrase structures: *is/are plant<u>ing</u>, plant<u>ed</u>, <u>will</u> <u>plant</u>, plant<u>s</u>, dig<u>s</u>, <u>dug</u>, grow<u>s</u>, <u>grew</u>, waters, water<u>ed</u>, <u>is</u> work<u>ing</u>, work<u>ed</u>*

Adjective/object descriptions: *little seed, big hole, yellow flower, dirty shovel, hard work*

Question structures: *what, how, where, when, who, what if, why, how many, which one*

Pronouns: *I, you, he, she, we, they, my, your, him, her, his, our, their, me, us, them*

Prepositions: *in, on, under, over, near, beneath, next to, beside, around, inside, outside*

Sounds: /k/ <u>c</u>ome, wor<u>k</u>; /l/ <u>l</u>ike, ye<u>ll</u>ow, fa<u>ll</u>; /s/ <u>s</u>eed, mi<u>ss</u>

Noting print has meaning: names on chairs and on cubbies, signs in dramatic play, words in books and on chalkboard

Noting sound–symbol associations: What sound does _____ start with?

Writing: letters, names, words

Social Skills Facilitated

Initiating interaction with peers and adults; responding to questions and requests from peers and adults

Negotiating with peers for toys and materials

Group cooperation: waiting for a turn in a group, taking a turn at the appropriate time

Cognitive Skills Facilitated

Problem-solving skills: how to plant seeds

Classification skills: things that grow in the ground

Sequencing skills: songs, stories

Narrative/story structure: labeling story

Motor Skills Facilitated

Large motor: outdoor play activities—jumping, running, hopping, pedaling, climbing

Small motor: writing, drawing, gluing

DRAMATIC PLAY **Earth—Gardening**

Type of Activity: Central

Objectives
1. Learn new, and employ familiar, vocabulary
2. Learn new, and employ a variety of, syntactic constructions
3. Interact with peers
4. Sequence familiar routines
5. Expand conceptual knowledge of the world

Settings
- Two or three garden areas
- Seed and gardening store (optional)
- Market (optional)

Props
- Two or three large boxes cut about 4"–6" deep
- Sand or soil
- Child-sized garden tools
- Gardening clothes (e.g., hats, gloves)
- Seeds or other small objects (e.g., lima beans, LEGOs)
- Plants (e.g., pretend flowers, pretend vegetables)
- Pails
- Watering can
- Counter (optional)
- Pretend cash register (optional)
- Pretend money (optional)

Roles
- Gardeners
- Store clerks (optional)
- Garden produce sellers (optional)
- Customers (optional)

General Description of Activity

Children work in a pretend garden, digging, planting seeds, and growing flowers or vegetables. Two or three large boxes (e.g., a refrigerator box) cut about 4"–6" deep and filled with sand or soil make a good garden. The children can use child-sized gardening tools to prepare the sand or soil. Lima beans or other small objects (e.g., LEGOs) make good "seeds." A seed and gardening store or a market for selling garden produce can be added to the play activity. (Be aware that the activity will need to be restarted after the plants have "grown" and have been "harvested.")

Verbal Productions

Level of linguistic complexity varies with the role or competency of the child playing the role.
- "Do you have any flower seeds?" or "Seeds, please"
- "Do you have any shovels or pails?" or "Diggers?"
- "He is digging a big hole" or "Dig hole"
- "I want a large, round, orange pumpkin" or "Big pumpkin, please"

Adult Facilitative Role

The adult is to facilitate role play and help expand language and literacy skills. Typical actions or strategies to use include

Playing a role: "I want to touch the dirt. It feels funny."

Asking an open question: "What do you think we should plant?"

Expanding a child's utterance: "Seeds" to "Yes, he is planting the seeds."

Modeling the reading of a sign: "the sign says *keep off*."

Identifying rhyming words: "The words *sand, band,* and *land* all rhyme."

ART **Sand Pictures**

Objectives
1. Express creativity
2. Develop small motor skills (e.g., drawing, painting, cutting, pasting)
3. Practice turn-taking skills
4. Converse with peers and adults

Materials
- Sand
- Paper
- Box lid
- Glue (white or colored)
- Glitter (optional)

General Description of Activity

Have children place a sheet of paper in a box lid. They drip glue in a pattern or a drawing (e.g., outline of a face or an animal or abstract object) on the paper, then sprinkle sand on top of the glue to form a texture. They tip the box around so that the sand sticks to the glue, then lift the paper out and shake out the excess sand into the box lid. The sand can be poured back into a container. Children can use glitter instead of sand.

GROUP **Planting Seeds**

Objectives
1. Improve listening skills
2. Improve sequencing ability
3. Learn appropriate group-interaction skills
4. Practice turn-taking skills

Materials
- *Pumpkin Pumpkin*
- 5-oz. paper cups or baby food jars, one for each child and one for you
- Lima bean seeds, one or two for each child, OR grass seed
- Plastic wrap and rubber bands
- Bag of soil

General Description of Activity

Read a story about seeds, such as *Pumpkin Pumpkin* by Jeanne Titherington, which tells about the planting and growth of a pumpkin seed. Then tell the children that they are going to plant a seed. Explain that they will need a container, some soil, and a seed. Show them a 5-oz paper cup or a baby food jar that is half full of soil. Put a seed under the soil.

Group Participation

Divide children into groups, with an adult in each group. Give each child a container half full of soil and then a seed or two (typically a bean seed; lima bean seeds work well). The children plant their seed in their cup or jar. If using paper cups, have children cover the cups with plastic wrap held on with a rubber band (if using baby food jars, have children place the lid on it). Have children put their container in their cubby to take home.

Variation

Have children plant grass seed instead of a bean seed.

Summary/Transition Activity

Discuss with the children what a seed needs to grow, such as soil, water, and sunshine. Water your own seed and place it where it will get some sunshine. The children can watch your seed grow as the days pass and also report on the growth of their plant at home.

WEEKLY PLANNING GUIDE

	Dramatic Play	Art	Group	Story	Song
Monday *Suggested Props and Materials*	Craft Fair *Craft fair scenario, booths for the exhibits, beads, strings, marbles, box lids, construction paper, paper strips for paper weaving, paint, paintbrushes, paper, cups, play cash registers, concession stand, play food items*	Macaroni Necklaces *String or yarn, macaroni, Cheerios (optional)*	Act out a Story *(The Wide-Mouth Frog)* *Story and props*	*The Wide-Mouth Frog*	"Going to Kentucky"
Tuesday *Suggested Props and Materials*	Car Racing *Car racing scenario, assortment of toy cars, tracks, checkered flag, tools, chairs for spectators, concession stand, cups, play food items, cash register*	Car Track Painting *Construction paper, tempera paint (three or four colors), smocks, small die-cast cars, shallow containers to hold the paint and cars (e.g., Styrofoam meat trays)*	Identifying *V, W,* and *X* *Alphabet letters V, W, and X, alphabet chart, paper and pencils or markers (optional), or chalkboard and chalk*	*Play It Safe*	"Twinkle, Twinkle, Traffic Light"
Wednesday *Suggested Props and Materials*	Baking *Baking scenario, play food items, dishes, spatula, silverware, pots and pans, dolls, baby food, bottles, brooms, mops*	Gingerbread Men *36 gingerbread men made out of brown construction paper, small circle cutouts, small triangle cutouts, glue*	Tap out Syllables *Drum*	*Mr. Cookie Baker*	"Do You Know the Muffin Man?"
Thursday *Suggested Props and Materials*	All About Pets *Pet store scenario, stuffed animals, pretend cash register, play money, shelves, pretend pet products (e.g., food, leashes, collars, toys), cages, aquariums, pet carriers, brushes, ribbons, show ring*	Paper Bag Puppets *Paper bags, construction paper cutouts (eyes, nose, mouth, ears), glue, markers*	Classify Pets and Zoo Animals *Toy house, toy fence, zoo mat, toy pets, toy zoo animals, pictures of animals (optional)*	*Franklin Wants a Pet*	"How Much Is that Doggy in the Window?"

NEWSLETTER

Vol. 1, No. 35

Date: _____

Hobbies

Monday

Today the children will have a craft fair. They will make and sell their wares (e.g., necklaces, weavings, paintings) in dramatic play. They may even have a picnic in the park along with attending the fair. They will make macaroni necklaces in art. The featured story is *The Wide-Mouthed Frog*. During group time, they will act out the story. Our song will be "Going to Kentucky."

Tuesday

Today our hobby is all about cars. There will be an exciting car race, with children pretending to be the racers, the mechanics, or the spectators. In art, children will make car track pictures. Our story is *Play It Safe*. During group time, we will focus on the letters *V*, *W*, and *X*. Our featured song is "Twinkle, Twinkle, Traffic Light."

Wednesday

Today the children will explore the hobby of baking. They will roll out the dough, cut out shapes, and of course pretend to bake tasty treats! We will also make real cookies to have at snack time. At the art center, children will decorate gingerbread men. The story for today is *Mr. Cookie Baker*. During group time, we will tap out the number of syllables in different words. In music, the children will sing "Do You Know the Muffin Man?"

Thursday

Today our hobbies are our pets. A pet store will be set up as well as a pet show, where the children's pets will perform and win ribbons. In art, the children will make paper bag puppets. Our story is *Franklin Wants a Pet*. The children will classify pets and zoo animals at group. Our song is "How Much Is that Doggy in the Window?"

Early Literacy in Action: The Language-Focused Curriculum for Preschool by Betty H. Bunce.

Monday

Dramatic Play	Art	Group	Story	Song
Craft Fair	Macaroni Necklaces	Act out a Story (The Wide-Mouth Frog)	The Wide-Mouth Frog	"Going to Kentucky"

DAILY PLANNING GUIDE

Language and Literacy Skills Facilitated

Vocabulary: *beads, marbles, paper weaving, paper strip, easel, drawings, crafts, necklace, macaroni, painting, selling*

Verb phrase structures: *is paint<u>ing</u>, paint<u>ed</u>, <u>are</u> fold<u>ing</u>, fold<u>ed</u>, weave<u>s</u>, <u>wove</u>, <u>has woven</u>, who's ready? I <u>am</u>*

Adjective/object descriptions: _____ *beads (e.g., blue, green,) narrow/wide strip, long/short neck- lace*

Question structures: *what, how, where, when, who, what if, why, how many, which one*

Pronouns: *I, you, he, she, we, they, my, your, him, her, his, our, their, me, us, them*

Prepositions: *in, on, under, over, near, beneath, next to, beside, around, inside, outside*

Sounds: /g/ <u>g</u>o, do<u>g</u>; /m/ <u>m</u>ake, co<u>m</u>e; /s/ <u>s</u>ee, ni<u>ce</u>

Noting print has meaning: names on chairs and on cubbies, signs in dramatic play, words in books and on chalkboard

Noting sound–symbol associations: What sound does _____ start with?

Writing: letters, names, words

Social Skills Facilitated

Initiating interaction with peers and adults; responding to questions and requests from peers and adults

Negotiating with peers for toys and materials

Group cooperation: waiting for a turn in a group, taking a turn at the appropriate time

Cognitive Skills Facilitated

Problem-solving skills: how to make necklaces

Classification skills: things that are crafts

Sequencing skills: story, songs

Narrative/story structure: adventure

Motor Skills

Large motor: outdoor play activities—jumping, running, hopping, pedaling, climbing

Small motor: writing, drawing, gluing, weaving, painting

DRAMATIC PLAY **Craft Fair**

Type of Activity: Related

Objectives
1. Learn new, and employ familiar, vocabulary
2. Learn new, and employ a variety of, syntactic constructions
3. Interact with peers
4. Sequence familiar routines
5. Expand conceptual knowledge of the world

Objectives

1. Learn new, and employ familiar, vocabulary
2. Learn new, and employ a variety of, syntactic constructions
3. Interact with peers
4. Sequence familiar routines
5. Expand conceptual knowledge of the world

Settings

- Booths for craft exhibits
- Concession stands

Props

- Beads or macaroni and strings
- Marbles, box lids, and paint
- Construction paper (for folding fans)
- Construction paper strips (for paper weaving)
- Paint, paintbrushes, and paper
- Cups
- Pretend soda pop dispenser
- Pretend cotton candy or popcorn
- Play cash registers

Roles

- Crafts people
- Customers (dolls may be included to play children)
- Concession stand workers
- Band members (optional)

General Description of Activity

Set up a craft fair for the children to make and sell their crafts. They can string beads and/or macaroni for necklaces, fold paper into paper fans, weave with paper, paint pictures, do marble painting (i.e., children dip marbles in paint and roll them back and forth on paper that is in a shoebox lid), draw pictures, and make stencils. Other children can be customers; some may make purchases, and others will merely browse. Provide a cash register to make change for those who do buy something. Concession stands may be available, and a band may play as well.

Verbal Productions

Level of linguistic complexity varies with the role or competency of the child playing the role.

- "Look! Please buy my special necklace. I worked hard to make it," "Look!" or "Buy this?"
- "I am making a ____" or "I made a ____"
- "What are you making?" or "What doing?"

Adult Facilitative Role

The adult is to facilitate role play and help expand language and literacy skills. Typical actions or strategies to use include

Playing a role: "I like to make necklaces. This one is yellow and white."

Modeling correct production of the /k/ sound in final position: "Jack can make the beads go around his neck."

Modeling the reading of a sign: "The sign says *craft fair*."

Recasting present tense and irregular past tense: "He buys all of Jane's mats" to "Last time he bought all of the pictures."

ART **Macaroni Necklaces**

Objectives

1. Express creativity
2. Develop small motor skills (e.g., drawing, painting, cutting, pasting)
3. Practice turn-taking skills
4. Converse with peers and adults

Materials
- Different kinds of macaroni (with holes big enough for a string to go through)
- String or yarn (with one end wrapped in tape to make threading easier)
- Pieces of paper
- Straws (cut up in 1" pieces)

General Description of Activity

Children make necklaces by stringing different kinds of macaroni. The macaroni can be dyed different colors. They can use small pieces of construction paper or straws cut to different lengths to string between the macaroni pieces. Tie one piece of macaroni to one end of the string so that the others will not fall off the string.

Variation

Have children use Cheerios instead of macaroni.

GROUP **Act out a Story (*The Wide-Mouth Frog*)**

Objectives
1. Improve listening skills
2. Improve sequencing ability
3. Increase knowledge of storytelling
4. Learn appropriate group-interaction skills
5. Practice turn-taking skills

Materials
- *The Wide-Mouth Frog*
- Props for the story

General Description of Activity

Read *The Wide-Mouth Frog*, or summarize it if children are familiar with the story.

Group Participation

Assign children roles from the story. Assure the children not chosen the first time that everyone will have a turn and that they have the very important job of being a good listening audience. Narrate the story as the children act it out. They should say as many of the lines as they can, with prompts given when needed. Repeat with new actors until all the children have had a turn.

Summary/Transition Activity

Compliment the children's acting, and ask the children what other stories they would like to act out another day.

Tuesday

Dramatic Play	Art	Group	Story	Song
Car Racing	Car Track Painting	Identifying *V, W,* and *X*	*Play It Safe*	"Twinkle, Twinkle, Traffic Light"

DAILY PLANNING GUIDE

Language and Literacy Skills Facilitated

Vocabulary: *transportation, vehicle, car, track, ramp, garage, truck, win, lose, flag, start, finish, wheels, square*

Verb phrase structures: *go<u>es</u> fast, win<u>s</u> the race, crash<u>ed</u> the car, push<u>ed</u> it, <u>was</u> rac<u>ing</u>, start<u>s</u>, stopp<u>ed</u>, <u>won</u>, <u>were</u> los<u>ing</u>*

Adjective/object descriptions: *race car, fast ____, slow ___, big/little ___, yellow flag, checkered flag*

Question structures: *what, how, where, when, who, what if, why, how many, which one*

Pronouns: *I, you, he, she, we, they, my, your, him, her, his, our, their, me, us, them*

Prepositions: *in, on, under, over, near, beneath, next to, beside, around, inside, outside*

Sounds: /r/ <u>r</u>ace, sta<u>r</u>te<u>r</u>, ca<u>r</u>; /s/ <u>s</u>ee, mi<u>ss</u>es, ra<u>ce</u>; /f/ <u>f</u>ast, o<u>ff</u>; /sh/ <u>sh</u>ape, fini<u>sh</u>; blends: <u>fl</u>ag, <u>tr</u>uck, <u>st</u>art

Noting print has meaning: names on chairs and on cubbies, signs in dramatic play, words in books and on chalkboard

Noting sound–symbol associations: What sound does _____ start with?

Writing: letters, names, words

Social Skills Facilitated

Initiating interaction with peers and adults; responding to questions and requests from peers and adults

Negotiating with peers for toys and materials

Group cooperation: waiting for a turn in a group, taking a turn at the appropriate time

Cognitive Skills Facilitated

Problem-solving skills: how to set up the tracks

Classification skills: vehicles/nonvehicles

Sequencing skills: song, racing the cars, art

Narrative/story structure: labeling

Motor Skills Facilitated

Large motor: outdoor play activities—jumping, running, hopping, pedaling, climbing

Small motor: writing, drawing, gluing, rubbings

DRAMATIC PLAY **Car Racing**

Type of Activity: Related

Objectives
1. Learn new, and employ familiar, vocabulary
2. Learn new, and employ a variety of, syntactic constructions
3. Interact with peers
4. Sequence familiar routines
5. Expand conceptual knowledge of the world

Settings
- Three or four different track areas (one with two tracks elevated on one end and other tracks that form circles or ovals)
- Garage or pit area
- Spectator area
- Portable slide elevated on one end (optional—another track)
- Concession stand (optional)

Props
- Assortment of toy cars
- Tracks
- Electric tracks (optional)
- Checkered flag
- Play stopwatch
- Tools (e.g., wrench, screwdriver, pretend batteries)
- Chairs for spectators
- Pretend drink machine
- Cups
- Pretend cotton candy (optional)

Roles
- Drivers
- Mechanics
- Timers or judges
- Spectators
- Concession stand workers

General Description of Activity

Arrange several tracks for the toy cars to race on, an area for the cars to be worked on, and an area for spectators. Children play the roles of drivers, mechanics, timers, and spectators. The drivers race the cars by releasing two cars simultaneously and watching as they race down the tracks, which are elevated on one end. (Electric tracks could also be used, particularly for children with physical disabilities so they could press the switches.) The activity could be expanded to include concession stands.

Verbal Productions

Level of linguistic complexity varies with the role or competency of the child playing the role.
- "Get your cars ready" or "Ready"
- "Your car needs a new engine" or "New car"
- "That car went very fast" or "Fast car"
- "I fixed it" or "Fix"

Adult Facilitative Role

The adult is to facilitate role play and help expand language and literacy skills. Typical actions or strategies to use include

Playing a role: "Do you want to race cars with me?"

Modeling a statement/vocabulary: "The green flag means the start of the race, and the checkered flag mean that I won the race."

Asking an open question: "Which car do you want to race?"

Expanding a child's utterance and providing corrective feedback: "My car go fast" to "Your car did go fast. My car went fast, too."

Modeling the reading of a sign: "The sign says *drinks for sale*."

ART **Car Track Painting**

Objectives
1. Express creativity
2. Develop small motor skills (e.g., drawing, painting, cutting, pasting)
3. Practice turn-taking skills
4. Converse with peers and adults

Materials
- 8" × 11" pieces of construction paper (at least one piece per child)
- Three or four colors of tempera paint
- Smocks
- Small die-cast cars
- Shallow containers to hold the paint and cars (e.g., Styrofoam meat trays)

General Description of Activity

The children each don a smock before sitting at the art table. Give each child an 8" × 11" piece of construction paper. On the art table are several shallow containers (e.g., small Styrofoam meat trays) containing tempera paints of various colors (one color per container) and small die-cast cars. The children dip the wheels of the cars into the paint and then roll the car along their paper to make designs. Before changing to a different color, the children return the cars they had been using to their original paint container.

GROUP **Identifying *V*, *W*, and *X***

Objectives
1. Improve listening skills
2. Increase knowledge of the alphabet and sounds
3. Learn appropriate group-interaction skills
4. Practice turn-taking skills

Materials
- Target alphabet letters on cards
- Alphabet chart
- Paper and pencils or markers (optional)
- Chalkboards, chalk (optional)

General Description of Activity

Lay the letters *V*, *W*, and *X* in front of the children. Have the children, in chorus, say the letters as you point to each one. Have one child come to the front and point to a specific letter.

Group Participation

Ask different children to point to specific letters, helping them as necessary. Vary the difficulty by having children identify letters in order or out of order, or by having some match a letter card to the letters on the floor instead of pointing to a designated letter. You can also ask them to match lowercase letters to uppercase letters. Children can also point to a letter and have the class label it.

Summary/Transition Activity

Say the whole alphabet with the children as you point to an alphabet chart. Then have everyone say the target alphabet letters (*V*, *W*, *X*) as you point to each letter in turn. An alternative activity is to have the children practice writing the three target letters.

Wednesday

Dramatic Play	Art	Group	Story	Song
Baking	Gingerbread Men	Tap out Syllables	*Mr. Cookie Baker*	"Do You Know the Muffin Man?"

DAILY PLANNING GUIDE

Language and Literacy Skills Facilitated

Vocabulary: *cook, house, food, soup, stew, muffins, babies, wash, table, clean, button, zip, teeth, toothbrush, dentist*

Verb phrase structures: *is cooking, was cooking, cooks, cooked, fixes, fixed, makes, made, do you have ___?, eats, ate, has eaten, washes, washed*

Adjective/object descriptions: *good food, hot/cold food, sweet/tart fruit, green vegetables, red apple, yellow banana, dirty/clean baby*

Question structures: *what, how, where, when, who, what if, why, how many, which one*

Pronouns: *I, you, he, she, we, they, my, your, him, her, his, our, their, me, us, them*

Prepositions: *in, on, under, over, near, beneath, next to, beside, around, inside, outside*

Sounds: /k/ *cook, cooking, make;* /l/ *lick, Jell-o, yell;* /s/ *see, cooks;* /r/ *roof, carrot, bar*

Noting print has meaning: names on chairs and on cubbies, signs in dramatic play, words in books and on chalkboard

Noting sound–symbol associations: What sound does _____ start with?

Writing: letters, names, words

Social Skills Facilitated

Initiating interaction with peers and adults; responding to questions and requests from peers and adults

Negotiating with peers for toys and materials

Group cooperation: waiting for a turn in a group, taking a turn at the appropriate time

Cognitive Skills Facilitated

Problem-solving skills: how to bake cookies

Classification skills: things we use to make and bake cookies

Sequencing skills: story, songs

Narrative/story structure: adventure

Motor Skills Facilitated

Large motor: outdoor play activities—jumping, running, hopping, pedaling, climbing

Small motor: writing, drawing, gluing, squeezing, swirling

DRAMATIC PLAY **Baking**

Objectives
1. Learn new, and employ familiar, vocabulary
2. Learn new, and employ a variety of, syntactic constructions
3. Interact with peers
4. Sequence familiar routines
5. Expand conceptual knowledge of the world

Settings
- Kitchen
- Baking area or sand/water table filled with flour in tubs
- Table
- Chairs

Props
- Play food cookies
- Flour
- Sifters
- Measuring cups
- Measuring spoons
- Baking tins
- Dishes
- Utensils
- Aprons
- Chef hats (optional)
- Spatula and other utensils
- Silverware
- Bowls, baking sheets, muffin tins
- Play oven

Roles
- Bakers
- Assistants
- Mommies
- Daddies
- Babies

General Description of Activity

A housekeeping area can be set up with a pretend kitchen including a stove, oven, refrigerator, and table. In addition, an area can be set up so that the children can sift real flour and use measuring cups. The area might be similar to a sand/water table area, only flour is used instead of sand/water. The flour could be put in dish tubs and then placed in the empty sand/water table so that the flour is less likely to spill on the floor. Real cookies could also be made in a separate area where the children decorate premade cookie dough, which is then baked in a toaster oven (outside of the classroom). The cookies could then be eaten at snack time.

Verbal Productions

Level of linguistic complexity varies with the role or competency of the child playing the role.
- "Do you want some more cookies?" or "Cookies?"
- "Put it in the oven" or "Cook it"
- "Look, the flour is coming out of the sifter" or "Flour out"

Adult Facilitative Role

The adult is to facilitate role play and help expand language and literacy skills. Typical actions or strategies to use include

Playing a role: "I am sifting a cup of flour. I am making bread."

Recasting present progressive with past tense: "I am baking the bread" to "I baked the bread in the oven."

Event casting a child's action: "You are sifting the flour. Now you are putting the flour in a bowl. You stirred the flour and put the flour in the muffin tins. You spilled some of the flour."

Modeling the correct production of the /k/ sound: "I can ma<u>k</u>e all of the muffins now."

Identifying rhyming words: "The words *cake, bake,* and *make* all rhyme."

ART : Gingerbread Men

Objectives
1. Express creativity
2. Develop small motor skills (e.g., drawing, painting, cutting, pasting)
3. Practice turn-taking skills
4. Converse with peers and adults

Materials
- 36 gingerbread men out of brown construction paper
- Small circle cutouts
- Small triangle cutouts
- Scissors
- Paper
- Glue

General Description of Activity

Children decorate gingerbread cookies (previously cut by staff from brown construction paper) by gluing or pasting small pieces of construction paper cut in various shapes onto the figures. The shapes should be placed in separate containers so that the children can easily choose the shapes that they want. Other items, such as yarn, extra paper, scissors, and markers are also available. Children can decorate their gingerbread cookies in any way they want by gluing various items on them or by drawing on them.

GROUP **Tap out Syllables**

Objectives
1. Improve listening skills
2. Improve sequencing ability
3. Learn appropriate group-interaction skills
4. Practice turn-taking skills

Materials
• Drum

General Description of Activity

Place a drum in front of the children. Explain that there are "beats" in words, called *syllables*. Tell children that you are going to make as many taps on the drum as there are syllables in your name. Say your name while tapping on the drum the appropriate number of times, one beat per syllable. Repeat this task once while the children listen again. Have one child come up to try the task using his or her own name. Assist the child if necessary.

Group Participation

Call up one child at a time and have the child tap out the number of syllables in his or her name. Continue until each child has had at least one turn.

Variation

If a drum is unavailable, have the children clap out the number of syllables in their name. You might also give the children other words to tap out, such as *rabbit, dinosaur, or caterpillar*.

Summary/Transition Activity

Remind children that the "beats" in words are syllables and that these syllables are important because we talk in syllables (not sounds).

Thursday

Dramatic Play	Art	Group	Story	Song
All About Pets	Paper Bag Puppets	Classify Pets and Zoo Animals	*Franklin Wants a Pet*	"How Much Is that Doggy in the Window?"

DAILY PLANNING GUIDE

Language and Literacy Skills Facilitated

Vocabulary: *dog, cats, birds, gerbils, Dalmatians, pets, rabbits, camera, ribbons, awards, phone, cash register, cages, podium*

Verb phrase structures: *takes a picture, is taking the pet home, fed the dog, gave a ribbon, petted the dog, walked the dog*

Adjective/object descriptions: *blue/red ribbon, first place, big/little _____, white/black _____, long/short leash*

Question structures: *what, how, where, when, who, what if, why, how many, which one*

Pronouns: *I, you, he, she, we, they, my, your, him, her, his, our, their, me, us, them*

Prepositions: *in, on, under, over, near, beneath, next to, beside, around, inside, outside*

Sounds: /k/ *catch, pack, trick;* /f/ *fed, off;* /r/ *rabbit, far*

Noting print has meaning: names on chairs and on cubbies, signs in dramatic play, words in books and on chalkboard

Noting sound–symbol associations: What sound does _____ start with?

Writing: letters, names, words

Social Skills Facilitated

Initiating interaction with peers and adults; responding to questions and requests from peers and adults

Negotiating with peers for toys and materials

Group cooperation: waiting for a turn in a group, taking a turn at the appropriate time

Cognitive Skills Facilitated

Problem-solving skills: how to take care of a pet

Classification skills: things at a pet show

Sequencing skills: story, songs, art activity

Narrative/story structure: adventure

Motor Skills Facilitated

Large motor: outdoor play activities—jumping, running, hopping, pedaling, climbing

Small motor: writing, drawing, constructing with playdough

DRAMATIC PLAY **All About Pets**

Type of Activity: Central

Objectives
1. Learn new, and employ familiar, vocabulary
2. Learn new, and employ a variety of, syntactic constructions
3. Interact with peers
4. Sequence familiar routines
5. Expand conceptual knowledge of the world

Settings
- Pet store
- Counter
- Children's houses (playhouses or dismantled cardboard boxes)

Props
- Stuffed animals
- Pretend cash register
- Play money
- Pretend credit cards
- Shelves of pretend pet products (e.g., food, leashes, collars, toys)
- Cages
- Aquariums
- Bowls for food and water
- Brushes for grooming
- Pet carriers
- Pretend cleaning supplies
- Ribbons
- Show ring area

Roles
- Clerks
- Cashier
- Judges
- Customers
- Animals

General Description of Activity

Children buy pets at the pet store. The store should have a variety of pets (stuffed animals or children pretending to be the animals), such as dogs, cats, birds, hamsters, turtles, and fish, in appropriate containers and cages. A clerk can ring up sales on a cash register and be given money for the purchases. Pretend pet food, leashes, collars, and pet toys can also be sold at the pet store. Children can then take the pets to their houses. Children can also be workers in the store, caring for the pets by feeding and grooming them. Children could also take their pets to a pet show and see if they win ribbons.

Verbal Productions

Level of linguistic complexity varies with the role or competency of the child playing the role.
- "How much is this dog?" or "Buy dog"
- "I need five pounds of cat food for Fuzzy" or "Cat food, please"
- "He is cleaning the dog's cage" or "Clean"
- "My turn to use the cash register" or "Mine"

Adult Facilitative Role

The adult is to facilitate role play and help expand language and literacy skills. Typical actions or strategies to use include

Playing a role: "I want to get a new cat at the pet store. I will need some food, too."

Modeling a statement/vocabulary: "I am taking my dog to the dog show. A dog show is where dogs do tricks or do what they are told to do. A judge decides who is the best at doing the tricks or following the owner's commands. The best dogs get special ribbons."

Redirecting a child to a peer: "Ask Maura for a turn with the cash register. Say, 'May I have a turn, please?'"

Expanding a child's utterance: "You best" to "You have the best dog."

ART **Paper Bag Puppets**

Objectives
1. Express creativity
2. Develop small motor skills (e.g., drawing, painting, cutting, pasting)
3. Practice turn-taking skills
4. Converse with peers and adults

Materials
- Paper bags, one for each child
- Construction paper
- Construction cutouts (e.g., circles, triangles)
- Scissors
- Glue or paste

General Description of Activity

Children make paper bag puppets by decorating small brown paper bags. The puppet might be a pet or other creature. The base fold of the paper bag will be the face so that when the child's hand is placed inside the bag, the fold can be used to open and close the mouth. Children may glue red construction paper inside the fold to represent the tongue. Other construction paper cutouts can be used for facial features, such as ears, a nose, and a mouth, or children can use markers to draw in the facial features. Yarn can be used for fur. When the puppets are finished, the children can stick their hands into the bag and make their puppets "talk."

GROUP **Classify Pets and Zoo Animals**

Objectives

1. Improve listening skills
2. Learn appropriate group-interaction skills
3. Practice turn-taking skills

Materials

- Toy house
- Toy fence
- Zoo mat
- Toy pets (e.g., dogs, cats, fish)
- Toy zoo animals
- Pictures of pets and zoo animals (optional)

General Description of Activity

Set up a home area (a toy house with a toy fence) and a zoo area (a plastic or cardboard mat with zoo scenes drawn on it). Tell the children that they are going to put the animals that can be pets by the house and the zoo animals in the zoo. Ask one child to put a toy dog in the home area and another child to place a toy elephant in the zoo area.

Group Participation

Distribute the different toy animals to the children. Have them come up one at a time to label their animal and decide whether it is a pet or lives at the zoo. You can also ask children to think of other animals that are not among the toys and tell the group where those animals live.

Variation

If toy animals are not available, use pictures of animals.

Summary/Transition Activity

Review the classifications of pets and zoo animals, renaming a few of the animals in each classification.

WEEKLY PLANNING GUIDE

	Dramatic Play	Art	Group	Story	Song
Monday *Suggested Props and Materials*	Doctor *Doctor scenario, table with telephone and appointment book, several tables or mats to represent examination rooms, doctor kits, bandages, X-ray machine, telephone in area representing patients' homes*	Chalk Drawings *Black construction paper, chalk*	Review Writing Numbers 1–10 *Cards with the numbers 1–10, chalkboards and chalk, paper and pencils (optional), whiteboard and markers, counting bears or other objects (optional)*	*Little Rabbit Goes to the Doctor*	"Baby Bear Has Chicken Pox"
Tuesday *Suggested Props and Materials*	Teacher *Teacher scenario, school area (different centers and circle area delineated), bus area, name cards, alphabet cards, flannel board and flannel board stories, books, small blackboard, paper and pencils, art materials, flashlight (to use in check-in), puzzles*	Easel Paintings *Tempera paint, brushes, easels, paper, smocks*	Identifying *Y* and *Z* *Target alphabet letters (Y, Z), alphabet chart, paper and pencils or markers (optional), chalkboards, chalk (optional)*	*Who Took the Cookies from the Cookie Jar?*	"The Alphabet Song"
Wednesday *Suggested Props and Materials*	Sanitation Engineer *Sanitation engineer scenario, sanitation truck (wheeled cart with large bags attached), wastebaskets, crunched-up garbage (newspaper), plastic containers, aluminum cans, desks, telephones, boxes (for trash to be dumped into for sorting)*	Trash Collage *Construction paper; scissors; "trashable" items including scrap paper, Styrofoam, metal pieces, etc.; glue*	Word Deletion *List of compound words (e.g., blackboard, sidewalk, toothbrush, toothpaste, groundhog, lighthouse, postcard, lifeguard, songbird, cupboard, flashcard, backyard, skateboard, doorknob, washrag)*	*Dear Garbage Man*	"Hokey Pokey"
Thursday *Suggested Props and Materials*	Police Officer *Police officer scenario, pretend motorcycles, tickets, pretend driver's licenses, pencils, traffic signs, play telephones, steering wheels (paper plates), seatbelts (men's ties or string loosely tied around chairs), microphones (for dispatcher's office) walkie-talkies*	Badges *Cardboard cut in the shape of badges, glue (or paste), scrap pieces of paper, pieces of string, foil (enough to cover the badges), masking tape, predrawn badges to color (optional), scissors (optional), crayons or markers (optional)*	What Is Your Address? *Address cards with children's addresses and phone numbers*	*Edward Hurts His Knee*	"Red Light, Red Light, What Do You Say?"

NEWSLETTER

Vol. 1, No. 36

Date: _____

Community Helpers

Monday

Today the children will pretend to be doctors, nurses, or patients. They will use stethoscopes, bandages, and other things found in a doctor's office. In art, they will make chalk drawings. Our story for the day is *Little Rabbit Goes to the Doctor*. During group time, we will focus on the number *10*. The children will write the number and count objects to 10. Our song of the day is "Baby Bear Has Chicken Pox."

Tuesday

Today we are focusing on teachers. There will be a miniature classroom set up in the dramatic play area. The children can be the teachers, the students, or the bus drivers. They will do easel painting in art. Our story is *Who Took the Cookies from the Cookie Jar?*. Children will identify, match, and write the letters *Y* and *Z* during group time. Our song of the day is "The Alphabet Song."

Wednesday

Today we are focusing on the job of a sanitation engineer. The children will drive the truck, pick up the trash, or even be the workers at the recycling plant. In art, children will make pictures using items that are disposable (Styrofoam, plastic, paper). Our story is *Dear Garbage Man*. During group time, children will be learning about compound words and what happens if part of the word is deleted. Our song of the day is "Hokey Pokey."

Thursday

Today our community helper is the police officer. The children can be the officer or the one who needs help. One of the children can also be the one who drives a bit too fast! In art, children will make badges. Our story is *Edward Hurts His Knee*. During group time, we will talk about safety rules and knowing our address and phone number. "Red Light, Red Light, What Do You Say?" is our song of the day.

Monday

Dramatic Play	Art	Group	Story	Song
Doctor	Chalk Drawings	Review Writing the Numbers 1–10	*Little Rabbit Goes to the Doctor*	"Baby Bear Has Chicken Pox"

DAILY PLANNING GUIDE

Language and Literacy Skills Facilitated

Vocabulary: *doctor, nurse, paramedic, ambulance, stethoscope, thermometer, fever, cast, X-ray, oxygen, accident, vehicle, arm, leg, ankle, bandage, forehead, hospital, hurt, stomachache*

Verb phrase structures: *is carrying the stretcher, drove the ambulance, rides, examines, gave oxygen, sets the leg*

Adjective/object descriptions: *broken leg, big ambulance, loud siren*

Question structures: *what, how, where, when, who, what if, why, how many, which one*

Pronouns: *I, you, he, she, we, they, my, your, him, her, his, our, their, me, us, them*

Prepositions: *in, on, under, over, near, beneath, next to, beside, around, inside, outside*

Sounds: /k/ *carry, doctor, broke*; /s/ *set, inside, us, ambulance*

Noting print has meaning: names on chairs and on cubbies, signs in dramatic play, words in books and on chalkboard

Noting sound–symbol associations: What sound does _____ start with?

Writing: letters, names, words

Social Skills Facilitated

Initiating interaction with peers and adults; responding to questions and requests from peers and adults

Negotiating with peers for toys and materials

Group cooperation: waiting for a turn in a group, taking a turn at the appropriate time

Cognitive Skills Facilitated

Problem-solving skills: What does a doctor do?

Classification skills: things in a doctor's office, body parts

Sequencing skills: story, songs

Narrative/story structure: labeling

Motor Skills Facilitated

Large motor: outdoor play activities—jumping, running, hopping, pedaling, climbing

Small motor: writing, drawing, gluing, cutting

DRAMATIC PLAY **Doctor**

Type of Activity: Central

Objectives

1. Learn new, and employ familiar, vocabulary
2. Learn new, and employ a variety of, syntactic constructions
3. Interact with peers
4. Sequence familiar routines
5. Expand conceptual knowledge of the world

Settings
- Several examination rooms
- Waiting room
- Patients' "homes"

Props
- Table with a telephone and appointment book
- Several tables or mats to represent examination rooms
- Doctor kits
- Bandages
- X-ray machine
- Telephone in area representing patients' "homes"

Roles
- Doctor
- Nurse
- Receptionist
- Patient
- Parent

General Description of Activity

A doctor's office with several examination rooms and a waiting room is set up. Children who are patients call the receptionist and make an appointment. When it is time for their appointment, they go into the examination room with the doctor. He or she examines them by looking into their mouth, ears, and eyes; checking reflexes; checking muscle tone; listening with the stethoscope; and so forth. A patient might have a broken bone that needs to be X-rayed, set in a cast, and wrapped with a bandage.

Verbal Productions

Level of linguistic complexity varies with the role or competency of the child playing the role.
- "Open your mouth, please" or "Open mouth"
- "Where does it hurt?" or "Hurt?"
- "I don't feel good. My tummy hurts" or "I sick"

Adult Facilitative Role

The adult is to facilitate role play and help expand language and literacy skills. Typical actions or strategies to use include

Playing a role: "Are you sick today? Maybe you have chicken pox."

Using a cloze procedure: "This is a real stethoscope, and this is a _____(pretend) stethoscope."

Asking an open question: "What do you think is wrong with my baby?"

Identifying rhyming words: "The words *hot, shot, cot,* and *lot* all rhyme."

Modeling the writing of names: "You write James's name in the appointment book so that he can be the next one to see the doctor."

ART : **Chalk Drawings**

Objectives
1. Express creativity
2. Develop small motor skills (e.g., drawing, painting, cutting, pasting)
3. Practice turn-taking skills
4. Converse with peers and adults

Materials
- Black construction paper
- White chalk
- Other chalk available
- Chalk fixative (sprayed on to keep pictures from smudging)

General Description of Activity

The children are given black construction paper and white chalk to draw pictures on the paper. Some children might like to draw X-ray pictures by making line drawings of skeleton-like people. Some of the X-ray pictures could be of "broken" arms and then could be incorporated into the dramatic play. (The artists could be the "radiologists.") Other children might want to draw general pictures that have nothing to do with the X-ray activity.

GROUP **Review Writing the Numbers *1–10***

Objectives
1. Improve listening skills
2. Increase conceptual knowledge
3. Learn appropriate group-interaction skills
4. Practice turn-taking skills
5. Practice recognition and writing of numbers

Materials
- Number cards or card strip with the numbers *1–10*
- Chalkboards and chalk
- Paper and pencils (optional)
- Whiteboard and markers
- Number line (optional)

General Description of Activity

Hold up a card strip with the numbers *1–10* written on it. Have children choose a number and come up and write it on the chalkboard. Repeat until all the numbers and rhymes have been reviewed.

1: Start at the top, go down and you're done, that's the way to make a *1*.

2: Around and back on the railroad track, *2, 2, 2*.

3: Around the tree, around the tree, that's the way to make a *3*.

4: Down and over and down once more, that's the way to make a *4*.

5: Down around, make a hat on it, and look what you've found. (*5*)

6: Down around until it sticks, that's the way to make a *6*.

7: Over and down and it's not heaven, over and down makes a *7*.

8: Make an S and go back straight, that's the way to make an *8*.

9: A balloon and a line make *9*.

10: Draw a line and a circle with your pen, that's the way to make a *10*.

Group Participation

Distribute individual chalkboards and chalk (or paper and pencils) to the children, and have them practice writing numbers.

Variation

Whiteboards and markers may be easier for some children to use.

Variation 2

To introduce the number, use a number line and have the children count up to the target number on the line. One child could place the target number on the number line.

Summary/Transition Activity

Ask children to hold up their chalkboards and show the group their numbers.

Tuesday

Dramatic Play	Art	Group	Story	Song
Teacher	Easel Paintings	Identifying Y and Z	Who Took the Cookies from the Cookie Jar?	"The Alphabet Song"

DAILY PLANNING GUIDE

Language and Literacy Skills Facilitated

Vocabulary: *school, bus, pencil, pen, paper, flashlight, check in, alphabet, sounds, cubes, shapes, numbers, paint*

Verb phrase structures: *is writing, reads the book, says the alphabet, goes to check in, drove the bus, painted a picture*

Adjective/object descriptions: *red, blue ____, big ____, little ____, pretty ____, dirty ____, fancy ____, nice ____, unusual ____*

Question structures: *what, how, where, when, who, what if, why, how many, which one*

Pronouns: *I, you, he, she, we, they, my, your, him, her, his, our, their, me, us, them*

Prepositions: *in, on, under, over, near, beneath, next to, beside, around, inside, outside*

Sounds: /s/ *say, pencil, bus;* /k/ *car, check-in, look;* /l/ *look, flashlight, pencil, school*

Noting print has meaning: names on chairs and on cubbies, signs in dramatic play, words in books and on chalkboard

Noting sound–symbol associations: What sound does ____ start with?

Writing: letters, names, words

Social Skills Facilitated

Initiating interaction with peers and adults; responding to questions and requests from peers and adults

Negotiating with peers for toys and materials

Group cooperation: waiting for a turn in a group, taking a turn at the appropriate time

Cognitive Skills Facilitated

Problem-solving skills: how to paint on an easel

Classification skills: things a teacher uses

Sequencing skills: songs, stories

Narrative/story structure: adventure and repetitive line

Motor Skills Facilitated

Large motor: outdoor play activities—jumping, running, hopping, pedaling, climbing

Small motor: writing, drawing, gluing, cutting

DRAMATIC PLAY **Teacher**

Type of Activity: Related

Objectives
1. Learn new, and employ familiar, vocabulary
2. Learn new, and employ a variety of, syntactic constructions
3. Interact with peers
4. Sequence familiar routines
5. Expand conceptual knowledge of the world

Settings
- School area (circle outlined on floor with masking tape)
- Bus (playhouse with cardboard door that opens and closes and a box and dashboard in front to make the cab)
- Art area
- Quiet area (books and puzzles)

Props
- Name cards
- Alphabet cards
- Flannel board and flannel board stories
- Books
- Small blackboard
- Paper and pencils
- Art materials
- Flashlight

Roles
- Bus driver
- Children
- Teacher
- Staff members
- Principal
- School nurse
- Custodian
- Parents

General Description of Activity

Set up the school area in imitation of the classroom. Include name cards, alphabet cards, flannel board stories, books, writing materials, and so forth. Also have a school bus. The children can board the bus, be driven to school, disembark, be checked in (the children who are playing the roles of staff check the "children's" throats to see if they are too sick to be in school), and then play the roles of teachers, staff, and students. When school is over, they can return home by riding on the bus again.

Verbal Productions

Level of linguistic complexity varies with the role or competency of the child playing the role.
- "He wrote his name on the paper" or "Write name"
- "I am the bus driver. You need to sit down" or "Sit down"
- "I want to drive the bus. He has driven it for a long time" or "Drive bus"
- "What does this letter say?" or "What sound?"

Adult Facilitative Role

The adult is to facilitate role play and help expand language and literacy skills. Typical actions or strategies to use include

Playing a role: "I want you to say the alphabet, please."

Event casting: "You are writing your name. You write *Suzie* at the top of the page. Now you are marking the papers."

Asking an open question: "What should we do next?"

Using a cloze procedure: "The word *apple* starts with the letter *a*, and the word *ball* starts with the letter ___(b)."

Expanding a child's utterance: "He teacher" to "He is the teacher. He says it is time for recess."

ART : **Easel Paintings**

Objectives
1. Express creativity
2. Develop small motor skills (e.g., drawing, painting, cutting, pasting)
3. Practice turn-taking skills
4. Converse with peers and adults

Materials
- Smocks
- Easels
- Different colors of tempera
- Paint cups to hold the paint
- Large paintbrushes
- 9" × 12" or 12" × 18" paper
- Wooden rack or other area for drying

General Description of Activity

Set up two easel boards with a large piece of paper clipped to each. Set out two to four cups filled with tempera paint and a paintbrush in each cup. (It is helpful to have cup covers with holes in them for the brushes. As children dip the brushes into the paint and pull them through the hole, some of the excess paint is removed. It is also helpful to place the easel over plastic or newspaper so that the paint drips do not stain the floor.)

Children put on their smocks, dip the brush into the paint, and paint shapes, objects, or anything else they want. Sometimes children will paint a picture and then experiment by painting other colors on top. Let the children experiment with the tempera for some projects. Sometimes you might have the children tell you about their painting, and you can label it for display. (Let the children decide if they want their paintings displayed.) Have a designated area for drying the pictures, such as a wooden clothes rack. Note: This is a large muscle activity, particularly appropriate for young children (3 years and up).

GROUP **Identifying *Y* and *Z***

Objectives
1. Improve listening skills
2. Increase knowledge of the alphabet and sounds
3. Learn appropriate group-interaction skills
4. Practice turn-taking skills

Materials
- Target alphabet letters
- Alphabet chart
- Paper and pencils or markers (optional)
- Chalkboard, chalk (optional)

General Description of Activity

Lay the letters *Y* and *Z* in front of the children. Have the children, in chorus, say the letters as you point to each one. Have one child come to the front and point to a specific letter.

Group Participation

Ask different children to point to specific letters, helping them as necessary. Vary the difficulty by having children identify letters in order or out of order, or by having some match a letter card to the letters on the floor instead of pointing to a designated letter. You can also ask them to match lower-case letters to uppercase letters. Children can also point to a letter and have the class label it.

Summary/Transition Activity

Say the whole alphabet with the children as you point to an alphabet chart. Then have everyone say the target alphabet letters (*Y, Z*) as you point to each letter in turn. An alternative activity is to have the children practice writing the two target letters.

Wednesday

Dramatic Play	Art	Group	Story	Song
Sanitation Engineer	Trash Collage	Word Deletion	*Dear Garbage Man*	"Hokey Pokey"

DAILY PLANNING GUIDE

Language and Literacy Skills Facilitated

Vocabulary: *trash, sanitation worker, garbage, recycle, plastic, cardboard, glass, newspaper, litter, cleanup*

Verb phrase structures: <u>are</u> pick<u>ing</u>/ pick<u>ed</u> up trash, throw away, litter<u>ed</u>, clean<u>ed</u>, <u>is</u> clean<u>ing</u>, <u>are</u> recycl<u>ing</u>, recycl<u>ed</u>

Adjective/object descriptions: *big truck, dirty/clean yard, plastic bottle, glass bottle*

Question structures: *what, how, where, when, who, what if, why, how many, which one*

Pronouns: *I, you, he, she, we, they, my, your, him, her, his, our, their, me, us, them*

Prepositions: *in, on, under, over, near, beneath, next to, beside, around, inside, outside*

Sounds: /l/ <u>l</u>itter, be<u>ll</u>; /f/ <u>f</u>ix, of<u>f</u>; /; /k/ <u>c</u>an, pi<u>ck</u> up; /s/ <u>s</u>ee, bu<u>s</u>

Noting print has meaning: names on chairs and on cubbies, signs in dramatic play, words in books and on chalkboard

Noting sound–symbol associations: What sound does _____ start with?

Writing: letters, names, words

Social Skills Facilitated

Initiating interaction with peers and adults; responding to questions and requests from peers and adults

Negotiating with peers for toys and materials

Group cooperation: waiting for a turn in a group, taking a turn at the appropriate time

Cognitive Skills Facilitated

Problem-solving skills: What does a sanitation worker do?

Classification skills: things we recycle

Sequencing skills: story, song

Narrative/story structure: repetitive line

Motor Skills Facilitated

Large motor: outdoor play activities—jumping, running, hopping, pedaling, climbing

Small motor: writing, drawing, gluing

DRAMATIC PLAY **Sanitation Engineer**

Type of Activity: Related

Objectives
1. Learn new, and employ familiar, vocabulary
2. Learn new, and employ a variety of, syntactic constructions
3. Interact with peers
4. Sequence familiar routines
5. Expand conceptual knowledge of the world

Settings
- Sanitation truck (wheeled cart with large bags attached)
- Houses with wastebaskets
- Road (floor marked with masking tape)
- Recycling plant office
- Sorting area

Props
- Sanitation truck (wheeled cart with large bags attached)
- Wastebaskets
- Crunched-up "garbage" (newspaper)
- Plastic containers
- Aluminum cans
- Desks
- Telephones
- Boxes (for trash to be dumped into for sorting)

Roles
- Sanitation workers
- Homeowners
- Truck drivers
- Workers at recycling plant

General Description of Activity

Children pretend to be sanitation workers who are picking up garbage from houses and from parks. They can ride a sanitation truck made out of a cart with wheels. Large bags can be attached so that children can stop at a house, empty trash cans into the large bag, and then go on to the next house. If the cart is sturdy enough, some of the children can actually ride on it while others push it. When the large bag is full, the truck goes to the plant to drop off the garbage. Some of the garbage can be taken to a recycling plant, where it can be sorted by workers to be made into new things. (Be aware that this activity requires that someone refill the wastebaskets so the play can continue.)

Verbal Productions

Level of linguistic complexity varies with the role or competency of the child playing the role.
- "He picked up three trash cans. It's my turn" or "My turn"
- "I want to ride the cart. He has ridden it a long time" or "Ride long time"
- "We have three piles—one for cans, one for paper, and one for plastic" or "Three piles"

Adult Facilitative Role

The adult is to facilitate role play and help expand language and literacy skills. Typical actions or strategies to use include

Playing a role: "I like driving the garbage truck. It is a big truck."

Providing confirmatory feedback: "Yes, that is a truck."

Redirecting a child to a peer: "Ask Jaden if you can dump the trash can. Say, 'May I have a turn, please?'"

Modeling phonological awareness: "The words *bag, box, big*, and *Bob* all start with the /b/ sound."

Recasting present tense to past tense: "He dumps the trash" to "Yesterday he dumped the trash."

ART **Trash Collage**

Objectives
1. Express creativity
2. Develop small motor skills (e.g., drawing, painting, cutting, pasting)
3. Practice turn-taking skills
4. Converse with peers and adults

Materials

- Construction paper
- Scissors
- "Trashable" items, (e.g., crumpled and torn paper, other scrap paper, Styrofoam, newspaper)
- Glue

General Description of Activity

Children paste a variety of trashable items to construction paper to make collages.

GROUP **Word Deletion**

Objectives

1. Improve listening skills
2. Increase knowledge of the alphabet and sounds
3. Learn appropriate group-interaction skills
4. Practice turn-taking skills

Materials

- List of compound words (e.g., *blackboard, sidewalk, toothbrush, toothpaste, groundhog, lighthouse, postcard, lifeguard, songbird, cupboard, flashcard, backyard, skateboard, doorknob, washrag*, etc.)

General Description of Activity

Tell the children that some words are made up of two smaller words and that the group is going to play a game guessing the little words. For example, the word *blackboard* is two words, *black* and *board*. The word *sidewalk* is made up of *side* and *walk*. After the children have separated several compound words into two words, ask what word would be left if they took away one of the smaller words in the compound word. For example, for the word *blackboard*, what would be left if they took away the word *black*? (answer—*board*) Do the same for another word, such as *sidewalk* without *side* (answer—*walk*).

Group Participation

Using your list of compound words, ask the children to provide, in chorus, the word that is left when one of the smaller words in a compound word is deleted. Initially, delete the first word of the compound word, then switch and delete the second. When switching to the second word deletion, warn the children that you are changing the game and see if they can figure out what word is left (e.g., *sidewalk* without the *walk*, etc.).

Variation

Have the children clap out the two words in a compound word, clapping once per word. Then delete one of the smaller words, clapping only to the word that is left. For example, have the children clap twice for the word *blackboard*. Then ask the children what *blackboard* is without *black*, and spread your hands as *black* is said, clapping only on the word *board*. The children answer the question (What is *blackboard* without *black*?) by saying only the word that is clapped (*board*).

Summary/Transition Activity

Provide one more example of deletion of the initial word and final word.

Thursday

Dramatic Play	Art	Group	Story	Song
Police Officer	Badges	What Is Your Address?	*Edward Hurts His Knee*	"Red Light, Red Light, What Do You Say?"

DAILY PLANNING GUIDE

Language and Literacy Skills Facilitated

Vocabulary: *police officer, ticket, speed limit, seatbelts, street, safety rules, motorcycle, handcuffs, one-way*

Verb phrase structures: *drive safely, ride motorcycle, write ticket, put on belt, drive car*

Adjective/object descriptions: *big ____, small ____, red ____, blue ____, purple ____*

Question structures: *what, how, where, when, who, what if, why, how many, which one*

Pronouns: *I, you, he, she, we, they, my, your, him, her, his, our, their, me, us, them*

Prepositions: *in, on, under, over, near, beneath, next to, beside, around, inside, outside*

Sounds: /s/ *see*, *poli<u>c</u>e;* /f/ *<u>f</u>ix, of<u>f</u>;* /k/ *<u>k</u>eep, ti<u>ck</u>et, ba<u>ck</u>;* /l/ *<u>l</u>ook, <u>l</u>ight, ru<u>l</u>e*

Noting print has meaning: names on chairs and on cubbies, signs in dramatic play, words in books and on chalkboard

Noting sound–symbol associations: What sound does _____ start with?

Writing: letters, names, words

Social Skills Facilitated

Initiating interaction with peers and adults; responding to questions and requests from peers and adults

Negotiating with peers for toys and materials

Group cooperation: waiting for a turn in a group, taking a turn at the appropriate time

Cognitive Skills Facilitated

Problem-solving skills: What are safety rules?

Classification skills: traffic signs

Sequencing skills: songs, story, art activity

Narrative/story structure: adventure

Motor Skills Facilitated

Large motor: outdoor play activities—jumping, running, hopping, pedaling, climbing

Small motor: writing, drawing, gluing, painting

DRAMATIC PLAY **Police Officer**

Type of Activity: Related

Objectives
1. Learn new, and employ familiar, vocabulary
2. Learn new, and employ a variety of, syntactic constructions
3. Interact with peers
4. Sequence familiar routines
5. Expand conceptual knowledge of the world

Settings
- Dispatch office
- Roads (floor marked by masking tape)
- Shopping areas
- Police station

Props
- Motorcycles (two paper plates together and affixed on each end of a yardstick)
- Tickets
- Pretend driver's licenses
- Pencils
- Traffic signs
- Play telephones
- Steering wheels (paper plates)
- Seatbelts (men's ties or string loosely tied around chairs)
- Microphones (for dispatch office)
- Walkie-talkies

Roles
- Police officers
- Police chief
- Dispatcher
- Parents
- Children
- Motorcycle riders
- Store clerks

General Description of Activity

The children enact different police officer scenarios. For example, police officers on motorcycles can stop those who speed or do not wear their seatbelts. They can help someone whose car has broken down. Other officers can help children who get separated from their parents in the shopping area and need help. The police station can be set up as a place to bring the "lost" children and a place to pay "tickets."

Verbal Productions

Level of linguistic complexity varies with the role or competency of the child playing the role.
- "Where is your mommy?" or "Where Mommy?"
- "I don't know. I'm lost" or "I lost"
- "I've lost my child. Please help me" or "Help me"
- "You ran the stop sign, and I must give you a ticket" or "Too fast"
- "I did not see the sign" or "Not see!"

Adult Facilitative Role

The adult is to facilitate role play and help expand language and literacy skills. Typical actions or strategies to use include

Playing a role: "You were driving too fast. I have to give you a ticket."

Modeling a statement/vocabulary: "A police officer is someone who keeps you safe. They will give tickets to remind people to slow down. A ticket means that you have to pay some money because you did something wrong."

Expanding a child's utterance: "He ticket" to "You are right. He needs a ticket because he didn't use the stop sign."

Using a cloze procedure: "The red light means stop, and the green light means __(go)."

Modeling the reading of a sign: "The sign says *stop*."

ART **Badges**

Objectives
1. Express creativity
2. Develop small motor skills (e.g., drawing, painting, cutting, pasting)
3. Practice turn-taking skills
4. Converse with peers and adults

Materials
- Cardboard cut in the shape of badges
- Glue (or paste)
- Scrap pieces of paper
- Pieces of string
- Foil (enough to cover the badges)
- Masking tape
- Predrawn badges to color (optional)
- Scissors (optional)
- Crayons or markers (optional)

General Description of Activity

The children glue pieces of paper and bits of string onto cardboard pre-cut in the shape of a badge. The paper and string give the badges texture. They then cover the "badge" with foil. Attach children's badges to their clothing with masking tape. An alternative is to have the children color pre-designed badges, cut them out, and glue them onto the cardboard cut in the shape of a badge.

GROUP **What Is Your Address?**

Objectives
1. Improve listening skills
2. Increase conceptual knowledge
3. Learn appropriate group-interaction skills
4. Practice turn-taking skills

Materials
- Address cards with children's addresses

General Description of Activity

Tell the children that it is important for them to know their addresses. Addresses tell where they live, and without addresses people cannot send letters to them and firefighters would not know where to come if there was a fire. Explain that an address has several parts. The first part is the house or apartment number, the second part is the name of the street, and the last part is the city (and state). Write a sample address on the board, pointing out each part.

Group Participation

Asks if anyone knows his or her address. Have those who do come to the front of the group and state their address. Give them a card with their address on it, and pass out address cards to the remaining children as well. Divide the class into smaller groups and have the other staff members help the children recite their address to their group.

Summary/Transition Activity

After all of the groups have practiced their addresses, have the children gather back in one large group and remind them of the different parts of an address. The children can take their index cards home and practice with their parents until they can recite their address.

May

MONTHLY PLANNING GUIDE

Activities	Monday	Tuesday	Wednesday	Thursday
Week 37 — The Five Senses				
Dramatic Play	Beauty Salon/Barber Shop (Touch)	Concert/Art in the Park (Hearing)	Pizza Parlor (Taste/Smell)	Movie/Puppet Show (Sight)
Art	Fingerpaint with Shaving Cream	Make Tambourines	Paper Plate Pizza	Mural
Group	Feely Box	Sound Pattern Sequencing	Shape Review	Act out a Story (The Berenstain Bears Get Stage Fright)
Story	*Here Are My Hands*	*Polar Bear, Polar Bear, What Do You Hear?*	*Pizza Party*	*The Berenstain Bears Get Stage Fright*
Song	"Teddy Bear, Teddy Bear, Turn Around"	"The Ants Go Marching"	"I Wish I Were a Pepperoni Pizza"	"Six Little Ducks"
Week 38 — Places People Work				
Dramatic Play	Office	Department Store	Construction Site	Veterinarian's Office
Art	Stamp Art	Catalog Collage	Crayon Rubbings: Tools	Doghouse and Dog Prints
Group	How Are ____ Alike?	ABC Bingo	Introduction to Unifix Cubes	Bring Your Favorite "Stuffy"
Story	*The ABC Mystery*	*At the Mall*	*Stop Those Painters*	*Have You Seen My Cat?*
Song	"My Hands" (fingerplay)	"Mary Wore Her Red Dress"	"Building Song" (fingerplay)	"Little Ducky Duddle"
Week 39 — Things Big Kids Do				
Dramatic Play	Babysitting	Newspaper Route	Fast-Food Job	Work on Cars
Art	Tissue Paper Collage	Newspaper Collage	Playdough	Car Track Painting
Group	Size Comparisons (Big, Medium, Little)	Make a Class Newsletter	Addition with Unifix Cubes	Review Numbers 1–20
Story	*Peter's Chair*	*Curious George Rides a Bike*	*Jamal's Busy Day*	*Go, Dog. Go!*
Song	"Shake Your Sillies out"	"Extra, Extra, Read All About It"	"On Top of Spaghetti"	"Twinkle, Twinkle, Traffic Light"
Week 40 — All About Food				
Dramatic Play	Garden/Farm	Grocery Store	Ice Cream Parlor/Sock Hop	Dinner Theater
Art	Vegetable Prints	Popcorn Letters	Ice Cream Cone Pictures	Watercolor Paintings
Group	Fruits and Vegetables	Counting to 20	Oddity Match	Act out a Story (The Wide-Mouth Frog)
Story	*The Surprise Garden*	*The Very Hungry Caterpillar*	*Ice Cream Soup*	*The Wide-Mouth Frog*
Song	"I Like to Eat Apples and Bananas"	"Peanut Butter and Jelly"	"1, 2, Bubble Gum Chew"	"If You're Happy and You Know It"

······································
: WEEKLY PLANNING GUIDE :
······································

	Dramatic Play	Art	Group	Story	Song
Monday *Suggested Props and Materials*	Beauty Salon/Barber Shop (Touch) *Beauty salon/barber shop scenario, salon chairs, pretend sink, telephone, appointment book, pencil, tables, curlers, combs, mirrors, pretend fingernail polish, pretend shampoo, towels, pretend hair dryer, shaving cream and rectangular plastic strips (for razors), smocks, cash register, money*	Fingerpaint with Shaving Cream *Shaving cream, formboards, wooden craft sticks*	Feely Box *Drawstring bags (or boxes), 10 to 20 toy objects contained in the bags (e.g., Nerf balls, spool, car, cup boat, bead, cotton ball, sandpaper, different types of plastic food)*	*Here Are My Hands*	"Teddy Bear, Teddy Bear, Turn Around"
Tuesday *Suggested Props and Materials*	Concert/Art in the Park (Hearing) *Park scenario, picnic area, bandstand area, music stand, musical instruments, micro-phones, baton, chairs for audience, arts and crafts display, play food, picnic baskets, concessions stand, pretend food, cash register, money*	Make Tambourines *Paper plates, dry beans or Cheerios, markers, stapler, tape, crepe paper streamers*	Sound Pattern Sequencing *Drum, keyboard (optional)*	*Polar Bear, Polar Bear, What Do You Hear?*	"The Ants Go Marching"
Wednesday *Suggested Props and Materials*	Pizza Parlor (Taste/Smell) *Pizza parlor scenario, pretend kitchen, restaurant area, dishes and cups, trays, soda pop dispenser, cash register, money, order form, pencils, menus, delivery van, English muffins, real pizza toppings, and micro-wave oven (optional)*	Paper Plate Pizza *Paper plates, cutouts for toppings, 3"–4" red circles for tomato sauce, yellow yarn for cheese*	Shape Review *Colored tape to make shape outlines (or draw outlines with chalk), variety of construction-paper shapes, small chalkboards and chalk*	*Pizza Party*	"I Wish I Were a Pepperoni Pizza"
Thursday *Suggested Props and Materials*	Movie/ Puppet Show (Sight) *Movie theater scenario, tickets, ticket booth, cash register, food items, TV monitor/VCR and movie, puppets, chairs and 8' × 5' tumbling mat (optional—fold mat to make risers for chairs)*	Mural *Large sheet of paper, smocks, tempera paint, paint cups, brushes, markers, appropriate cutout pictures, glue*	Act out a Story *(The Berenstain Bears Get Stage Fright)* *Story and props*	*The Berenstain Bears Get Stage Fright*	"Six Little Ducks"

NEWSLETTER

Vol. 1, No. 37

Date: _____

The Five Senses

Monday

Today the classroom will be full of busy barbers and beauticians. The children will shampoo, cut, and style hair during dramatic play. Then they will fingerpaint with shaving cream at the art center. *Here Are My Hands* is the story for today, and the group activity will be identifying items by touch. The theme song for music will be "Teddy Bear, Teddy Bear, Turn Around."

Tuesday

The children continue the senses theme today by listening to and making the sounds of music. They will enjoy a concert in the park where they can picnic as well as listen to the music (or be the musicians). In art, the children will create their own tambourines. At storytime, we will read *Polar Bear, Polar Bear, What Do You Hear?* The group activity will be listening to sound patterns and then repeating them in the correct sequence on a drum. "The Ants Go Marching" is this day's theme song.

Wednesday

This is the day for pizza parlor. The children will enjoy the taste and smell of pizza during dramatic play. In art, they will make paper plate pizzas. The story is *Pizza Party*. In group, the children will review different shapes, including triangle, circle, square, rectangle, and diamond. "I Wish I Were a Pepperoni Pizza" will be a featured song during music.

Thursday

The children will be learning about the sense of sight today in dramatic play. They will pretend to watch movies or a puppet show at the theater while enjoying movie snacks. Painting a mural is the activity in art. *The Berenstain Bears Get Stage Fright* is Thursday's story. In group, the children will act out the story. Our featured song will be "Six Little Ducks."

Monday

Dramatic Play	Art	Group	Story	Song
Beauty Salon/Barber Shop (Touch)	Fingerpaint with Shaving Cream	Feely Box	*Here Are My Hands*	"Teddy Bear, Teddy Bear, Turn Around"

DAILY PLANNING GUIDE

Language and Literacy Skills Facilitated

Vocabulary: *comb, brush, hair, wash, cut, set, curl, dry, blow-dry, fix, shave, shaving cream, emery board, customer, appointment*

Verb phrase structures: *curls her hair, is curling, curled, dries, is drying, dried, will dry, cuts, is cutting, cut*

Adjective/object descriptions: *soft/hard _____, wet/dry hair, cold/hot ___, long/short hair, rough/smooth ___*

Question structures: *what, how, where, when, who, what if, why, how many, which one*

Pronouns: *I, you, he, she, we, they, my, your, him, her, his, our, their, me, us, them*

Prepositions: *in, on, under, over, near, beneath, next to, beside, around, inside, outside*

Sounds: /k/ cut, back; /s/ set, cuts; /sh/ shave, brush; /l/ long, curl

Noting print has meaning: names on chairs and on cubbies, signs in dramatic play, words in books and on chalkboard

Noting sound–symbol associations: What sound does _____ start with?

Writing: letters, names, words

Social Skills Facilitated

Initiating interaction with peers and adults; responding to questions and requests from peers and adults

Negotiating with peers for toys and materials

Group cooperation: waiting for a turn in a group, taking a turn at the appropriate time

Cognitive Skills Facilitated

Problem-solving skills: how to fix hair

Classification skills: things found in a beauty shop

Sequencing skills: songs, stories

Narrative/story structure: labeling

Motor Skills Facilitated

Large motor: outdoor play activities—jumping, running, hopping, pedaling, climbing

Small motor: writing, drawing, gluing

DRAMATIC PLAY **Beauty Salon/Barber Shop (Touch)**

Type of Activity: Central

Objectives
1. Learn new, and employ familiar, vocabulary
2. Learn new, and employ a variety of, syntactic constructions
3. Interact with peers
4. Sequence familiar routines
5. Expand conceptual knowledge of the world

Settings
- Salon chair (use a highchair for dolls to sit in)
- Chairs (for children)
- Sink to "wash" hair
- Reception area with telephone, appointment book, and pencil or crayon
- Barber chair

Props
- Curlers and clips (put children's names on curlers and clips so they use only theirs, and disinfect at the end of play)
- Combs (put children's names on the combs so they use only theirs, and disinfect at the end of play)
- Mirrors
- Fingernail polish bottles (filled with water)
- Pretend shampoo and conditioner
- Pretend hairspray
- Pretend hair dryer (made out of two toilet paper rolls and a cottage cheese container, with a twisted pipe cleaner to represent the cord)
- Plastic strips (razors)
- Shaving cream
- Smocks (typically used when children paint)
- Pretend nail polish remover
- Nail files
- Towels
- Toy cash register
- Pretend money

Roles
- Customers
- Receptionist
- Beautician
- Barber
- Manicurist

General Description of Activity

Children play beauty/barber shop and get their hair shampooed, cut, dried, and styled. They also might get a manicure (hair salon) or a shave (barber shop). Children can use their fingers in a cutting motion to pretend to cut hair.

Verbal Productions

Level of linguistic complexity varies with the role or competency of the child playing the role.
- "I'm washing her hair" or "Wash hair"
- "Do you want your hair to be cut?" or "Cut?"
- "Your hair is wet" or "Wet"
- "Cut my hair, please" or "Cut hair"
- "He is shaving" or "He shaved"

Adult Facilitative Role

The adult is to facilitate role play and help expand language and literacy skills. Typical actions or strategies to use include

Playing a role: "I think I will cut my hair short."

Contrasting two sounds: "Do you mean 'fine' or 'sign?'"

Modeling a statement/vocabulary: "A manicure is when you get your nails filed with an emery board and then painted with fingernail polish."

Using a cloze procedure: "The emery board is rough, and the ribbon is _____(smooth)."

Providing confirmatory feedback: "You are right. The word is *hair*."

ART : **Fingerpaint with Shaving Cream**

Objectives
1. Express creativity
2. Develop small motor skills (e.g., drawing, painting, cutting, pasting)
3. Practice turn-taking skills
4. Converse with peers and adults

Materials
- Shaving cream
- Formboards
- Wooden craft sticks
- Other tools for "drawing" in the shaving cream

General Description of Activity

Put a dab of shaving cream on each child's formboard. The children can use their hands and fingers to smear the cream all over the board, then use their fingers to draw and write in the shaving cream. The children can also make abstract designs, make full handprints, or use their fingers to practice writing letters or numbers. Fingerpainting is a good excuse to get messy and gooey. Some children love this; others may need some coaxing to get their fingers dirty.

GROUP **Feely Box**

Objectives
1. Improve listening skills
2. Increase conceptual knowledge
3. Learn appropriate group-interaction skills
4. Practice turn-taking skills

Materials
- Boxes, one per group of children
- 10–20 toy objects in the boxes (e.g., Nerf ball, spool, car, cup, boat, bead, cotton ball, sandpaper, different types of plastic food)

General Description of Activity

Tell the children that this week they are going to be learning about different senses. Hold up a "feely" box that contains several objects. Tell the children that they are going to try to guess what an object is by using their sense of touch. To demonstrate, have a staff member put a hand into the box and, without looking, try to identify an object. He or she problem-solves out loud by saying something like "It feels sort of round, it is soft, I know—it is a Nerf ball!"

Group Participation

Invite one child to come to the front of the class and try to identify an object by feeling it in the box. The child makes a guess and then holds up the object so all can see. Other children come one at a time and try to identify the objects by touch. After identifying an object, the child can either put it back in the box or set it aside. In order to facilitate turn taking, have children do this activity in two or three small groups.

Variation

Instead of putting the object aside or back in the box after it has been identified, children could categorize the object and make piles for those that feel rough, smooth, sharp, sticky, and so on.

Summary/Transition Activity

Ask children, "What was easy and what was hard about guessing the object?" Then ask, "What sense were we using to guess the object?" Remind the children that the sense of touch is only one of the senses we have.

Tuesday

Dramatic Play	Art	Group	Story	Song
Concert/Art in the Park (Hearing)	Make Tambourines	Sound Pattern Sequencing	*Polar Bear, Polar Bear, What Do You Hear?*	"The Ants Go Marching"

DAILY PLANNING GUIDE

Language and Literacy Skills Facilitated

Vocabulary: *music, drum, instruments, picnic, barbecue, parade, march, fun, lemonade, three-legged race*

Verb phrase structures: *barbecu<u>es</u> hamburgers, <u>made</u> lemonade, cook<u>s</u>, cook<u>ed</u>, <u>is</u> march<u>ing</u>, march<u>ed</u>, play<u>ed</u> an instrument*

Adjective/object descriptions: *loud/soft music; little/big drum; red, white, and blue flag; spicy barbecue; sour lemonade*

Question structures: *what, how, where, when, who, what if, why, how many, which one*

Pronouns: *I, you, he, she, we, they, my, your, him, her, his, our, their, me, us, them*

Prepositions: *in, on, under, over, near, beneath, next to, beside, around, inside, outside*

Sounds: /l/ *lemonade, ba<u>ll</u>;* /r/ *<u>r</u>ace, hambu<u>r</u>ger, ca<u>r</u>;* /k/ *<u>c</u>ar, par<u>k</u>;* /f/ *<u>f</u>un, o<u>ff</u>*

Noting print has meaning: names on chairs and on cubbies, signs in dramatic play, words in books and on chalkboard

Noting sound–symbol associations: What sound does _____ start with?

Writing: letters, names, words

Social Skills Facilitated

Initiating interaction with peers and adults; responding to questions and requests from peers and adults

Negotiating with peers for toys and materials

Group cooperation: waiting for a turn in a group, taking a turn at the appropriate time

Cognitive Skills Facilitated

Problem-solving skills: how to play the instruments

Classification skills: things that make noise, different kinds of noises

Sequencing skills: songs, dramatic play (picnic), patterns

Narrative/story structure: repetitive line

Motor Skills Facilitated

Large motor: outdoor play activities—jumping, running, hopping, pedaling, climbing

Small motor: writing, drawing, gluing, cutting

DRAMATIC PLAY : **Concert/Art in the Park (Hearing)**

Type of Activity: Related

Objectives
1. Learn new, and employ familiar, vocabulary
2. Learn new, and employ a variety of, syntactic constructions
3. Interact with peers
4. Sequence familiar routines
5. Expand conceptual knowledge of the world

Settings
- A gazebo (marked off with masking tape)
- Trash can area
- Concession stands
- Picnic area

Props
- Trash cans
- Trash paper bags
- Music stand
- Musical instruments
- Microphones
- Baton (for the director)
- Chairs for audience

- Pretend food and picnic basket
- Pretend cash register
- Pretend money
- Lemonade (can have a real lemonade stand)
- Stuffed dogs
- Leashes

Roles
- Cleanup workers
- Band members
- Director

- Audience members
- Picnic goers
- Concession stand workers

General Description of Activity

A day in the park might include an outdoor concert and an art show. The children can play musical instruments or sell their art. The children could also go on a picnic, walk their dogs, or buy pretend food at a concession stand.

Verbal Productions

Level of linguistic complexity varies with the role or competency of the child playing the role.
- "Bobby will sing the 'Alphabet Song" or "Here's Bobby!"
- "Look at this one—lots of red! Would you like to buy it?" or "Buy this one"
- "He played the music too loudly!" or "Too loud"

Adult Facilitative Role

The adult is to facilitate role play and help expand language and literacy skills. Typical actions or strategies to use include

Playing a role: "I like to listen to the music in the park, but I'm thirsty, so let's go get a lemonade."

Event casting an adult's actions: "Look, Miss Jane is giving Suzie a lesson on playing the maracas. Now she is showing Sally how to play the drums. Now she is playing the guitar."

Asking an open question: "What do you want to do at the park?"

Expanding a child's utterance: "Play drums" to "He plays the drums."

Redirecting a child to a peer: "Go ask Ying if you can play the drums. Say, 'Can I play the drums with you?'"

ART **Make Tambourines**

Objectives
1. Express creativity
2. Develop small motor skills (e.g., drawing, painting, cutting, pasting)
3. Practice turn-taking skills
4. Converse with peers and adults

Materials
- Paper plates (at least two per child)
- Dry beans or other small items (e.g., Cheerios)
- Small containers to hold the beans
- Markers or crayons
- Stapler
- Tape (optional)
- Crepe paper streamers (optional)

General Description of Activity

Give each child two paper plates to use to create a tambourine. Have children decorate the bottom side of each plate with markers or crayons; the bottom of each plate will form the outer portions of the tambourine. After children finish decorating the plate, have them place a few dry beans or other small items (e.g., Cheerios) on the inside of one of the plates. They turn the other plate over, so that its bottom is facing upward, and put it on top of the first one. They then staple or tape the plates together along the rims (with assistance, if necessary). Additional decorations such as crepe paper streamers may be added.

GROUP : **Sound Pattern Sequencing**

Objectives

1. Improve listening skills
2. Increase ability to recognize and sequence patterns
3. Learn appropriate group-interaction skills
4. Practice turn-taking skills

Materials

- Drum
- Keyboard (optional)

General Description of Activity

Place a drum is placed in front of the children. Tap out a simple pattern while the children listen. Repeat the pattern while they listen again. One child is invited to come up to the front of the class and try to make the same pattern. (The child can be helped if necessary so that the sound pattern matches the teacher's.)

Group Participation

A different pattern is played and another child tries to match it. This continues until all the children have had at least one turn. The patterns can vary from two short taps to complicated patterns involving a series of taps grouped in two or three sequences. For example, one pattern might be *tap-tap-pause-tap*. Another might be *tap-tap-tap-pause-tap-tap*. Other sample patterns include the following:

Tap-tap (pause) *tap-tap*

Tap-tap-tap (pause) *tap*

Tap (pause) *tap-tap*

Loud tap (pause) *soft tap*

Two loud taps (pause) *two soft taps*

Variation

A keyboard can be used to set a rhythm and the children could clap to the rhythm.

Summary/Transition Activity

The teacher plays one more pattern and has the children clap the pattern, or the teacher can play a rhythm from a song that is to be sung during music time and have the children clap out that rhythm.

Wednesday

Dramatic Play	Art	Group	Story	Song
Pizza Parlor (Taste/Smell)	Paper Plate Pizza	Shape Review	*Pizza Party*	"I Wish I Were a Pepperoni Pizza"

DAILY PLANNING GUIDE

Language and Literacy Skills Facilitated

Vocabulary: *fast food, soft drinks, pizza, tomato sauce, cheese, cartons, cook, cashier, customer, order, pizza parlor, delivery*

Verb phrase structures: *place*s *an order, buy*s *a pizza, pay*s *money,* eat *out,* is *mak*ing *a pizza, serve*s*/serv*ed *the customer, choose*s *a drink,* are *mak*ing *pizzas*

Adjective/object descriptions: *large drink, small pizza, paper hat, red cup*

Question structures: *what, how, where, when, who, what if, why, how many, which one*

Pronouns: *I, you, he, she, we, they, my, your, him, her, his, our, their, me, us, them*

Prepositions: *in the cash register, on the plate, near the stove (in, on, under, over, near, beneath, next to, beside, around, inside, outside)*

Sounds: /p/ *p*izza *p*arlor, *p*a*p*er *p*late; /m/ *m*oney, *m*enus

Noting print has meaning: names on chairs and on cubbies, signs in dramatic play, words in books and on chalkboard

Noting sound–symbol associations: What sound does _____ start with?

Writing: letters, names, words

Social Skills Facilitated

Initiating interaction with peers and adults; responding to questions and requests from peers and adults

Negotiating with peers for toys and materials

Group cooperation: waiting for a turn in a group, taking a turn at the appropriate time

Cognitive Skills Facilitated

Problem-solving skills: setting up a restaurant, remembering items

Classification skills: things on a pizza

Sequencing skills: putting a pizza together, words to song

Narrative/story structure: adventure

Motor Skills Facilitated

Large motor: outdoor play activities—jumping, running, hopping, pedaling, climbing

Small motor: writing, drawing, gluing

DRAMATIC PLAY **Pizza Parlor (Taste/Smell)**

Type of Activity: Central

Objectives
1. Learn new, and employ familiar, vocabulary
2. Learn new, and employ a variety of, syntactic constructions
3. Interact with peers
4. Sequence familiar routines
5. Expand conceptual knowledge of the world

Settings
- Restaurant kitchen
- Dining area
- Counter
- Carry-out window
- Salad bar (optional)

Props
- Tables and chairs
- Menus
- Pretend pizzas (plastic facsimiles, or cardboard circles for pizza crusts; variety of construction paper cutouts for toppings, such as pepperoni, green peppers, and mushrooms; pieces of yellow yarn for cheese)
- Dishes and cups
- Trays
- Pretend soda pop dispenser
- Pretend cash register
- Pretend money
- Order form and pencils
- Delivery van (optional)
- Roads (area of floor marked with masking tape—optional)
- English muffins, real pizza toppings, and microwave oven (optional)

Roles
- Customers
- Waiters and waitresses
- Cashier
- Cooks
- Delivery van driver (optional)

General Description of Activity

Children run a pizza parlor. The waiter or waitress seats the guests and gives them menus. The guests order their pizzas, with various toppings, and possibly other items, such as spaghetti or bread sticks. Children who are the cooks must construct the pizzas, which are then taken to the customers by the waiter or waitress. A pizza delivery van can also be used to deliver pizzas to homes. Note: Real pizzas can be made at snack time by using English muffins as the crust. The children can add different toppings and cook the pizzas in a microwave oven.

Verbal Productions

Level of linguistic complexity varies with the role or competency of the child playing the role.
- "We have two kinds of pizza, pepperoni and cheese. Which do you want?" or "Which one?"
- "Cheese?" or "More pizza?"
- "You ate my pizza" or "My pizza!"
- "You bought two pizzas and I bought one" or "One pizza"

Adult Facilitative Role

The adult is to facilitate role play and help expand language and literacy skills. Typical actions or strategies to use include

Playing a role: "I am going to have a cheese pizza and a soda. What are you having?"

Modeling the reading of a menu: "The menu says *large pizza*."

Contrasting error and correct /pl/ blend: "Did you say peas or please?"

Using a cloze procedure: "Here is one pizza. Over there are _____ (pizzas)."

Expanding a child's utterance: "I make big pizza" "Yes, you made a big pizza. I made a big pizza, too."

ART **Paper Plate Pizza**

Objectives
1. Foster creativity
2. Foster small motor development (e.g., drawing, painting, cutting, pasting skills)
3. Practice turn-taking skills
4. Converse with peers and adults

Materials

- Paper plates
- Large red construction paper circles (tomato sauce)
- Gray construction paper mushrooms
- Green construction paper peppers
- White construction paper onions
- Small red circles (pepperoni)
- Glue sticks
- Yellow yarn for cheese

General Description of Activity

Children are to glue pizza ingredients on a paper plate crust to make their own pizza art. Ingredients are made out of construction paper. Children can paste red circles for tomato sauce and then paste mushrooms, green peppers, pepperoni, onions, and cheese (yellow yarn) on top of a paper plate to make their pizzas. They can also cut out their own ingredients.

Variation

Pizza could be served in dramatic play activities.

GROUP **Shape Review**

Objectives

1. Improve listening skills
2. Increase sequencing ability
3. Learn appropriate group-interaction skills
4. Practice turn-taking skills

Materials

- Colored tape to make shape outlines
- Variety of shapes out of construction paper
- Small chalkboards and chalk

General Description of Activity

From previous activities, circle, square, triangle, rectangle and diamond shapes should already be taped on the floor. Point to the different outlines on the floor and label each one (e.g., circle, square, triangle, rectangle, diamond). Ask a child to name his or her favorite shape. Stand in the outlined area of the shape named.

Group Participation

Ask different children to stand on a particular shape. Vary the difficulty of the requests by asking some children to find only the shape and others to find a shape of a particular size (large or small). Color can be included in the requests as well if tape of different colors was used to make the outlines (e.g., "Find the big red square"). The task can be made more challenging by having children place a hand in one shape area and a foot in another. It may be necessary to have children do this activity in smaller groups.

Variation

Give children individual whiteboards (or chalkboards) and ask them to draw the various shapes. You might also give children cutout shapes and ask them to place them inside the matching shapes on the floor.

Summary/Transition Activity

Review the shape labels by pointing to or standing in the outlined area as you identify them.

Thursday

Dramatic Play	Art	Group	Story	Song
Movie/Puppet Show (Sight)	Mural	Act out a Story (The Berenstain Bears Get Stage Fright)	The Berenstain Bears Get Stage Fright	"Six Little Ducks"

DAILY PLANNING GUIDE

Language and Literacy Skills Facilitated

Vocabulary: *movie, film, picture show, screen, ticket, watch, puppet, Oscar, Miss Piggy, dog, cat, popcorn, soft drink, actor, actress, costume, prop*

Verb phrase structures: <u>act</u> *like a dog,* <u>watch</u> *the film,* <u>act</u> *in the show,* <u>put</u> *on costumes*

Adjective/object descriptions: *good picture, pink piggy, noisy/quiet show, funny/sad puppet*

Question structures: *what, how, where, when, who, what if, why, how many, which one*

Pronouns: *I, you, he, she, we, they, my, your, him, her, his, our, their, me, us, them*

Prepositions: *in, on, under, over, near, beneath, next to, beside, around, inside, outside*

Sounds: /f/ <u>f</u>ix, o<u>ff</u>; /s/ <u>s</u>it, talk<u>s</u>; /l/ <u>l</u>ittle, be<u>ll</u>

Noting print has meaning: names on chairs and on cubbies, signs in dramatic play, words in books and on chalkboard

Noting sound–symbol associations: What sound does _____ start with?

Writing: letters, names, words

Social Skills Facilitated

Initiating interaction with peers and adults; responding to questions and requests from peers and adults

Negotiating with peers for toys and materials

Group cooperation: waiting for a turn in a group, taking a turn at the appropriate time

Cognitive Skills Facilitated

Problem-solving skills: how to act out the story, what to do with the props

Classification skills: things in a movie theater

Sequencing skills: story, songs

Narrative/story structure: adventure

Motor Skills Facilitated

Large motor: outdoor play activities—jumping, running, hopping, pedaling, climbing

Small motor: writing, drawing, gluing

DRAMATIC PLAY : **Movie/Puppet Show (Sight)**

Type of Activity: Related

Objectives
1. Learn new and employ familiar vocabulary
2. Learn new and employ a variety of syntactic constructions
3. Interact with peers
4. Sequence familiar routines
5. Expand conceptual knowledge of the world

Settings
- Ticket booth
- Concession stand
- Spectator seats
- Stage or puppet area

Props
- Tickets
- Cash register
- Chairs and mat for making risers
- Food items (e.g., pretend popcorn, candy, soft drinks)
- TV monitor/VCR and movie
- Puppets

Roles
- Cashier
- Ticket taker
- Customers
- Concession workers
- Puppeteers

General Description of Activity

Set up a movie theater with a ticket booth area, a spectator section, a concession area, and a stage. The children can purchase tickets, buy their popcorn and other food, find their seats, and prepare to watch a movie or puppet show. It is helpful if the spectator area is raised (this can be accomplished by folding over a tumbling mat and putting chairs on one level and a second row on a higher level). Set up a TV monitor and a short film for the children to watch. You could also add a puppet area—a shelf with a blanket thrown over it so that the children can use hand puppets on the shelf and hide behind the shelf while they are doing the puppet actions.

Verbal Productions

Level of linguistic complexity varies with the role or competency of the child playing the role.

- "I need tickets for three adults and two children, please" or "Tickets, please"
- "I'll be Big Bird, you be Elmo" or "Big Bird"
- "Do you want popcorn and a coke?" or "Popcorn?"
- "I watched that at my birthday party" or "Watch at party"

Adult Facilitative Role

The adult is to facilitate role play and help expand language and literacy skills. Typical actions or strategies to use include

Playing a role: "I like to play with puppets. My puppet is a little cat."

Modeling a statement/vocabulary: "A puppet is a kind of glove with a face and body. You can put it on your hand, and then you hide behind the table and just let your hand be seen. You can have the puppet talk by moving your fingers."

Identifying rhyming words: "The words *pup, cup,* and *up* all rhyme."

Using a cloze procedure: "The puppet's body feels soft, but the puppet's head feels _____(hard)."

Recasting a child's utterance (present progressive with third person singular): "He is playing" to "Yes, he plays with the puppet."

ART **Mural**

Objectives
1. Express creativity
2. Develop small motor skills (e.g., drawing, painting, cutting, pasting)
3. Practice turn-taking skills
4. Converse with peers and adults

Materials
- Large sheet of paper (e.g., 3' × 8')
- Masking tape (optional)
- Plastic or newsprint to protect the floor
- Smocks
- Tempera paint
- Paint cups
- Paintbrushes
- Crayons or markers (optional)
- Small bowls of water to rinse brushes
- Appropriate pictures to be pasted

General Description of Activity

Tape a large piece of paper to a wall, or lay it on the floor on top of plastic or newsprint. The children don smocks and paint pictures or designs on the paper using tempera paint. The children may choose to draw with crayons or markers instead of using tempera paint, or they may paste previously produced pictures on the mural. For example, a mountain mural might include a mountain range drawn onto the paper. The children can add snow on the top of the mountains, trees, different animals, a river, and so forth. The items could be drawn or different pictures could be pasted to the mural. Another example could be to illustrate a story such as the *Three Little Pigs* and have the teacher outline the figures and have the children paint them. Again, different houses could be drawn or pictures could be pasted to the mural.

Variation

If painting scenery for a program or for a dramatic play theme, outline the objects on the mural and have the children fill them in with paint. For example, you might outline a house or tree, and the children can add the colors to the outline.

GROUP **Act out a Story (*The Berenstain Bears Get Stage Fright*)**

Objectives
1. Improve listening skills
2. Improve sequencing ability
3. Increase knowledge of storytelling
4. Learn appropriate group-interaction skills
5. Practice turn-taking skills

Materials
- *The Berenstain Bears Get Stage Fright*
- Props for the story

General Description of Activity

Read *The Berenstain Bears Get Stage Fright*, or summarize it if children are familiar with the story.

Group Participation

Assign children roles from the story. Assure the children not chosen the first time that everyone will have a turn and that they have the very important job of being a good listening audience. Narrate the story as the children act it out. They should say as many of the lines as they can, with prompts given when needed. Repeat with new actors until all the children have had a turn.

Summary/Transition Activity

Compliment the children's acting, and ask children what other stories they would like to act out another day.

WEEKLY PLANNING GUIDE

	Dramatic Play	Art	Group	Story	Song
Monday *Suggested Props and Materials*	Office *Office scenario, desks, computer keyboards (or real computer setup), typewriters, hole punches, staplers, tape, envelopes, stationery, file folders, binders, telephones, paper, pencils, calendars*	Stamp Art *Construction paper, inkpads, rubber stamps, smocks, markers or crayons (optional)*	How Are ____ Alike? *Paper, things that hold paper together (stapler, paper clips, tape, folder, glue, rubber bands, binder clips, paper fasteners, etc.), things used to write (pen, marker, chalk, crayon, pencil, typewriter, etc.)*	*The ABC Mystery*	"My Hands" (fingerplay)
Tuesday *Suggested Props and Materials*	Department Store *Department store scenario, dressing rooms, elevator, clothes rack, clothes, bags, shoes, purses, toys, play money, cash registers*	Catalog Collage *Construction paper, scissors, catalogs*	ABC Bingo *ABC Bingo cards, bags, chips, large Bingo card*	*At the Mall*	"Mary Wore Her Red Dress"
Wednesday *Suggested Props and Materials*	Construction Site *Construction site scenario, cardboard construction area, tools, hardhats, wooden pegs, roof to shingle, shingles, wallpaper, glue, paintbrushes, sketch of scenery*	Crayon Rubbings: Tools *Paper, tool cutouts, crayons with paper removed*	Introduction to Unifix Cubes *10 Unifix cubes (or small blocks in sets of 10) per child, small mats or boards (at least one per child)*	*Stop Those Painters*	"Building Song" (fingerplay)
Thursday *Suggested Props and Materials*	Veterinarian's Office *Veterinary scenario, chairs, reception desk, play telephone, doctor kits, scrubs, stuffed animals, X-ray machine, cash register, play money*	Doghouse and Dog Prints *Paper, large paper squares to make a doghouse, paper triangles to form a roof, markers, paint, shallow dishes to hold the paint, inkpads (optional)*	Bring Your Favorite "Stuffy" *Variety of stuffed animals (have some available for children who do not bring one from home)*	*Have You Seen My Cat?*	"Little Ducky Duddle"

NEWSLETTER

Vol. 1, No. 38

Date: _____

Places People Work

Monday

The dramatic play area will become an office today. The children will answer the phones, type on computers, and write letters. The art activity will be using stamps to make designs. *The ABC Mystery* is our story. During group time, the children will discuss how different office items are alike. Our fingerplay is "My Hands."

Tuesday

On Tuesday, the dramatic play area will become a department store. The children will help customers with their shopping and will be the customers as well. In art, the children will make a catalog collage. *At the Mall* will be our featured storybook. During group time, the children will play ABC Bingo. "Mary Wore Her Red Dress" will be our featured song.

Wednesday

The children will spend their day working at a construction site. In dramatic play, they will use hammers, saws, and other tools to experience activities that builders do. In art, the children will make rubbings with tool cutouts. Our story today is *Stop Those Painters*. During group time, children will learn about Unifix cubes. The "Building Song" will be our special music activity.

Thursday

Today the dramatic play setting will be a veterinarian's office. The children can be the vet, the owners of the pets, or the receptionist/assistant. In art, children will make a doghouse and dog prints. *Have You Seen My Cat?* is our story for the day. During group time, children will talk about their favorite stuffed animal (children can bring their favorite "stuffy" from home). Our song for the day is "Little Ducky Duddle."

Monday

Dramatic Play	Art	Group	Story	Song
Office	Stamp Art	How Are ___ Alike?	*The ABC Mystery*	"My Hands" *(fingerplay)*

DAILY PLANNING GUIDE

Language and Literacy Skills Facilitated

Vocabulary: *office, mail, letter, typewriter, computer, bills, tape, paper clip, stapler, three-hole punch, file, envelope, file cabinet, secretary, telephone, paste, folder, glue, copier, adding machine*

Verb phrase structures: *is/was typing, types, typed, Who's typing? I am, punching, punches, punched, is/was calling, calls, called*

Adjective/object descriptions: *fast/slow typing, big/little ___, two-hole/three-hole punch*

Question structures: *what, how, where, when, who, what if, why, how many, which one*

Pronouns: *I, you, he, she, we, they, my, your, him, her, his, our, their, me, us, them*

Prepositions: *in, on, under, over, near, beneath, next to, beside, around, inside, outside*

Sounds: /t/ *type, computer, letter, at;* /k/ *call, ticket, back;* /l/ *lick, calling, bill*

Noting print has meaning: names on chairs and on cubbies, signs in dramatic play, words in books and on chalkboard

Noting sound–symbol associations: What sound does _____ start with?

Writing: letters, names, words

Social Skills Facilitated

Initiating interaction with peers and adults; responding to questions and requests from peers and adults

Negotiating with peers for toys and materials

Group cooperation: waiting for a turn in a group, taking a turn at the appropriate time

Cognitive Skills Facilitated

Problem-solving skills: What does an office worker do?

Classification skills: things in an office

Sequencing skills: story, songs, alphabet

Narrative/story structure: adventure

Motor Skills Facilitated

Large motor: outdoor play activities—jumping, running, hopping, pedaling, climbing

Small motor: writing, drawing, gluing, stapling, cutting

DRAMATIC PLAY : **Office**

Type of Activity: Related

Objectives
1. Learn new, and employ familiar, vocabulary
2. Learn new, and employ a variety of, syntactic constructions
3. Interact with peers
4. Sequence familiar routines
5. Expand conceptual knowledge of the world

Settings
- Offices
- Reception area
- Break room area
- Conference room
- Elevator

Props
- Desks and chairs
- Play telephones
- Paper
- Rubber bands
- Pretend (or real) stapler
- Lists
- Folders

- Computers, typewriters, or keyboards
- Envelopes
- Stamps and scale
- Pencils or crayons
- Wastebasket
- Mop and broom
- Pretend coffeemaker

Roles
- Receptionist
- Office workers
- Boss
- Custodian

General Description of Activity

Children pretend to be people who work in an office. They might use computers or typewriters to write letters and reports. They can sit at a desk and answer a telephone, have meetings, make notes, address and weigh envelopes, staple papers together, and put papers in file folders or notebooks. They might dictate notes to other office workers, or play a receptionist who answers the telephone and makes appointments.

Verbal Productions

Level of linguistic complexity varies with the role or competency of the child playing the role.
- "Here's your file" or "Need file"
- "I want a turn on the computer now" or "My turn"
- "He typed a *J* for my name" or "*J*"
- "She stapled all of the papers" or "Staple papers"
- "That letter needs a stamp" or "Need stamp"

Adult Facilitative Role

The adult is to facilitate role play and help expand language and literacy skills. Typical actions or strategies to use include

Playing a role: "I have to work on the computer. Then I will file these papers."

Modeling phonological awareness: "Yes, the words *type, toe, table,* and *tea* all begin with the /t/ sound."

Expanding a child's utterance and providing corrective feedback: "Them type computer" to "They type on the computer."

Providing confirmatory feedback: "That's right, that is the biggest desk."

ART · **Stamp Art**

Objectives
1. Express creativity
2. Develop small motor skills (e.g., drawing, painting, cutting, pasting)
3. Practice turn-taking skills
4. Converse with peers and adults

Materials

- 8½" × 11" sheets of construction paper
- Inkpads
- Rubber stamps
- Smocks
- Markers or crayons (optional)

General Description of Activity

Have children put on smocks before participating in this activity, and give each child a sheet of 8½" × 11" construction paper. Place a variety of inkpads and rubber stamps on the art table. The children use the stamps and ink to create scenes on their papers (e.g., scenes of dinosaurs, farm animals, trucks, cars). Children may use markers or crayons to further decorate their pictures if they wish (e.g., by adding trees, volcanoes, barns, houses).

GROUP : **How Are _____ Alike?**

Objectives

1. Improve listening skills
2. Increase conceptual knowledge
3. Learn appropriate group-interaction skills
4. Practice turn-taking skills

Materials

- Paper
- Stapler
- Paper clips
- Other objects that hold paper together (e.g., tape, folder, glue, rubber bands, binder clips, paper fasteners)
- Objects used to write (e.g., pen, marker, chalk, crayon, pencil, typewriter)

General Description of Activity

Place a stapler and a paper clip in front of the children, and ask them what is alike about the two items. Help the children determine that both can be used to hold paper together. Ask a child to come to the front of the group to demonstrate how each item works to hold paper together.

Group Participation

Add a variety of other objects to the display. Ask the children to decide whether each one can be used to hold paper together. The children should demonstrate how paper could be held together with each item. (This demonstration is particularly important if other children question whether an item really holds paper together.) After all of the items have been discussed and classified, note that the rejected items can all be used to write. Other office items can also be classified according to function. For example, some items are used to cut (e.g., scissors, hole punch) or to transfer messages (e.g., phone, computer e-mail, notes).

Variation

Note that items can be alike in function even though they look quite different. For example, a paper clip and a stapler do not look similar to each other, but they perform similar purposes.

Summary/Transition Activity

List the items that hold paper together and also those that can be used to write. A vertical line can be drawn between the two lists.

Tuesday

Dramatic Play	Art	Group	Story	Song
Department Store	Catalog Collage	ABC Bingo	*At the Mall*	"Mary Wore Her Red Dress"

DAILY PLANNING GUIDE

Language and Literacy Skills Facilitated

Vocabulary: *shopping, mall, department store, salesclerks, cash register, money, clothes, shoes, pants, dress, hangers*

Verb phrase structures: *shops, is shopping, shopped, pays, paid, tries on, tried on*

Adjective/object descriptions: *big/small _____, pretty _____, too tight, too big, too _____*

Question structures: *what, how, where, when, who, what if, why, how many, which one*

Pronouns: *I, you, he, she, we, they, my, your, him, her, his, our, their, me, us, them*

Prepositions: *in, on, under, over, near, beneath, next to, beside, around, inside, outside*

Sounds: /f/ *find, off;* /k/ *cash, jacket, sack;* /l/ *little, mall*

Noting print has meaning: names on chairs and on cubbies, signs in dramatic play, words in books and on chalkboard

Noting sound–symbol associations: What sound does _____ start with?

Writing: letters, names, words

Social Skills Facilitated

Initiating interaction with peers and adults; responding to questions and requests from peers and adults

Negotiating with peers for toys and materials

Group cooperation: waiting for a turn in a group, taking a turn at the appropriate time

Cognitive Skills Facilitated

Problem-solving skills: how to make a fabric collage, what to buy

Classification skills: letters of the alphabet

Sequencing skills: song, story, buying things at a store

Narrative structure: adventure

Motor Skills Facilitated

Large motor: outdoor play activities—jumping, running, hopping, pedaling, climbing

Small motor: writing, drawing, gluing

DRAMATIC PLAY **Department Store**

Type of Activity: Central

Objectives
1. Learn new, and employ familiar, vocabulary
2. Learn new, and employ a variety of, syntactic constructions
3. Interact with peers
4. Sequence familiar routines
5. Expand conceptual knowledge of the world

Settings

- Department store
- Counters and racks
- Shelves and other display areas
- Dressing rooms
- Check-out area
- Elevator (optional)

Props

- Clothes, including shoes, belts, and ties
- Hangers
- Purses
- Mirror
- Pretend cash register
- Pretend money
- Pretend credit cards

Roles

- Clerks
- Customers (dolls may be included for children)
- Custodians
- Cashiers

General Description of Activity

Children shop at a department store, choosing from a variety of items, including clothes. They can try on the clothes and purchase them. Store clerks can help the customers in purchasing the clothes and in hanging up clothes that are tried on but not purchased. Cashiers can take the customers' money or credit cards.

Verbal Productions

Level of linguistic complexity varies with the role or competency of the child playing the role.

- "This dress is too big. I need a smaller size" or "Too big"
- "He is working at the cash register now" or "He there"
- "She has had a long turn. I want a turn now" or "My turn"

Adult Facilitative Role

The adult is to facilitate role play and help expand language and literacy skills. Typical actions or strategies to use include

Playing a role: "I want to get a new pair of shoes. I want a red pair of shoes."

Redirecting a child to a peer: "Ask Emma for a turn on the cash register. Say, 'May I have a turn, please?'"

Recasting a present tense with past tense irregular form: "She wears a dress to go to the store" to "She wore the same dress yesterday."

Contrasting /s/ with /sl/: "Did you say 'side' or 'slide?'"

Redirecting a child to a peer: "Go ask Mary if you can have a turn trying on the clothes. Say, 'May I have a turn, please?'"

ART Catalog Collage

Objectives

1. Express creativity
2. Develop small motor skills (e.g., drawing, painting, cutting, pasting)
3. Practice turn-taking skills
4. Converse with peers and adults

Materials

- Construction paper
- Scissors
- Catalogs

General Description of Activity

Children will cut out pictures of clothes and other items from a catalog. The children then paste these pictures on construction paper. Children can choose from a variety of pictures.

GROUP **ABC Bingo**

Objectives
1. Improve listening skills
2. Improve sequencing ability
3. Learn appropriate group-interaction skills
4. Practice turn-taking skills

Materials
- Large replica of Bingo card
- Bag of alphabet letters (either all uppercase or all lowercase)
- Alphabet Bingo cards (either all uppercase or all lowercase)
- Markers or chips with container

General Description of Activity

Hold up a large Bingo card with letters of the alphabet in the columns. Reach into the bag holding the 26 letters and pull out one letter. Announce the letter to the children as you hold it up. Then place a chip or marker on that letter on the card. Explain that the group is going to play the Bingo game, and when each child or group of children has markers in a line, either across or diagonal, they are to shout "BINGO!"

Group Participation

Hand out a Bingo card and markers to each child or to a group of children. Pull out a letter and announce and show it to the children. Children who have that letter on their card place a marker on it. Continue to announce the letters until someone shouts "BINGO!" If time permits, play the game again.

Variation 1

Play the game until everyone has won the game or until someone's whole card is covered with markers.

Variation 2

Use both upper- and lowercase letters on the card and in the bag.

Summary/Transition Activity

Have the children place the Bingo cards in the box and the markers in the container. Review the alphabet one more time. The children can sing the alphabet song (optional).

Wednesday

Dramatic Play	Art	Group	Story	Song
Construction Site	Crayon Rubbings: Tools	Introduction to Unifix Cubes	*Stop Those Painters*	"Building Song" (fingerplay)

DAILY PLANNING GUIDE

Language and Literacy Skills Facilitated

Vocabulary: *construction, build, building, hammer, nail, fix, make, work, hardhat, safety, paint, screw, saw*

Verb phrase structures: *is building, constructed, built, hammered, Who is building? I am, makes, carries, carried*

Adjective/object descriptions: *large/small _____, heavy/light _____, hard/soft material*

Question structures: *what, how, where, when, who, what if, why, how many, which one*

Pronouns: *I, you, he, she, we, they, my, your, him, her, his, our, their, me, us, them*

Prepositions: *in, on, under, over, near, beneath, next to, beside, around, inside, outside*

Sounds: /f/ *fix, fun, off;* /s/ *size, walks;* /k/ *construct, can, make*

Noting print has meaning: names on chairs and on cubbies, signs in dramatic play, words in books and on chalkboard

Noting sound–symbol associations: What sound does _____ start with?

Writing: letters, names, words

Social Skills Facilitated

Initiating interaction with peers and adults; responding to questions and requests from peers and adults

Negotiating with peers for toys and materials

Group cooperation: waiting for a turn in a group, taking a turn at the appropriate time

Cognitive Skills Facilitated

Problem-solving skills: how to make a building

Classification skills: tools used to construct things

Sequencing skills: songs, steps in building, stories

Narrative/story structure: adventure

Motor Skills Facilitated

Large motor: outdoor play activities—jumping, running, hopping, pedaling, climbing

Small motor: writing, drawing, gluing, pounding

DRAMATIC PLAY **Construction Site**

Type of Activity: Related

Objectives
1. Learn new, and employ familiar, vocabulary
2. Learn new, and employ a variety of, syntactic constructions
3. Interact with peers
4. Sequence familiar routines
5. Expand conceptual knowledge of the world

Settings
- Street (area of the floor marked with masking tape) lined with houses made from a variety of materials (e.g., blocks, cardboard)

Props
- Playhouse
- Cardboard box additions that can be taped to the playhouse
- LEGOs
- Blocks
- Play bricks
- Paper strips of various colors for roof or siding
- Glue

- Tools (e.g., plastic hammers, wrenches, saws, screwdrivers, screws)
- Tool belts
- Pegs for pounding (wooden clothespins that can be pounded into cardboard)
- Play hardhats
- Masking tape

Roles
- Carpenters
- Architects
- Homeowners
- Other construction workers

General Description of Activity

Children participate in a construction/repair dramatic play involving putting together different materials to make buildings. A variety of materials can be used. One area can be set up for constructing buildings with LEGOs or other blocks. Another area can be designated for a new addition to the playhouse (using big boxes). A third area can utilize play bricks and boxes to make another house. The children can problem-solve how to construct houses or apartments by rearranging the boxes, bricks, and blocks. (Some of the houses could be doll-size; others could be large enough for the children to play in).

Houses may also need to be repaired. Children can replace a roof by making "shingles" out of paper bag strips. The strips could be laid on top of cardboard. (You might suggest that children start at the outer edge and overlay the shingles so that "rain" will roll off the roof and not under the shingles.) The children can put new siding on a house by using strips of colored paper and glue, and they could even put up wallpaper on the inside of a house.

Verbal Productions

Level of linguistic complexity varies with the role or competency of the child playing the role.
- "I'm building a big house" or "Me build house"
- "We need to make that side higher. Call the carpenter" or "Higher"
- "Look, I pounded the nail into the wall" or "Look"

Adult Facilitative Role

The adult is to facilitate role play and help expand language and literacy skills. Typical actions or strategies to use include

Playing a role: "I want to fix the roof. The shingle is coming loose. Do you want to help?"

Using a cloze procedure: "This window is broken, and this window is _____(not broken)."

Expanding a child's utterance: "He want paint" to "Yes, he wants to paint the house."

Modeling a statement/vocabulary: "Sandpaper is used to make things smooth. You rub the paper over the wood until it is smooth."

Modeling the reading of a sign: "The sign says *construction site*."

ART : **Crayon Rubbings: Tools**

Objectives
1. Express creativity
2. Develop small motor skills (e.g., drawing, painting, cutting, pasting)
3. Practice turn-taking skills
4. Converse with peers and adults

Materials
- Newsprint
- Cardboard tool cutouts
- Other cutouts
- Crayons with paper removed
- Container to hold crayons

General Description of Activity

Cut outlines of various tools from cardboard. Children place these cutouts under a sheet of newsprint and rub a crayon (laid flat on the paper) back and forth on the paper to slowly reveal the shape underneath the paper. A variety of other cutouts can be used to add to the picture (e.g., vehicle shapes, animal shapes).

GROUP **Introduction to Unifix Cubes**

Objectives
1. Improve listening skills
2. Increase knowledge about counting and grouping into sets
3. Learn appropriate group-interaction skills
4. Practice turn-taking skills

Materials
- 10 Unifix cubes (or small blocks in sets of 10) per child
- Small mats or boards (at least one per child)

General Description of Activity

Hold up 10 interlocked Unifix cubes and shows the class how the cubes come apart. Separate them, counting them one by one. Give each child 10 cubes and a mat or board on which to lay them.

Group Participation

Have the children count their cubes while laying them, one at a time, on the mat. Then have them arrange them in groups of two. The children should note how many groups of two there are. Ask the children to do other groupings (e.g., "How many groups of three can you make? Of four?"). Encourage children to experiment with forming different groups. (Some of the children may just play with the cubes; however, you can periodically count the number of cubes the child has laid out).

Summary/Transition Activity

Ask children to link all of their cubes. Have the class count their cubes together, making sure everyone still has 10 cubes. Have children put the cubes back into the box.

Thursday

Dramatic Play	Art	Group	Story	Song
Veterinarian's Office	Doghouse and Dog Prints	Bring Your Favorite "Stuffy"	*Have You Seen My Cat?*	"Little Ducky Duddle"

DAILY PLANNING GUIDE

Language and Literacy Skills Facilitated

Vocabulary: *dog, cats, birds, gerbils, Dalmatians, pets, sick, veterinarian, shot, bandage, medicine, phone, appointment, fleas, rabies shot*

Verb phrase structures: *gives a shot, is taking the pet to the vet, fed the dog, gave medicine, petted the dog, took an X ray*

Adjective/object descriptions: *examining table, high fever, sick cat, yellow cat, big dog, little rabbit*

Question structures: *what, how, where, when, who, what if, why, how many, which one*

Pronouns: *I, you, he, she, we, they, my, your, him, her, his, our, their, me, us, them*

Prepositions: *in, on, under, over, near, beneath, next to, beside, around, inside, outside*

Sounds: /v/ *vet, gave;* /f/ *fed, fever, off;* /r/ *rabbit, far*

Noting print has meaning: names on chairs and on cubbies, signs in dramatic play, words in books and on chalkboard

Noting sound–symbol associations: What sound does _____ start with?

Writing: letters, names, words

Social Skills Facilitated

Initiating interaction with peers and adults; responding to questions and requests from peers and adults

Negotiating with peers for toys and materials

Group cooperation: waiting for a turn in a group, taking a turn at the appropriate time

Cognitive Skills Facilitated

Problem-solving skills: how to take care of pets

Classification skills: equipment and instruments a veterinarian uses

Sequencing skills: songs, stories

Narrative/story structure: adventure

Motor Skills Facilitated

Large motor: outdoor play activities—jumping, running, hopping, pedaling, climbing

Small motor: writing, drawing, gluing, cutting

DRAMATIC PLAY **Veterinarian's Office**

Type of Activity: Central

Objectives
1. Learn new, and employ familiar, vocabulary
2. Learn new, and employ a variety of, syntactic constructions
3. Interact with peers
4. Sequence familiar routines
5. Expand conceptual knowledge of the world

Settings
- Reception/waiting area
- Examining rooms
- Cages/kennels

Props
- Chairs in the reception area
- Reception desk
- Play telephone
- Doctor kit collage
- White coats
- Stuffed animals
- Pet food
- X-ray machine
- Chalk pictures (simulating X-rays)
- Play cash register
- Play money

Roles
- Veterinarians
- Receptionist
- Customers
- Animals
- Kennel attendants

General Description of Activity

Children bring their sick or injured animals to the veterinarian for treatment. There might be a waiting room set up, with a receptionist to assist pet owners. The veterinarian's office might include an examining table, a sink, pet supplies, medicines, syringes, cotton balls, and other medical supplies. There might be cages for animals who must stay overnight.

Verbal Productions

Level of linguistic complexity varies with the role or competency of the child playing the role.
- "What is wrong with your cat?" or "What matter?"
- "Cat sick" or "He needs a shot"
- "Your dog needs some stitches" or "Need stitches"
- "Your cat has fleas and needs a flea bath," "Fleas," or "Needs bath"
- "The doctor will see you now" or "You're next"

Adult Facilitative Role

The adult is to facilitate role play and help expand language and literacy skills. Typical actions or strategies to use include

Playing a role: "My cat has ear mites. He needs to get some medicine."

Identifying rhyming words: "The words *vet, pet, let*, and *met* all rhyme."

Asking an open question: "What's the matter with your dog?"

Providing confirmatory feedback: "Yes, that is the big gray cat."

Redirecting a child to a peer: "Ask Joe if you can have the stethoscope. Say, 'Can I have a turn, please?'"

ART **Doghouse and Dog Prints**

Objectives
1. Express creativity
2. Develop small motor skills (e.g., drawing, painting, cutting, pasting)
3. Practice turn-taking skills
4. Converse with peers and adults

Materials
- Paper
- Large paper squares to make a doghouse
- Paper triangles to form a roof
- Markers
- Paint
- Shallow dishes to hold paint
- Inkpads (optional)

General Description of Activity

Children paste squares and triangles on a piece of paper to make a doghouse. Then they make "dog prints" with tempera paint by dipping the tips of their fingers and thumb into the paint and pressing on the paper. (Ink pads could be used instead of paint.) The children can also draw dogs or other animals. The children can also add other items such as people, trees, and sun.

GROUP : Bring Your Favorite "Stuffy"

Objectives
1. Improve listening skills
2. Increase conceptual knowledge
3. Learn appropriate group-interaction skills
4. Practice turn-taking skills

Materials
- Variety of stuffed animals (have some available for those children who do not bring one)

General Description of Activity

Hold up a favorite stuffed animal and ask the children if they can guess the name. After a few guesses, tell the children the animal's name and why you like your "stuffy."

Group Participation

Have each child, in turn, show his or her favorite stuffed animal to the group and tell a little bit about it. Let children who have not brought an animal from home choose one from the classroom.

Variation

Do this activity in smaller groups.

Summary/Transition Activity

Have the children group the animals according to type (e.g., bears in one pile).

```
................................................
:          WEEKLY PLANNING GUIDE                :
................................................
```

	Dramatic Play	Art	Group	Story	Song
Monday *Suggested Props and Materials*	Babysitting *Babysitter scenario, play stove, refrigerator, tables, chair, dolls, doll highchairs, dishes, bottles, doll beds, blankets, pillow, baby carriage, bathtub, pretend soap*	Tissue Paper Collage *Precut forms, glue, 1" tissue paper squares (several colors), pencils or crayons*	Size Comparisons (Big, Medium, Little) *Big tub, little tub, medium-sized tub, 15 groups of items of different sizes*	*Peter's Chair*	"Shake Your Sillies out"
Tuesday *Suggested Props and Materials*	Newspaper Route *Newspaper carrier scenario, at least two to three house areas with a "porch," paper bag, carrier bags, rubber bands, comics, newspapers*	Newspaper Collage *Strips of paper to make comic strip, scissors to cut out comics, newspapers, sheets of paper with columns*	Make a Class Newsletter *Large sheet of paper, markers, pictures (optional)*	*Curious George Rides a Bike*	"Extra, Extra, Read All About It"
Wednesday *Suggested Props and Materials*	Fast-Food Job *Fast-food restaurant scenario, counters, drink counter, hamburgers, french fries, other pretend food, cash register(s), play money, dishes, soda pop dispenser, menu, trays, walkie-talkie, pretend cars*	Playdough *Playdough, cookie cutters, plastic knives, rolling pins*	Addition with Unifix Cubes *Unifix cubes, whiteboard, markers, eraser, paper strips similar to Unifix cubes (optional)*	*Jamal's Busy Day*	"On Top of Spaghetti"
Thursday *Suggested Props and Materials*	Work on Cars *Cars, car track, mechanic tools, car wash scene, cars for painting, story props*	Car Track Painting *Paper, small cars, tempera paint, shallow dishes to hold paint*	Review Numbers 1–20 *Number lines from 1–10 and 11–20, two sets of number cards from 1–20, 1–100 number chart, whiteboard, markers*	*Go, Dog. Go!*	"Twinkle, Twinkle, Traffic Light"

MY NOTES

NEWSLETTER

Vol. 1, No. 39

Date: _____

Things Big Kids Do

Monday

What a fun week for the children! They will pretend to be teenagers. They will be babysitters during dramatic play and take care of babies and children. In art, they will make tissue paper collages. The story will be *Peter's Chair*. During group time, we will focus on different sizes—little, medium, and big. Our song for today is "Shake Your Sillies out."

Tuesday

This is another great day to learn about jobs for big kids. The children will be newspaper carriers. They will roll newspapers and deliver them to their customers. In art, the children will create a newspaper collage with comics. Our Tuesday story is *Curious George Rides a Bike*. During group time, we will write a class "newspaper" story. Our song is "Extra, Extra, Read All About It."

Wednesday

In dramatic play today, the children will be fast-food workers. They will cook food and sell it to hungry people. The food theme continues in art, where the children will make "food" items out of playdough. The story for Wednesday is *Jamal's Busy Day*. Group time will focus on addition activities with Unifix cubes. "On Top of Spaghetti" is the featured song for today.

Thursday

Teenagers like cars, and today the children will work on cars. They will pretend to be mechanics and fix cars, and they could also take their cars to a car show. At art, children will make car track paintings. Our story is *Go, Dog. Go!* During group time, children will review numbers *1–20*. They might even practice writing the numbers. Our featured song is "Twinkle, Twinkle, Traffic Light."

Monday

Dramatic Play	Art	Group	Story	Song
Babysitting	Tissue Paper Collage	Size Comparisons (Big, Medium, Little)	*Peter's Chair*	"Shake Your Sillies out"

DAILY PLANNING GUIDE

Language and Literacy Skills Facilitated

Vocabulary: *sitter, babysitter, babies, bath, story, highchair, crib, spoon, knife, fork, play, cry, feed, bottle, diaper*

Verb phrase structures: <u>is</u> crying, cr<u>ies</u>, cr<u>ied</u>, <u>will</u> cry, play<u>s</u>, play<u>ed</u>, eat<u>s</u>, <u>ate</u>, <u>has</u> <u>eaten</u>, sleep<u>s</u>, slept

Adjective/object descriptions: *happy baby, crying baby, cute baby, hungry baby, wet baby, funny toy*

Question structures: *what, how, where, when, who, what if, why, how many, which one*

Pronouns: *I, you, he, she, we, they, my, your, him, her, his, our, their, me, us, them*

Prepositions: *in, on, under, over, near, beneath, next to, beside, around, inside, outside*

Sounds: /k/ <u>c</u>over, ba<u>ck</u>; /t/ <u>t</u>op, si<u>tt</u>er, sa<u>t</u>; /f/ <u>f</u>our, o<u>f</u>ten, o<u>ff</u>

Noting print has meaning: names on chairs and on cubbies, signs in dramatic play, words in books and on chalkboard

Noting sound–symbol associations: What sound does _____ start with?

Writing: letters, names, words

Social Skills Facilitated

Initiating interaction with peers and adults; responding to questions and requests from peers and adults

Negotiating with peers for toys and materials

Group cooperation: waiting for a turn in a group, taking a turn at the appropriate time

Cognitive Skills Facilitated

Problem-solving skills: how to take care of babies

Classification skills: things that are big, medium-sized, and little

Sequencing skills: songs, story

Narrative/story structure: adventure

Motor Skills Facilitated

Large motor: outdoor play activities—jumping, running, hopping, pedaling, climbing

Small motor: writing, drawing, gluing, constructing

DRAMATIC PLAY **Babysitting**

Type of Activity: Central

Objectives
1. Learn new, and employ familiar, vocabulary
2. Learn new, and employ a variety of, syntactic constructions
3. Interact with peers
4. Sequence familiar routines
5. Expand conceptual knowledge of the world

Settings
- House(s)
- Park (optional)

Props
- Play stove
- Play refrigerator
- Tables and chairs
- Highchairs
- Cupboards, dishes, utensils, and bottles
- Play food
- Beds, blankets, and pillows
- Dolls
- Dolls' clothes
- Books
- Baby carriage
- Play bathtub
- Washcloths and towels
- Pretend soap
- Bath toys (e.g., rubber duck)

Roles
- Babysitters
- Children
- Babies
- Parents

General Description of Activity

Children act as babysitters and take care of babies and children. They might feed and bathe the children, read them stories, play with them, take them for walks, and put them to bed.

Verbal Productions

Level of linguistic complexity varies with the role or competency of the child playing the role.

- "It's time for bed, now" or "Bed, now"

- "The baby needs a bottle. Please get it from the table" or "Bottle!"

- "First, I'll read you the story, and then you go to bed" or "Story, bed"

Adult Facilitative Role

The adult is to facilitate role play and help expand language and literacy skills. Typical actions or strategies to use include

Playing a role: "I am taking care of two children. One is a baby and one is a little girl."

Event casting an adult's actions: "I am getting a bottle ready for the baby. Now I am fixing supper for the little girl. She likes cheese sandwiches and milk. Oh no, the baby is crying."

Expanding a child's utterance: "Feed baby" to "He feeds the baby the bottle."

Asking an open question: "How do we get the baby to stop crying?"

Contrasting two sounds: "Did you say 'sit' or 'fit?'"

ART **Tissue Paper Collage**

Objectives
1. Express creativity
2. Develop small motor skills (e.g., drawing, painting, cutting, pasting)
3. Practice turn-taking skills
4. Converse with peers and adults

Materials
- Precut construction paper shapes (e.g., fish, flowers)
- Paste or glue
- 1" tissue paper squares in several colors
- Pencils or crayons

General Description of Activity

Children crush the 1" pieces of tissue paper and paste them onto a precut construction paper form. One way to crush the paper is to wrap it around the eraser end of a pencil (or one end of a crayon)

and push it off onto glue or paste that is already on the form. Or children can just crumple the squares and then paste them on the paper. When the form is completely covered, the result is a three-dimensional picture, or a picture with texture.

GROUP **Size Comparisons (Big, Medium, Little)**

Objectives
1. Improve listening skills
2. Increase conceptual knowledge
3. Learn appropriate group-interaction skills
4. Practice turn-taking skills

Materials
- Big tub
- Little tub
- Medium-size tub
- 15 groups of items of different sizes

General Description of Activity

Place a big, a medium-size, and a little tub in front of the children. Hold up a big object, a medium-size object, and a little object (e.g., a big toy horse, a medium-size toy horse, and a little toy horse). Then put the big object in the big tub, the medium-size object in the medium-size tub, and the little object in the little tub. Tell the children that they are going to help sort some objects into big, medium-size, and little tubs.

Group Participation

Hold up other items that are the same except for size, and have different children put the items in the three tubs. Ask them to tell why they put the items where they did ("I put it there because it is a big ____, a medium-size ____, or a little ____"). The class proceeds through several item groups. Have a variety of sizes available so children begin to understand that it is the comparison between the items that determines whether something is big or not.

Summary/Transition Activity

Have three children come to the front of the group. Ask the rest of the children to say who is big, who is medium-size, and who is little. The child who is little sits down. Have another child who is taller than the "big" child come up, and also a child who is smaller than the first child. Ask the children to decide who is biggest, then who is medium-size, and finally who is smallest. You (or another adult) stand by the last child and ask who is bigger. Be careful not to choose the smallest child in the class or a child who is particularly sensitive about his or her size.

Tuesday

Dramatic Play	Art	Group	Story	Song
Newspaper Route	Newspaper Collage	Make a Class Newsletter	*Curious George Rides a Bike*	"Extra, Extra, Read All About It"

DAILY PLANNING GUIDE

Language and Literacy Skills Facilitated

Vocabulary: *newspaper carrier, bag, rubber band, porch, payment, list, newsprint, headline, advertisement, bundle*

Verb phrase structures: *delivers papers, is tossing on porch, collected payment, was folding papers, carried paper bag, wrote story*

Adjective/object descriptions: *heavy papers, light load, funny papers, white paper, black ink, big _____, little ____*

Question structures: *what, how, where, when, who, what if, why, how many, which one*

Pronouns: *I, you, he, she, we, they, my, your, him, her, his, our, their, me, us, them*

Prepositions: *in, on, under, over, near, beneath, next to, beside, around, inside, outside*

Sounds: /k/ *carry, ink*; /s/ *sit, beside, toss*; /r/ *road, car, paper*

Noting print has meaning: names on chairs and on cubbies, signs in dramatic play, words in books and on chalkboard

Noting sound–symbol associations: What sound does _____ start with?

Writing: letters, names, words

Social Skills Facilitated

Initiating interaction with peers and adults; responding to questions and requests from peers and adults

Negotiating with peers for toys and materials

Group cooperation: waiting for a turn in a group, taking a turn at the appropriate time

Cognitive Skills Facilitated

Problem-solving skills: how to fold a newspaper

Classification skills: things that go in an newspaper

Sequencing skills: story, chant

Narrative/story structure: adventure

Motor Skills Facilitated

Large motor: outdoor play activities—jumping, running, hopping, pedaling, climbing

Small motor: writing, drawing, gluing, folding

DRAMATIC PLAY **Newspaper Route**

Type of Activity: Sequential

Objectives
1. Learn new, and employ familiar, vocabulary
2. Learn new, and employ a variety of, syntactic constructions
3. Interact with peers
4. Sequence familiar routines
5. Expand conceptual knowledge of the world

Settings
- Newspaper office
- Homes (Each home could be represented by a chair with a doll or another child. A mat placed in front of the chair could represent the porch.)
- Streets (area of floor marked with masking tape)

Props
- Bags (two grocery bags cut in half with straps attached so that there is a bag in front and a bag in back)
- Newspapers
- Rubber bands
- Homes (chairs with dolls or children seated in them and mats placed as the porches)
- Play money
- Route lists
- Play telephones
- Desk (for newspaper office)
- Paper and pencils

Roles
- Carriers
- Customers
- Office workers

General Description of Activity

The children pretend to be newspaper carriers by counting newspapers, folding them, securing them with rubber bands, putting them in their delivery bag, and then delivering them to homes. It is important that the newspapers be delivered on the porch or placed in front of the door at each house or apartment. Children might have to call the newspaper office to have more papers delivered and collect money from the subscribers. The carrier also goes to the newspaper office each month to pay the bill for the number of papers delivered.

Verbal Productions

Level of linguistic complexity varies with the role or competency of the child playing the role.
- "Here's your paper" or "Paper"
- "I need five more papers at 124 Lawrence Street" or "More paper"
- "He is collecting money for the newspaper. You owe $10" or "Money, please"

Adult Facilitative Role

The adult is to facilitate role play and help expand language and literacy skills. Typical actions or strategies to use include

Playing a role: "I am rolling the papers. Do you want to help me?"

Modeling a statement/vocabulary: "The papers need to be delivered to each doorstep along the route. The papers are rolled and then put in the big bag. Then you deliver them to the houses."

Recasting present tense and irregular past tense forms: "I throw the newspapers every day onto the doorsteps" to "I threw 20 newspapers yesterday."

Modeling phonological awareness: "The words *paper, page, put,* and *pet* all start with the letter *p*."

ART **Newspaper Collage**

Objectives
1. Express creativity
2. Develop small motor skills (e.g., drawing, painting, cutting, pasting)
3. Practice turn-taking skills
4. Converse with peers and adults

Materials
- White paper
- Scissors
- Newspapers (including cartoons)
- Sequence stories (optional)

General Description of Activity

Lay out white paper on the art table. Children can cut letters, cartoons, or pictures from newspaper and paste them on the paper to make a collage.

Variation

Draw lines on the paper so children can paste their "articles" in columns. The children can also use the cartoon pictures to tell a story.

GROUP **Make a Class Newsletter**

Objectives
1. Improve listening skills
2. Increase knowledge about newsletters
3. Improve sequencing skills
4. Learn appropriate group-interaction skills
5. Practice turn-taking skills

Materials
- Poster paper with columns drawn on it
- Tape
- Blackboard or chart holder
- Markers and crayons

General Description of Activity

On the blackboard, tape a large piece of poster paper with columns drawn on it to resemble a newspaper. Tell the children that they are going to write a class newsletter to tell their parents what has been happening in the class. Have the children come up with a title for the newsletter (e.g., "LAPlines"), and write the title at the top along with the date. Then ask children for ideas about what to write.

Group Participation

Write down the children's ideas. Have children come up two or three at a time to sign the articles or to draw pictures. You could write two or three news stories and write/illustrate a couple of advertisements.

Variation

Add comic strips, drawn by the children.

Summary/Transition Activity

Reread all of the stories, pointing out the headlines, bylines, and illustrations.

Wednesday

Dramatic Play	Art	Group	Story	Song
Fast-Food Job	Playdough	Addition with Unifix Cubes	*Jamal's Busy Day*	"On Top of Spaghetti"

DAILY PLANNING GUIDE

Language and Literacy Skills Facilitated

Vocabulary: *fast food, hamburger, french fries, soft drinks, shakes, wrappers, cartons, cook, cashier, customer, order, pizza parlor, pizza*

Verb phrase structures: *place*s *an order, buy*s *a hamburger, pay*s *money,* eat *out,* is *mak*ing *a burger, serv*ed *the customer, flipp*ed *a burger, choose*s *a drink,* are *mak*ing *pizzas*

Adjective/object descriptions: *large drink, small hamburger, paper hat, red cup*

Question structures: *what, how, where, when, who, what if, why, how many, which one*

Pronouns: *I, you, he, she, we, they, my, your, him, her, his, our, their, me, us, them*

Prepositions: *in, on, near, beneath, next to, beside, around, inside, outside*

Noting print has meaning: names on chairs and on cubbies, signs in dramatic play, words in books and on chalkboard

Noting sound–symbol associations: What sound does _____ start with?

Writing: letters, names, words

Social Skills Facilitated

Initiating interaction with peers and adults; responding to questions and requests from peers and adults

Negotiating with peers for toys and materials

Group cooperation: waiting for a turn in a group, taking a turn at the appropriate time

Cognitive Skills Facilitated

Problem-solving skills: setting up a restaurant, remembering items

Classification skills: things in a fast-food restaurant

Sequencing skills: putting a hamburger together, words to song

Narrative/story structure: adventure

Motor Skills Facilitated

Large motor: outdoor play activities—jumping, running, hopping, pedaling, climbing

Small motor: writing, drawing, gluing

DRAMATIC PLAY : **Fast-Food Job**

Type of Activity: Central

Objectives
1. Learn new, and employ familiar, vocabulary
2. Learn new, and employ a variety of, syntactic constructions
3. Interact with peers
4. Sequence familiar routines
5. Expand conceptual knowledge of the world

Settings
- Counter (or facsimile)
- Kitchen
- Eating area (booths or tables and chairs)
- Drive-up window (optional)

Props
- Cash register(s)
- Pretend money
- Dishes (plastic or Styrofoam)
- Soda pop dispenser (box lid with pretend levers)
- Posted menu
- Variety of pretend food (e.g., hamburgers, french fries)
- Pretend "Kids' Meals" (small boxes with little toys and pretend food inside)
- Paper bags
- Trays
- Dolls
- Walkie-talkie for the drive-up window cashier
- Pretend cars

Roles
- Customers
- Cooks
- Cashiers
- Custodians
- Drive-up window cashier

General Description of Activity

Children act out eating and working at a fast-food restaurant. They may have customers order food at a counter from a posted list of items. Cashiers could ring up the food order on a cash register, then place the prepared food on a tray or in a bag. The customer would pay for the food and either consume it at a table or booth or take it somewhere else to eat it. The restaurant might serve hamburgers, hot dogs, chicken sandwiches, roast beef sandwiches, french fries, salads, pizza, and so forth. Drinks may include soda pop, milk, coffee, milkshakes, and so forth. The dishes and utensils could be made of plastic or Styrofoam. The customers could bus their own dishes.

Verbal Productions

Level of linguistic complexity varies with the role or competency of the child playing the role.
- "May I take your order?" or "Yes?"
- "I want a hamburger, french fries, and a Coke" or "Coke, please"
- "He is cooking the french fries now" or "Cooking now"

Adult Facilitative Role

The adult is to facilitate role play and help expand language and literacy skills. Typical actions or strategies to use include

Playing a role: "Do you want some french fries with your hamburgers?"

Modeling the reading of a menu: "The menu says *chicken*."

Recasting present progressive with past progressive: "He is eating a hamburger" to "He was eating chicken yesterday."

Asking an open question: "How can we make this work?"

Modeling phonological awareness: "The words *yet*, *yes*, and *yellow* all start with the letter *Y*."

ART **Playdough**

Objectives
1. Express creativity
2. Develop small motor skills (e.g., drawing, painting, cutting, pasting)
3. Practice turn-taking skills
4. Converse with peers and adults

Materials
- Smocks
- Playdough
- Rolling pins
- Cookie cutters
- Cookie presses
- Wooden craft sticks
- Rolling boards or individual cutting boards

General Description of Activity

Children wash their hands and put on smocks to explore playdough at the art table, using various presses, cutters, rolling pins, wooden craft sticks, and other tools. Children can make pretend food or any other objects by rolling, cutting, or making pressing motions. They can form animals or people by rolling a main body and then adding heads, arms, and legs. Yarn can be used for hair (if children want to take their creations home). When children are finished, they roll the dough into a ball, wash their hands, and take off and fold their smocks.

GROUP : **Addition with Unifix Cubes**

Objectives

1. Improve listening skills
2. Increase knowledge about counting and grouping into sets
3. Learn appropriate group-interaction skills
4. Practice turn-taking skills

Materials

- 10 Unifix cubes (or small blocks in sets of 10) per child or paper blocks in appropriate colors
- Small mats or boards (at least one per child)
- Number cards

General Description of Activity

Hold up 10 interlocked Unifix cubes and break them apart into one set of five interlocking cubes and five single cubes. Place the number 5 card by the set of five interlocking cubes, and have the children count the cubes to check that there are five.

Put each single block below the five interlocking cubes, counting as you place each block. Point to each set of cubes and say, "Here are five cubes [interlocked ones] and here are five cubes [five singles]." Then put two of the single cubes together and three of the single cubes together to form one set of two and one set of three cubes. Place a number 2 card above the set of two cubes and a number 3 card under the set of three cubes. Then ask the children, "How many cubes are there if we put a set of two cubes and a set of three cubes together?" Lay the two-cube set and the three-cube set together, and have the children count the number of cubes. The two sets are equal to the set of five interlocking cubes. Then put the number cards 2 + 3 = 5 above the sets and say, "Two plus three equals five." Note: Paper block cutouts in appropriate colors can be used instead of cubes (e.g., white = 1, red = 2, green = 3, purple = 4, and brown = 5). Five 1s can be the size of one brown strip and so forth.

Group Participation

Give each child one set of five interlocked cubes, one set of five single cubes, and a mat on which to lay the cubes. Have the children make sets like yours and then check that 2 + 3 = 5. Then ask the children to take the five single cubes and make another grouping to make five (e.g., one cube and four cubes). Give children a few minutes to experiment with groupings before demonstrating that 1 + 4 = 5. You can put down number cards, if desired, that say 1 + 4 = 5. The children can again count the two sets to make sure that both equal five.

Summary/Transition Activity

On the board, write 2 + 3 = 5 and 1 + 4 = 5. Have the children point to their groupings that show each equation. Then have them interlock both sets of five cubes to make one set of 10 to be collected and put in the box.

Thursday

Dramatic Play	Art	Group	Story	Song
Work on Cars	Car Track Painting	Review Numbers 1–20	*Go, Dog. Go!*	"Twinkle, Twinkle, Traffic Light"

DAILY PLANNING GUIDE

Language and Literacy Skills Facilitated

Vocabulary: *transportation, vehicle, car, track, garage, mechanic, truck, finish, battery, brakes, ignition, hose, tools, engine, wheels, shapes, rectangle, square, circle, triangle*

Verb phrase structures: *works, is working, crashed the car, pushed it, was racing, starts, stopped, fixed the car*

Adjective/object descriptions: *broken part, dead battery, big/little _____*

Question structures: *what, how, where, when, who, what if, why, how many, which one*

Pronouns: *I, you, he, she, we, they, my, your, him, her, his, our, their, me, us, them*

Prepositions: *in, on, under, over, near, beneath, next to, beside, around, inside, outside*

Sounds: /r/ *race, starter, car*; /s/ *see, misses, miss*; /sh/ *shape, finish*; blends: *flag, truck, start*

Noting print has meaning: names on chairs and on cubbies, signs in dramatic play, words in books and on chalkboard

Noting sound–symbol associations: What sound does _____ start with?

Writing: letters, names, words

Social Skills Facilitated

Initiating interaction with peers and adults; responding to questions and requests from peers and adults

Negotiating with peers for toys and materials

Group cooperation: waiting for a turn in a group, taking a turn at the appropriate time

Cognitive Skills Facilitated

Problem-solving skills: how to fix the cars

Classification skills: things that go on cars

Sequencing skills: song, art, numbers

Narrative/story structure: labeling

Motor Skills Facilitated

Large motor: outdoor play activities—jumping, running, hopping, pedaling, climbing

Small motor: writing, drawing, gluing

DRAMATIC PLAY **Work on Cars**

Type of Activity: Central

Objectives
1. Learn new, and employ familiar, vocabulary
2. Learn new, and employ a variety of, syntactic constructions
3. Interact with peers
4. Sequence familiar routines
5. Expand conceptual knowledge of the world

Settings

- Garage/repair shop
- Desk
- Cashier's station
- Gas pumps
- Car lift (cardboard blocks holding a plastic truck high enough for a child to slide under)
- Car wash (optional)

Props

- Appointment book and pencil or crayon
- Toy cash register
- Pretend money
- Hoses for pumps
- Car with hood, which can be made out of cardboard
- Dashboard
- Tools
- Pretend battery
- Pretend computer
- Pretend cans for oil change
- Play telephones
- Hoses
- Sponges

Roles

- Mechanics
- Customers
- Receptionist
- Sales clerk
- Cashier

General Description of Activity

Children take their vehicle to a gas station or garage to be repaired, gassed up, or tuned up. The oil in the car may need to be changed or the battery recharged. Customers can call ahead and make appointments. In one area, a receptionist/cashier desk is arranged. Another area might have a wooden or cardboard facsimile of a car with a hood that opens so that the mechanics can work under the hood if needed. Also, blocks or a vehicle Erector Set may be placed in one area to build cars. An optional activity is to have a parts counter or store.

Verbal Productions

Level of linguistic complexity varies with the role or competency of the child playing the role
- "May I please have the wrench?" or "Wrench, please"
- "Please start the car now" or "Start"
- "My car needs a new battery" or "Battery"

Adult Facilitative Role

The adult is to facilitate role play and help expand language and literacy skills. Typical actions or strategies to use include

Playing a role: "My tire is low. I'd better get it filled with air."

Redirecting a child to a peer: "Why don't you give the screwdriver to James? He needs to fix the car. Say, 'Here is the screwdriver.'"

Event casting an adult's actions: "I am changing the tire. I am taking the screws out. Now I can take the tire off. Now I am putting a new tire on. See, it is fixed."

Expanding a child's utterance: "She driving" to "Yes, she is driving the red car."

ART : **Car Track Painting**

Objectives

1. Express creativity
2. Develop small motor skills (e.g., drawing, painting, cutting, pasting)
3. Practice turn-taking skills
4. Converse with peers and adults

Materials
- 8" × 11" pieces of construction paper (at least one piece per child)
- Three or four colors of tempera paint
- Smocks
- Small die-cast cars
- Shallow containers to hold the paint and cars (e.g., Styrofoam meat trays)

General Description of Activity

The children each don a smock before sitting at the art table. Give each child an 8" × 11" piece of construction paper. On the art table are several shallow containers (e.g., small Styrofoam meat trays) containing tempera paints of various colors (one color per container) and small die-cast cars. The children dip the wheels of the cars into the paint and then roll the car along their paper to make designs. Before changing to a different color, the children return the cars they had been using to their original paint container.

GROUP **Review Numbers 1–20**

Objectives
1. Improve listening skills
2. Increase knowledge of the numbers and quantities
3. Learn appropriate group-interaction skills
4. Practice turn-taking skills

Materials
- Number cards 1–20 (one number per card)
- Box to hold number cards
- Counting items (e.g., counting bears, small blocks, etc.)
- Whiteboard (or chalkboard)
- Whiteboard markers (or chalk)
- 1–100 number chart
- 1–10 number line
- 11–20 number line

General Description of Activity

Place the 1–20 number lines in front of the children. Tell the children that we are going to match numbers up to the number 20. Refer to the 1–100 number chart, pointing out that the 20 is called "twenty," and show the relationship of the ones column, twos column, etc. Have a child come up and find the number 20 on the big number chart.

Group Participation

Have one child pick a number card out of a box and place the card below the corresponding number on the number lines. Have other children repeat the activity until both 1–10 and 11–20 number lines are created on the floor. You can use additional sets of number cards so that more children can participate in recognizing and labeling the numbers. The children can place their numbers on top of the ones that match. Note: It is not expected that all children will be able to do this activity without assistance. This activity is to alert children that counting goes on beyond 10. Also, the children will now notice the big number chart displayed in the room.

Variation

Have children point out the matching number of their card on the 1–100 number chart.

Summary/Transition Activity

Quickly point to different number cards as children, as a group, label the number indicated.

··
: WEEKLY PLANNING GUIDE :
··

	Dramatic Play	Art	Group	Story	Song
Monday *Suggested Props and Materials*	Garden/Farm *Garden/farm scenario, sandbox, sand, toy tractors, plows, farm animals, barn, garden tools, pretend food for animals, pretend plants, seeds*	Vegetable Prints *Cutouts on potatoes, celery stalks, green pepper cutouts, paint in shallow dishes, paper*	Fruits and Vegetables *Plastic fruit (e.g., apple, oranges, bananas), plastic vegetables (e.g., carrot, corn), two tubs*	*The Surprise Garden*	"I Like to Eat Apples and Bananas"
Tuesday *Suggested Props and Materials*	Grocery Store *Grocery store scenario, shelves, canned goods, other play box food items, fruit and vegetable area, play fruit and vegetables, play cash register, play money, shopping carts, grocery bags*	Popcorn Letters *Outlines of letters on construction paper, glue, popcorn*	Counting to *20* *Counting chart, counting book, chalkboard, chalk or whiteboard and markers*	*The Very Hungry Caterpillar*	"Peanut Butter and Jelly"
Wednesday *Suggested Props and Materials*	Ice Cream Parlor/Sock Hop *Ice cream parlor, ice cream scoops, different colored LEGOs to represent ice cream, pretend cones and/or cardboard dishes, cash register, CDs, CD player, cleaning supplies (e.g., broom, mop, vacuum cleaner)*	Ice Cream Cone Pictures *Sheets of paper with outlines of ice cream cone, crayons or colored pencils, scissors, glue, cutouts of ice cream scoops*	Oddity Match *Several items that are exact matches (and some that are not), several items that are similar (and some that don't match), several items that are related, cardboard X (optional)*	*Ice Cream Soup*	"1, 2, Bubble Gum Chew"
Thursday *Suggested Props and Materials*	Dinner Theater *Dinner theater scenario, play food, dishes, kitchen area, customer area, stage, menus, costumes and props appropriate to story acted out*	Watercolor Paintings *Watercolor paints, brushes, paper, water*	Act out a Story *(The Wide-Mouth Frog)* *Props for story, story*	*The Wide-Mouth Frog*	If You're Happy and You Know It"

MY NOTES

NEWSLETTER

Vol. 1, No. 40

Date: _____

All About Food

Monday
Today the children will be gardeners or farmers in dramatic play. They can plow the field, plant the seeds, feed the animals, milk the cow, and gather the eggs. They will make vegetable prints in art. The story is *The Surprise Garden*. During group time, the children will classify fruits and vegetables. Our featured song is "I Like to Eat Apples and Bananas," which involves changing the vowels in the words.

Tuesday
Today the children will focus on food at the grocery store. They will pretend to be the grocery story clerks, the stockers, the customers, and the bakers. They will make popcorn letters at art. *The Very Hungry Caterpillar* is the featured story. The children will have fun counting to 20 during group time. Our featured song is "Peanut Butter and Jelly."

Wednesday
The children will have fun at the ice cream parlor/sock hop today in dramatic play. They will dance, eat ice cream, or be the DJ. In art, they will make ice cream cone pictures. The story is *Ice Cream Soup*. During group time, the children will learn to choose the item that does not go with the others. Our featured song is "1, 2, Bubble Gum Chew."

Thursday
The children will enjoy going to a dinner theater in dramatic play. They might be the waiters, the customers, the cooks, or the actors. At art, they can make water-color paintings. The story of the day is *The Wide-Mouth Frog*. During group time, children will act out a favorite story (*The Wide-Mouth Frog*). Our song for the day is "If You're Happy and You Know It."

Monday

Dramatic Play	Art	Group	Story	Song
Garden/Farm	Vegetable Prints	Fruits and Vegetables	*The Surprise Garden*	"I Like to Eat Apples and Bananas"

DAILY PLANNING GUIDE

Language and Literacy Skills Facilitated

Vocabulary: *farm, barn, cow, horse, pig, feed, hay, fence, corral, milk, pail, silo, pen, tractor, corn, wheat, potatoes, apples*

Verb phrase structures: *feeds, is feeding, fed the animals, milks, milked the cow, is baling the hay, stacked the hay, plants the corn, planted the corn, is harvesting the wheat, harvested the wheat/corn, plowing the fields, plowed*

Adjective/object descriptions: *big/little _____, hungry _____, milking pail, white/brown/___ cow; yellow/____ chicken*

Question structures: *what, how, where, when, who, what if, why, how many, which one*

Pronouns: *I, you, he, she, we, they, my, your, him, her, his, our, their, me, us, them*

Prepositions: *in, on, under, over, near, beneath, next to, beside, around, inside, outside*

Sounds: /k/ cow, chicken, milk; /f/ farm, off; /m/ milk, hammer, them

Noting print has meaning: names on chairs and on cubbies, signs in dramatic play, words in books and on chalkboard

Noting sound–symbol associations: What sound does _____ start with?

Writing: letters, names, words

Social Skills Facilitated

Initiating interaction with peers and adults; responding to questions and requests from peers and adults

Negotiating with peers for toys and materials

Group cooperation: waiting for a turn in a group, taking a turn at the appropriate time

Cognitive Skills Facilitated

Problem-solving skills: how to be a farmer, how to take turns

Classification skills: square/circle

Sequencing skills: story, song

Narrative/story structure: labeling story

Motor Skills Facilitated

Large motor: outdoor play activities—jumping, running, hopping, pedaling, climbing

Small motor: writing, drawing, cutting, pasting

DRAMATIC PLAY **Garden/Farm**

Type of Activity: Central

Objectives
1. Learn new, and employ familiar, vocabulary
2. Learn new, and employ a variety of, syntactic constructions
3. Interact with peers
4. Sequence familiar routines
5. Expand conceptual knowledge of the world

Settings
- Farm house (playhouse or dismantled cardboard boxes)
- Barn (playhouse or dismantled cardboard boxes)
- Field (floor area marked with masking tape or pretend fences)
- Planting area (wading pool filled with sand or soil)

Props
- Pretend tractor
- Pretend machinery
- Cow to be milked (latex gloves filled with milky water)
- Horses (yardsticks)
- Blocks for fencing
- Farm animals (stuffed animals)
- Hats
- Pretend seeds
- Scarecrow
- Cardboard trees (with removable Ping-Pong balls for fruit)

Roles
- Farmer(s)
- Farmer's helper(s)
- Farm animals (the children pretend to be animals)
- Tractor operator
- Other machinery operators
- Milker (optional)
- Fruit pickers (optional)

General Description of Activity

Children act out the different roles and activities found on a farm. There may be animals to care for, such as cows, horses, pigs, and chickens. Children may grow crops or run a dairy farm. Different types of activities can be designed around the farm theme. For example, this week the focus is on food, so provide an area with soil in which to plant and then harvest crops. (Painted Ping-Pong balls can become apples to be harvested, particularly if Velcro is attached so the balls will stick to a cardboard tree.) Pretend tractors and other machinery could also be available.

Verbal Productions

Level of linguistic complexity varies with the role or competency of the child playing the role.
- "It's my turn to feed the chickens" or "Feed chickens"
- "I plowed the field and then planted corn" or "Plow field"
- "My horse wants some hay" or "Horse eat"

Adult Facilitative Role

The adult is to facilitate role play and help expand language and literacy skills. Typical actions or strategies to use include

Playing a role: "I am milking the cow. Do you want to help?"

Contrasting two location terms: "This cow is in the barn. The other cow is in front of the barn."

Expanding a child's utterance: "Find eggs" to "He did find the eggs."

Contrasting present and past tense: "He plows the fields" to "He plowed the fields."

Redirecting a child to a peer: "Ask Jules for a turn on the tractor. Say, 'May I have a turn, please?'"

ART **Vegetable Prints**

Objectives
1. Express creativity
2. Develop small motor skills (e.g., drawing, painting, cutting, pasting)
3. Practice turn-taking skills
4. Converse with peers and adults

Materials
- Assortment of vegetables, sliced (e.g., peppers, carrots, broccoli, cauliflower, celery)
- Cutout shapes on a halved potato (e.g., carve out a cross, triangle, or square on each half of the potato)
- Tempera paint
- Shallow container (e.g., meat tray)
- Light-colored construction paper
- Smocks

General Description of Activity

Pour small amounts of tempera paint into shallow containers, such as Styrofoam meat trays. Children touch the vegetable piece to the paint and then press it on their paper, making a print of the vegetable's shape. The more choice of vegetables and colors, the more creative and colorful the prints will turn out.

GROUP **Fruits and Vegetables**

Objectives
1. Improve listening skills
2. Increase conceptual knowledge
3. Learn appropriate group-interaction skills
4. Practice turn-taking skills

Materials
- Plastic fruits (e.g., apple)
- Plastic vegetables (e.g., carrot)
- Two tubs

General Description of Activity

Hold up a plastic apple and a plastic carrot and ask the children to tell you which one is the fruit and which is the vegetable. If they do not know or do not respond, label each item and put each in a different tub.

Group Participation

Give each child a plastic fruit or vegetable. One at a time, each child labels the item as a fruit or a vegetable and places it into the appropriate tub. If a child makes an error, remove the item from the tub and have the child place it in the correct tub.

Variation

Rather than give each child an item, have children choose their own item from an assortment. (Explain that the tomato is often labeled as a vegetable; however, it is really a fruit.)

Summary/Transition Activity

Ask the group to label the items in the fruit category and then label the items in the vegetable category.

Tuesday

Dramatic Play	Art	Group	Story	Song
Grocery Store	Popcorn Letters	Counting to 20	*The Very Hungry Caterpillar*	"Peanut Butter and Jelly"

DAILY PLANNING GUIDE

Language and Literacy Skills Facilitated

Vocabulary: *groceries, cart, cereal, shop, checker, buy, sell, bag, sack, shelf, money, change*

Verb phrase structures: *eats, is eating, ate, has eaten, pushes, is pushing, pushed, buys, bought, checks, is checking, checked*

Adjective/object descriptions: *big/little bag, full/empty shelf*

Question structures: *what, how, where, when, who, what if, why, how many, which one*

Pronouns: *I, you, he, she, we, they, my, your, him, her, his, our, their, me, us, them*

Prepositions: *in, on, under, over, near, beneath, next to, beside, around, inside, outside*

Sounds: /sh/ *shelf, push*; /k/ *cart, sack*; /s/ *sell, carts*

Noting print has meaning: names on chairs and on cubbies, signs in dramatic play, words in books and on chalkboard

Noting sound–symbol associations: What sound does _____ start with?

Writing: letters, names, words

Social Skills Facilitated

Initiating interaction with peers and adults; responding to questions and requests from peers and adults

Negotiating with peers for toys and materials

Group cooperation: waiting for a turn in a group, taking a turn at the appropriate time

Cognitive Skills Facilitated

Problem-solving skills: what to buy

Classification skills: fruits, vegetables, meats

Sequencing skills: songs, story

Narrative/story structure: adventure

Motor Skills Facilitated

Large motor: outdoor play activities—jumping, running, hopping, pedaling, climbing

Small motor: writing, drawing, gluing

DRAMATIC PLAY **Grocery Store**

Type of Activity: Sequential

Objectives
1. Learn new, and employ familiar, vocabulary
2. Learn new, and employ a variety of, syntactic constructions
3. Interact with peers
4. Sequence familiar routines
5. Expand conceptual knowledge of the world

Settings

- Grocery store
- Shelves and aisles
- Check-out stand
- Customers' homes

Props

- Shelves
- Canned goods and other food items
- Fruit and vegetable area
- Pretend cash register
- Pretend money
- Pretend credit cards
- Pretend coupons
- Shopping carts
- Grocery bags
- Pencil and paper for making lists
- Table for checkout area

Roles

- Shoppers
- Cashiers
- Stockers
- Baggers

General Description of Activity

The children pretend to be grocery shopping. They can make lists, take their "children" with them, choose the items on the list to put in their carts, pay, bag their groceries, and go home. Other children can be the grocery store workers. Some can keep the shelves stocked; others can be checkers and baggers.

Verbal Productions

Level of linguistic complexity varies with the role or competency of the child playing the role.

- "Will that be all? Your total is $5" or "All? $5!"
- "Milk, please" or "Milk"
- "Do you have any cereal?" or "Want cereal"

Adult Facilitative Role

The adult is to facilitate role play and help expand language and literacy skills. Typical actions or strategies to use include

Playing a role: "That will be $50 for the groceries."

Event casting an adult's actions: "I am putting groceries in my cart. I put some fruit, a bottle of milk, and some cheese in the cart. Now I will go to the checkout counter."

Expanding a child's utterance: "Buy chicken" to "I forgot to buy the chicken."

Providing confirmatory feedback: "That's right. The word *cart* starts with the /k/ sound."

ART : **Popcorn Letters**

Objectives

1. Express creativity
2. Develop small motor skills (e.g., drawing, painting, cutting, pasting)
3. Practice turn-taking skills
4. Converse with peers and adults

Materials
- Various colors of construction paper (8½" × 11")
- Popped popcorn
- White glue

General Description of Activity

Have children choose a letter, perhaps the initial in their first name. Drizzle glue, or have children drizzle it, on the paper in the shape of the letter chosen. Children put popped popcorn on the glue line.

It might be fun to make a large chart of all 26 letters and let children cross off the letter they made until the whole class creates the entire alphabet. This makes a nice bulletin board display and gives children a chance to practice the alphabet.

GROUP **Counting to *20***

Objectives
1. Improve listening skills
2. Increase conceptual knowledge
3. Increase ability to count and recognize numbers
4. Learn appropriate group-interaction skills
5. Practice turn-taking skills

Materials
- *Count* by Denise Fleming
- Chalkboard and chalk
- Number chart

General Description of Activity

Show children the book *Count* by Denise Fleming, pointing to the title and the author's name. Tell the children that they are going to count zoo animals today, but there is a trick at the end of the lesson.

Group Participation

As you read the book, have the children repeat the numbers and names of the animals. As the numbers get higher, have a child come up and count the animals on the page. When *10* is reached, tell the children that now they will count by tens. Write the numbers from *1* to *10* across the chalkboard in a horizontal line. Write the "teen" numbers underneath these numbers (*11* under the *1*, *12* under the *2*, etc.). Under the *10* write *20*, and under the *20* write *30*, under the *30* write *40*, and under the *40* write *50*. From the book, show children the pictures of *20* animals, *30* animals, and so on. Wow, that is a lot of animals!

Variation

The *20* could be written under the *2* and the *30* under the *3* and the *40* under the *4* and the *50* under the *5* to show how to count by tens.

Summary/Transition Activity

Have the whole class count again from *1–20*.

Wednesday

Dramatic Play	Art	Group	Story	Song
Ice Cream Parlor/ Sock Hop	Ice Cream Cone Pictures	Oddity Match	*Ice Cream Soup*	"1, 2, Bubble Gum Chew"

DAILY PLANNING GUIDE

Language and Literacy Skills Facilitated

Vocabulary: *ice cream, sundaes, banana split, cones, vanilla, chocolate, strawberry, nuts, sauce, records, music, dance, jitterbug, sock hop*

Verb phrase structures: <u>*is*</u>/<u>*are*</u> *eat<u>ing</u>, <u>ate</u>, danc<u>ing</u>, danc<u>ed</u>, <u>was</u>/<u>were</u> mak<u>ing</u>*

Adjective/object descriptions: *plain ice cream, big/little scoops, gooey ice cream, chocolate sauce*

Question structures: *what, how, where, when, who, what if, why, how many, which one*

Pronouns: *I, you, he, she, we, they, my, your, him, her, his, our, their, me, us, them*

Prepositions: *in, on, under, over, near, beneath, next to, beside, around, inside, outside*

Sounds: /k/ <u>*c*</u>*ream, ma<u>k</u>ing;* /s/ <u>*s*</u>*it, walk<u>s</u>, dan<u>ce</u>;* /f/ <u>*f*</u>*inds, <u>f</u>un, of<u>f</u>*

Noting print has meaning: names on chairs and on cubbies, signs in dramatic play, words in books and on chalkboard

Noting sound–symbol associations: What sound does _____ start with?

Writing: letters, names, words

Social Skills Facilitated

Initiating interaction with peers and adults; responding to questions and requests from peers and adults

Negotiating with peers for toys and materials

Group cooperation: waiting for a turn in a group, taking a turn at the appropriate time

Cognitive Skills Facilitated

Problem-solving skills: how to run an ice cream parlor

Classification skills: different flavors of ice cream

Sequencing skills: story, songs

Narrative/story structure: adventure

Motor Skills Facilitated

Large motor: outdoor play activities—jumping, running, hopping, pedaling, climbing

Small motor: writing, drawing, gluing

DRAMATIC PLAY **Ice Cream Parlor/Sock Hop**

Type of Activity: Related

Objectives
1. Learn new, and employ familiar, vocabulary
2. Learn new, and employ a variety of, syntactic constructions
3. Interact with peers
4. Sequence familiar routines
5. Expand conceptual knowledge of the world

Settings
- Counter with tubs for the pretend ice cream
- Pretend freezer
- Cashier's area
- Dance area with CD player (pretend jukebox)

Props
- Ice cream scoops
- Colored LEGOs to represent ice cream
- Pretend cones and/or cardboard dishes
- Cash register
- CDs
- Cleaning supplies (e.g., broom, mop, vacuum cleaner)

Roles
- Customers
- Counter workers
- Cashier
- Custodian

General Description of Activity

Children go to an ice cream parlor, where they can buy different kinds of ice cream in a cone or in a dish. Set up an area for dancing to a jukebox or CD. The children can dance to the music on the jukebox or CD, even taking off their shoes so it is a "sock hop." The children can be the workers, the cashier, the customers, the cleanup crew, or the dancers.

Verbal Productions

Level of linguistic complexity varies with the role or competency of the child playing the role
- "He wants vanilla ice cream cone, and I want a chocolate one" or "Vanilla"
- "I danced very fast and fell down" or "I dance"
- "You need to clean up this mess" or "Clean up"
- "That will cost you $2" or "$2"

Adult Facilitative Role

The adult is to facilitate role play and help expand language and literacy skills. Typical actions or strategies to use include

Playing a role: "That will be $1 for the ice cream."

Event casting an adult's actions: "I am buying my ice cream at the counter. I am eating my ice cream. Now I am dancing very fast to the music."

Expanding a child's utterance: "Ice cream" to "I would like to buy some ice cream."

Modeling the reading of a sign: "The sign says *ice cream*."

ART Ice Cream Cone Pictures

Objectives
1. Express creativity
2. Develop small motor skills (e.g., drawing, painting, cutting, pasting)
3. Practice turn-taking skills
4. Converse with peers and adults

Materials
- Sheets of paper with outline of ice cream cone
- Crayons or colored pencils
- Scissors (optional)
- Glue (optional)
- 8½" × 11" sheets of construction paper (optional)

General Description of Activity

Give each child a picture of an outline of an ice cream cone with scoops of ice cream on it. As children color in the cone and scoops of ice cream with crayons or colored pencils, talk about what they are doing (e.g., "Yum! That ice cream is pink, like strawberry ice cream. I like to eat strawberry ice cream"). The finished ice cream pictures may be cut out and pasted on larger sheets (e.g., 8½" × 11") of construction paper.

Variation

Provide an outline of only the cone, and have children draw the scoops of ice cream themselves before coloring them in.

GROUP **Oddity Match**

Objectives
1. Improve listening skills
2. Increase sequencing ability
3. Learn appropriate group-interaction skills
4. Practice turn-taking skills

Materials
- Several items that are exact matches (and some that are not)
- Several items that are similar (and some that do not match)
- Several items that are related
- Cardboard X (optional)

General Description of Activities

Lay out four items. Three of the items should be identical and one should be different (e.g., three red cars and one doll). Ask the children to look for the item that does not belong with the others. Then point to the item that is different and say, "This one does not go with the others." Lay out another set, this time with three items that are not identical but are the same kind of item, and one that is different from the others (e.g., three different dolls, one boat). Ask one child to come to the front and find the one that is different (or that does not go with the others).

Group Participation

Continue to present three items that are the same and one that is different until each child has had a turn identifying the different item. Be sure to vary the placement of the different item so that the children do not think it is always the second item or the last item. The difficulty of the task can be varied depending on the children's abilities (some children may need exact matches, others can recognize relationships or that the items go together even though one is bigger than the other). The children also could put a cardboard X on top of the item that does not belong rather than say or point to the item. Note: You may want to do this activity after the lesson on same and different.

Variation

One way to vary the items is to put them in a 2 × 2 matrix instead of in a row. Another procedure would be to use related items instead of the same kind of items. For example, of the following items, coat, hat, fork, and mitten, the coat, hat, and mitten are the items that go together and the fork does not belong. Another variation is to use color or function as the identifying feature (e.g., all the red items go together and the blue item is the one that is different, or all the of writing instruments go together and the scissors are the item that is different).

Summary/Transition Activity

Lay out one more group of items and have the children, in unison, say which one does not go with the others.

Thursday

Dramatic Play	Art	Group	Story	Song
Dinner Theater	Watercolor Paintings	Act out a Story (*The Wide-Mouth Frog*)	*The Wide-Mouth Frog*	"If You're Happy and You Know It"

DAILY PLANNING GUIDE

Language and Literacy Skills Facilitated

Vocabulary: *restaurant, plate, food, meat, waiter, waitress, menu, stage, acting, play, story*

Verb phrase structures: <u>eat</u> *meat,* <u>drink</u> *milk,* <u>act</u> *in a play,* <u>wait</u> *tables,* <u>order</u> *from the menu*

Adjective/object descriptions: *good play, tall actor, little pigs, good food, big/little plate*

Question structures: *what, how, where, when, who, what if, why, how many, which one*

Pronouns: *I, you, he, she, we, they, my, your, him, her, his, our, their, me, us, them*

Prepositions: *in, on, under, over, near, beneath, next to, beside, around, inside, outside*

Sounds: /f/ *fix, off;* /s/ *sit, talks;* /l/ *little, bell*

Noting print has meaning: names on chairs and on cubbies, signs in dramatic play, words in books and on chalkboard

Noting sound–symbol associations: What sound does _____ start with?

Writing: letters, names, words

Social Skills Facilitated

Initiating interaction with peers and adults; responding to questions and requests from peers and adults

Negotiating with peers for toys and materials

Group cooperation: waiting for a turn in a group, taking a turn at the appropriate time

Cognitive Skills Facilitated

Problem-solving skills: how to act in a play

Classification skills: things at a restaurant

Sequencing skills: story, songs

Narrative/story structure: adventure

Motor Skills Facilitated

Large motor: outdoor play activities—jumping, running, hopping, pedaling, climbing

Small motor: writing, drawing, gluing

DRAMATIC PLAY **Dinner Theater**

Type of Activity: Central

Objectives
1. Learn new, and employ familiar, vocabulary
2. Learn new, and employ a variety of, syntactic constructions
3. Interact with peers
4. Sequence familiar routines
5. Expand conceptual knowledge of the world

Setting

- Stage area
- Dining area, with several tables around the stage area
- Kitchen area
- "Wait to be seated" area

Props

- Play food
- Dishes
- Menus
- Costumes and props appropriate to story acted out
- Scenery (optional)

Roles

- Customers
- Wait staff
- Actors
- Host/Hostess

General Description of Activity

Set up a dinner theater, with dining tables arranged around a stage area. A play is performed on the stage as the "diners" have dinner. The play can be one of the stories that the children have acted out in group activities (e.g., *The Three Little Pigs*, *The Three Billy Goats Gruff*, *The Tiger's Surprise*). The children can pretend to be the customers, the waiters and waitresses, or the actors.

Verbal Productions

Level of linguistic complexity varies with the role or competency of the child playing the role.

- "I am the Big Bad Wolf, and I am going to get you" or "Bad Wolf"
- "Do you want the steak or chicken?" or "Chicken?"
- "I am anxious to see the play" or "See play"
- "Please be seated, and your waiter will be right with you" or "Sit"

Adult Facilitative Role

The adult is to facilitate role play and help expand language and literacy skills. Typical actions or strategies to use include

Playing a role: "I am going to be a big bad wolf in the play."

Modeling the reading of a menu: "The menu says *steak* and *salad*."

Event casting of a child's actions: "Johnny is cooking the food, now he is putting it on the plate to take to Suzie."

Contrasting location terms: "This dish is on the table. That dish is in the sink. This spoon is behind the glass."

Asking an open question: "What story should we act out?"

Contrasting two sounds: "Did you say 'fish' or 'fit?'"

ART : Watercolor Paintings

Objectives

1. Express creativity
2. Develop small motor skills (e.g., drawing, painting, cutting, pasting)
3. Practice turn-taking skills
4. Converse with peers and adults

Materials

- Watercolor paints
- Brushes
- Tubs of water
- White construction paper

General Description of Activity

Lay out white construction paper, watercolor paint boxes, and brushes on the art table. Place tubs of water to clean the brushes above the paper. The children put on smocks and sit down in front of the paper, paint box, and water tub. Each child selects a brush, wets it, and chooses the paint color. The children paint on the paper, rinsing the brush before selecting a new color. Children can paint a collage of colors, animals, people, scenery, and so on. You may want to be close by so children can talk about their paintings.

GROUP **Act out a Story (*The Wide-Mouth Frog*)**

Objectives
1. Improve listening skills
2. Increase sequencing ability
3. Increase knowledge of story telling
4. Learn appropriate group-interaction skills
5. Practice turn-taking skills

Materials
- Book of *The Wide-Mouth Frog*
- Props for the story

General Description of Activity

Read or summarize the story of *The Wide-Mouth Frog* for the children. The children will act out the story.

Group Participation

Assign children roles from the story. Assure the children who are not chosen the first time that everyone will have a turn and that they have the very important job of being a good listening audience. Narrate the story as the children act it out. They should say as many of the lines as they can, with prompts given when needed. Repeat the story with new actors until all the children have had a turn.

Summary/Transition Activity

Compliment the children's acting. Discuss past stories the children have enjoyed acting out.

III

Resources

Blank Planning Guides and Lesson Plans

- Blank Monthly Planning Guide
- Blank Weekly Planning Guide
- Blank Daily Planning Guide
- Blank Lesson Plans for
  - Dramatic Play Activities
  - Art Activities
  - Group Activities

_____ SEMESTER

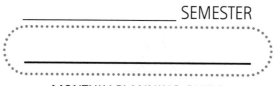

MONTHLY PLANNING GUIDE

Activities	Monday	Tuesday	Wednesday	Thursday
Week 1 Theme: _____				
Dramatic Play				
Art				
Group				
Story				
Song				
Week 2 Theme: _____				
Dramatic Play				
Art				
Group				
Story				
Song				
Week 3 Theme: _____				
Dramatic Play				
Art				
Group				
Story				
Song				
Week 4 Theme: _____				
Dramatic Play				
Art				
Group				
Story				
Song				
Week 5 Theme: _____				
Dramatic Play				
Art				
Group				
Story				
Song				

WEEKLY PLANNING GUIDE

	Dramatic Play	Art	Group	Story	Song
Monday *Suggested Props and Materials*					
Tuesday *Suggested Props and Materials*					
Wednesday *Suggested Props and Materials*					
Thursday *Suggested Props and Materials*					

MY NOTES

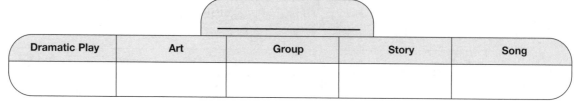

Dramatic Play	Art	Group	Story	Song

DAILY PLANNING GUIDE

Language and Literacy Skills Facilitated

Vocabulary_____

Verb phrase structures _____

Adjective/object descriptions _____

Question structures _____

Pronouns _____

Prepositions _____

Sounds _____

Noting print has meaning _____

Noting sound–symbol associations _____

Writing _____

Social Skills Facilitated _____

_____

Cognitive Skills Facilitated

Problem-solving skills _____

Classification skills_____

Sequencing skills _____

Narrative/story structure _____

Motor Skills Facilitated

Large motor _____

Small motor _____

Type of Activity _____
_____
_____
_____

Objectives _____
_____
_____
_____

Settings _____
_____
_____
_____

Props _____
_____
_____
_____

Roles _____
_____
_____
_____

General Description of Activity _____
_____
_____
_____

Verbal Productions _____
_____
_____
_____

Adult Facilitory Role _____
_____
_____
_____

Objectives _____
_____
_____
_____

Materials _____
_____
_____
_____
_____
_____
_____
_____

General Description of Activity _____
_____
_____
_____
_____
_____
_____
_____

Objectives _____

_____

_____

_____

Materials _____

_____

_____

_____

_____

_____

_____

General Description of Activity _____

_____

_____

_____

_____

_____

_____

Group Participation _____

_____

_____

_____

_____

_____

_____

Summary/Transition Activity _____

_____

_____

_____

_____

_____

_____

Early Literacy in Action: The Language-Focused Curriculum for Preschool by Betty H. Bunce.

B

Learning Observation Guide (LOG)

Individual Observation of Developmental
Skills in Relationship to the
Language-Focused Curriculum

Skills Include:
Motor
Social
Language
Cognition
Emergent Literacy

Use to Develop:
Present Level of Progress
Classroom Accommodations
Individualized Interventions

Date(s) of Observation:_____ Name: _____

LEARNING OBSERVATION GUIDE (LOG)

Children who are 3–5 years old are developing skills in many areas, including motor, social, language, cognitive, and emergent literacy.

All children have the right to a general curriculum. Children's development of skills within the language-focused curriculum can be assessed by relating them to the four types of activities: 1) those that change daily and are teacher led, 2) those that are routine and teacher led, 3) those that change daily and are child centered, and 4) those that are routine and child centered. The activities are assessed as to whether there is a need to modify classroom procedures to accommodate a child or whether there needs to be individualized intervention devised.

	Teacher Led	Child Centered
Changes Daily	Group time Storytime Music time	Dramatic play Art
Routine	Circle time Sharing time	Arrival time Snack time Outside playtime Block area Quiet area

Directions: Observe the child as he/she participates in activities across the curriculum. Observations may take place over a 1–2 week period of time. Use the forms to provide an overall summary of observations of a child's areas of need within the four categories of activities during the week-long observation period. A scale of 1–7 is used to judge behavior that is typical versus that where there is need to make curriculum adaptations or where there is need for individualized interventions. A rating of 5 and above indicates typical behavior; a rating of 3–4 may signal a need for some accommodations; and a rating of 1 or 2 indicates individualized interventions are needed.

1	2	3	4	5	6	7
Major Concerns		Some Concerns		Typical		Above Average

Date(s) of Observation:_____ Name: _____

CHANGE DAILY/TEACHER-LED ACTIVITIES
(Story, Group, Music)

Rating	Activity Focus	NOTES
	General Motor Skills	
	Sitting on floor/chair	
	Posture righting response	
	Manipulation of own body/space	
	Manipulation of materials	
	General Social Skills/Attention	
	Listening to teacher/children	
	Following directions	
	Appropriate initiating/responding	
	Turn-taking skills	
	General Language Skills	
	Vocabulary understanding	
	Vocabulary production	
	Speech	
	Language structure	
	General Cognitive Skills	
	Imitation	
	Matching	
	Sequencing	
	Classification	
	Problem solving	
	Emergent Literacy Skills	
	Left–right orientation	
	Story grammar (types)	
	Phonemic awareness (e.g., rhyming, sound matching)	
	Alphabet knowledge	
	Sight word recognition	

Date(s) of Observation:_____ Name: _____

ROUTINE/TEACHER-LED ACTIVITIES

Rating	Activity Focus	NOTES
	General Motor Skills	
	Sitting on floor/chair	
	Manipulation of own body/space	
	Manipulation of materials	
	General Social Skills/Attention	
	Listening to teacher/children	
	Responding when called upon	
	Initiating (e.g. sharing questions)	
	Turn-taking skills	
	General Language Skills	
	Vocabulary comprehension	
	Vocabulary production	
	Speech	
	Language structure	
	Requesting/commenting	
	General Cognitive Skills	
	Imitation	
	Matching	
	Sequencing (e.g., calendar, sharing question format)	
	Decision making	
	Emergent Literacy Skills	
	Recognizing names (e.g., roll call)	
	Rote counting	
	Identifying numbers	
	Letter identification	
	Name-sign recognition	

Date(s) of Observation:_____ Name: _____

CHANGE DAILY/CHILD-CENTERED ACTIVITIES

Rating	Activity Focus	NOTES
	Fine Motor Skills	
	Tactile stimulation tolerance	
	Pencil grip	
	Pencil/marker control (e.g., drawing)	
	Cutting	
	Pasting	
	Knob rotation, stacking, pouring	
	Manipulation of toys/props/body	
	General Social Skills	
	Sharing materials with peers	
	Turn-taking skills	
	Appropriate initiating/responding	
	General Language Skills	
	Commenting/describing	
	Making requests	
	Negotiating	
	Sentence structure	
	Vocabulary	
	Speech sounds	
	General Cognitive Skills	
	Imitation/matching	
	Sequencing of action/schemes	
	Classifying/pattern recognition	
	Problem solving	
	Emergent Literacy Skills	
	Pretend play (e.g., pioneer, space)	
	Writing letters/words /numbers	

Date(s) of Observation: _____ Name: _____

ROUTINE/CHILD-CENTERED ACTIVITIES
(Arrival, Block, Quiet, Outdoor, Snack)

Rating	Activity Focus	NOTES
	General Motor Skills	
	Movement changes (e.g., sit/stand)	
	Sequencing of actions	
	Chewing/swallowing	
	Carrying/pouring	
	Running, sliding	
	Hopping, jumping	
	Pedaling, spinning	
	Social Skills	
	Listening to others	
	Initiating/responding appropriate	
	Sharing toys/objects	
	General Language Skills	
	Verb structures	
	Prepositions (*in/under/between*)	
	Politeness terms	
	Question/answer forms	
	Size/shape/quantity/color terms	
	General Cognitive Skills	
	Matching/imitation/observing	
	Creativity	
	Sequencing	
	Classification/pattern recognition	
	Problem solving	
	Emergent Literacy Skills	
	Names on chairs/cubbies	
	Recognition of common words (*stop*)	
	Writing on paper/chalkboard	

Date(s) of Observation: _____ Name: _____

SUMMARY

Divide total score by number of observations per category to get average rating per category.

      5+ = No Concerns
      3–4 = Some Concerns—*at risk (accommodations may help)*
      1–2 = Major Concerns *(intervention needed)*

	Total Score	Number of Observations	Average Rating	Level of Concern
Motor Skills		/21 =		
Social Skills/Attention		/14 =		
Language Skills		/20 =		
Cognitive Skills		/18 =		
Emergent Literacy Skills		/15 =		

Any discrepancies in skills between activities that change daily and routine activities?

_____
_____
_____
_____
_____
_____

Any discrepancies in skills between activities that are teacher led and those that are child centered?

_____
_____
_____
_____
_____
_____

Summary of strengths:

_____
_____
_____
_____
_____

Summary of weaknesses:

_____
_____
_____
_____
_____

Bibliography of Children's Books

Accorsi, W. (1992). *Friendship's first Thanksgiving.* New York: Scholastic.

Ahlberg, J., & Ahlberg, A. (1986). *The jolly postman.* Boston: Little, Brown.

Amery, H. (1988). *Cinderella.* London: Usborne Publishing.

Amery, H., & Cartwright, S. (1984). *At the seaside.* London: Usborne Publishing.

Andreae, G., & Wojtowycz, D. (1998). *Commotion in the ocean.* New York: Scholastic.

Andriani, V. (1994). *Peanut butter rhino.* New York: Scholastic.

Arnosky, J. (1987). *Raccoons and ripe corn.* New York: Scholastic.

Asch, F. (1985). *Bear shadow.* New York: Scholastic.

Asch, F. (1992). *Little fish, big fish.* New York: Scholastic.

Baer, E., & Bjorkman. (1995). *This is the way we eat our lunch.* New York: Scholastic.

Barbaresi, N. (1984). *Jenny's in the hospital.* Racine, WI: Western Publishing.

Barchas, S.E. (1975). *I was walking down the road.* New York: Scholastic.

Barkan, J. (1991). *Whiskerville grocery.* New York: Grosset & Dunlap.

Barton, B. (1981). *Building a house.* New York: Greenwillow Books.

Berenstain, S., & Berenstain, J. (1983). *The Berenstain bears and the messy room.* New York: Random House.

Berenstain, S., & Berenstain, J. (1991). *The Berenstain bears don't pollute.* New York: Random House.

Berenstain, S., & Berenstain, J. (1996). *The Berenstain bears get stage fright.* New York: Random House.

Berger, M., & Hafner, M. (1985). *Germs make me sick!* New York: HarperCollins.

Blackaby, S. (2003). *The princess and the pea.* Mankato, MN: Picture Window Books.

Blackstone, M., & O'Brien, J. (1993). *This is baseball.* New York: Scholastic.

Bond, F. (1983). *The Halloween performance.* New York: Scholastic.

Bottner, B. (1987). *Zoo song.* New York: Scholastic.

Bourgeois, P. (1989). *Big Sarah's little boots.* New York: Scholastic.

Bourgeois, P., & Clark, B. (1995). *Franklin wants a pet.* New York: Scholastic.

Brandenberg, A. (1989). *My five senses.* New York: Harper Collins.

Branley, F.M. (1960). *Big tracks, little tracks.* New York: Scholastic.

Bridwell, N. (1966). *Clifford's Halloween.* New York: Scholastic.

Brown, M. (1984). *Arthur goes to camp.* Boston: Little, Brown.

Brown, M.W. (1947). *Goodnight moon.* New York: Scholastic.

Brown, M.W. (1992). *Red light, green light.* New York: Scholastic.

Brown, R. (1994). *What rhymes with snake?* New York: Tambourine Books.

Buckley, C. (1987). *The greedy grey octopus.* Portsmouth, NH: Heinemann.

Burningham, J. (1970). *Mr. Gumpy's outing.* New York: Holt, Rinehart & Winston.

Burton, V.L. (1943). *Katy and the big snow.* New York: Scholastic.

Calhoun, M. (1979). *Cross-country cat.* New York: Mulberry Books.

Calmenson, S. (1995). *Kinderkittens: Who stole the cookie.* New York: Scholastic.

Capucilli, A.S., & Arnold, T. (1995). *Inside a barn in the country.* New York: Scholastic.

Carle, E. (1969). *The very hungry caterpillar.* New York: Scholastic.

Carle, E. (1987). *A house for hermit crab.* New York: Scholastic.

Carle, E. (1997). *Have you seen my cat?* New York: Simon & Schuster.

Children's Television Workshop. (1986). *Sesame Street learning about letters* [Videotape]. New York: Random House.

Chisholm, J., & Reid, S. (1995). *Who built the pyramids?* London: Usborne Publishing.

Christelow, E. (1989). *Five little monkeys jumping on the bed.* New York: Clarion Books.

Civardi, A. (1992a). *Going on a plane.* Tulsa, OK: EDC Publishing.

Civardi, A. (1992b). *Going to the doctor.* London: Usborne Publishing.

Cohen, M. (1967). *Will I have a friend?* New York: Scholastic.

Craig, J., & Harvey, P. (1982). *Now I know what's under the ocean.* Mahwah, NJ: Troll Associates.

Crews, D. (1968). *Ten black dots.* New York: Scholastic.

Cushman, D. (1993). *The ABC mystery.* Columbus, OH: Newfield Publications.

Day, A. (1985). *Good dog, Carl.* New York: Scholastic.

DePaola, T. (1983). *The legend of Bluebonnet.* New York: Scholastic.

Eastman, P.D. (1960). *Are you my mother?* New York: Random House.

Eastman, P.D. (1961). *Go, dog. Go!* New York: Random House.

Edwards, P. (1998). *The grumpy morning* [Audiobook]. New York: Scholastic.

Ehlert, L. (1987). *Growing vegetable soup.* New York: Scholastic.

Ehlert, L. (1991). *Red leaf, yellow leaf.* New York: Scholastic.

Elliott, D. (1982). *Grover goes to school.* New York: Random House/Children's Television Workshop.

Evans, J. (1979). *The three bears.* Allen, TX: Developmental Learning Materials.

Evans, J. (1982). *The gingerbread man.* Allen, TX: Developmental Learning Materials.

Faulkner, K., & Lambert, J. (1996). *The wide-mouthed frog*. New York: Dial Books.

Fleming, D. (1992). *Count*. New York: Scholastic.

Ford, B.G. (1993). *Don't forget the oatmeal! A word book*. New York: Reader's Digest.

Frasier, D. (2002). *Out of the ocean*. New York: Harcourt.

Freeman, D. (1968). *Corduroy*. New York: Scholastic.

Freeman, D. (1978). *A pocket for Corduroy*. New York: Viking.

Gelman, R., & Gergerg, M. (1998). *Stop those painters!* New York: Scholastic.

Gretz, S. (1984). *Teddy bear cures a cold*. New York: Scholastic.

Grodin, C. (1993). *Freddie the fly*. New York: Random House.

Guarino, D. (1989). *Is your mama a llama?* New York: Scholastic.

Hall, Z., & Halpern, S. (1996). *The apple pie tree*. New York: Scholastic.

Hall, Z., & Halpern, S. (1998). *The surprise garden*. New York: Scholastic.

Hall, Z., & Halpern, S. (1999). *It's pumpkin time*. New York: Scholastic.

Henderson, K. (1988). *Don't interrupt*. London: Frances Lincoln.

Hennessy, B.G. (2001). *Corduroy at the zoo*. New York: Scholastic.

Herman, G. (1988). *The fire engine*. New York: Random House.

Herman, G., & Alley R.W. (1990). *Ice cream soup*. New York: Random House.

Herriot, J. (1984). *Moses the kitten*. New York: St. Martin's Press.

Hoberman, M.A. (1986). *A house is a house for me*. Richmond Hill, Ontario, Canada: Scholastic TAB.

Holland, M. (1988). *Monsters don't scare me*. Worthington, OH: Willowisp Press.

Howe, J., & Hall, Z. (1999). *It's pumpkin time*. New York: Scholastic.

Huston, W. (1991). *Jamal's busy day*. New York: Scholastic.

Hutchins, H., & Ohi, R. (1992). *And you can be the cat*. North York, Ontario: Annick Press.

Hutchins, P. (1987). *Rosie's walk*. New York: Scholastic.

Johnson, A. (1990). *Do you like Kayla?* New York: Scholastic.

Keats, E.J. (1978). *The trip*. New York: Greenwillow Books.

Keats, E.J. (1967). *Peter's chair*. New York: Scholastic.

Keats, E.J. (1968). *A letter to Amy*. New York: HarperCollins.

Kimmel, E., & Stevens, J. (1988). *Anansi and the moss-covered rock*. New York: Holiday House.

Korman, J. (1993). *Working hard with the mighty loader*. New York: Scholastic.

Kovalcik, T. (1993). *What's under your hood, Orson?* New York: Scholastic.

Kroll, S., & Hoban, L. (1993). *Will you be my valentine?* New York: Scholastic.

Kuhn, D. (1993). *My first book of nature*. New York: Cartwheel Books.

Lass, B., & Sturgis, P. (2000). *Who took the cookies from the cookie jar?* New York: Scholastic.

Lionni, L. (1974). *Fish is fish*. New York: Dragonfly Books.

London, J., & Remkiewicz, F. (2001). *Froggy eats out*. New York: Puffin Books.

Loomis, C., & Poydar, N. (1993). *At the mall*. New York: Scholastic.

Maccarone, G., & Carter, D.A. (1995). *Cars! Cars! Cars!* New York: Scholastic.

Maccarone, G., & McCully, E.A. (1994). *Pizza party!* New York: Scholastic.

Maestro, B. (1989). *Snow day*. New York: Scholastic.

Martin, B., Jr. (1985). *Here are my hands*. New York: Scholastic.

Martin, B., Jr., & Archambault, J. (1989). *Chicka chicka boom boom*. New York: Simon & Schuster.

Martin, B., Jr., & Carle, E. (1967). *Brown bear, brown bear, what do you see?* New York: Holt, Rinehart & Winston.

Martin, B. Jr., & Carle, E. (1991). *Polar bear, polar bear, what do you hear?* New York: Scholastic.

Mayer, G., & Mayer, M. (1993). *Trick or treat little critter*. Racine, WI: Western Publishing.

Mayer, M. (1986). *Just me and my little sister*. Racine, WI: Western Publishing.

Mayer, M. (1987). *Just a mess*. Racine, WI: Western Publishing.

Mayer, M. (1989). *Just shopping with mom*. New York: Golden Book Publishing.

Mayer, M. (2001). *All by myself*. Racine, WI: Western Publishing.

McNaught, H. (1978). *The truck book*. New York: Random House.

McPhail, D. (1987). *Emma's vacation*. New York: Scholastic.

McQueen, L. (1985). *The little red hen*. New York: Scholastic.

Merrill, B. (2004). *How much is that doggy in the window?* Watertown, MA: Charlesbridge Publishing.

Miller, J.P. (1987). *Little rabbit goes to the doctor*. New York: Random House.

Moché, D.L. (1982a). *My first book about space*. Racine, WI: Western Publishing.

Moché, D.L. (1982b). *We're taking an airplane trip*. Racine, WI: Western Publishing.

Moffatt, J. (2000). *Trick or treat faces*. New York: Scholastic.

Moncure, J.B. (1973). *Try on a shoe*. Elgin, IL: The Child's World.

Morgan, M., & Porter, S. (1988). *Edward hurts his knee*. New York: E.P. Dutton.

Morris, A. (1989). *Bread, bread, bread*. New York: Scholastic.

Most, B. (1990). *The cow that went oink*. New York: Scholastic.

Nister, E. (1991). *Our farmyard*. New York: Penguin Books.

Numeroff, L.J. (1985). *If you give a mouse a cookie*. New York: Scholastic.

Packard, M. (1991). *A visit to China*. Racine, WI: Western Publishing Co.

Parker, V., & Bolam, E. (1999). *Bearobics*. New York: Scholastic.

Pfister, M. (1993). *Rainbow fish*. New York: North-South Books, Scholastic.

Pfister, M. (2001). *Rainbow fish to the rescue*. New York: North-South Books, Scholastic.

Preller, J., & Wilhelm H. (1994). *Hiccups for elephant*. New York: Scholastic.

Quinn, G.H., & Shiffman, L. (1995). *The garden in our yard*. New York: Scholastic.

Rader, L. (1998). *Chicken Little*. New York: HarperCollins.

Rey, H.A. (1952). *Curious George rides a bike*. New York: Scholastic.

Robbins, K. (1989). *Boats*. New York: Scholastic.

Rockwell, A. (1989). *Apples and pumpkins*. New York: Scholastic.

Rockwell, A., & Rockwell, L. (1997). *Halloween day*. New York: HarperCollins.

Rosen, M. (1989). *We're going on a bear hunt*. New York: Margaret K. McElderry Books.

Rowe, J. (1990). *Scallywag*. New York: Ashton Scholastic.

Ryder, J. (1987). *Chipmunk song*. New York: Dutton.

Rylant, C., & Gammell, S. (1985). *The relatives came*. New York: Scholastic.

Seibert, P. (2001). *The three little pigs*. New York: McGraw Hill.

Sendak, M. (1963). *Where the wild things are*. New York: Scholastic.

Serfozo, M. (1988). *Who said red?* New York: Scholastic.

Sharmat, M. (1980). *Gregory, the terrible eater*. New York: Four Winds Press.

Shaw, C.G. (1947). *It looked like spilt milk*. New York: HarperCollins.

Shone, V. (1990). *Wheels*. New York: Scholastic.

Silverstein, S. (1964). *The giving tree*. New York: Harper Collins.

Strickland, H., & Strickland, P. (1994). *Dinosaur roar!* New York: Scholastic.

Sykes, J., & Warnes, T. (1999). *Little tiger's big surprise*. Waukesha, WI: Little Tiger Press.

Tafuri, N. (1986). *Who's counting?* New York: Scholastic.

Titherington, J. (1990). *Pumpkin pumpkin*. New York: HarperTrophy.

Waber, B. (1972). *Ira sleeps over*. New York: Scholastic.

Webb, J. (1986). *Play it safe*. Racine, WI: Western Publishing.

Weinberger, K. (2000). *Our Thanksgiving*. New York: Scholastic.

Wellington, M. (2006). *Mr. Cookie Baker*. New York: Dutton Children's Books.

Wilson-Max, K. (2000). *Big silver space shuttle*. New York: Scholastic.

Yoshi, A.C. (1988). *Big Al*. New York: Scholastic.

Zion, G. (1988). *Dear garbage man*. New York: Trumpet Club.

References

Anderson, L.A., & Anderson, D. (2001). *The change leader's roadmap: How to navigate your organization's transformation.* San Francisco: Jossey-Bass/Pfeiffer.

Baker, N., & Nelson, K.E. (1984). Recasting and related conversational techniques for triggering syntactic advances by young children. *First Language, 5*(1), 3–22.

Bandura, A. (1986). *Social foundations of thought and action: A social cognitive.* Englewood Cliffs, NJ: Prentice Hall.

Bergen, D. (2002). The role of pretend play in children's cognitive development. *Early Childhood Research & Practice, 4*(1). Retrieved March 12, 2007, from http://www.ecrp.uluc.edu/

Bunce, B., & Leibhaver, G. (1989). *Language Acquisition Preschool (LAP) curriculum.* Unpublished staff manual for the LAP, University of Kansas, Lawrence.

Bunce, B. (1998, March). *Implementing naturalistic language intervention.* Paper presented at the Cimarron Conference on Communication Disorders, Oklahoma State University, Stillwater, OK.

Bunce, B. (1999, February 25–26). *Developing language for literacy.* Two-day inservice presented at EDIS/DoDDS tri-country conference, Weinheim, Germany.

Bunce, B. (1999, April). *Using a language-focused curriculum in a preschool classroom.* Paper presented at the Core Knowledge National Conference, Orlando, FL.

Bunce, B.H. (1995a). *Building a language-focused curriculum for the preschool classroom: A planning guide* (Vol. 2). Baltimore: Paul H. Brookes Publishing Co.

Bunce, B.H. (1995b). Children learning English as a second language. In M.L. Rice & K.A. Wilcox (Eds.), *Building a language-focused curriculum for the preschool classroom: A foundation for lifelong communication* (pp. 91–103). Baltimore: Paul H. Brookes Publishing Co.

Bunce, B.H. (2003). Children with culturally diverse backgrounds. In L. McCormick, D. Frome-Loeb, & R. Schiefelbusch (Eds.), *Early language intervention: Supporting children in inclusive settings* (2nd ed., pp. 367–407). Boston: Allyn & Bacon.

Bunce, B.H. (2005, March). *Using a language-focused curriculum to promote language and literacy in preschools.* Workshop sponsored by Wayne State University and presented to Head Start teachers, Detroit, MI.

Bunce, B.H., Rice, M.L., & Wilcox, K.A. (2000, October). *Language acquisition preschool update: Celebrating 15 years of curriculum development, intervention, research, and training.* Paper presented at the Kansas Speech-Language-Hearing Association Convention, Wichita, KS.

Bunce, B.H., & Watkins, R.V. (1995). Language intervention in a preschool classroom: Implementing a language-focused curriculum. In M.L. Rice & K.A. Wilcox (Eds.), *Building a language-focused curriculum for the preschool classroom: A foundation for lifelong communication* (Vol. 1, pp. 39–71). Baltimore: Paul H. Brookes Publishing Co.

Bunce, B.H., Watkins, R.V., Eyer, J., Torres, S. Ray, T., & Ellsworth, J. (1995). Language-focused curriculum in other settings. In M. Rice & K. Wilcox (Eds.), *Building a language-focused curriculum for the preschool classroom: A foundation for lifelong communication* (Vol. 1, pp. 199–220). Baltimore: Paul H. Brookes Publishing Co.

Camarata, S., & Nelson, K.E. (2006). Conversational recast intervention with preschool and older children. In R.J. McCauley & M.E. Fey (Eds.), *Treatment of language disorders in children* (pp. 237–264). Baltimore: Paul H. Brookes Publishing Co.

Camarata, S.M., Nelson, K.E., & Camarata, M.N. (1994). Comparison of conversational-recasting and imitative procedures for training grammatical structures in children with specific language impairment. *Journal of Speech and Hearing Research, 37*(6), 1414–1423.

Christie, J., & Stone, S. (1999). Collaborative literacy activity in print-enriched play centers: Exploring the "zone" in same age and multi-age groupings. *Journal of Literacy Research, 31,* 109–131.

Connor, C.M., Morrison, F.J., & Slominski, L. (2006). Preschool instruction and children's emergent literacy growth. *Journal of Educational Psychology, 98*(4), 665–689.

Constable, C.M. (1986). The application of scripts in the organization of language intervention contexts. In K. Nelson (Ed.), *Event knowledge: Structure and function in development* (pp. 205–230). Hillside, NJ: Lawrence Erlbaum Associates.

Davidson, J. (1996). *Emergent literacy and dramatic play in early education.* Albany, NY: Delmar Publishers.

Dickinson, D. (1984). First impressions: Children's knowledge of words gained from a single exposure. *Applied Psycholinguistics, 5*(4), 359–373.

Dickinson, D.K., & Tabors, P.O. (Eds.). (2001). *Beginning literacy with language: Young children learning at home and school.* Baltimore: Paul H. Brookes Publishing Co.

Dunn, L.M., & Dunn, L.M. (1981). *Peabody Picture Vocabulary Test–R.* Circle Pines, MN: American Guidance Services.

Dunn, L.M., & Dunn, L.M. (1997). *Peabody Picture Vocabulary Test–III.* Circle Pines, MN: American Guidance Services.

Ellis Weismer, S., & Robertson, S. (2006). Focused stimulation approach to language intervention. In R.J. McCauley & M.E. Fey (Eds.), *Treatment of language disorders in children* (pp. 175–202). Baltimore: Paul H. Brookes Publishing Co.

Ferguson, C.J. (1999). Building literacy with child constructed sociodramatic play centers. *Dimensions of Early Childhood, 27*(3), 23–29.

Fey, M. (1986). *Language intervention with young children.* San Diego, CA: College Hill Press.

Fey, M., & Loeb, D. (2002). An evaluation of facilitative effects of inverted yes-no questions on the acquisition of auxiliary verbs. *Journal of Speech and Hearing Research, 45,* 160–174.

Fey, M.E., Cleave, P.L., Long, S.H., & Hughes, D.L. (1993). Two approaches to the facilitation of grammar in children with language impairment: An experimental evaluation. *Journal of Speech, Language, and Hearing Research, 36,* 141–157.

Fivush, R., & Slackman, E.A. (1986). The acquisition and development of scripts. In K. Nelson (Ed.), *Event knowledge: Structure and function in development* (pp. 71–96). Hillsdale, NJ: Lawrence Erlbaum Associates.

Fluharty, N.B. (2001). *Fluharty Preschool Speech and Language Screening Test, Second Edition.* Austin, TX: Pro-Ed, Inc.

French, L.A., Lucariello, J., Seidman, S., & Nelson, K. (1985). The influence of discourse content and context on preschoolers' use of language. In L. Galda & A.D. Pellegini (Eds.), *Play, language and stories* (pp. 1–27). Norwood, NJ: Ablex.

Gillum, H., Camarata, S., Nelson, K.E., & Camarata, M. (2003). A comparison of naturalistic and analog treatment effects in children with expressive language disorder and poor preintervention imitation skills. *Journal of Positive Behavior Interventions, 5*(3), 171–178.

Girolametto, L., Pearce, P., & Weitzman, E. (1997). Effects of lexical intervention on the phonology of late talkers. *Journal of Speech, Language, and Hearing Research, 40,* 338–348.

Girolametto, L., & Weitzman, E. (2002). Responsiveness of child care providers in interactions with toddlers and preschoolers. *Language, Speech, and Hearing Services in Schools, 33,* 268–281.

Girolametto, L., Weitzman, E., & Greenberg, J. (2003). Training day care staff to facilitate children's language. *American Journal of Speech-Language Pathology, 12,* 299–311.

Goldman, R., & Fristoe, M. (2000). *Goldman-Fristoe Test of Articulation* (2nd ed.). Circle Pines, MN: American Guidance Services.

Goldstein, H., & Cisar, C.L. (1992). Promoting interaction during sociodramatic play: Teaching scripts to typical preschoolers and classmates with disabilities. *Journal of Applied Behavior Analysis, 25,* 265–280.

Gray, S. (2003). Word-learning by preschools with specific language impairment. *Journal of Speech Language Hearing Research, 46,* 56–67.

Guralnick, M.J. (1997). *The effectiveness of early intervention.* Baltimore: Paul H. Brookes Publishing Co.

Hadley, P.A., & Rice, M.L. (1993). Parental judgments of preschoolers' speech and language development: A resource for assessment and IEP planning. *Seminars in Speech and Language, 14,* 278–288.

Haynes, N.M. (1998). Lessons learned. *Journal of Education for Students Placed at Risk, 3,* 87–99.

Heath, S.B. (1986). Separating "things of the imagination" from life: Learning to read and write. In W. Teale & E. Sulzby (Eds.), *Emergent literacy* (pp. 156–172). Norwood, NJ: Ablex.

Justice, L.M., & Ezell, H.K. (1999). Knowledge of syntactic structures: A comparison of speech-language pathology graduate students to those in related disciplines. *Contemporary Issues in Communication Science and Disorders, 26,* 119–127.

Justice, L.M., Mashburn, A., Hamre, B., & Pianta, R.C. (2007). *Quality of language and literacy instruction in prekindergarten programs serving at-risk pupils.* Manuscript in review.

Karoly, L.A., Kilburn, M.R., & Cannon, J.S. (2005). *Early childhood interventions: Proven results, future promise.* Santa Monica, CA: RAND Corporation.

Keys, P.M. (2005). Are teachers walking the walk or just talking the talk in science education? *Teachers and Teaching: Theory to Practice, 11,* 499–516.

Kouri, T.A. (2005). Lexical training through modeling and elicitation procedures with late talkers who have specific language impairment and developmental delays. *Journal of Speech, Language, and Hearing Research, 48,* 157–171.

Lederer, S.H. (2002). Collaborative pretend play: From theory to therapy. *Child Language Teaching and Therapy, 18*(3), 233–255.

Leonard, L.B. (1981). Facilitating linguistic skills in children with specific language impairment. *Applied Psycholinguistics, 2,* 89–118.

Lucariello, J., Kyratzis, A., & Engel, S. (1986). The influence of discourse content and context on preschooler's use of language. In L. Galda & A.S. Pellegrini (Eds.), *Play, language and stories* (pp. 1–27). Norwood, NJ: Ablex.

Lyons, S. (2000). *A comparison of reading ability in middle grades of children identified with a specific speech-language impairment in preschool and their typically developing peers.* Unpublished thesis. University of Kansas, Lawrence.

Miller, J., & Chapman, R. (1986–2000). *The systematic analysis of language transcripts.* Madison, WI: Language Analysis Laboratory, Waisman Research Center.

Neeley, P.M., Neeley, R.A., Justen, J.E., & Tipton-Sumner, C. (2001). Scripted play as a language intervention strategy for preschoolers with developmental disabilities. *Early Childhood Education Journal, 28*(4), 243–246.

Nelson, K. (1981). Social cognition in a script framework. In J. H. Flavell & L. Ross (Eds.), *Social cognitive development* (pp. 97–118). Cambridge, UK: Cambridge University Press.

Nelson, K. (Ed.). (1986). *Event knowledge: Structure and function in development.* Hillsdale, NJ: Lawrence Erlbaum Associates.

Nelson, K., & Seidman, S. (1984). Playing with scripts. In I. Bretherton (Ed.), *Symbolic play: The development of social understanding* (pp. 45–71). New York: Academic Press.

Nelson, K.E., Camarata, S.M., Welsh, J., Butkovsky, L., & Camarata, M. (1996). Effects of imitative and conversational recasting treatment on the acquisition of grammar in children with specific language impairment and young language-normal children. *Journal of Speech and Hearing Research, 39,* 850–859.

Pellegrini, A.D. (1984). The effect of classroom ecology on preschoolers' functional uses of language. In A.D. Pellegrini & T.D. Yawkey (Eds.), *The development of oral and written language in social contexts* (pp. 129–141). Norwood, NJ: Ablex.

Pellegrini, A.D., & Galda, L. (2000). Cognitive development, play, and literacy: Issues of definition and developmental function. In K. Roskos and J. Christie (Eds.), *Play and literacy in early childhood: Research from multiple perspectives* (pp. 63–74). Mahwah, NJ: Lawrence Erlbaum Associates.

Pence, K.L, Justice, L.M., & Wiggins, A.K. (2007). *Preschool teachers' fidelity in implementing a comprehensive language-rich curriculum.* Manuscript under review.

Proctor-Williams, K., Fey, M., & Loeb, D. (2001). Parental recasts and production in copulas and articles by children with specific language impairment and typical language. *American Journal of Speech-Language Pathology, 10,* 155–168.

Quill, K.A. (1997). Instructional considerations for young children with autism: The rationale for visually cued instruction. *Journal of Autism & Developmental Disorders, 27*(6), 697–714.

Reynell, J.R., & Gruber, C.P. (1991). *Reynell Developmental Language Scales–U.S. Edition.* Los Angeles: Western Psychological Services.

Rice, M.L. (1990). Preschoolers' QUIL: Quick incidental learning of words. In G. Conti-Ramsden & C. Snow (Eds.), *Child language* (Vol. 7, pp. 171–195). Hillsdale, NJ: Lawrence Erlbaum Associates.

Rice, M.L. (1993). "Don't talk to him: He's weird": A social consequences account of language and social interactions. In A.P. Kaiser & D.B. Gray (Eds.), *Enhancing children's communication: Research foundations for intervention* (pp. 139–158). Baltimore: Paul H. Brookes Publishing Co.

Rice, M.L. (1998, May). *Preschool language intervention in group settings: Principles, practices, and precedents.* Paper presented at the Speech Pathology Australia National Conference, Perth, Australia.

Rice, M.L., Buhr, J., & Nemeth, M. (1990). Fast mapping word-learning abilities of language-delayed preschoolers. *Journal of Speech and Hearing Disorders, 55*(1), 33–42.

Rice, M.L., & Hadley, P. (1995). Language outcomes of the language-focused curriculum. In M.L. Rice & K.A. Wilcox (Eds.), *Building a language-focused curriculum for the preschool classroom: A foundation for lifelong communication* (pp. 155–169). Baltimore: Paul H. Brookes Publishing Co.

Rice, M.L., Oetting, J., Marquis, J., Bode, J., & Pae, S. (1994). Frequency of input effects on word comprehension of children with specific language impairment. *Journal of Speech and Hearing Research, 37*, 106–122.

Rice, M.L., Sell, M.A., & Hadley, P.A. The Social Interactive Coding System (SICS): An on-line, clinically relevant descriptive tool. *Language, Speech, and Hearing Services in Schools, 21*, 2–14.

Rice, M.L., & Wilcox, K.A. (Eds.). (1995). *Building a language-focused curriculum for the preschool classroom: A foundation for lifelong communication* (Vol. 1). Baltimore: Paul H. Brookes Publishing Co.

Rice, M.L., Wilcox, K.A., Bunce, B.H., & Liebhaber, G.K. (1989, October). *LAP: A model preschool for language disordered and ESL children.* Paper presented at the Kansas Speech-Language-Hearing Association meeting, Lawrence, KS.

Robertson, S.B., & Ellis Weismer, S. (1999). Effects of treatment on linguistic and social skills in toddlers with delayed language development. *Journal of Speech, Language, and Hearing Research, 42*, 1234–1248.

Roskos, K., & Christie, J. (Eds.). (2000). *Literacy-enriched play settings: A broad-spectrum instructional strategy.* Mahwah, NJ: Lawrence Erlbaum Associates.

Saville-Troike, M. (1988). Private speech: Evidence for second language learning strategies during the "silent period." *Journal of Child Language, 15*, 567–590.

Sawyer, R.K. (1997). *Pretend play as improvisation.* Hillsdale, NJ: Lawrence Erlbaum Associates.

Schuele, M., Rice, M., & Wilcox, K. (1995). Redirects: A strategy to increase peer initiations. *Journal of Speech Language Hearing Research, 38*, 1319–1333.

Schweinhart, L.J., & Weikart, D.P. (1988). Education for young children living in poverty: Child-initiated learning or teacher-directed instruction? *Elementary School Journal, 89*, 213–225.

Shirk, A. (1993). *English proficiency of children learning English as a second language: A descriptive study.* Unpublished masters thesis, University of Kansas, Lawrence, KS.

Silliman, E.R., & Wilkinson, L.C. (1991). *Communicating for learning: Classroom observation and collaboration.* Gaithersburg, MD: Aspen Publishers, Inc.

Smith, A., & Camarata, S. (1999). Increasing language intelligibility of children with autism within regular classroom settings using teacher implemented instruction. *Journal of Positive Behavior Intervention, 1*(3), 141–151.

Sobeck, J.L., Abbey, A., & Agius, E. (2006). Lessons learned from implementing school-based substance abuse prevention curriculums. *Children and Schools, 28*, 77–85.

Stanovich, P.J., & Stanovich, K.E. (2003). *Using research and reason in education: How teachers can use scientifically-based research to make curricular instructional decisions.* Washington, DC: The Partnership for Reading.

Stipek, D. (2006). No Child Left Behind come to preschool. *Elementary School Journal, 106*, 455–466.

Stipek, D., Feiler, R., Bykler, P., Ryan, R., Milburn, S., & Salmon, S.M. (1998). Good beginnings: What differences does a program make in preparing young children for school? *Journal of Applied Developmental Psychology, 19*, 41–66.

Vedeler, L. (1997). Dramatic play: A format for "literate" language. *British Journal of Educational Psychology, 67*(2), 153–167.

Wasik, B.A., Bond, M.A., & Hindman, A. (2006). The effects of a language and literacy intervention on Head Start children and teachers. *Journal of Educational Psychology, 98*, 63–74.

Watkins, R.V., & Bunce, B.H. (1996). Natural literacy: Theory and practice for preschool intervention programs. *Topics in Early Childhood Special Education, 16*(2), 191–212.

Wiederholt, J., & Bryant, R. (1992). *Gray Oral Reading Test–III.* Austin, TX: Pro-Ed.

Wilcox, K.A., & Morris, S. (1995). Speech outcomes of the language-focused curriculum. In M.L. Rice & K.A. Wilcox (Eds.), *Building a language-focused curriculum for the preschool classroom: A foundation for lifelong communication* (Vol. 1). Baltimore: Paul H. Brookes Publishing Co.

Woodcock, R.W. (1987). *Woodcock Reading Mastery Tests–R.* Circle Pines, MN: American Guidance Services.

Wong-Fillmore, L. (1989). Teachability and second language acquisition. In M.L. Rice & R.L. Schiefelbusch (Eds.), *The teachability of language* (pp. 311–332). Baltimore: Paul H. Brookes Publishing Co.

Index

Page references to figures, tables, and footnotes are indicated by *f*, *t*, and *n*, respectively.